Glamour
An Extraordinary History

85 YEARS OF WOMEN BREAKING BOUNDARIES

"PLEASE MAKE ME OVER"...

Is it WORTH IT for women?

OUR BODIES, OUR SELF-RESPECT

INSTEAD OF THE PILL

The Girl with a Job stands at the Crossroads

This is Glamour

YOU CAN DO IT YOURSELF!

WHAT'S NEW

Superiority of women

GLAMOUR GIRLS HAVE MORE FUN

WHAT GOES ON AT GLAMOUR

NEW PERSPECTIVE ON FEMININITY

real stories

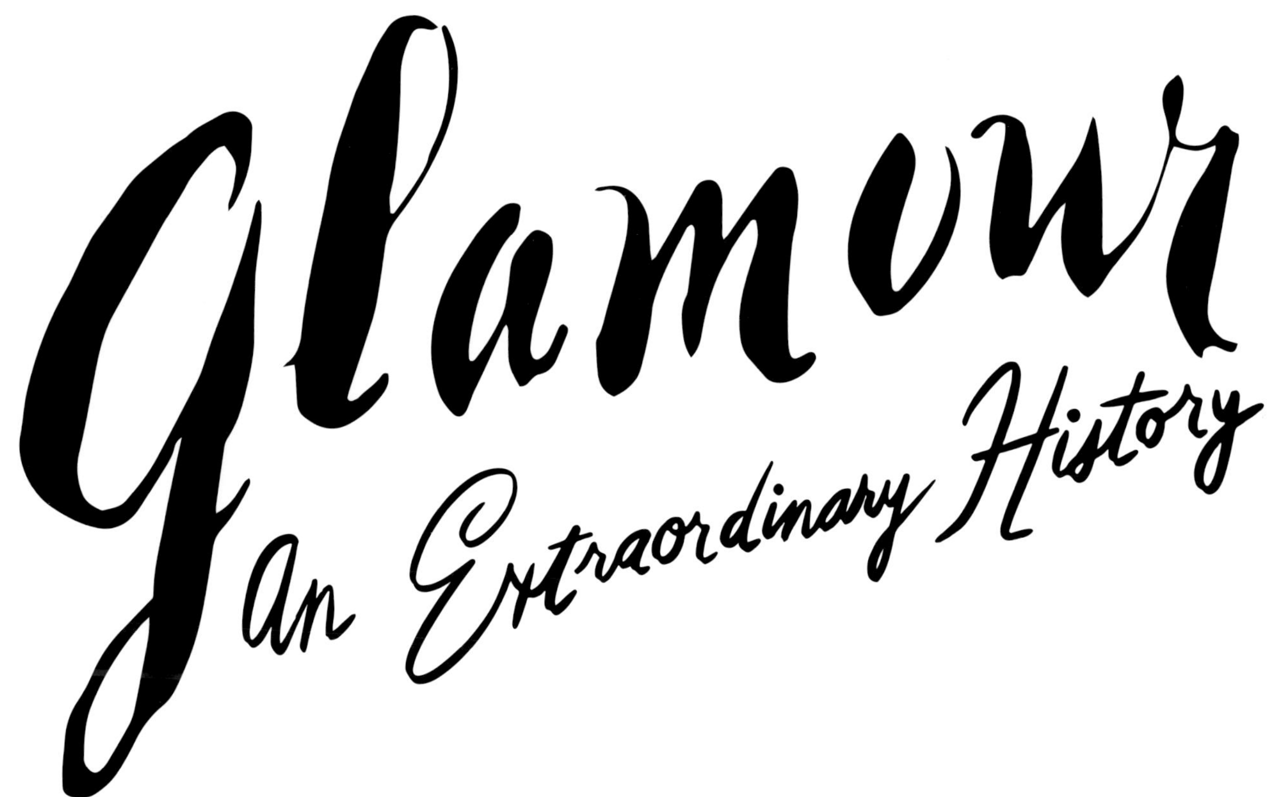

Glamour
An Extraordinary History

85 YEARS OF WOMEN BREAKING BOUNDARIES

BY NATASHA PEARLMAN

WITH RUHAMA WOLLE AND ANNA MOESLEIN

INTRODUCTION BY SAMANTHA BARRY

To Everyone Who Loves the
Magic of Magazines

The Importance of Glamour

IN THE ENGLISH LANGUAGE, the word *glamour* came from the Scots. In the early 1700s they altered the Scottish word grammar to "glamour," and it meant "a magic spell." The meaning of the word grew and evolved, and in 1825 it appeared in a dictionary with the description "the power of enchant-ment…applied to female fascination."

While today the word is more commonly used to mean "an exciting and often illusory and romantic attractiveness" and "alluring or fascinating attraction," to me it retains magic, especially when thinking about *Glamour*, the title I serve as editor in chief. The magic of *Glamour*'s origin story is what drew me in. I wanted to be at the helm of a magazine that could tackle female fascination, one that could talk to women about changing the world as confidently as they talked to each other about changing their look, a title that understood that a woman could be as motivated to read a piece about reality television as she was about reproductive rights.

Because of this, *Glamour* has, in every iteration over the course of its 85 years, been so much more than a magazine. It's been a place for women to celebrate and commiserate, a home for service and sexiness, a source of entertainment and enlightenment.

It's always been a destination and a community, bringing women together in its pages, online, and in person. You can see these communities come together again and again through the decades, standing on the shoulders of the women and the storytelling that came before them. In the 1970s *Glamour* reported on the women fighting for reproductive rights, and the legal right to an abortion. Today, the *Glamour* team is fighting alongside our readers to lobby politicians to pass the country's first paid family and medical leave act. In the 1990s *Glamour* got hundreds of letters about race in America in the wake of groundbreaking articles addressing racism towards the Black community. Today, our audience comments on and shares our videos when we report on the need to pass The Crown Act and end hair discrimination against Black people in the workplace. The beating heart of *Glamour*, since its inception, has been both the content we create for people to read and the community we create with our content.

I get a thrill every time someone tells me what *Glamour* means to them. I could be anywhere in the world—Dublin, Rome, LA, or Austin—and when I talk about my role, women of all generations tell me about their favorite *Glamour* cover, story, or video.

They tell me how their mom was a model in the pages, how their aunt was a College Woman of the Year, or that their neighbor wrote us letters in the '80s. They tell me that their mom saved the *Glamour* issue from the month that they were born. They talk

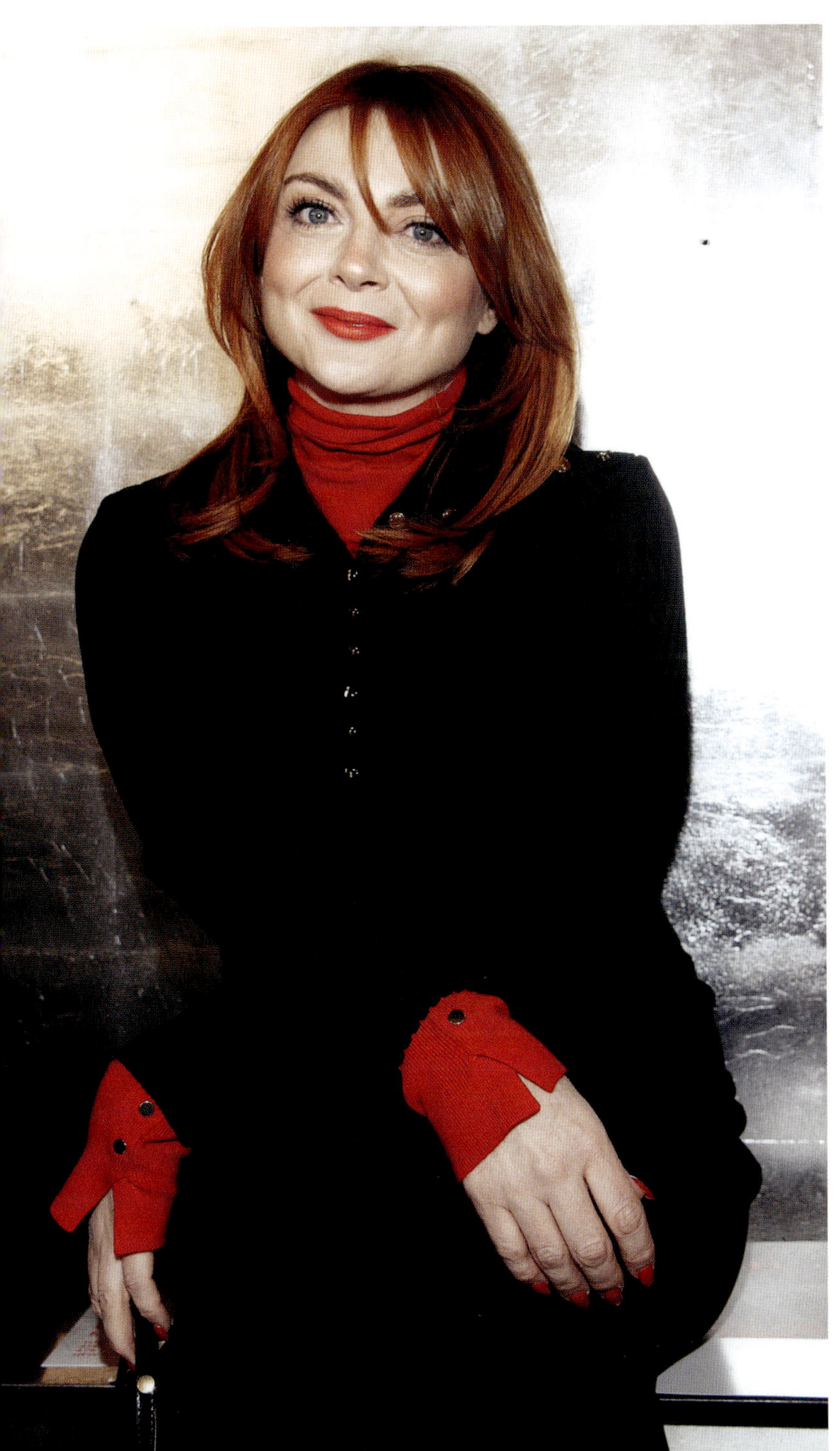

about a story they loved, or a Woman of the Year they admired, or an outfit they adored in our pages or online.

That thrill is magnified when I am in the presence of cover stars and Women of the Year. If it happened during my time at *Glamour* we reminisce about the time on set, our favorite quote, and the readers' reaction to the release. If their *Glamour* cover predates my time at the title, I soak up their stories of time with Ruth Whitney or Cindi Leive. The connection and community is palpable in every conversation.

This is why I know this book is so special. Not only does it chart the extraordinary changes in women's lives over the past eight decades, it gives me even more hope about the future of women and the future of *Glamour*.

Our service and storytelling is as vital today as it was in the 1940s. It may appear in very different ways (hi TikTok!) but that doesn't make it any less valuable or impactful. As women we've fought many fights over the decades—for the right to own a credit card in our own name, for the right to a legal abortion, and against sexual harassment—many of which are laid out in this book. I'm delighted to see how much progress we've made, even though the fights for true equality and representation still aren't over. *Glamour* will continue to advocate for our readers, and continue to grow our community.

I hope you will all treasure this book we have worked so hard to make. It is a living, breathing, beautiful history of all that has come before, and the possibility of what's still in store for women. I want those that pick up this book to be delighted by a fashion shoot, enraged by the fights of the past, and forever inspired by the storytelling.

Samantha Barry

EDITOR IN CHIEF, 2018–PRESENT

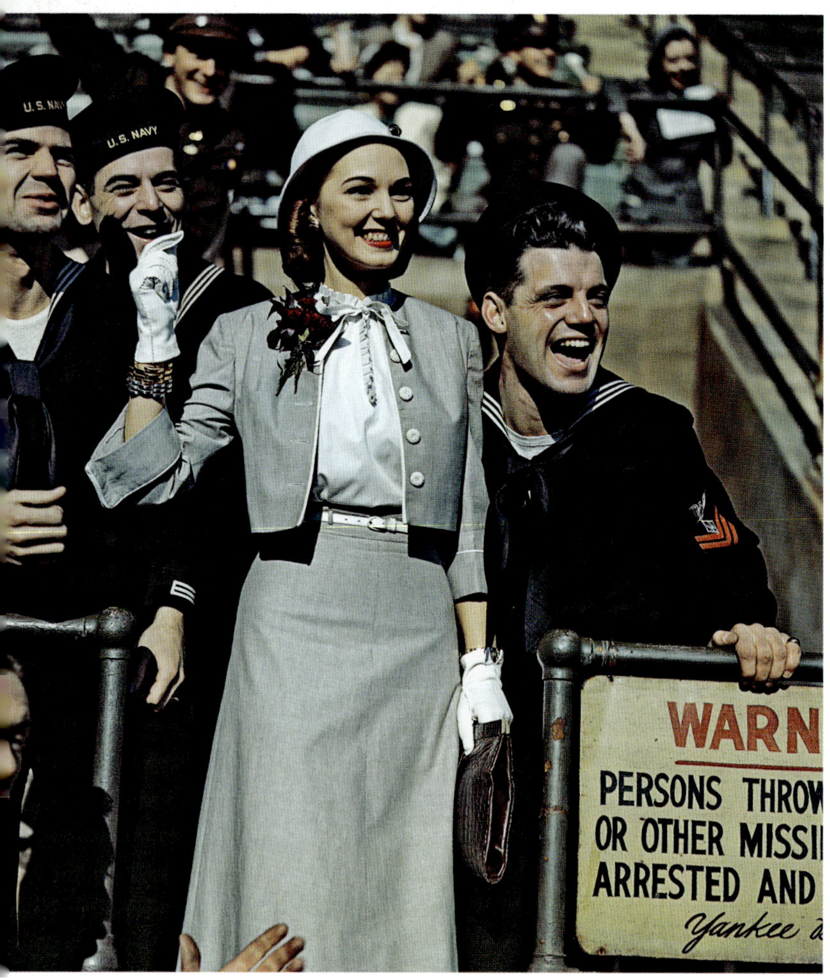

CHAPTER 1

The Girl With a Job

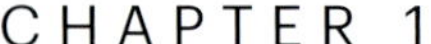

1939–1949

INTRODUCTION	24
THE FIRST ISSUE	28
GLAMOUR'S HOLLYWOOD STARS	30
WAR BEGINS	34
YOUR JOB IS OUR JOB	40
WOMEN WHO WRITE THE WAR	42
EQUAL RIGHTS AMENDMENT	44
FASHION OF THE ERA	46
LIFE AFTER WAR	54
QUOTES OF THE ERA	56
TACKLING PREJUDICE	58
A SEXUAL AWAKENING	60
GLAMOUR STAFF	62
NOTABLE CONTRIBUTORS	64
ICONIC COVERS	68

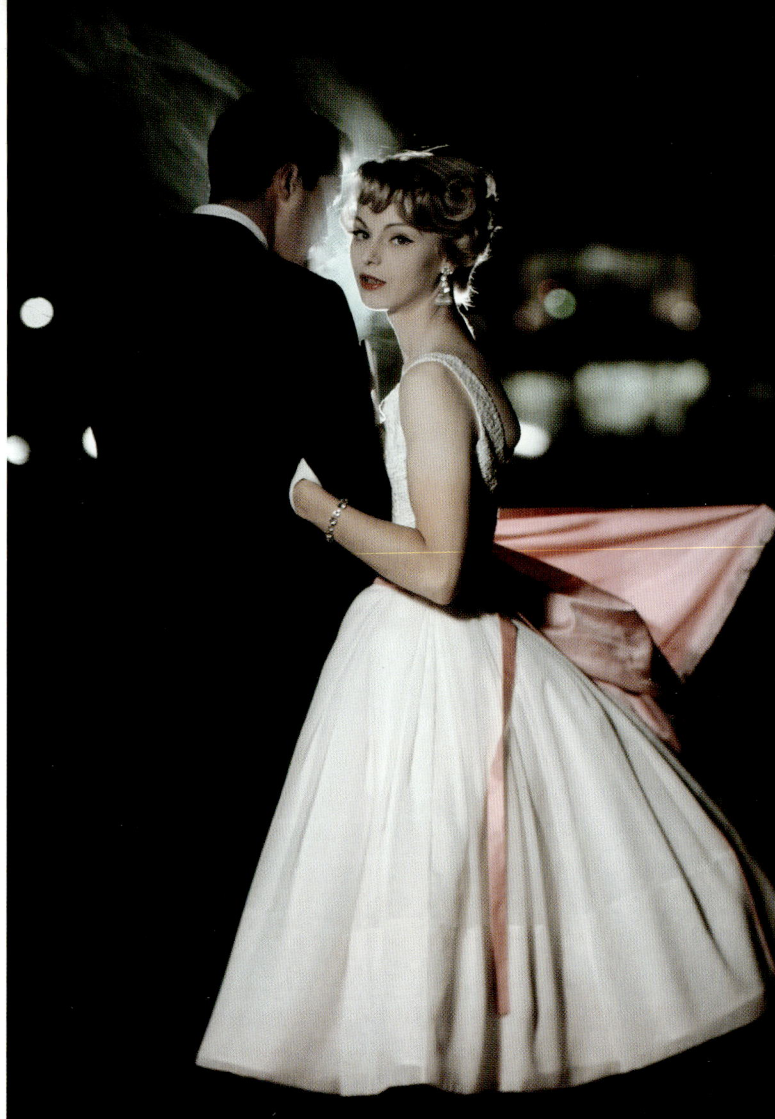

CHAPTER 2

The "Perfect" Housewife

1950–1963

INTRODUCTION	72
BODY IMAGE	76
QUOTES OF THE ERA	80
A GLOBAL *GLAMOUR*	82
WOMEN: THE SUPERIOR SEX	84
JAKE	86
FASHION OF THE ERA	88
NENA VON SCHLEBRÜGGE	96
MARRIAGE AND MOTHERHOOD	98
WHAT IS THE PERFECT WIFE?	102
ICONIC COVERS	104

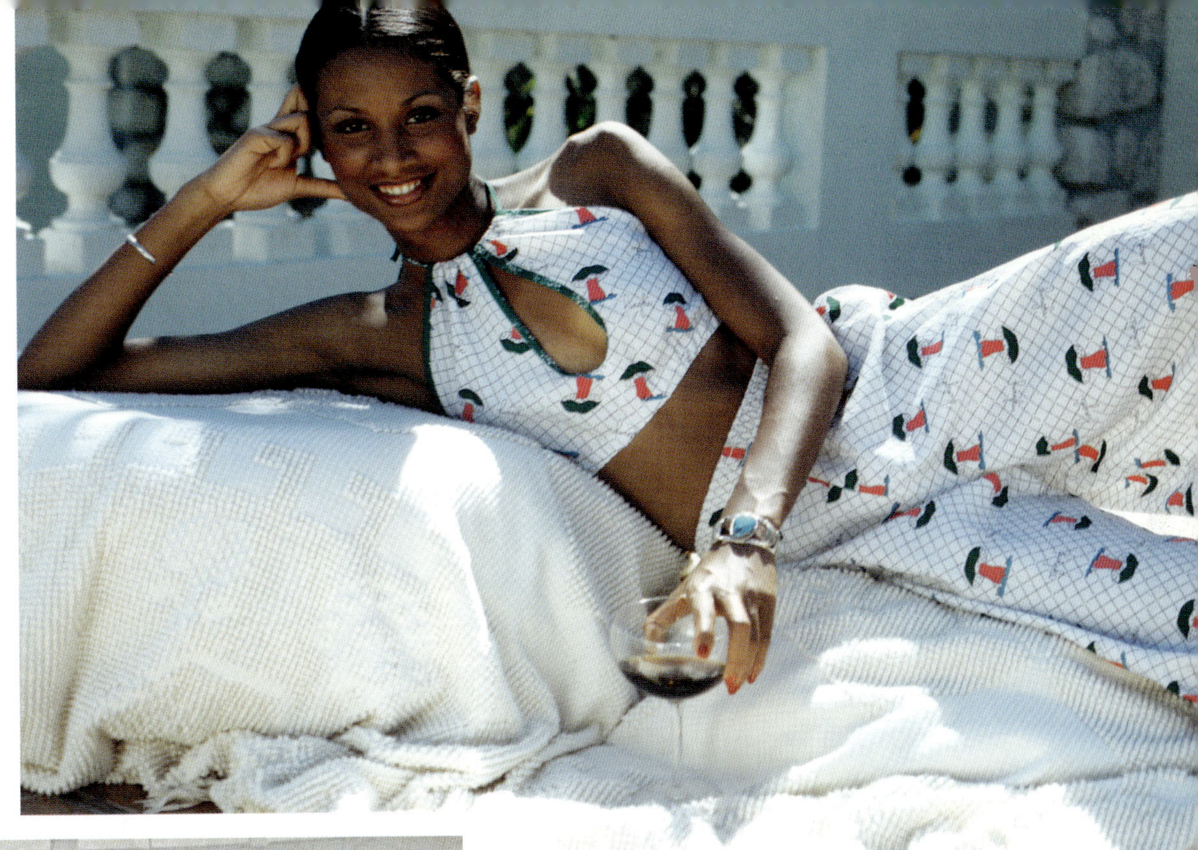

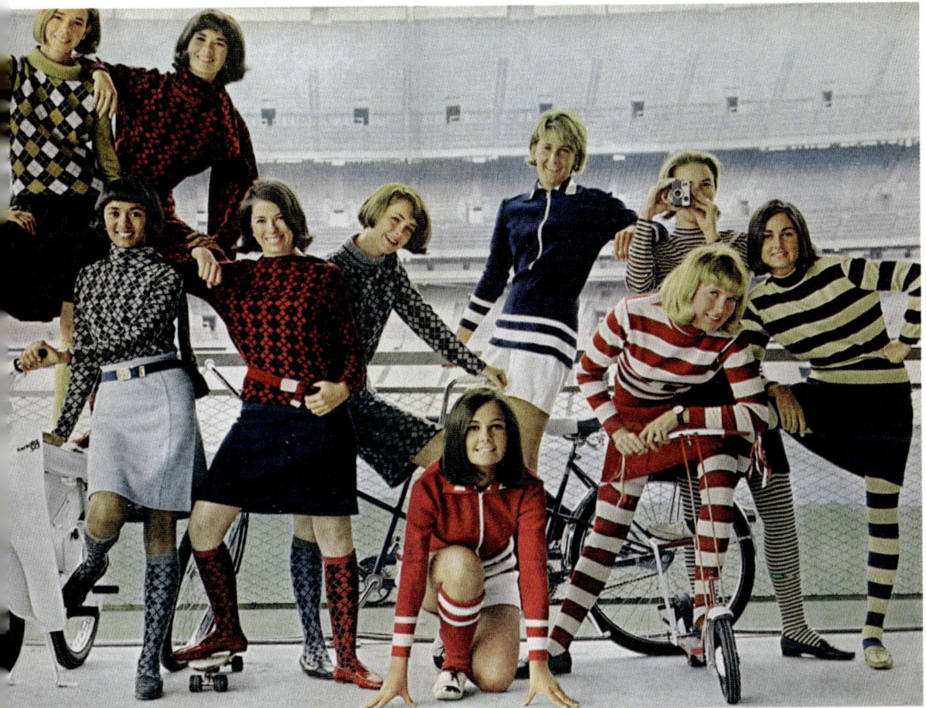

College Women of the Year
— 108

CHAPTER 3

The Liberated Woman

1964–1979

INTRODUCTION	120
THE NEW ERA	124
FASHION OF THE ERA	126
RISE UP FOR *ROE*	134
THE GLORIA DAYS	138
RUTH WHITNEY	142
KATITI KIRONDE	144
THE SEXUAL REVOLUTION	146
PLAYBOY AND WOMEN'S LIB	148
GIVING VOICE TO BLACK WOMEN	150
SHIFTING VIEWS ON MARRIAGE	152
A YOUNG LESBIAN TALKS	154
BEVERLY JOHNSON	156
SHIRLEY CHISHOLM	160
ICONIC COVERS	162
FAMOUS FACES	164

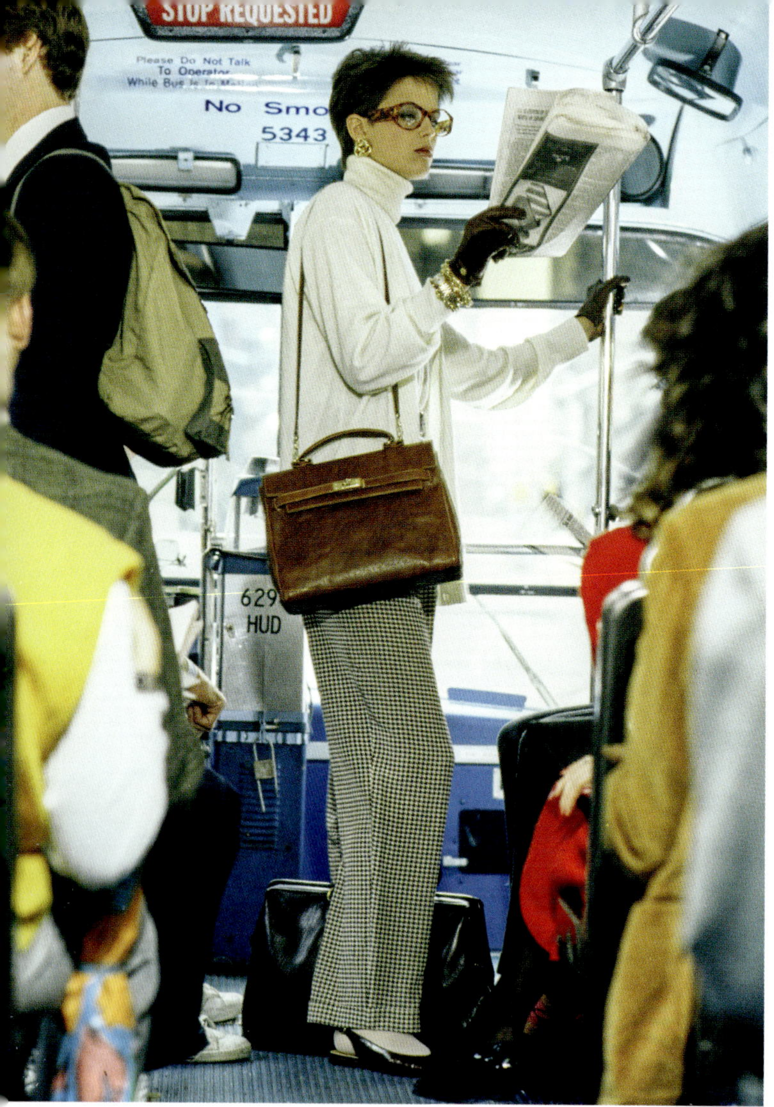

CHAPTER 4

Out on Your Own

1980–1998

INTRODUCTION —— 166
SUCCESS AND SINGLEDOM —— 170
OUTSTANDING YOUNG WORKING WOMEN —— 174
WASHINGTON REPORT —— 176
WOMEN-CENTERED SEX —— 178
DIET CULTURE —— 180
WHAT THE STARS EAT IN BED —— 182
MAKEOVERS —— 184
FASHION OF THE ERA —— 186
QUOTES OF THE ERA —— 196
NOT JUST ANOTHER PROM —— 198
DRIVING FORWARD ON RACE —— 200
CAMPUS RAPE —— 204
THE REPRODUCTIVE BATTLEGROUND —— 206
ICONIC COVERS —— 208
FAMOUS FACES —— 212

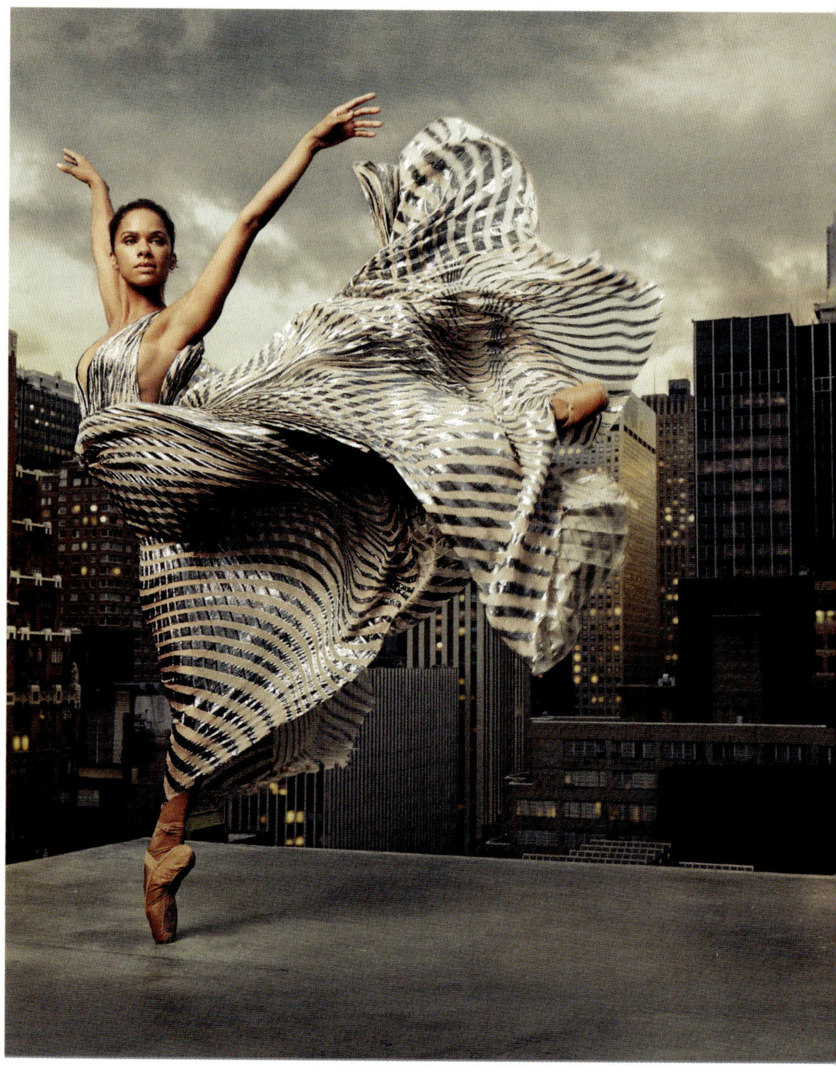

A CLOSER LOOK AT

Women of the Year

214

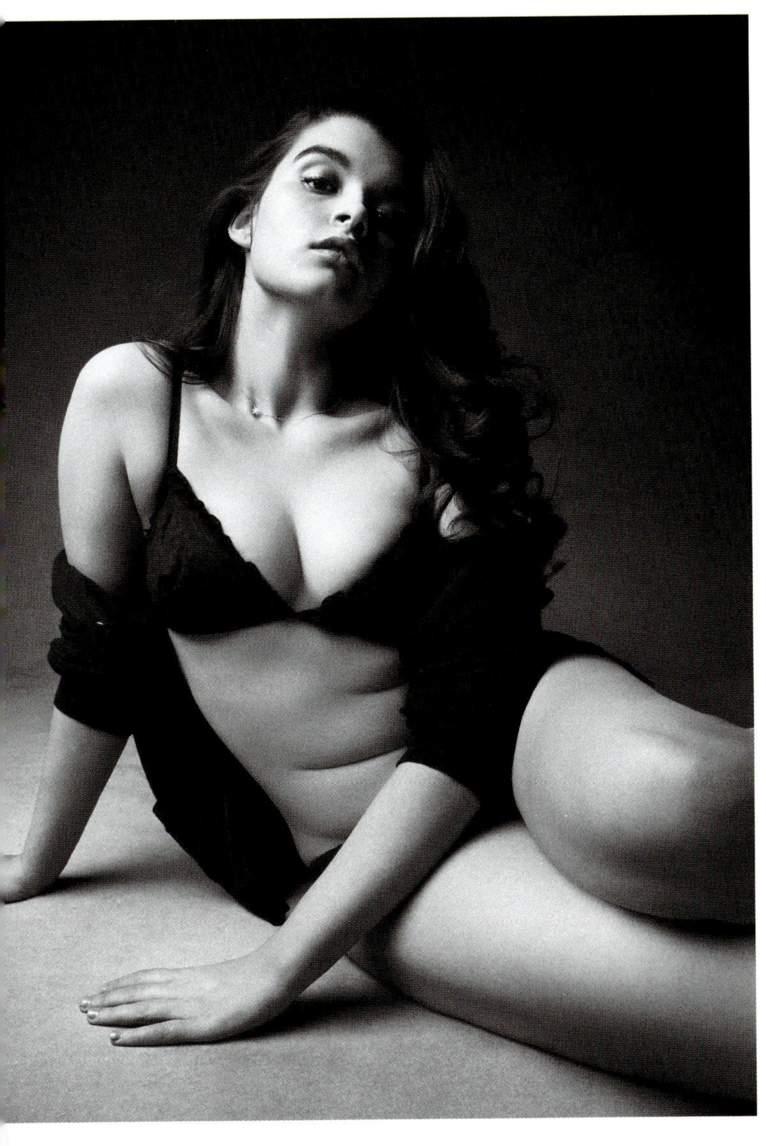

CHAPTER 5

All About You

1999–2009

INTRODUCTION — 226
THE CELEBRITY REVOLUTION — 230
POLITICS AND PRESIDENTS — 238
9/11 — 244
CINDI LEIVE — 248
SEX GOES SUPERSIZED — 250
CONTRACEPTION CONUNDRUM — 254
FASHION OF THE ERA — 256
PLASTIC SURGERY — 264
A BODY IMAGE RECKONING — 266
THE *GLAMOUR* GIRLS — 268
ENGAGEMENT CHICKEN — 270
SPORTING SUPERHEROES — 272

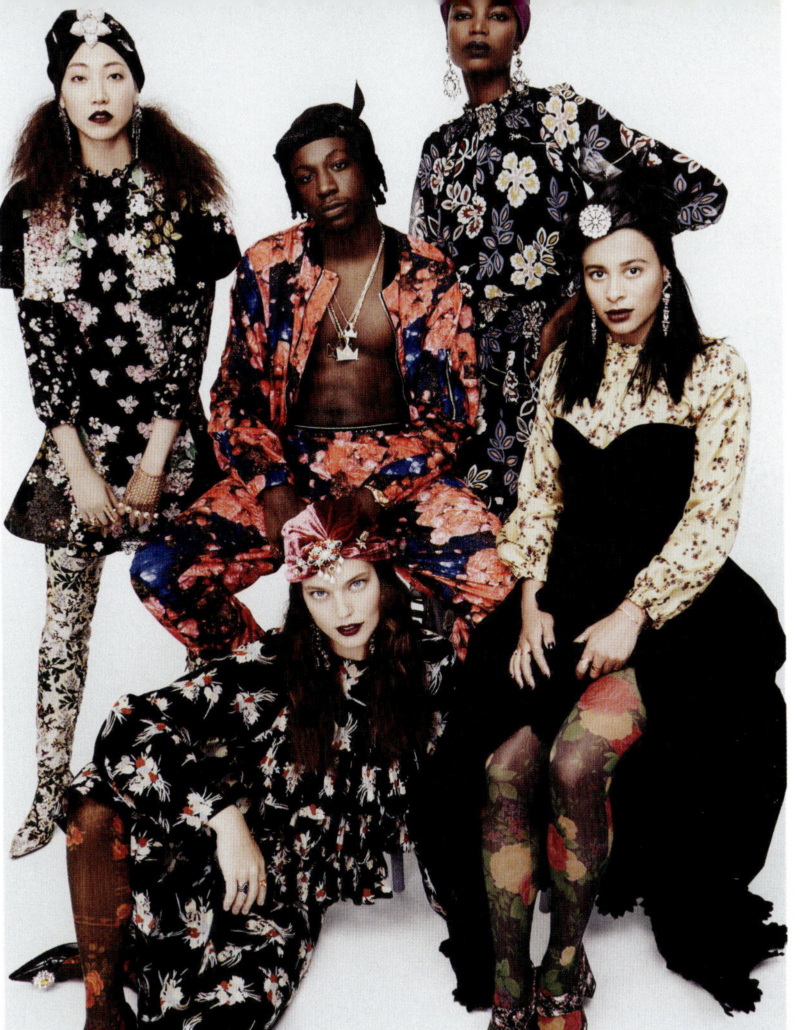

CHAPTER 6

Stronger Together

2010–PRESENT DAY

INTRODUCTION — 276
THE SOCIAL INFLUENCE — 280
ICONIC COVERS — 282
DOS AND DON'TS — 286
WOMEN AND POLITICS — 290
OBAMA: THIS IS WHAT A FEMINIST LOOKS LIKE — 294
QUOTES OF THE ERA — 298
A FEMINIST DEBATE — 300
THE F-WORD — 302
SAMANTHA BARRY — 304
GLAMOUR GOES DIGITAL — 306
FASHION OF THE ERA — 308
UNIQUE BEAUTY — 316
REPORTAGE AND ACTIVISM — 318

ACKNOWLEDGEMENTS — 328
PHOTOGRAPHY CREDITS — 332

"Glamour.

What Is It?
Who Has It?

"CAN WE GET IT? CAN WE USE IT? Capitalizing on this clamor for glamour, a new fashion magazine flashes on the publishing horizon—a magazine dedicated to the reporting of fashion, beauty and the mode of living of those cinema stars whose ways are envied and copied by millions of women throughout the entire world. 'Glamour', the magazine, will portray for age and youth alike, every fashion, every device, every product that will add to the 'bewitching power' of the reader."

So read an internal company memo in March 1939, announcing the launch of Condé Nast's brand-new magazine, *Glamour of Hollywood*. The first issue was a roaring success: "I don't think any of us have appreciated what an extraordinary accomplishment it was to sell 152,622 copies of the first issue of *GLAMOUR*," read a note to staff.

Glamour was, it seemed, the magazine that the women of America had been waiting for. But history is never so cut-and-dried. Within two years, the profound global impacts of the Second World War would alter the course of women's lives—with millions joining the workforce like never before—and the purpose and future of *Glamour* as well. No longer would a magazine solely about Hollywood's frivolities satisfy its readers (as rocky sales figures attested). American women wanted more from their lives—jobs, advancement, independence—and more from their publications. *Glamour* responded, with a remarkable transformation of its own to the magazine "for the girl with a job." Resolutely feminist, even before the word became widely used in the magazine's pages, the writers and editors of *Glamour* tackled equal rights, premarital sex, the importance of college and education, how to get a job (and how to dress for it), and (if imperfectly) race and prejudice. They'd finally hit on a winning formula, and, even more significantly, they'd tapped into a new generation of women with a completely new mindset: free-thinking, ambitious, and desperate to break through the many societal and legal barriers still holding them back.

It wouldn't be a straightforward path to equality, though, and in many ways the history of *Glamour* is irrevocably intertwined with the history of women's empowerment and liberation—not least because the female staff were themselves living through, and often fighting for, their own revolution, as well as documenting it.

In the 1940s, for example, they created a truly groundbreaking magazine for ambitious career women who entered the workforce during the war. But when the war ended, the women who'd fought so hard for their jobs were often displaced by returning men—and a patriarchal push to return to the status quo of old. *Glamour* struggled with this reality and, for a time, even bent to the moment. One notable 1956 cover declared the magazine to be filled with "special fashions picked to please men."

But as the women's liberation and student power movements rose up, and the sexual revolution transformed society, *Glamour* too broke free—exploring sex and sexuality, celebrating outstanding young career women, and embracing liberated fashion and beauty. Writers offered abortion advice, and told stories of vital national interest on the availability of reproductive services. When the Equal Credit Opportunity Act passed in 1974, the magazine celebrated women living—and spending their money—independently. Then, as the technological and social media revolutions put women in control of their own images, and amplified their voices in ways that had never been accessible before, *Glamour* found its own voice online—and grew into its new life as a digital publication. At the same time, movements such as Black Lives Matter and #MeToo began to tear down historic barriers to advancement. The women leading these organizations, as well as those whose lives were transformed by their existence, were featured prominently in *Glamour*. From the launch of the magazine in 1939 to today, *Glamour* has chronicled the most important evolutions of women's lives and freedoms.

Glamour, of course, hasn't been perfect. The staff strived to open a meaningful discourse on race and prejudice in the 1940s, yet it wasn't until the late 1960s that women of color were the authors of these vitally important pieces, were members of staff, or appeared on the covers. The magazine also, for example, offered broad support to all women when it came to finding success in the workplace, but over the course of several decades had a painfully narrow definition of physical attractiveness.

But there are also many achievements in *Glamour*'s lifetime that belong, for the right reasons, in the history books. It was the first American magazine to have a Black woman cover star—Katiti Kironde, in August 1968. It was one of the first American magazines to publish and grow the work of a young writer by the name of Gloria Steinem, who was a *Glamour* contributing editor from 1963 to 1970. It was one of the first magazines to publish early illustrations by Andy Warhol. Presidents John F. Kennedy, Lyndon B. Johnson, Richard Nixon, Ronald Reagan, George W. Bush, and Barack Obama have all appeared in its pages, sharing unique insights into their lives with *Glamour*'s readers. The now iconic Women of the Year Awards, launched in 1990, have become the beating heart of *Glamour* annually. And the magazine has won its own national accolades—becoming in 1981 the first women's magazine ever to win the General Excellence category at the National Magazine Awards, for a publication with over a million readers. The magazine received many more awards and nominations over the subsequent decades. But for all this seriousness, what *Glamour* knew—and still knows—best is that women are multifaceted. Over the course of the last 85 years, what makes *Glamour* so memorable is that it has successfully balanced decades of advocacy for women with glamorous yet affordable fashion for working women on a budget, accessible beauty, practical life advice, and iconic franchises, like the Jake column—giving a man's view on sex and relationships from 1956 to 2016—and the famous Dos and Don'ts, which appeared in the first ever issue in 1939, and were only laid to rest in 2018 (an extraordinary run of nearly 80 years). This unique mix has remained at the heart of *Glamour* to this day.

Eighty-five years of publishing, over 900 print issues, and tens of thousands of articles can't easily be distilled, but we hope this book does justice to *Glamour*'s dedication to women, and the evolution of women's lives and power.

Glamour's editor in chief, Alice Thompson, starts to spend increasing amounts of time in Hollywood, much to the frustration of senior executives at Condé Nast—who are struggling with *Glamour*'s inconsistent sales, and readers' lack of interest in the lives of Hollywood stars. A memo from Dr. Agha, the art director of Condé Nast publications, from February 1940 lamented:

"

The trouble with Glamour is that Mrs. Thompson is not on the job in New York but spends most of her time in Hollywood.... The absence of Mrs. Thompson from New York is a very serious matter.... In New York, the magazine is running without anybody actually editing it.

A new era begins, focusing on women in the workplace and their careers.

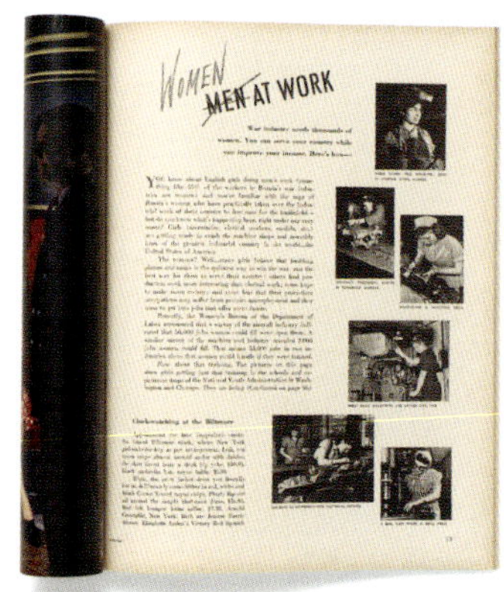

1939

1940

1941

1942

1943

The first issue of *Glamour of Hollywood* is published. Just three names appeared on the first masthead: editor in chief Alice Thompson, associate editor Irene Kittle, and art editor Charlotte Getleson (though it grew to add a fourth, merchandise editor Ottilie Aks, by the second issue).

On February 28, 1941, the same day Condé Nast announces the appointment of Elizabeth Penrose as *Glamour*'s new managing editor, *Glamour*'s editor in chief Alice Thompson is asked for her resignation.

Glamour becomes the magazine "for the girl with a job." Women were encouraged to pursue whatever jobs they were most passionate about, including flying.

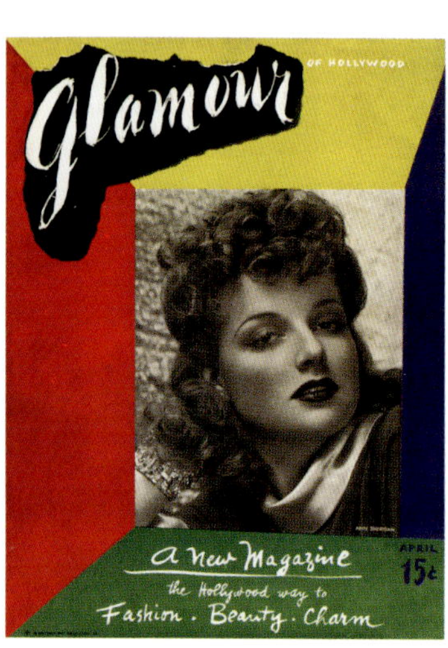

February 28, 1941

Dear Alice:

You know, I think, that during the past six weeks, all of my time has been given to a study of GLAMOUR'S editorial situation. The object of this study has been twofold: (1) To get an accurate appraisal of the manner in which GLAMOUR, through its editorial treatment, has succeeded in satisfying the group of young women we thought waiting for such a periodical: In a word, to obtain an appraisal of the journalistic skill and judgment that had been applied to the development of GLAMOUR; (2) To make a fair and just appraisal of your own responsibility for the journalistic short-comings that, from the beginning, were evident in the accomplishment of that purpose.

You will recall my frank conference with you when I began to make these studies. In that conference, I told you that my discussions with you, on editorial and business problems, had always left me most favorably impressed with your intelligence and judgment, but that your accomplishment, as editor of GLAMOUR, did not support such a favorable impression, in fact, in many instances, contradicted it. I was, I admitted, puzzled and confused.

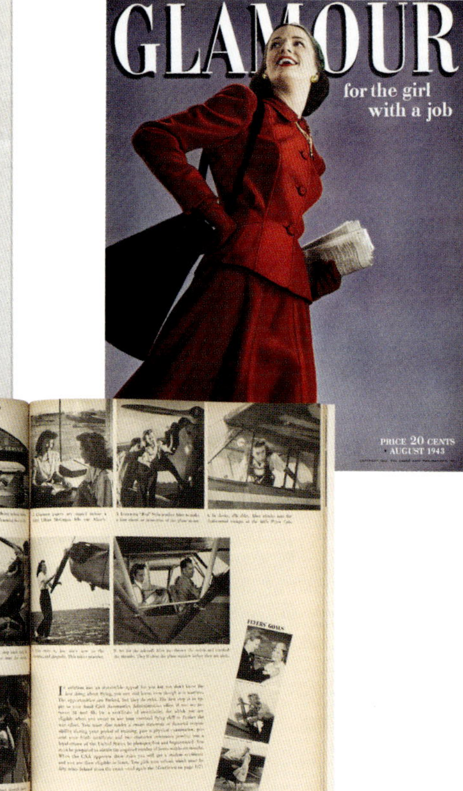

In September, *Glamour* publishes Andy Warhol's first illustration for the magazine.

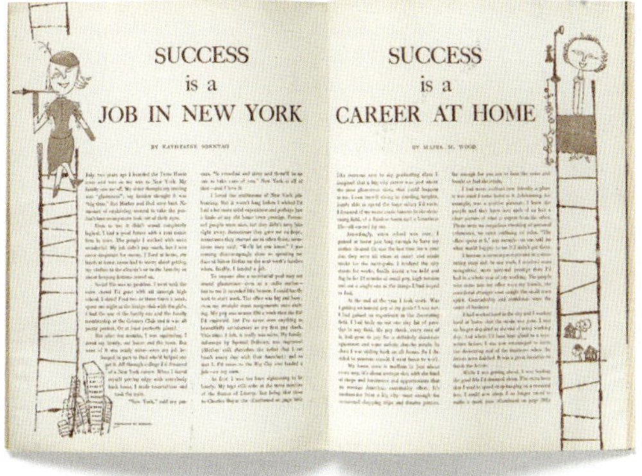

In February, *Glamour* introduces a new anonymous columnist, "Jake." His role was to tell women what men really thought about love, sex, dating, and more. The column ran for 60 years.

1948

1949

1953

1956

1957

During the 1940s, the legendary Black photographer Gordon Parks worked for *Glamour*, capturing fashion and reportage, including "Ceiling and Visibility Unlimited," a portfolio of aviation careers that *Glamour*'s job editor, Mary E. Campbell, sought him out for. This image of a model wearing a dress in Dupont polka dot fabric is from June 1948.

Elizabeth Penrose steps down due to illness. Kathleen Aston Casey takes the helm as the new editor in chief. Penrose's fiercely feminist *Glamour* begins to fade, as increasing numbers of articles focus on women through the lens of men.

The 10 Best-Dressed College Girls competition launches.

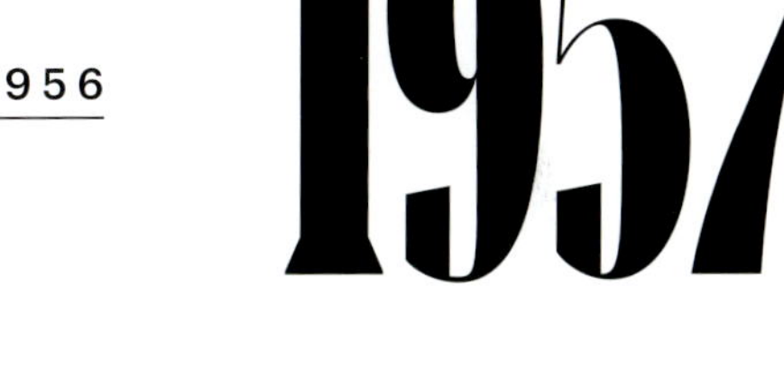

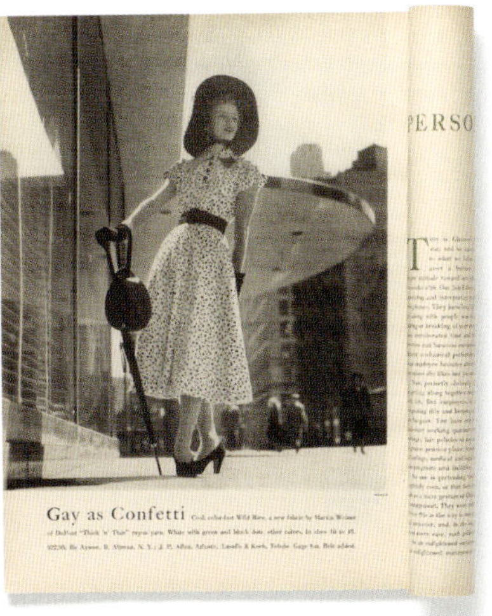

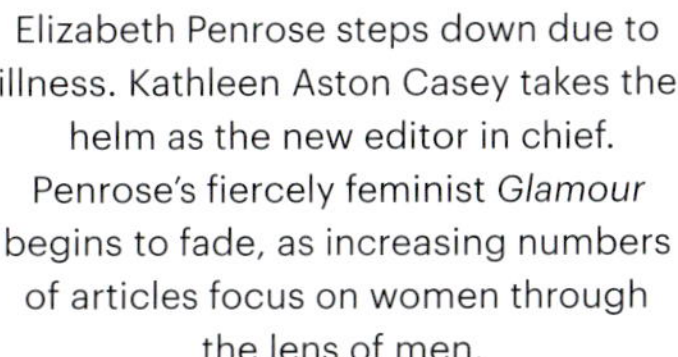

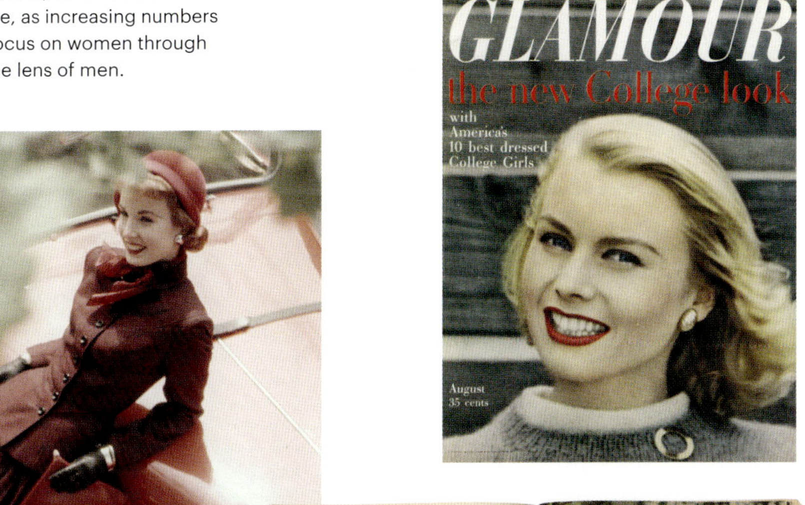

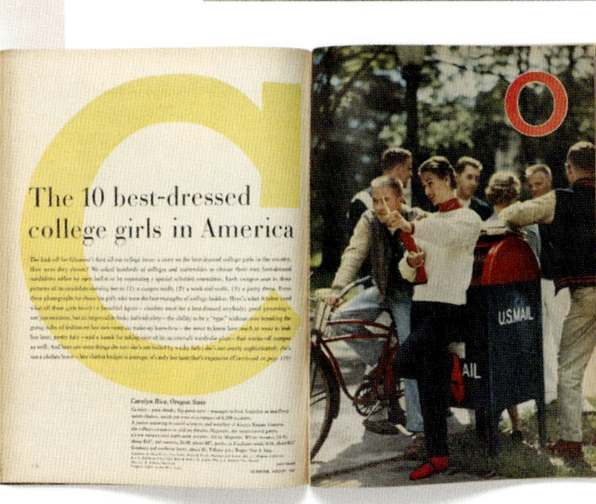

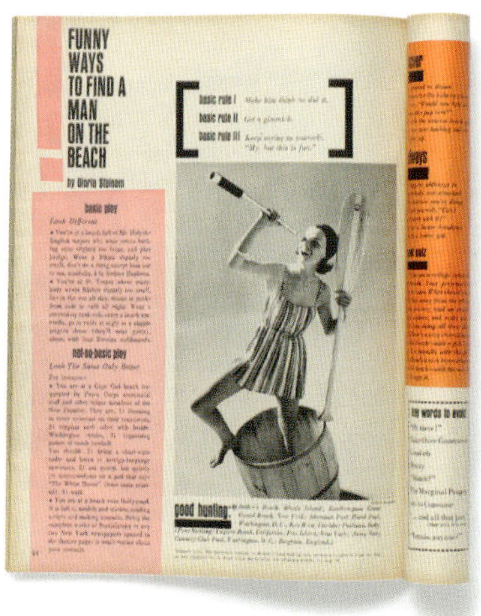

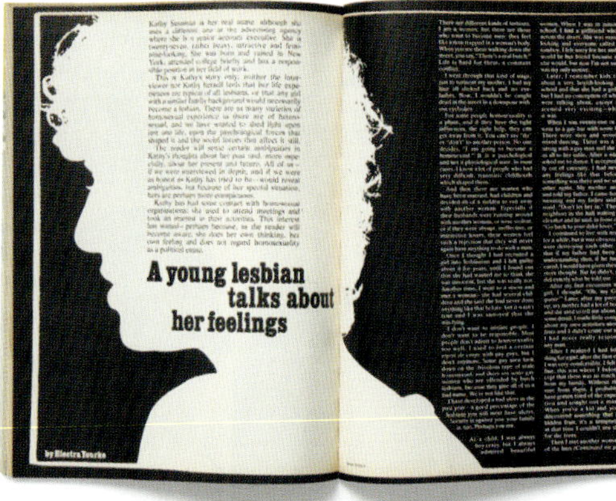

Ruth Whitney
becomes *Glamour*'s
fourth editor in chief.

"

The problems and lives of women are always changing. Making an impact on those lives, keeping pace with and addressing those problems is what makes editing *Glamour* an endless, everlasting thrill.

An early piece about the LGBTQ+ experience is published in *Glamour*, titled "A young lesbian talks about her feelings."

1963

1967

1968

1971

1972

Gloria Steinem's writing first appears in *Glamour*. She remained a contributing editor until 1970.

Katiti Kironde is honored as one of *Glamour*'s 10 Best-Dressed College Girls, and makes history as the first Black woman to cover an American magazine. The issue becomes a bestseller.

Beverly Johnson makes her modeling debut in *Glamour,* and becomes one of the magazine's most prolific cover stars (with 15 covers in all).

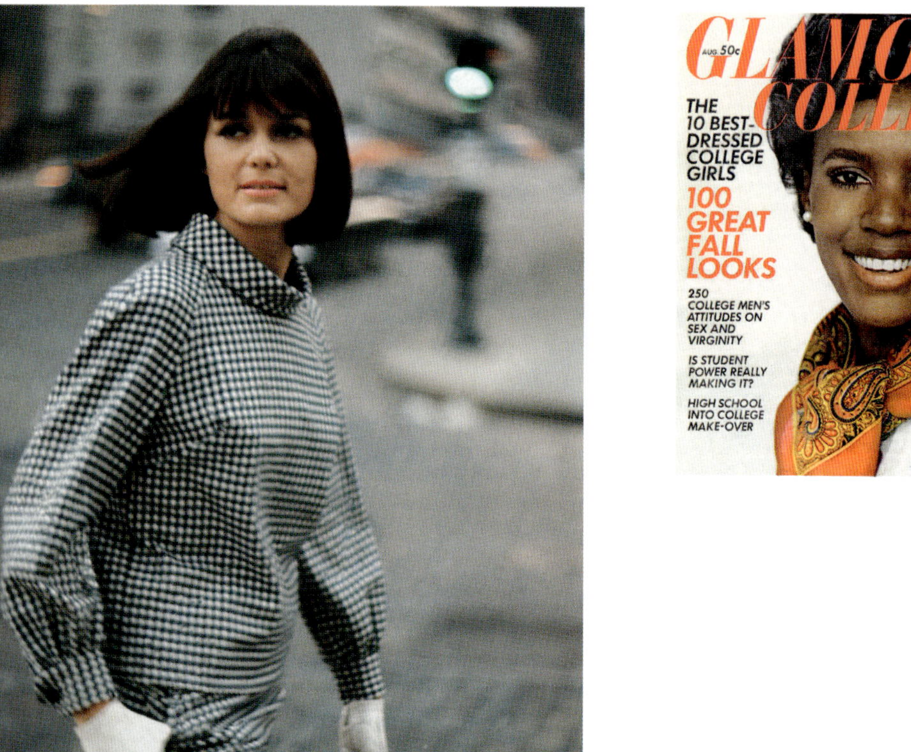

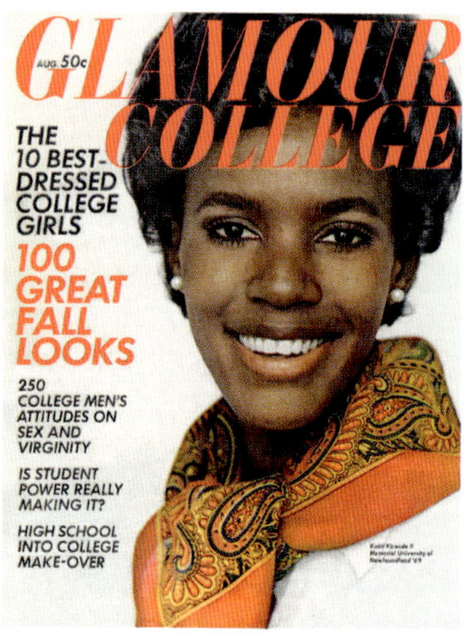

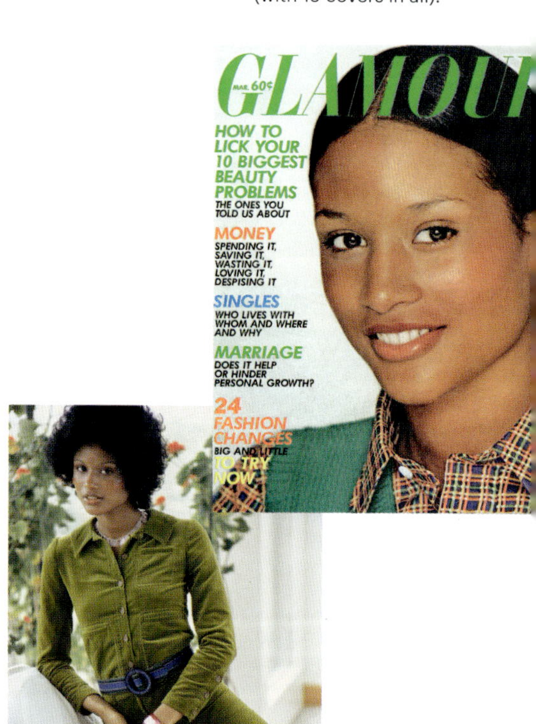

Glamour launches the first Washington Report column. A year later, *Glamour* wins the National Magazine Award for General Excellence, one-million-plus circulation category, for the first time. At the time it was the only women's magazine ever to have won.

Glamour publishes "Black Working Women: A report from the front," an important examination of how Black women were being discriminated against in the workforce.

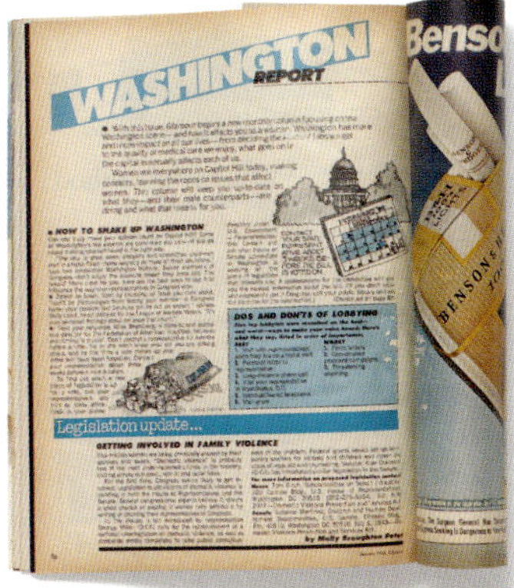

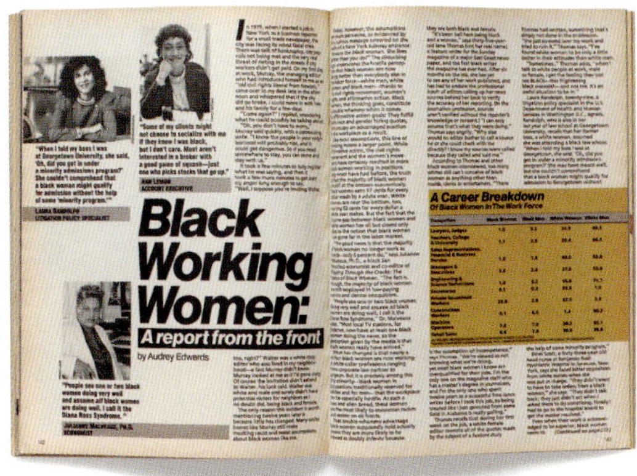

1975

1980

1984

1987

1990

Glamour launches the Outstanding Young Working Women competition.

A 20-year-old singer and former teen model by the name of Whitney Houston is photographed for *Glamour*. She tells the magazine she wants to embrace an image that's "young, kind of innocent but sexy."

The first ever Woman of the Year Awards launches.

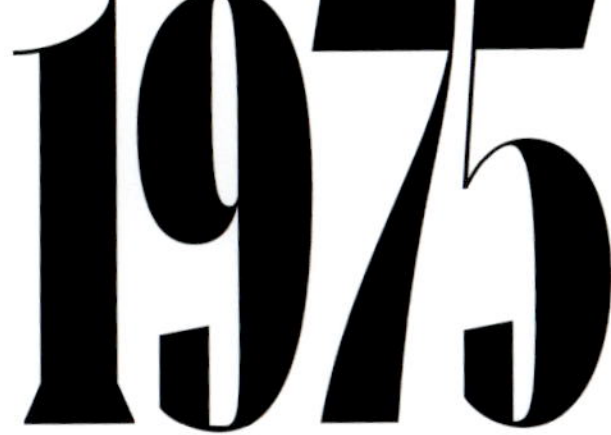

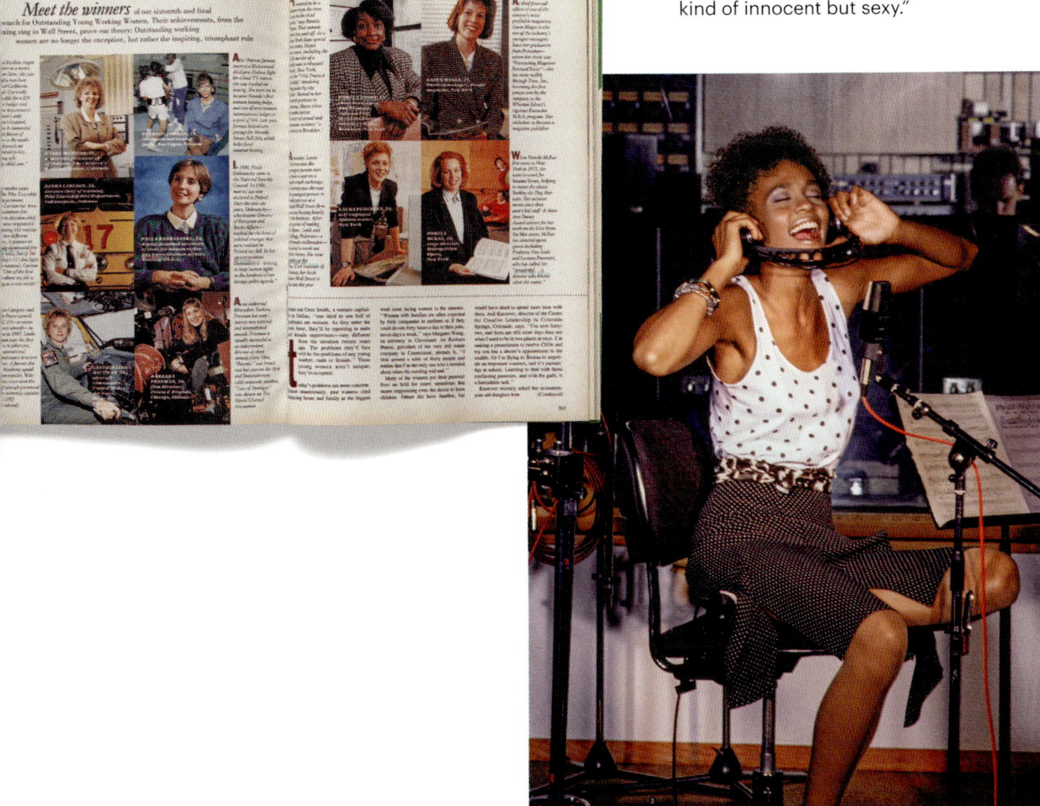

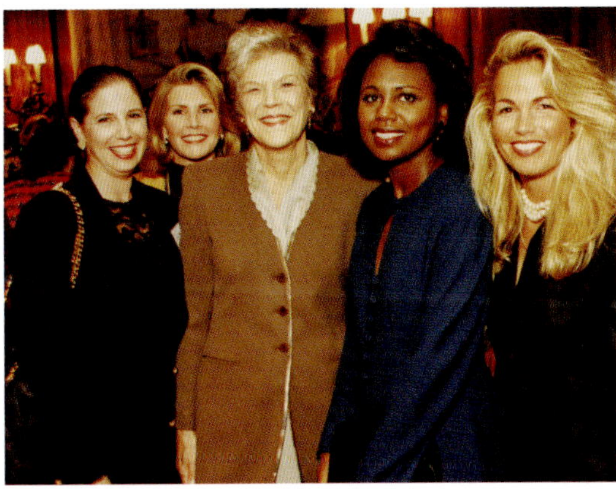

↑

Ruth Whitney and guests at the 1991 Women of the Year Awards.

Glamour wins the public interest category at the National Magazine Awards for a trio of articles on abortion.

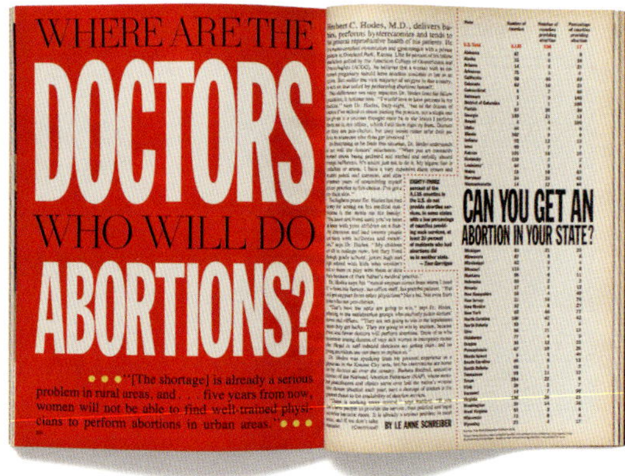

Bonnie Fuller becomes editor in chief of Glamour. A year later, George W. Bush is interviewed by *Glamour* on board his presidential campaign plane. He gets into a verbal altercation with the reporter. The interview receives significant press coverage. That same year, Beyoncé Knowles, Kelly Rowland, and Michelle Williams, the members of Destiny's Child, are first photographed and interviewed for *Glamour*.

1990

1992

1993

1999

2001

Ruth Whitney shares her rules for editing in a speech to the Magazine Publishing Congress. She writes, memorably:

year eliminate some of the worst dogs. The middle kind of takes care of itself.

7. The risks. Try ideas you've never tried before – cover changes, design changes, idea changes, columnist changes.

8. Be willing to offend. If you haven't offended either your advertisers or your readers in the past 6 months, chances are you're not doing your job.

9. Don't underestimate the importance of packaging. Your design, photography and layout speak for your magazine before anyone reads a word. A good idea can seem great with the right packaging. A great idea will only be good in mediocre packaging.

Ruth Bader Ginsburg is interviewed in October, the same year she was appointed as the Supreme Court's second-ever woman justice. She tells her interviewer, Rice University senior and 1993 *Glamour* College Women of the Year winner Angela Hunt, "The days of not hiring women are over. I don't know how many times I've had the experience of people laughing at me. You don't give up. You keep trying." In the same issue, a doctor writes for *Glamour* about why she chose to become an abortion provider.

Cindi Leive, who began her career as a writer *Glamour,* is appointed editor in chief.

As she is sending her first issue as editor in chi press, two planes are flown into the World Tra Center on 9/11. Production is paused while t *Glamour* team reports on the attack.

The actor, writer, and director Olivia Wilde performs a headline-grabbing monologue at a *Glamour*-hosted event. She tells the crowd of her failed first marriage:

"

Sometimes your vagina dies. Then you know it's time to go. There's no reason to sacrifice your womanhood and femininity for some sort of weird feeling of responsibility to something that may not be right. I feel like far too many women do that…. [Men] are not allowed to be the only ones thinking with their genitals."

Jane Fonda revisits her iconic 1959 cover. Later that year, *Glamour* launches its award-winning paid leave campaign.

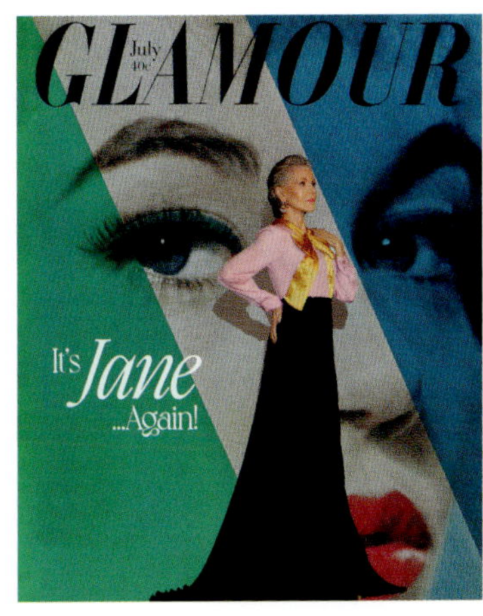

2008

2012

2018

2022

2024

Barack Obama is interviewed by *Glamour* as he campaigns for a historic presidency.

Samantha Barry is appointed editor in chief. A year later, *Glamour* publishes its final print issue. The same year, it launches a suite of hit podcasts and its critically acclaimed F-Word series, tackling the lack of size representation for women in fashion.

Glamour turns 85!

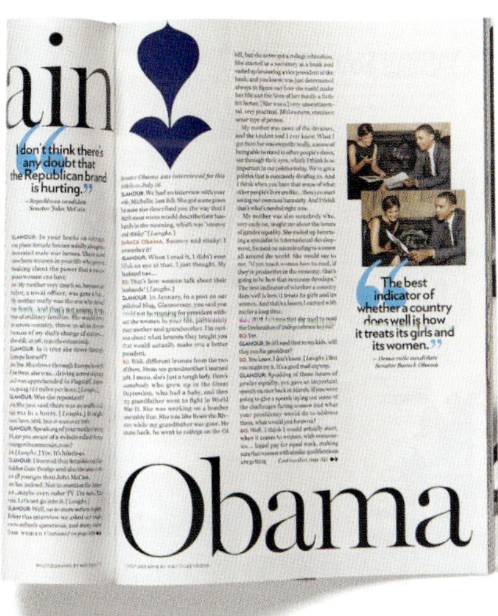

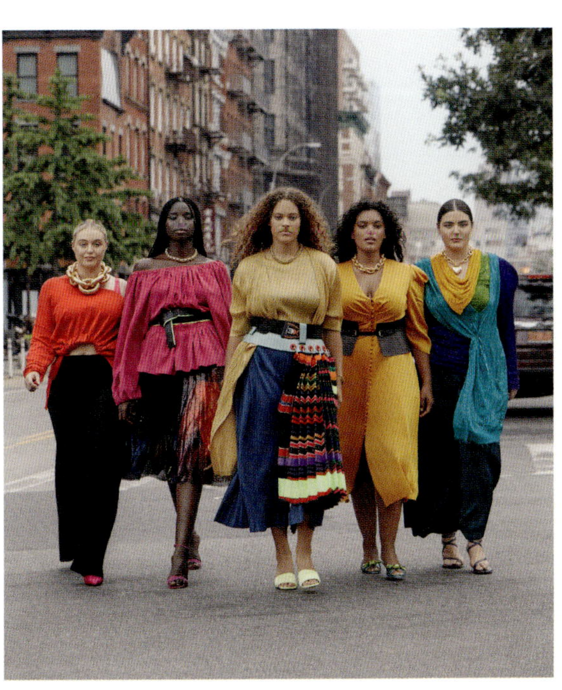

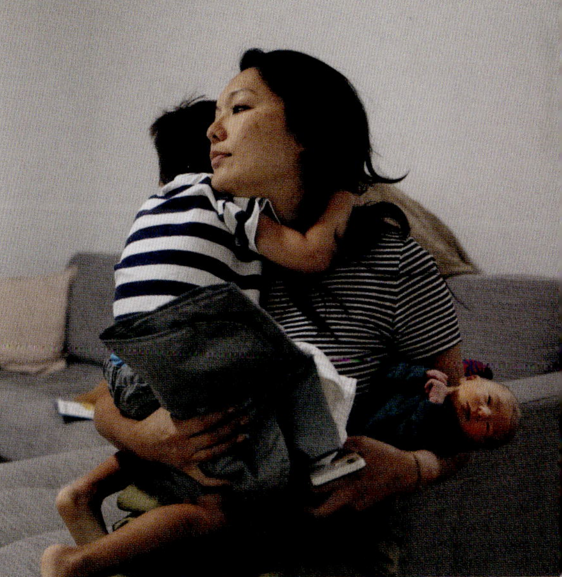

↑

Tiffany Mrotek, from the award-winning paid leave project.

The Glamour Bookshelf

A
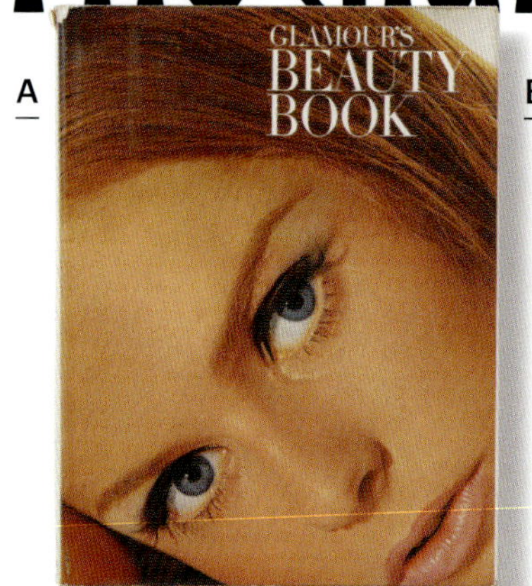

B
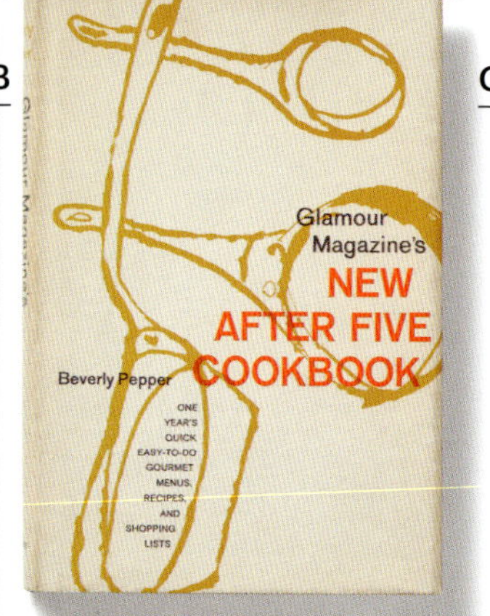

C
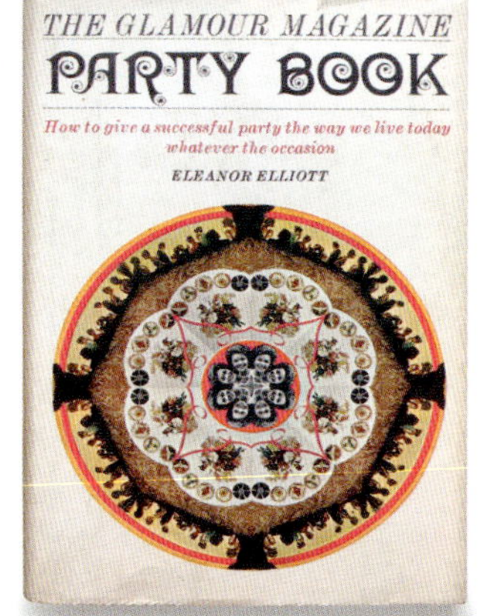

D
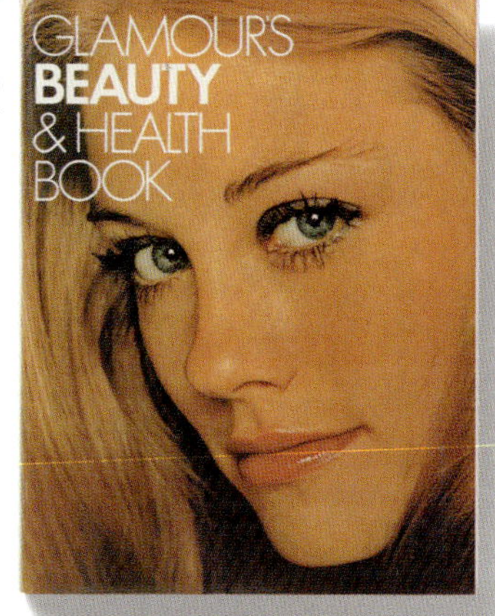

E
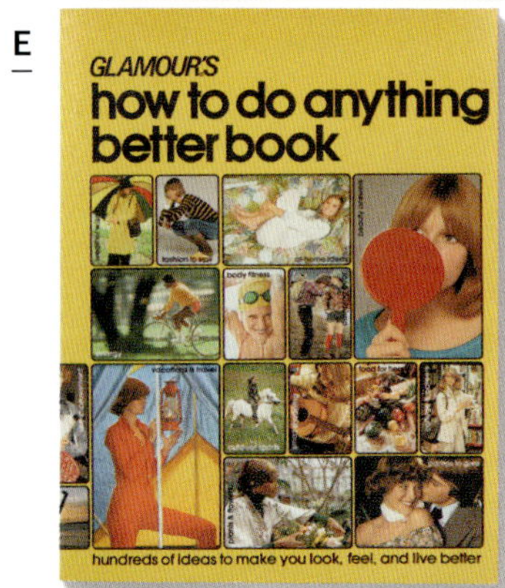

F
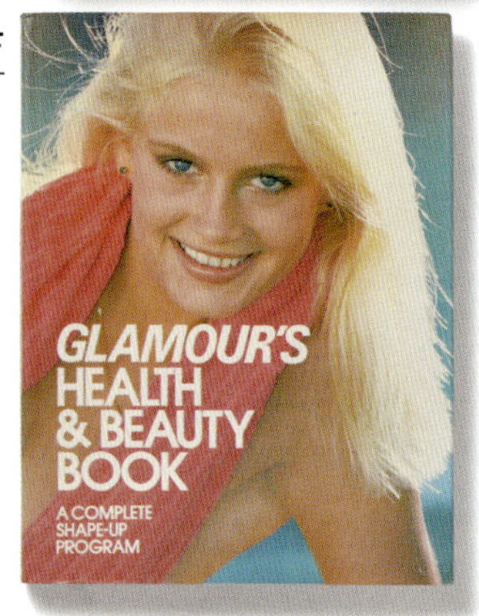

G
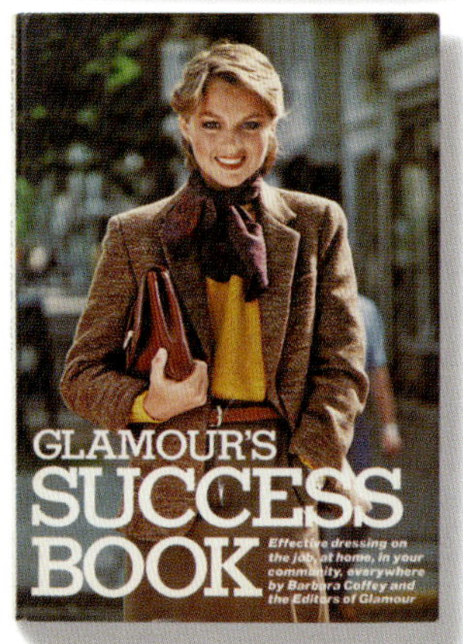

H
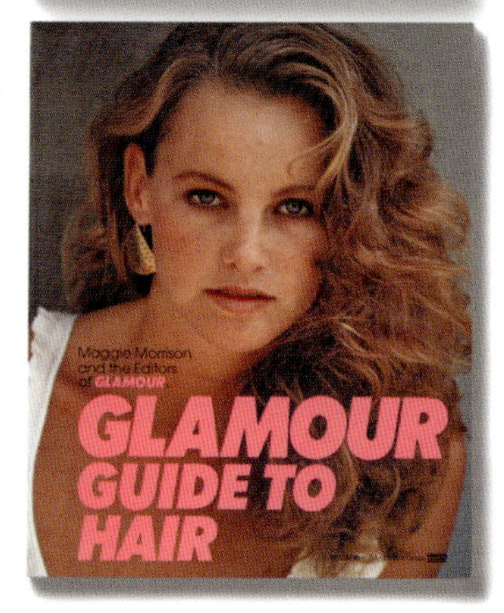

I
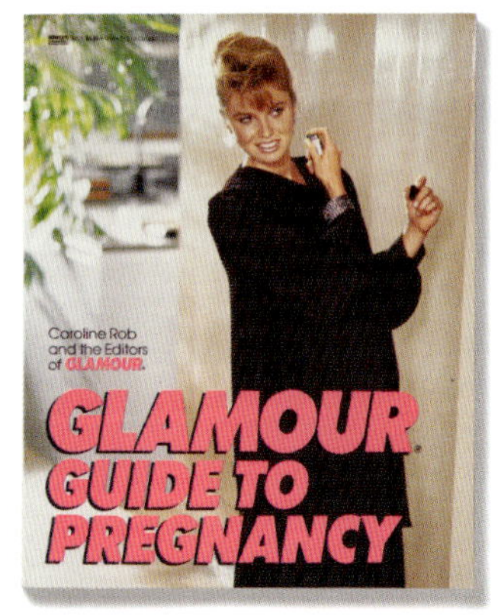

J
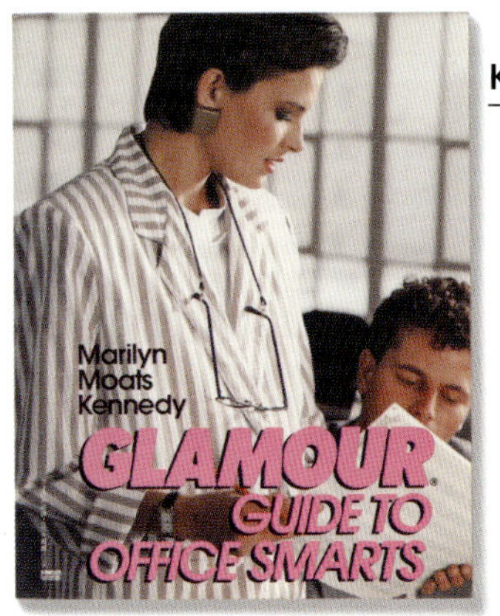

K
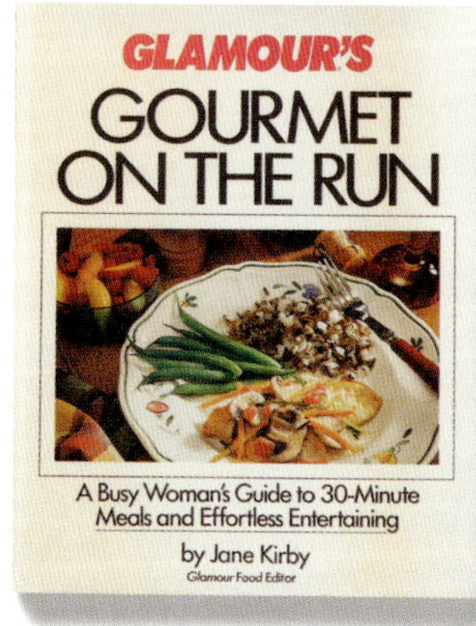

L
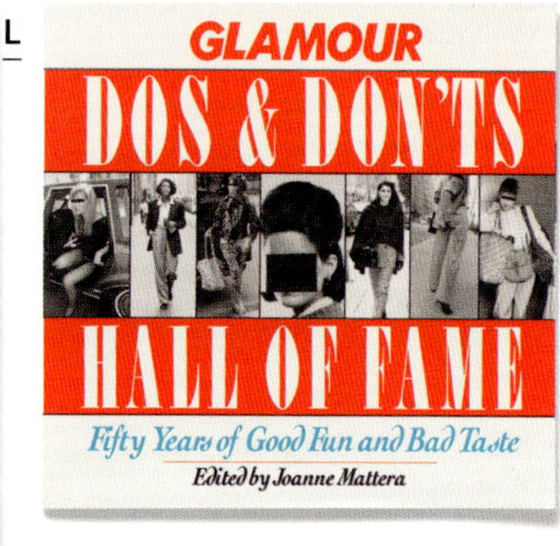

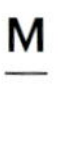

M
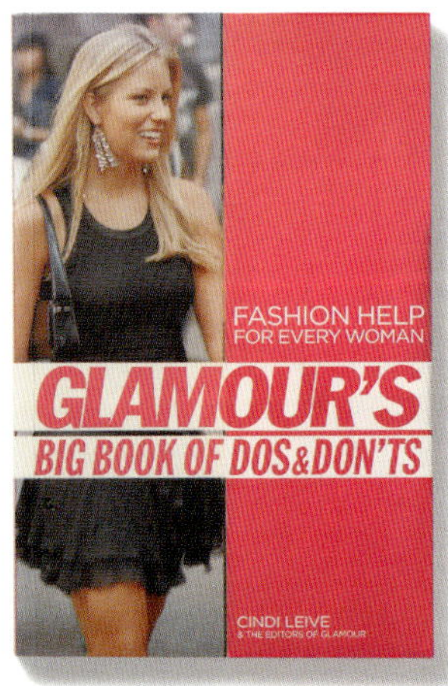

N
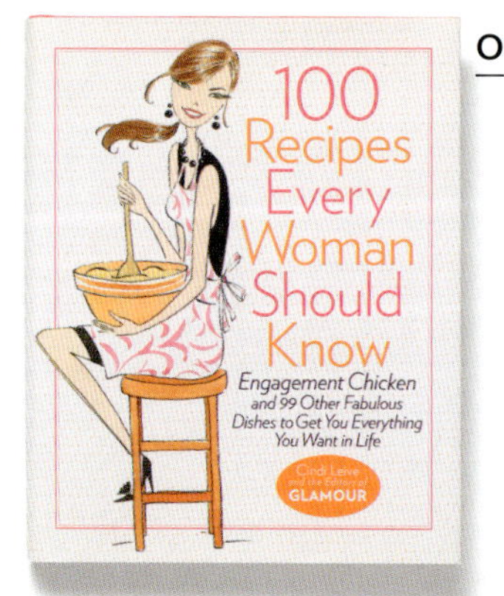

O
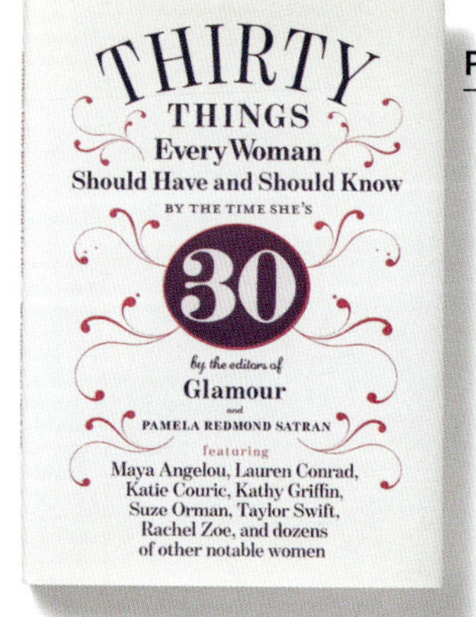

P
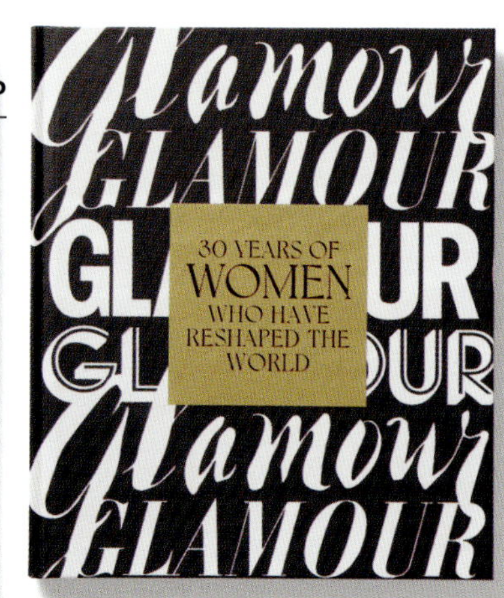

"

Glamour Goes Global

Since we're diving into the history books, this isn't the first book *Glamour* has published. Take a look at some of the most iconic from the archives.

Glamour's Beauty Book, 1957 (A). *Glamour Magazine's New After Five Cookbook,* 1963 (B). *The Glamour Magazine Party Book,* 1965 (C). *Glamour's Beauty & Health Book,* 1968 (D). *Glamour's How to Do Anything Better Book,* 1971 (E). *Glamour's Health & Beauty Book: A Complete Shape-Up Program,* 1973 (F). *Glamour's Success Book: Effective dressing on the job, at home, in your community, everywhere,* 1979 (G). *Glamour Guide to Hair,* 1986 (H). *Glamour Guide to Pregnancy,* 1986 (I). *Glamour Guide to Office Smarts,* 1986 (J). *Glamour's Gourmet on the Run: A Busy Woman's Guide to 30-Minute Meals and Effortless Entertaining,* 1987 (K). *Glamour Dos & Don'ts Hall of Fame: Fifty Years of Good Fun and Bad Taste,* 1992 (L). *Glamour's Big Book of Dos & Don'ts: Fashion Help for Every Woman,* 2006 (M). *100 Recipes Every Woman Should Know,* 2011 (N). *Thirty Things Every Woman Should Have and Should Know By the Time She's 30,* 2012 (O). *30 Years of Women Who Have Reshaped the World,* 2021 (P).

1976

The Italian edition of *Glamour* launches, under the title *Lei* (She), but is officially renamed *Glamour* in 1992

1998

Glamour Mexico/Latin America launches

2001

Glamour UK and Germany launch

2002

Glamour Spain launches

2003

Glamour Poland launches

2004

Hungary, France, South Africa, and Russia launch their editions of *Glamour*

2005

Glamour Netherlands launches

2006

Glamour Romania launches

2009

Glamour Bulgaria launches

2012

Glamour Brazil launches

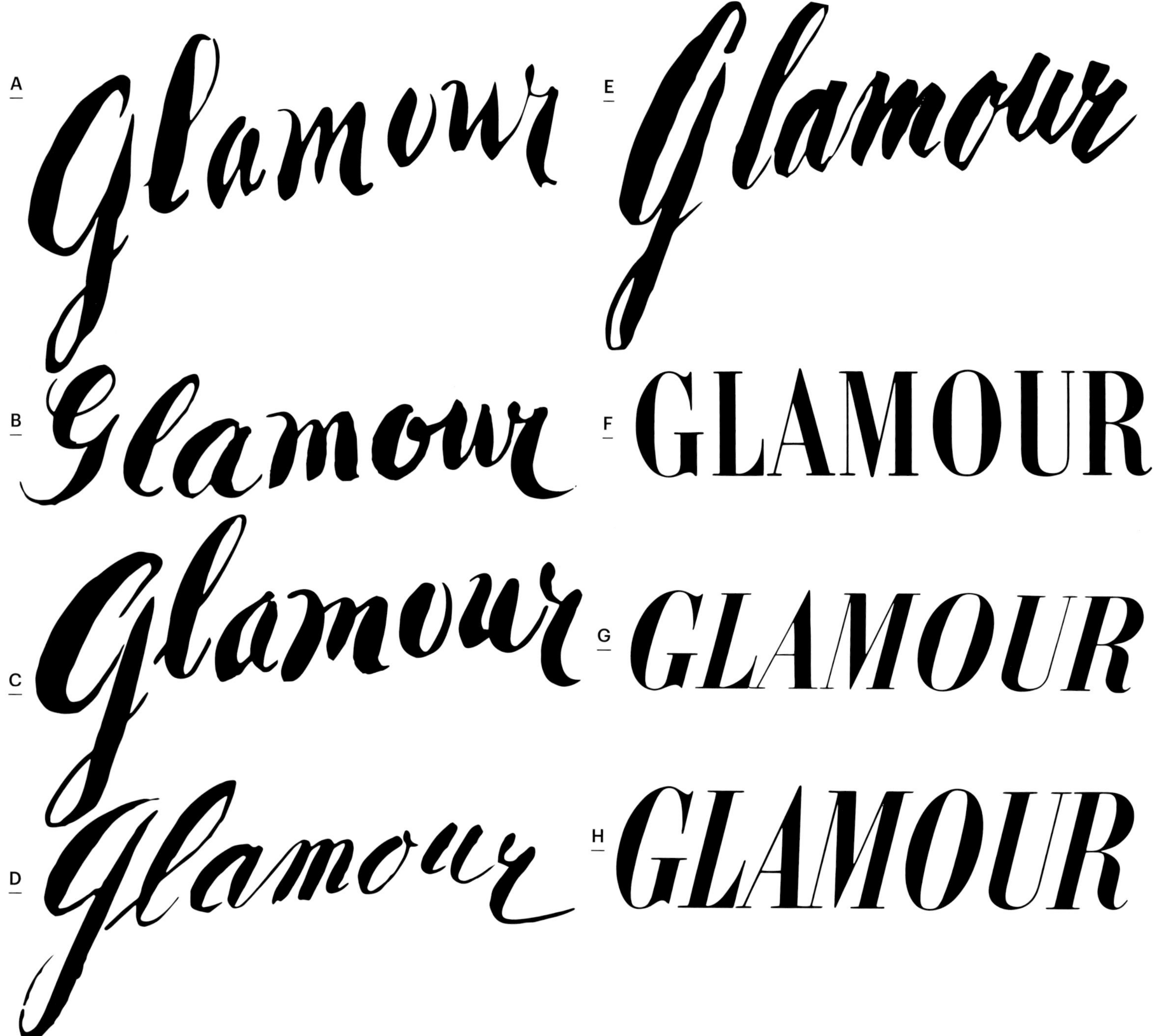

IT'S FASCINATING TO CHART the evolution of *Glamour*'s logo over the course of the title's lifetime. During the first few months of the magazine's existence, the word *Glamour* was hand-lettered on each issue's cover. There were some issue-to-issue variances (A, B, C, and D) depending on the overall cover design, but they largely adhered to the original style. In November 1939, logo E began to be used more consistently. March 1943's Career Issue introduced *Glamour*'s new typeset logo, all in caps (F), aligning with the magazine's evolving identity as a publication for working women. Later that year it would rebrand as the magazine "for the girl with a job."

Less than a year later, on the April 1944 cover, the same typography was shifted and set in italics—a small tweak that stood the test of time, becoming the longest-standing logo in *Glamour*'s history (G). Throughout the 1950s and 1960s, the *Glamour* logo did not change, except for a brief stint in 1953 and 1954 when designers experimented with stretching the typography taller (H) and taller (I) before ultimately coming back to where they began. The March

GLAMOUR (I)

GLAMOUR (J)

GLAMOUR (K)

GLAMOUR (L)

GLAMOUR (M)

GLAMOUR (N)

GLAMOUR (O)

GLAMOUR (P)

GLAMOUR (Q)

GLAMOUR (R)

1976 cover marked a more substantial shift in branding when the existing serif typography was replaced with sans serif letters (J). The changes that followed over the course of the next two and a half decades were subtle, bolding and refining the type like on the March 1980 (K) and February 1989 (L) covers, and experimenting with typesetting the letters in italics (N) versus standard (M).

The May 2000 issue featured a new sans serif condensed logo (O), which would be used globally over the course of the next two decades during a time of expansion as new international editions of *Glamour* launched. Meanwhile, the US edition of *Glamour* switched back to their previous logo for several years before replacing it with a heavier-faced, shorter logo on the cover of the September 2008 issue (P). In May 2018, the US edition unveiled a logo (Q), bridging the gap between the design experience of *Glamour*'s print issue and online features. With the further aim of aligning the brand under one unified aesthetic, in March 2023 the latest *Glamour* logo (R) was released and is now used globally across its 11 regions.

THE GIRL WITH A JOB

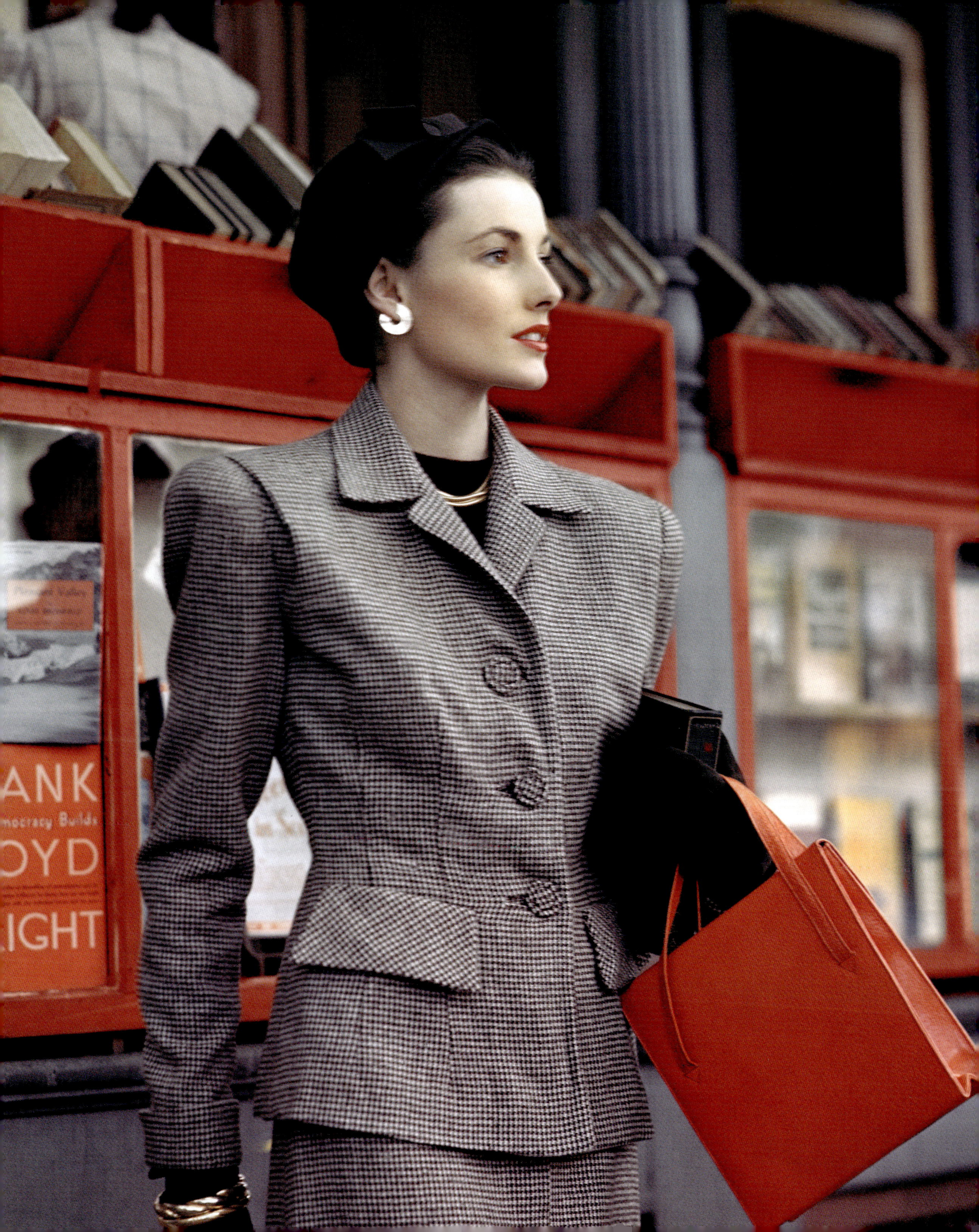
ANK
mocracy Builds
OYD
RIGHT

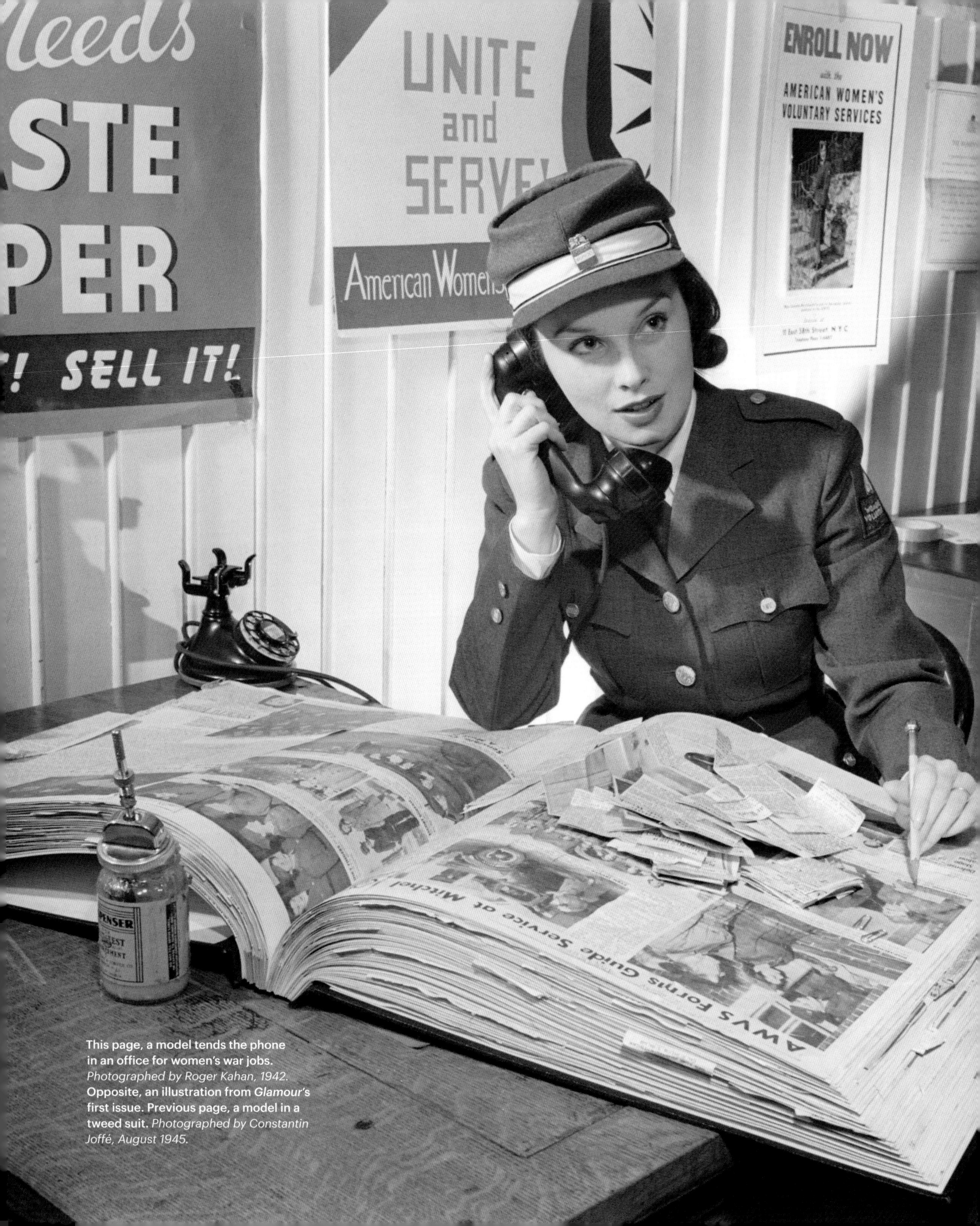

This page, a model tends the phone in an office for women's war jobs. *Photographed by Roger Kahan, 1942.* Opposite, an illustration from *Glamour*'s first issue. Previous page, a model in a tweed suit. *Photographed by Constantin Joffé, August 1945.*

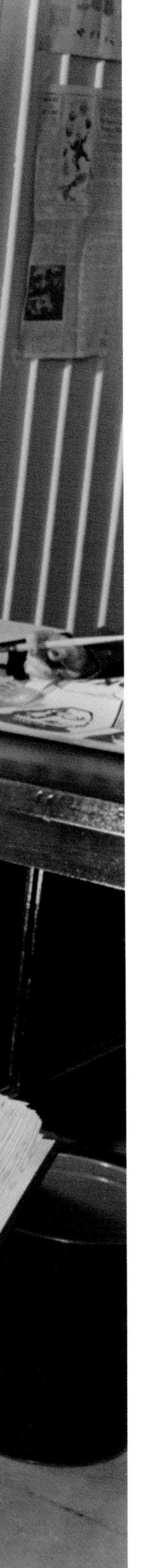

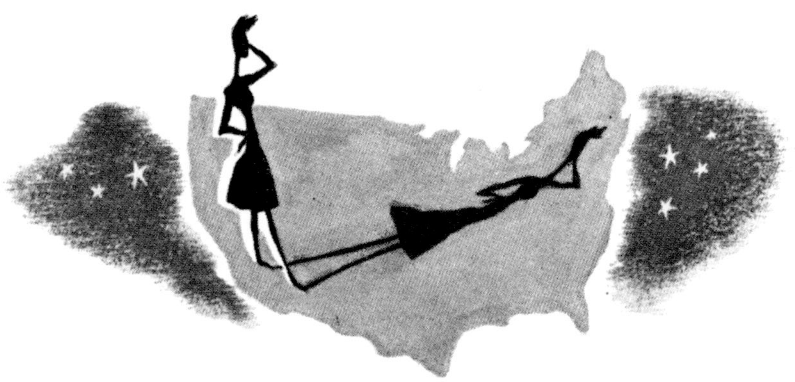

"This new magazine, *Glamour*, first admits what all of us know—that most of the happy experiences in daily living come to the attractive woman. It may not be fair or right—but it's true." This was the bold opening gambit of America's brand-new magazine, *Glamour of Hollywood*, in April 1939.

THE GOAL OF THE MAGAZINE WAS TO DELIVER "feminine loveliness" for every reader, but especially those "who count the dollars." Hollywood stars, like Oscar-winning actor Olivia de Havilland, were called upon to share their glamorous secrets, and the staff, under the editorship of Alice Thompson, took readers through the dos and don'ts of Hollywood style—which became a franchise that would define *Glamour* for generations to come.

But glamorous as the magazine was, its approach to womanhood was reductive. And reflective as it may have been of the times, it didn't deliver the consistent big sales the team had hoped for. Women clearly wanted more. Their lives were changing—the outbreak of the Second World War in 1939 called men to service, and women to the workplace. As the *Glamour* team itself noted in an internal brainstorm meeting, millions of women were now at work, and an opportunity to deliver a different kind of publication presented itself. A new editor, Elizabeth (Betty) Penrose, was appointed in 1941 and brought with her a bold new approach.

Work, career, and education became a huge focus. And as American women were increasingly called into the workplace, *Glamour* didn't just report on this evolution, it argued for a recalibration of the status quo. In March 1942, an article by Gladys Schultz celebrated the huge advances made by women: "A hundred years ago there was no question about a woman's place being in the home…. Today it's commonplace for women to plan cities, probe crime, produce plays, perform appendectomies, perfect patents and pay taxes—to say nothing of wearing pants. They sit on judges' benches, in the President's cabinet, at the head of large industries, at the helm of newspapers and magazines, and it's as natural to them as breathing. That picture of the female as a frail creature designed for communing with the poets or gently playing the pianoforte in the parlor was a neat hoax perpetrated on us by the Victorians."

As early as 1941, the magazine had started to become a strident call to arms for the working girl—with a literal jobs manual in its biannual careers issues—a magazine that tackled ambition, college, race relations, even sex before marriage and divorce. It was feminist before feminism became a commonly used term. And while it wasn't perfect, it was revolutionary. It is a true piece of history chronicling the rise and fortunes of "America's blessing, America's heroine, America's own—the Girl With a Job."

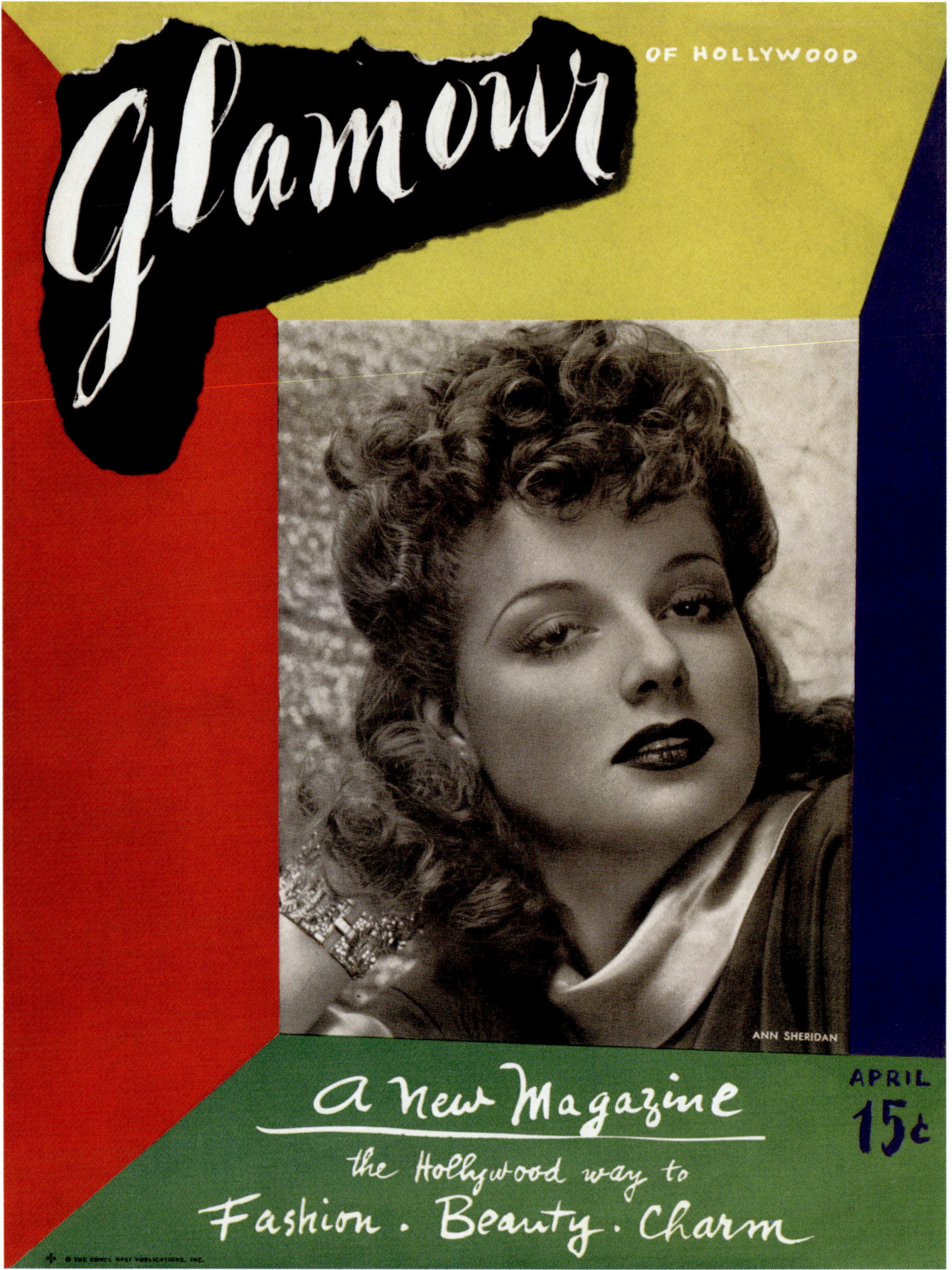

1939

Welcome to the first issue of *Glamour of Hollywood*. While this Hollywood-focused iteration of the magazine ended up being short-lived, the original hand-drawn sketches for the dummy issue of the magazine are a precious piece of history, likely drawn by Charlotte Getleson (*Glamour*'s original art editor), Cipe Pineles (art editor from 1941 to 1946), and other members of the creative team under then art director Dr. M. F. Agha. Here, they sit side by side with the final printed pages from the first issue.

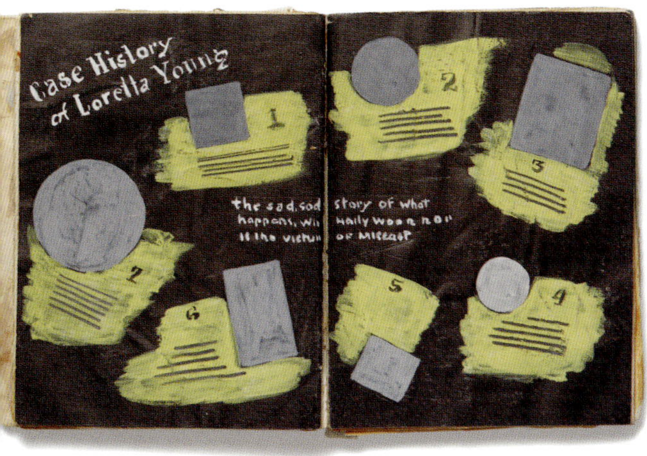
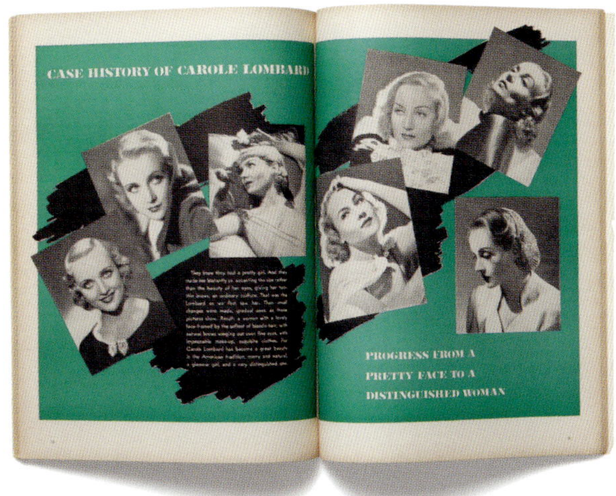
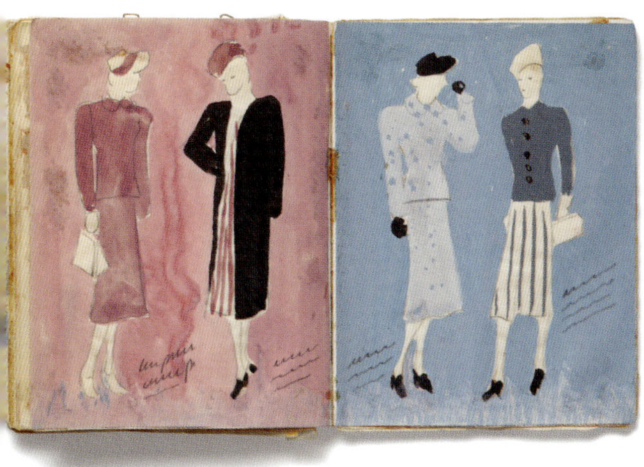
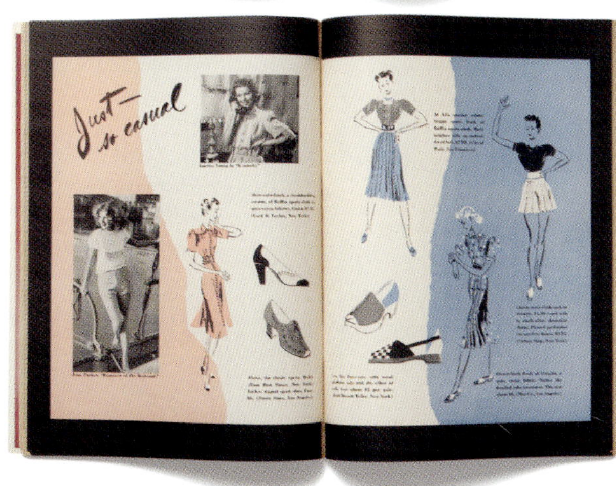
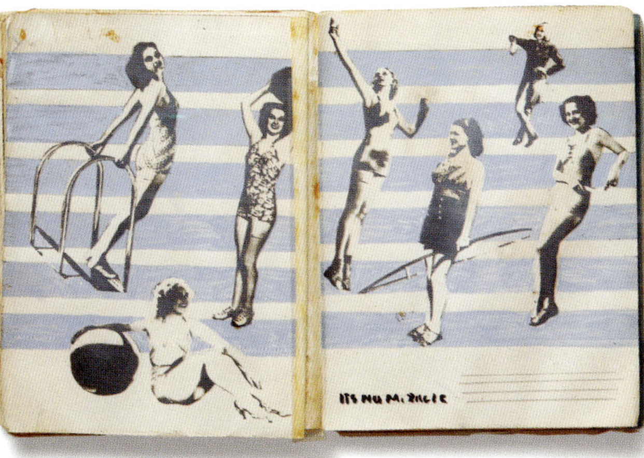
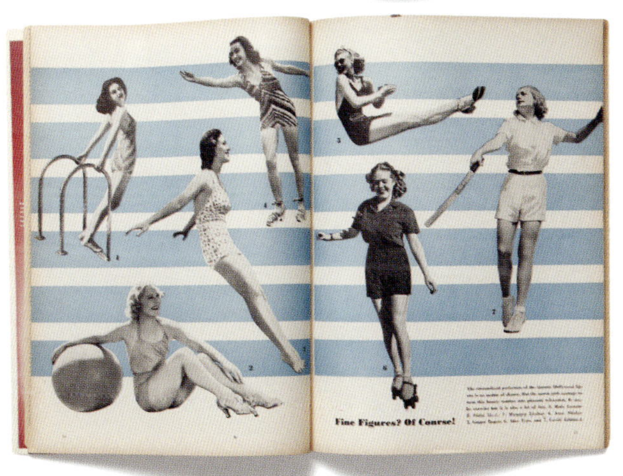
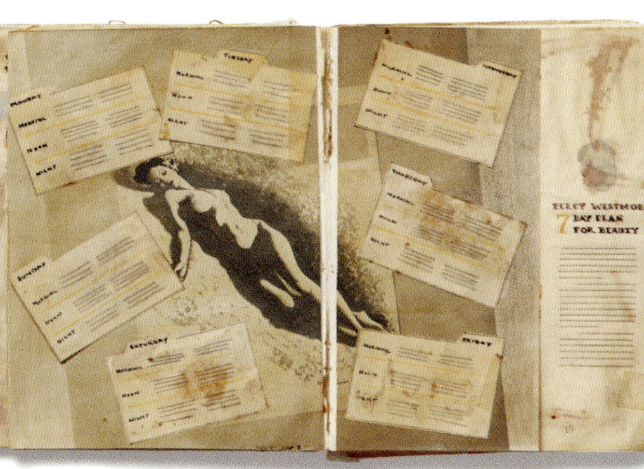
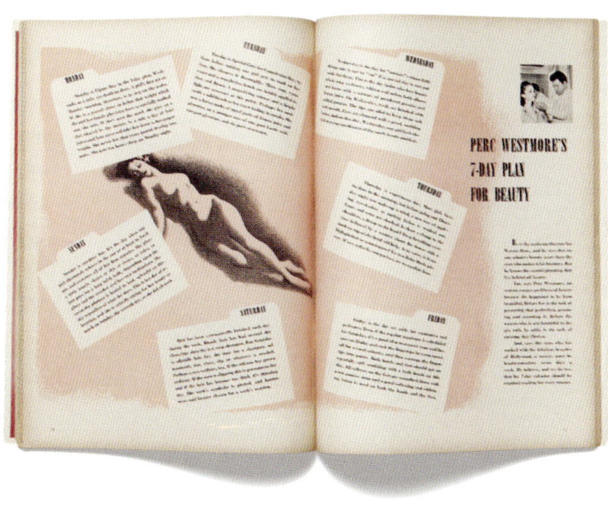

From top row, a draft layout of "Case History of Loretta Young: The sad, sad story of what happens when a Hollywood doll is the victim of miscast." Right, the layout that appeared in print, which had a notably kinder approach: "Progress from a pretty face to a distinguished woman."

A sketch of a fashion spread, and how it appeared in the first issue.

A draft layout of Hollywood stars exercising and the almost identical printed result.

Perc Westmore was a famous makeup artist of the day. Here is his seven-day guide to beauty, from the magazine's dummy issue to print.

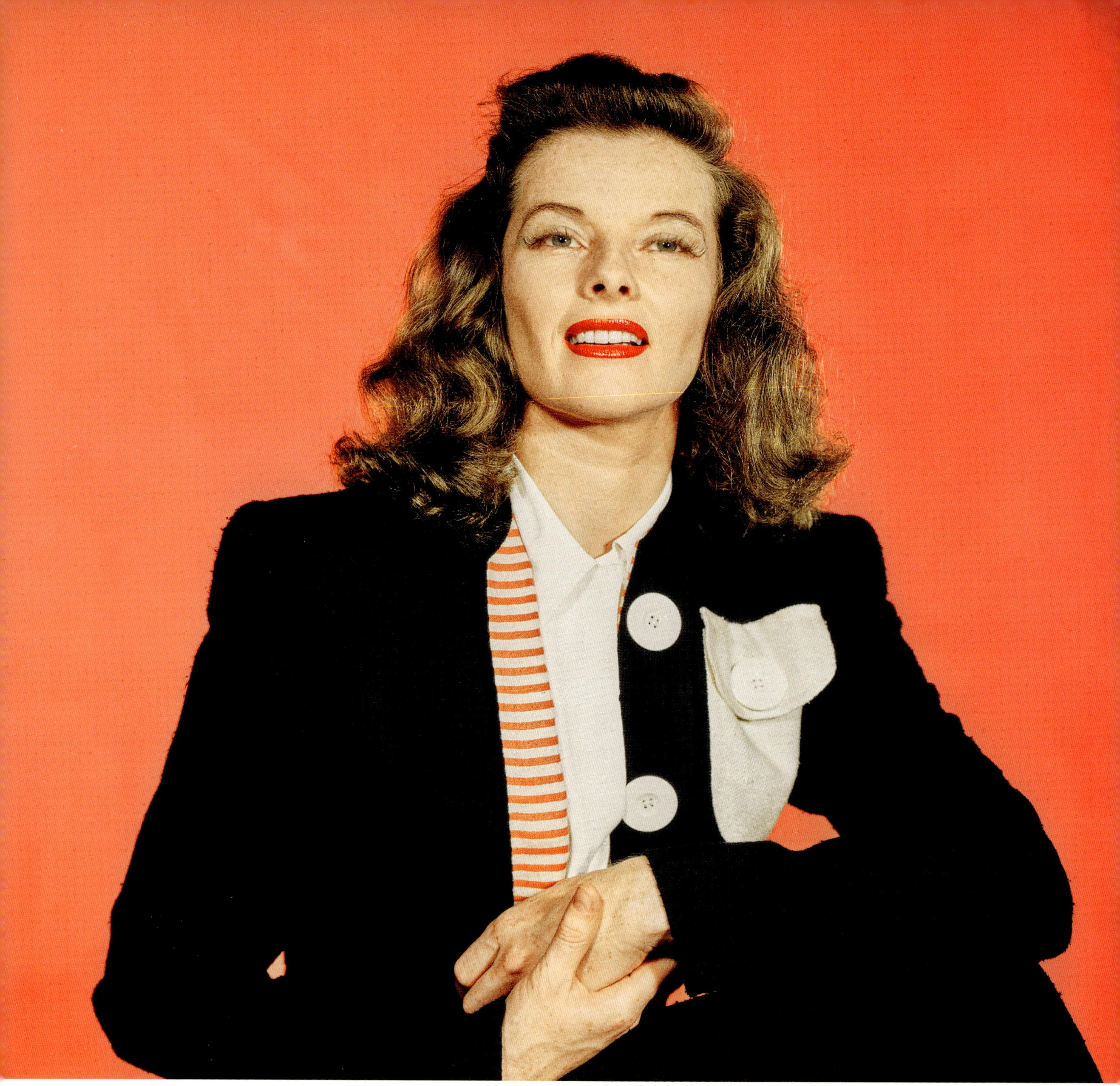

COVERS OF THE ERA

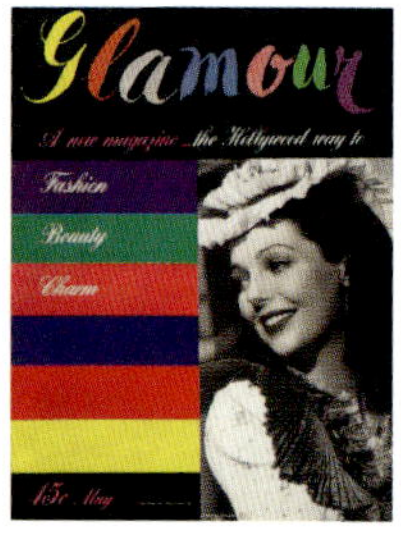

Loretta Young in costume from
the film *The Story of Alexander
Graham Bell*, May 1939.

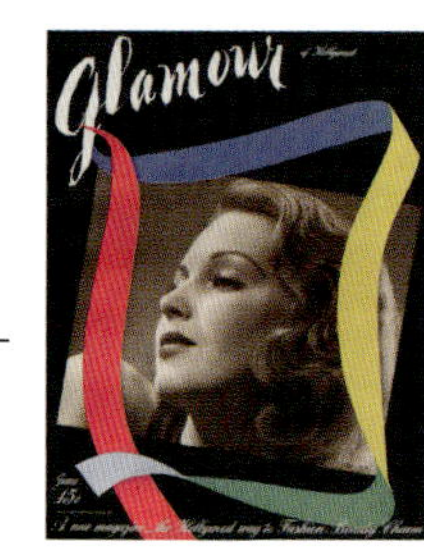

June Lang of *Captain Fury*,
June 1939.

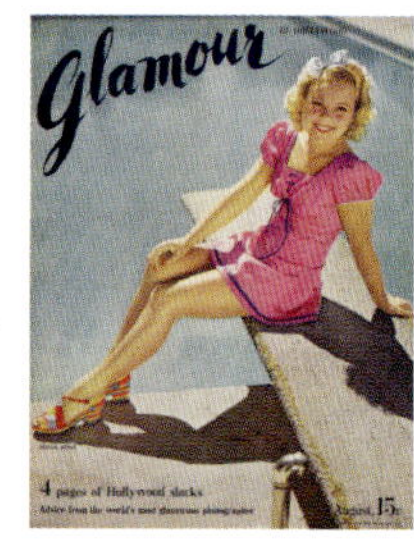

Sonja Henie of *Second Fiddle*
on a diving board,
August 1939.

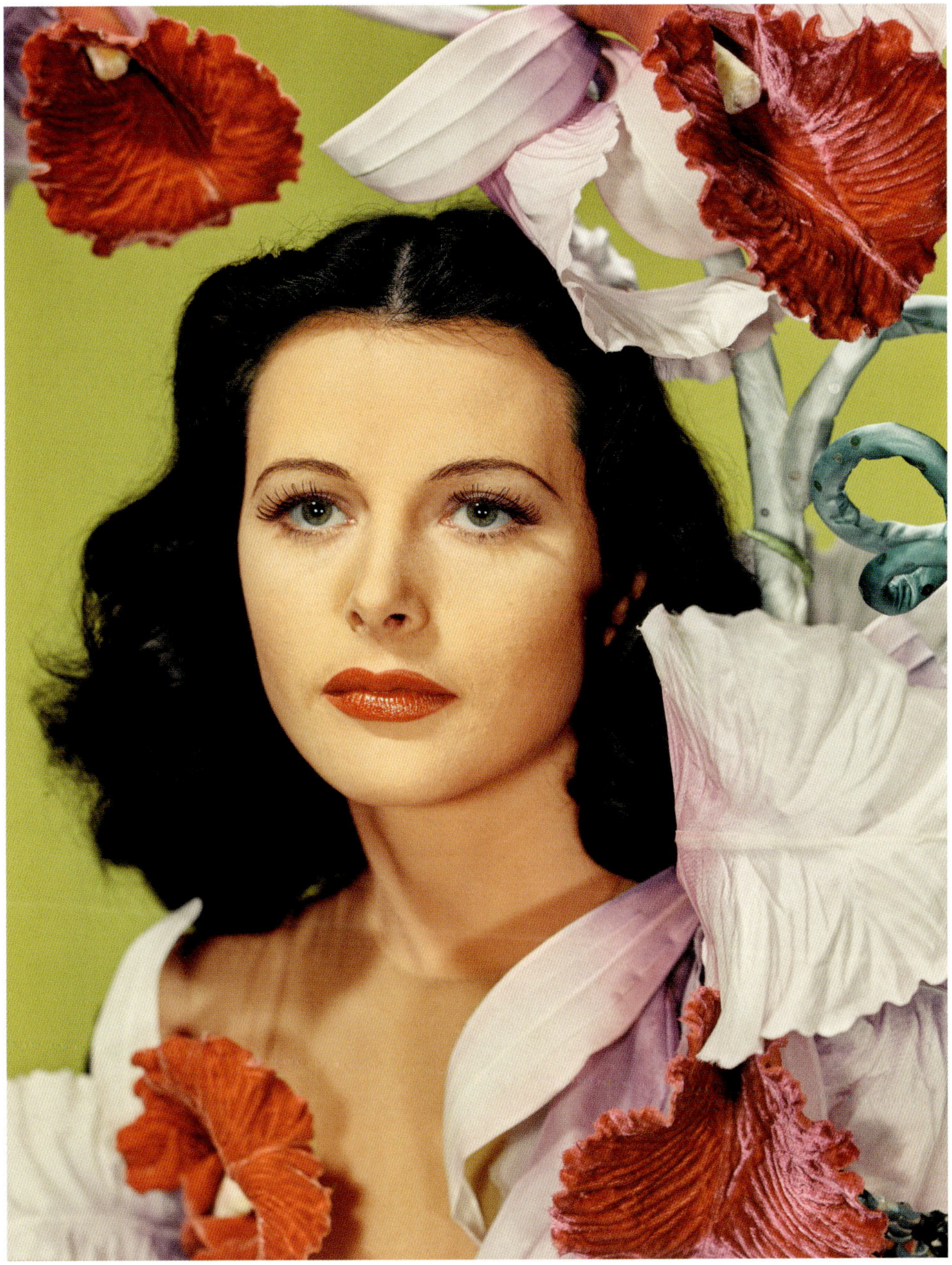

The ambition of *Glamour of Hollywood* was to showcase the lives and fashions of Hollywood's most glamorous actresses. And each month, the magazine aimed to print at least one full-color photograph of a prominent Hollywood star. Often, the photograph was one of only a handful of color pages in an issue—such was the expense and rarity of color printing. The stunning image of Katharine Hepburn opposite, then star of the newly released *The Philadelphia Story*, was shot by Clarence Sinclair Bull and appeared in the April 1941 issue of *Glamour*. And this image of Hedy Lamarr, photographed by Eddie Cronenweth, appeared in the May 1941 issue. Other iconic Hollywood stars to grace early issues of *Glamour* included Joan Bennett, Bette Davis, Loretta Young, Olivia de Havilland, and Vivien Leigh.

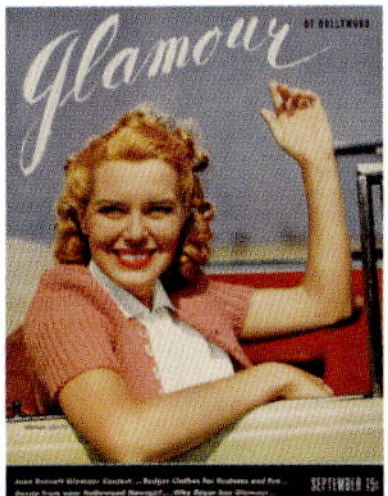

Brenda Joyce of *The Rains Came,* September 1939.

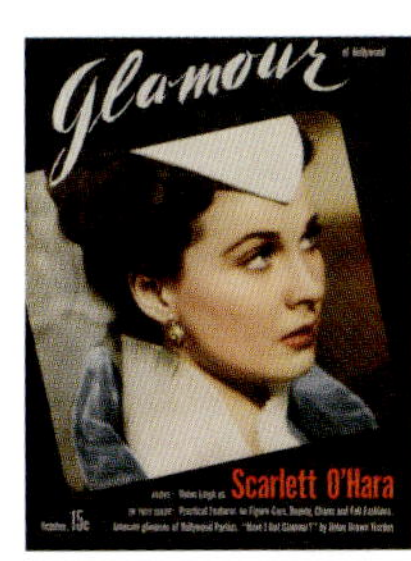

Vivien Leigh as Scarlett O'Hara in *Gone With the Wind,* October 1939.

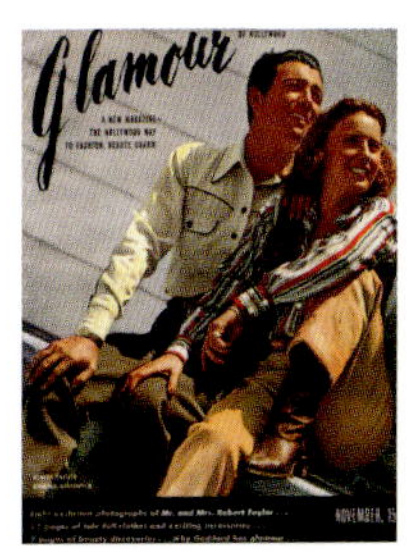

Married couple and actors Robert Taylor and Barbara Stanwyck, November 1939.

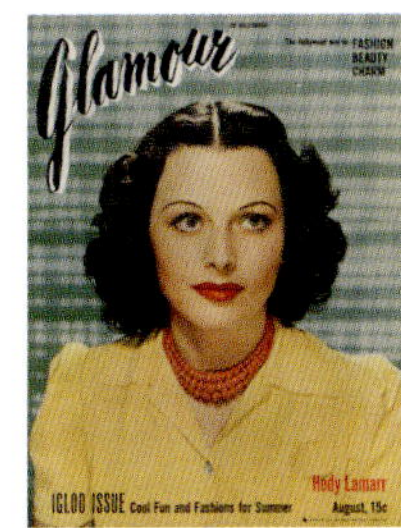

Hedy Lamarr from *Boom Town,* August 1940.

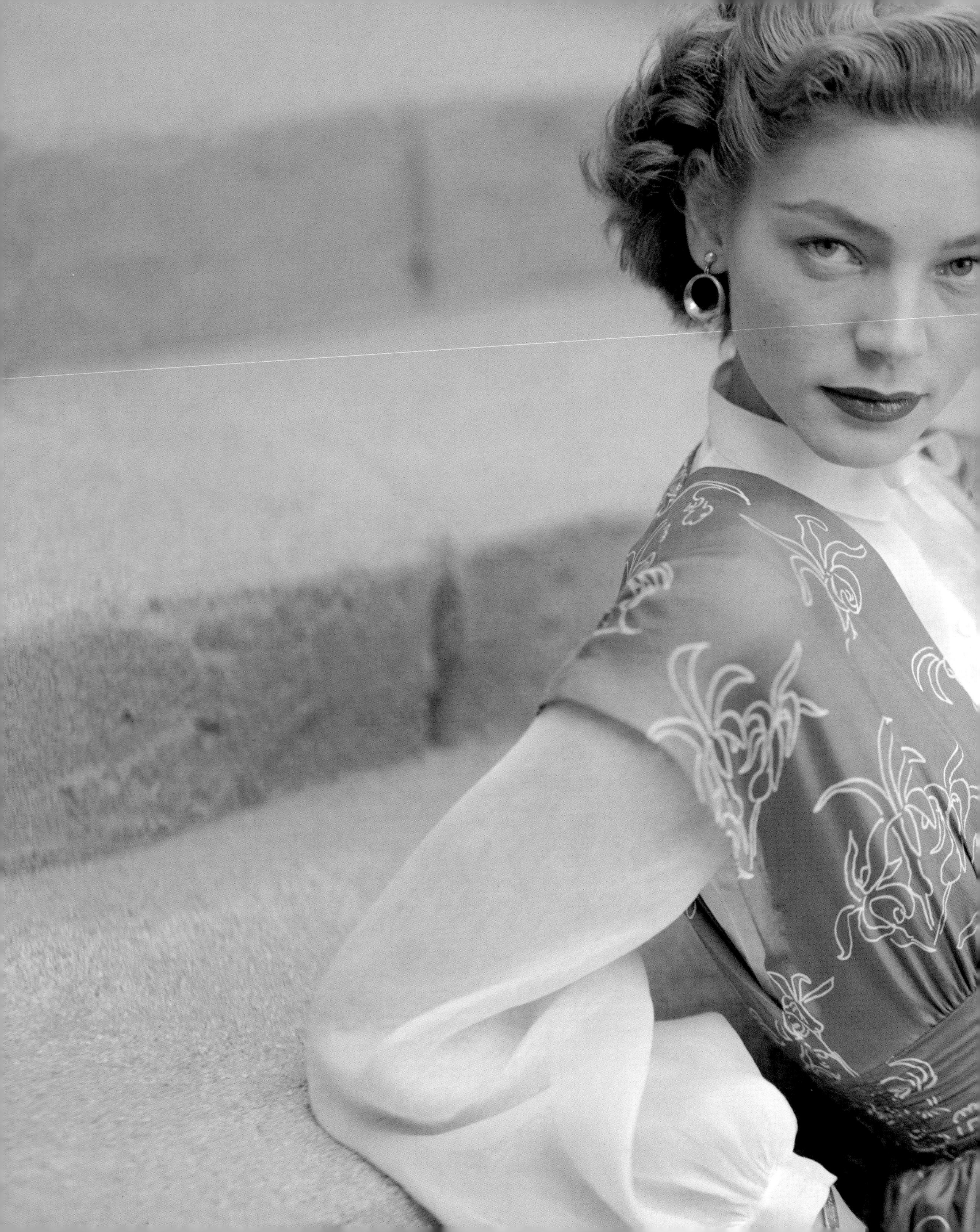

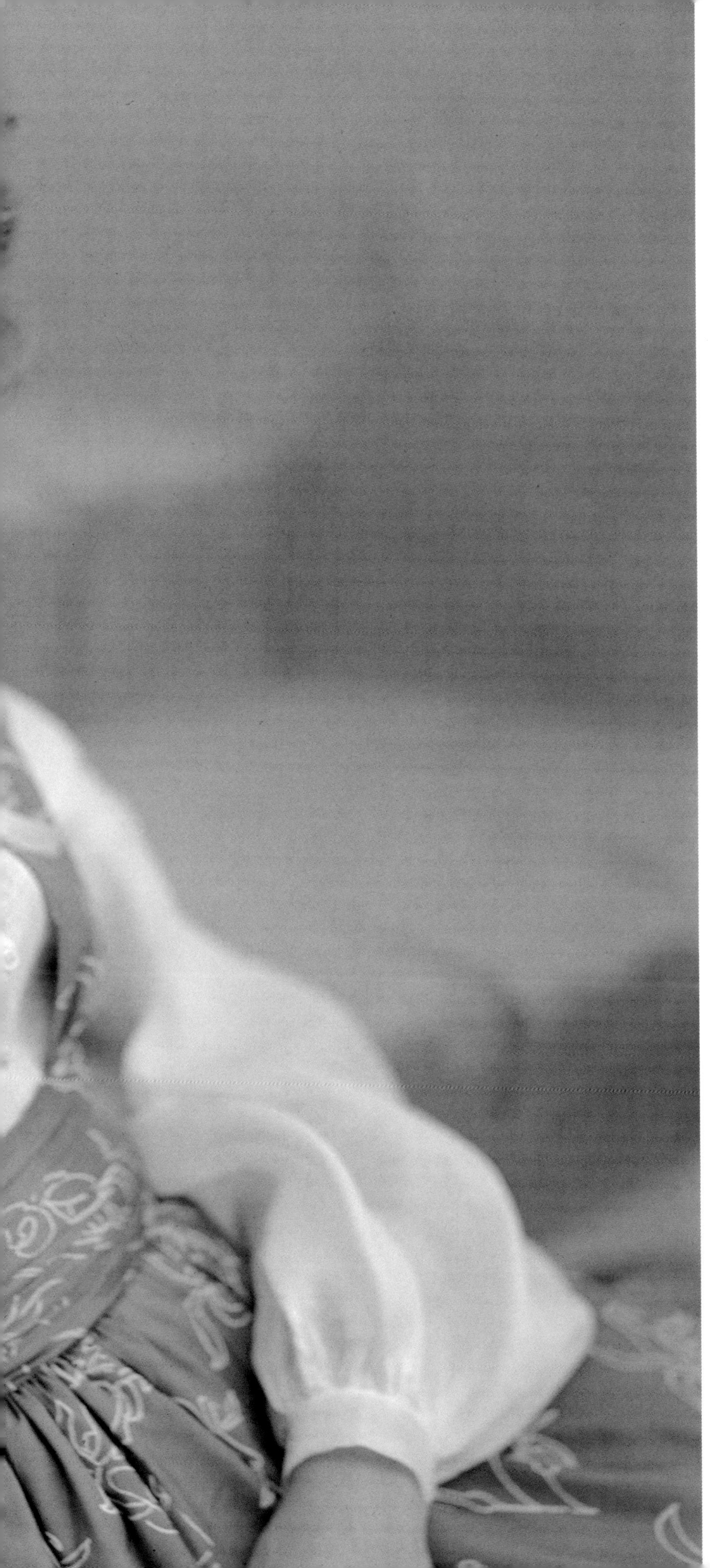

1949

The legendary American actor Lauren Bacall
was photographed for *Glamour* in August 1949
by Clifford Coffin. While the magazine had
shifted from a Hollywood fashion and beauty
bible to a life and style manual for working
women, Hollywood stars still held an appeal.
And few were as mesmerizing as Bacall—by
then the star of *To Have and
Have Not, Key Largo,* and *The Big Sleep.*
This entire shoot was ultimately never
published, until now.

GLAMOUR

for the girl with a job

Uncle Sam
wants <u>you</u>

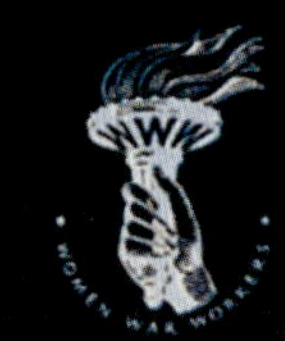

PRICE **20** CENTS
SEPTEMBER 1943

MEDICAL ILLUST[…]

Waneeta Stevic of [...]

admires human inte[...]

"THE inside of a human [...] as beautiful to me as a [...] head," writes *Glamour's* Care[…] Waneeta Stevic, who has [...] out of being an artist. She [...] and lung tumors and stomac[...] for medical journals, textbo[...] charts and lantern slides.

"I studied art all th[...] from kindergarten up, and be[...] ested in medicine while work[...] tor's office. I became the first [...] trator at the University of Ca[...] the Board of Regents create[...] for me.

"I studied under Max [...] country's most famous medica[...] for two years, and learned [...] quick sketches at the scene [...] tion, standing in cap and gow[...] side the surgeon. I also w[...] morgue, the dissecting roo[...] bedsides of patients.

"One may wonder why ph[...] not used for this purpose. Be[...] even in competent hands, ca[...] duce exactly what is before [...] freehand drawing must be of [...] accuracy to be of scientific us[...] artist is able to eliminate th[...] and emphasize the interest[...]

"Many interesting and [...] canny experiences come in [...] course of this work—there [...] for each problem is different. [...] years' experience I never rem[...] the same thing twice. That[...] I like this strange career."

Among Miss Stevic's [...] the retina of a rabbit's ey[...] sides of several monkeys [...] the stomach of a man who die[...] ing an anti-freeze solution.

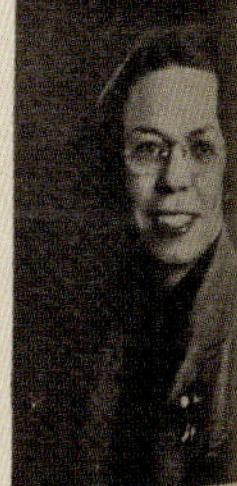

Councillor Waneeta [...] likes to do drawing for [...]

GLAMOUR ENROLLS FOR DEFENSE

GLAMOUR ENROLLS FOR DEFENSE

A message from the Editor who previously edited British Vogue through the first impact of war in Europe

IN September, 1939, when England declared war on Germany, I had been living in London for seven years—working on British *Vogue*, sister publication of American *Vogue* and of *Glamour*.

In December, 1941, when Japan attacked the United States, I had been home editing *Glamour* for almost a year. So, for the second time in my life, it has become necessary for me to adjust the editorial formula of a feminine magazine from a peace-time to a war-time tempo.

As I set myself to the task of making *Glamour* useful to you, the reader, now, I do so with the profound conviction that the principles to which this publication is dedicated—namely, the business of living, looking and dressing attractively on a modest budget, are among the stoutest weapons at the command of embattled young American womanhood.

It has been said that "an army fights on its stomach." It has been said with equal certitude that "man does not live by bread alone." Morale is as important as munitions. And morale is women's work.

It is up to people like you—the career girls of the United States— and to people like us, the women journalists of the country—to keep the fighting spirit of America high and healthy. We can best do it by maintaining within the limits of suitability and necessity, the standards of civilization by which we have lived in peace. These, in themselves, are the very issues over which the war is being fought.

I saw it happen in England. I am sure that I shall see it happen here. When your soldier comes home on leave he will count on you to look your prettiest. Your rôle is to be, at all costs, your most charming, feminine, attractively dressed self—as he remembers you in peace-time.

Because of this fundamental human urge to cling to the visible signs of a good way of life, British *Vogue*—veteran of the First World War, now a combatant in the Second—is today more avidly read throughout the British Empire than ever before. Thus we know that fashion needs no apology in war-time. Suitably applied, it can and must militate for the good of the common morale.

So flaunt your lipstick bravely. Tilt your hat debonairly. Keep the corners of your mouth as well as your chin up. See that your home—wherever or whatever it may be—is, above all else, bright, cozy, restful.

Then—and only then—can you face each working day, each extra hour of defense effort with the invincible spirit you have to give to the job.

Elizabeth Penrose

↗

"*Glamour* Enrolls for Defense," February 1942.

←

A model poses in front of the iconic Uncle Sam poster. The issue outlined various careers where women were most needed, September 1943.

IN SEPTEMBER 1939, WAR WAS DECLARED ON GERMANY, AND THE WORLD changed forever. When the US entered the war in 1941, *Glamour* had to pivot. With millions of women called to work, a magazine about beauty and Hollywood no longer reflected the lives of readers. The founding editor in chief, Alice Thompson, was fired in 1941. In her place, Condé Nast appointed Elizabeth Penrose, former editor in chief of British *Vogue*. Penrose was the antithesis of Thompson, and her intentions for the magazine were clear from the get-go: She recognized what the moment meant for her readers, her women— opportunity—and *Glamour* was reborn. It was ambitious, it was smart, and it was there to do a duty. The letter published here was written by Penrose for the February 1942 issue. In it, she declares, "It is up to people like you—the career girls of the United States—and to people like us, the women journalists of the country—to keep the fighting spirit of America high and healthy." The stage was set—this was a new era. The era of the career woman, of the girl with a job.

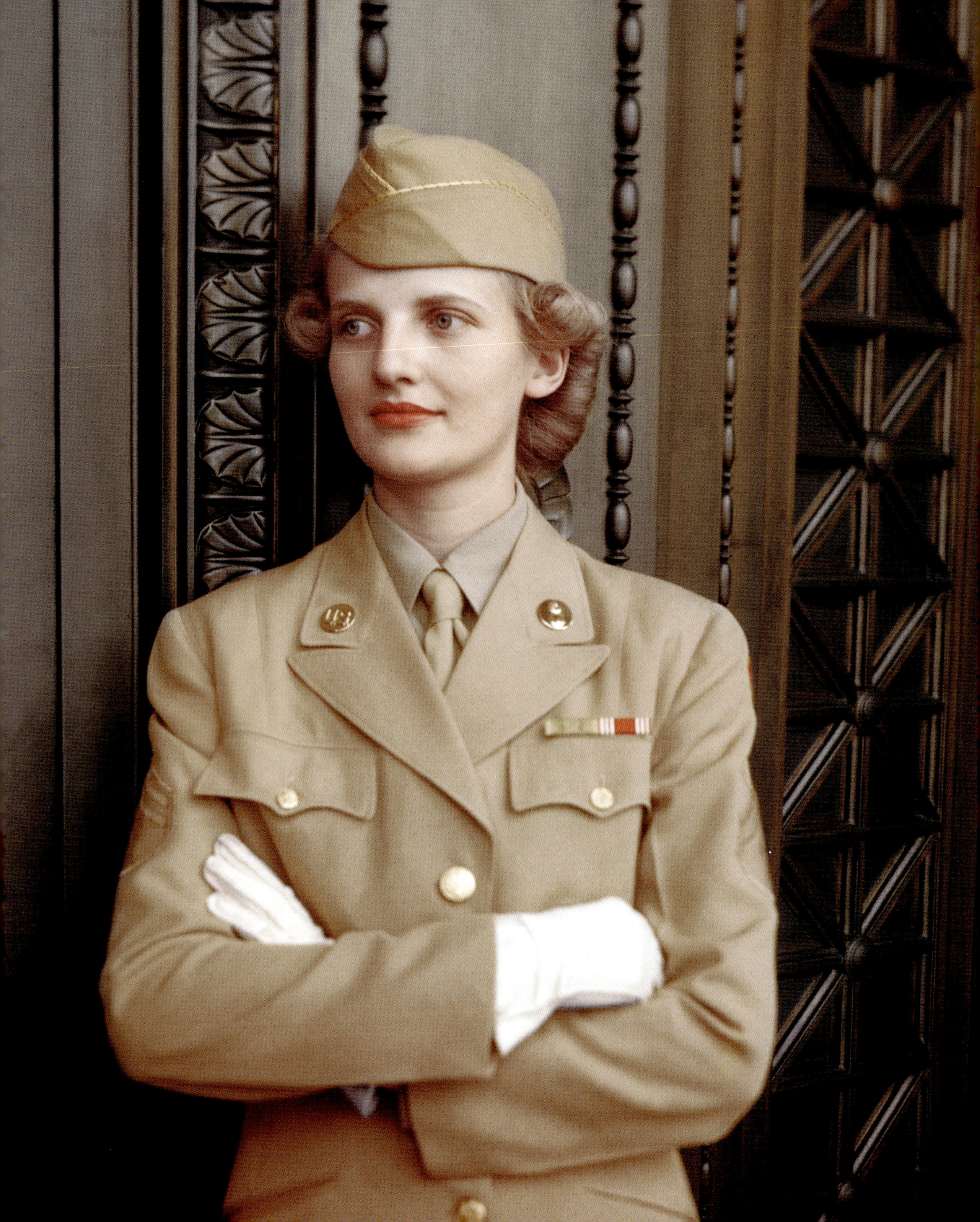

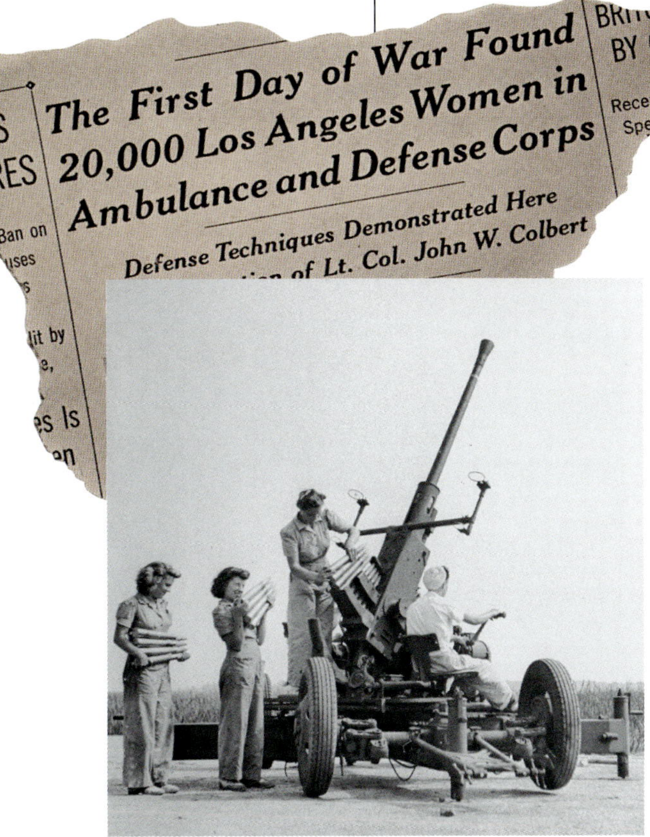

Women weapons testers at Aberdeen Proving
Ground, Maryland, 1942.

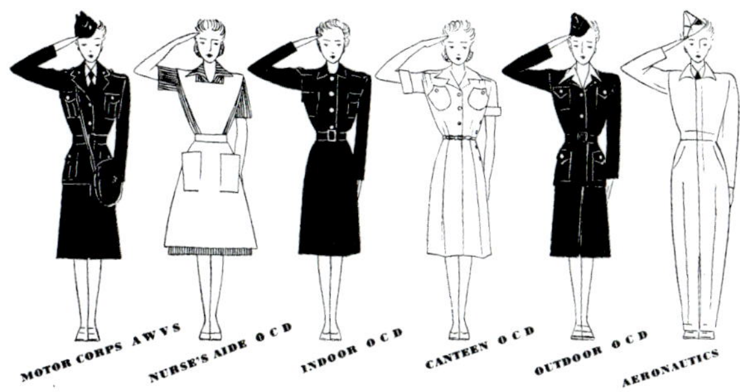

Illustration of volunteer opportunities in the Red Cross,
Office of Civilian Defense, American Women's Voluntary
Services, and American Women's Hospital Reserve Corps
from the February 1942 issue.

AUGUST

1944

Corporal Clara Grundon, 23, was photographed in her Women's Army
Corps uniform for the August 1944 issue of *Glamour*, by Horst P. Horst.
Grundon was celebrated in the monthly "We Name for Glamour"
feature that recognized a different extraordinary woman in each issue.
In the short biography that accompanied her photograph, *Glamour*
lauded her "because her gift for science made her one of 60 girls
chosen for a blitz course in higher mathematics. Because she operates
the dizzyingly complicated Differential Analyzer at the Ballistic
Research Laboratory, Aberdeen Proving Grounds."

←

While *Glamour*'s coverage of working women during the war was
admirable, it fell short in its recognition of the importance and
contribution of women of color. More than half a million Black
women worked in shipyards, factories, and administrative offices,
but received little acknowledgment. It's important to note their
vital contributions today even though the magazine at the time
didn't. Pictured here, a woman at Vultee-Nashville, Tennessee,
working on an A-31 Vengeance dive-bomber.

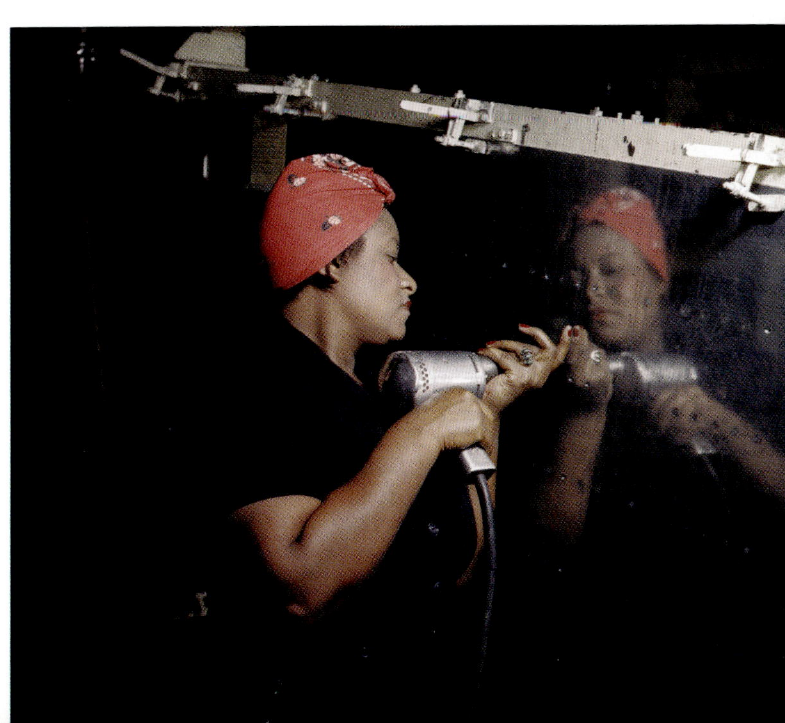

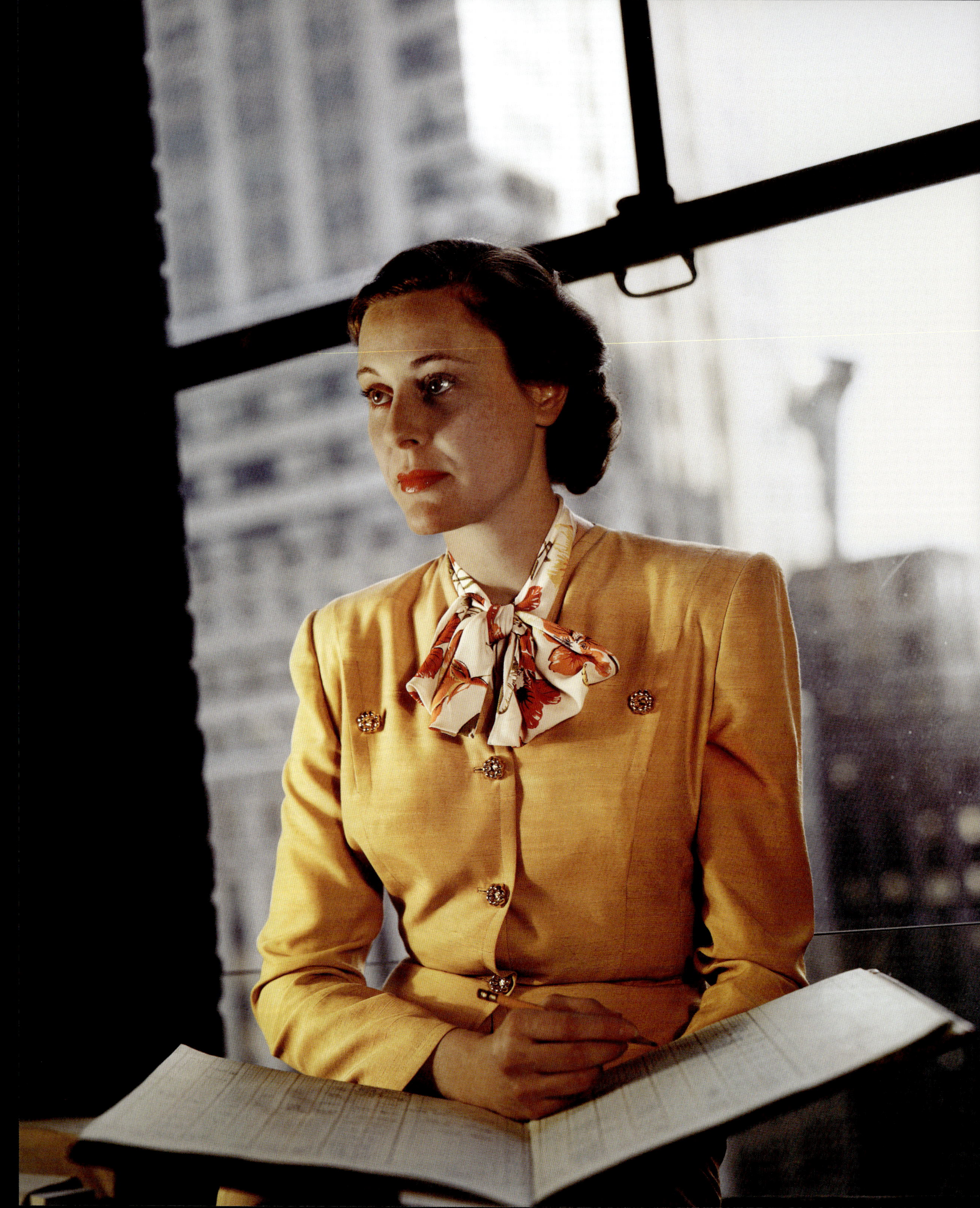

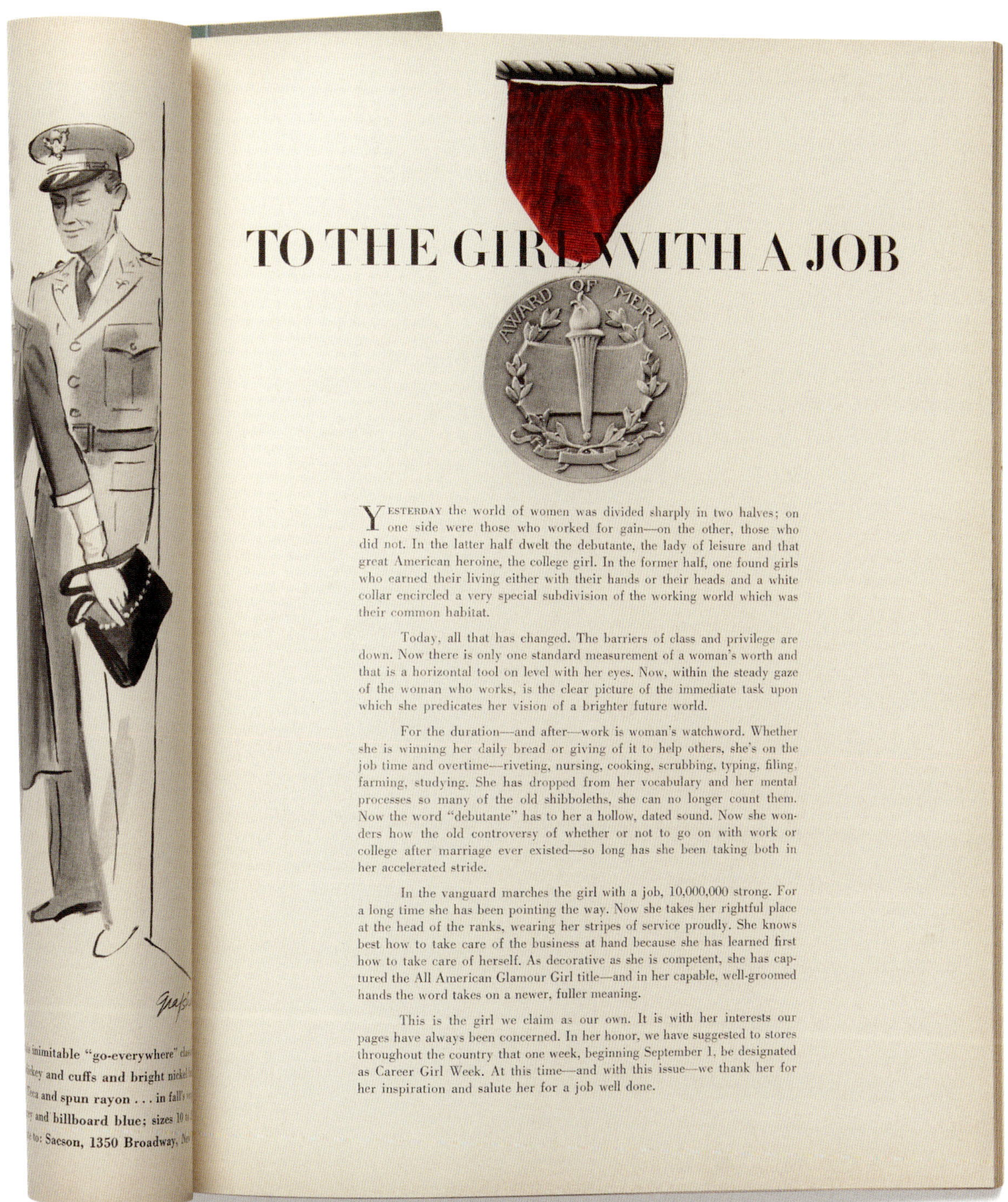

YESTERDAY the world of women was divided sharply in two halves; on one side were those who worked for gain—on the other, those who did not. In the latter half dwelt the debutante, the lady of leisure and that great American heroine, the college girl. In the former half, one found girls who earned their living either with their hands or their heads and a white collar encircled a very special subdivision of the working world which was their common habitat.

Today, all that has changed. The barriers of class and privilege are down. Now there is only one standard measurement of a woman's worth and that is a horizontal tool on level with her eyes. Now, within the steady gaze of the woman who works, is the clear picture of the immediate task upon which she predicates her vision of a brighter future world.

For the duration—and after—work is woman's watchword. Whether she is winning her daily bread or giving of it to help others, she's on the job time and overtime—riveting, nursing, cooking, scrubbing, typing, filing, farming, studying. She has dropped from her vocabulary and her mental processes so many of the old shibboleths, she can no longer count them. Now the word "debutante" has to her a hollow, dated sound. Now she wonders how the old controversy of whether or not to go on with work or college after marriage ever existed—so long has she been taking both in her accelerated stride.

In the vanguard marches the girl with a job, 10,000,000 strong. For a long time she has been pointing the way. Now she takes her rightful place at the head of the ranks, wearing her stripes of service proudly. She knows best how to take care of the business at hand because she has learned first how to take care of herself. As decorative as she is competent, she has captured the All American Glamour Girl title—and in her capable, well-groomed hands the word takes on a newer, fuller meaning.

This is the girl we claim as our own. It is with her interests our pages have always been concerned. In her honor, we have suggested to stores throughout the country that one week, beginning September 1, be designated as Career Girl Week. At this time—and with this issue—we thank her for her inspiration and salute her for a job well done.

Above, "To the Girl With a Job," September 1942. Left, Dorothy Rodgers, who was spotlighted by *Glamour* for her work at the Writers War Board, gathering "every sort of written entertainment for presentation by and for the Armed Forces." *Photographed by Constantin Joffé, June 1944.*

IN SEPTEMBER 1942, AFTER MONTHS OF TEASING THE TITLE'S NEW CAREERS-driven purpose, *Glamour* published one of its most famous editorials in the form of a letter, "To the Girl With a Job." From this moment forth, there was no mistaking who the magazine was courting, and the vital importance it placed on her as the future of the country. *Glamour* threw itself into supporting the woman, one of a millions-strong army, taking "her rightful place at the head of the ranks." "This is the girl," the magazine states, "we claim as our own." It is no overstatement to say that this new direction set the tone for the future of *Glamour*, not just while Penrose was editor, but for the magazine's entire life up until today (although the 1950s took a little detour). The magazine would still carry fashions and beauty tips—for the budget-conscious working woman, of course—but every subsequent issue was marked by a focus on women's rights, women's advancement, women's access to education, and women's autonomy in marriage, relationships, and sex. It was groundbreaking.

ONE OF THE MORE EXTRAORDINARY FOOTNOTES IN *Glamour*'s history was the creation of the magazine's job department. With the pivot from Hollywood to careers came a new monthly column: Your Job is our job. In each issue, the job department would suggest a career idea to its readers. It would list the description, attributes needed, and likely salary, and invite readers to write in for advice. The jobs editor would then answer readers' questions, with detailed and heavily researched responses. It became a runaway success, and such was the importance of the column that by 1948 it had become one of *Glamour*'s largest departments. In the January 1948 issue, the magazine published an article specifically highlighting this. "When *Glamour*'s job department was inaugurated in 1942…it boasted a one-woman staff," the editorial began. "In the intervening years, it has seemed that every time we looked up from our work the Job Department had doubled its staff and tripled its services. Now, because of your interest, it is one of *Glamour*'s largest departments." Pictured beneath were the department's dedicated 12 staff members. Unmatched by any rival, this team offered true service journalism and became a pillar of the magazine for decades.

→

"For the girl with a job," August 1943.

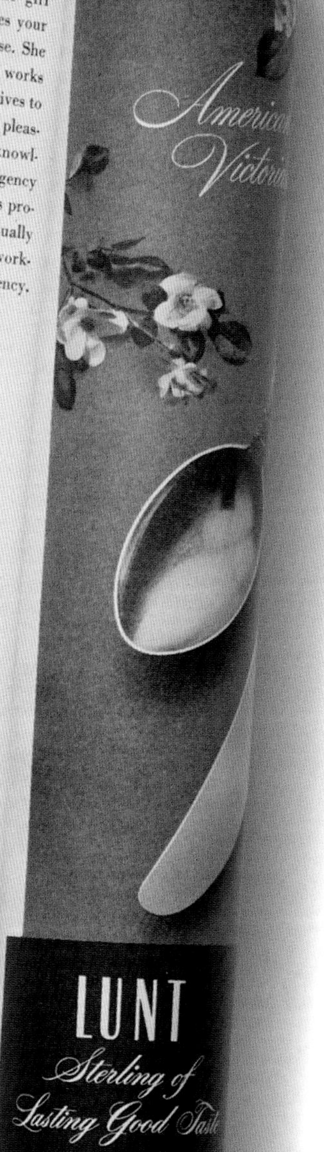

242

October Job Idea Travel Agent, the girl who works with wanderlust. She plans and arranges your vacation, honeymoon, business trip or cruise. She lines up lower berths and rooms-with-views, works closely with transportation and hotel representatives to assure your pleasant passage. She must have a pleasing manner, a talent for accurate detail and a knowledge of passport and visa regulations. A large agency may train her for her job. In a smaller firm she's promoted from receptionist or stenographer. Salary: usually $150 to $175 a month. She stands a good chance of working up to agency manager, or starting her own agency.

Your Job
is our job

GLAMOUR will help you to make the most of the job you have…or give you advice on how to get started on the career you've chosen. Every letter with a job problem is answered personally; those of unusual general interest are printed anonymously on this page.

WRITE TO THE JOB PROBLEM DEPARTMENT, GLAMOUR, 420 LEXINGTON AVENUE, NEW YORK 17, NEW YORK.

Dear Job Editor:

This letter may not merit your attention; even so that will not affect my regard for your fine magazine.

I am a twenty-seven-year-old negro woman with two years of college training in teacher's college. I know typing and shorthand.

I am interested in getting into journalism. I would like eventually to work up to critical, editorial work. Will you suggest the best school? I'm particularly eager to learn about correspondence courses…T. H., Indiana.

Dear Mrs. H:

We're delighted to hear of your high regard for GLAMOUR. Your letter and every other reader letter merits our personal attention, and we're happy to make suggestions about your career and the training you'll need for it.

Your request that we select the best school for you is a large order. As you know the school situation now is very tight. There's unprecedented enrollment everywhere and veterans, of course, are being given preference. Try applying to small colleges in your vicinity (your state board of education can tell you whether they're accredited) or your state university. Two well-known schools of journalism in your part of the country are Indiana University School of Journalism, Bloomington, Indiana; and Medill School of Journalism, Northwestern University, Evanston, Illinois. At Indiana, there is a full day program. Medill offers evening courses leading to a degree. Write for catalogs, details of entrance requirements, tuition, housing.

Correspondence courses may be your solution. The secretary of the American University Extension Association, Bloomington, Indiana, will be glad to send you information about such study.

We're sure you understand that work as an editor or critic takes a lot of working up to. It requires ability to judge writing which can be based only on having done a great deal of writing yourself; a thorough knowledge of literary markets; and the many contacts with publishers, editors, agents and writers which you naturally acquire through working in publishing.

To approach this sort of work, get a job—any job— in publishing. (See *Do You Want a Job in Publishing?* in the September issue of GLAMOUR). Your knowledge of stenography should make it easy for you to break in, either on a magazine or in a book publishing firm. Or if you prefer a newspaper, there are beginning jobs especially on small town papers.

Meanwhile, you'll want to get acquainted with the books on the trade … *Writer's Market*, published by the Writer's Digest Publishing Co., 22 East 12th Street, Cincinnati 10, Ohio. $3; and (Continued on page 253)

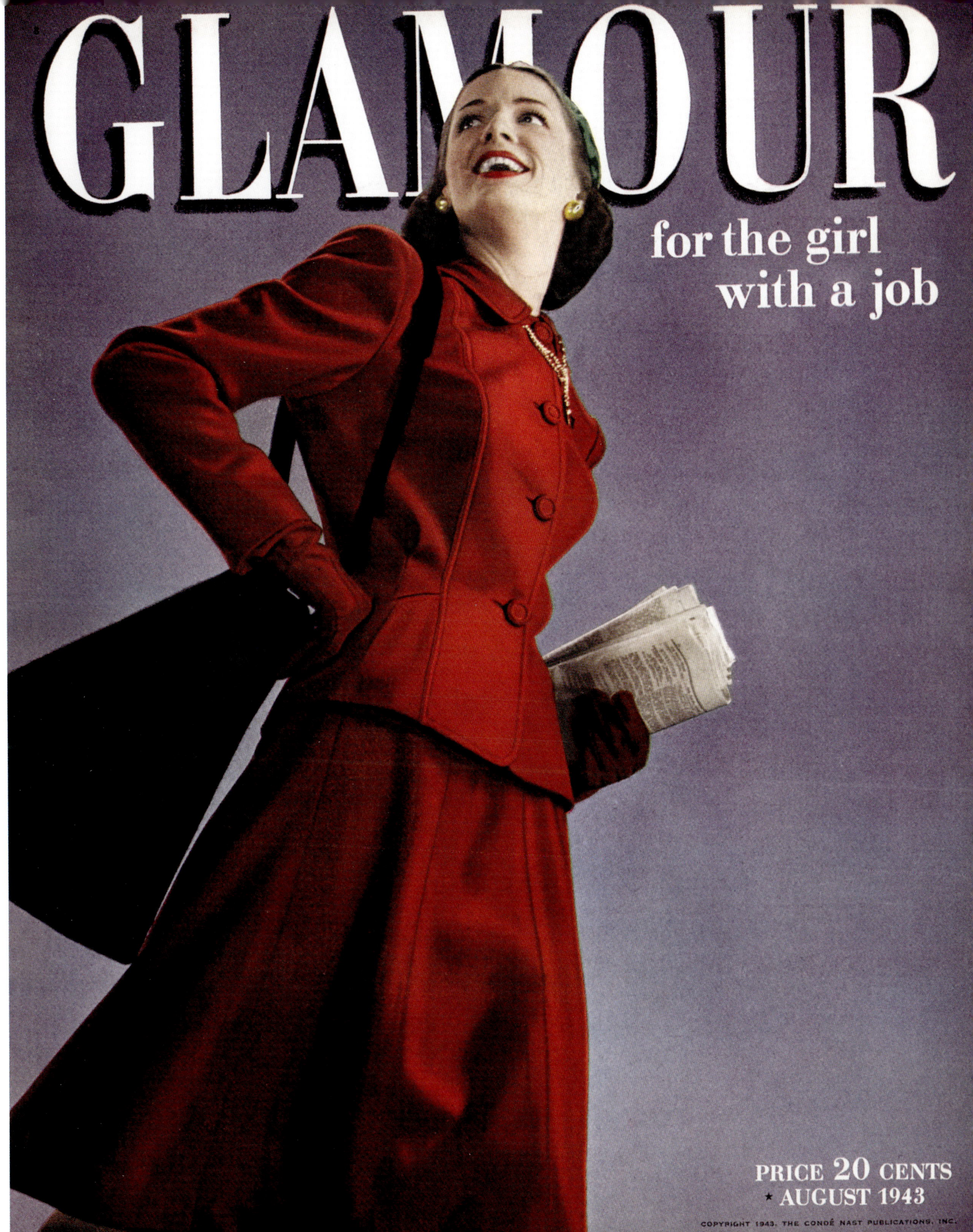

GLAMOUR
for the girl
with a job
PRICE 20 CENTS
★ AUGUST 1943
COPYRIGHT 1943, THE CONDÉ NAST PUBLICATIONS, INC.

 with a job took its mission seriously. Each month, its staff highlighted a woman of achievement, and most issues contained features on working women in a wide variety of careers—from aiding the war effort, to television and radio writing and production, nursing, factory work, government, and more. The women were always exceptional, but arguably few more so than the women war correspondents, who often risked their lives to report on the horrors from the front line. Today, we republish the extraordinary article "Women Who Write the War," from the September 1945 issue, featuring, among others, the celebrated photojournalist and war correspondent Lee Miller, and Betty M. Phillips, the only Black female overseas war correspondent during the Second World War.

> **Betty had to cover her beat from a hospital bed.**
>
> "WOMEN WHO WRITE THE WAR,"
> SEPTEMBER 1945

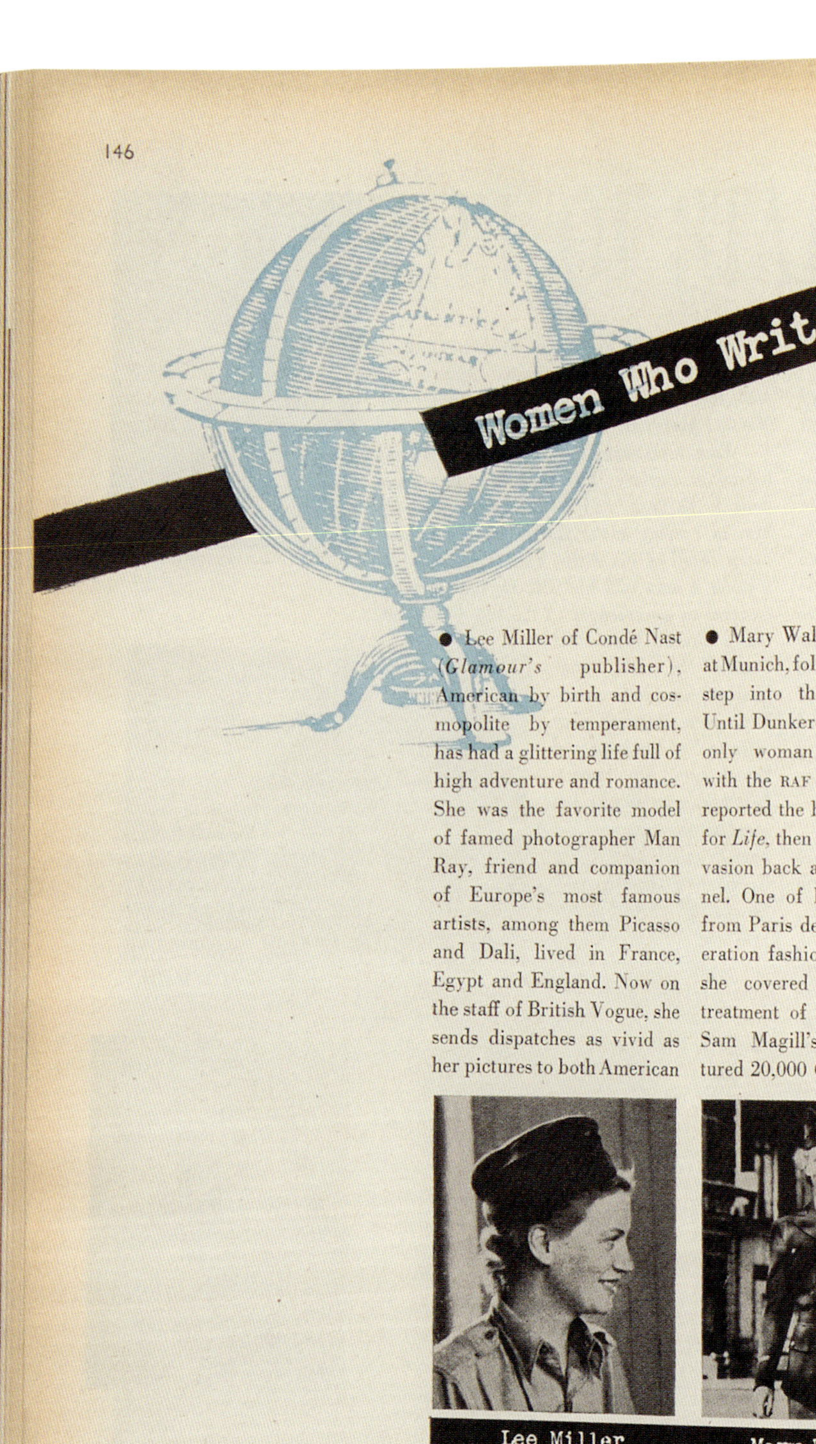

● Lee Miller of Condé Nast (*Glamour's* publisher), American by birth and cosmopolite by temperament, has had a glittering life full of high adventure and romance. She was the favorite model of famed photographer Man Ray, friend and companion of Europe's most famous artists, among them Picasso and Dali, lived in France, Egypt and England. Now on the staff of British Vogue, she sends dispatches as vivid as her pictures to both American

● Mary Walsh of *Time* at Munich, followed the go... step into the Sudetenla... Until Dunkerque she was... only woman correspon... with the RAF in France. ... reported the battle of Bri... for *Life*, then followed the... vasion back across the ch... nel. One of her first ca... from Paris described the ... eration fashions, but usu... she covered the war— ... treatment of casualties, ... Sam Magill's platoon c... tured 20,000 Germans. M...

Lee Miller

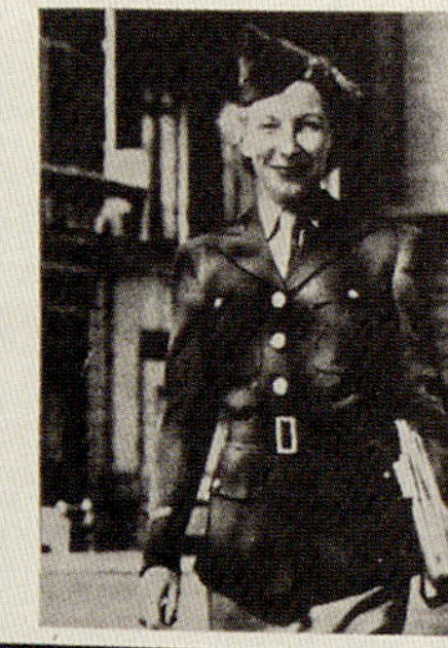

Mary Walsh

and British Vogue. Lee went into Germany, documented her report of the horrors of Dachau with pictures not intended to spare tender feelings. Her current assignment, the whole Continent.

is a Minnesota girl who m... good in England's big c... From a five-year stint on ... *Chicago Daily News,* ... went to the *London D... Express,* then to *Time.* ... current whereabouts. Pa...

World War II has opened a new career front to women journalists
These correspondents write under fire in bombed cities, on battlefields
Cover what used to be a man's assignment—war where it's happening

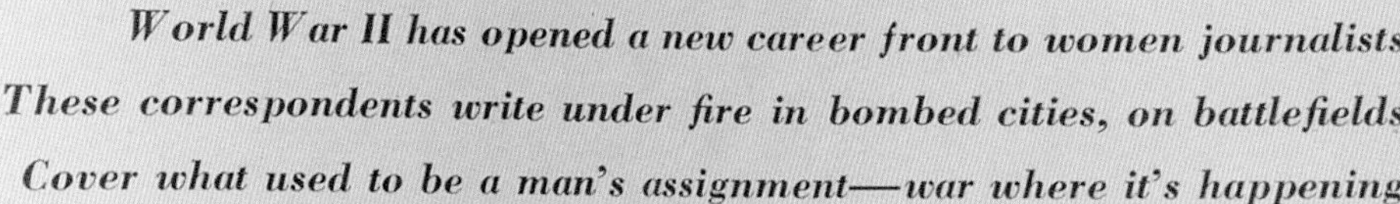

● Ruth Cowan of Associated Press used to be a school marm. A weekly movie column for San Antonio's *Evening News* gave her a permanent taste for printer's ink, and she dropped teaching, began to freelance for the news services. Then she landed a job at AP's Chicago office. Her first assignments were gangster funerals and Al Capone's trial—both from the woman's angle. Then she reported the 1936 presidential election, later went to Washington to cover Mrs. FDR. Came the war, and Ruth braved submarines to sail to Africa with the WAC, worked under fire on the Normandy beachhead. Presently she's home awaiting reassignment.

● Bettye M. Phillips, of Afro-American Newspapers, was sent overseas to get into places a man couldn't—WAC barracks, nurses' quarters. But Bettye had to cover her beat from a hospital bed, recuperating from a crippling attack of neuralgia. Since she couldn't go after the stories, the stories came to her, in the form of unwelcome V-bombs and welcome visitors. She held open house in her hospital room, lent a sympathetic reporter's ear to the adventures, gripes, questions of dozens of GIS every day, saw that the home front learned what the boys were thinking about post-war America, the GI Bill, jim crow. Home now, Bettye hopes soon to return.

● Rita Hume, of International News Service, left her radio program and her job on the *Seattle Times* to become a Red Cross correspondent. She landed in Africa with the first nine Red Cross workers to go overseas. After Africa, Rita was assigned to cover Anzio and Cassino for INS. She worked side by side with Sgt. Bill Mauldin, learned about the infantry from him. She was bombed out of her apartment in Naples, witnessed the Milan demonstration after the death of Mussolini, had a thirty-two vehicle German convoy surrender to her. In Yugoslavia, Rita delved into underground intrigue. Her present beat, reporting in Italy.

● Helen Kirkpatrick of the *Chicago Daily News* made Phi Beta Kappa at Smith, snagged a job with the Foreign Policy Association in Geneva. Geneva was a hotbed of intrigue, teeming with correspondents. Helen was soon touring Europe for the *Herald Tribune* and half a dozen British newspapers. She founded and edited the famous *Whitehall News Letter*, a weekly news digest. She was bombed out of her London home, blown bodily through a doorway, almost blasted to bits in the street, but she got the story of London at War. From freed Paris she cabled an eye-witness account of the attempt on De Gaulle's life. Next stop, home, lecturing.

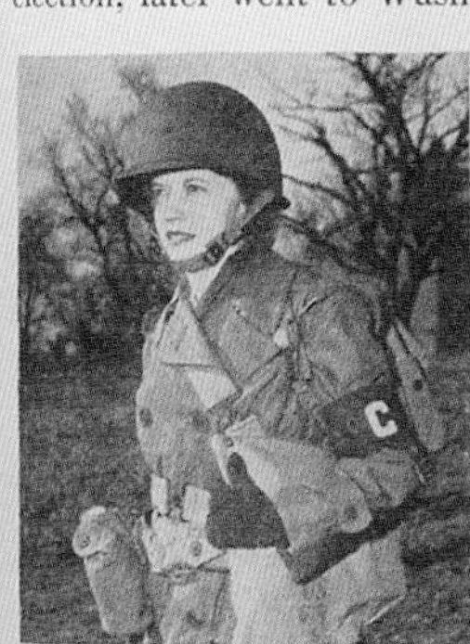

Ruth Cowan

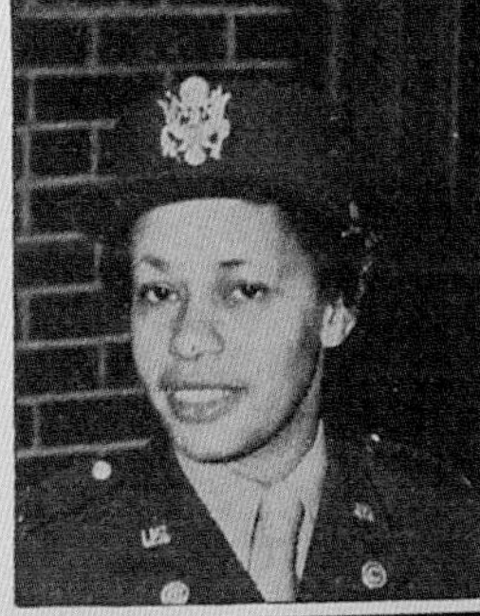

Bettye M. Phillips

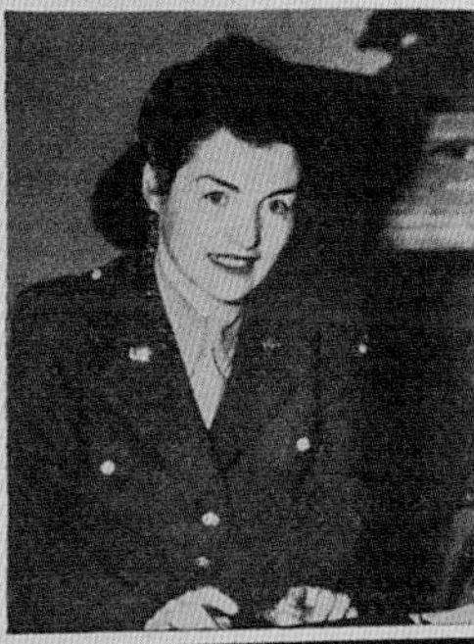

Rita Hume

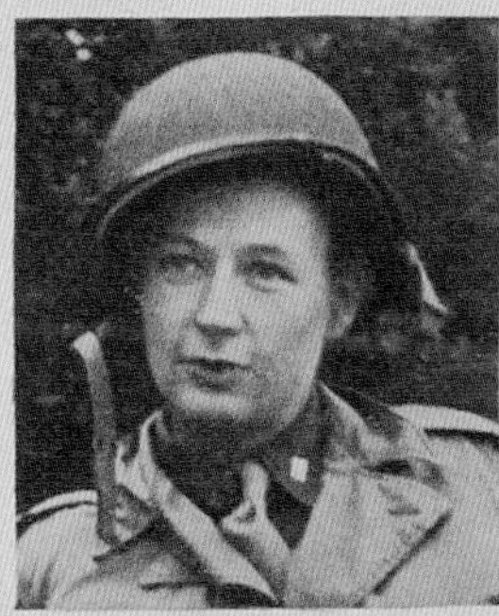

Helen Kirkpatrick

IN THE **FEBRUARY 1944** ISSUE:

How legally limited are your rights as a woman? That was the question *Glamour* posed in the February 1944 issue. The answer was very. Which was why the magazine published the piece reprinted here, arguing the importance of passing the Equal Rights Amendment to the Constitution. Even 80 years on, with the ERA still not ratified, readers will find the article deeply resonant. BY RICHARD DE BROWN

THE FEMININE HALF OF THE NATION... that thinks equal rights for women have already been won in the invasion of the polls, the smoking car, the army and the assembly line, is living in the bliss of ignorance.

For the shattering truth reveals that of the twelve demands drawn up by the first Equal Rights convention at Seneca Falls, N.Y., in 1848, only one, the right to vote, has been completely won. More than one thousand laws in the various states still discriminate against women on the other eleven demands: equal rights in education, industry, the professions, in political office, marriage, personal freedom, in control of property, guardianship of children, in making contracts, in church, and in the leadership of all moral and public movements.

No woman favors comparison with a cow, but under many of these laws women are relegated to the status of chattel, an old French spelling of cattle, meaning, according to Webster: "1. Any item or movable or immovable property except real estate, or the freehold, or the things which are parcel of it. 2. Sometimes a slave."

The young thing who complains to her husband that she "hasn't a thing to wear" isn't kidding if she lives in South Carolina. By the laws of that state, a woman's clothes are held to be the property of her husband.

And just in case this gives the impression that such carryings-on occur only in the Deep South, there is that center of all that is civilized and cultured, New York. In the Empire State, the little woman who strains her eyes with home dressmaking or who stands over a hot stove all day cooking for boarders is entitled legally to none of her hard-won pennies. For the law says all earnings from a project in the home belong to her husband unless the brute chooses to relinquish them in her favor.

Many states consider women incompetent for jury service and bar them from it. Of the states where women may serve on juries, only nine have the same requirements for women as they have for men.

When Ma Ferguson was elected the first woman governor of Texas, she had to petition the court to set aside an indefinite something known by law as "disabilities as a married woman" in order that her acts for the state might be legal. The court solemnly entered a decree reciting that her husband's consent having been obtained, her disabilities were removed. And in certain states a favorite legal classification has referred to "idiots, lunatics, minors and married women."

A career girl in California and Nevada thinks twice before accepting a husband if she wishes to continue operating a separate business. For no matter whether she has run a successful beauty shop or real estate office for twenty years, the moment she marries she must go through a complicated court procedure to convince a judge that she is competent to engage in business.

Massachusetts, Michigan and New York are among states where the services and earnings of a minor child—be he prodigy or delivery boy—belong to the father. Alabama and Georgia prefer the father as guardian of a child's property and person while Idaho, Virginia and Texas hold that an unmarried mother can claim no funds to support her child—even though she bears the burden of the expense.

Inheritance laws in Nevada and New Mexico allow a husband to will away one-half of the common property, but the wife cannot will away one dollar, even to her children, while the husband is still alive.

In Texas, a husband may secure a divorce if his wife slips even once from her marital vows. A wife, on the other hand, must prove that her husband has deserted her and indeed is living in unfaithful sin to secure release. Kentucky accepts wifely drunkenness as sufficient reason to grant a divorce to the husband, but a wife who wants a divorce must also prove property waste and non-support on the part of her spouse.

In 1923 Senator Charles E. Curtis of Kansas, later vice president of the United States, and Representative Daniel Anthony of Kansas introduced an amendment in Congress which stated: "Men and women shall have equal rights throughout the United States and every place subject to its jurisdiction."

In the 21 years since, this same amendment has been back before each succeeding Congress but never passed. Opposition to the measure has come chiefly from two groups. One bases its opposition on traditional prejudice, which cannot be removed by laws but can be overcome eventually only by women's increasing excellence in business and professions.

The other, which includes many national women's organizations headed by the National League of Women Voters, has more concrete reasons for its opposition. The League contends that "The mischievous vagueness of the amendment means that every law treating men and women differently would be subject to challenge in the courts." The League cites, as one example, the fact that in some states the husband's failure to support his wife is cause for divorce, and asks, "Under equal rights, may a husband divorce his wife if she does not support him?"

Those opposing the passage of the Equal Rights Amendment believe that the only direct, certain and effective method for removing the laws that discriminate against women is by educating the citizenry in general and by changing the statutes state by state, by vote.

Supporters of the amendment, headed by the National Woman's Party, hold that the Equal Rights Amendment is the Bill of Rights for American women and that its passage will enable the United States, after the war, to go the Peace Conference "as a nation which has removed the bondage of chattel laws and the hazard of discriminatory legislation from its women, thus proving its belief in democratic government."

Before any woman can decide whether she is for or against the Equal Rights Amendment, she must first inform herself on the pros and cons of this large and vital question. Both the National League of Women Voters, 726 Jackson Place, Washington, DC, and the National Woman's Party, 144 B Street, NE, Washington, DC, will supply excellent literature on request. Having studied the problem, every woman who can vote should then write to her congressman, urging them to pass or drop the amendment, depending on her own personal conviction.

World War I gave women the right to vote. Perhaps World War II yet will give them completely equal rights with men—including, of course, the right to vie for that last seat in the bus, ladies.

While the headline isn't one we would use today, the article remains deeply relevant.

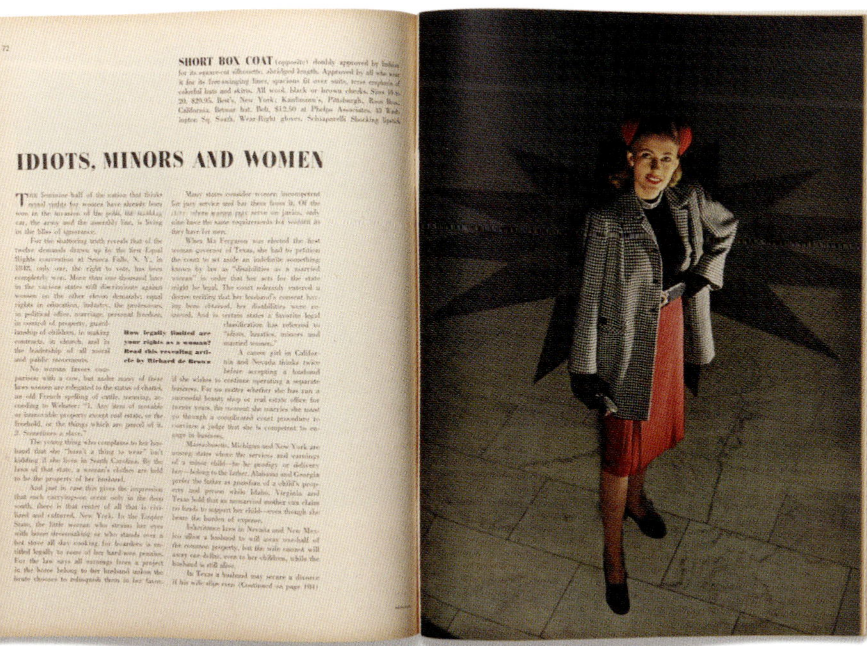

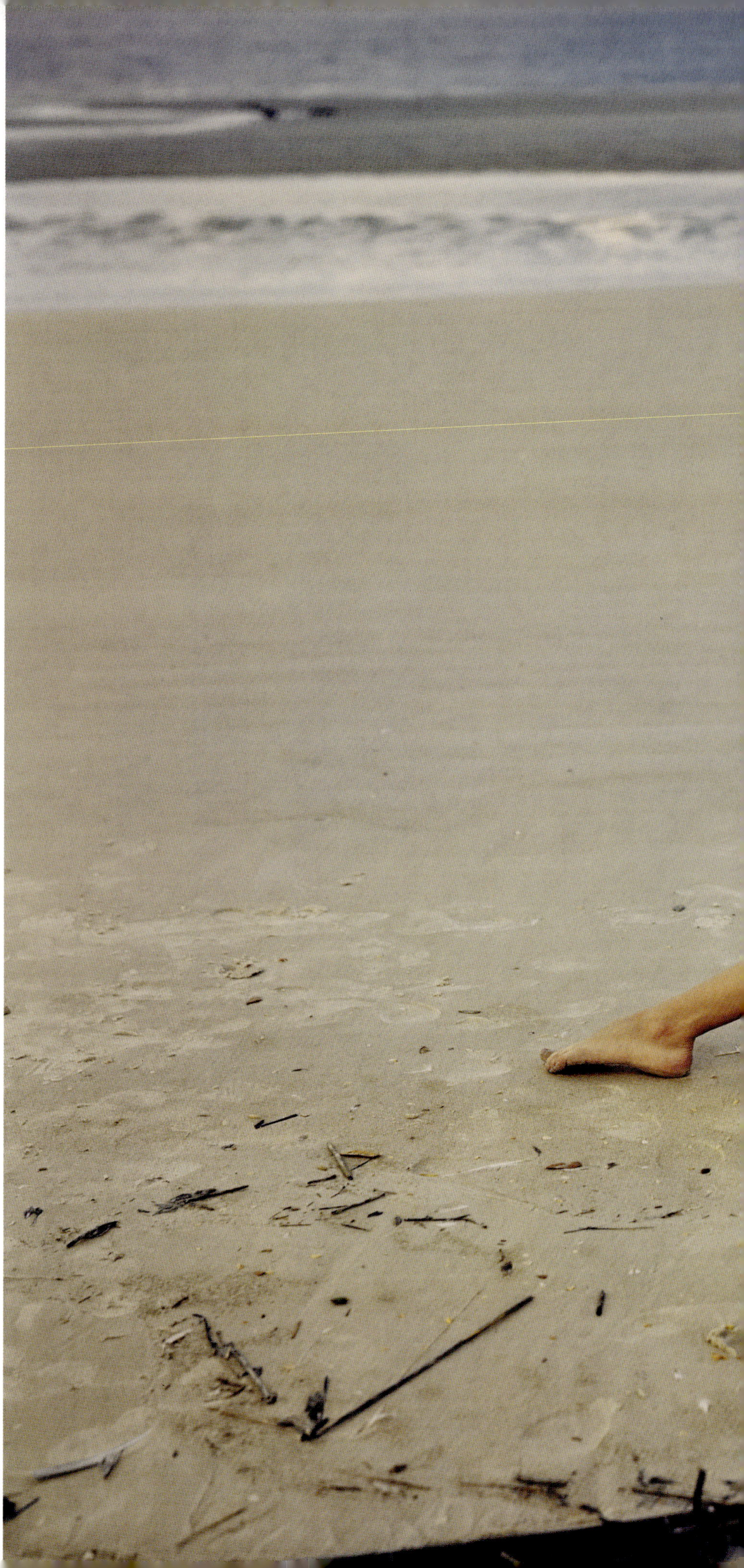

GLAMOUR'S FASHION PERSPECTIVE
was always affordable style for the career
woman. Many articles were dedicated to ward-
robes on a budget. But while the emphasis was
on keeping prices low, there was never a compromise on inspiring imagery. In the 1940s,
Glamour worked with some of America's most
important and influential photographers, men
and women alike—Diane and Allan Arbus,
Frances McLaughlin-Gill, Richard Rutledge,
Norman Parkinson, and Toni Frissell—who all
brought a unique and important lens to the era.

→

A model wrapped in a pink towel,
designed by Brigance. *Photographed
by Frances McLaughlin-Gill, July 1949.*

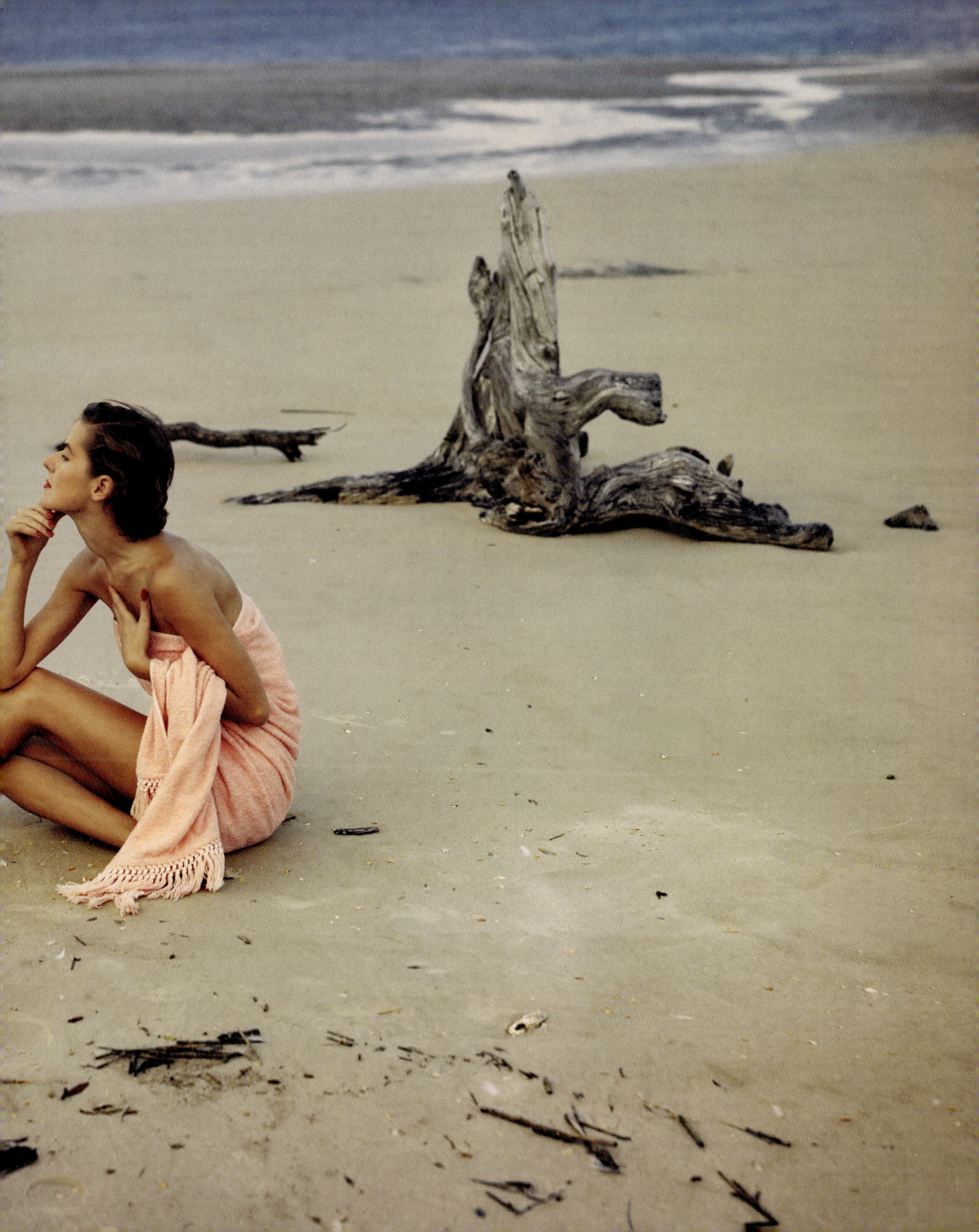

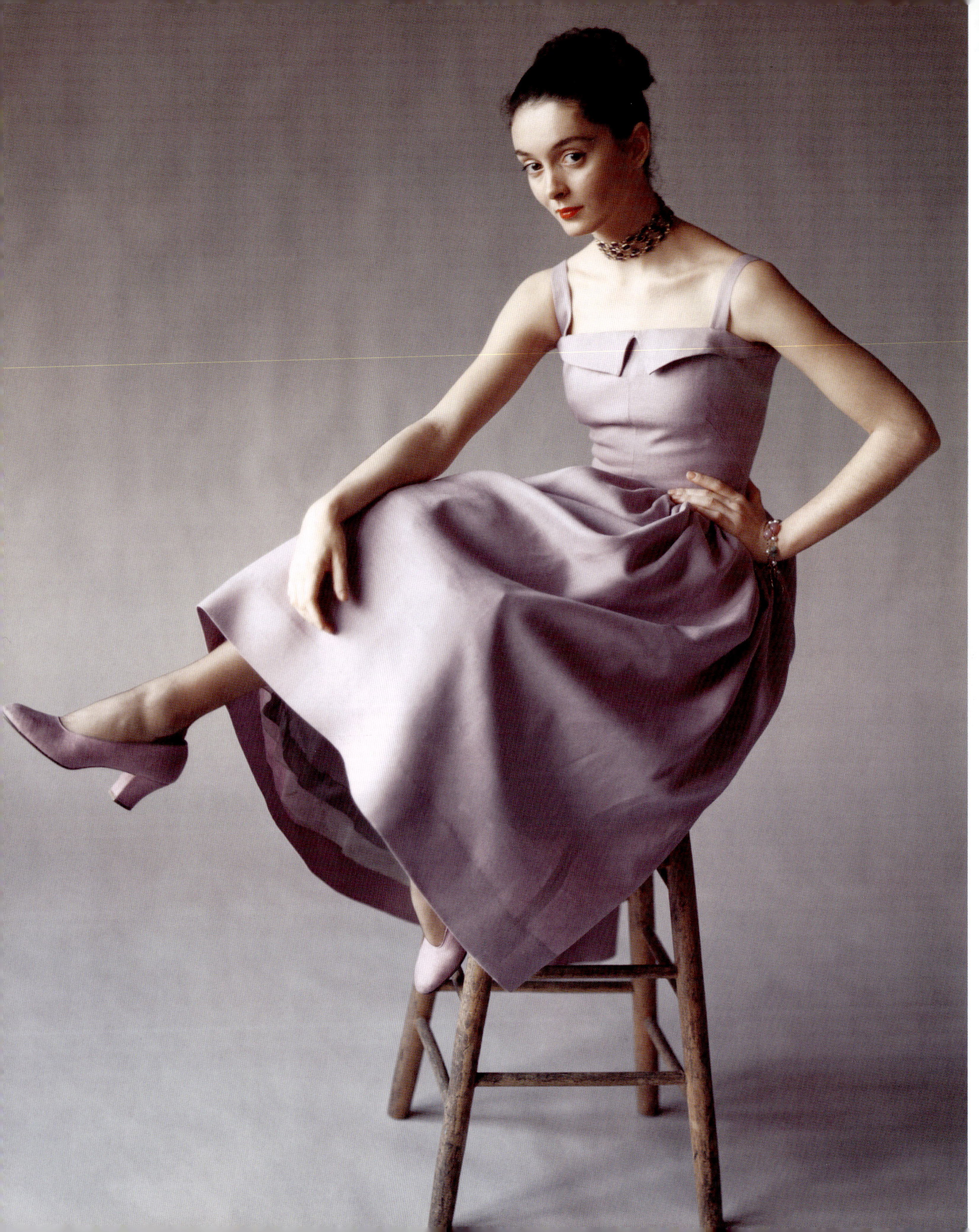

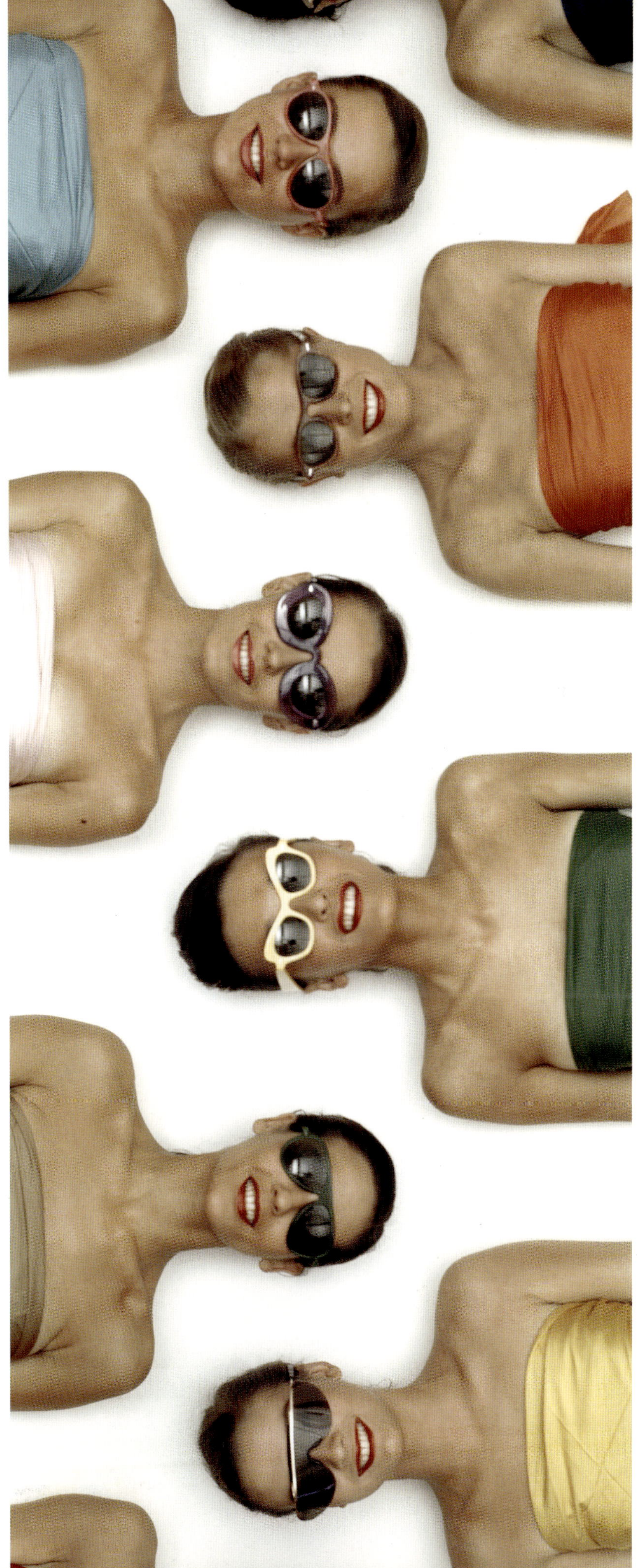

←

A model seated on a stool, wearing a mauve linen sundress based on Jr. Vogue Pattern #3206. *Photographed by Richard Rutledge, April 1948.*

→

Two rows of models lying on their backs wearing bright, strapless bodices, and each featuring a different pair of sunglasses. *Photographed by Richard Rutledge, July 1947.*

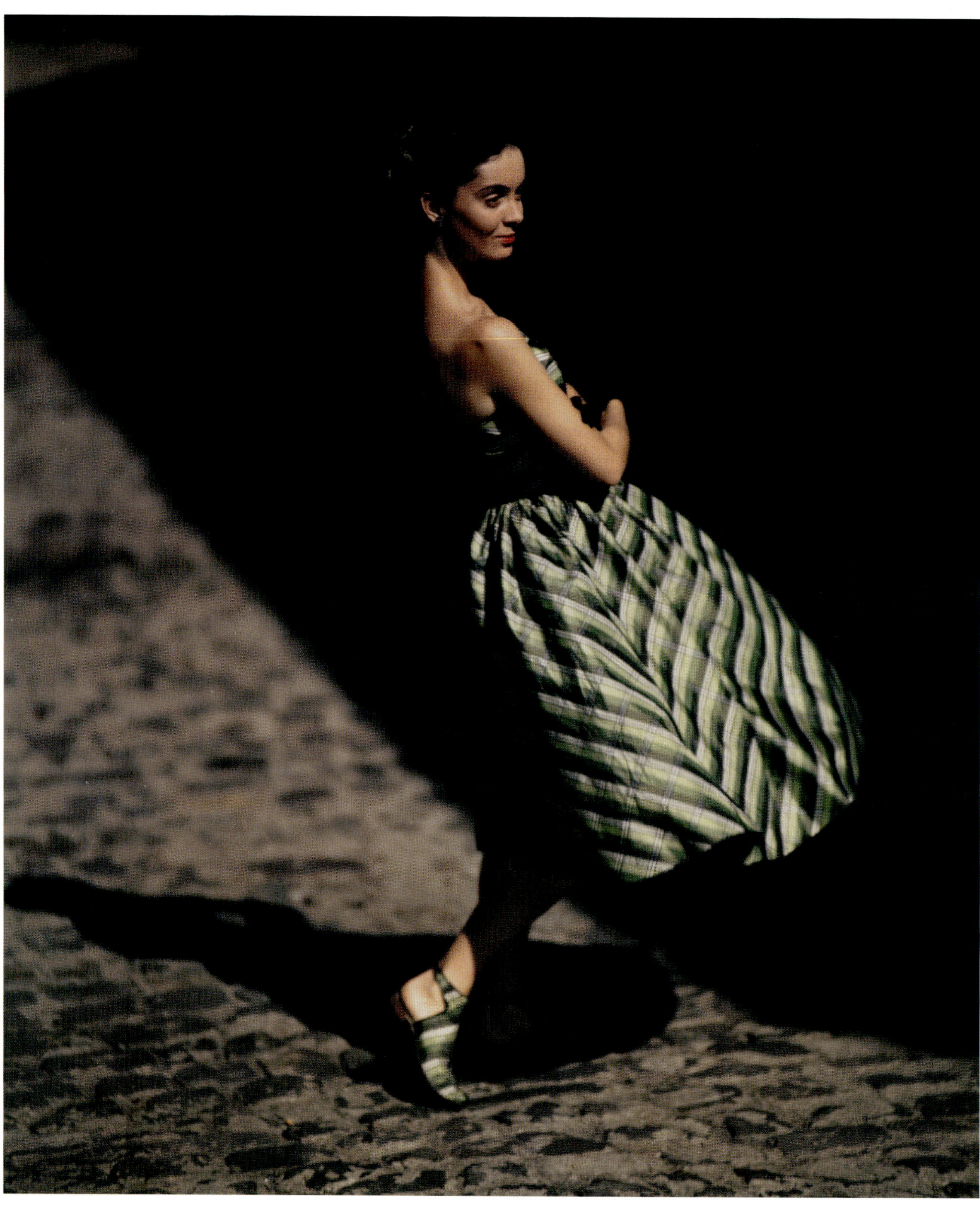

A model in a green rayon plaid taffeta dress with Capezio's matching boots. *Photographed by Frances McLaughlin-Gill, November 1946.*

Model Dovima in New York, wearing a Venetian wool broadcloth coat by Swansdown, a leopard stencil lapin muff by Winter Furs, and a cloche by Tret Marli. *Photographed by Norman Parkinson, October 1949.*

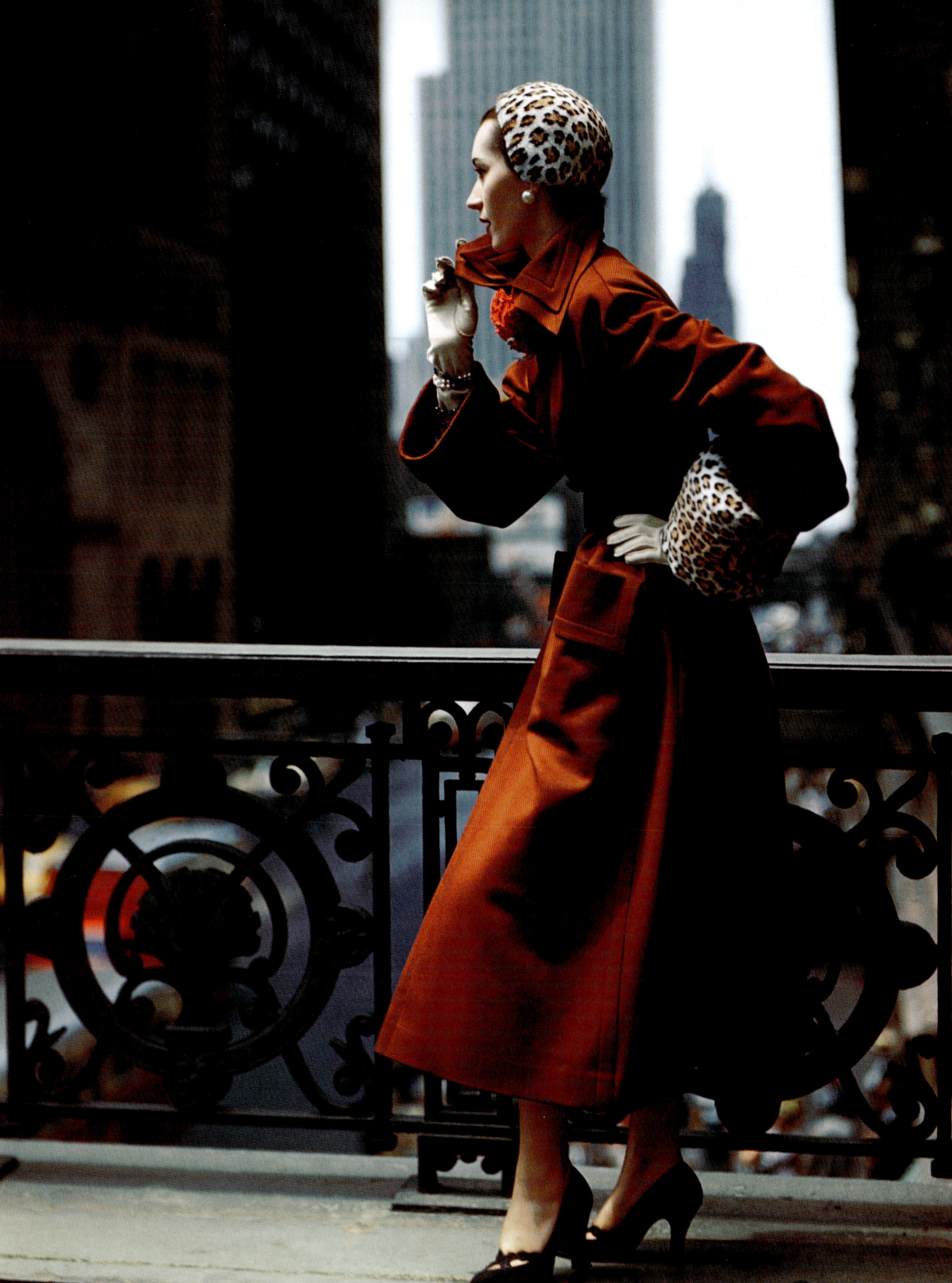

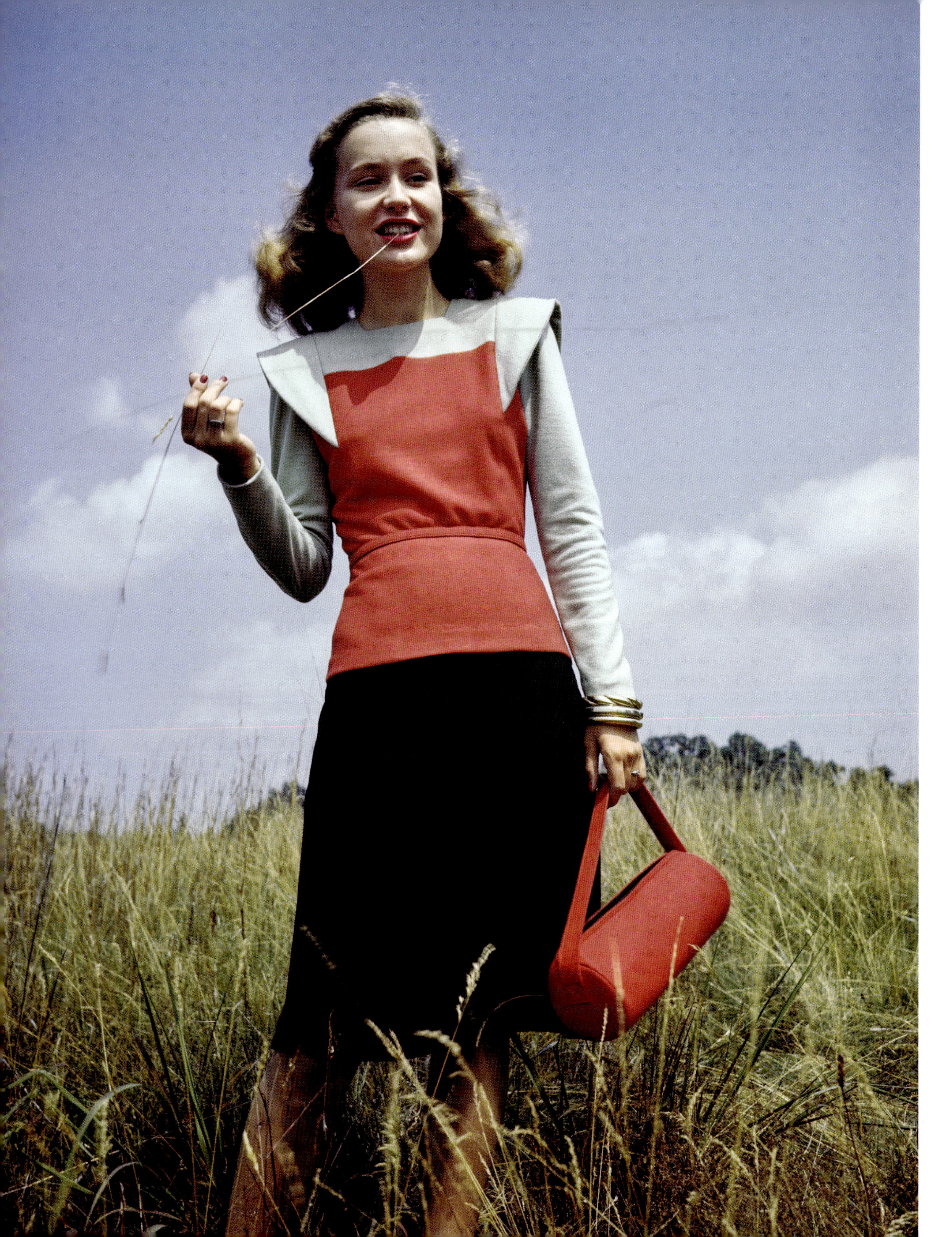

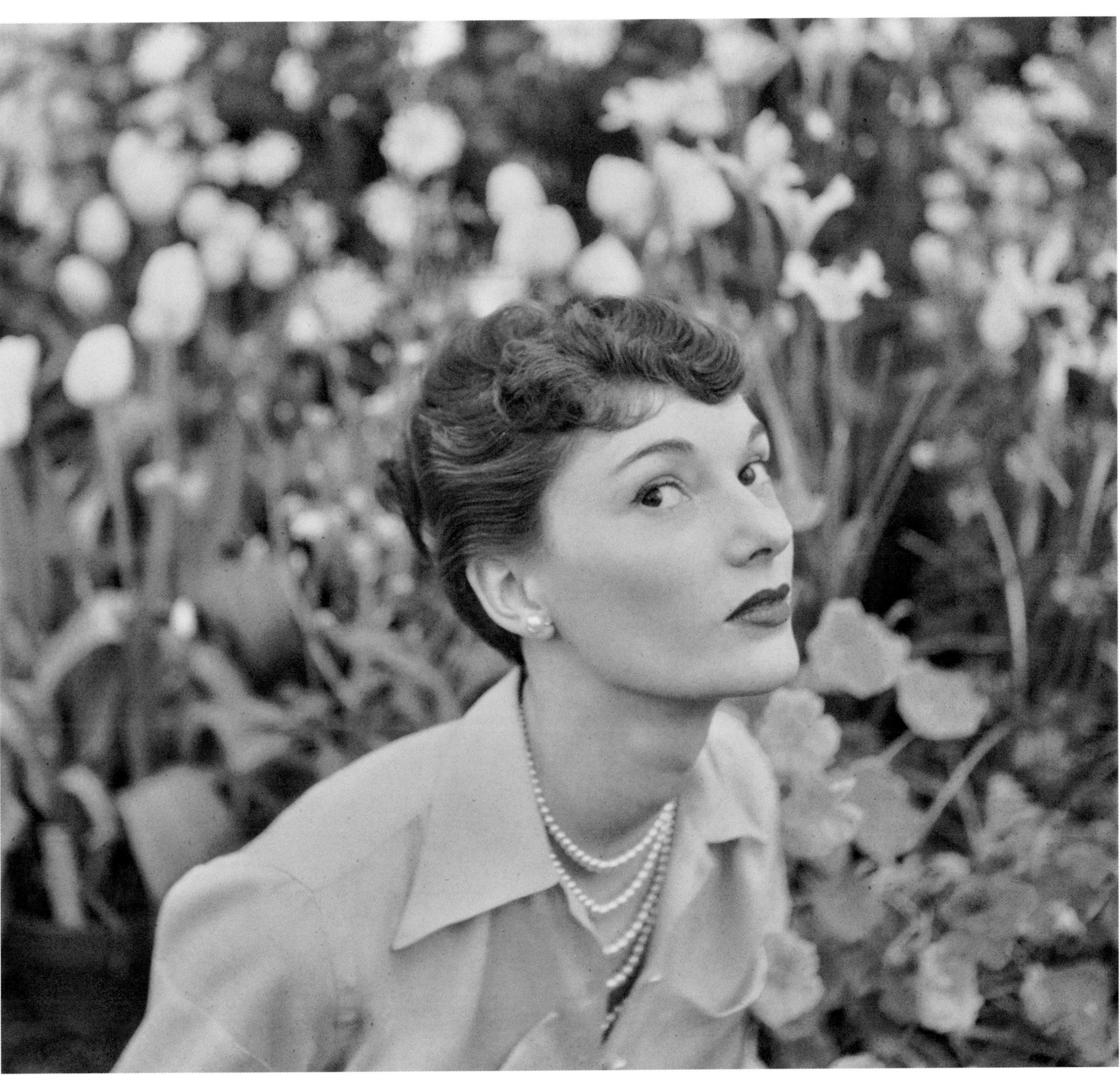

A model in a field wearing a
two-piece wool jersey back-
buttoned blouse with wide
shoulders and black skirt, both by
Carlwynn, with a carryall barrel
bag in red felt by Betmar.
*Photographed by Toni Frissell,
October 1944.*

A model in front of a flower
bed, wearing a blouse by
Claire Potter and strands of
pearls by D. Lisner, with a
tinted shingle coiffure by
Christian Frederick Jungst.
*Photographed by Diane and
Allan Arbus, July 1949.*

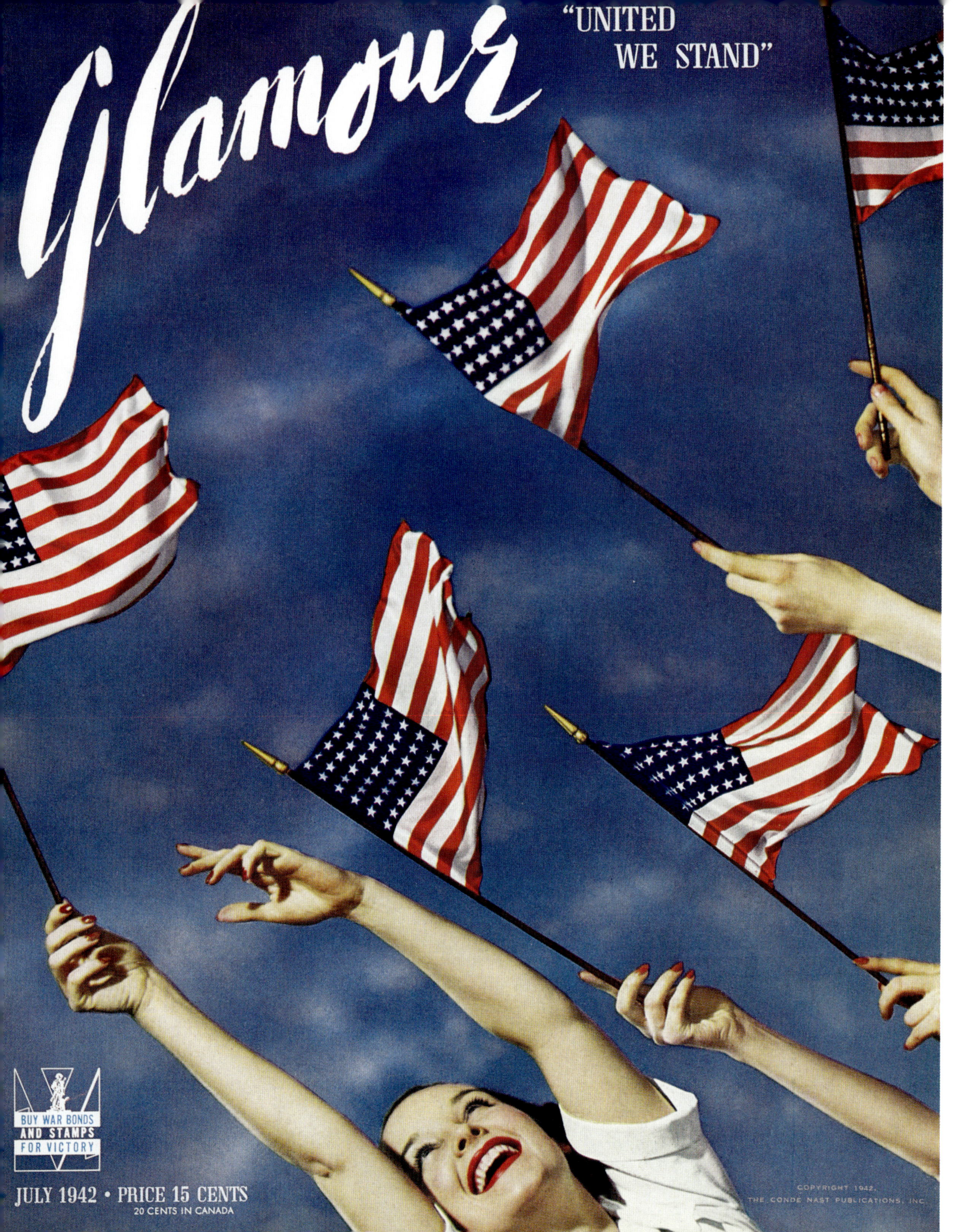

Glamour
"UNITED WE STAND"
BUY WAR BONDS AND STAMPS FOR VICTORY
JULY 1942 • PRICE 15 CENTS
20 CENTS IN CANADA
COPYRIGHT 1942,
THE CONDE NAST PUBLICATIONS, INC.

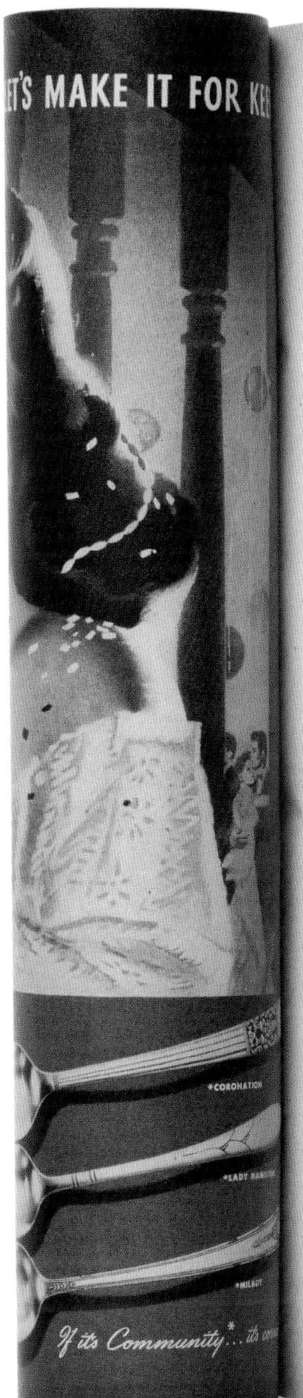

GLAMOUR
March 1947 · Careers and Spring Shopping

The·Girl with a Job stands at the Crossroads

BY ELIZABETH WESTON

THE young woman who earns her living has come a long way since the day, a very few decades ago, when she put on her hat, squared her shoulders and marched into the hostile world of business. She has surprised everyone with her progress, surpassed even the wildest dreams of her early pioneer sisters in the pinnacle she's reached and the money she's earned. She has proved her mettle over and over again, won acceptance from the doubtingest of the Thomases, past and present. She has had many triumphs. She has also made mistakes.

Today she stands at a critical juncture in her progress. The years just past have been hysterical, hire-anybody years. Personnel-starved employers have been unable to demand adequate training or truly professional performance. Salaries have been deceptively high, and business methods, of necessity, static. Now the hysteria is quieting down to normalcy, jobs are fewer, employers more exacting. What the career woman does *right now* will decide her status for a long time to come. If she can hold her own, measure up to the increased responsibility the war temporarily earned her, she will go ahead to new professional heights. If she fails to come through, she'll lose ground it may take her years to regain. So the business woman with her wits about her is taking stock, consolidating her gains and cutting her losses, looking at her future with a realistic eye.

On the whole, she finds the career picture bright. She sees business expanding, firm after firm in field after field branching out to operate on an international scale. She notes evidence of a swords-to-ploughshares activities, watches business converting war-born discoveries to peacetime uses. And she sees employment back on a healthy competitive basis...employers demanding thorough schooling qualifications and well-rounded experience for the jobs that lead places.

She looks, naturally, for the fields of work that hold special promise for women. If she's a beginner, she recognizes the wisdom of applying a general skill like stenography to a trade with a future for her. These, she finds, fall into three categories: The first, the traditional professions of women—teaching, social work, library work, nursing and retailing. These are familiar occupations, the ones in which her predecessors gained their first foothold—but they are also developing professions. She discovers each reformed or reforming, each offering new opportunity and challenge to the thoroughly equipped applicant.

The second group consists of the partially-pioneered fields of art and science. In (Continued on page 210)

***GLAMOUR* COVERED THE WAR FOR** nearly six years, during which time women found workplace success, social freedom, and financial independence. They were thriving. And *Glamour* stood with them, cheering. But if wartime victory were to come, could women hold on to their wins? This had first been contemplated as a hypothetical in February 1942 by writer Samuel Grafton, who observed, "The American woman has a terrible, creative responsibility. She has to see to it that after taking her classes faithfully, and 'helping out' until the last day of war, she is not then fobbed off with a pat on the head and a 'well done' and a one-way ticket back to peacetime complacency." By 1947, this struggle was a reality, as *Glamour* copy editor Elizabeth Weston observed in her piece above: "On the one hand she sees brilliant possibilities for the woman who wants success enough to work for it; on the other, employment offices filled with returning veterans with whom she'll be competing." It was, as the oncoming decade would show, a competition women struggled to win.

← "United We Stand," July 1942.

" **Today it's commonplace for women to... sit on judges' benches, in the President's cabinet, at the head of large industries, at the helm of newspapers and magazines, and it's as natural to them as breathing. That picture of the female as a frail creature designed for communing with the poets or gently playing the pianoforte in the parlor was a neat hoax perpetrated on us by the Victorians.**

"CAREER GIRLS, THEN AND NOW" BY GLADYS SHULTZ, MARCH 1942

" A job has become more than a weekly paycheck—it's our guarantee of confidence in ourselves. We can never be frightened again by the nightmare of utter dependence upon some other human being.

EDITORIAL, CAREER ISSUE, 1941

" NOW, GLAMOUR STANDS IN THE RECORDS OF PUBLISHING AS THE FIRST MAGAZINE TO HAVE RECOGNIZED THAT THE GIRLS WHO EARN THEIR OWN WAY AND PAY THEIR OWN BILLS ARE THE MOST VITAL ELEMENT IN THE FASHION-FOLLOWING PUBLIC. WE BELIEVE IN SUCH SMART GIRLS FOR THEY BELONG TO THE SELECT COMPANY OF THOSE WHO GO PLACES.

EDITORIAL, MARCH 1949

" A GIRL MUST GO ABOUT HER COLLEGE WORK EXACTLY AS IF HER WHOLE FUTURE HANGS ON IT PRECISELY THE WAY HER BROTHER'S FUTURE HANGS ON HIS....

"WHY DOES A GIRL GO TO COLLEGE?"
BY DIANA TRILLING, AUGUST 1948

" You are the young American women of today, belonging to no one group. You have no family crest; you don't usually have a family fortune. You may be earning a salary, or you may be stretching a young husband's salary. You may be doing both. Until recently you have had no magazine dedicated to you or the role you play in American life.

EDITORIAL, APRIL 1941

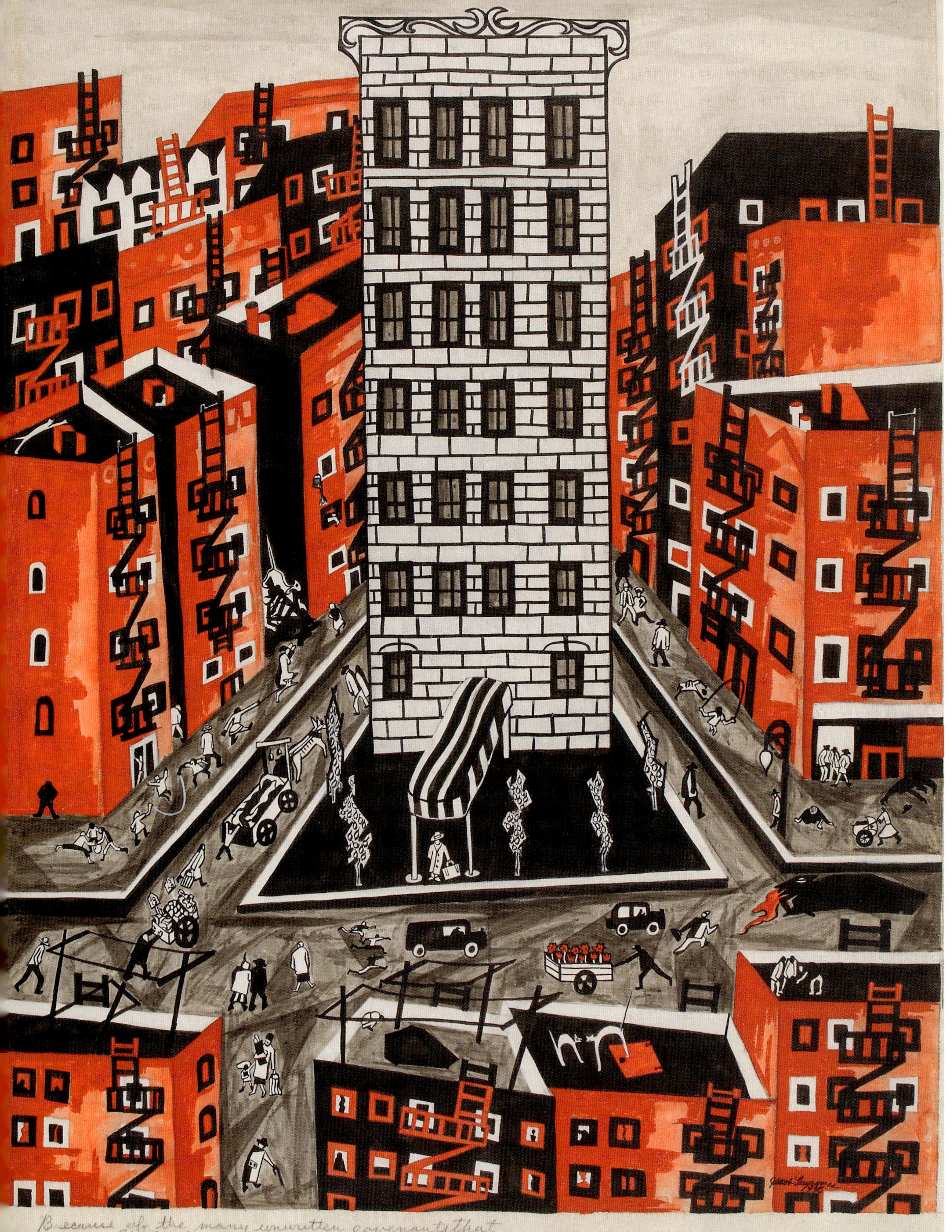

Because of the many unwritten covenants that exist in N.Y.C. Vacant living quarters are

Tackling Prejudice

This watercolor, *Harlem*, by award-winning Black artist Jacob Lawrence was printed in *Glamour*'s July 1946 issue. © 2023 The Jacob and Gwendolyn Knight Lawrence Foundation, Seattle / Artists Rights Society (ARS), New York. Jule Collins Smith Museum of Fine Art, Auburn University; Advancing American Art Collection.

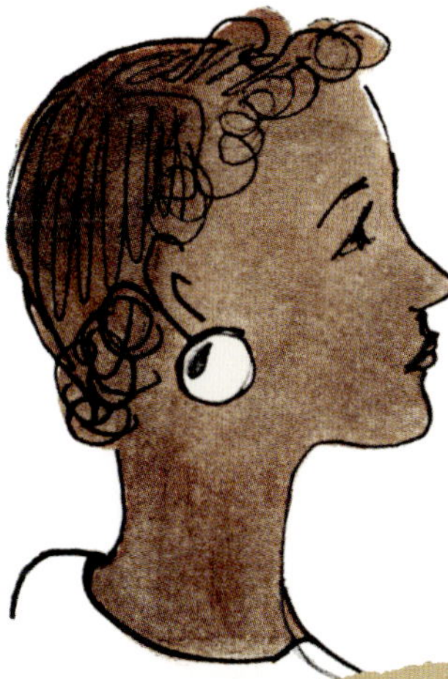

An illustration from a fashion story, July 1946. "Tolerance Begins at Home," July 1945. A headline confronting antisemitism, July 1946.

IN THE JULY 1945 ISSUE, amid the devastation of the Second World War, *Glamour* posed a thought-provoking question to its readers: "How Tolerant Are You?" Without sugarcoating, the magazine stated: "This quiz is designed to measure your unconscious and unfounded prejudices. A score of 100% means that you are an unprejudiced, well-informed, and world-minded citizen. Below 80% means you are fine Fascist soil for the seeds of another war." As well as tackling antisemitism, the questionnaire challenged readers to name three bestselling authors tackling interracial problems, and asked whether they were aware that for every dollar spent educating white children, only 35 cents were allocated to Black students. The accompanying piece also denounced the Ku Klux Klan, advocated for interfaith relations between Jews and Christians, exposed the pernicious effects of Jim Crow laws, and reported on the Mayor's Committee on Race Relations in Chicago, which backed unsegregated and cooperative housing.

Glamour was by no means a beacon of inclusivity—its cover stars remained 100% white until August 1968, with only occasional appearances by women of color inside—but editor in chief Elizabeth Penrose was dedicated to challenging readers and promoting a more enlightened perspective on race relations. In August 1946, the magazine featured a report on "A New Kind of School," without quotas, where students of all races studied together. And two years later, in August 1948, *Glamour* published an article about International House, student living quarters "where young people of every color, culture and country on earth have learned to live and work together." But perhaps the most significant contribution from the magazine came in July 1946, with an entire issue dedicated to helping readers better understand their world. An up-front editorial argued: "America has grown great through the efforts of the many—and can stay great only if the many have equal respect and opportunity." A few pages later, tackling "Beauty…and the color of a skin," readers were told, "Even if you are limited to 'white'…and what a limitation!…there are eleven kinds of white skin…. As for the differences, thank heaven for them. So throw away those labels. Beauty…like hope and laughter…can't be type-cast." And just a few pages further on, in a piece called "The Harlem Nobody Knows," the author Bucklin Moon wrote about the "injustices of segregation" and the deeply flawed misconceptions about the Black community in Harlem. That same issue also called on readers to confront antisemitism, and featured artwork by the award-winning Black painter Jacob Lawrence and the Jewish artist Marc Chagall. It is vitally important to note that these articles from the era were written from a white perspective, and none by Black authors. But despite the magazine's shortcomings, the staff were not blind to the inequalities and injustices inflicted on marginalized populations—and they used their voice to shed light on these issues.

A Sexual Awakening

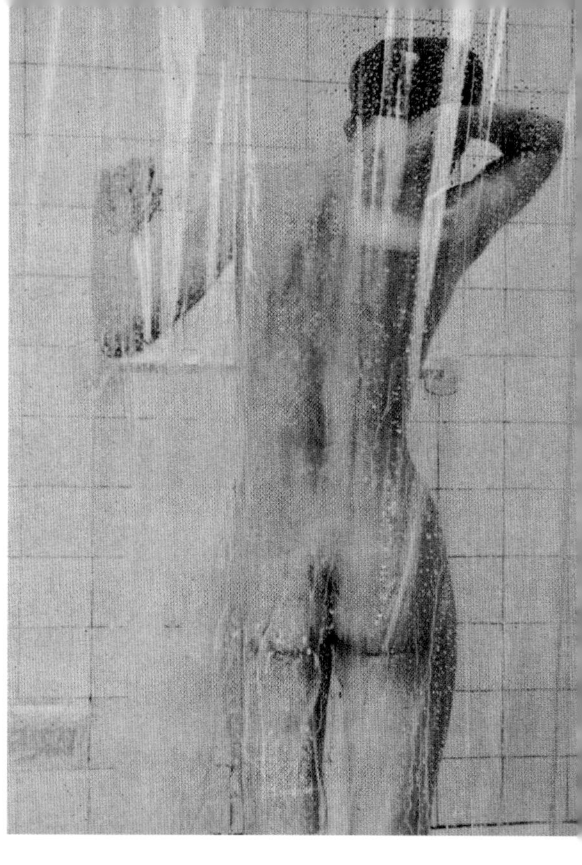

THE ISSUES OF SEX, MARRIAGE, RELATIONSHIPS, AND divorce featured prominently—and often surprisingly progressively—over the course of the first decade of *Glamour*'s existence. In the May 1943 issue, writer Louise Fox Connell explored the topic of "promiscuity" during wartime. Regarding unmarried sexual relations, she argued that women "have the perfect right to pooh-pooh the whole idea if you think it foolish and unwise. But it is equally your privilege to grant such little favors if you find him attractive and know him well enough to feel like it." And in the December 1947 issue Marynia F. Farnham, MD, discussed the sanctity, or not, of sex before marriage: "As women have gradually become more and more emancipated, the general conception of what is acceptable moral conduct for them has become more liberal…. The world in which we live today is one where women are thrown into easy contact with men, where young women are taught to regard premarital relations as dangerous and immoral, and yet where they eventually discover that such rules are constantly violated…. There is no one answer to the premarital sex question. Each individual must answer it for herself."

And as many questions about sex as there were on the agenda, there were also many about rising divorce rates. It presented *Glamour* with a dilemma: how to tackle the question of marriage. But, as ever, *Glamour*'s editor in chief Elizabeth Penrose thrived in the face of a challenge. In an up-front editorial entitled "Our Marriage Problem," she wrote: "Traditionally, bridal issues of magazines are pretty to look at, sentimental to read. But planning this issue, we could not escape the cold and sobering facts concerning marriage in America today. In 1945, one out of every three marriages in this country ended in divorce. When the 1946 figures are complete, the rate is expected to jump to one divorce for every two, or two and one-half marriages…. There can be no doubt that the failure of American marriage is not a threat, but an actuality." The team took it upon themselves to offer their readers advice from successfully married women—but with typical *Glamour* irreverence: "I proposed to my husband," the writer Page H. Dougherty begins. "I think it is as important for a woman to marry the man of her choice as it is for a man to marry the woman of his choice, so I took the initiative."

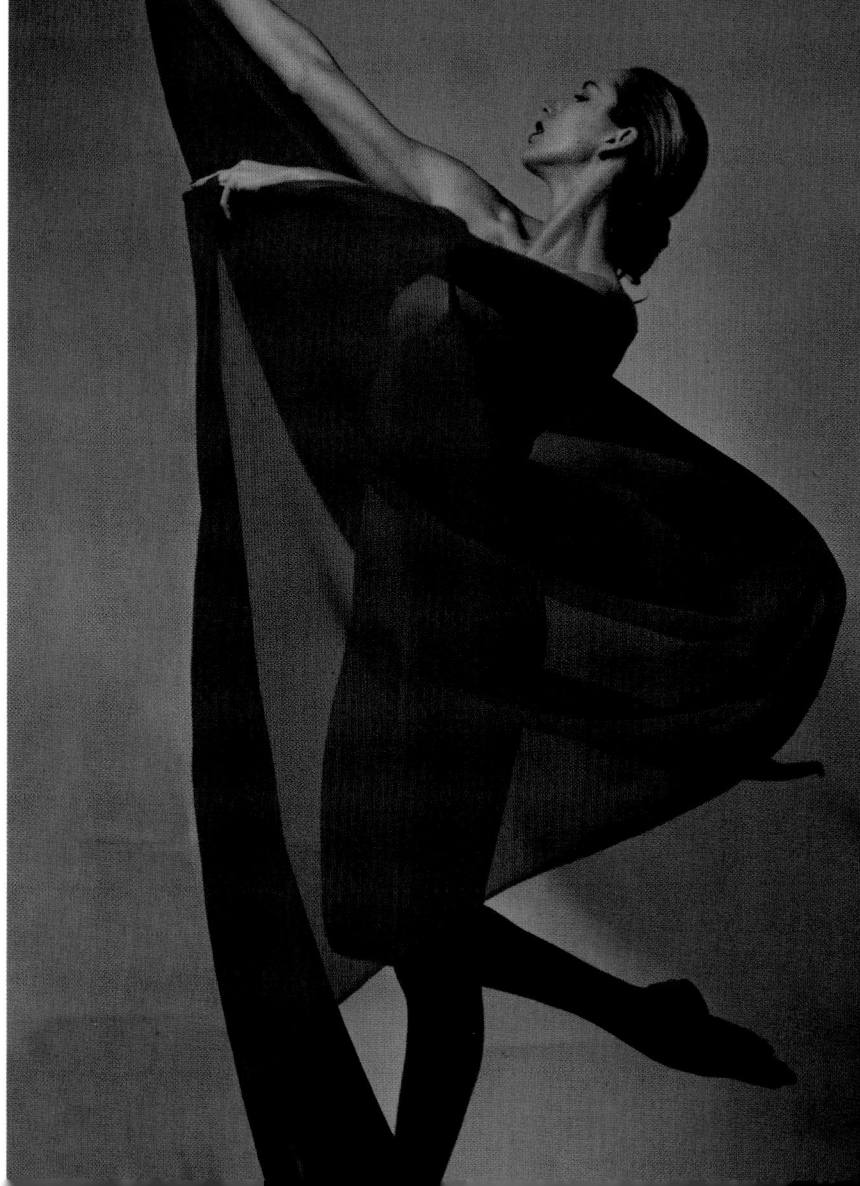

Right, a nude model stretching in a red Claire McCardell scarf. *Photographed by Gjon Mili, May 1946.* **Above, a model in the shower.** *Photographed by Frances McLaughlin-Gill, July 1944.*

The Problem of
Pre-marital Sex Relations

BY MARYNIA F. FARNHAM, M. D.

EDITOR'S NOTE: Dr. Farnham, psychiatrist and co-author of the widely debated book, "Modern Woman, the Lost Sex," is choosing as her subjects for this series of articles those problems which letters from readers reveal to be their most troubling problems. All letters are answered personally and complete anonymity is preserved. However, all any conscientious adviser can attempt to do by correspondence, and with only a superficial knowledge of the individual and her difficulties, is to give counsel in broad terms or, if necessary, to direct the writer to sources in her vicinity where competent guidance may be obtained. All letters should be addressed to Marynia F. Farnham, M.D., GLAMOUR, *420 Lexington Ave., N. Y. 17.*

For the past three months, this department has sought to give you briefly the basic information you should have on the subject of psychiatry in order to be able to understand better your emotions and the personal problems that grow out of them. In the September issue, we told you that psychiatry is the medical study of man's personality, or inner self, as opposed to his person, or outer self. In October we discussed the elements that go to make up the personality, or non-physical aspect of man—that is, the id, ego and super-ego that are responsible for one's feelings and behavior. And finally, last month, we explained the real meaning of happiness, and pointed out the essential causes of unhappiness—the fundamental requirements for happiness.

With the foregoing articles as background, we now come to the real purpose of these articles, which is to try to help readers solve their special personal problems.

WHAT ARE THE TROUBLESOME
ASPECTS OF THE PROBLEM?

In the letters addressed to this department, among the subjects that predominate are the problems related to pre-marital sexual relations. Some of the questions asked are: "Is sex play, without fulfillment, physically harmful?" "Is chastity physically harmful?" "Do pre-marital relations interfere with physical satisfaction in marriage?" "Do sexual relations before marriage make it difficult for men to respect a girl,

and therefore decrease her chances for marriage?" "Can a girl have dates and hold a man's interest without satisfying his wish for sexual relations?"

These questions present no problem to the many young women with firm, positive, religious or ethical convictions. This article is addressed to those without a strong, reliable authority to guide them, for to these young women the question of sex before marriage is a highly perturbing personal problem.

HOW SOCIAL CHANGES HAVE
ALTERED SEX CONVENTIONS

Up to the first World War, young women generally were not exposed to any doubt. Prior to this period, woman's position was clearly defined, morally and economically. If she was not chaste, she was "bad"; if she did not marry, keep house and bear children, she was considered something of a failure—an old maid, and thus a subject for mild jibes and ridicule. Women, by and large, did not work for their living. It was not until the war of 1914-1918 brought women out of chaperonage that the "double standard"—one code of sexual behavior for men and another for women—was questioned for the first time.

Today, we are in a transitional period in which we see a conflict between the strict moral code of Victorian times and a freer kind of behavior on the part of women. As women have gradually become more and more emancipated, the general conception of what is acceptable moral conduct for them has become more liberal. Now, from earliest school days on, females meet males on a freer, more casual basis. Chaperonage for young girls has all but disappeared. Moreover, a very large proportion of women, both married and single, have jobs. Probably as a direct result of the fact that women today are trained to support themselves and there is no social stigma against so doing, many are marrying, not of social necessity, but of choice. For many this means postponement of marriage.

The world in which we live today is one where women are thrown into easy contact with men, where young women are taught to regard pre-marital relations as dangerous and immoral, and yet where they (Continued on page 130)

> **"**
> **There is no one answer to the premarital sex question.**
> **Each individual must answer it for herself.**
>
> MARYNIA F. FARNHAM, MD

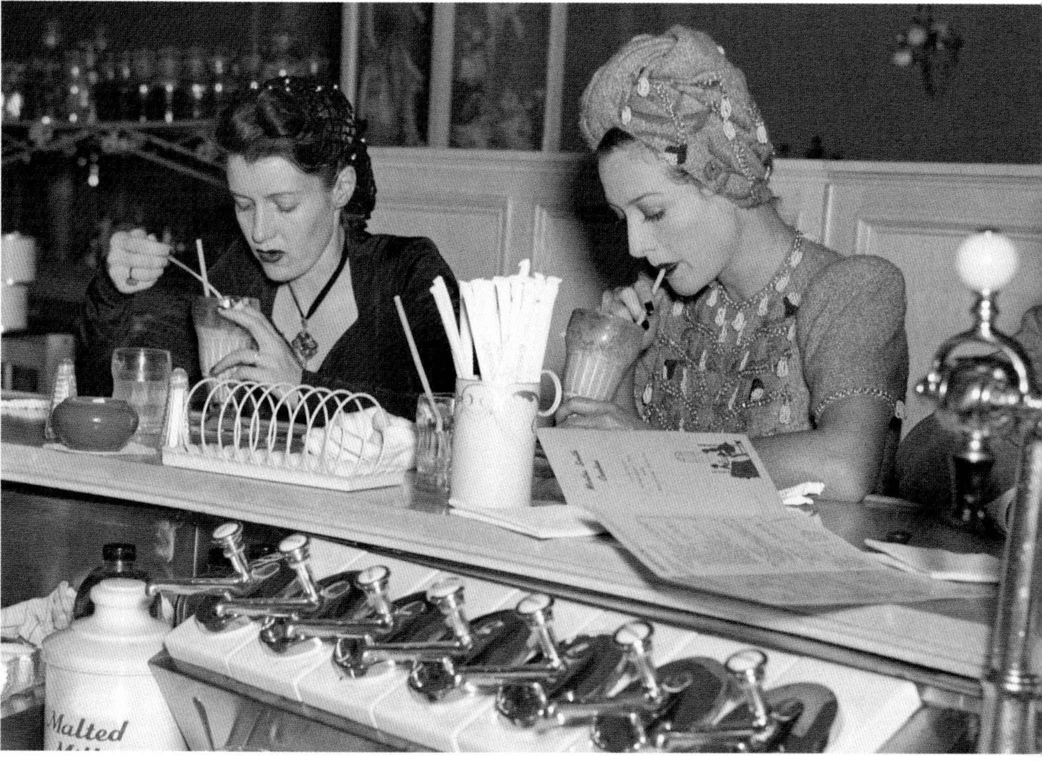

→

Actor Joan Crawford in an embroidered sweater and matching turban with editor Alice Thompson at a malt shop. *Photographed by Alexander Paal, December 1939.*

Glamour Staff

WHILE *GLAMOUR*'S STAFF MASTHEAD MAY HAVE BEEN small, at least in the first few years, this was not reflective of the numerous staff members who were crucial parts of the team over the course of the decade. Some were employed by Condé Nast when *Glamour* was simply an idea, others joined as the magazine swelled in influence and size. Many were introduced to readers via their writing. Others—job department editors, illustrators, fashion editors, secretaries—toiled hard behind the scenes bringing covers to life, answering reader letters, or plotting fashion shoots that would influence the working girl's wardrobe. Regardless, they were all of vital import. Here, you'll find some of *Glamour*'s staff from the era.

Two years ago *Glamour* started as a voice for you—the young American woman.

EDITORIAL, APRIL 1941

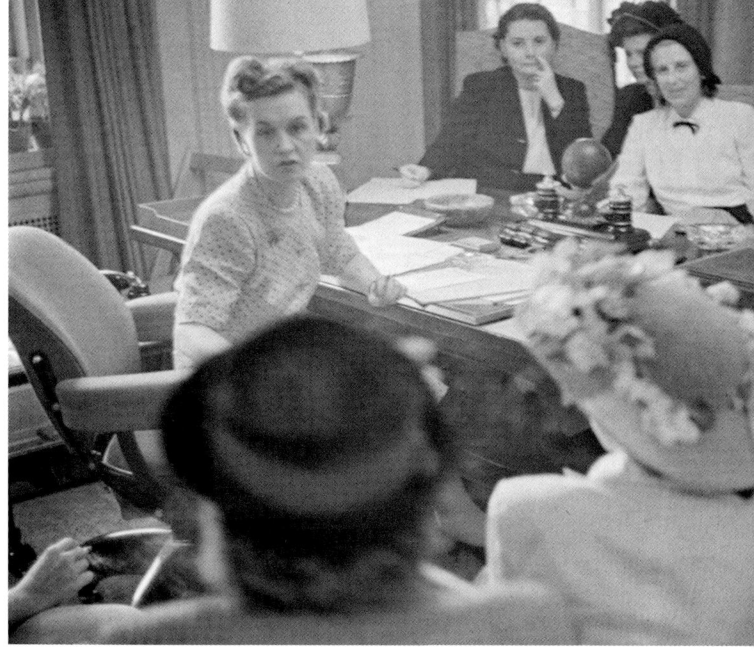

↑

Glamour staff, including editor in chief Elizabeth Penrose, at the Condé Nast offices in the Graybar Building in midtown Manhattan. *Photographed by Luis Lemus, September 1946.*

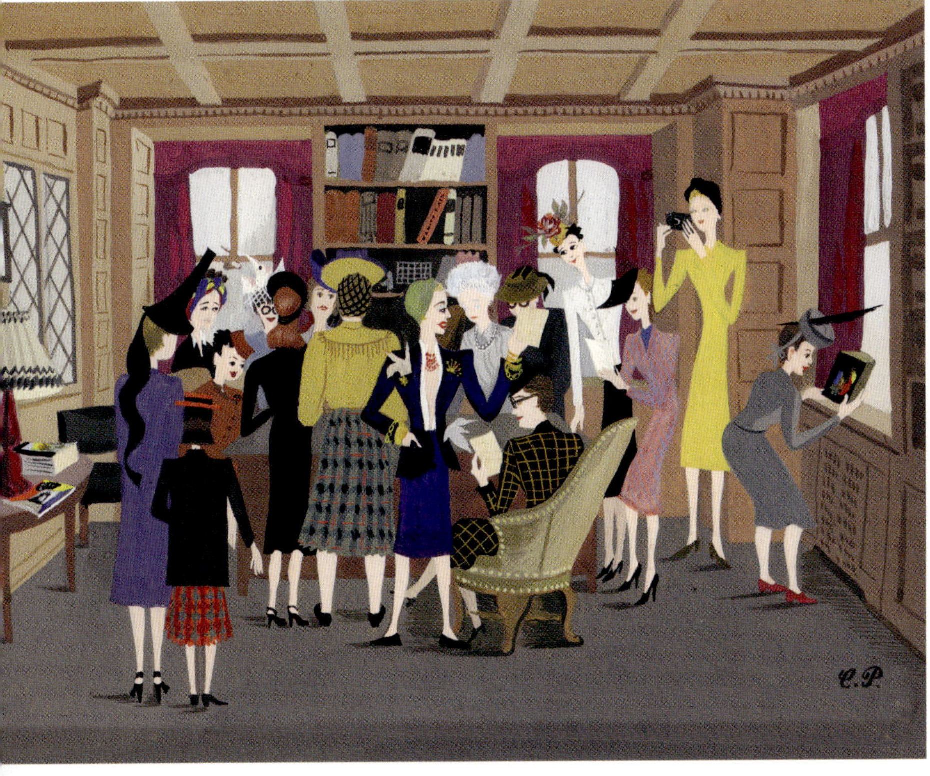

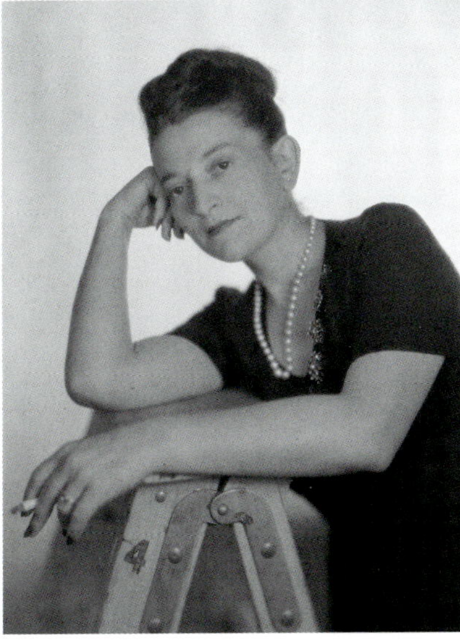

Glamour's art editor and graphic designer, Cipe Pineles. *Photographed by Constantin Joffé, August 1945.*

This 1939 painting, by *Glamour*'s art editor, Cipe Pineles, depicts editors around the desk of Condé Nast's then art director Dr. Agha.

Glamour's art director, Alexander Liberman, and art department staffer Tina Safranski at the Condé Nast offices. *Photographed by Luis Lemus, September 1946.*

Glamour's managing editor, Irene Kittle. *Photographed by Glenn Green, 1941.*

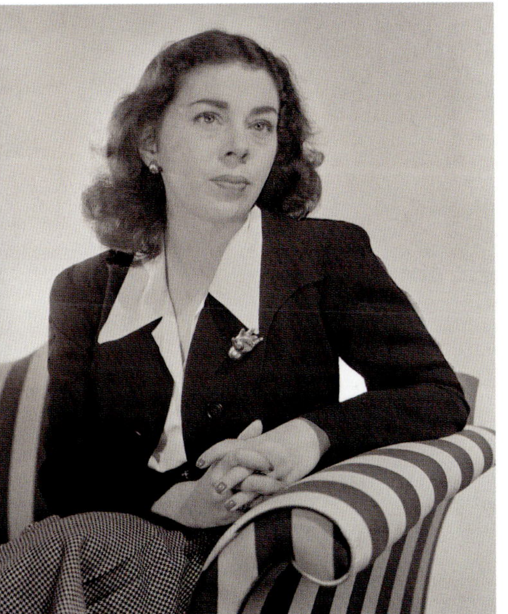

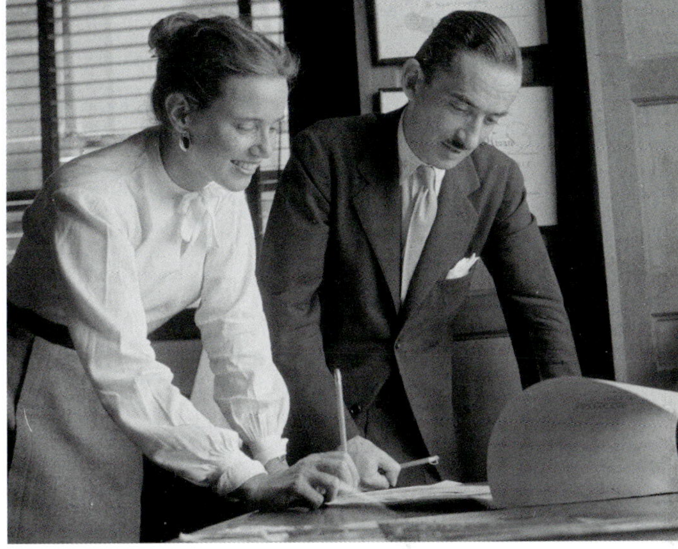

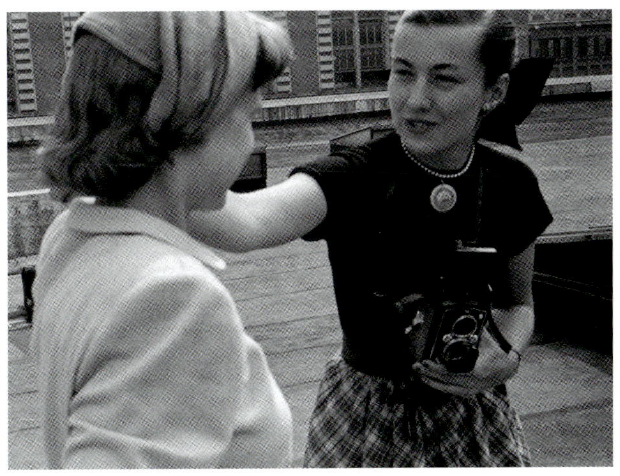

Photographer Frances McLaughlin-Gill arranging a model's outfit on the rooftop of the Graybar Building. *Photographed in July 1946 by Luis Lemus.*

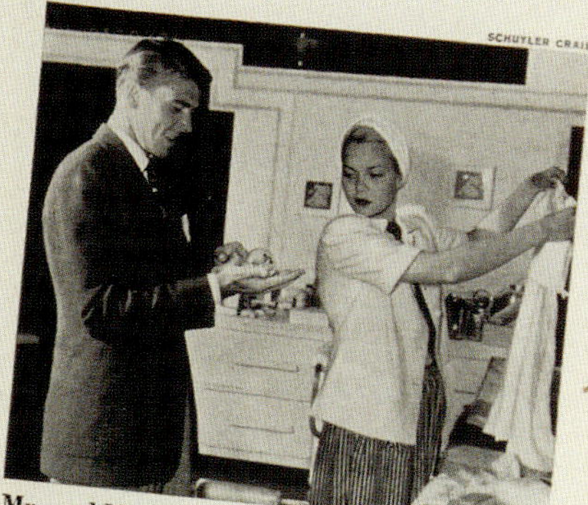

Mr. and Mrs. Reagan go a-shopping. She wears a slim stripe skirt, a light longer-length jacket

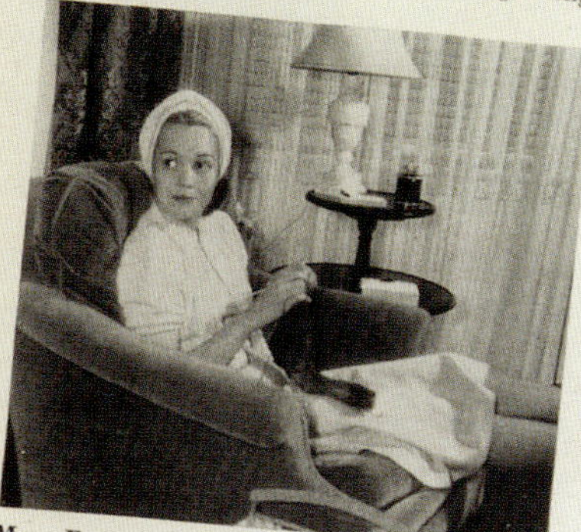

Mrs. Reagan, just finished a picture, enjoys knitting (the conventional tiny garments?)

You're going to have a baby?

...so are the Reagans

THE idea that baby-having is to glamour what laryngitis is to a soprano is fast going down the drain. Just look at Hollywood. Everyone—practically—is having a baby.

On this page we show you some happy mother-and-father-to-be photographs of Mr. and Mrs. Ronald Reagan, both talented young Warner Bros.' stars. "Santa Fé Trail" is Mr. Reagan's latest film, and the two will appear together in "Tugboat Annie Sails Again." Mrs. Reagan is Jane Wyman, professionally speaking, and has just finished "Honeymoon for Three." That's right—*just* finished.

The coming young one has slowed down Mrs. Reagan not a whit. Her maternity clothes and activities are as unselfconscious as those dated pre-blessed event. Her "condition" is definitely not to be referred to as "delicate." She intends to keep up her normal life until The Day, and takes a special pride in her maternity evening clothes.

Her young philosophy that having a baby should be taken in stride is reflected in the next two pages of smart, young mother-to-be clothes, chosen for glamour-plus by *Glamour*.

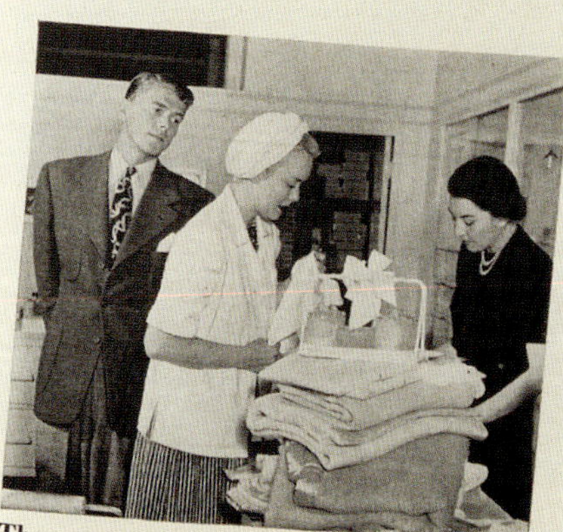

The prospective parents assemble the bassinet, although Mr. R. obviously prefers sporting goods

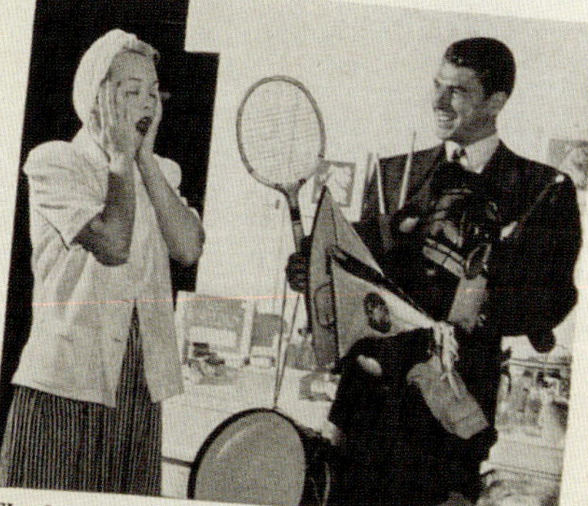

The head of the house seems to think the baby will be playing tennis with him pretty soon

---

GLAMOUR WASN'T JUST A chronicler of women's fashion and women's issues; it was also an incredible incubator for young artistic talent—and a documenter of society. In this republished set of photographs from the November 1940 issue, you will find the young Hollywood actor, and future president of the United States, Ronald Reagan with his pregnant first wife, Jane Wyman. Andy Warhol was also an important contributor to the magazine. Before he reached his extraordinary levels of fame, he got a break illustrating articles for *Glamour*. His first set was published in the September 1949 issue, opposite. He continued contributing to the magazine, and even illustrated the April 1955 cover.

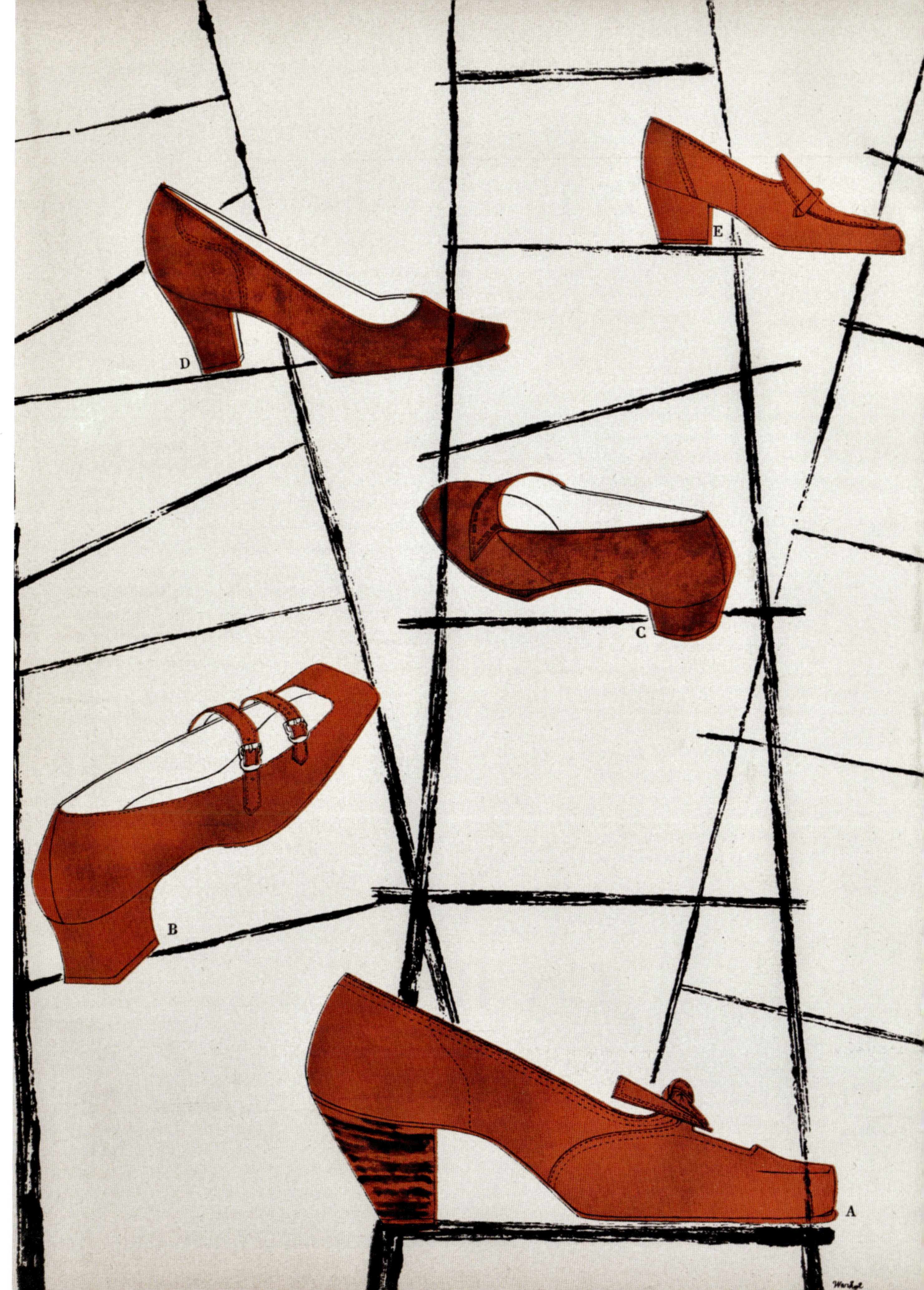

E
D
C
B
A

La Conga — How to do the basic steps in that popular dance

IT has its origin in the native dances of Cuba, its music and steps in authentic Afro-Cubana rhythms. After civilization added its polite veneer, the throbbing Conga swept the country—with more verve than veracity, as any night-clubbing editor can see even without her glasses. To speed up Conga lines, we give you directions for basic Conga steps. Stars Rita Hayworth and Glenn Ford, who appear in Columbia's "The Lady in Question," show you variations.

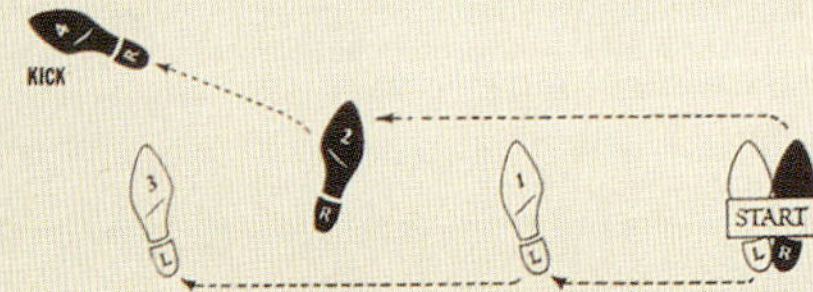

The basic Conga step, illustrated above, is simple as one, two, three, four. That's what it is—with a kick on the fourth beat. This diagram is for the man. The girl's step is simply the reverse. *Directions:* 1) Step left with left foot. 2) Cross right foot over left, continuing the walk in the same direction. 3) Step to left with left foot again. 4) Swing or kick right foot across left. 5) Repeat in opposite direction. Master this, and you have practically "arrived."

The Conga Rock is an easy variation for the fourth beat of the basic step. It is danced with the first three basic steps taken either straight ahead for the man (backwards for the girl) or sideways. In either case, the man starts on his left foot, the girl on her right. On the *fourth* beat, the man rocks back on his *right* foot, kicking up his left. The girl rocks back on her left foot, kicking up her right. This can go on indefinitely. It's a good change from regular kick.

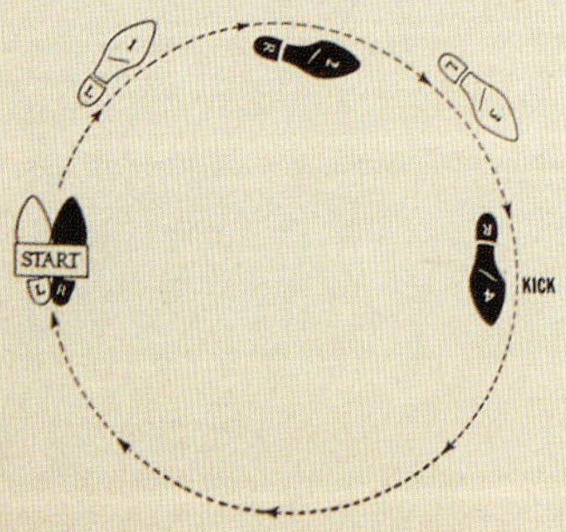

The Conga Turn, illustrated at left, is a simple deviation from the basic step. It, like the Rock, is woven into the pattern of La Conga when prompted by music or mood. The man walks in a circular direction for three steps, then makes the characteristic Conga kick on the fourth beat. The girl dances at her partner's *side*, and as he kicks *forward* on each fourth beat, she kicks in the direction from which they have danced. These three steps, plus the weaving Conga line in which dancers do La Conga with a hand on the shoulder of the next person, are the essentials of the dance . . . a simple technique plus rhythm. Easy, with a bit of living-room practice.

Diagrams and directions for La Conga, courtesy Arthur Murray

In the November 1940 issue, Glenn Ford and Rita Hayworth teach *Glamour* readers how to conga dance, in a set of step-by-step images.

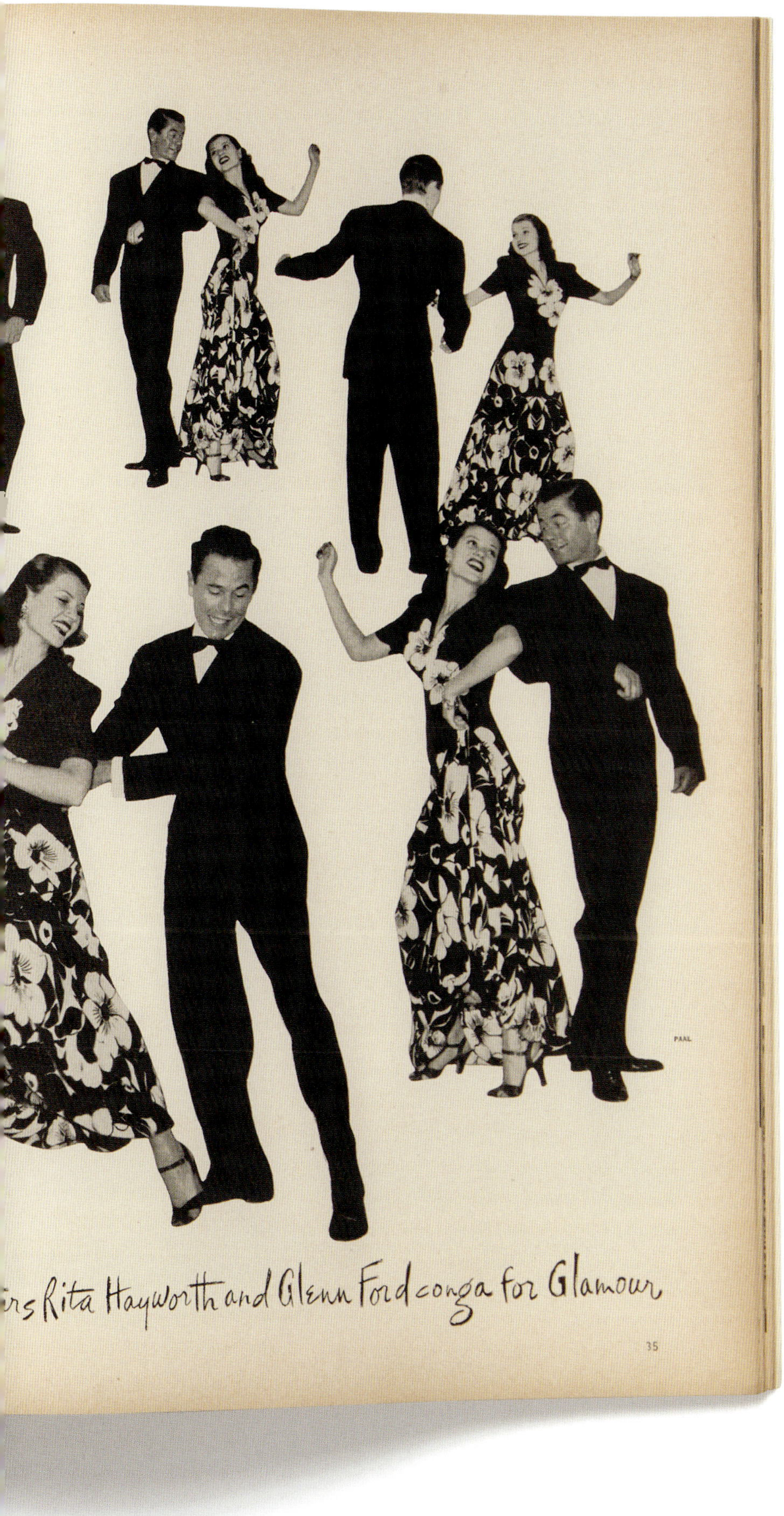

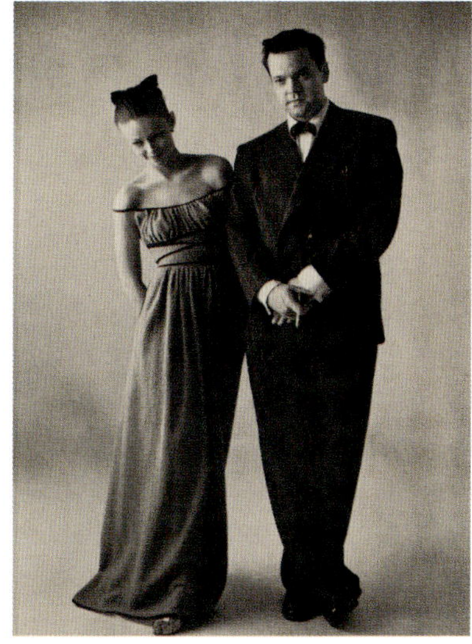

The actor and director Orson Welles photographed with the model Ron Compton. *Photographed by Irving Penn, November 1946.*

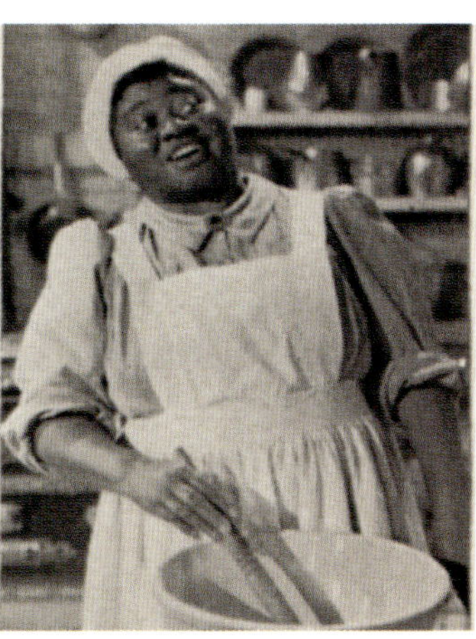

This image of actor Hattie McDaniel as Violet in *The Great Lie*, from the April 1941 issue, was the first time a woman of color appeared in *Glamour*. In 1949, she became the first Black American to win an Oscar.

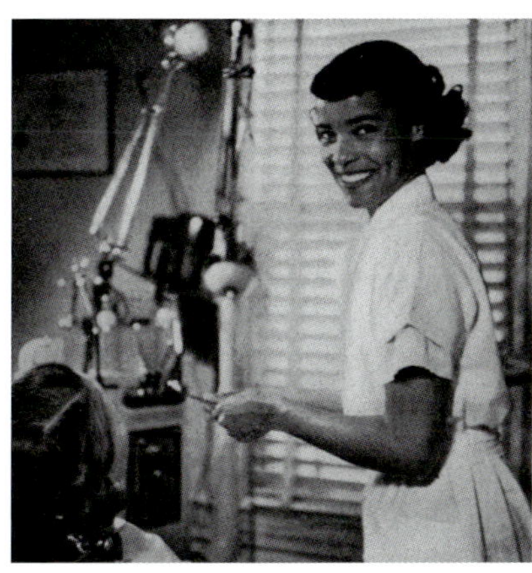

Thelma Porter, the first Black Miss Subways New York, a psychology major at Brooklyn College, and a dentist's office worker, appeared in an article entitled "How to beat the high cost of college." *Photographed by William Grigsby, August 1948.*

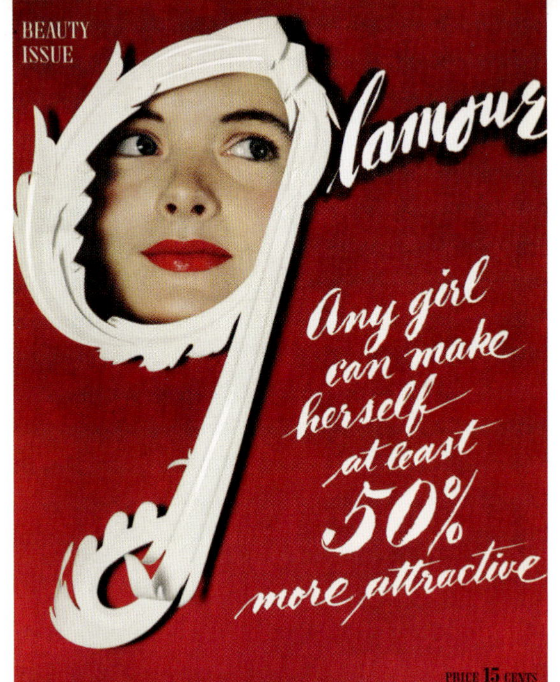

→

A model wearing a Franklin Simon bathing suit and Helena Rubinstein makeup, standing inside an exercise wheel, June 1942.

←

The Beauty Issue, with a woman's face shown in the *g* of *Glamour* wearing Chanel lipstick, November 1942.

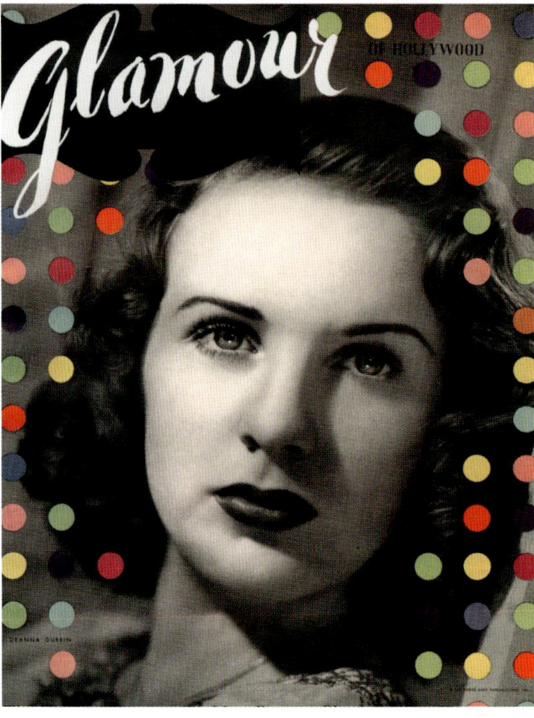

←

Actor Deanna Durbin, July 1939.

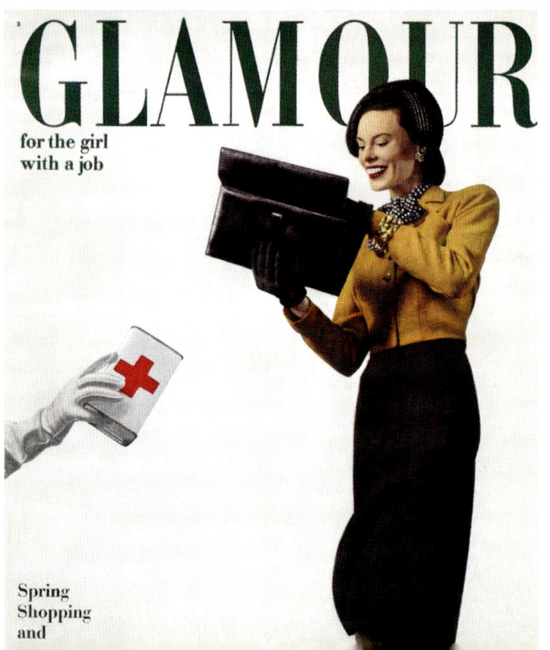

←

Model Meg Mundy in a two-piece wool suit with polka-dot ascot and straw bonnet paying a Red Cross worker, March 1944.

THE COVERS OF *GLAMOUR*'S FIRST decade were visually creative and compositionally ambitious. From the short-lived Hollywood years— where celebrities were briefly the cover stars—to the war and beyond, each issue had a clear message, be it a call to service, solving fashion dilemmas for the working woman, college advice, or even how to meet men. Here are some of the era's most iconic and historic covers.

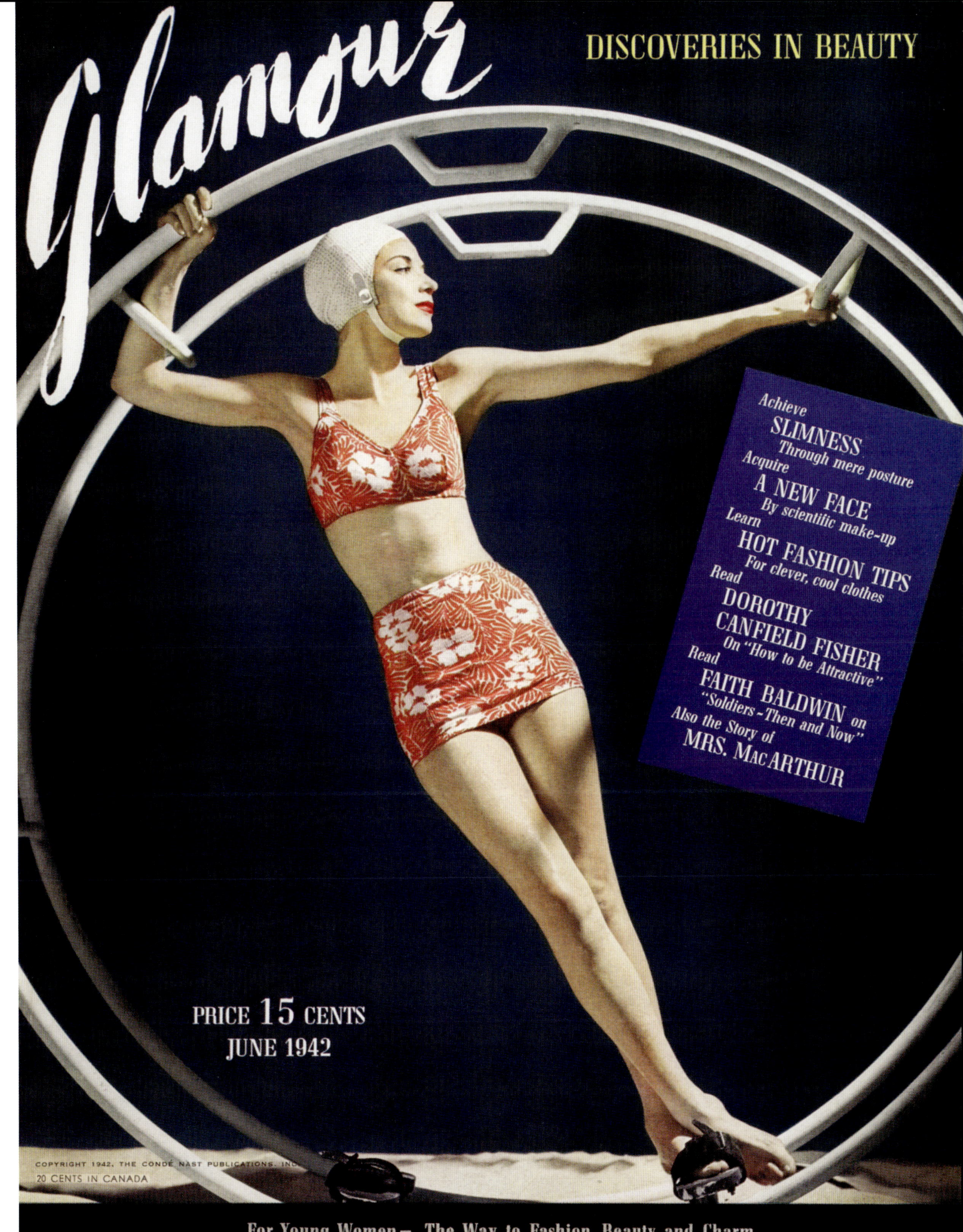
Glamour
DISCOVERIES IN BEAUTY
Achieve
SLIMNESS
Through mere posture
Acquire
A NEW FACE
By scientific make-up
Learn
HOT FASHION TIPS
For clever, cool clothes
Read
DOROTHY
CANFIELD FISHER
On "How to be Attractive"
Read
FAITH BALDWIN on
"Soldiers – Then and Now"
Also the Story of
MRS. MacARTHUR
PRICE 15 CENTS
JUNE 1942
COPYRIGHT 1942, THE CONDÉ NAST PUBLICATIONS, INC.
20 CENTS IN CANADA
For Young Women – The Way to Fashion Beauty and Charm

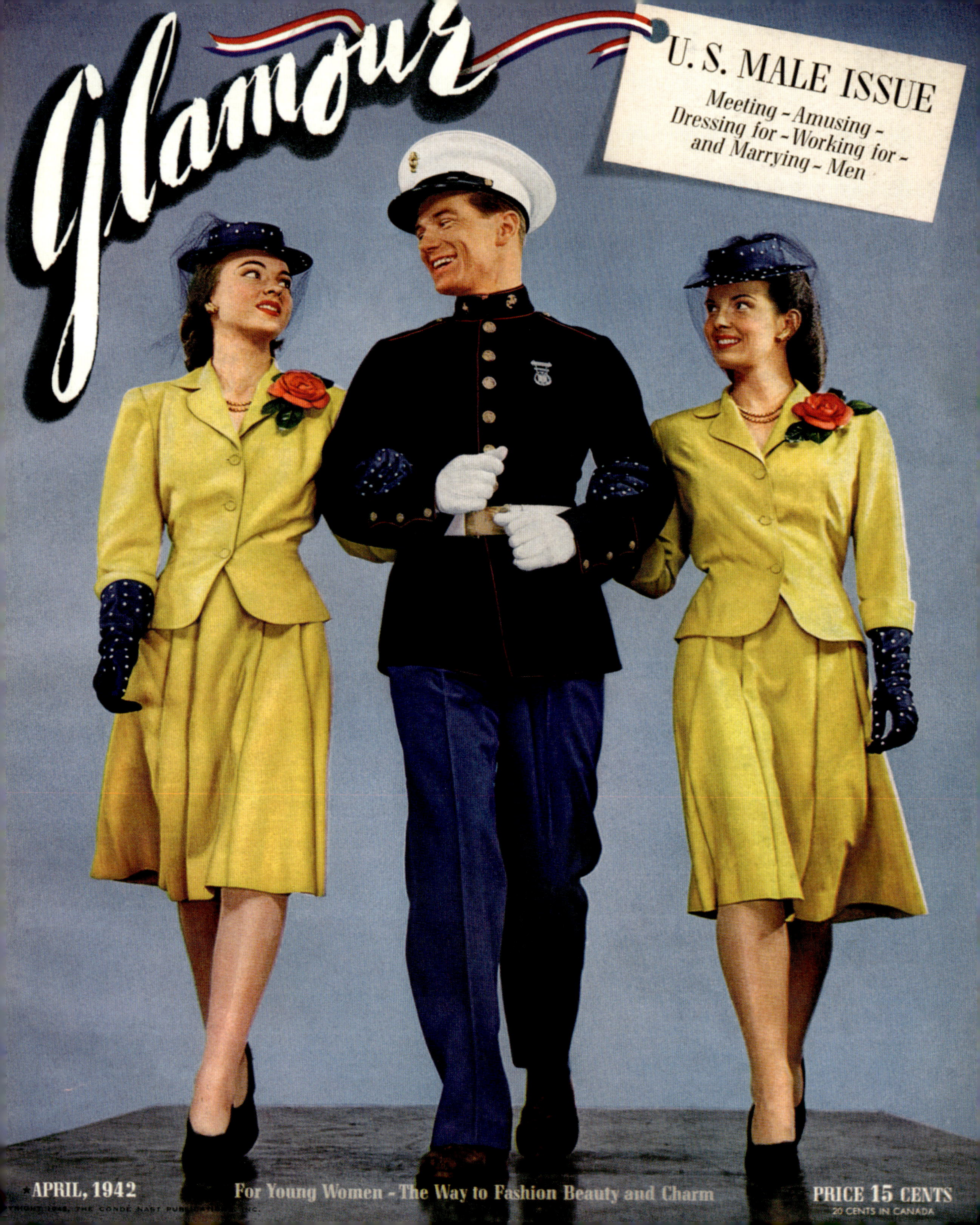

Glamour
U. S. MALE ISSUE
Meeting - Amusing -
Dressing for - Working for -
and Marrying - Men
APRIL, 1942
For Young Women - The Way to Fashion Beauty and Charm
PRICE 15 CENTS
20 CENTS IN CANADA
COPYRIGHT 1942, THE CONDÉ NAST PUBLICATIONS, INC.

← Two models in yellow suit dresses and navy polka-dot accessories, walking arm in arm with a sailor, April 1942.

→ Model Ricki VanDusen imposed on an image of a rose lying on a poem, July 1948.

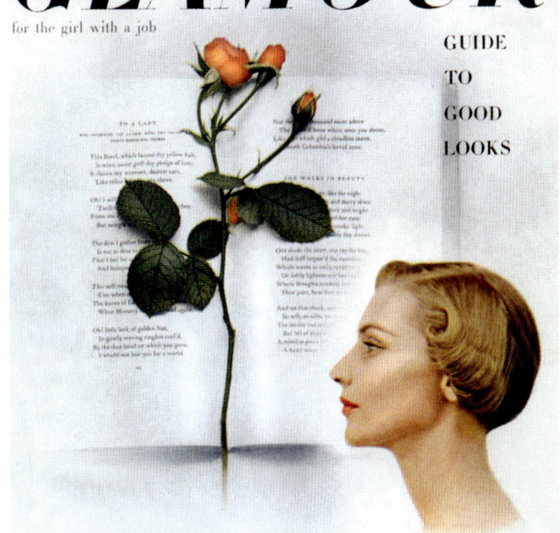

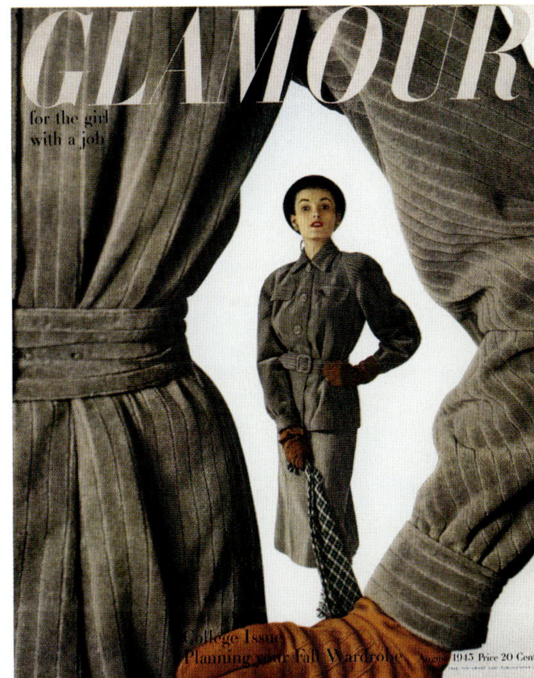

→ Model Elise Daniels in a barrel-shouldered suit by McArthur Ltd., August 1945.

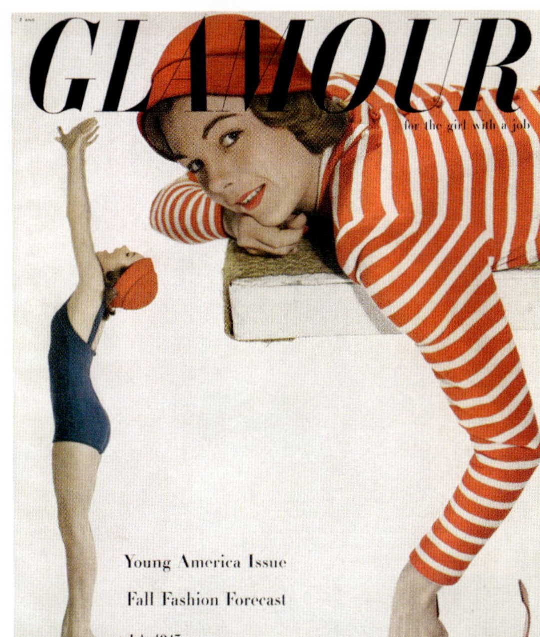

→ A model in a blue bathing suit and cap and a model in a striped red and white sweater and red cap, July 1947.

THE "PERFECT" HOUSEWIFE

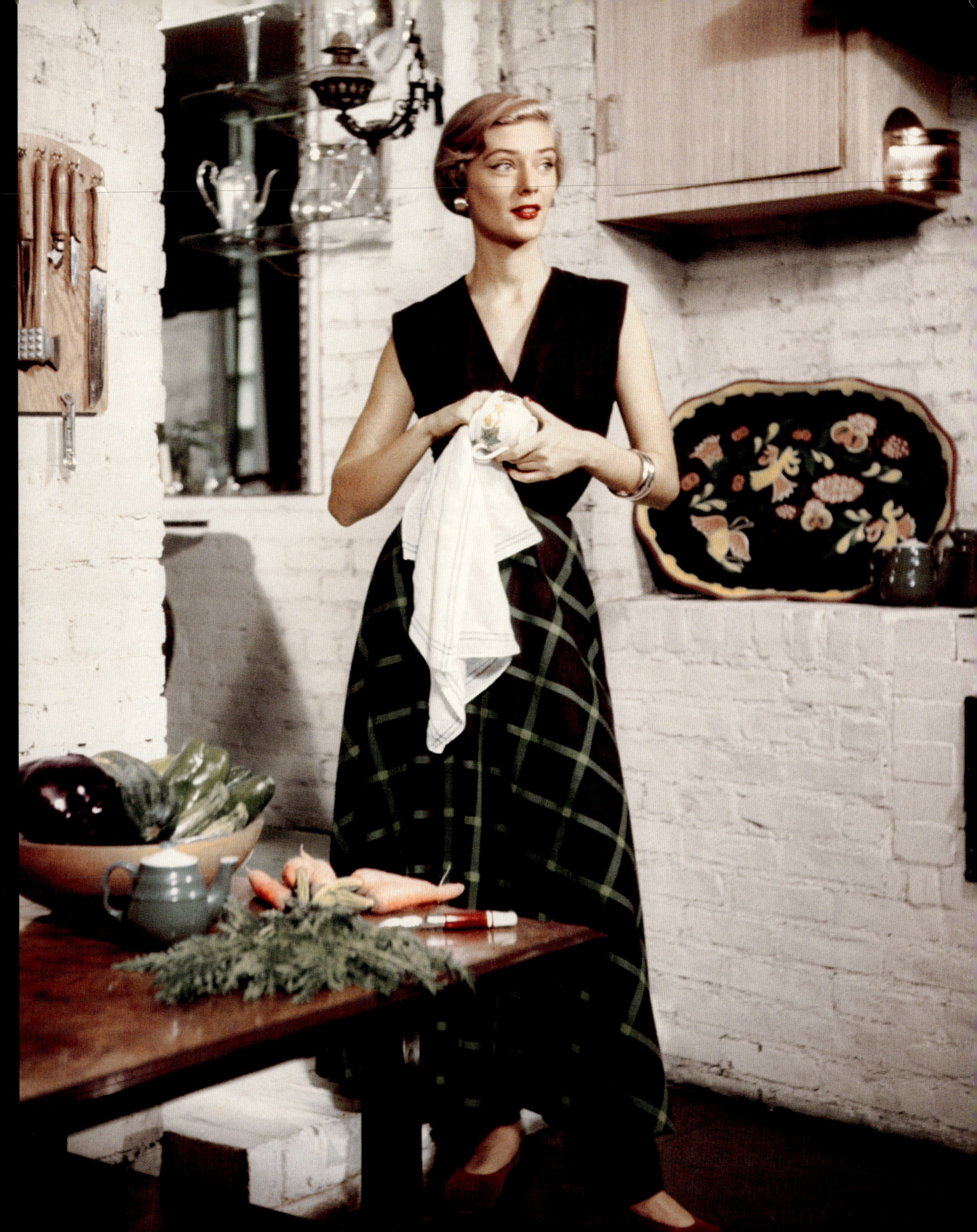

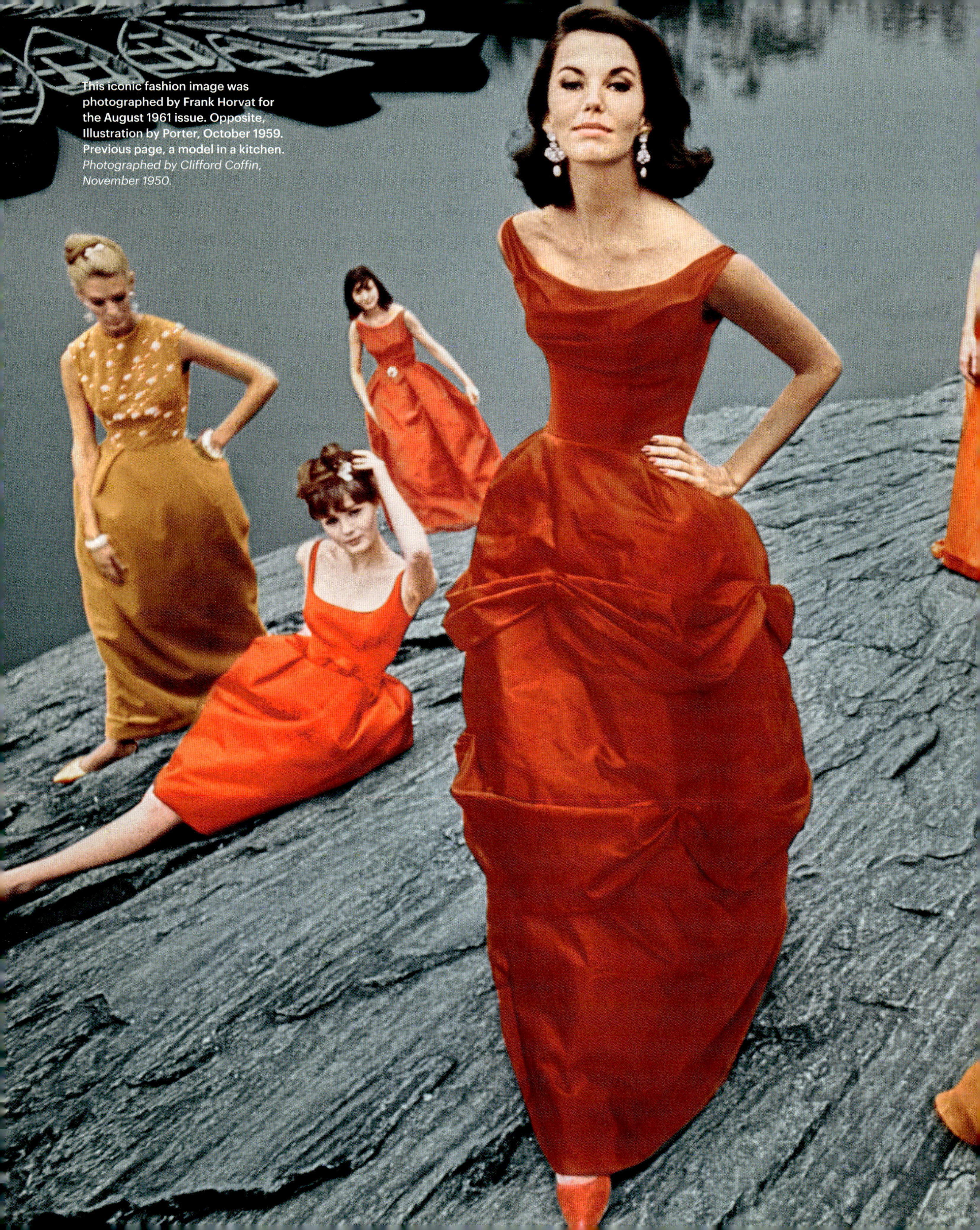

This iconic fashion image was photographed by Frank Horvat for the August 1961 issue. Opposite, Illustration by Porter, October 1959. Previous page, a model in a kitchen. Photographed by Clifford Coffin, November 1950.

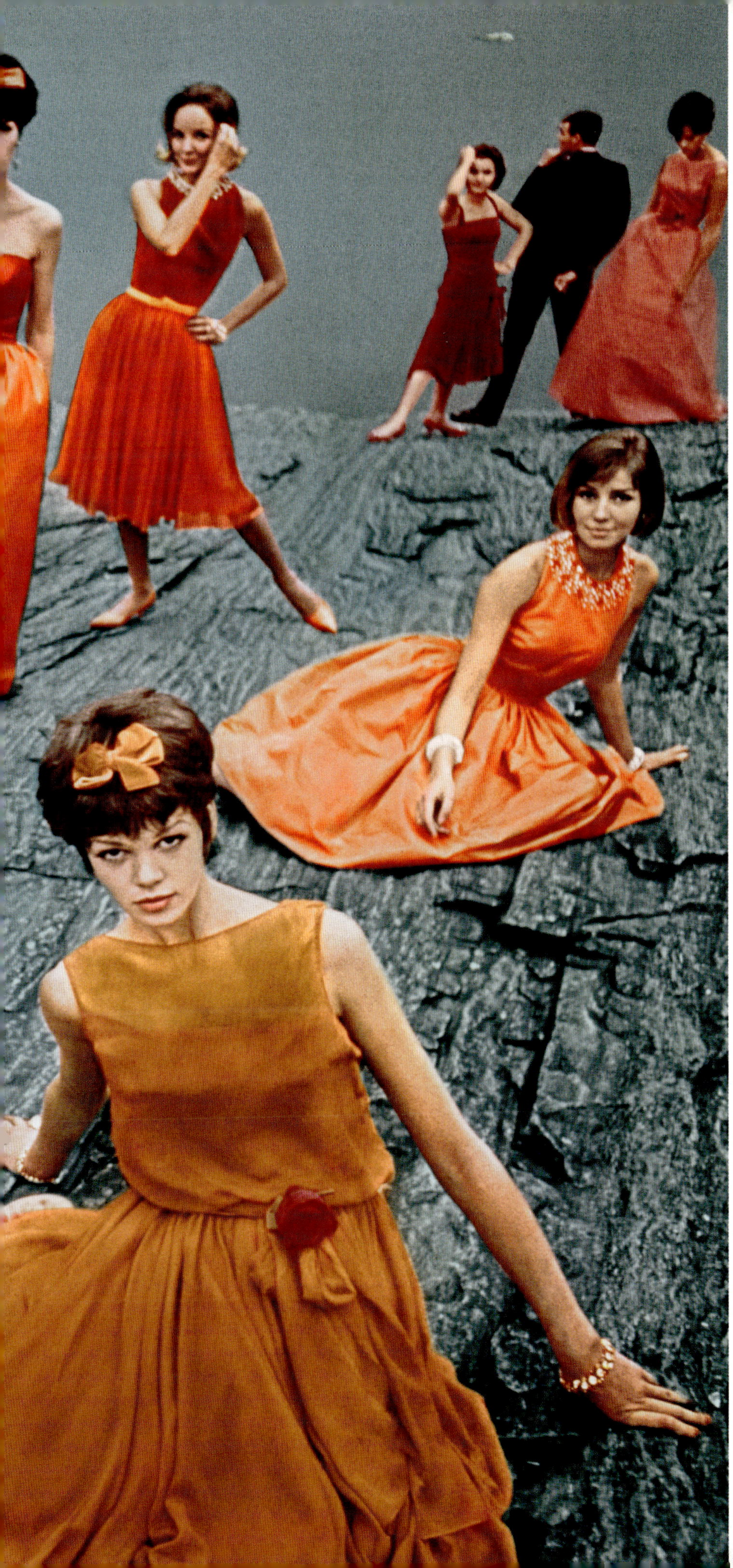

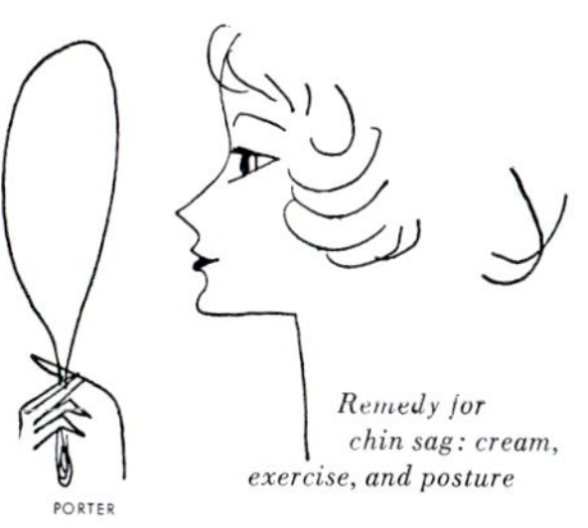

In the 1940s, *Glamour* posed the question: Could women retain the gains they had made in wartime when the men came home?

THE 1950S ANSWERED: no. This global struggle played out in the pages of the magazine. Under the editorship of Elizabeth Penrose, *Glamour* had followed the lives of women in the workplace—with Frances Perkins speaking at a *Glamour* seminar on "A Half Century of Progress for the Girl With a Job," and in November 1953 reporting on "India's radiant rebel," Lady Dhanvanthi Rama Rau, founder of India's Planned Parenthood Federation. But the November issue would be Penrose's last, after ill health forced her to step down.

The shift under her replacement, Kathleen Aston Casey, was stark. Almost immediately, women's lives were reframed under the gaze of men. In an August 1956 article, the model Ann Klem explained that every job she took had to be completed by late afternoon so that she could get home in time to make her husband's dinner.

In March 1956 the famous tagline "for the girl with a job" was replaced with "the fashion magazine for young women—a guide to good taste at home, at play, on the job"—a reflection of the diminishing importance of women's careers.

Body-image coverage became more reductive, and fashion became physically more restrictive. These were not styles to suit a working woman, but, as the November 1956 cover stated, "Special fashions picked to please men." Women were no longer, as Penrose had said in 1942, "at the head of the ranks." Instead the "perfect" housewife was born.

WHEN IT CAME TO DIETING and body image, *Glamour*'s approach was disappointing, but not surprising for the time. In fact, it took many more decades to shift away from calorie counting and equating beauty or success with attaining a certain body shape or weight. Throughout the 1950s—and even before the magazine became focused on fashion above careers—thinness was prioritized. Numerous issues featured diets to follow, calories to count, pounds to lose, and how to dress to look good, not just for yourself but for men's pleasure. It's certainly not an approach for today's world, but we would be remiss to gloss over the emphasis placed, however wrongly, on body shape during the 1950s—and what it said about the pressures on women to conform to a society constructed under the male gaze.

This cover, featuring model Phyllis Newell, is emblematic of the era, with the prominent cover line, "Special fashions picked to please men," November 1956.

Photograph of a calorie counting handkerchief, which cost $1. It was featured in a Christmas gifts roundup. The 13-inch square gave a calorie count for 60 different foods. *Photographed by William Grigsby, November 1952.*

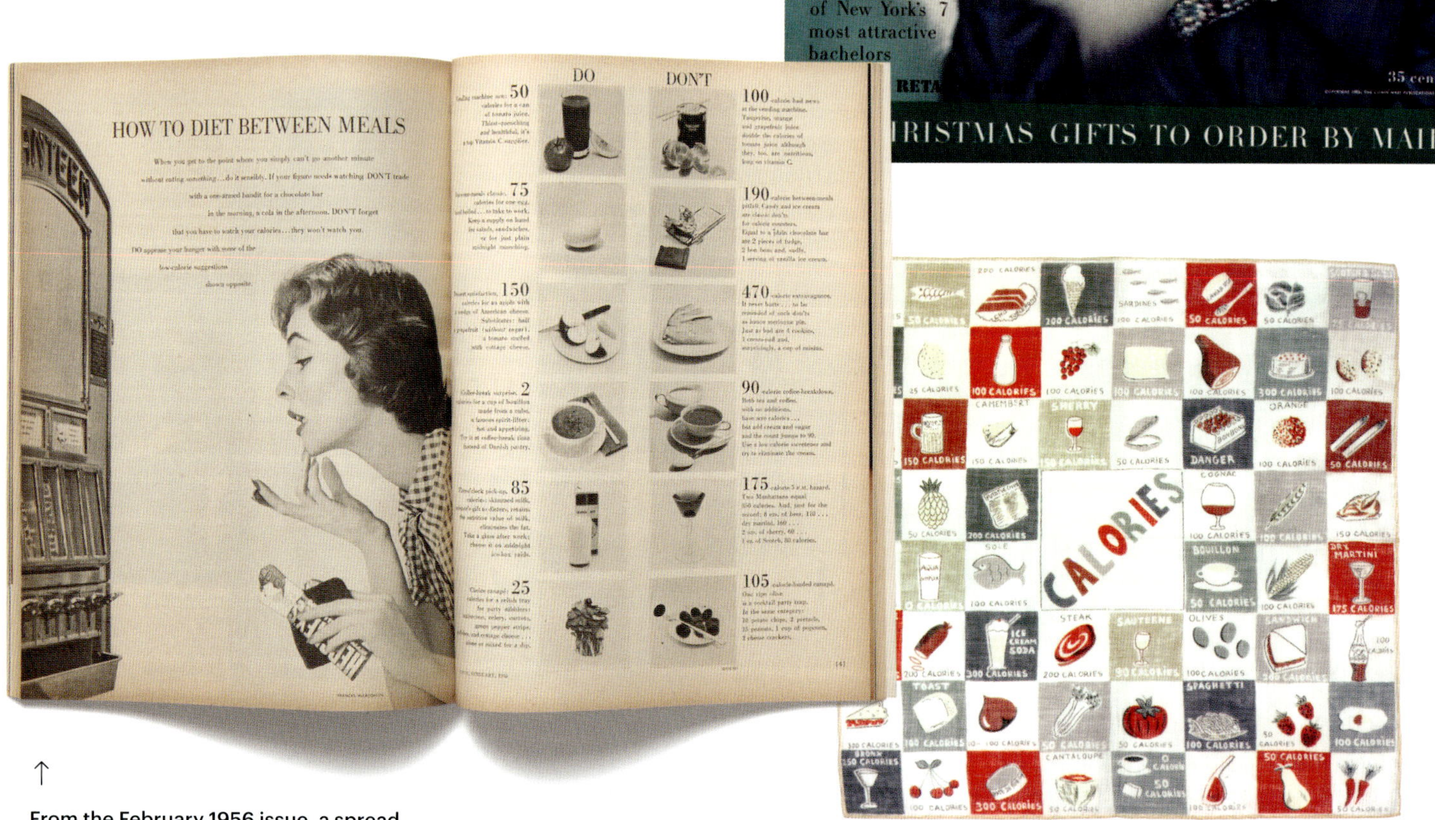

From the February 1956 issue, a spread explaining "How to Diet Between Meals."

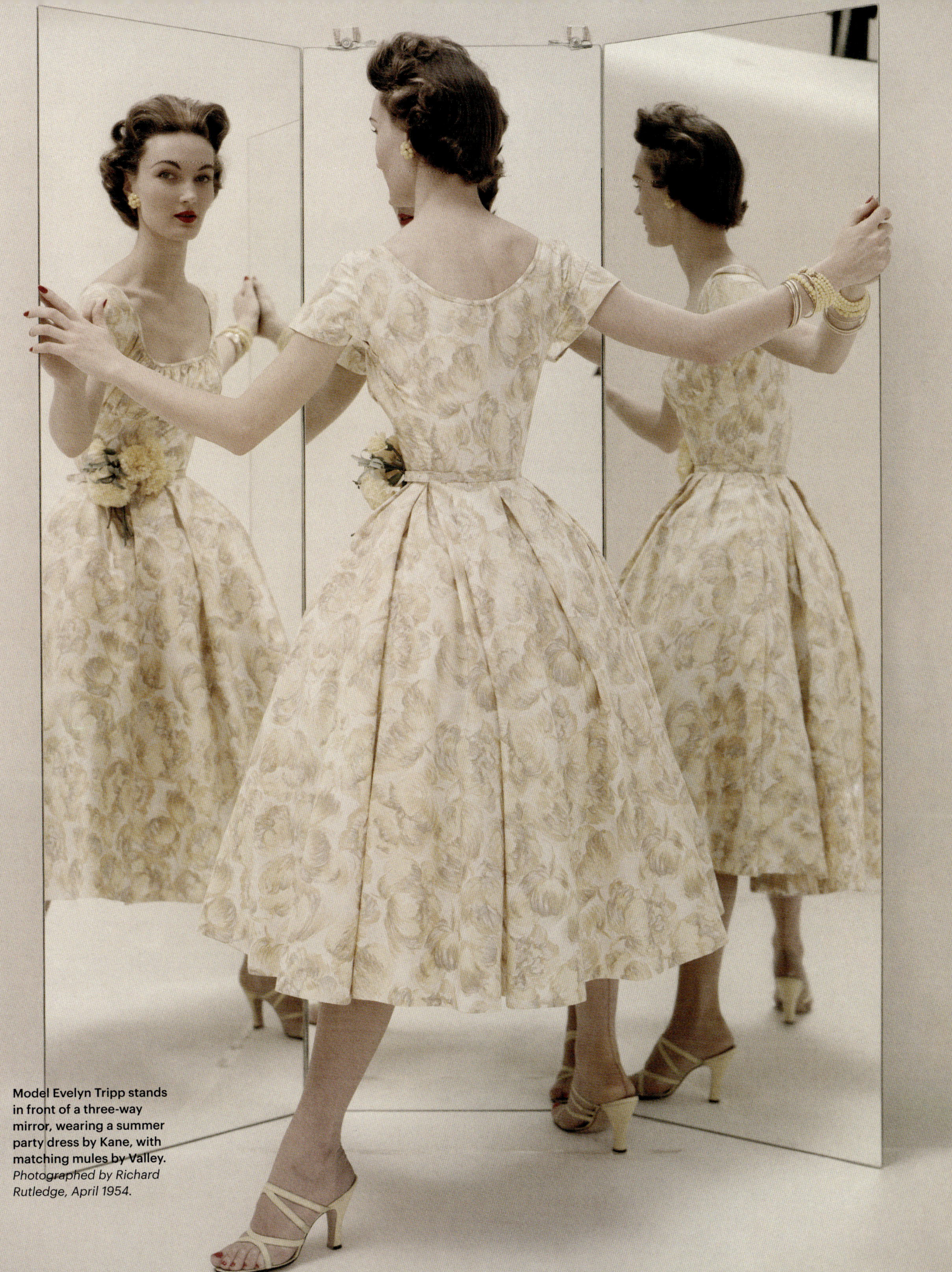

Model Evelyn Tripp stands in front of a three-way mirror, wearing a summer party dress by Kane, with matching mules by Valley. *Photographed by Richard Rutledge, April 1954.*

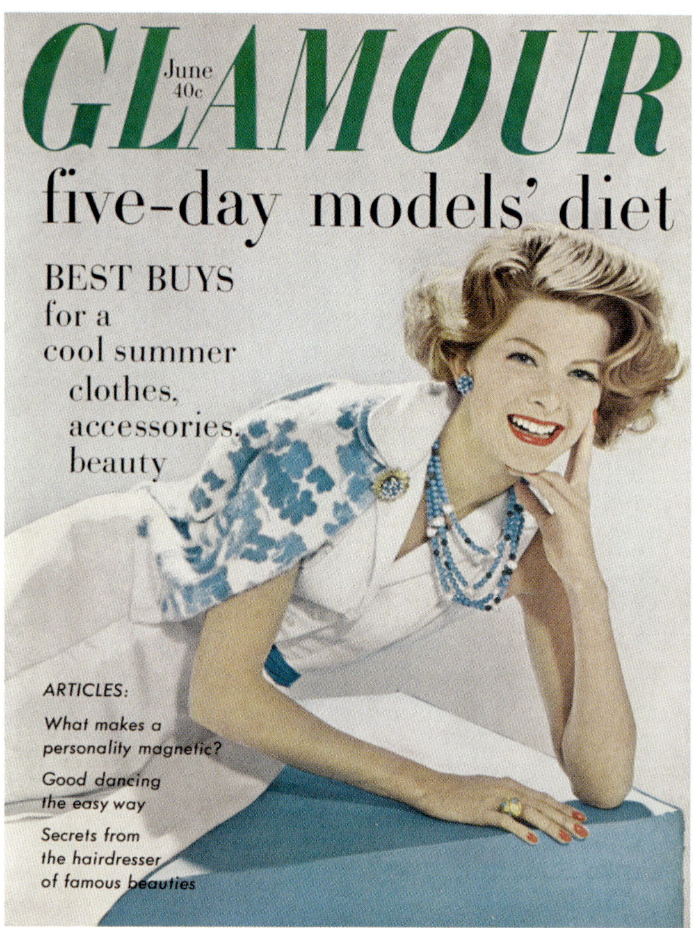

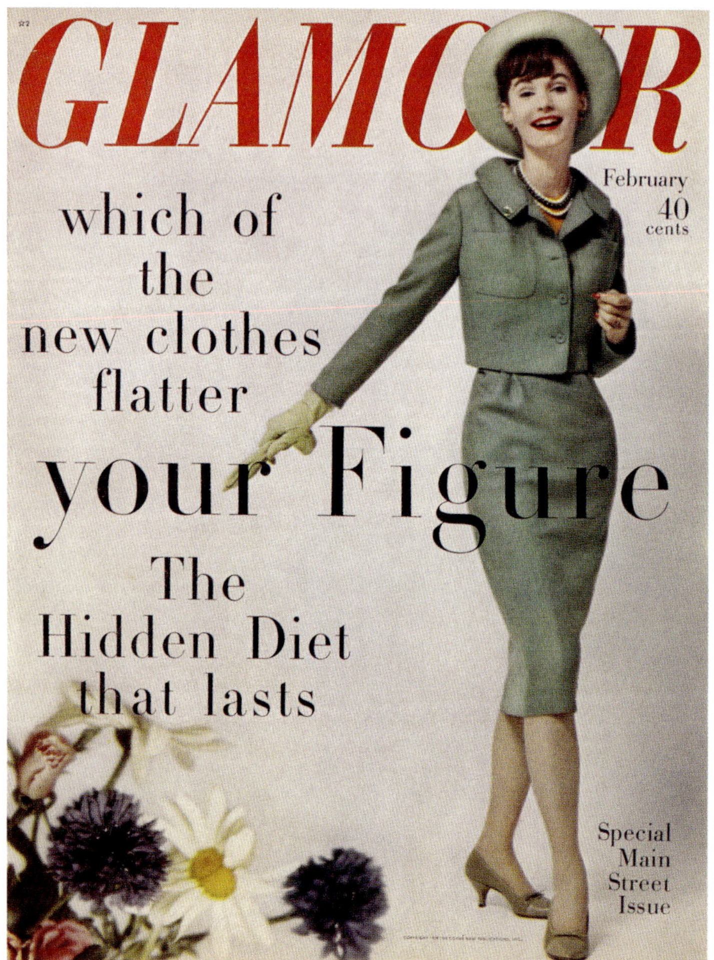

1958

In the May 1958 issue, *Glamour* published its "Pinch Test"—a readers' guide to discovering problem areas, followed by a feature on how best to camouflage them in swimwear. The photographic how-to illustrations are as comic as they are jaw-droppingly out of touch. But as much as we might deride the concept, this feature gives a vital insight into the shifting expectations placed on women: to present themselves in as pleasing a way as possible to the opposite sex.

Model Sandra Wright, below bold-type dieting cover lines, June 1959.

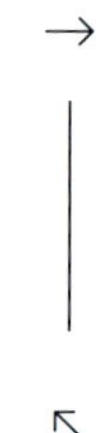

For bathing suits, it's not your measurements, but your soft spots that need camouflaging.

GLAMOUR EDITORIAL

Model Romaine Simenson, February 1958.

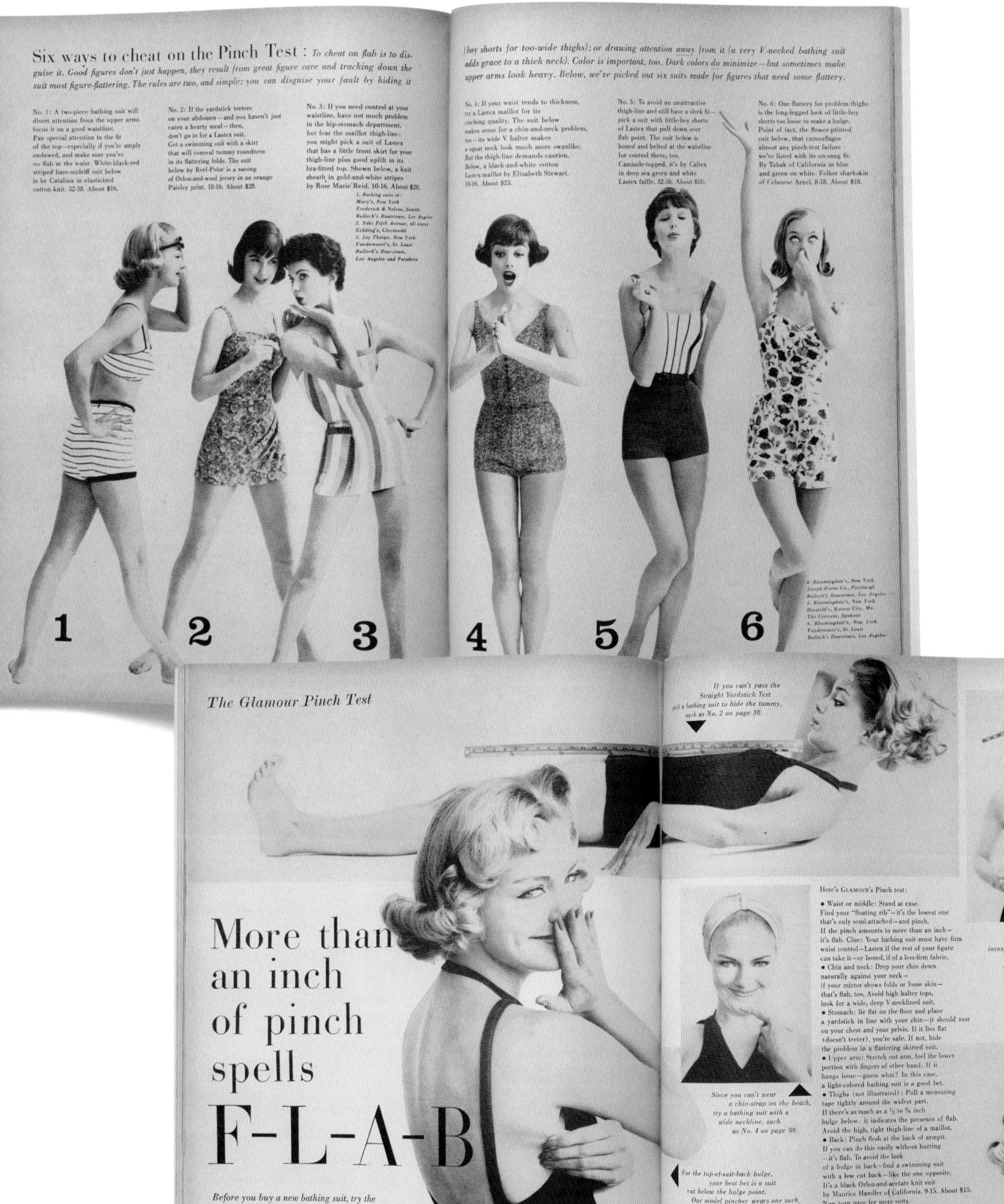

Six ways to cheat on the Pinch Test

To cheat on flab is to disguise it. Good figures don't just happen, they result from great figure care and tracking down the suit most figure-flattering. The rules are two, and simple: you can disguise your fault by hiding it (boy shorts for too-wide thighs); or drawing attention away from it (a very V-necked bathing suit adds grace to a thick neck). Color is important, too. Dark colors do minimize—but sometimes make upper arms look heavy. Below, we've picked out six suits made for figures that need some flattery.

No. 1: A two-piece bathing suit will divert attention from the upper arms, focus it on a good waistline. Pay special attention to the fit of the top—especially if you're amply endowed, and make sure you've no flab at the waist. White-black-red striped bare-midriff suit below is by Catalina in elasticized cotton knit. 32-38. About $16.

No. 2: If the yardstick teeters on your abdomen—and you haven't just eaten a hearty meal—then, don't go in for a Lastex suit. Get a swimming suit with a skirt that will conceal tummy roundness in its flattering folds. The suit below by Reel-Poise is a sarong of Orlon-and-wool jersey in an orange Paisley print. 10-16. About $28.

No. 3: If you need control at your waistline, have not much problem in the hip-stomach department, but fear the maillot thigh-line: you might pick a suit of Lastex that has a little front skirt for your thigh-line plus good uplift in its bra-fitted top. Shown below, a knit sheath in gold-and-white stripes by Rose Marie Reid. 10-16. About $20.

1. Bathing suits at:
Macy's, New York
Frederick & Nelson, Seattle
Bullock's Downtown, Los Angeles
2. Saks Fifth Avenue, all stores
Gidding's, Cincinnati
3. Jay Thorpe, New York
Vandervoort's, St. Louis
Bullock's Downtown,
Los Angeles and Pasadena

No. 4: If your waist tends to thickness, try a Lastex maillot for its cinching quality. The suit below makes sense for a chin-and-neck problem, too—its wide V halter makes a squat neck look much more swanlike. But the thigh-line demands caution. Below, a black-and-white cotton Lastex maillot by Elisabeth Stewart. 10-16. About $23.

No. 5: To avoid an unattractive thigh-line and still have a sleek fit—pick a suit with little-boy shorts of Lastex that pull down over flab point. The suit below is boned and belted at the waistline for control there, too. Camisole-topped, it's by Caltex in deep sea green and white Lastex faille. 32-38. About $25.

No. 6: One flattery for problem thighs is the long-legged look of little-boy shorts too loose to make a bulge. Point of fact, the flower-printed suit below, that camouflages almost any pinch-test failure we've listed with its un-snug fit. By Tabak of California in blue and green on white. Folker sharkskin of Celanese Arnel. 8-18. About $18.

4. Bloomingdale's, New York
Joseph-Horne Co., Pittsburgh
Bullock's Downtown, Los Angeles
5. Bloomingdale's, New York
Herpolsheimer's, Kansas City, Mo.
The Crescent, Spokane
6. Bloomingdale's, New York
Vandervoort's, St. Louis
Bullock's Downtown, Los Angeles

1   2   3   4   5   6

If you can't pass the Straight Yardstick Test get a bathing suit to hide the tummy, such as No. 2 on page 98.

More than an inch of pinch spells F-L-A-B

Before you buy a new bathing suit, try the Glamour Pinch Test. It's a can't-miss test that works for all figure types and tells which suits flatter you. (For bathing suits, it's not your measurements, but your soft spots that need camouflaging.) On the following pages, six bathing-suit shapes in fashion this summer. Take the test; then, take your pick.

Since you can't wear a chin-strap on the beach, try a bathing suit with a wide neckline, such as No. 4 on page 99.

For the top-of-suit-back bulge, your best bet is a suit cut below the bulge point. Our model pincher wears one such, on the opposite page.

Here's GLAMOUR's Pinch test:

• Waist or middle: Stand at ease. Find your "floating rib"—it's the lowest one that's only semi-attached—and pinch. If the pinch amounts to more than an inch—it's flab. Clue: Your bathing suit must have firm waist control—Lastex if the rest of your figure can take it—or boned, if of a less-firm fabric.

• Chin and neck: Drop your chin down naturally against your neck—if your mirror shows folds or loose skin—that's flab, too. Avoid high halter tops, look for a wide, deep V-necklined suit.

• Stomach: lie flat on the floor and place a yardstick in line with your chin—it should rest on your chest and your pelvis. If it lies flat (doesn't teeter), you're safe. If not, hide the problem in a flattering skirted suit.

• Upper arm: Stretch out arm, feel the lower portion with fingers of other hand. If it hangs loose—guess what? In this case, a light-colored bathing suit is a good bet.

• Thighs (not illustrated): Pull a measuring tape tightly around the widest part. If there's as much as a ½ to ⅜ inch bulge below, it indicates the presence of flab. Avoid the high, tight thigh-line of a maillot.

• Back: Pinch flesh at the back of armpit. If you can do this easily without hurting—it's flab. To avoid the look of a bulge in back—find a swimming suit with a low cut back—like the one opposite. It's a black Orlon-and-acetate knit suit by Maurice Handler of California. 9-15. About $15. Now turn page for more suits.

Bathing suit, left, at: Lit Brothers, Philadelphia; Frederick & Nelson, Seattle; Bullock's Downtown, Los Angeles

For middle flab, don't investigate a snugly-fitting Lastex suit on the following pages.

For arm-top flabbiness, try unobtrusive tailoring, low-cut armholes, such as in suit Nos. 1 or 6 on the following pages.

IF THERE IS ONE CHARACTERISTIC THAT MAKES A GIRL ATTRACTIVE TO MEN...IT'S THE ART OF BEING YOURSELF.

IT'S ALL JAKE, SEPTEMBER 1956

What is needed in politics is the spirit that prompted Mary Norton in a debate in the House of Representatives to remind one of her masculine colleagues who had repeatedly referred to her patronizingly as 'the lady' that she was not 'the lady,' but a member of Congress, elected as he was, and entitled to the same consideration.

"LET 'EM LICK STAMPS! WHAT REALLY HAPPENS TO WOMEN IN POLITICS, AND WHAT CAN THEY DO ABOUT IT?" BY LORENA A. HICKOK, MARCH 1952

It would be a good thing for the country if we had a charming, mature woman as our Chief Executive. The kind of woman I have in mind has that indefinable quality that a man doesn't, and makes a man want to do anything he can for her.

"WHY SHOULD THE NEXT PRESIDENT BE A WOMAN?" BY WALTER K. GUTMAN, SEPTEMBER 1960

SEX APPEAL DOESN'T CHANGE WITH THE YEAR, THE ERA, OR THE FASHION. IT IS A QUESTION OF SUBTLETY.... NOT ALL WOMEN OFFER IT, NOR SHOULD THEY, IN THE SAME WAY.

"SECRETS OF SEX APPEAL" BY ALFRED HITCHCOCK, OCTOBER 1956

" If she's serious about working, she's read that she's aggressive, and what is it doing to her children? If she stays home in the suburbs, she's a boring do-gooder.... The question of whether or not she should work has been chasing its tail since the end of World War II: for many, the question has been made obsolete by fact. One third of the labor force is female.

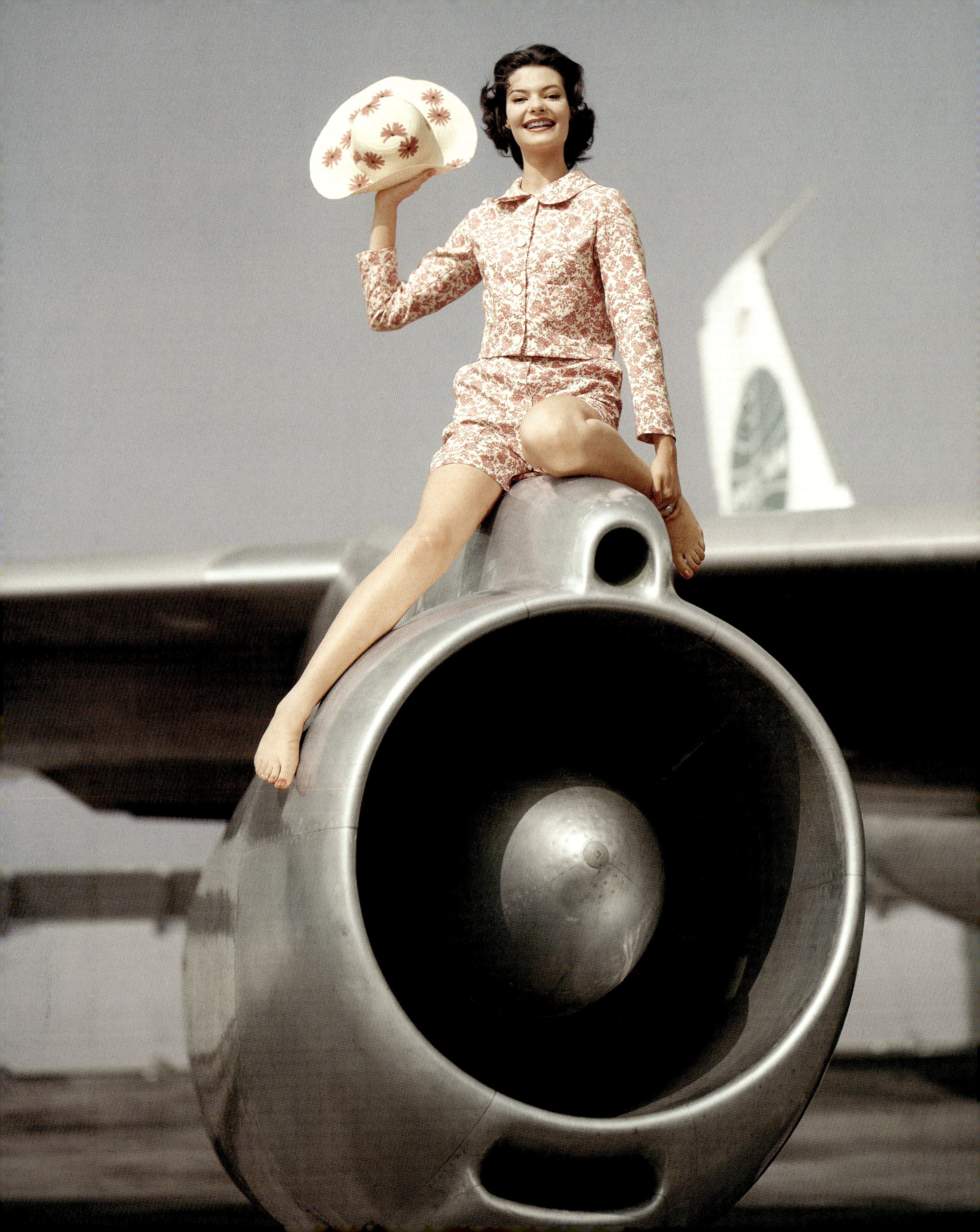

AFTER THE SECOND WORLD WAR, *GLAMOUR* **BEGAN TO TAKE A MUCH**

more global view—introducing readers to stories of life abroad, travel possibilities, and women's experiences in different countries. Unique reports included a May 1956 piece called "Russia, Girl-to-Girl," by Pulitzer Prize–winning journalist Marguerite Higgins, who interviewed two young Russian girls who had befriended the United Press acting Russia bureau chief, and a striking, if somewhat American-lensed, dispatch from a post-Hiroshima Japan in the May 1961 issue. Other pieces outlined the benefits to young American women of traveling and adventuring in Europe alone ("A girl on her own can be constructively selfish"), and the women from around the world—China, the United Kingdom, Belgium, Turkey, Burma, and more—working at the United Nations in New York. While unquestionably America-centric, the magazine aimed to open up a world of possibilities and knowledge to its readers.

←

A model sits atop the engine of a Pan Am Boeing 707.
Photographed by Sante Forlano, January 1959.

↓

The opening spread of "Women at work in the U.N." from the June 1952 issue.

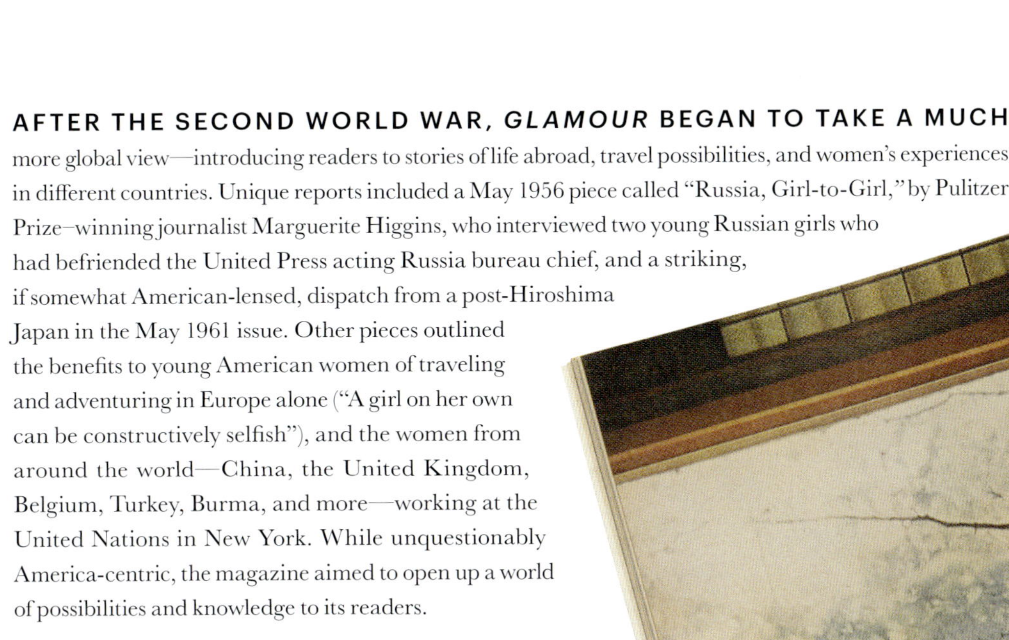

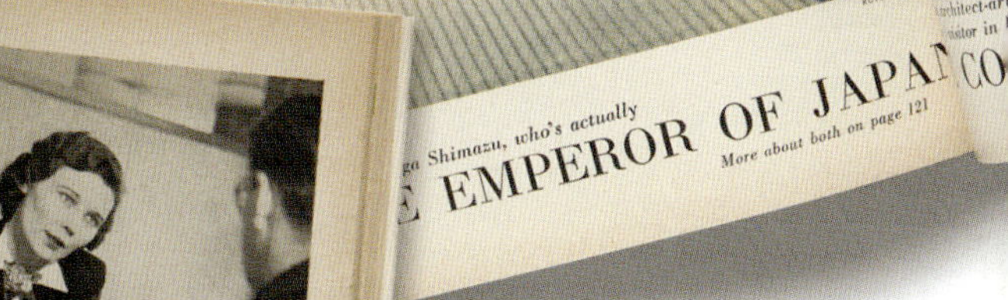

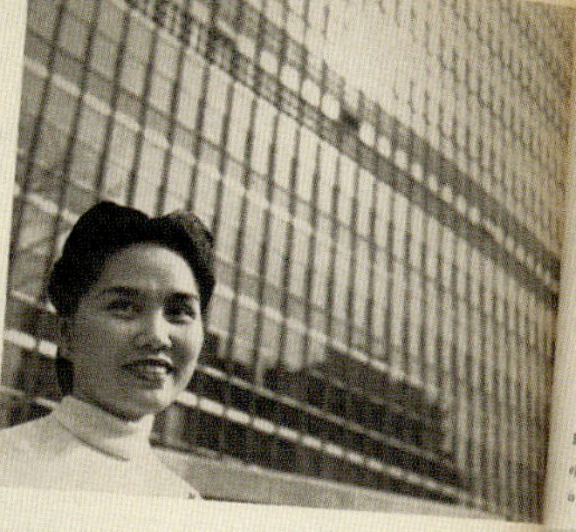

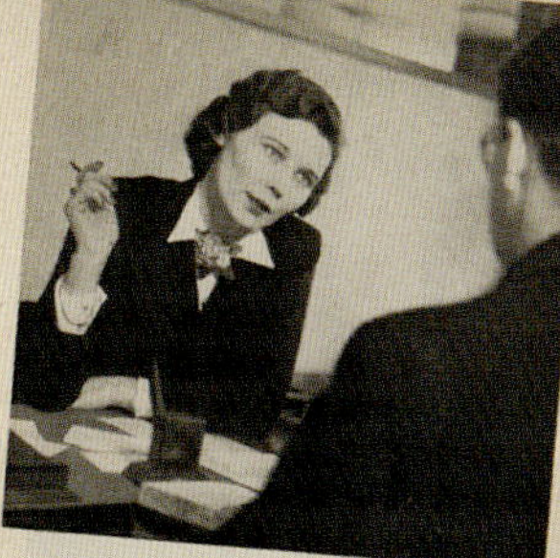

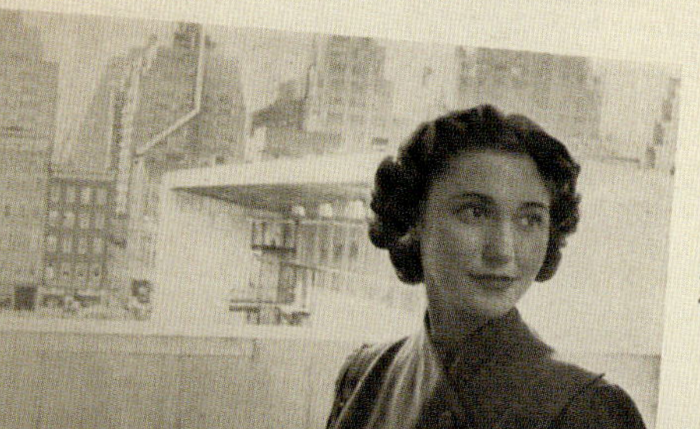

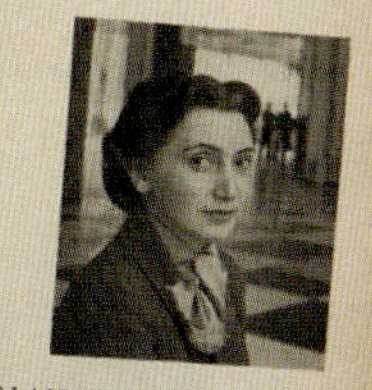

↑

The Emperor of Japan's daughter, Mrs. Hisanaga Shimazu, in traditional Japanese dress with a model (right) wearing a butterfly print silk dress and textured silk coat, both by Mr. Gee.
Photographed by Richard Rutledge, May 1961.

1953

In the penultimate issue of *Glamour* under the editorship of Elizabeth Penrose, the magazine ran an extraordinary piece by scholar and author Ashley Montagu, inspired by his book *The Natural Superiority of Women,* arguing that women are the superior sex.
We reprint it here.

why waste the natural superiority of women?

● During the greater part of history one half of the human race has been held in subjugation by the other. Men, for the most part, have deliberately prevented women from realizing their potentialities and prevented their participation in contributing to the common good.

From time immemorial men have been unconsciously jealous of women's natural capacities and enforced the myth of feminine inferiority by virtue of their greater muscular strength. Both men and women have come to accept this myth as the law of nature. Throughout history every stereotype in the racist's vocabulary has been applied to women. Women were alleged to have smaller brains, less intelligence. It was said they couldn't manipulate figures or handle accounts, that they were like children, that they were emotional and incapable of doing man's work. The list of stereotypes is both lengthy and absurd.

These ideas have no more truth than the beliefs of our nineteenth century ancestors that the "inferior races" could never learn to read or accomplish anything resembling the achievements of the "superior races". All scientific evidence today points in the opposite direction. By the one really significant test that an anthropologist or social biologist can apply, women are superior to men in all those traits which confer survival benefits upon their possessor. Deaths from almost all causes are more frequent in males at all ages. Women are fundamentally more resistant than men. They not only suffer

By Ashley Montagu

Man and all humanity would reap the benefits of a realistic assess-

ment of women's skills in the professions, in industry and in politics.

much less frequently than men from serious diseases which affect mankind, but with the exception of India, women everywhere live longer than men. Even in the much-vaunted muscular superiority of the male we have a trait which, by the biological test of superiority, is actually an inferior trait. Muscular superiority is held by the male at the price of higher metabolic rate; that is to say, a more rapid utilization and expenditure of energy, which causes the poor male to burn out more rapidly than does the female. Furthermore, in an age when over 90 per cent of the work that was formerly done by muscle is now done by machines, the possession of greater muscular power is certainly a questionable advantage.

Practically every test shows that women at all ages are more intelligent than men. All through the school years girls are about one or two years ahead of boys in their ability to grasp and handle school subjects, and are generally more adept and adroit than boys. In college, statistics show they do just as well as men, and among those levels of little education they show a constant level of higher intelligence, with the sole exception of tests for mathematical or mechanical ability.

Certainly in that supreme form of human intelligence, the passion for humanity, women so far outdistance men that it is high time we commenced utilizing this great store of socially creative energy for the constructive betterment and future welfare of society. It is in their capacity to love that the superiority of women to men is most clearly demonstrated. Women are the cherishers of life, the lovers of humanity. And the destiny of the human species, in fact its very survival, lies in the direction of love, universal peace and cooperation. It is my firm conviction as a scientist that women, by virtue of their feminine and maternal qualities, are destined to take the leading role in preparing humanity for such a future. Meanwhile, every day that we continue to ignore this inexhaustibly rich reservoir for the betterment of the human race is a lost day.

Dr. Ashley Montagu, a distinguished, soft-spoken scholar, became the center of a loud controversy when his book, The Natural Superiority of Women, was published recently by Macmillan. Now Chairman of the Department of Anthropology at Rutgers and Director of Research of the New Jersey Committee of Mental Health and Physical Development, he once taught anatomy at New York University; supports his thesis with psychological and physical data as well as anthropological evidence. His aim: to teach humanity "to accept superiority not in this group or that one, in this sex or the other, but in the person . . . . regardless of sex."

If the natural superiority of women reaches full expression, will this be the result?

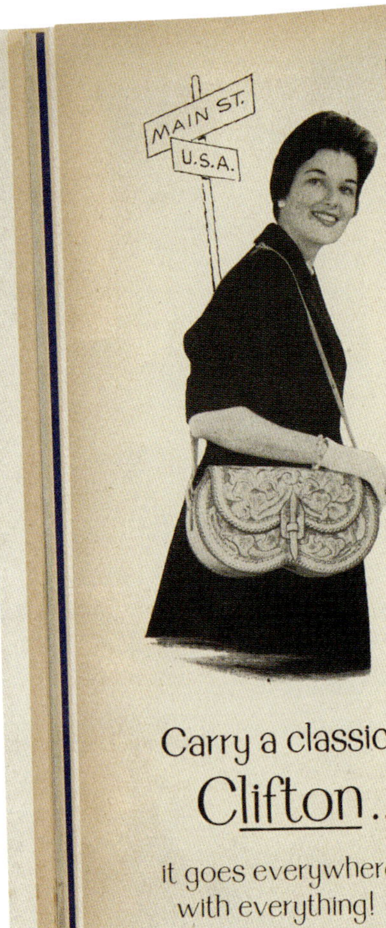

A MAN'S OPINION
IT'S ALL JAKE

Since we couldn't do without the men in our lives, since we dress, think, entertain and go overboard for them, we plan to bring a man's point of view into each issue of GLAMOUR. Choosing the most attractive, genial, and worldly bachelor we know—Jake Bellamy—we asked him to answer questions of manners, morals, taste . . . you name it.

"You've set me up as the world's greatest expert. Period," he remarked, running a nervous finger under the collar of his fine-striped black and white shirt as we sat over the veal piccata he ordered us in Romeo Salta's delicious Italian restaurant.

We've done just that. Let us know what you would like him to discuss in future issues.

To start the series off, we said to Jake, "Let's talk about dates. Dinner dates, specifically. What does a man expect of his guest at a rather expensive form of entertainment?" From here on, it's all Jake. . . .

It's usually a man's fault when a dinner date doesn't come off. It's up to him to choose the girl, the restaurant, the wine (if any). But there are times when the young lady contributes her full share to a general disaster. Here are half a dozen instances in my own experience that may give you some idea of what a man doesn't want facing him across the linen and silverware—and indirectly, what he does.

There was Laura who arrived forty-five minutes late, her eyes dancing with amusement at someone else's stories, her cheeks flushed with someone else's liquor. Our table and my temper were gone. No number of side-splitting anecdotes about the cocktail party she had just left, the important people met, the advances repulsed, helped recapture the magic spell that a tête-à-tête with a beautiful, bright young woman should cast.

Advice to Laura: If you must have too many cocktails, at least do it in the company of your dinner partner. No man likes second-hand hilarity. Fashionable tardiness is a thing of the past, and it is just as important, in these days of crowded restaurants and prompt curtains, to be punctual in a café as it is for dinner in a private house. And if you have been to a party that your escort didn't attend, please don't discuss it in loving detail. He may get the idea that you'd rather be elsewhere.

There was Madge who arrived on the dot but might as well have taken the extra three-quarters of an hour for window shopping. After a promisingly warm greeting there was a twenty-minute "time-out" in the powder room, followed by a brief reunion during which we held hands long enough for me to furnish her with some silver for a few "absolutely imperative" telephone calls. Thirty minutes later we went into dinner only to find that half the tables were occupied by her dearest friends (those that she hadn't already called). Nothing would do but for her to greet, and me to meet, them all. Lightning visits to and fro continued throughout dinner while soup, small birds, *crêpes maison* and I sat cooling.

Advice to Madge: It's great to be popular but the young man who is buying your dinner deserves priority. Table hopping is strictly for the pogo-stick set. A wide smile, a cordial wave of the hand will serve as well in most cases and spare innumerable men from the contortionist agonies of trying to stand at a table in a crowded restaurant. Telephone calls should be brief and really necessary. The powder room is not the place for elaborate cosmetic operations while your man friend is being jostled in the foyer; curl your eyelashes, glaze your furs, and lacquer your nails before you leave home.

There was Alice who had been told when she pouted she looked like Susan Hayward. The martinis, she announced to the bartender petulantly, weren't nearly dry enough. She looked at the waiter smokily and accused him of rudeness when he groaned at her changing her order for the umpteenth time. There was a hair in her minestrone; and the other patrons, she told me with a terrifying little *moue*, were staring at her as though they had never seen a girl before.

Advice to Alice: You couldn't be cuter, and agreed there is a time and a place for a girl to be difficult, but it isn't over dinner in one of your date's favorite off-beat restaurants. He may want to take someone else there some day. Don't send the food back out of pique. If you don't want to be stared at, don't wear an inadequate gold lamé sheath and mesh stockings when you've been invited out to "an unassuming little *ristorante* with checked tablecloths and the best pizza west of Naples." And Alice, if you don't want hair in your minestrone, then never, never comb your locks at the table, no matter how long, red and tangled they may be.

There was Lavinia from the S⸺ a share-the-calories girl. She was⸺ that didn't prevent her from ⸺ Cal ginger ale and then gulping ⸺ Alexander "just for a teenie ⸺ minute steak languished on her ⸺ her vagrant fork toyed with my ⸺ veau; and the *crème brûlée* that ⸺ gorically refused disappeared ⸺ on her spoon in "itty bitty sm⸺

Advice to Lavinia: You could⸺ er or more cuddly, dear. I love ⸺ making a wall seat for one do for ⸺ ing steady my hand when I li⸺ rette, but give up the delusion ⸺ the appetite of a bird. You're ⸺ as Grace whose eyes are half ⸺ chocolate soufflé bigger than ⸺

And then there was Lisette ⸺ girl, whose behavior was impecc⸺ conversation (as important an in⸺ a successful dinner as good mann⸺ "What a day," she sighed as we ⸺ our corner booth. "Really, was it ⸺ I replied jovially and those ⸺ words. With cocktails we had ⸺ of the difficult clients. With ⸺ ment's headaches. With the ent⸺ ies of employer relations, and ⸺ and coffee, a reprise of her last ⸺ with her psychoanalyst. "But ⸺ talked of you at all," Lisette said ⸺ her over to the doorman of her ⸺ glass apartment house. "True, ⸺ tered in response and stalked aw⸺

Advice to Lisette: Escorts, ⸺ shrinkers, like to talk about them⸺

There was Vera the little ⸺ Vera's insistent recommendation ⸺ first and last Scarlett O'Hara ⸺ involved two ounces of South⸺ some crème de menthe and a ⸺ served peach. Vera somehow ⸺ changed from the secluded corner ⸺ taurant's rear which I had ⸺ up-front spot where we could ⸺ and be seen. Ordering was no ⸺ Vera; she had been in the resta⸺ dred times before (all the waiters ⸺ were Jacques, Vito, Kurt, and D⸺ She knew exactly what we sh⸺ ordered it in French. At a snap ⸺ gers the *sommelier* who was prof⸺ wine list withdrew it in her fav⸺ nificent Burgundy resulted. All ⸺ things sputtered, flamed, crackled ⸺ dishes and platters all around us ⸺ ered, captains wrung their hands ⸺ of concern. For one dreadful mom⸺ the check was about to be placed ⸺ elbow, but an almost invisible ⸺ eyelid directed it to its proper ⸺ After a momentary flurry over ⸺ removed a bill from the tray ⸺ much," and crushed it surreptit⸺ my hand), we departed amid ⸺ and bows.

Advice to Vera: Forget ever⸺ know. Your wisdom is your own ⸺

Advice to readers: If you ha⸺ or problems for Jake, send them ⸺ 420 Lexington Avenue, New Yor⸺

IN THE FEBRUARY 1956 ISSUE, A NEW COLUMNIST WAS INTRODUCED: Jake Bellamy. His purpose? To tell readers what men really thought—about love, dating, sex, marriage, and more. You name it, *Glamour* asked it, and Jake (a pseudonym) told it exactly as he saw it. What the *Glamour* team wasn't to know back in 1956 was how iconic the column would become—the Jake column ran for 60 years, with more than a dozen men taking on the role. In 2012, "Jake" even published a book of "Secret Rules to Get the Love Life You Want." The column was finally retired in 2016: "The concept of a faceless male advice columnist suddenly seems as dated as tanning oil and the cassette tape," ran an editorial upon its ending. "We want our men to have names and own their opinions." The original Jake, John "Bud" Palmer—a Navy pilot, sports announcer, and pioneer of the jump shot—passed away in 2013 at the age of 91. Here, you'll find his first ever Jake column.

→

An image for a Jake column. *Photographed by Lionel Kazan, November 1960.*

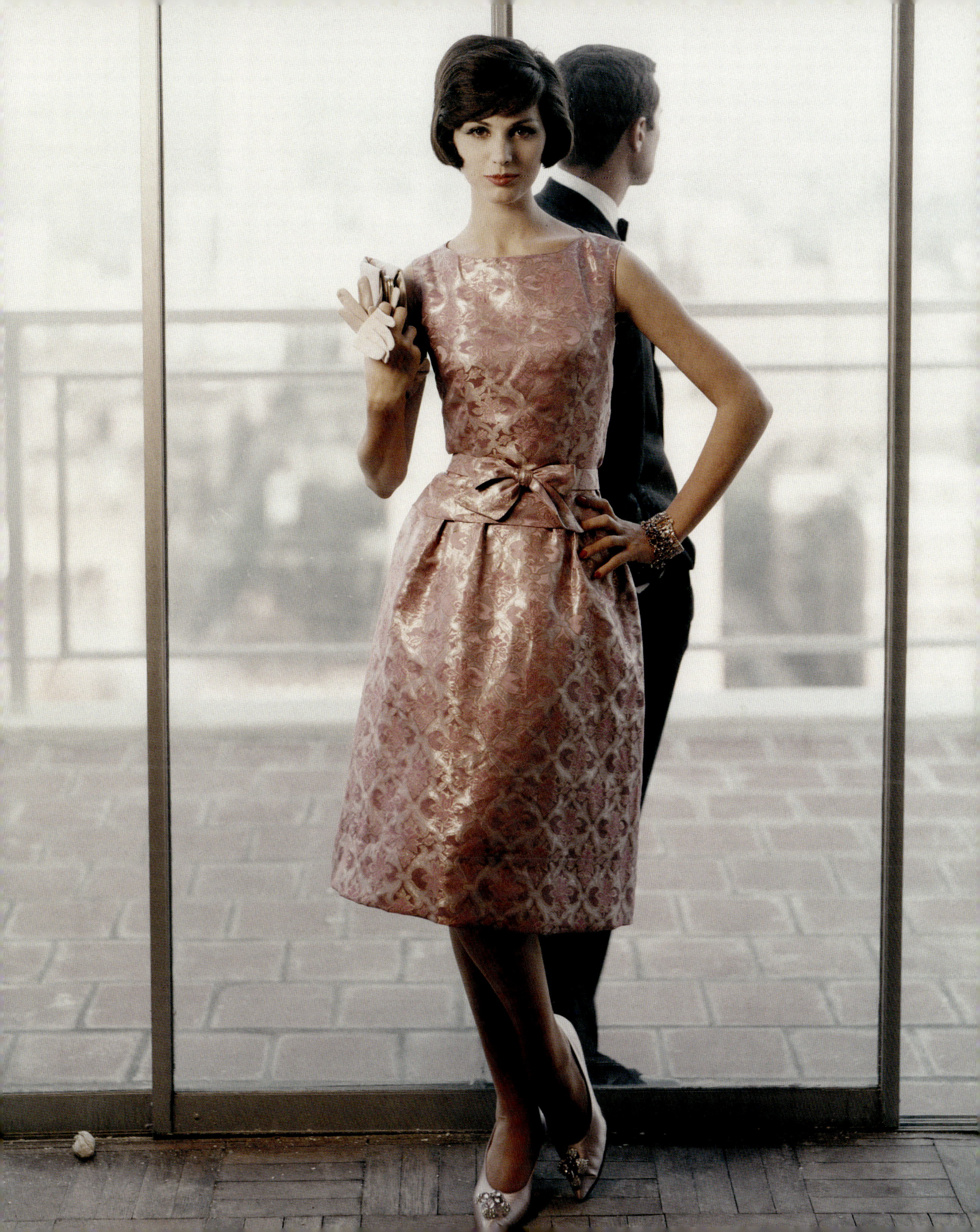

1952

The shifting silhouette of the 1950s and early '60s made for some of the most memorable fashion imagery in *Glamour*'s history. But the nipped-in waists and slightly more constricting designs didn't serve the working woman like the fashions of the war-era *Glamour* did—and perhaps reflected some of the wider post-war pressures on women to be servile rather than forthright. Nevertheless, these images, by some of the most important photographers of the century, remain timeless in their beauty.

→

Eleven models, including Sunny Harnett and Theo Graham, wear ensembles by rising designers Anne Fogarty, Mary Blair, Lotte Werner, Jenny Belle, Jeanne Campbell, Leisa Kolling, John Weitz, Betse Cann, Lee Evans, and Ruth Fair. *Photographed by Frances McLaughlin-Gill, April 1952.*

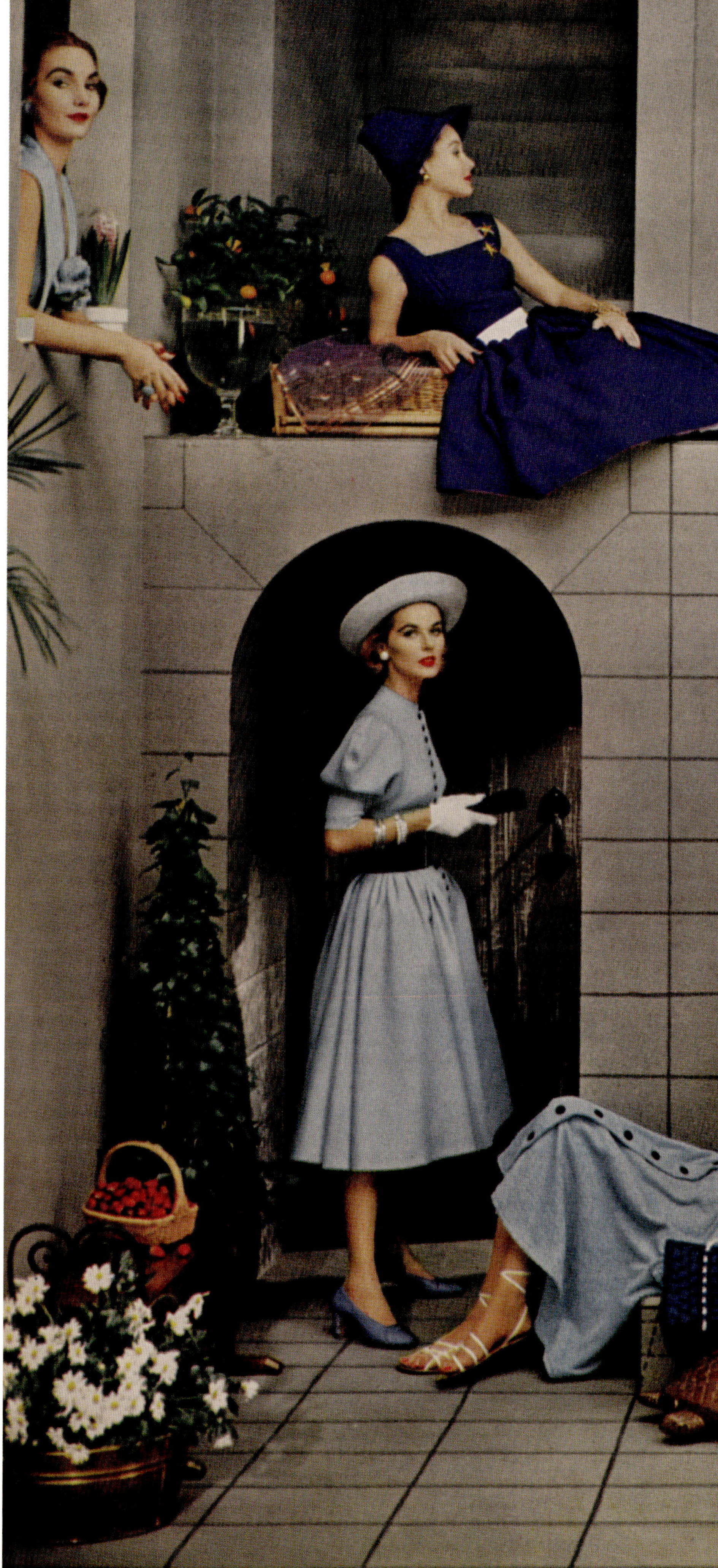

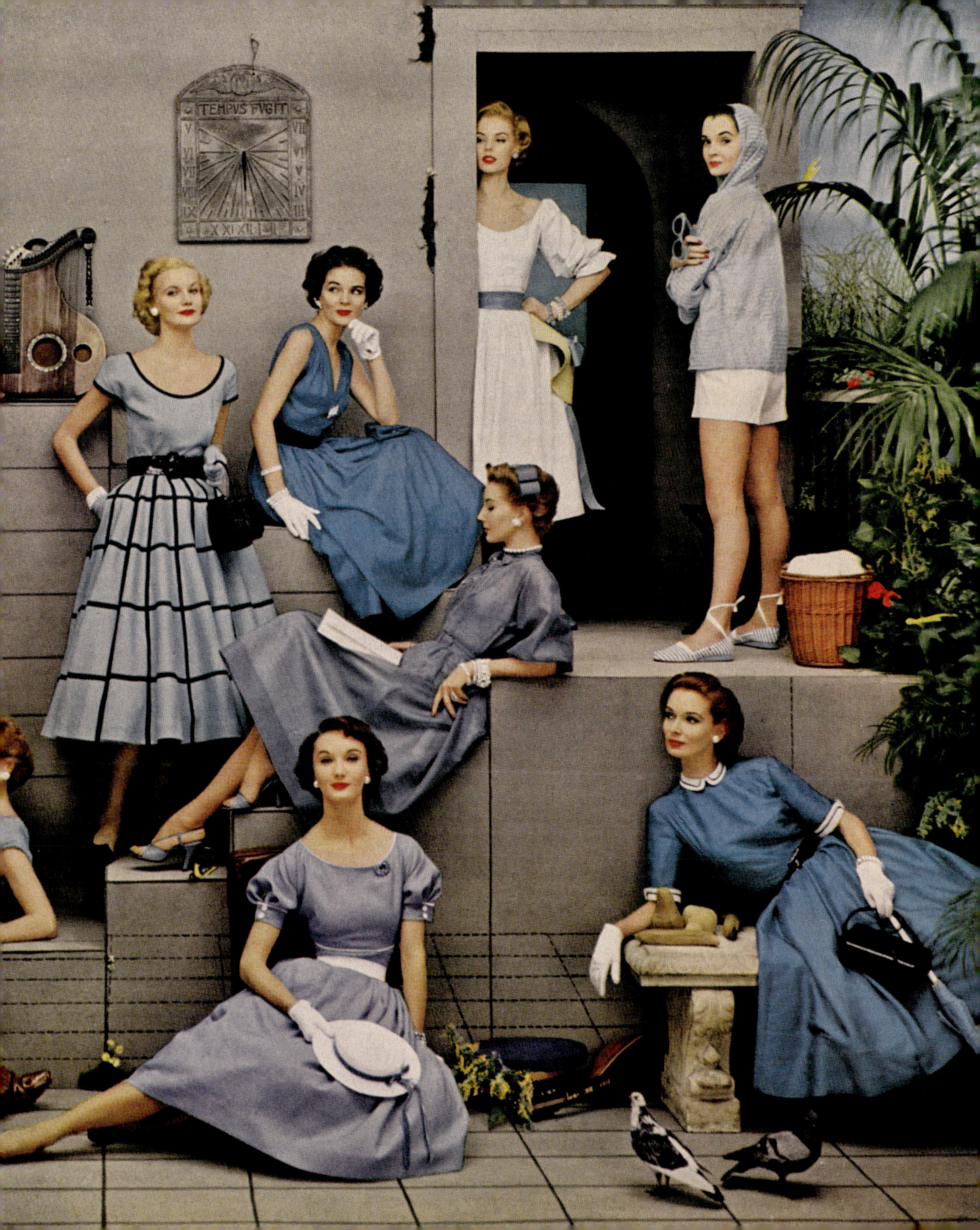

TEMPVS FVGIT

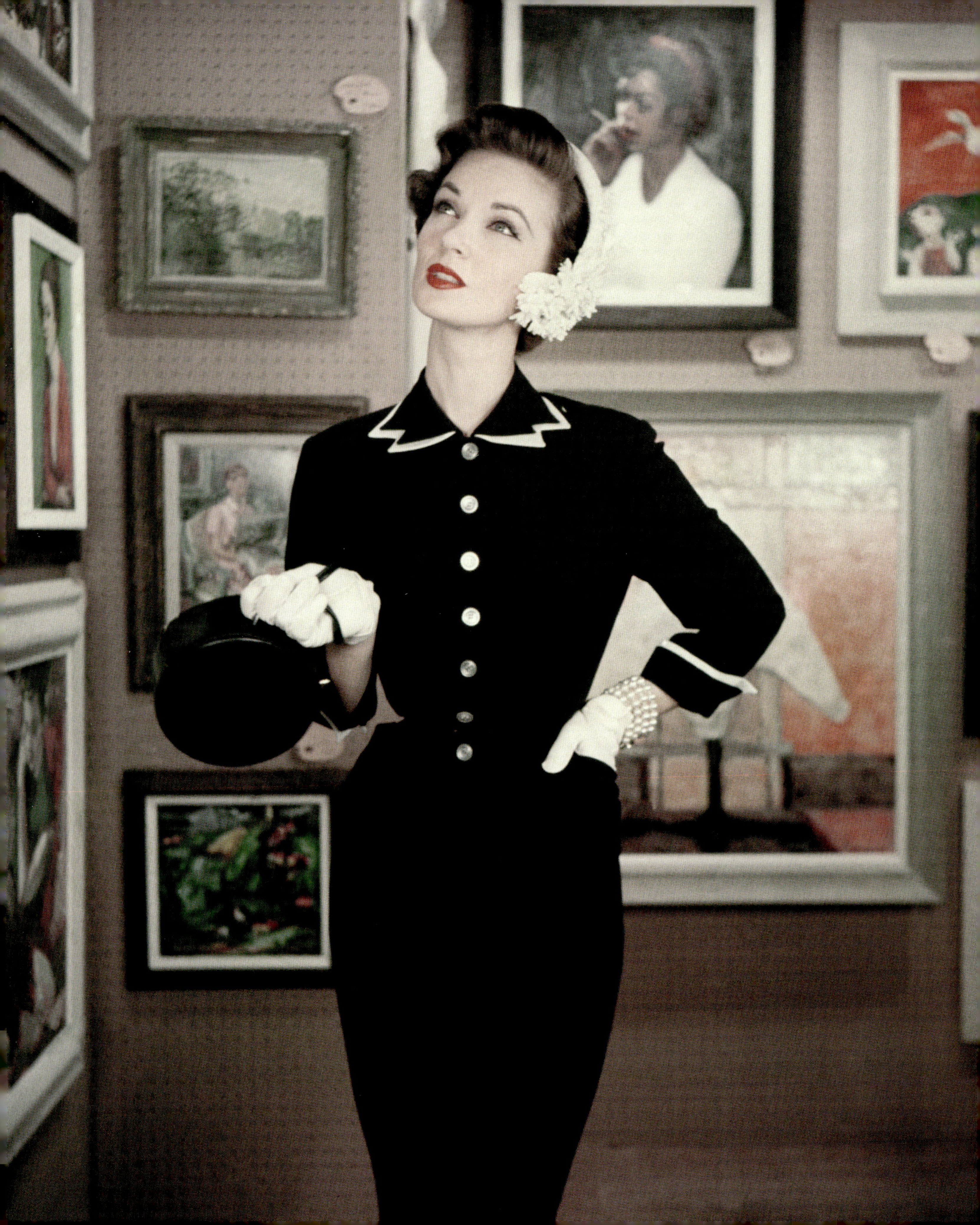

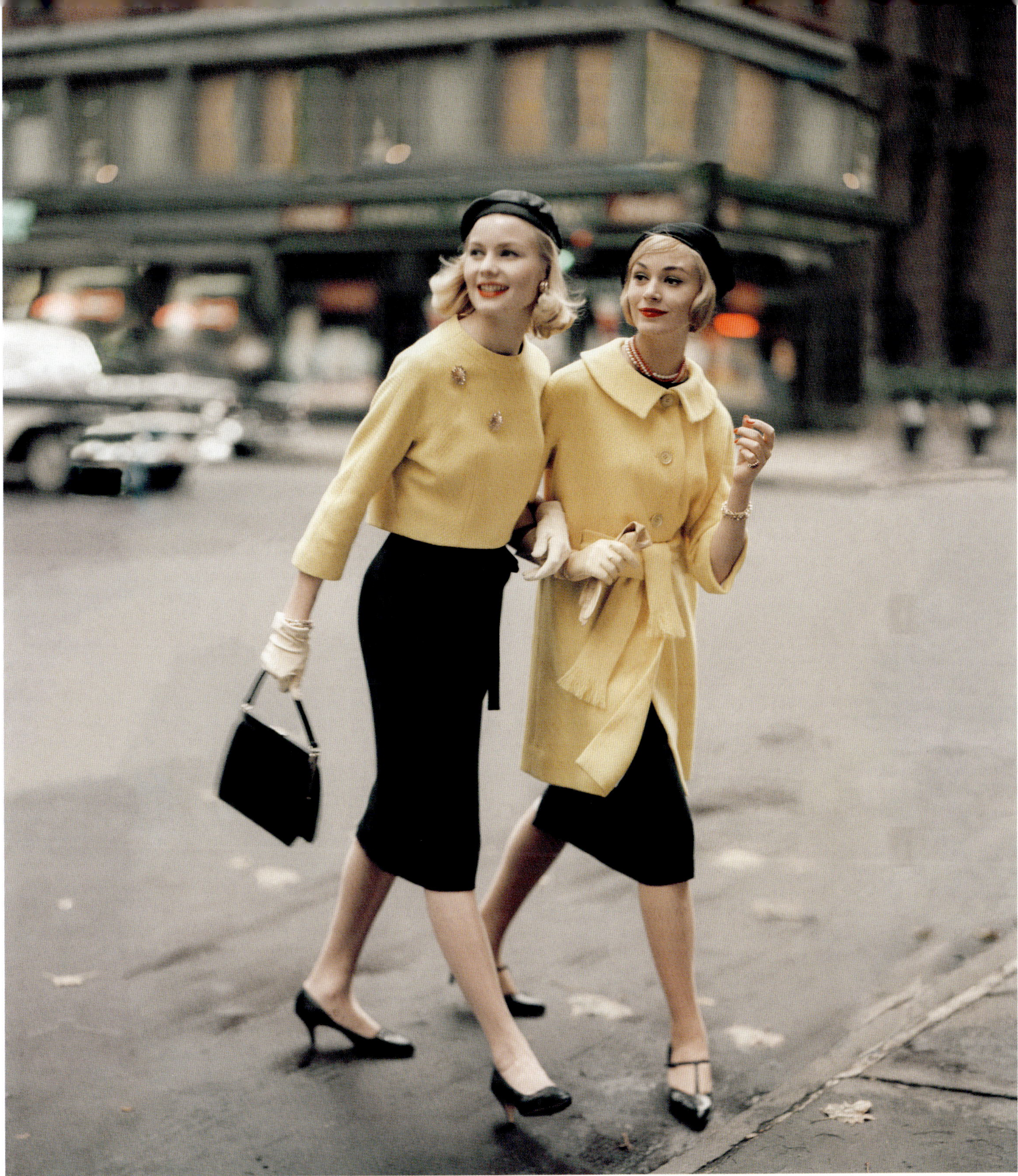

A model wears a navy blue suit by Glenhaven, profile cap by Joe Cohn, and hatbox bag by Lennox. *Photographed by Donald Honeyman, March 1953.*

Two models crossing the street, one wearing a classic navy sheath with short yellow jacket (left) by Jeanne Campbell for Sportwhirl, beret by John Frederics Charmer, pins by Tiffany and Co., and I. Miller pumps; while the other wears a knee-length coat and sleeveless chemise by Jeanne Campbell for Sportwhirl, T-strap shoes by Fortunet, necklace by Colette, Kislav gloves, and Capador beret. *Photographed by Sante Forlano, February 1958.*

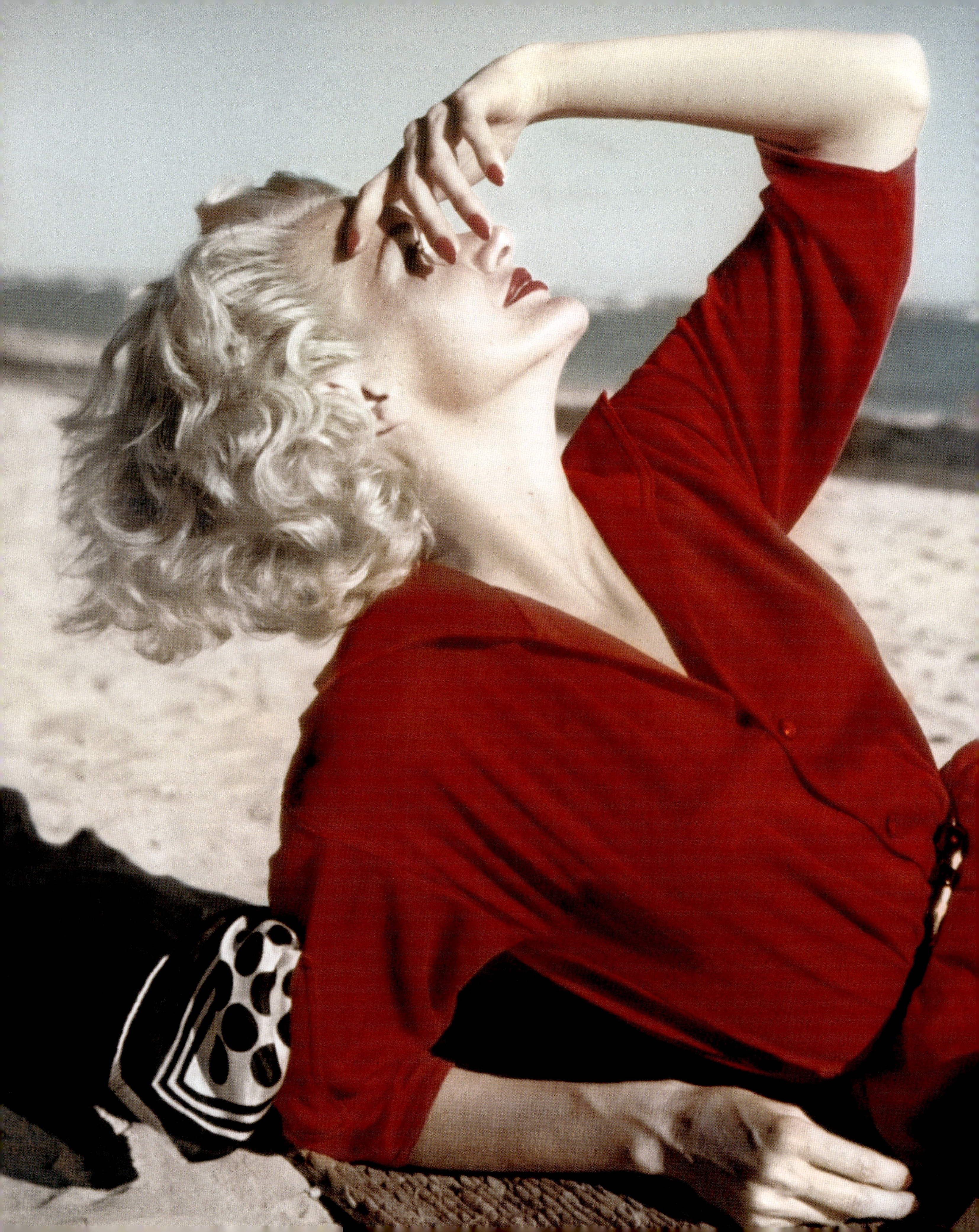

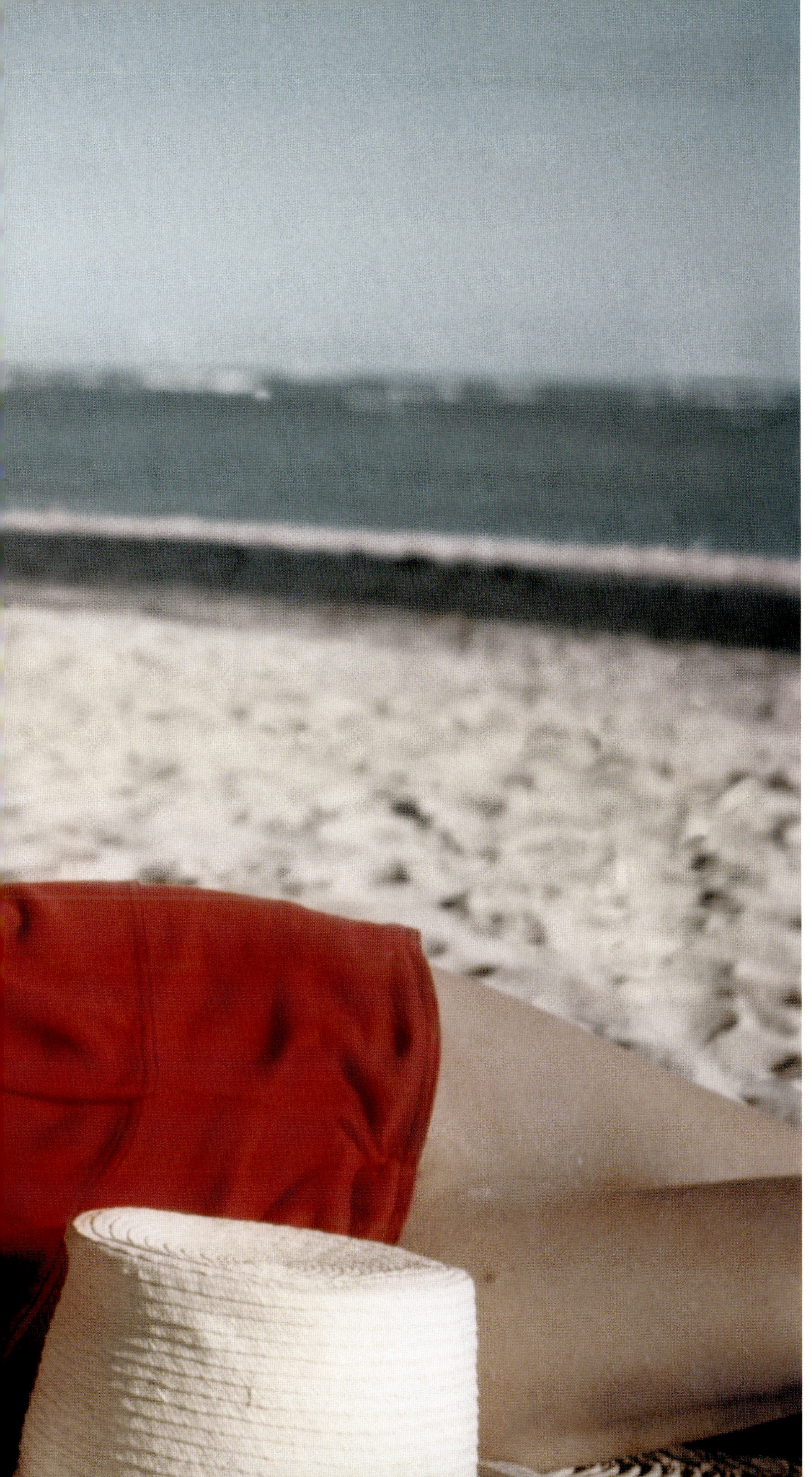

←

Famed model Sunny Harnett on the beach in a red shirt and shorts with a black patent leather belt. *Photographed by Joseph Leombruno and Jack Bodi, May 1954.*

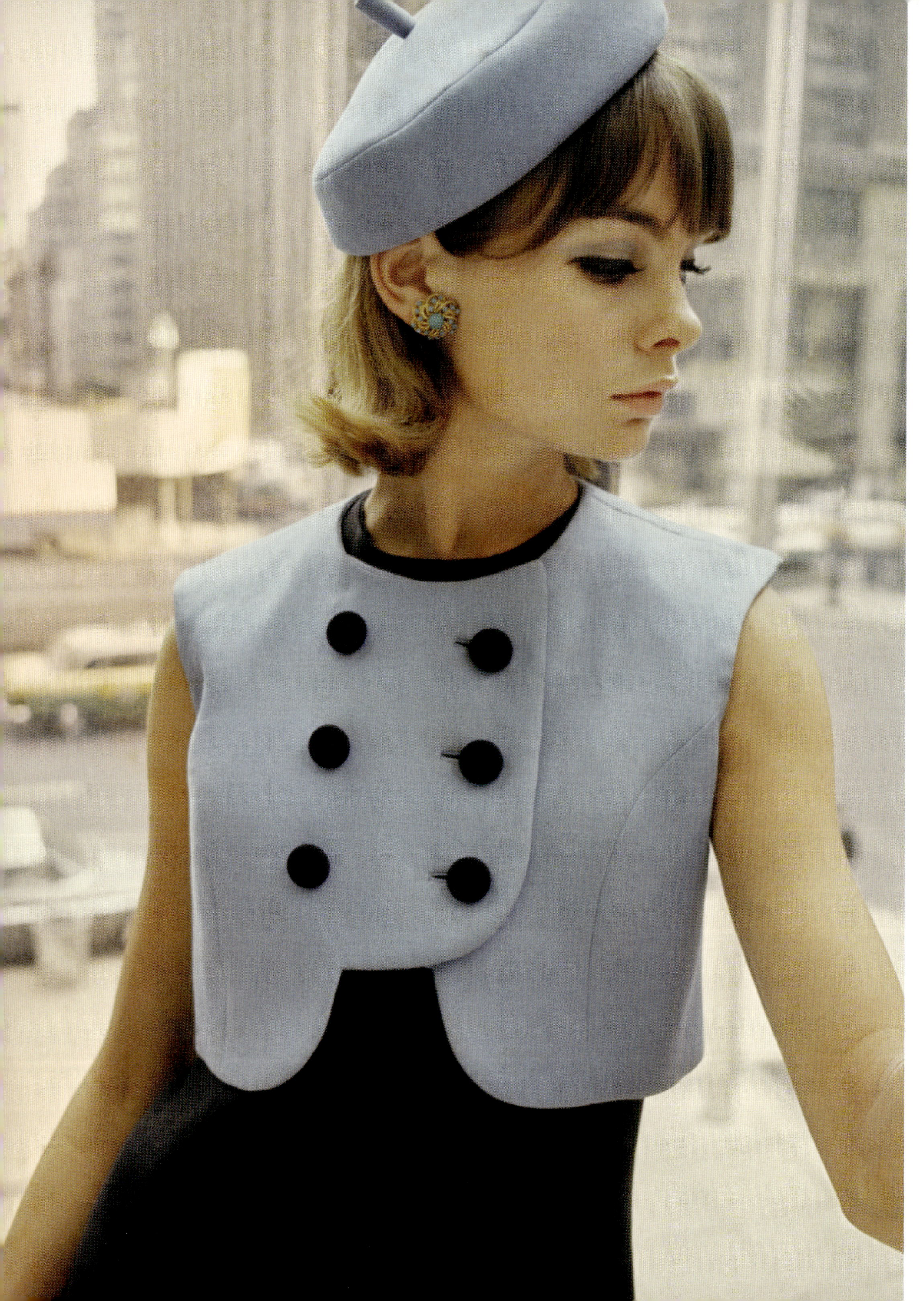

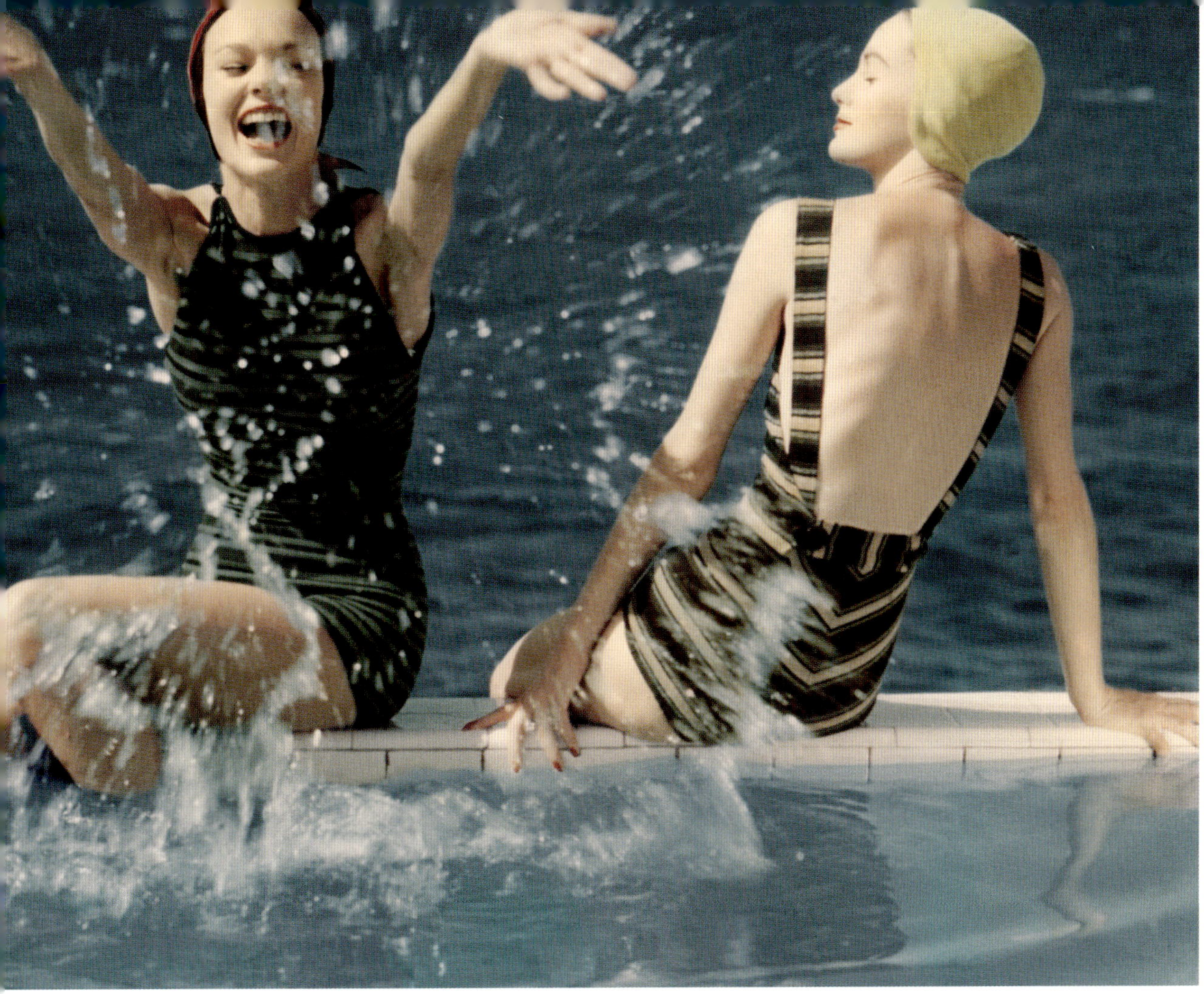

← Two splashing models, wearing a striped suit by Claire McCardell (left) and a black, blue, and gold suit by Annis International. *Photographed by Frances McLaughlin-Gill, April 1957.*

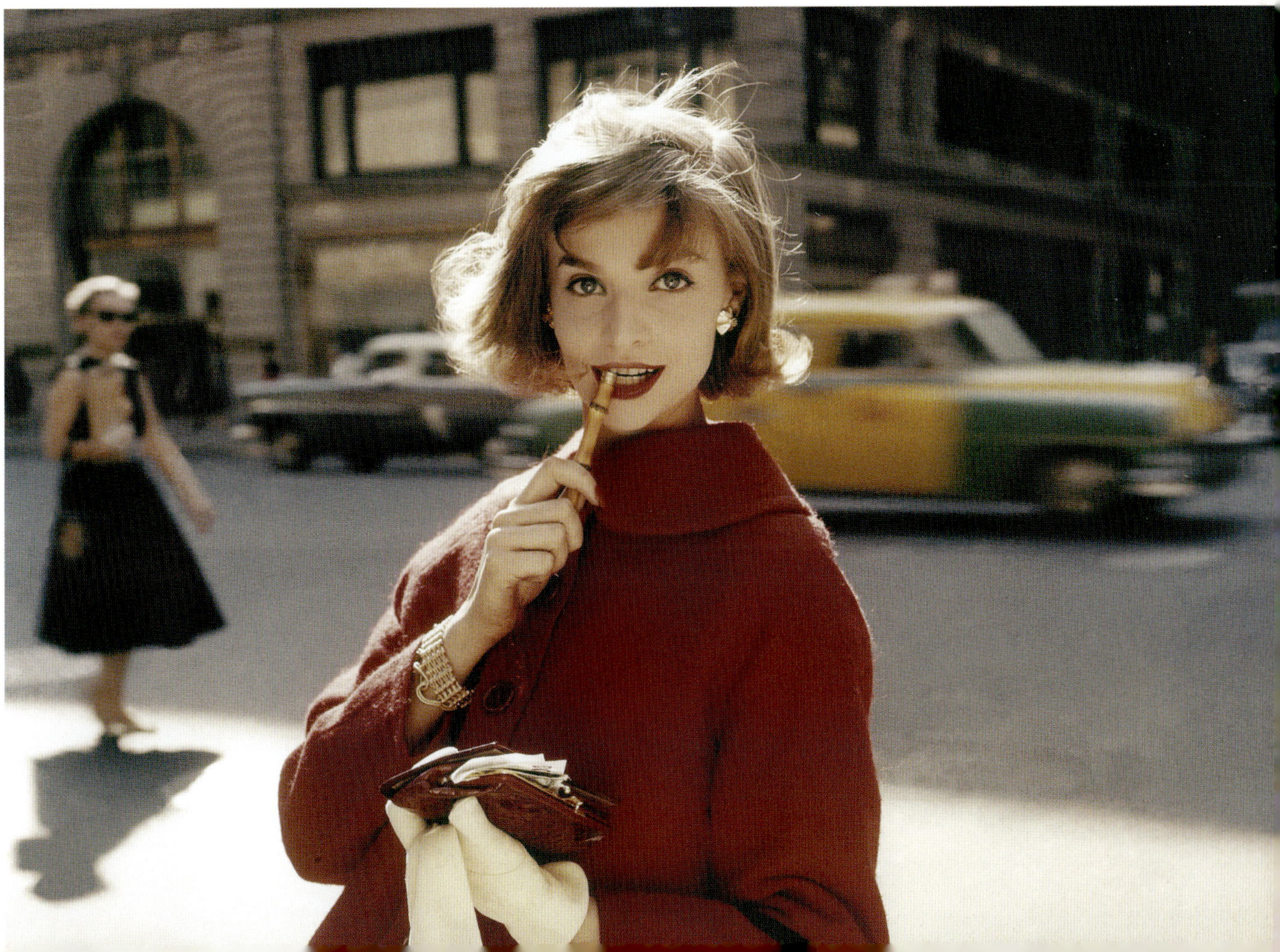

← Model Jean Shrimpton wears a curved jacket with black dress beneath by Townley, beret to match by Adolfo, and Richelieu earrings. *Photographed by David Bailey, June 1963.*

→ A model on a New York street. *Photographed by Otto Maya and Jess Brown, November 1957.*

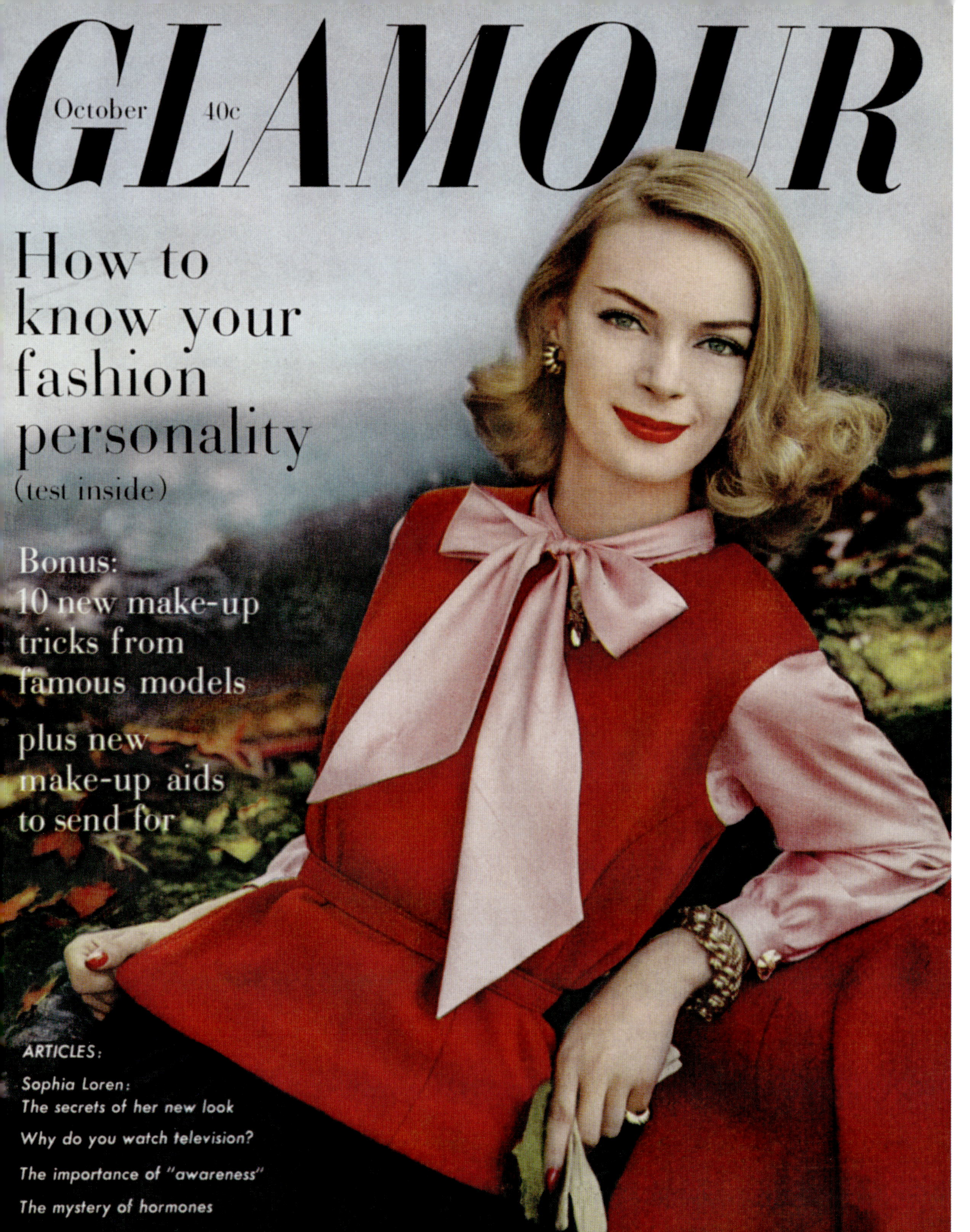

GLAMOUR
October
40c
How to know your fashion personality
(test inside)
Bonus:
10 new make-up tricks from famous models
plus new make-up aids to send for
ARTICLES:
Sophia Loren:
The secrets of her new look
Why do you watch television?
The importance of "awareness"
The mystery of hormones

Nena von Schlebrügge

You might recognize a familiar glint in the eyes and a famous smile: *Glamour*'s October 1959 cover model was 18-year-old Nena von Schlebrügge, known today as Nena Thurman—mother to actor Uma and grandmother to Maya Hawke. She was newly arrived in America from Sweden. Here, she recalls her early years in New York.

"MODELING WAS NEVER MY GOAL. MODELING WAS my vehicle…. It was just something that accidentally happened to me, but I grabbed that opportunity as a vehicle for going out into the big world, because what I was actually looking for, what I was pursuing, was the perennial question: the meaning of life.

The photographer Norman Parkinson was responsible for my career—in the sense that he discovered me in Sweden at the tender age of 14 when he was over there with his wife Wenda on a trip…. They wanted to find some unknown young person. And then there happened to be me, through all amazing circumstances and chance.

He said to me, if you ever do want to come to London and have a career in modeling, I think you would do very well, and here's my number…here's my address and so on, and let me know and I will arrange everything.

So when I was 16, I really didn't know what I wanted to do in life…. And so I contacted him and then I came to London and he arranged everything. I worked for him, and for *Vogue* magazine. Some of the photos I did with photographer Henry Clarke, from the collections in Paris, attracted the attention of Eileen Ford [the model and founder of global agency Ford Models]. She saw these pictures in a Chanel suit, and she contacted me and said, 'Do you want to come to New York?' At the time, New York was more or less the center of this sort of photographic fashion world. I took the *Queen Mary* [ocean liner] to New York in March of 1958, and that was it! Since I already had a bunch of photos, it was easier to make an album, and they would send me on go-sees.

In New York, I met the editors. If there was something like a cover, the editor often came to the studio. One thing that was amazing, which I don't know if you know, but we models had to do our own makeup and hair. So I would walk around with a rather big heavy bag—we all did. We had different types of makeup and then different kinds of eye shadows and different kinds of foundations and powders and eyebrows and false eyelashes, the works. I also had, in that bag, some full hairpieces as well, and some longer pieces of hair. We all became like makeup artists and hairdressers. And it was expected that you would be really good at doing all of this—it was part of your job to be able to do this.

I worked for *Vogue* and *Harper's Bazaar*, as well as my cover for *Glamour*. I did a cover with John Rawlings. And then I did a cover with Avedon, and a cover for *Bazaar* where I was called the 'Golden Girl.'

It was wonderful, but I still wanted to answer the question, is there a meaning to life?

Modeling became how I traveled, and how I was independently taking care of myself, making tons of money so I could live well and do what I wanted and so on. And then I actually did find the answer to all of my questions when I met my husband [the Buddhist academic and author Robert Thurman]. And then I was sort of finished with modeling at around 26 years old, and I ended up having four children. I enjoyed motherhood a great deal and I lost my hankering to do more modeling—it ultimately was not that meaningful to me."

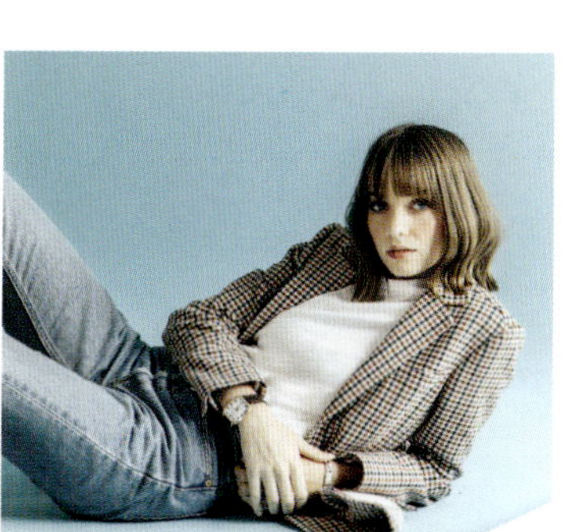

← **Uma Thurman.** *Photographed by Mark Abrahams, July 2006.*

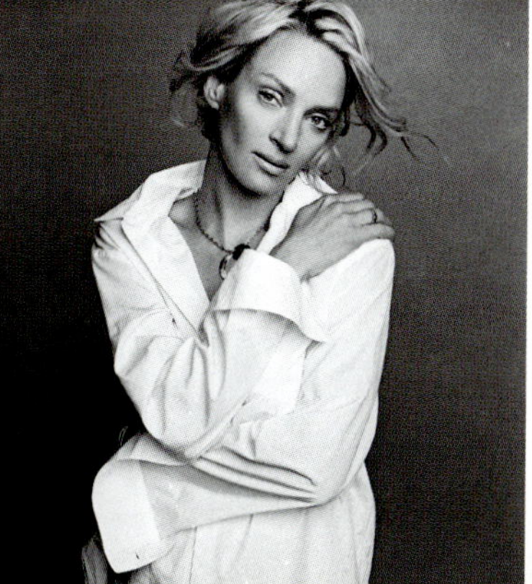

↖ **Maya Hawke.** *Photographed by Joel Barhamand, July 2019.*

"IF I HAD A DAUGHTER WHO'D REACHED THE AGE of thirty in a state of 'single blessedness,' I'd urge her to get married, even if I felt reasonably sure that the marriage wouldn't last." This was the provocative answer given by then beauty editor (later a romantic novelist) Helen Van Slyke to the question "Is Any Marriage Better Than None?" Writer Evelyn Harris, who took the opposing view, argued that her daughter "doesn't need—and I think she will never need—as a sop to her ego, the fact that a man made her a wife." That this debate even existed in the pages of *Glamour* indicates the weight of the societal pressures on women of the post-war era to marry, and then, of course, to marry "well," a topic explored in a January 1957 article by Georgia Gray titled "Should you marry for money?" The author told *Glamour*'s readers "it is just pure childishness to pretend that money doesn't matter in marriage." "One should marry for money," she continues. "Or more specifically, one should hope to find a mate with a similar attitude toward acquiring, keeping, and spending family finances." Whichever way *Glamour* readers fell in the debate, marriage surrounded them on the pages of the magazine more than ever before—even down to the front covers, including this unique December 1953 issue (left), shot by Joseph Leombruno and Jack Bodi, featuring two models posing as a married couple.

Above, the December 1953 issue. Near right, "Is Any Marriage Better Than None?" by Helen Van Slyke and Evelyn Harris. Far right, a model with bandleader Peter Duchin. *Photographed by Milton H. Greene, November 1963.*

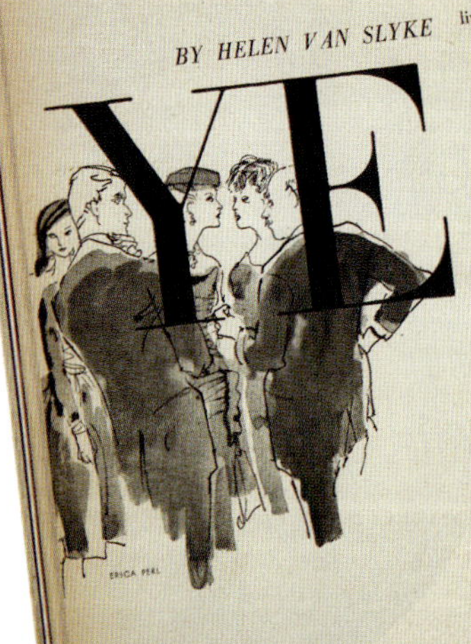

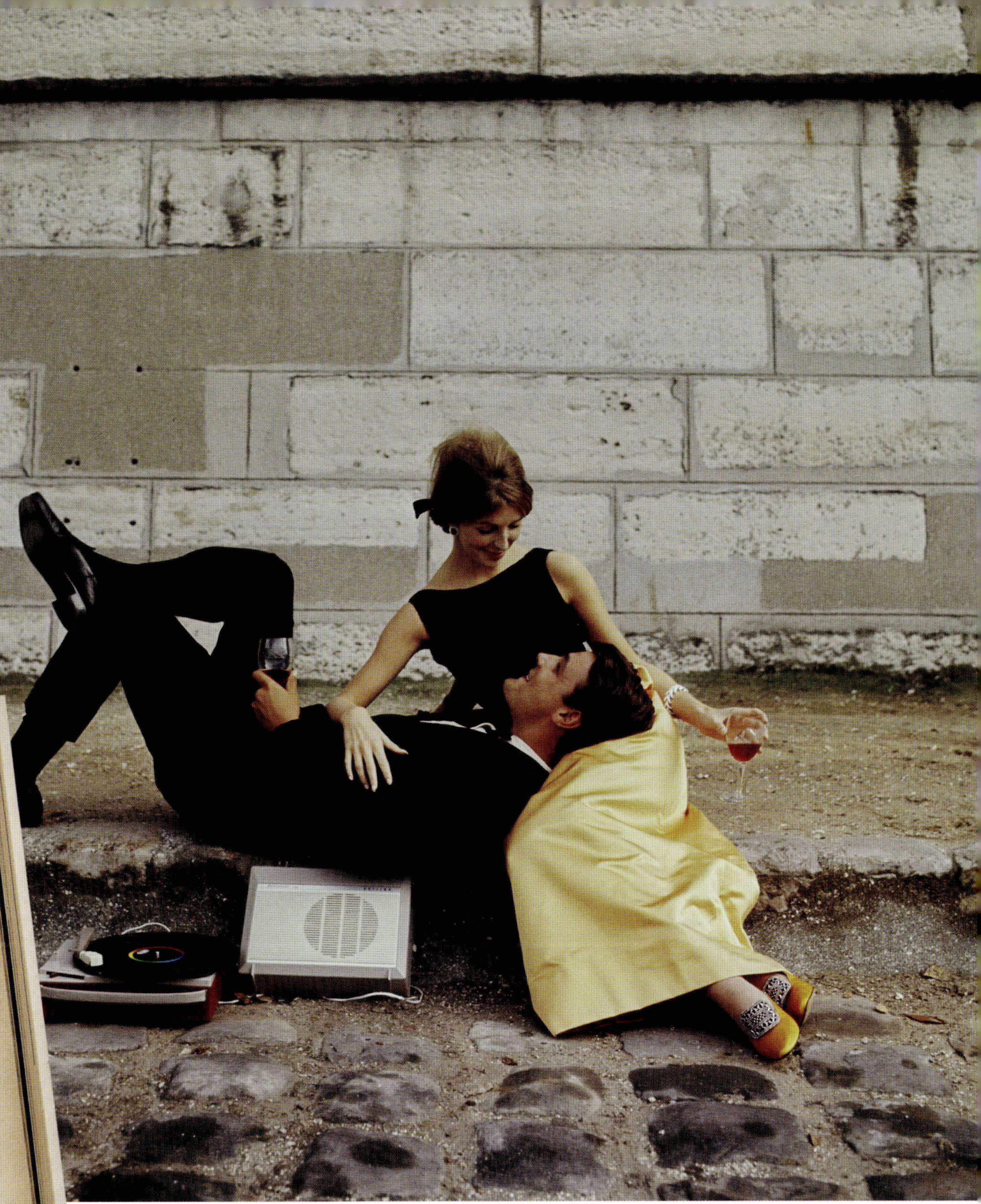

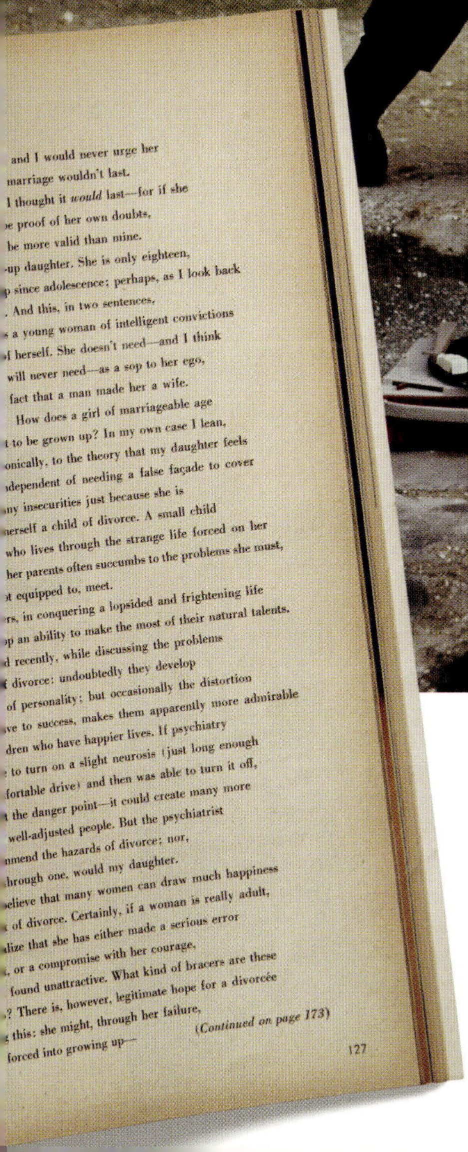

and I would never urge her
marriage wouldn't last.
I thought it *would* last—for if she
e proof of her own doubts,
be more valid than mine.
-up daughter. She is only eighteen,
p since adolescence; perhaps, as I look back
. And this, in two sentences,
a young woman of intelligent convictions
f herself. She doesn't need—and I think
will never need—as a sop to her ego,
fact that a man made her a wife.
How does a girl of marriageable age
t to be grown up? In my own case I lean,
onically, to the theory that my daughter feels
ndependent of needing a false façade to cover
ny insecurities just because she is
erself a child of divorce. A small child
who lives through the strange life forced on her
her parents often succumbs to the problems she must,
t equipped to, meet.
rs, in conquering a lopsided and frightening life
p an ability to make the most of their natural talents.
d recently, while discussing the problems
f divorce: undoubtedly they develop
of personality; but occasionally the distortion
ve to success, makes them apparently more admirable
dren who have happier lives. If psychiatry
to turn on a slight neurosis (just long enough
fortable drive) and then was able to turn it off,
t the danger point—it could create many more
well-adjusted people. But the psychiatrist
nmend the hazards of divorce; nor,
hrough one, would my daughter.
elieve that many women can draw much happiness
of divorce. Certainly, if a woman is really adult,
lize that she has either made a serious error
, or a compromise with her courage,
found unattractive. What kind of bracers are these
? There is, however, legitimate hope for a divorcée
this: she might, through her failure,
forced into growing up—

(*Continued on page 173*)

"

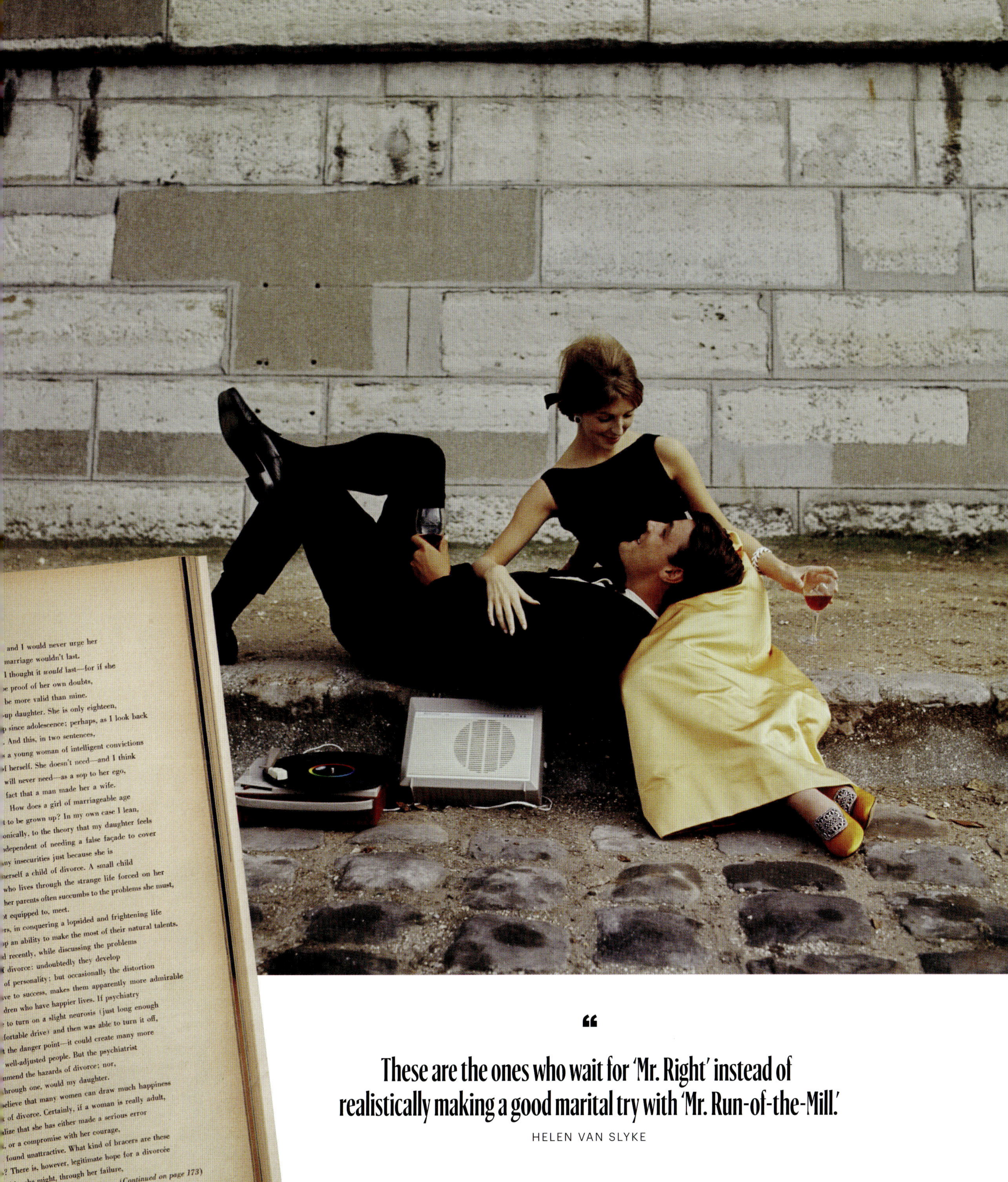

These are the ones who wait for 'Mr. Right' instead of realistically making a good marital try with 'Mr. Run-of-the-Mill.'

HELEN VAN SLYKE

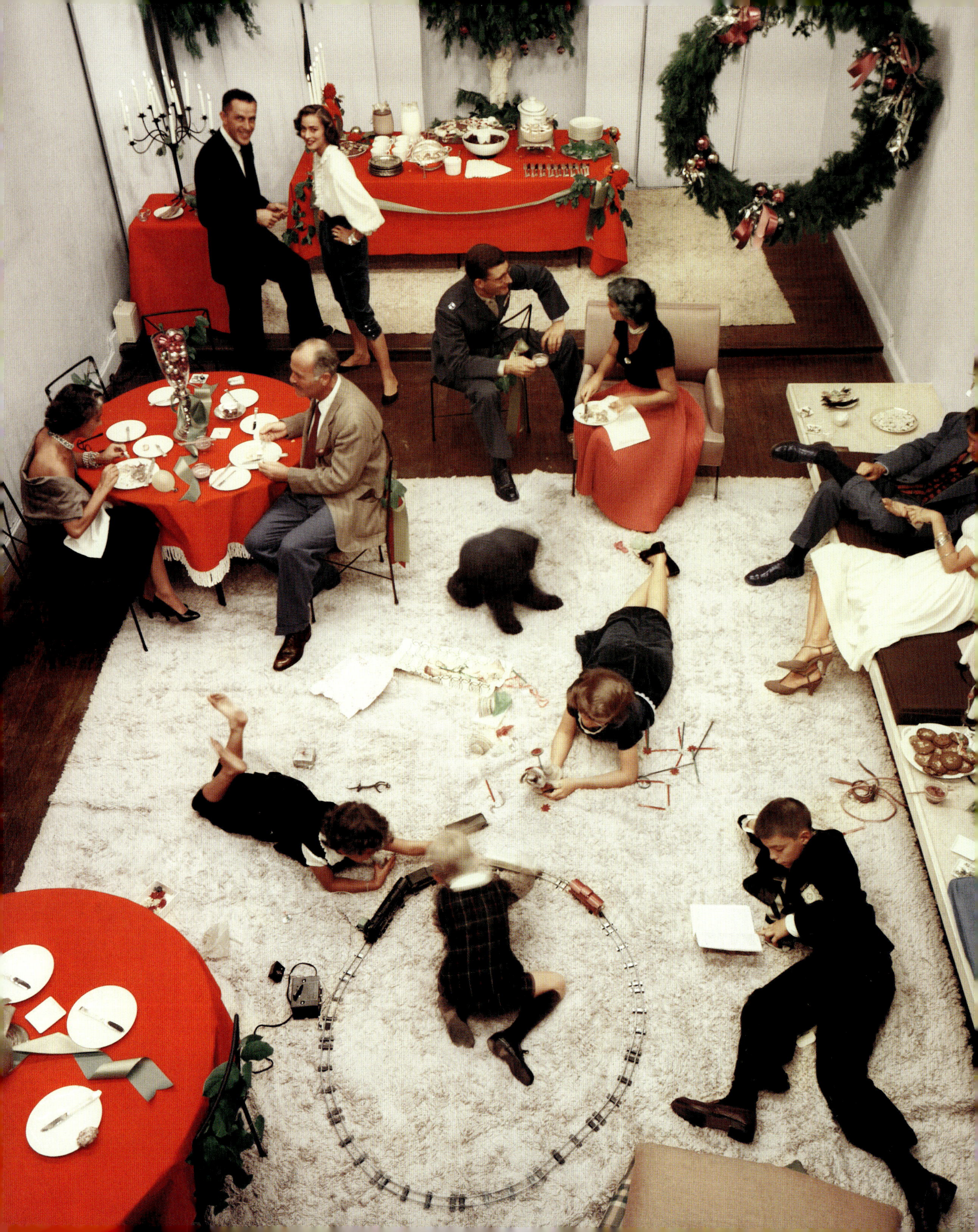

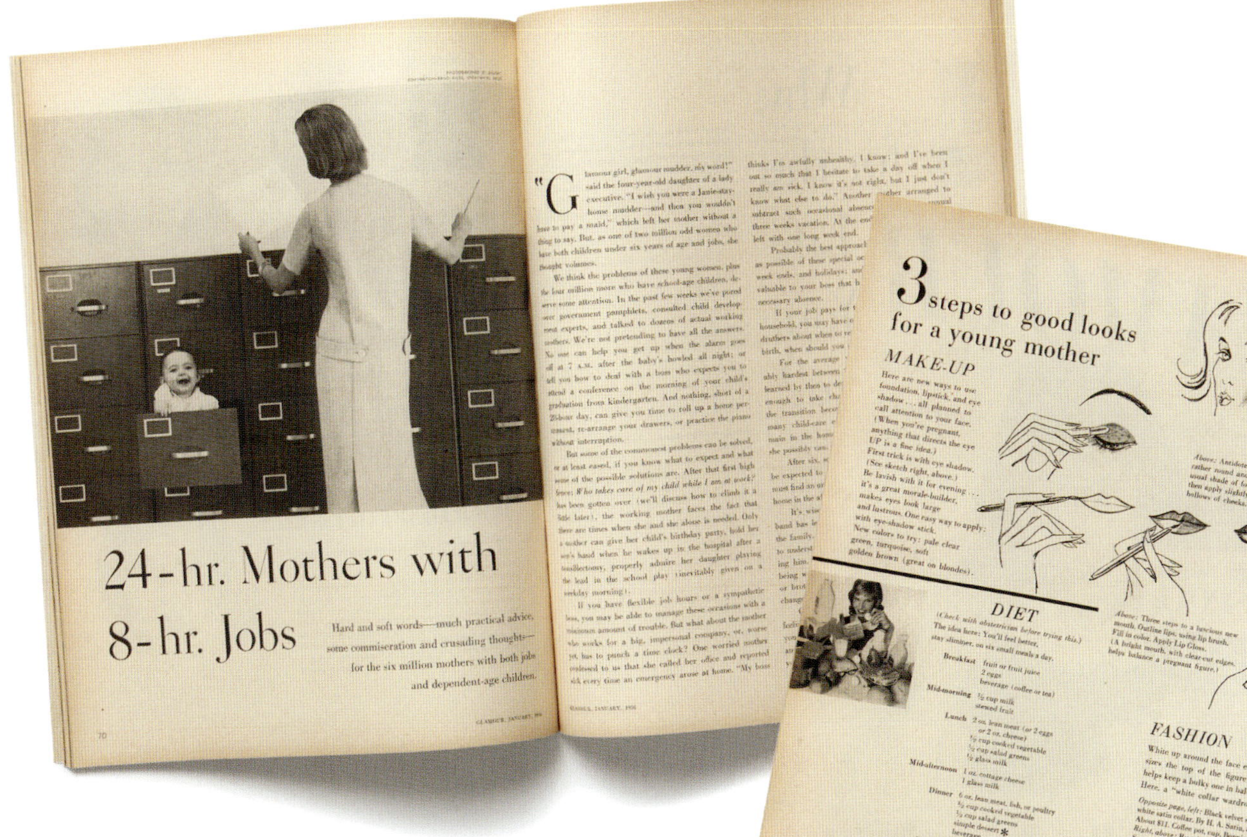

JUGGLING MOTHERHOOD, FAMILY,
and work was a new reality for American women, and in January 1956, the magazine published the article "24-hr. Mothers with 8-hr. Jobs." It noted that "nothing, short of a 28-hour day" would solve the problem of women's multiple responsibilities. *Glamour* readers were urged "to make yourself so invaluable to your boss that he'll condone an occasional necessary absence." Throughout the decade, *Glamour* had spotlighted women managing it all, as in the February 1951 article "How Do They Do It?" about four mothers "combining good-sized jobs with good-sized families." But as the decade came to a close, the focus on working mothers lessened. In 1958, a special section launched called "Glamour for Young Mothers." "We plan to give you the best fashions for pregnancy and for new babies, to say nothing of diet, beauty, health, and organizing life with a new baby."

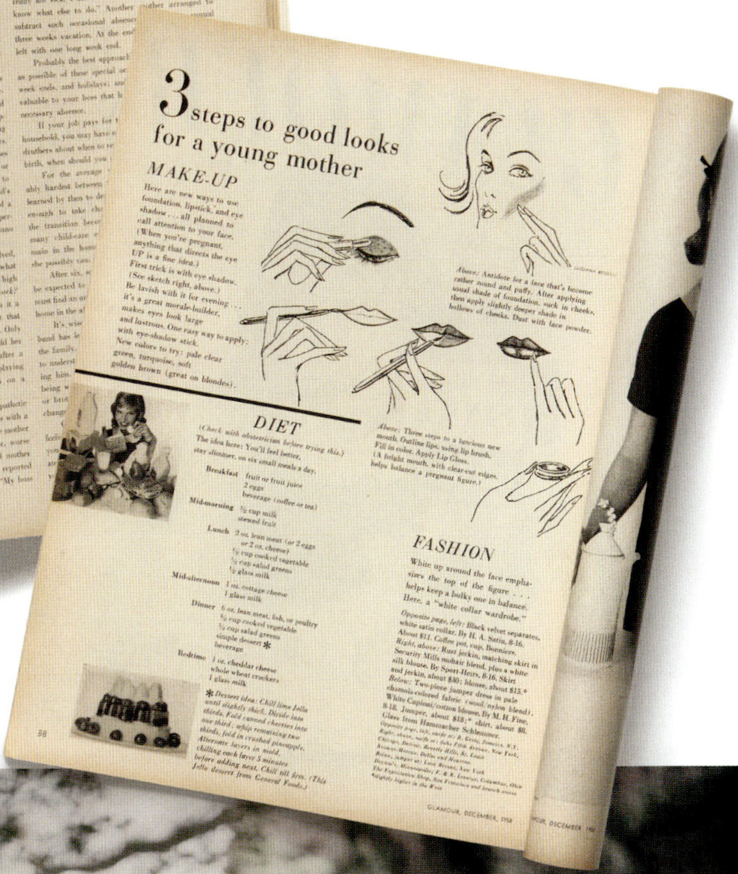

A family Christmas scene.
Photographed by Diane and Allan Arbus, December 1952.

A model and a young boy.
Photographed by Clifford Coffin, April 1953.

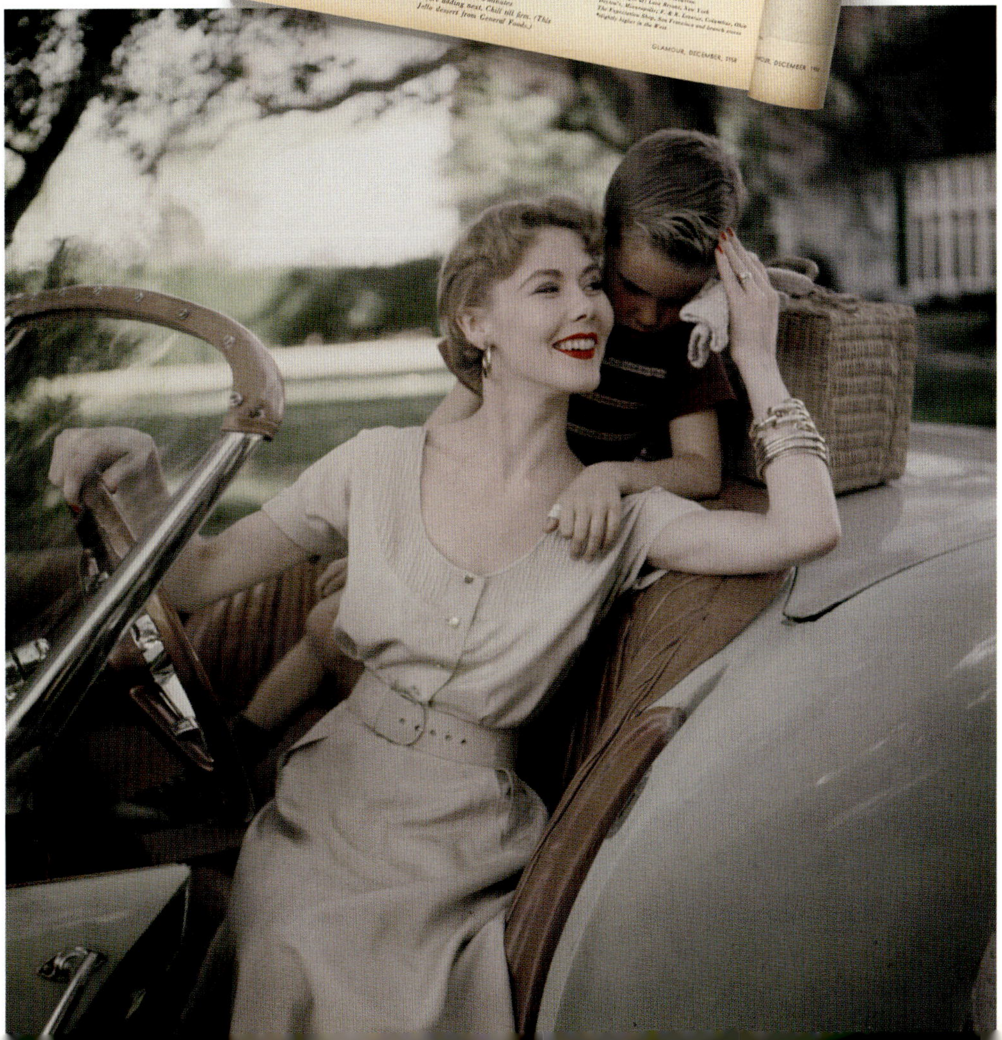

THE PERFECT WIFE

We asked for it, and got it—what they are really looking for, from some of the most eligible bachelors, divorcés, widowers we could find. We got some funny answers ("A deaf and dumb blonde whose father owns a liquor store," from a smug wag; " 'perfect wife' is a contradiction in terms," from a disillusioned one.) Seriously, their dream girls range from Jacqueline Kennedy to a lady scientist; they like long hair and short phone conversations. Almost unanimously they turn thumbs down on career women, stand together against togetherness, even take a dim view of separate but equal. Will they find what they want? Do they know what they want? Do they really want wives at all? For answers, we consulted marriage counselor Jane Mayer, who is secretary of the New York chapter of the American Association of Marriage Counselors, President of the Tri-State Council of Family Relations. If you don't make our bachelors' grade, find her consoling words on page 186.

ARTIST

*"I'm a romantic. I believe
in love, and I'm waiting for it."*

Fred R., twenty-five, is a layout man in an advertising agency, and a talented painter as well. He's tall, attractive, seemingly reserved, until he gets started on the subject of women.

"What lets me know that a woman's a romantic, too? The way she dresses, her joy in living. None of this melancholy, droopy, supposed romanticism.

"Actually, artists should never love and get married. As a rule, they're selfish. My wife would have to be terribly tolerant of me and my hours—sometimes I like to paint all night.

"I'd like her to be stylish looking. Not necessarily expensive clothes, but clothes that suit her. I'd like her to be graceful, rather sexy. She should have a certain amount of mystery to her. Even if it's frustrating to a man, there's a certain pleasure in never knowing what she's thinking.

"I like a woman who's secure, because she was loved as a child. I'd want her to be able to make decisions in what to do, where to have dinner—a man has more important things to decide. I want her interests to be different from mine. I get bored talking about the same things all the time.

"I don't think about a family at this point—that will come naturally. Although I can imagine loving a woman who doesn't want children. Love conquers all."

SCIENTIST

*"I want an intellectual;
it's unlikely that she'd be chic."*

Pete K. is a promising young scientist, twenty-three, simultaneously working in industry and for his Ph.D. He's tall, gangly, careless in his dress (with Adlai Stevenson holes in his shoes), passionately dedicated to his work.

"She wouldn't have time to spend on her adornment. She'd have to have an inner glow. I want a wife who has a career, but isn't a career girl. There should be equal status between husband and wife. I'd like her to have a career close to mine so that I could get some feedback from her. Since, with my doctorate, I'll be headed towards the psychology section of electrical engineering, it would be nice if she were in the biological sciences. She should be analytical rather than intuitive—it would be hard to deal with someone who reaches conclusions without reasons behind them. Warm, human qualities? I'll believe she has them because I'm in love with her.

"I have no prejudices about appearance, but I'm attracted to short, dark girls. I'd like a girl reasonably independent of her family, who has good girl and men friends but isn't a social butterfly. I'd like her to be able to enjoy life on a surface level—above all, like riding on my motor scooter. And I'd be perturbed if she really smoked a lot.

"I'm looking more for a companion now; I don't feel any pressure to get married. I don't feel very fatherly yet—maybe it's my age.

"There's not *THE* one woman I could marry—on the other hand, there aren't too many women who have a healthy conception of a career, a willingness to apply logical, scientific thinking even to themselves."

NEWSPAPERMAN

*"There are plenty of girls who have
read Proust, but it's hard
to find a good homemaker."*

Kenneth J., thirty-eight, is a newspaperman; once divorced and twice shy,

Who does the man you will—or did—
marry envision secretly as The Perfect
Wife? Is she you? Does she even exist?
Here, some highly eligible males of varying ages, in various occupations, give
their definitions, and a lady marriage
counselor evaluates them for us.

BY MARILYN MERCER

husband relax at home. I like
air and can't stand long telephone

The best wife is one who enjoys
a wife, not doing something else."

E-LAW STUDENT

like a wife who's an athlete.
doesn't scare me at all."

ck S., in his senior year at college,
athlete himself. He's going on to
hool, plans to go into politics.
'd like a wife who is active, lively,
One who likes skiing, sailing,
ing. What should she look like?
to my size (he's a six-footer) than
tive. Features strong, rather than
e or chic.
The person I have in mind would
o do a lot of things. I don't want
an dominate; I want her to have
as of her own. I enjoy an open,
ic relationship. I wouldn't mind
rking.
d like a wife who plays one or
usical instruments. I don't, but
to have a wife who's interested
arts, not because of me, but so
ld pass this training along to the
n. She should have a healthy at-
owards sex.
dislike phoniness. Superficiality.
on who hides her emotion too
About children, I'm intellectually
ted to the small family, because
overpopulation problem, but I
large family would be fun.
ostly I want a wife with a mind
wn. I'd be bored if my wife were
e me."

PSYCHIATRIST

"A woman . . . is a member of the anatomically feminine sex who enjoys a man for his own sake. And that definition rules out most American women under thirty."

Dr. Stanley M. is a psychiatrist, twenty-eight and single, halfway through his residency in a New England hospital. A witty and articulate young man, he's especially so on the subject of women, from both a professional and personal viewpoint.

"I make a distinction between an anatomical female and a woman. The classical example is the model. You want to look at her, but wouldn't want to muss her $50 hairdo.

"I've noticed a change in my own life on the subject of women. In high school, I liked girls with pretty faces. Then I liked girls with pretty faces and pretty figures. The ideal girl could be identified at 100 yards, and often was. Then, on a boat, I met a girl who was clearly not gorgeous. Not being particularly interested in looking at her, we began to talk. I discovered a tremendously bright girl. The more I talked to her, the prettier she seemed. Now I'm in a position to defend her beauty. Unfortunately, she's the one that got away.

"This is not supposed to be a consolation for homely girls. This 'homely girl' is a rationalization. A girl would rather think of herself as homely than frigid, arid, uninteresting. That way it's

(Continued on page 178)

IN A MAY 1961 ARTICLE THAT couldn't be more reflective of the era, writer Marilyn Mercer on behalf of *Glamour* interviewed "highly eligible males of varying ages" about what they were looking for in "the perfect wife." From a prelaw student who wanted "a wife with a mind of her own," and who "wouldn't mind her working," to a newspaperman who believed "the perfect wife would find all her satisfaction in making a home and smoothing the path for her husband," it's an enlightening—if somewhat exasperating—look at how men perceived relationships and marriage, and the hurdles facing women who wanted to break out of homemaking.

"

She should have a good sense of humor and a certain tolerance for Louis Armstrong records, especially at three in the morning.

KENNETH J., "THE PERFECT WIFE"

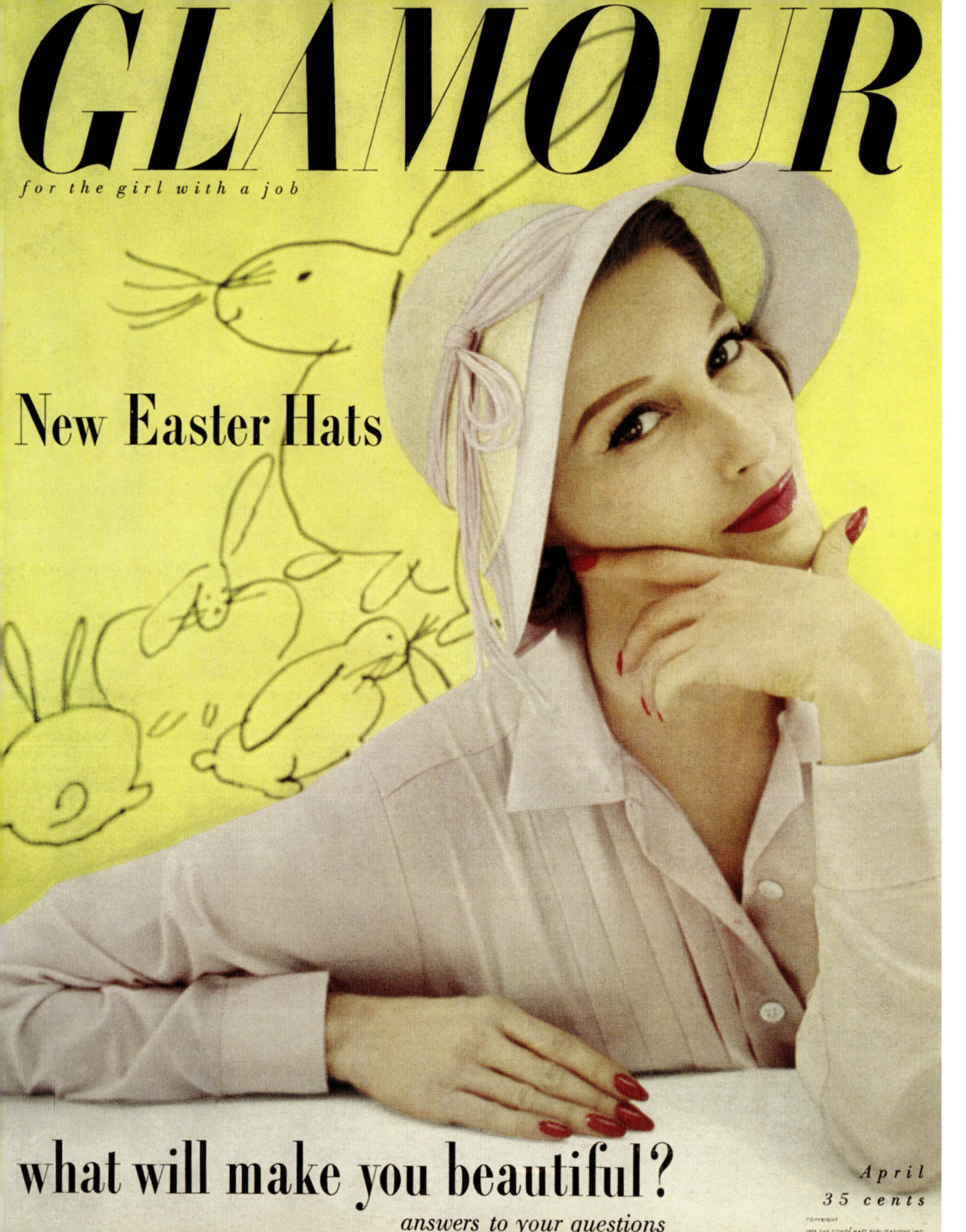

GLAMOUR
for the girl with a job
New Easter Hats
what will make you beautiful?
answers to your questions
April
35 cents

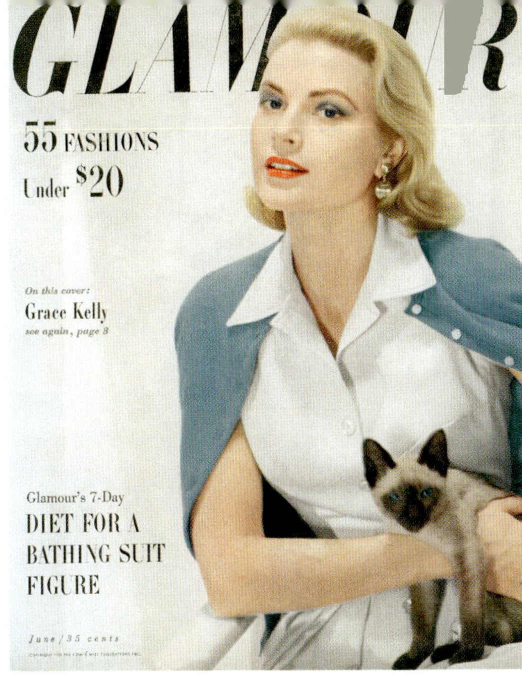

←

Actor Grace Kelly and a Siamese cat, June 1955.

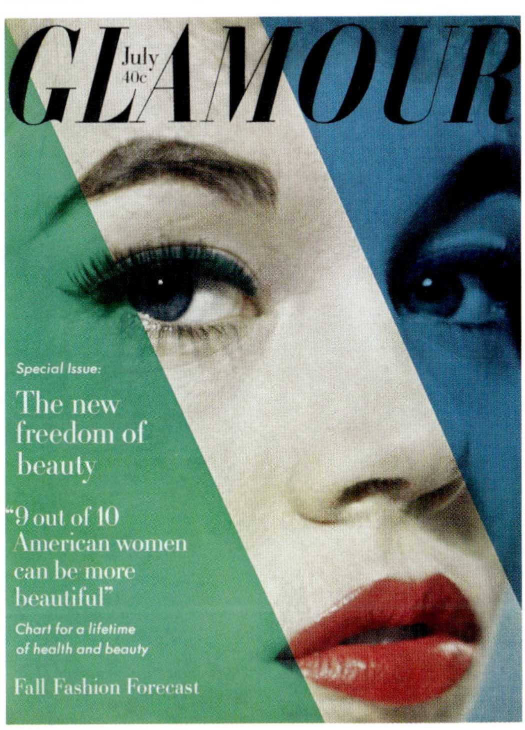

←

Actor Jane Fonda on her first ever cover for the magazine, July 1959. Fonda was photographed again for a 2023 *Glamour* cover, in front of a projection of this original (see page 284).

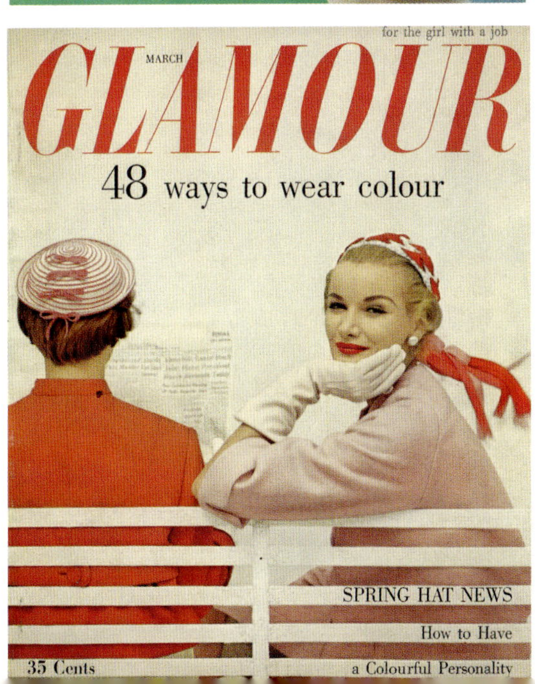

↙

Two models in pink on a bench, March 1954.

From Grace Kelly and Jane Fonda as cover stars to Andy Warhol illustrations and a hairstylist du jour so famous he could go simply by his first name (Kenneth, whose hands became *Glamour* cover stars of their own), the covers of this era were certainly memorable. Here are some of the standouts.

Opposite, model Mary Jane Russell alongside drawings of rabbits by Andy Warhol, April 1955.

A model with a blue bow and hair styled by Kenneth of Lilly Daché, July 1963.

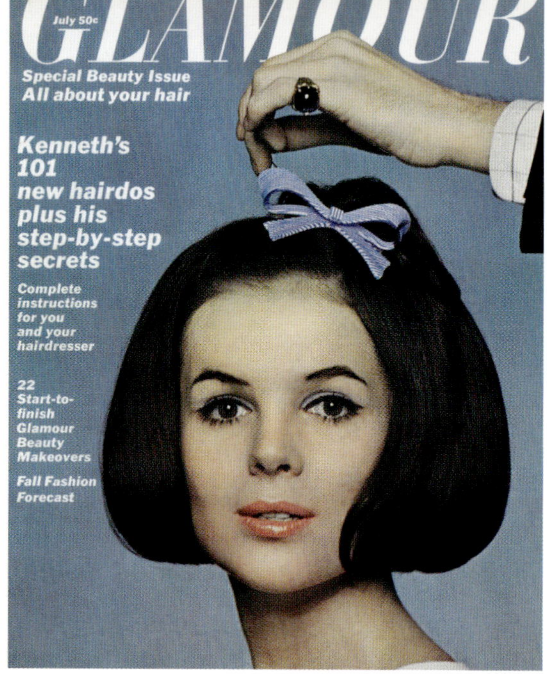

Model Monique Chevalier having her hair coiffed by Kenneth, July 1962.

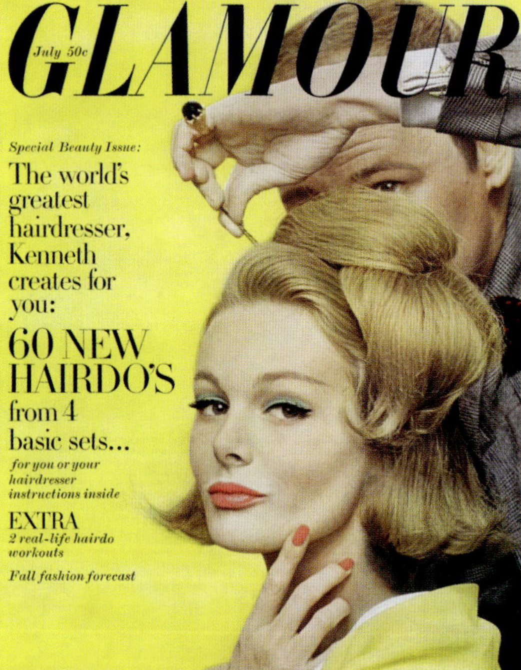

Model Monique Chevalier wearing a pink hat by Emme Inc., July 1961.

Opposite, model Dorothy McGowan with soapy hair styled by Kenneth. He was hairstylist to Jackie Kennedy, Marilyn Monroe, and Judy Garland, among others, and became a *Glamour* cover star in his own right (or at least his hands did!—see above), February 1962.

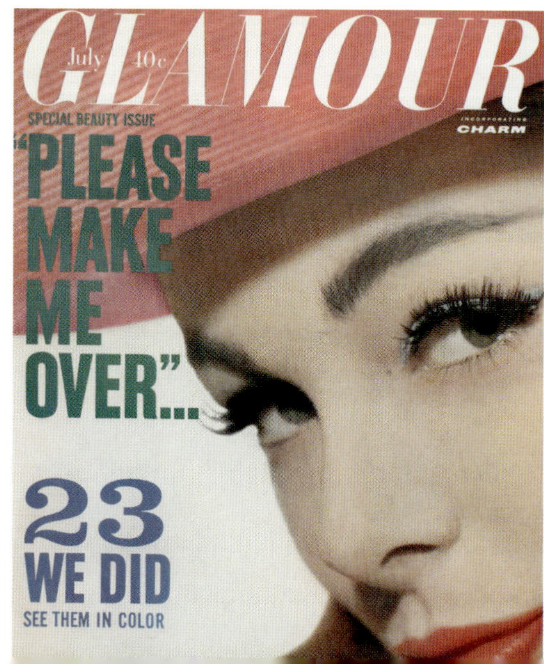

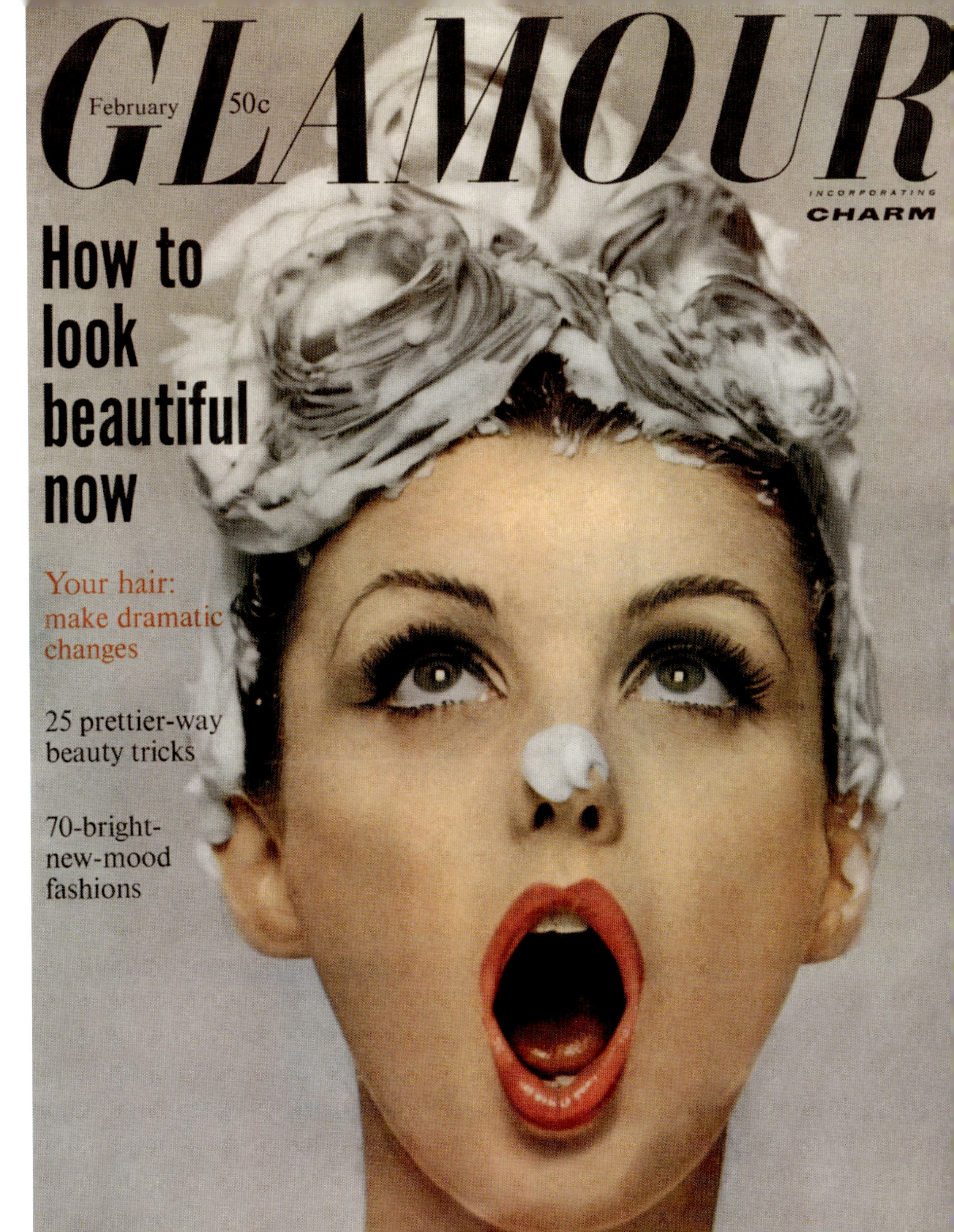

February 50c
GLAMOUR
INCORPORATING CHARM
How to look beautiful now
Your hair: make dramatic changes
25 prettier-way beauty tricks
70-bright-new-mood fashions

COLLEGE WOMEN *of the* YEAR

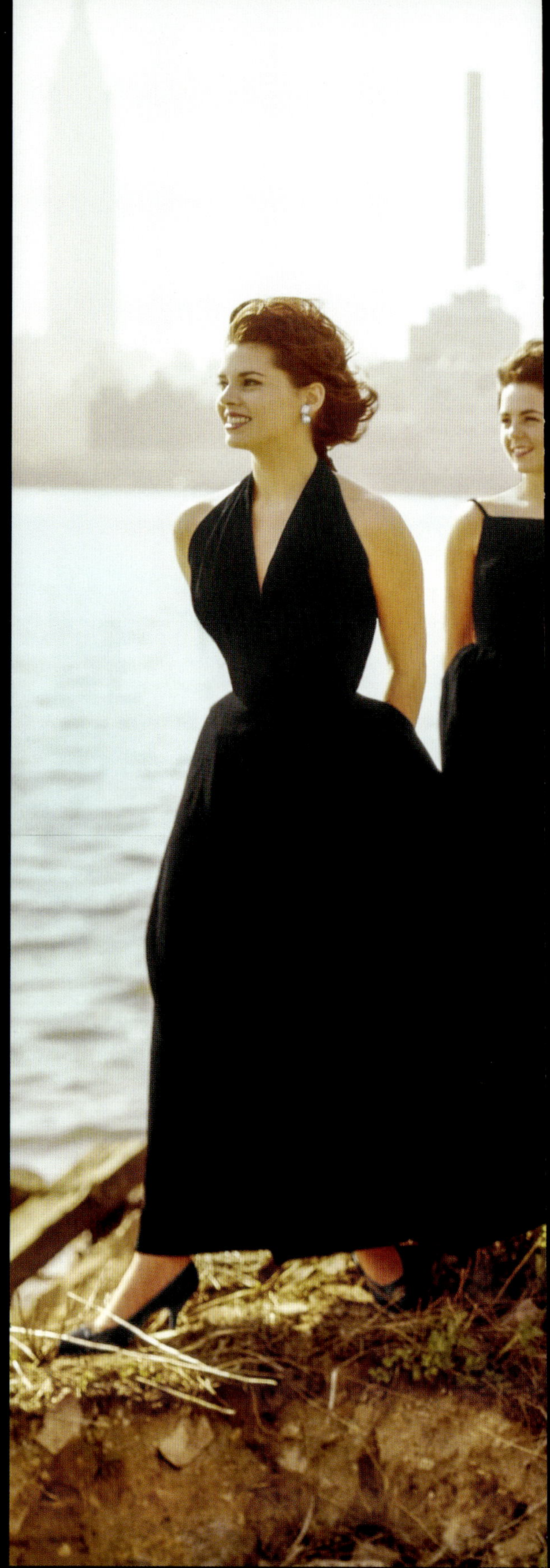

THE AUGUST 1957 ISSUE OF *GLAMOUR* UNVEILED
the magazine's first ever 10 Best-Dressed College Girls in
America. "We asked hundreds of colleges and universities to
choose their own best-dressed candidates either by open
ballot or special selection committee," explained the
magazine's editorial. Nominees were required to showcase their
best campus, weekend, and party outfits. Superficial as it was
to judge women on their looks and fashion alone—a too
frequent mark of the era in *Glamour*—it did acknowledge that
women were now a permanent fixture on campus. In 1969, with
Glamour under the editorship of Ruth Whitney, it was renamed
Glamour's Top Ten College Girls Contest, celebrating the
students fighting to make the American dream "a reality to all
people." Today, the annual awards—now called College Women
of the Year—are 67 years old. And the mission has stayed true
to Whitney's 1969 focus: spotlighting the next generation of

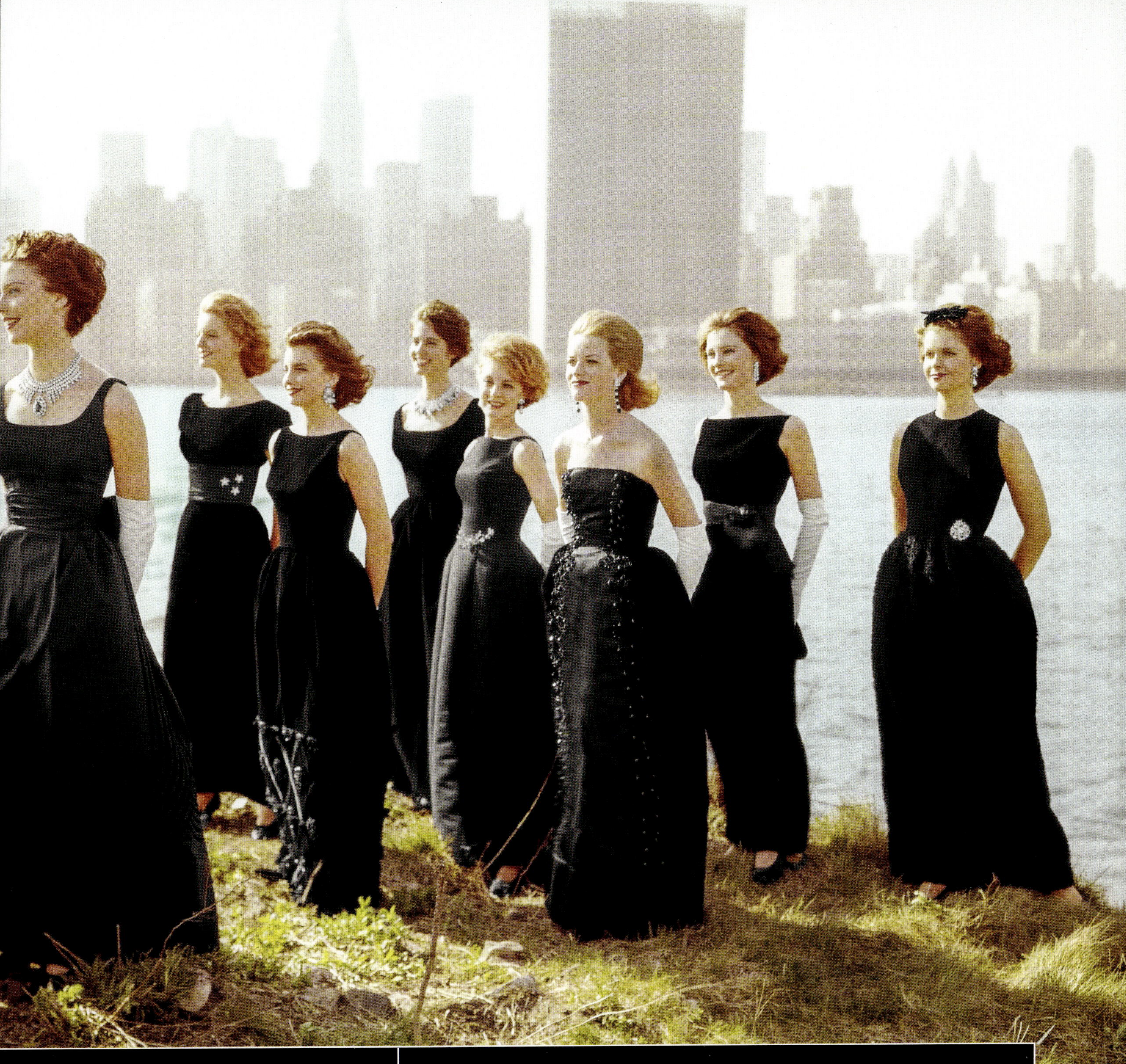

Glamour's 1962 10 Best-Dressed College Girls in America winners were **CAROLYN OLNEY** (Simmons College, Massachusetts), **SHARON FOSTER** (Randolph-Macon Woman's College, Virginia), **ANNETTE GRANT** (Pembroke College, Rhode Island), **SUNNY GRIFFIN** (Hood College, Maryland), **LISA THOMSIC** (Colorado State University), **SALLY LYON** (Seton Hill College, Pennsylvania), **CAROLYN TAYLOR** (Baylor University, Texas), **ANDREA QUINN** (Good Counsel College, New York), **LINDA CLARK** (Wisconsin State College), and **MARY ANNE EASTERLING** (University of South Carolina). *Photographed by Frank Horvat, August 1962.*

How does a college girl become one of the 10 best-dressed? In the August 1963 issue, *Glamour* outlined the list of attributes they were judged on. Each girl was rated for:

FIGURE AND POSTURE

GROOMING

BEAUTIFUL HAIR

SKILL WITH MAKEUP

UNDERSTANDING HER
   FASHION TYPE

CLOTHES BUDGETING

WARDROBE PLANNING

INDIVIDUALITY IN USE OF
   COLORS AND ACCESSORIES

AN APPROPRIATE LOOK
   ON CAMPUS AND
   OFF CAMPUS

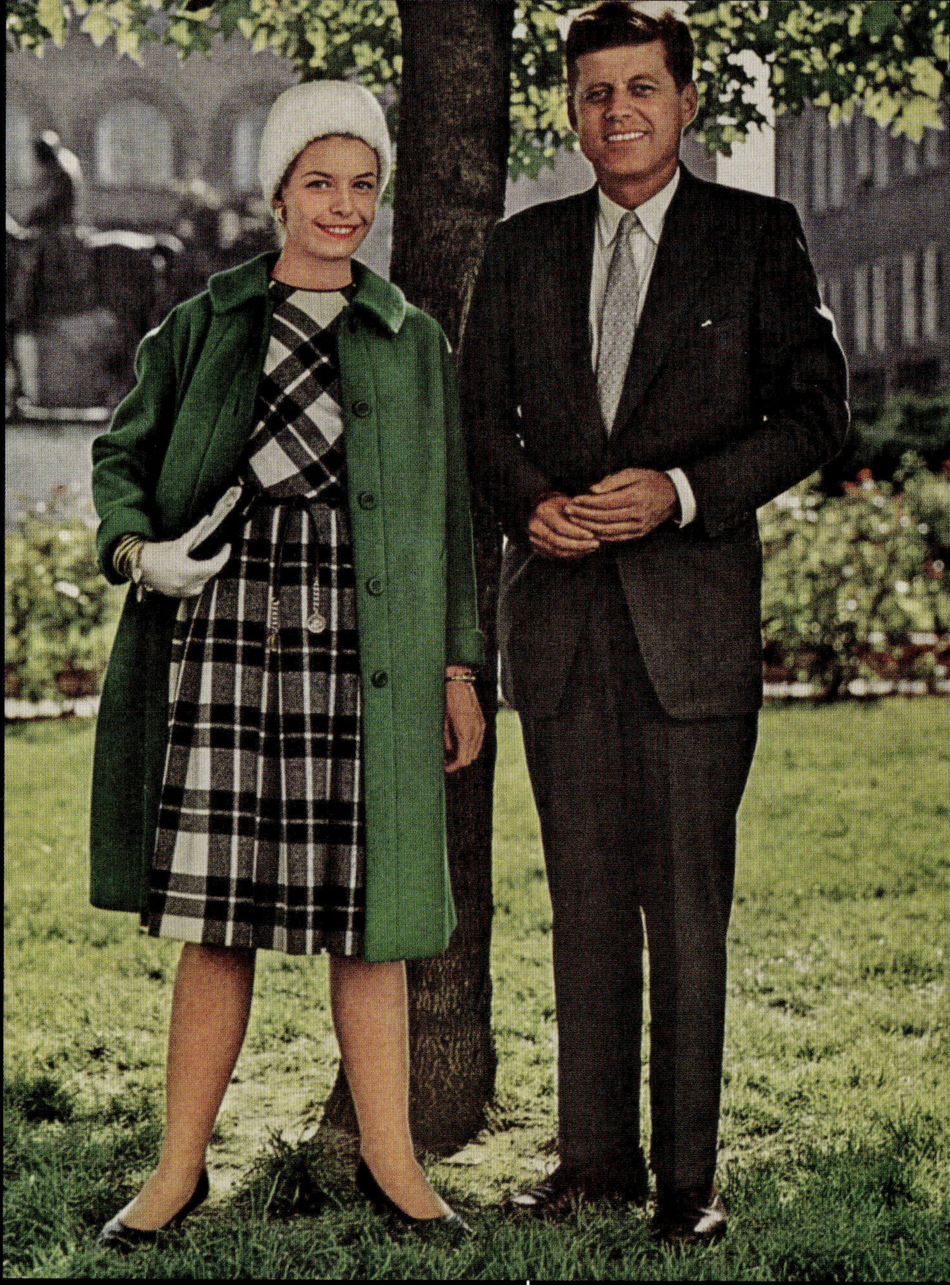

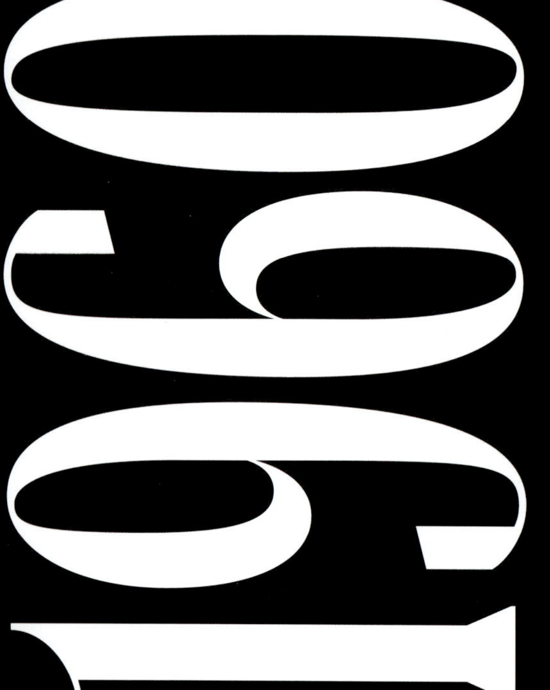

Glamour's 1960 Best-Dressed College Girls were given a unique opportunity—"to meet and exchange views with government leaders from their home states." Those leaders included Richard Nixon, Lyndon B. Johnson, and John F. Kennedy, all photographed by Milton H. Greene for the August 1960 issue. "These extraordinary portraits combine the authority of men who shape change," the editorial continued, "with the promise of young women who find their prize-winning fashion sense a true but subordinate clause in the prospectus of their lives." The winners asked the politicians this: "What single piece of advice would you offer to a young woman graduating from college today?"

JANET DAY, who attended Hood College in Maryland, met her then senator John F. Kennedy in West Virginia on his way to speak at her college. His succinct, and somewhat condescending advice: "Marry a politician—it's an interesting life!" Later that same year, he was elected the 35th president of the United States.

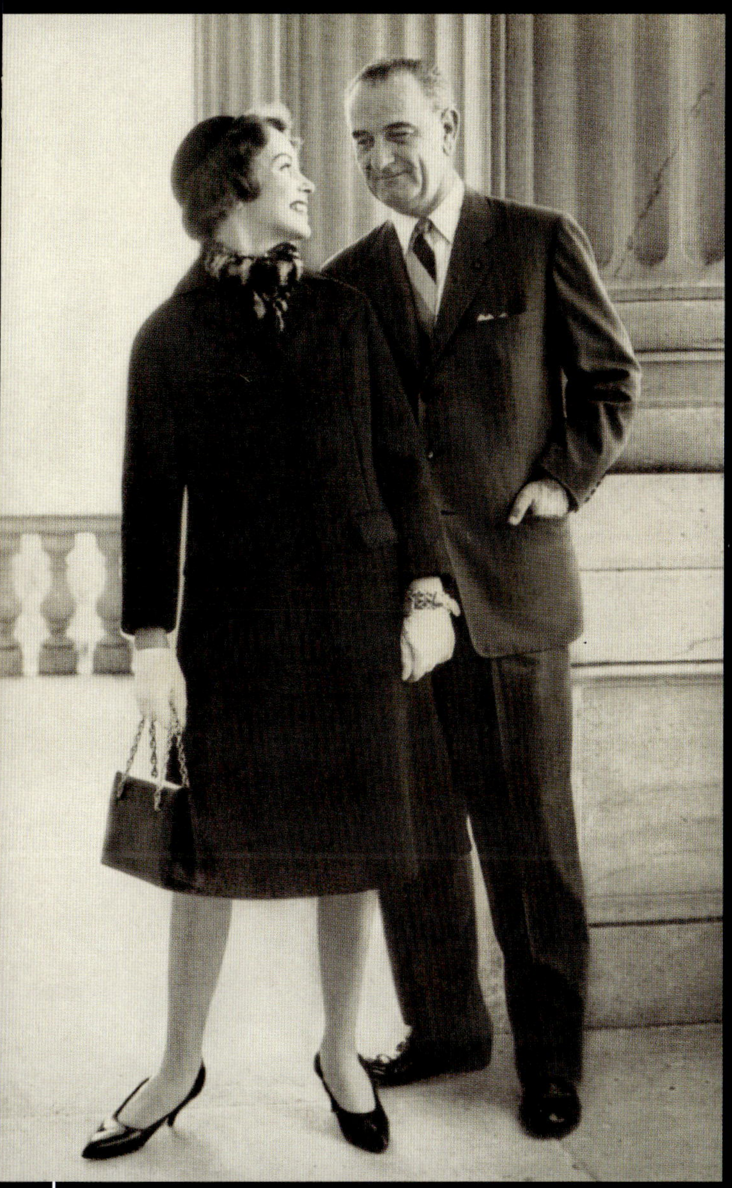

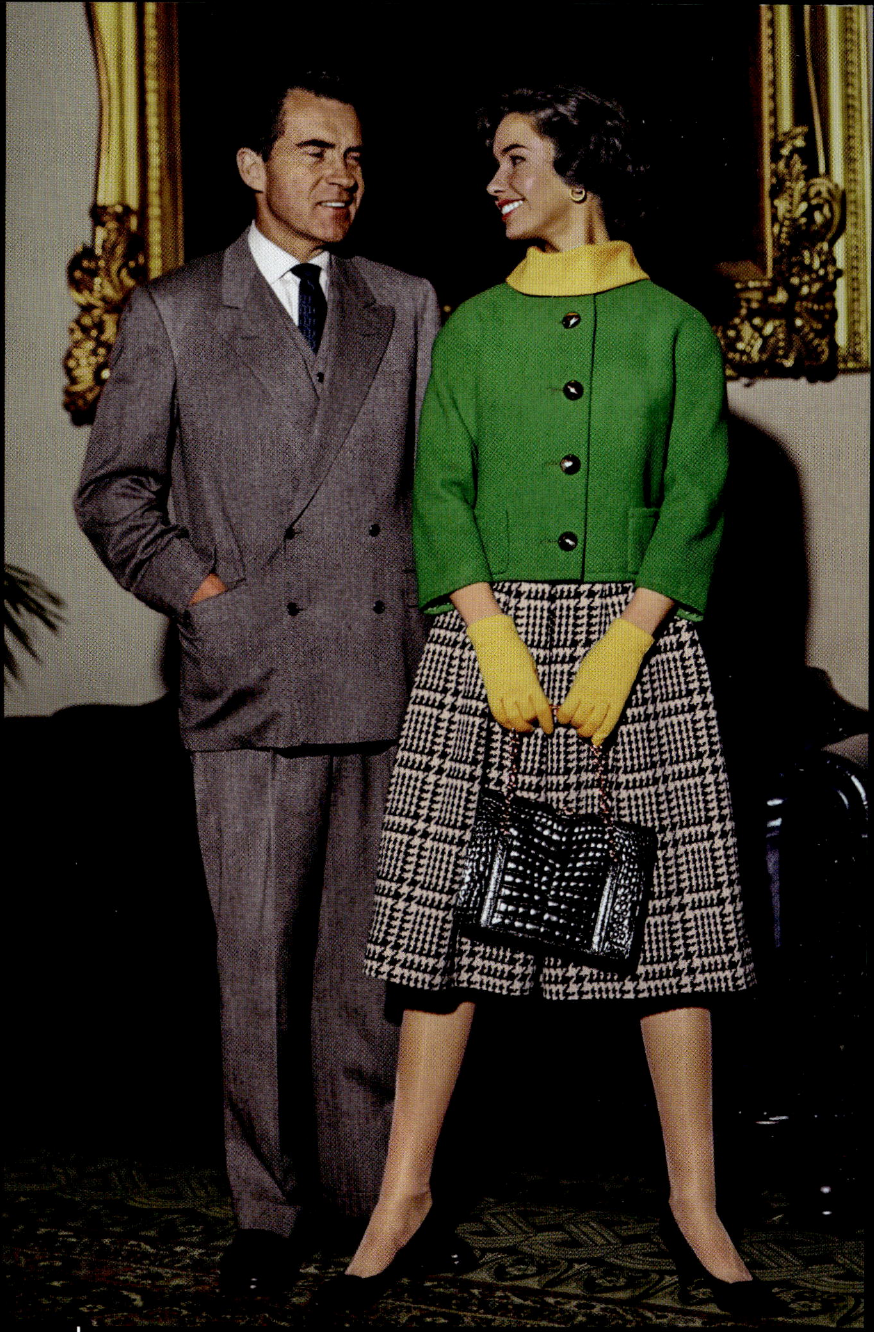

1961

One of the magazine's 1961 Best-Dressed College Girls was none other than Martha Kostyra, now known as **MARTHA STEWART.** A student at Barnard College in New York, she told readers, "I'd like to write a book on art, visit Pakistan, and help improve education." Martha also revealed to *Glamour* that, given her preference, she would opt to be an architect. As it turned out, she chose otherwise. *Photographed by Frank Horvat, August 1961.*

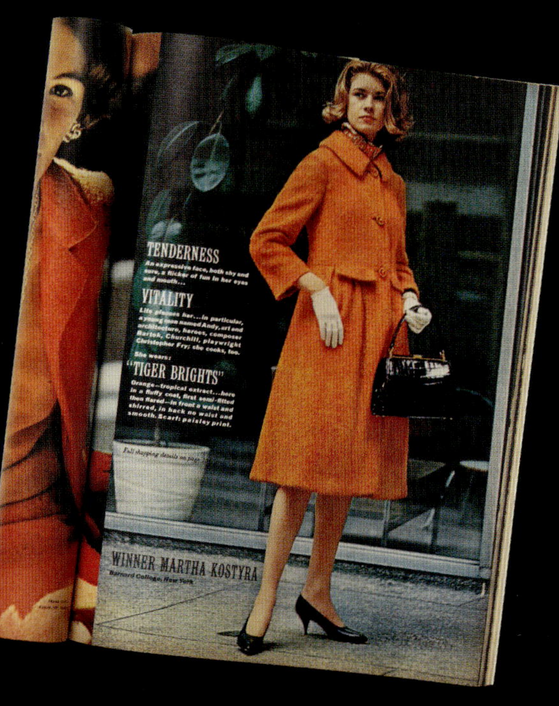

In the same 1961 issue, *Glamour*'s Best-Dressed winners were photographed by Milton H. Greene beneath the American flag. "Art, science, politics—in each, we have tried to imagine the new frontiers that will be met, and crossed, by today's college girls, in tomorrow's world," said the editorial. Martha Stewart stands at the top of the pole.

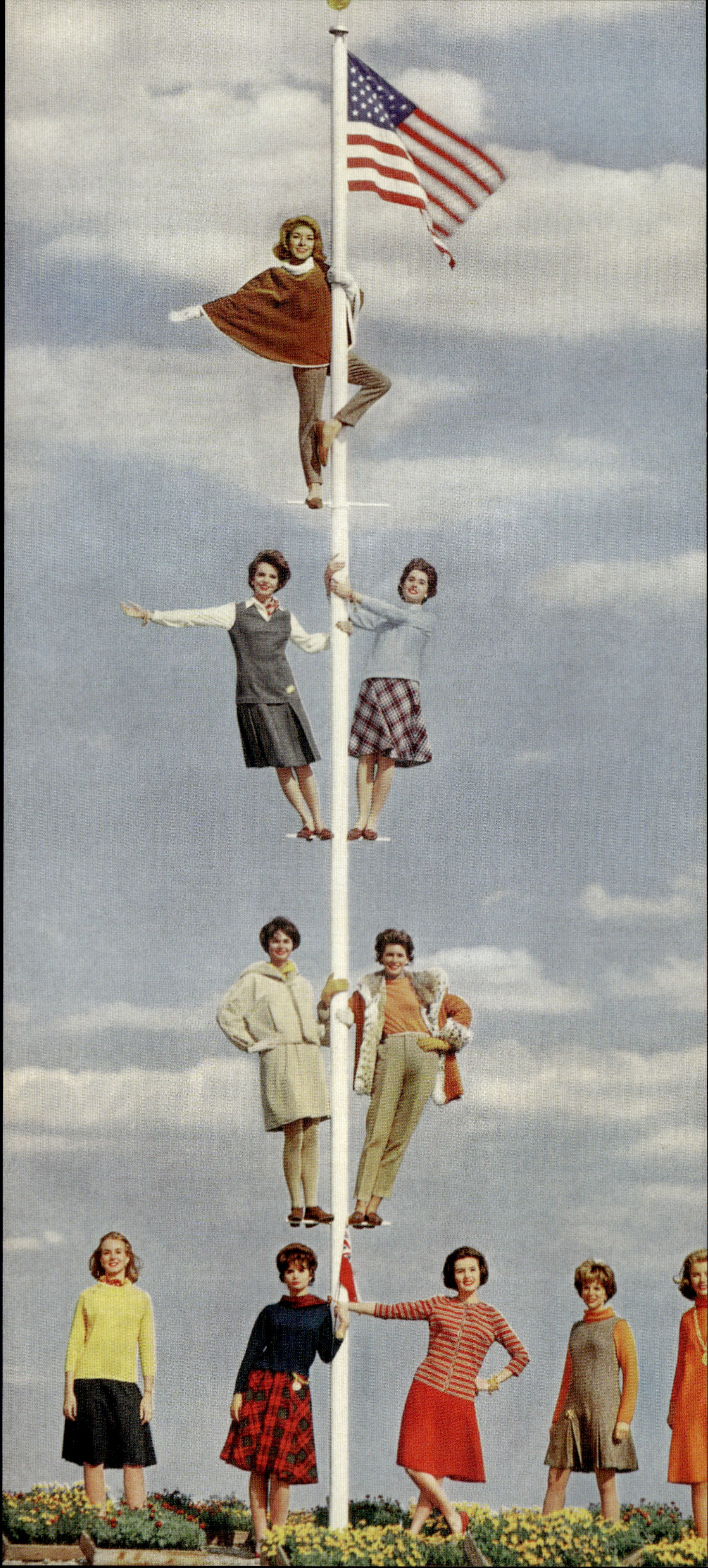

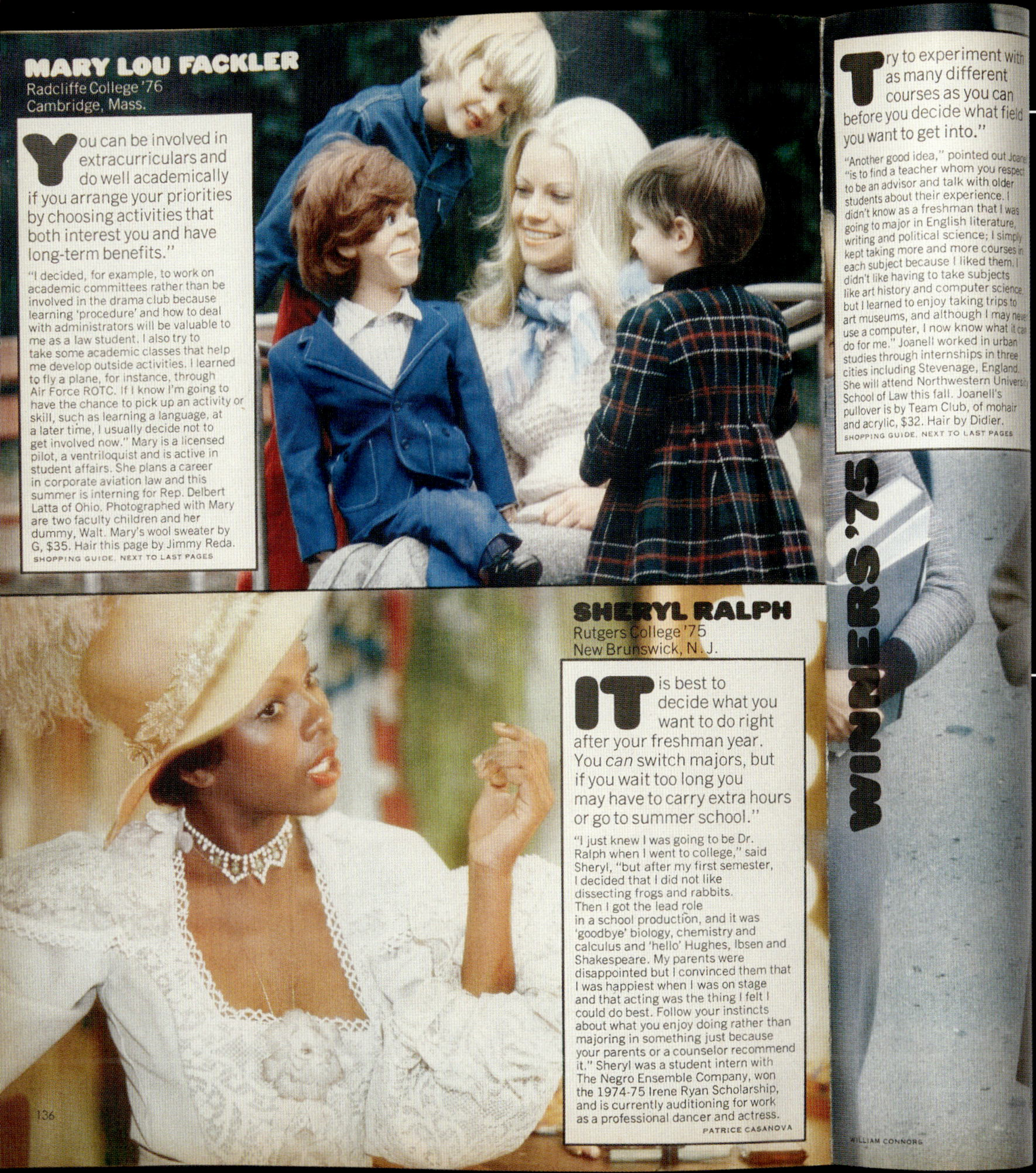

WINNERS '75

MARY LOU FACKLER
Radcliffe College '76
Cambridge, Mass.

"**Y**ou can be involved in extracurriculars and do well academically if you arrange your priorities by choosing activities that both interest you and have long-term benefits."

"I decided, for example, to work on academic committees rather than be involved in the drama club because learning 'procedure' and how to deal with administrators will be valuable to me as a law student. I also try to take some academic classes that help me develop outside activities. I learned to fly a plane, for instance, through Air Force ROTC. If I know I'm going to have the chance to pick up an activity or skill, such as learning a language, at a later time, I usually decide not to get involved now." Mary is a licensed pilot, a ventriloquist and is active in student affairs. She plans a career in corporate aviation law and this summer is interning for Rep. Delbert Latta of Ohio. Photographed with Mary are two faculty children and her dummy, Walt. Mary's wool sweater by G, $35. Hair this page by Jimmy Reda.
SHOPPING GUIDE, NEXT TO LAST PAGES

"**T**ry to experiment with as many different courses as you can before you decide what field you want to get into."

"Another good idea," pointed out Joan, "is to find a teacher whom you respect to be an advisor and talk with older students about their experience. I didn't know as a freshman that I was going to major in English literature, writing and political science; I simply kept taking more and more courses in each subject because I liked them. I didn't like having to take subjects like art history and computer science, but I learned to enjoy taking trips to art museums, and although I may never use a computer, I now know what it can do for me." Joanell worked in urban studies through internships in three cities including Stevenage, England. She will attend Northwestern University School of Law this fall. Joanell's pullover is by Team Club, of mohair and acrylic, $32. Hair by Didier.
SHOPPING GUIDE, NEXT TO LAST PAGES

SHERYL RALPH
Rutgers College '75
New Brunswick, N.J.

IT is best to decide what you want to do right after your freshman year. You *can* switch majors, but if you wait too long you may have to carry extra hours or go to summer school."

"I just knew I was going to be Dr. Ralph when I went to college," said Sheryl, "but after my first semester, I decided that I did not like dissecting frogs and rabbits. Then I got the lead role in a school production, and it was 'goodbye' biology, chemistry and calculus and 'hello' Hughes, Ibsen and Shakespeare. My parents were disappointed but I convinced them that I was happiest when I was on stage and that acting was the thing I felt I could do best. Follow your instincts about what you enjoy doing rather than majoring in something just because your parents or a counselor recommend it." Sheryl was a student intern with The Negro Ensemble Company, won the 1974-75 Irene Ryan Scholarship, and is currently auditioning for work as a professional dancer and actress.
PATRICE CASANOVA

WILLIAM CONNORS

1975

MARY LOU FACKLER, a Top 10 College Winner in 1975, attended Radcliffe College in Massachusetts. At the time a ventriloquist and licensed pilot, she went on to become inspector general of the United States Department of Transportation (DOT). In subsequent roles, she handled Foreign Intelligence Surveillance Act (FISA) requests, served as a special assistant to then US attorney general Edwin Meese, and worked in labor management standards at the United States Department of Labor. Notably, Fackler Schiavo (as she became known) also criticized the work of the 9/11 Commission.

Emmy Award–winning actor **SHERYL LEE RALPH** was also honored as one of *Glamour*'s Top 10 College Winners in 1975. In an interview with the magazine, Ralph recounted her experience at Rutgers College in New Jersey: "I just knew I was going to be Dr. Ralph when I went to college, but after my first semester, I decided that I did not like dissecting frogs and rabbits." A pivotal moment came when she landed the lead role in a school production, prompting a shift from biology, chemistry, and calculus to the world of Ibsen and Shakespeare. *Both photographs by Patrice Casanova, August 1975.*

1972

SHEILA STAINBACK was one of *Glamour*'s 1972 winners. Then a student at Fordham University in New York, she told the magazine: "I spent 18 years growing up in East Harlem, and the enormous helplessness that abounds in areas like this is still with me. That's why I've been studying the urban problem." Stainback later became a TV anchor and analyst at Court TV.
Photographed by Mike Reinhardt, August 1972.

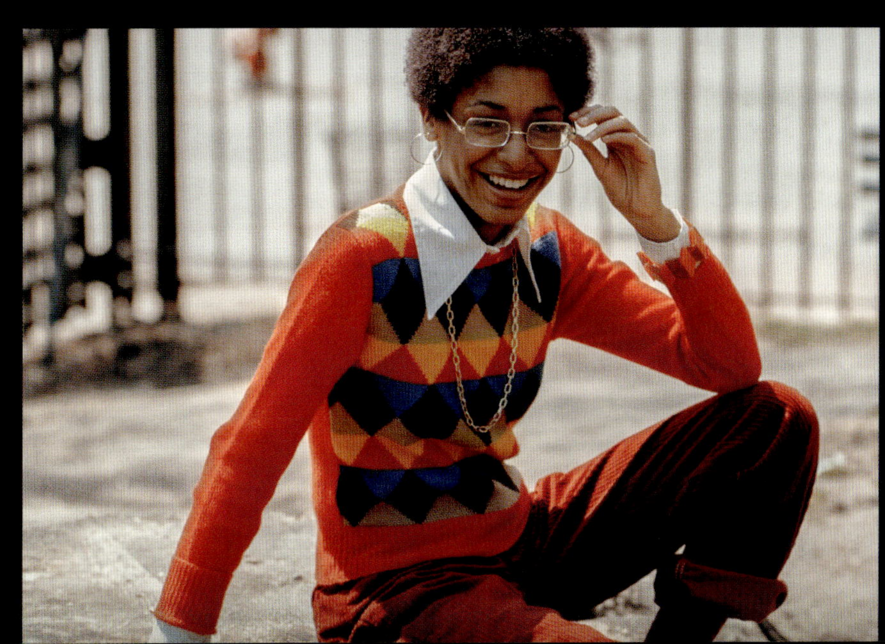

The October 1995 issue marked 38 years of honoring college students. While the image of the women harked back to the 1962 photograph found on pages 108–109, the focus had shifted squarely to their college achievements. The 10 honorees forged direct paths to success in medicine, politics, science, sports, and music—a powerful transition from taking advice to wielding power themselves. From left to right, **E. STACY PARKER, VANESSA POTKIN, REBECCAH BENNETT, SUSANNE AMHARI, ALLISON YURI IWAOKA, NIKKI NICHOLSON, AZRA MEDJEDOVIC, JANIS M. POTTER, CYNTHIA D. JOHNSON,** and **MICHELLE MUNSON.** *Photographed by Noel Sutherland, October 1995.*

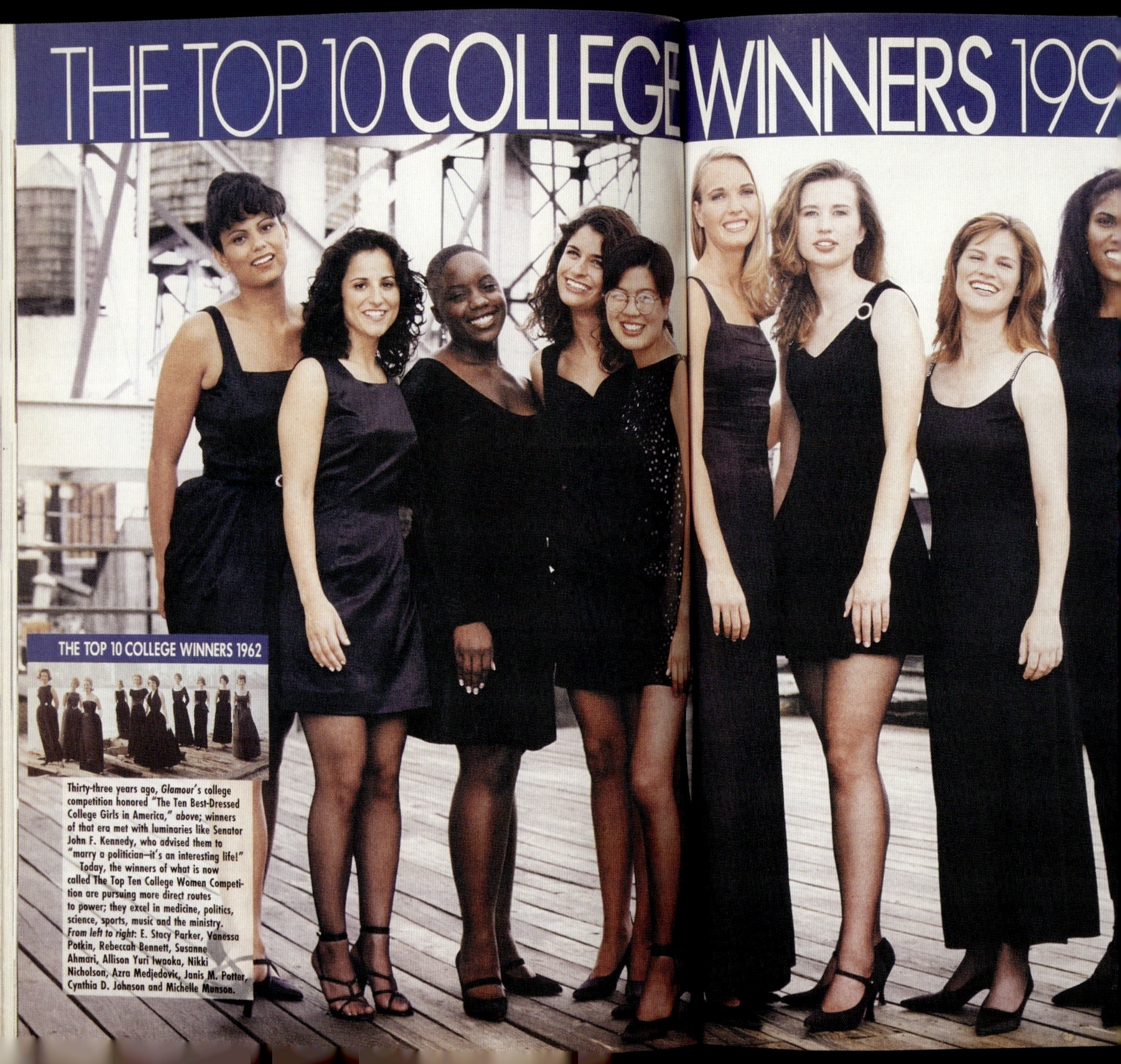

THE TOP 10 COLLEGE WINNERS 1962

Thirty-three years ago, *Glamour's* college competition honored "The Ten Best-Dressed College Girls in America," above; winners of that era met with luminaries like Senator John F. Kennedy, who advised them to "marry a politician—it's an interesting life!"

Today, the winners of what is now called The Top Ten College Women Competition are pursuing more direct routes to power; they excel in medicine, politics, science, sports, music and the ministry. *From left to right:* E. Stacy Parker, Vanessa Potkin, Rebeccah Bennett, Susanne Ahmari, Allison Yuri Iwaoka, Nikki Nicholson, Azra Medjedovic, Janis M. Potter, Cynthia D. Johnson and Michelle Munson.

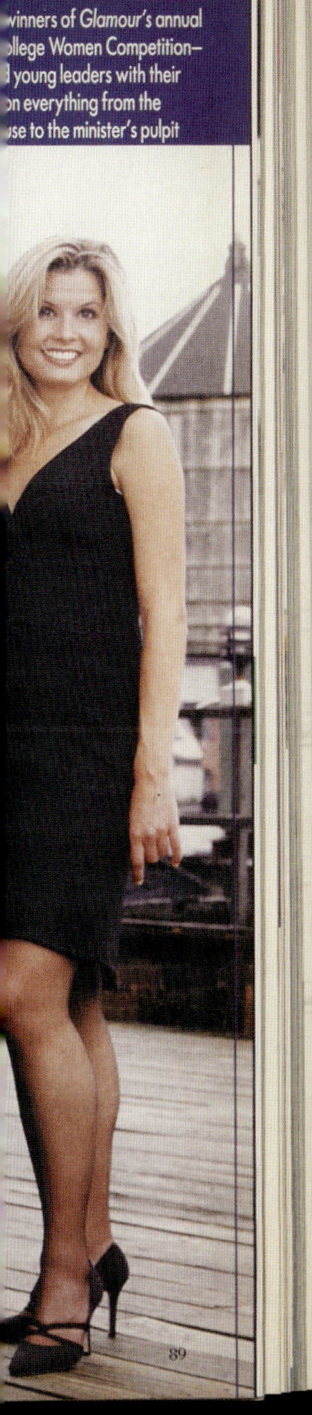

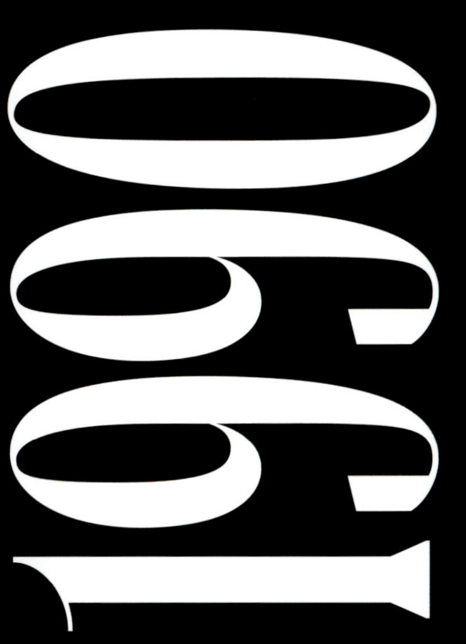

1990

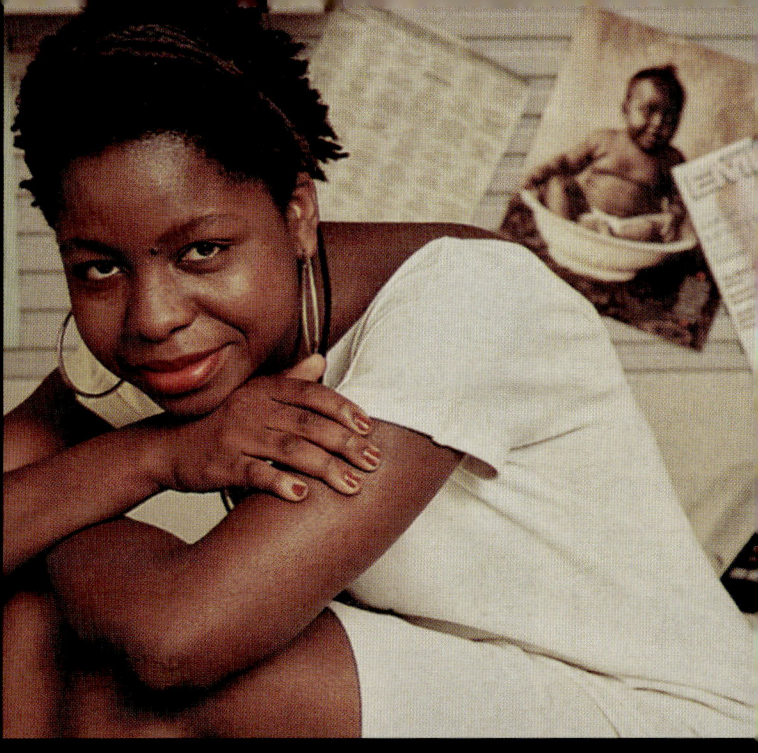

VERONICA CHAMBERS, a literature major at Simon's Rock College in Massachusetts, was praised by *Glamour* for maximizing her internship experiences at *Sassy, Seventeen, Essence, Life,* and MTV, and for speaking up on racism and cultural awareness both on and off campus, aiming to foster understanding and appreciation for diverse cultures. Today, she is a celebrated children's author and has co-written a *New York Times* bestseller with television anchor Robin Roberts.

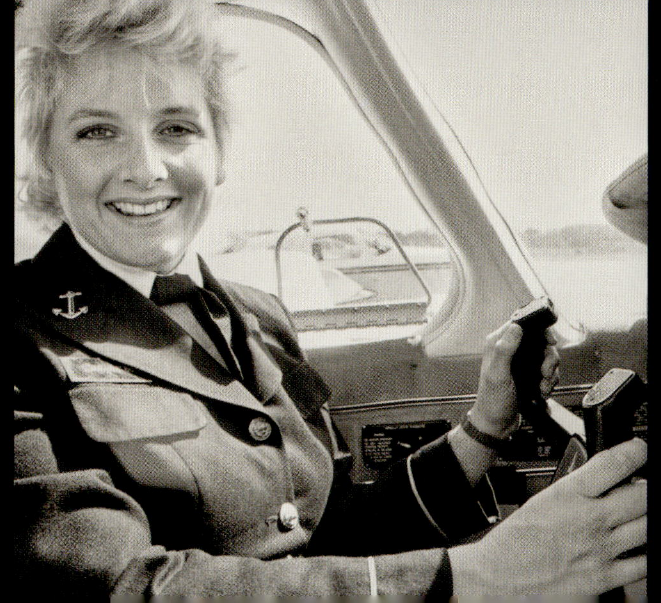

1988

MISSY CUMMINGS attended the United States Naval Academy in Maryland. Her passion for flying led her to become one of the top-ranking women accepted into the highly competitive naval air program. While at the academy, Cummings served as the editor in chief of its magazine, *The Log.* Afterwards, she became a naval officer and military pilot, and eventually one of the Navy's first female fighter pilots. She continued

ICONIC COLLEGE COVERS

August 1960
NORMA COLLIER of Wilson College (left) and **ELIZABETH NEWSOM** of Pembroke College.

August 1963
Clockwise from left, **DORRIE PENNISTON KAVANAGH** of Hollins University, **GINNY MARTIN** of Baylor, **SUSAN MCARTHUR** of San Diego State, **NANCY TOLLEY** of Randolph-Macon College, and **SANDY PRICE** (center) of Ohio State.

August 1968
KATITI KIRONDE, a freshman at the Memorial University of Newfoundland.

August 1970
ANN FONCANNON of Kansas State University.

August 1976
CATHERINE LAFLECHE of the University of Kentucky.

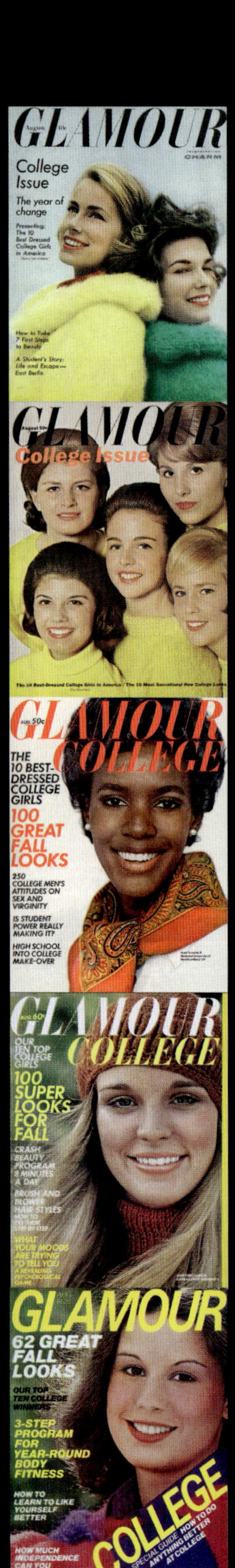

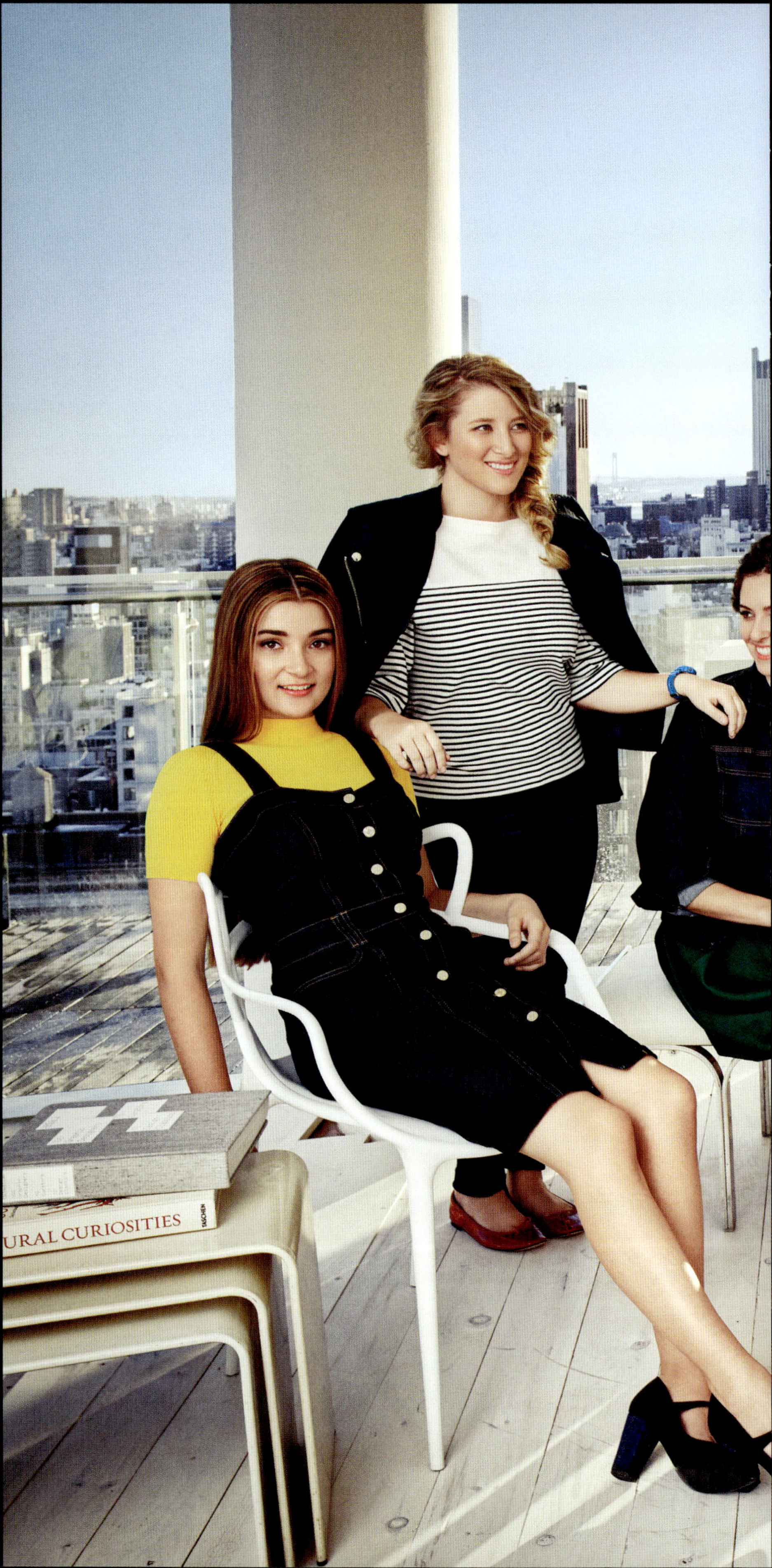

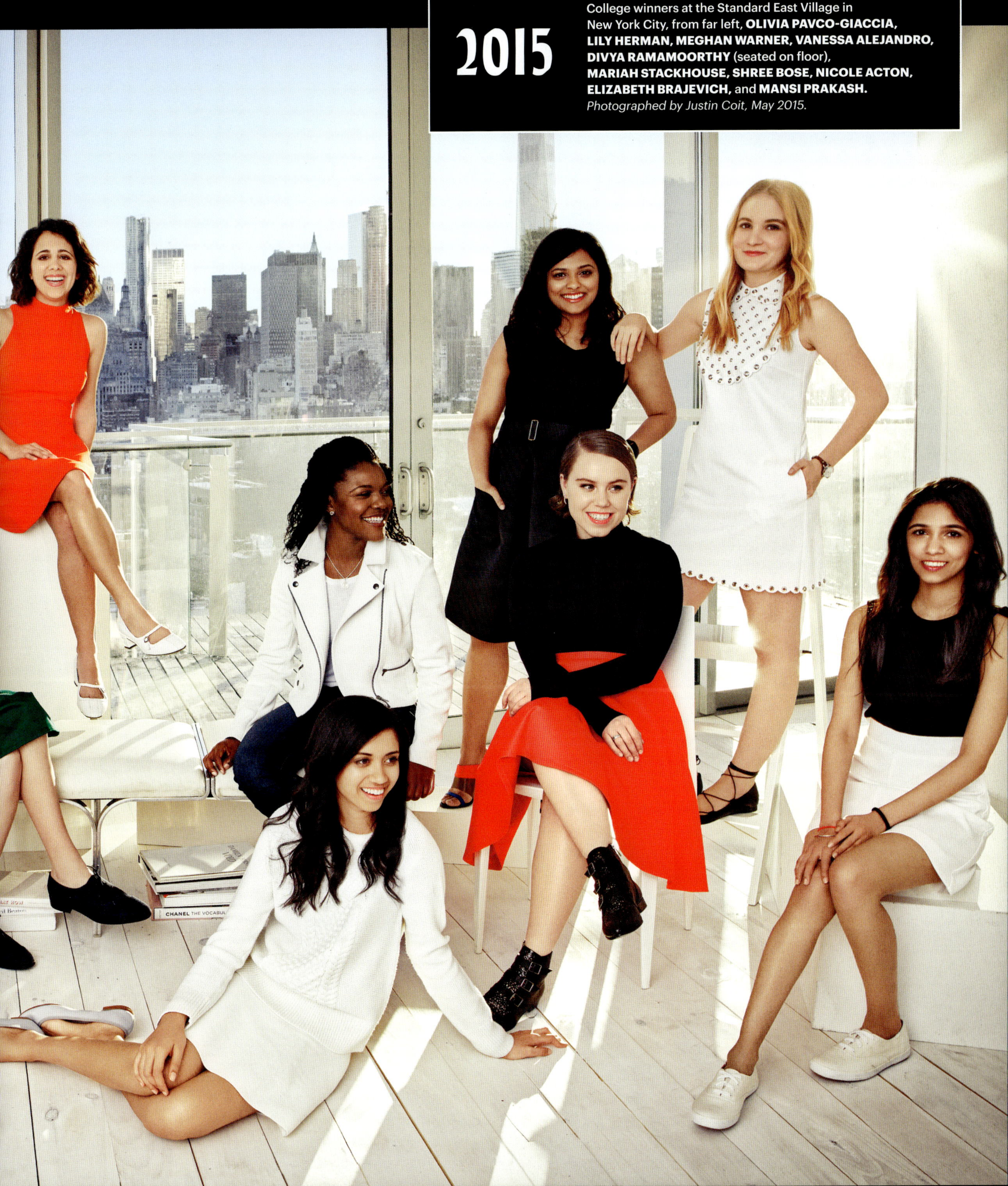

2015
College winners at the Standard East Village in New York City, from far left, OLIVIA PAVCO-GIACCIA, LILY HERMAN, MEGHAN WARNER, VANESSA ALEJANDRO, DIVYA RAMAMOORTHY (seated on floor), MARIAH STACKHOUSE, SHREE BOSE, NICOLE ACTON, ELIZABETH BRAJEVICH, and MANSI PRAKASH.
Photographed by Justin Coit, May 2015.

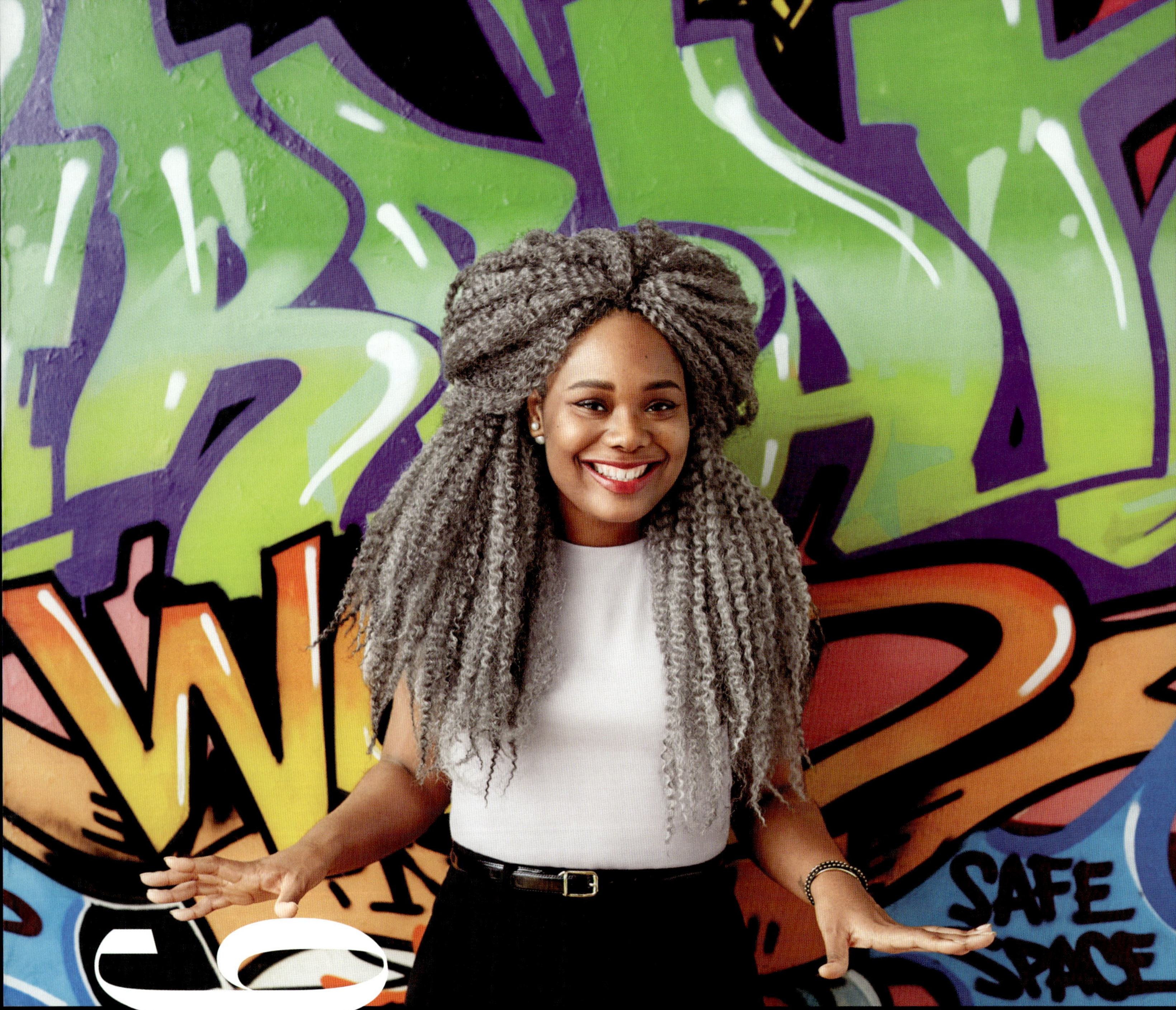

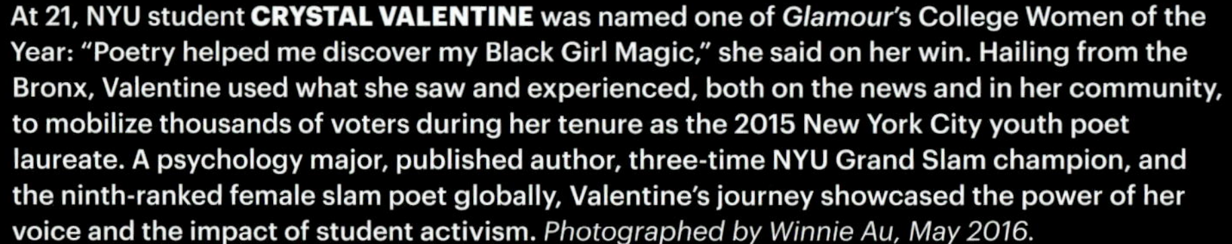

2016

At 21, NYU student **CRYSTAL VALENTINE** was named one of *Glamour*'s College Women of the Year: "Poetry helped me discover my Black Girl Magic," she said on her win. Hailing from the Bronx, Valentine used what she saw and experienced, both on the news and in her community, to mobilize thousands of voters during her tenure as the 2015 New York City youth poet laureate. A psychology major, published author, three-time NYU Grand Slam champion, and the ninth-ranked female slam poet globally, Valentine's journey showcased the power of her voice and the impact of student activism. *Photographed by Winnie Au, May 2016.*

2018

In 2018, another extraordinary poet laureate was named as one of *Glamour*'s College Women of the Year: **AMANDA GORMAN.** The then Harvard sociology major had recently been named the first ever youth poet laureate, and her poem "In This Place (An American Lyric)" was acquired by the Morgan Library and Museum in New York City. In January 2021, she wrote and recited "The Hill We Climb" at President Joe Biden's inauguration, and later that year became the first ever College Woman of the Year also honored as one of *Glamour*'s Women of the Year. *Photographed by Shaniqwa Jarvis, November 2021.*

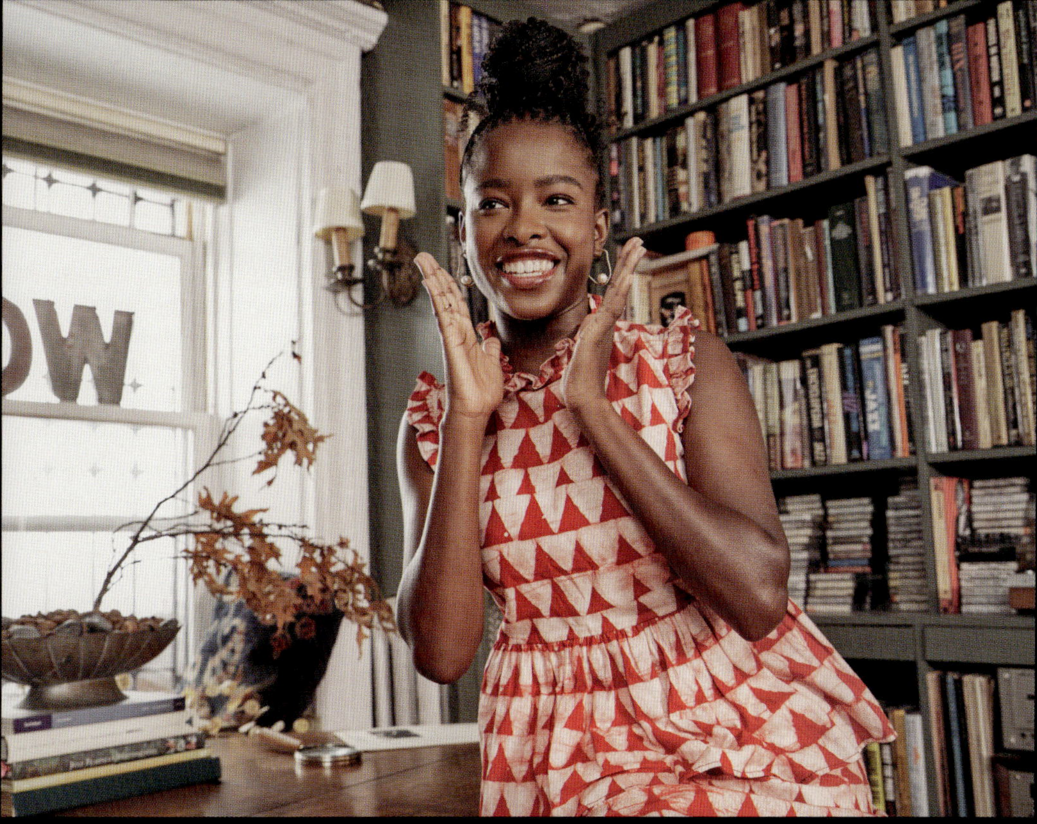

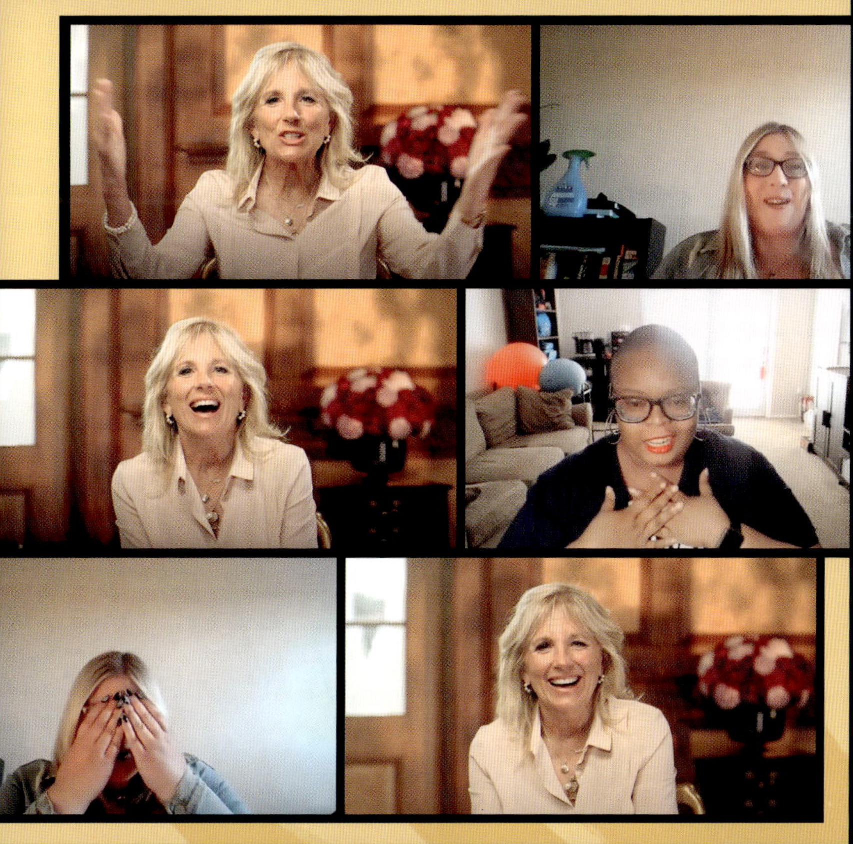

2021

Glamour organized a unique surprise for our College Women of the Year in 2021. For the first time, the competition focused on the achievements of community college students. First lady Jill Biden, EdD, a lifelong educator and community college instructor, surprised two finalists on a special Zoom call: **TAY MOSELY,** 46, from Sinclair Community College in Ohio, and **KATHERINE HALEY,** 29, from Bristol Community College in Massachusetts. Mosely and Haley joined five other honorees, ranging from 17 to nearly 80 years old, highlighting the diverse and impactful role of community colleges.

THE LIBERA

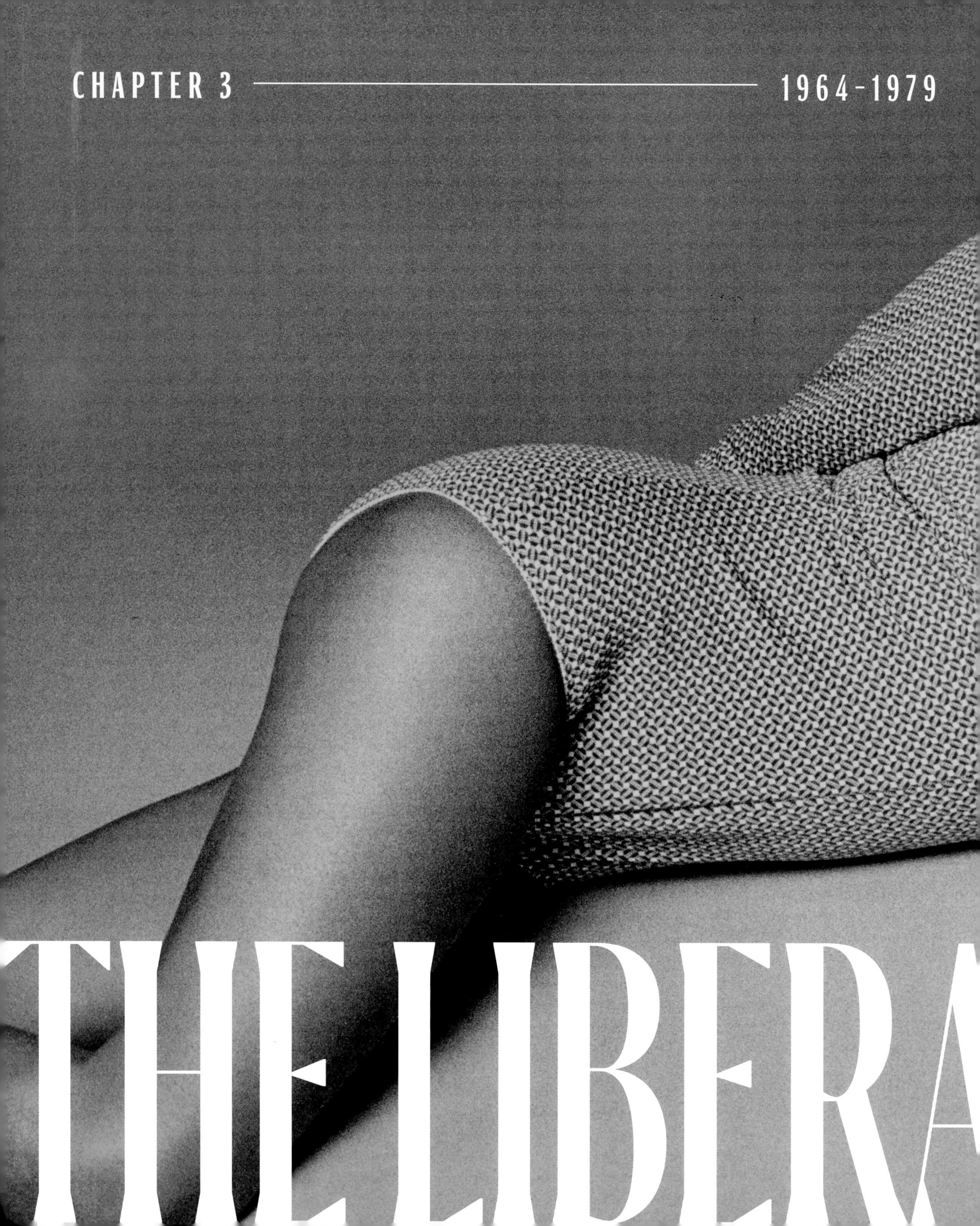

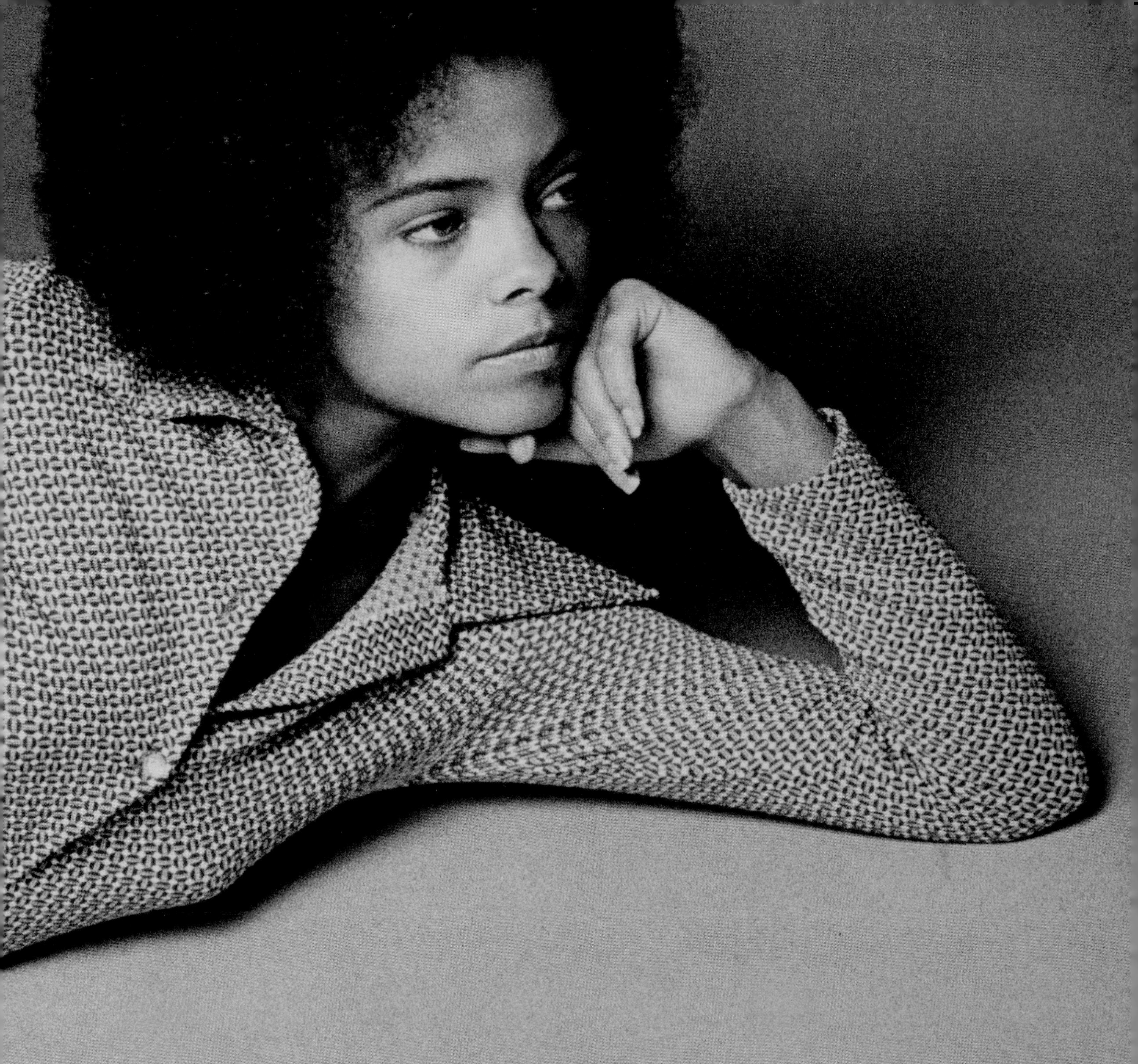
TED WOMAN

Revolution was afoot.

THE 1950S was a decade when women were constrained by men's expectations. But the mid-'60s brought a loosening of women's ties to their expected wifely duties, and the exploration of so much more than what men had deemed appropriate for them. And the 1970s? A throwing off of the last shackles of marital, sexual, and professional oppression. The woman of this era wanted to be free, and *Glamour* came to meet her in the moment. The "perfect" housewife had been left far behind. In her place stood a liberated woman—one who went to college, one who had thrown off her bra, one who wanted to explore sexuality and sex unapologetically, one who wanted the right to an abortion in every state in America, who argued for the legalization of marijuana, and who was ready to protest, to tackle questions of race, of queerness, of political ambition. It was in this era that *Glamour* hired a young contributing editor by the name of Gloria Steinem, whose voice became a mainstay in its pages. But to say it was just societal changes that inspired the new *Glamour* would be to dismiss the importance and influence of the magazine's new editor in chief, Ruth Whitney, appointed in 1967. A fearless advocate for women, she made it her mission to reimagine the magazine—publishing articles on interracial relationships, abortion, divorce, and more. In 1968, she also featured a young student by the name of Katiti Kironde, who became the first ever Black woman on the cover of an American fashion magazine—an issue that became one of the best-selling of the time. It's no overstatement to say that this era marked a turning point in *Glamour*'s history: The white-gloved domesticity of the 1950s was banished, and fighting for women's empowerment was firmly at the core.

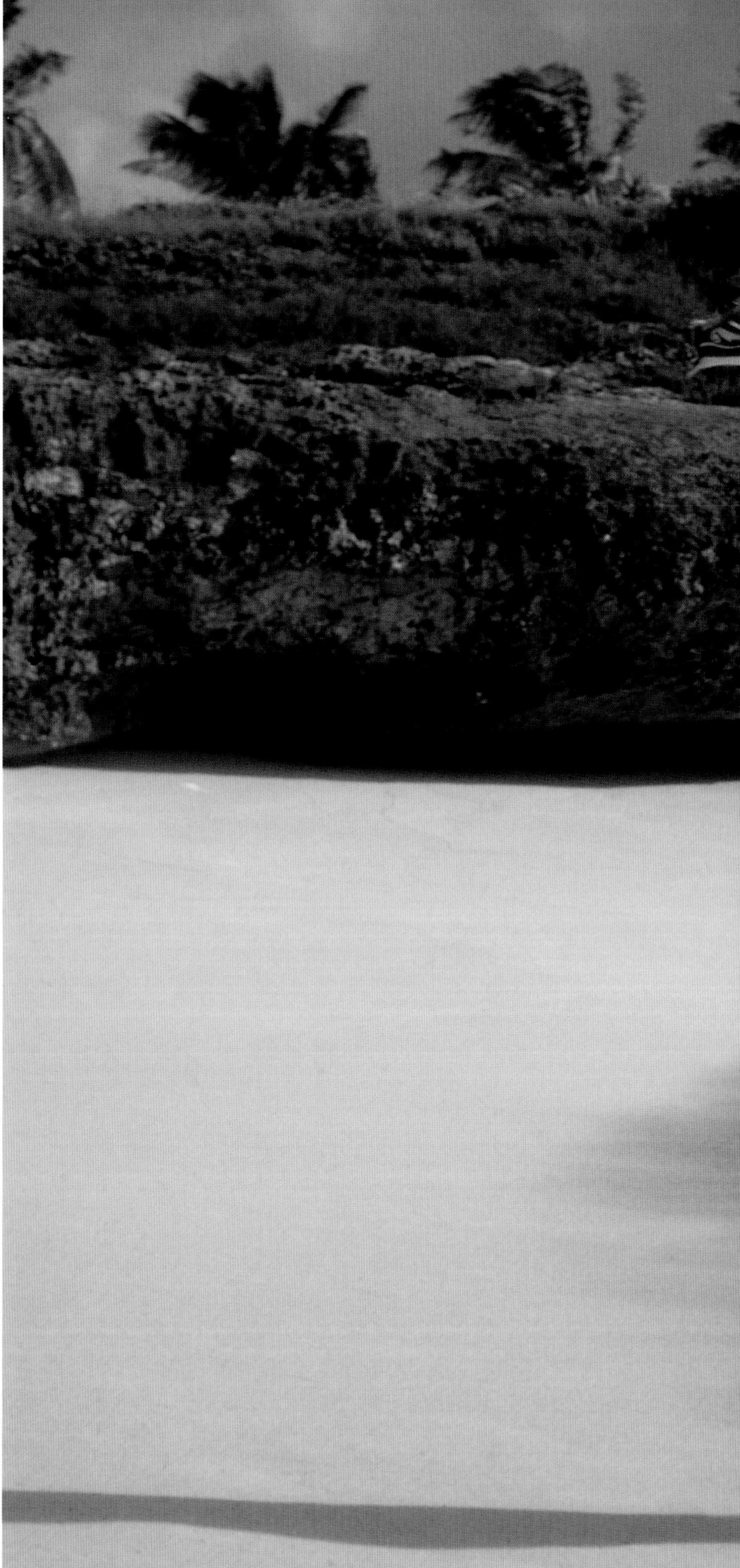

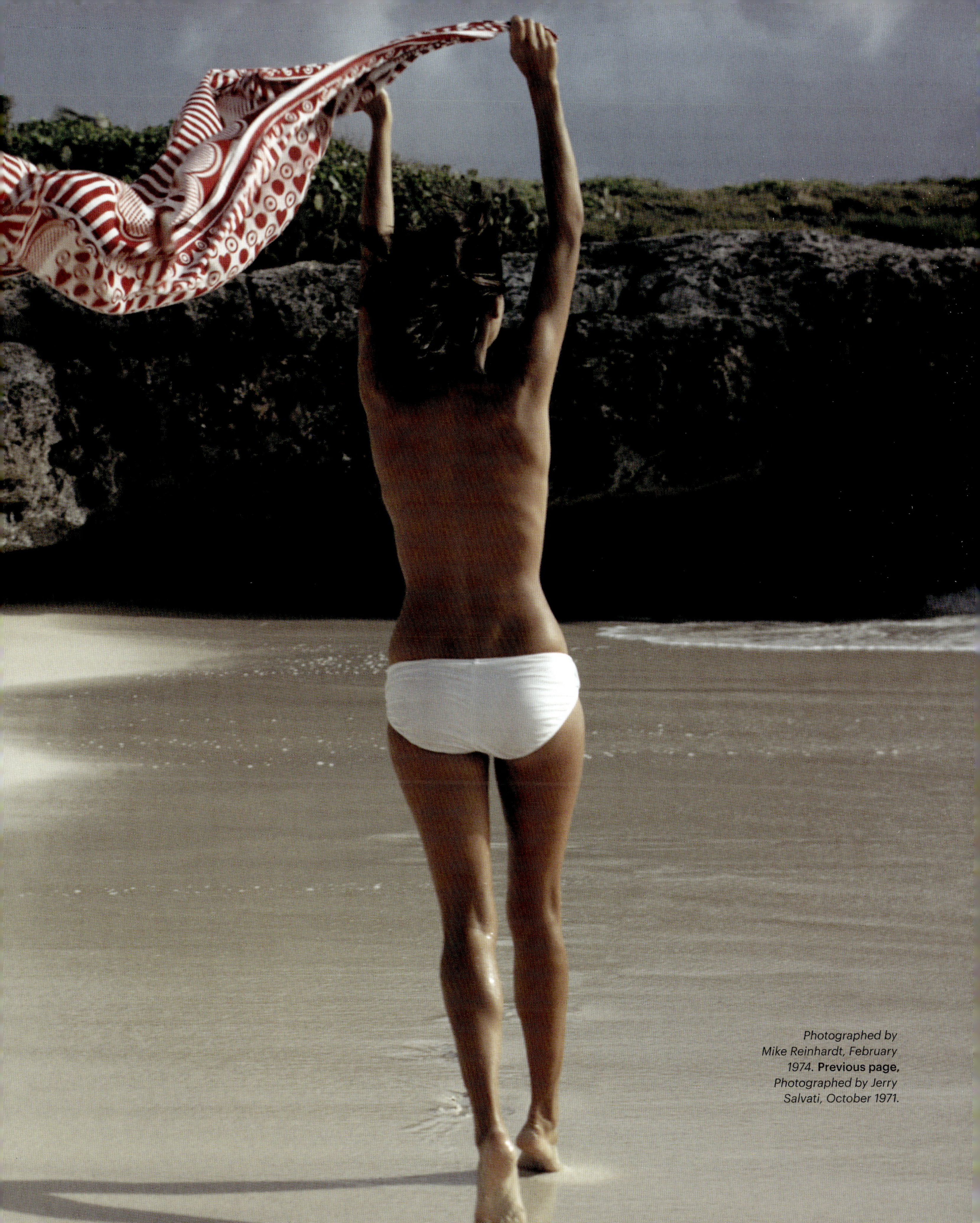

Photographed by
Mike Reinhardt, February
1974. **Previous page,**
Photographed by Jerry
Salvati, October 1971.

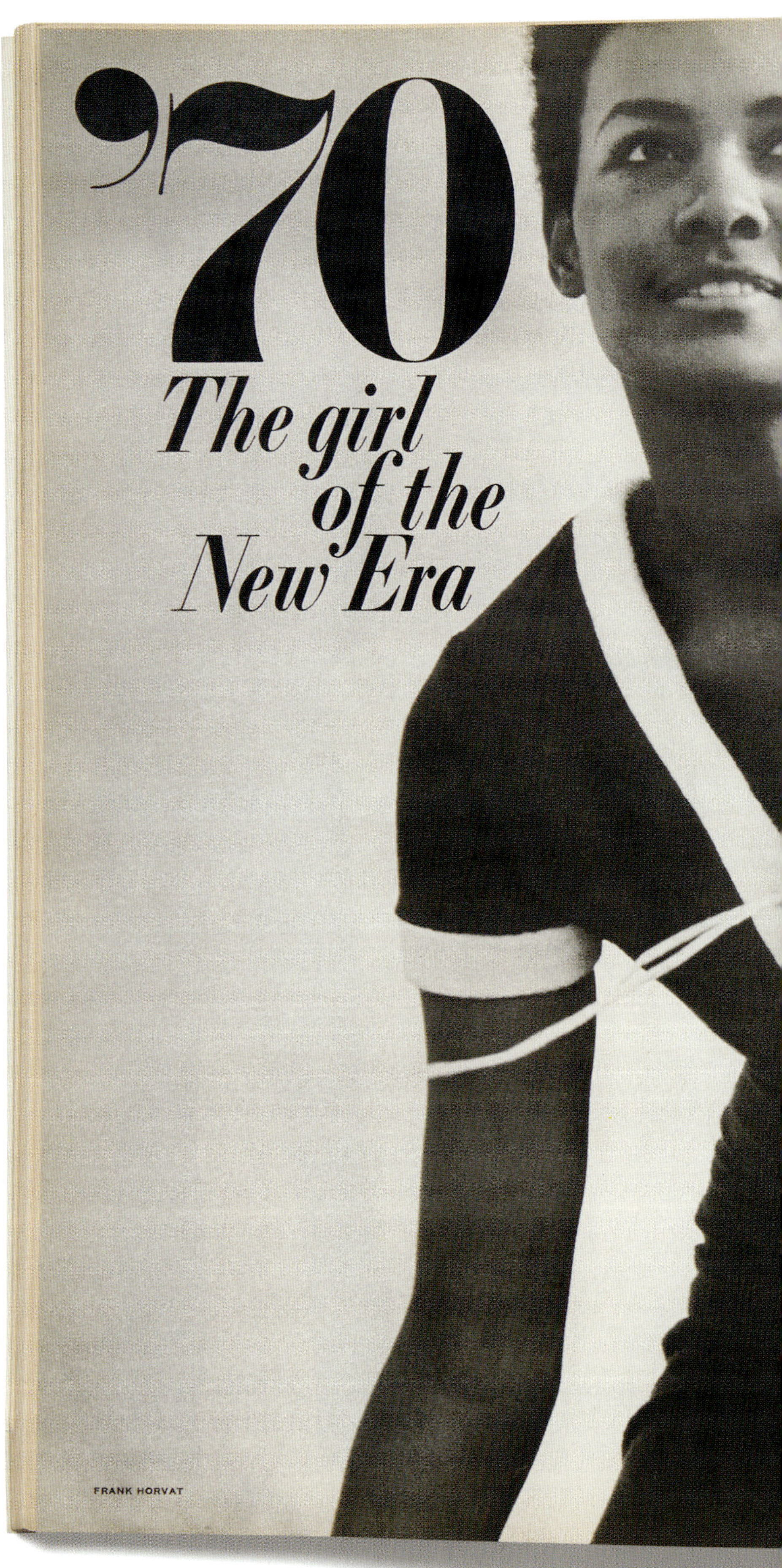

1970

Glamour's January 1970 issue was one of
new beginnings, in every sense. The staff
chronicled the new music to listen to, the
new books to read, the new hairstyles, the
new makeup. But it was the new-look fashion
that really embodied the extraordinary
cultural shift affecting women's lives—"her
clothes tell the story of her new liberation."
She was "unaffected, unafraid," and, most
importantly, "unsensationalized." This was
"The girl of the New Era"—revolutionized
in fashion, yes, but also in life: free and
unconstrained by so many
strictures of the past.

Her clothes tell the story of her new liberation. In their uncontrived lines they say: a total acceptance of her body and sex, neither flaunting it nor hiding it. A new shift of interest to the bosom — the no-bra look, unsensationalized by padding or nakedness, but not unnoticed under the soft cling of the new clothes — is part of the story. And if the fashion historian James Laver is right, that women dress for seduction and up to the position of their men, who themselves dress for power or status—the royal robes of kings, the brass of generals, the gallant clothes of the hippies and motorcycle boys, the self-styled kings of the road—it is a new kind of seduction: unaffected, unafraid and much more human.

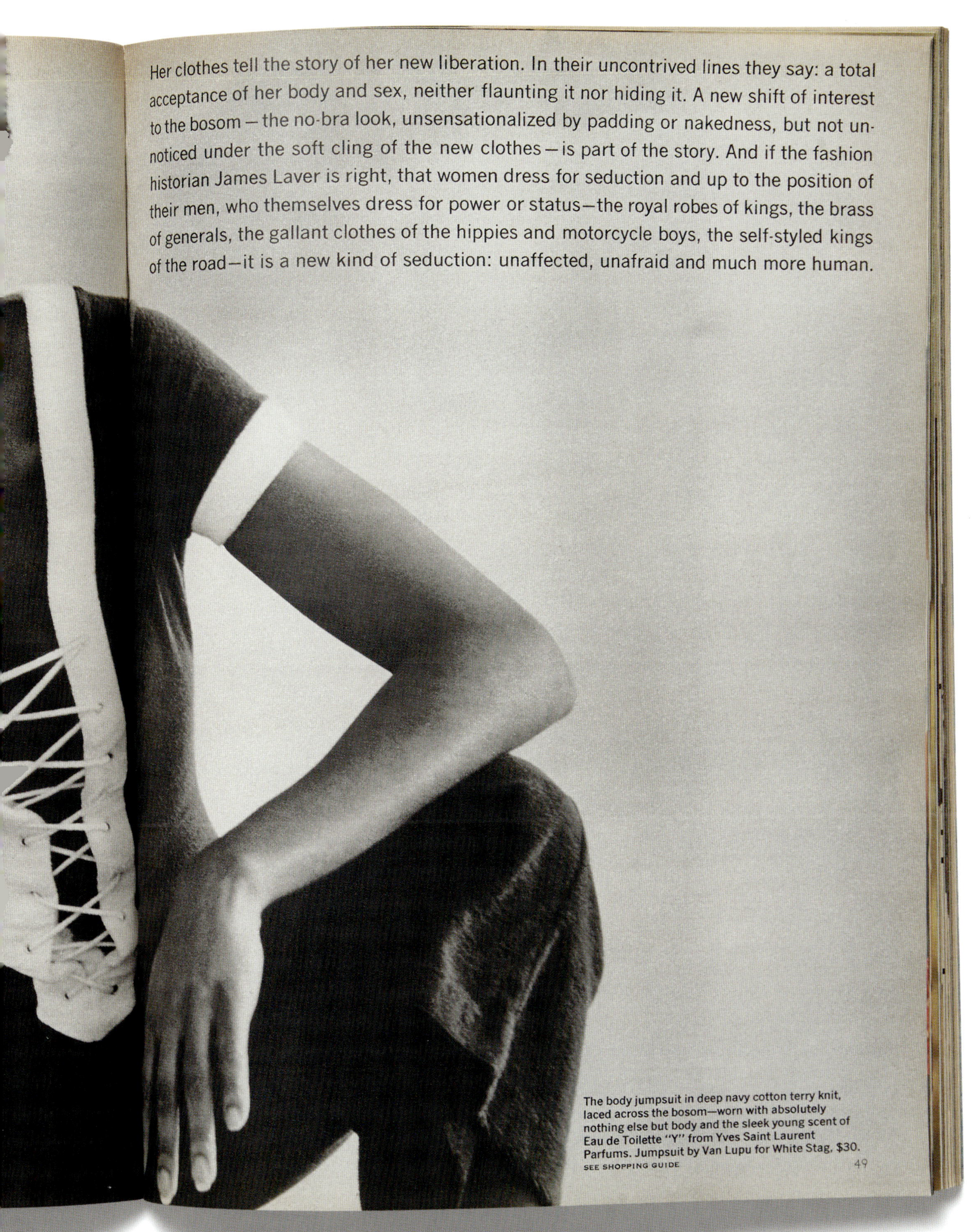

The body jumpsuit in deep navy cotton terry knit, laced across the bosom—worn with absolutely nothing else but body and the sleek young scent of Eau de Toilette ''Y'' from Yves Saint Laurent Parfums. Jumpsuit by Van Lupu for White Stag, $30.
SEE SHOPPING GUIDE

49

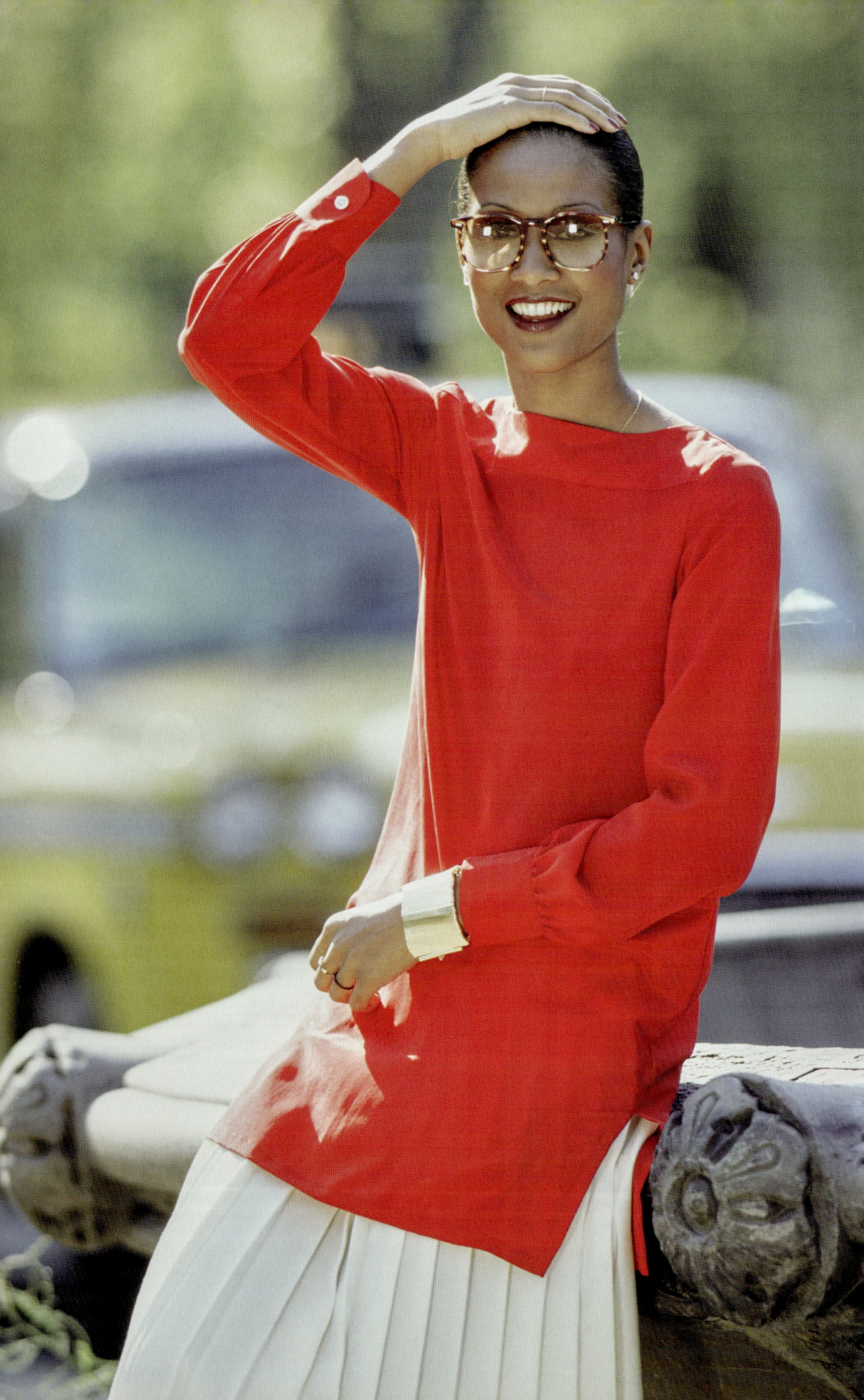

Beverly Johnson.
Photographed by Frank Horvat, January 1977.

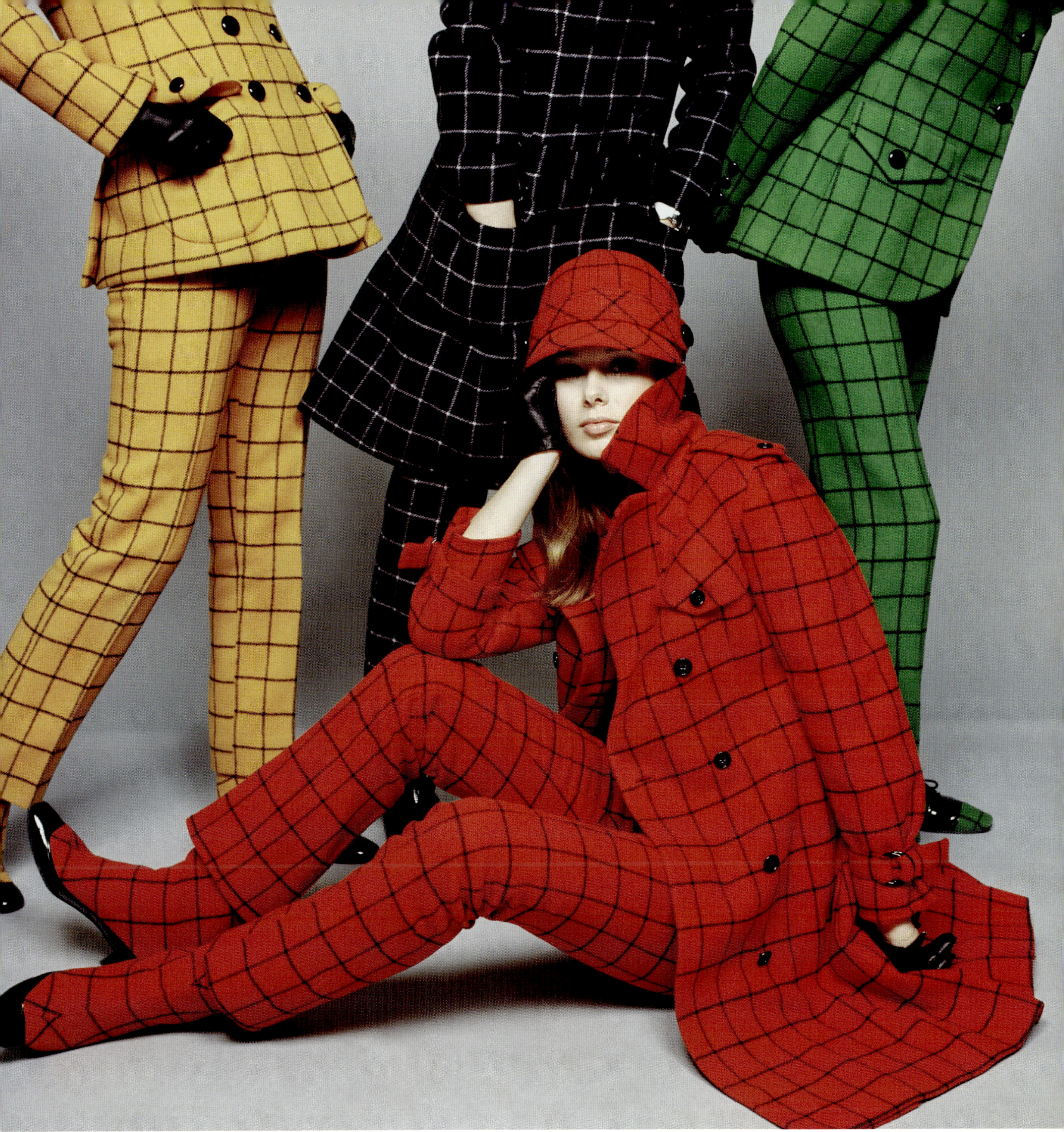

British photographer David Bailey shot these four models for the July 1966 issue, all wearing wool pantsuits by Luba for Elite, with matching schoolboy caps by Halston. Bailey shot nine *Glamour* covers through the '60s and '70s, six of which were of his muse and then girlfriend Jean Shrimpton.

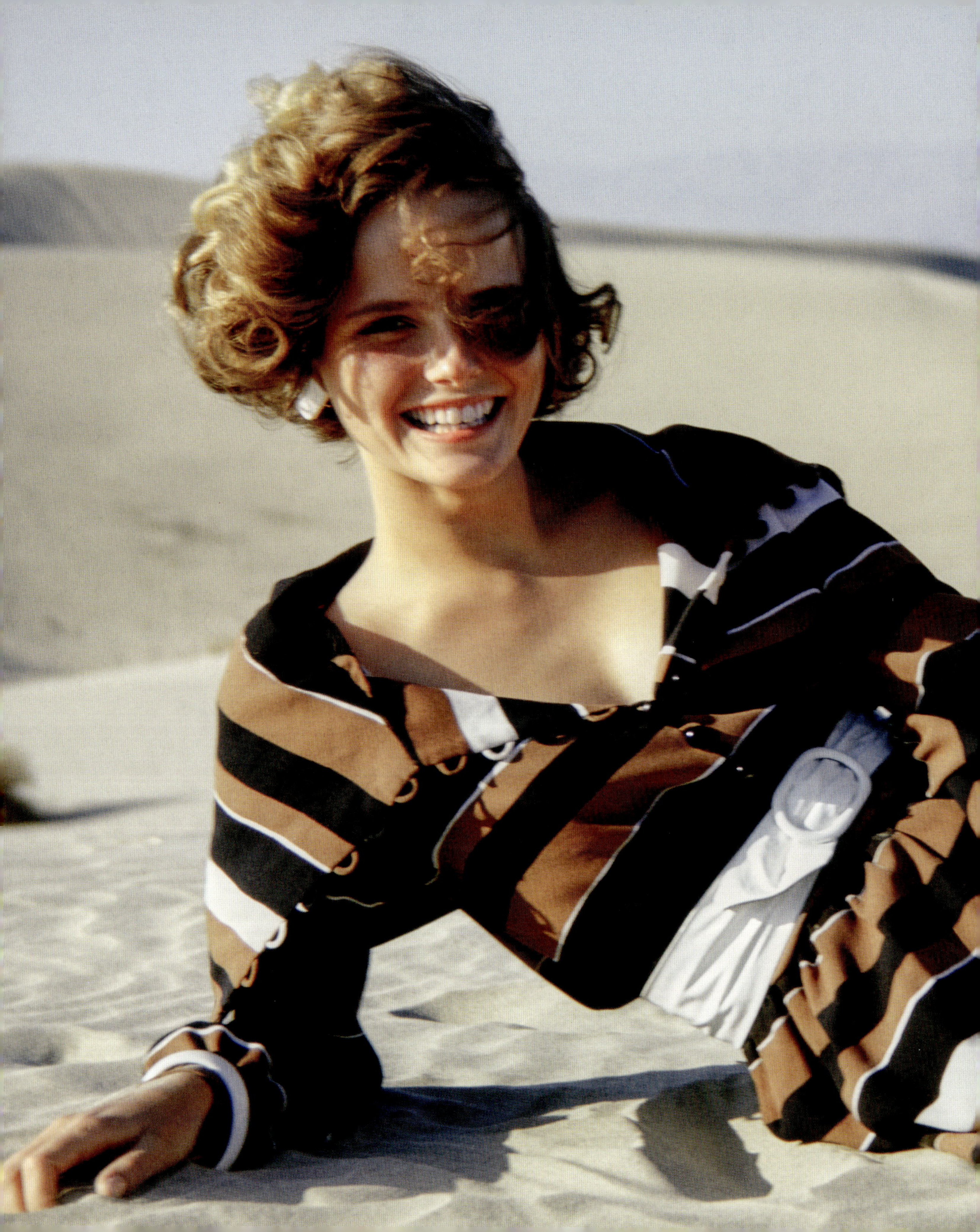

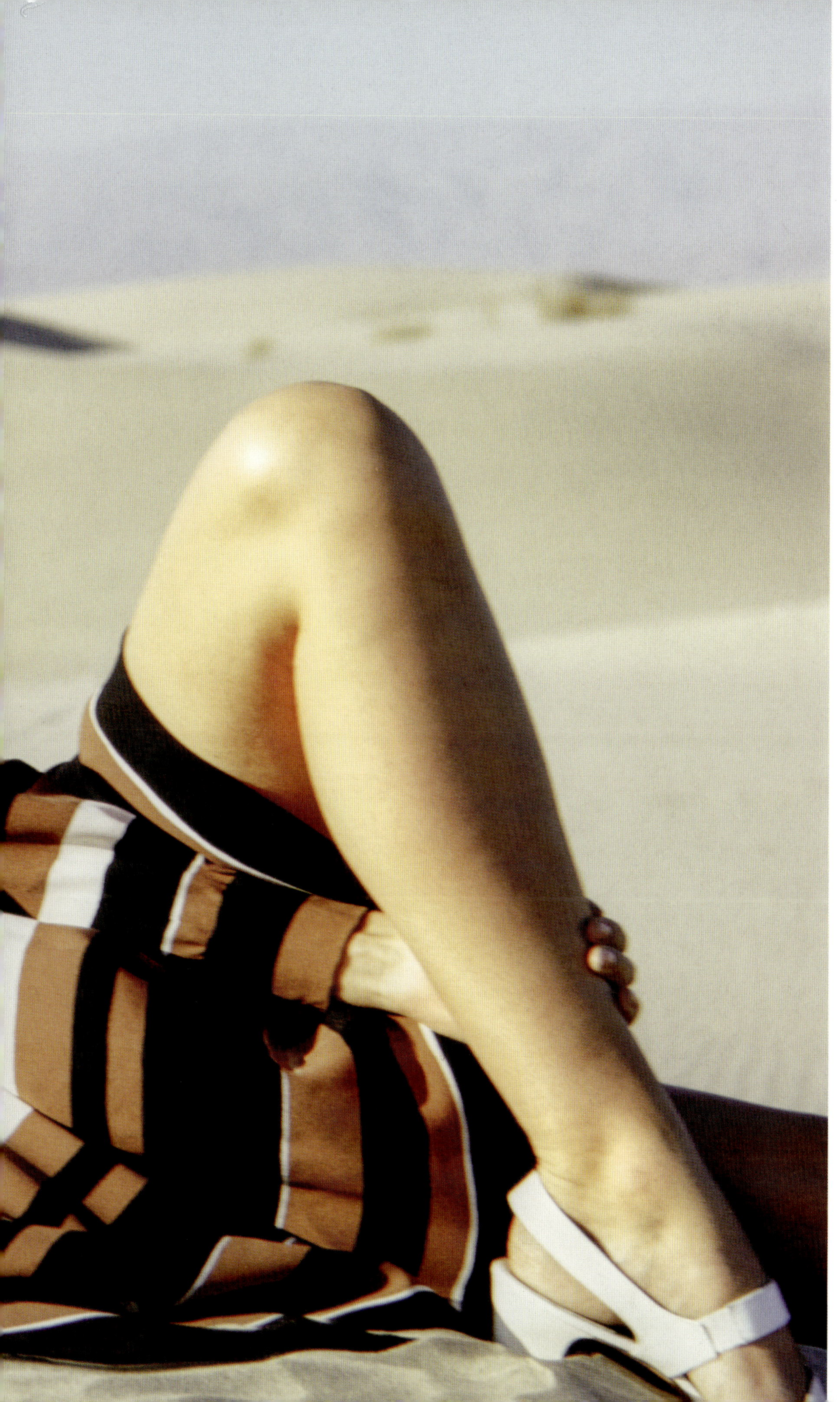

Model Cheryl Tiegs appeared on 24 *Glamour* covers. *Photographed by Sante Forlano, June 1967.*

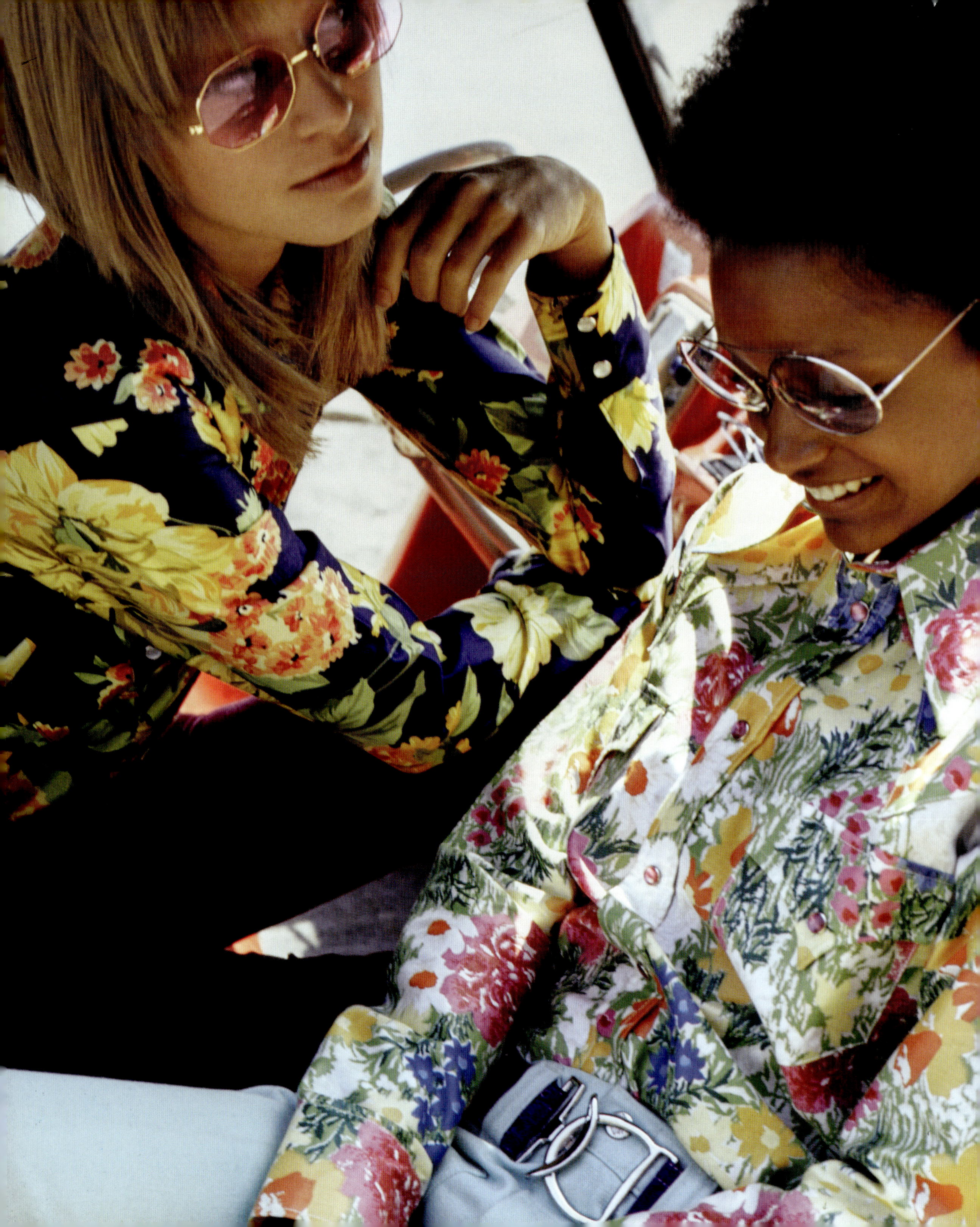

Evocative fashion of the new era. Two models wear floral print long-sleeve shirts by Andrew Jansen and John Eding for Smiling Crows Adventures. *Photographed by Marc Hispard, July 1971.*

→

Patti Hansen, the model and actor. *Photographed by Frank Horvat, January 1973.*

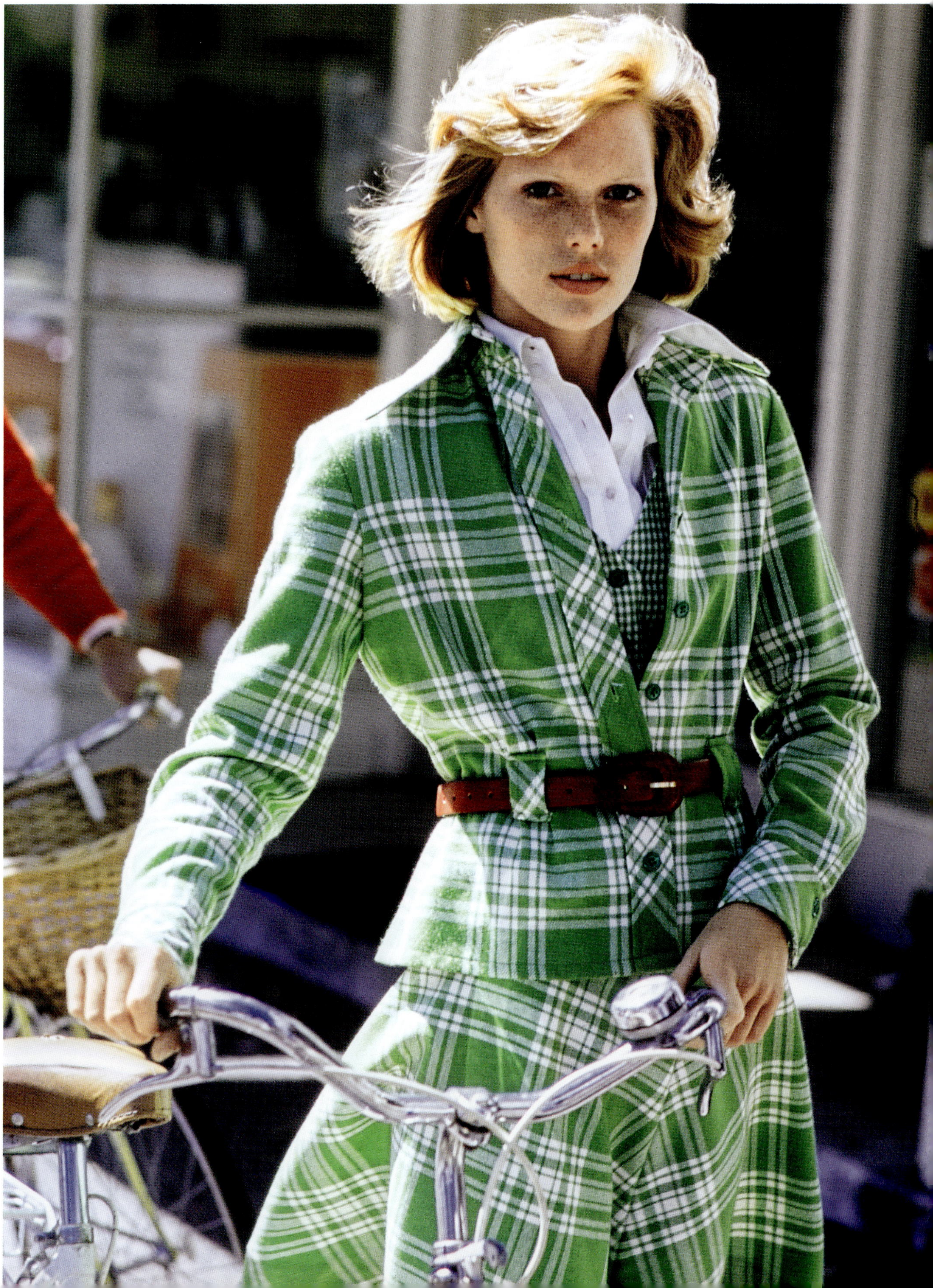

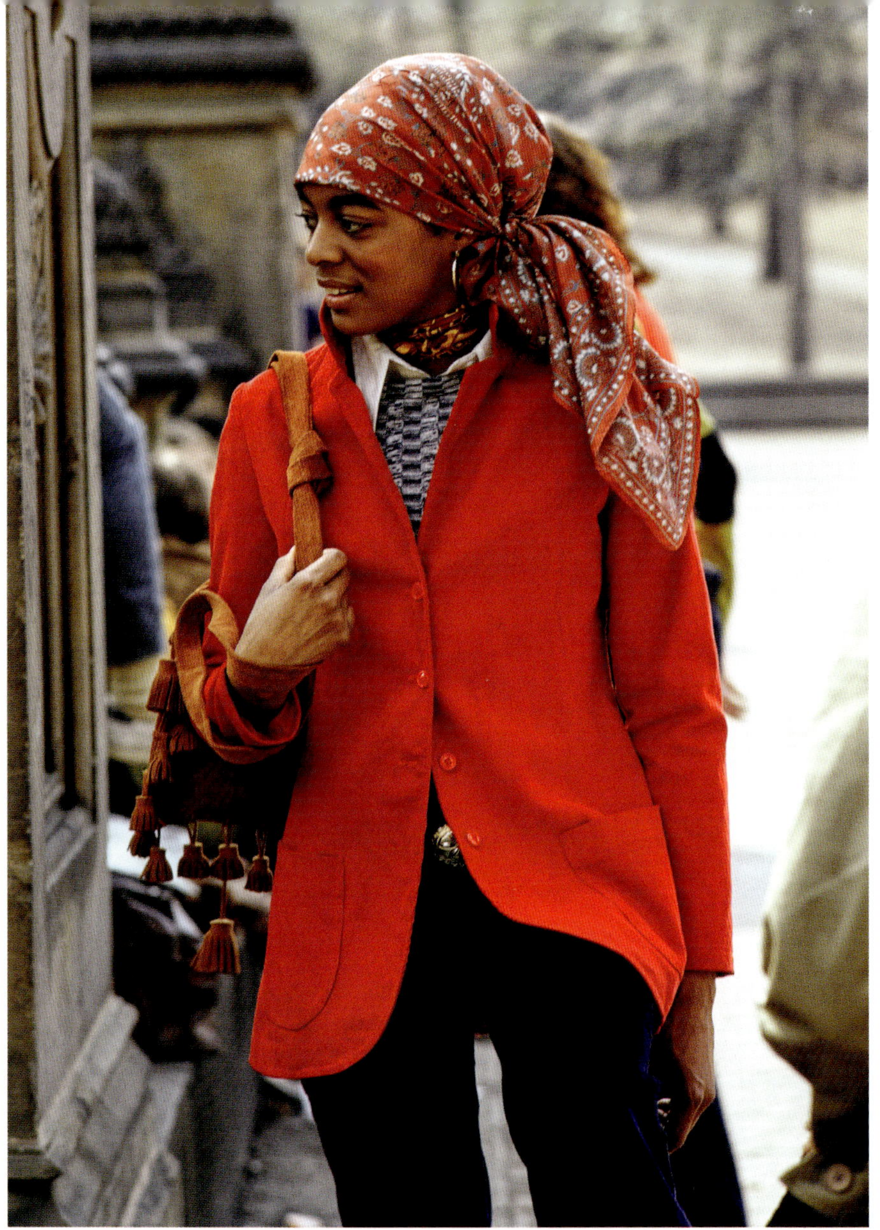

One of *Glamour*'s Top Ten College
Girls of 1970, Ava Campbell, a student
at Radford College in Virginia, wearing
both a head scarf and neck scarf.
*Photographed by William Connors,
August 1970.*

→

Actor and model Lauren Hutton, who
began modeling in the mid-1960s.
*Photographed by William Connors,
December 1970.*

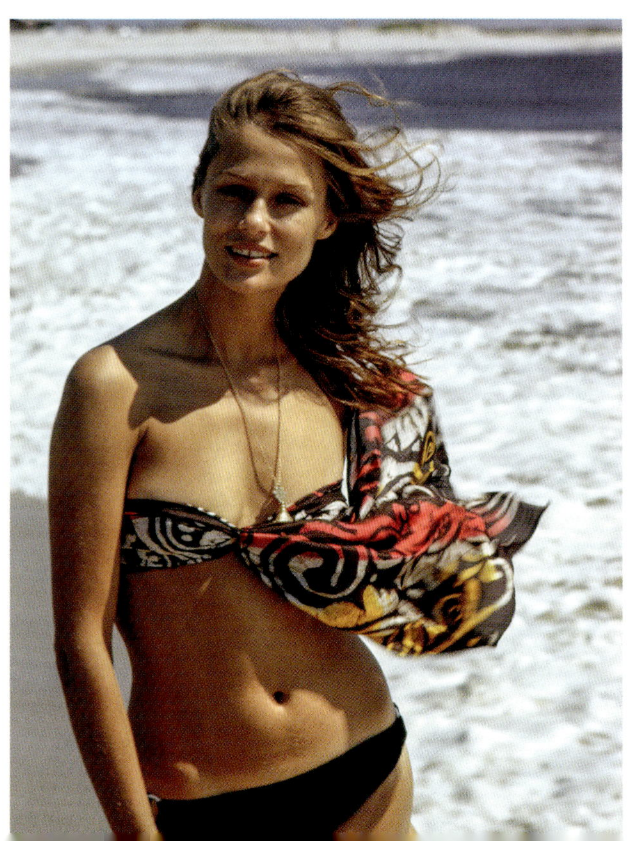

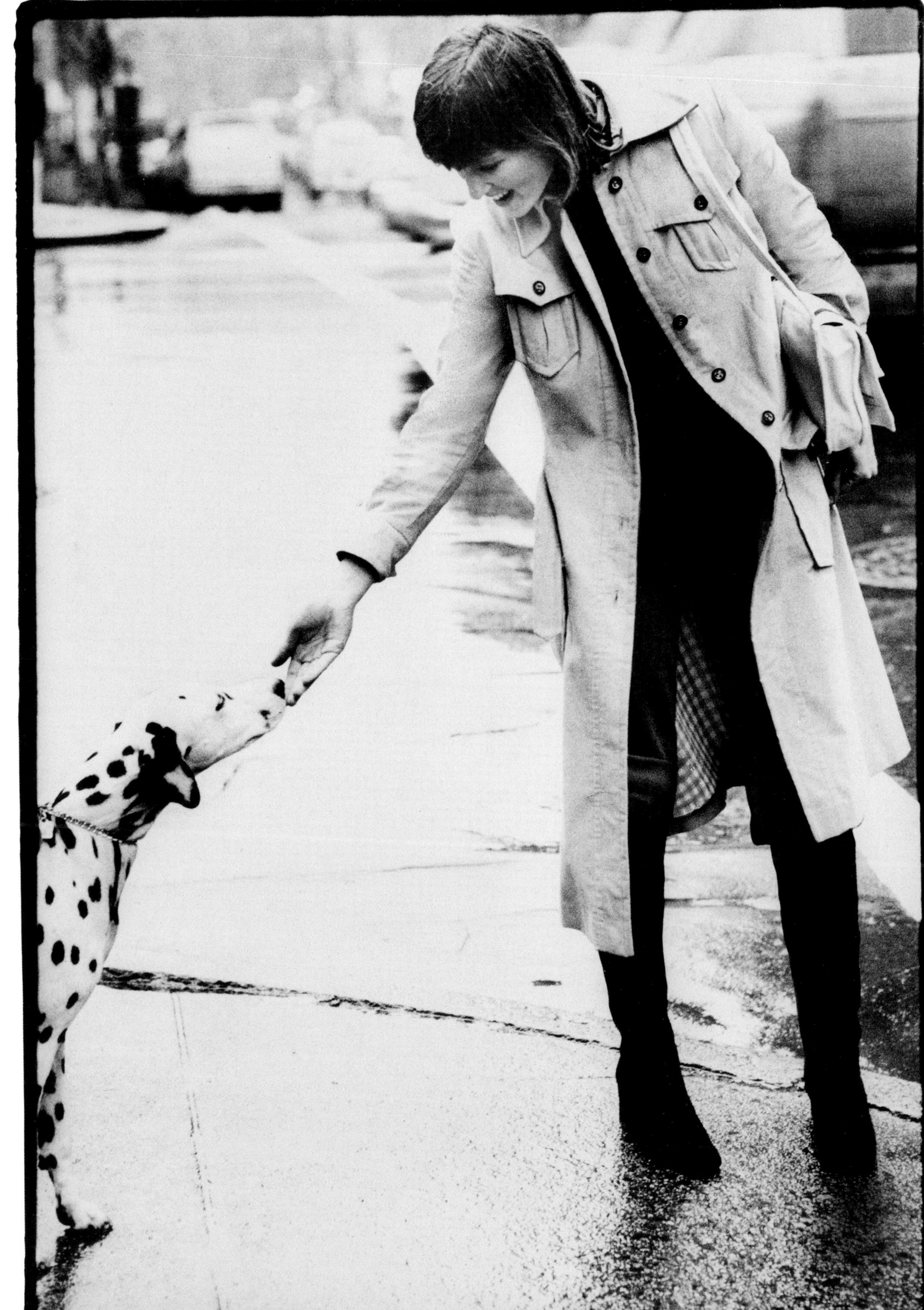

→
Bob Stone, who
regularly shot
for Condé Nast
in the 1970s,
captured this
moment
between a
model and a
dalmatian for
the March
1972 issue.

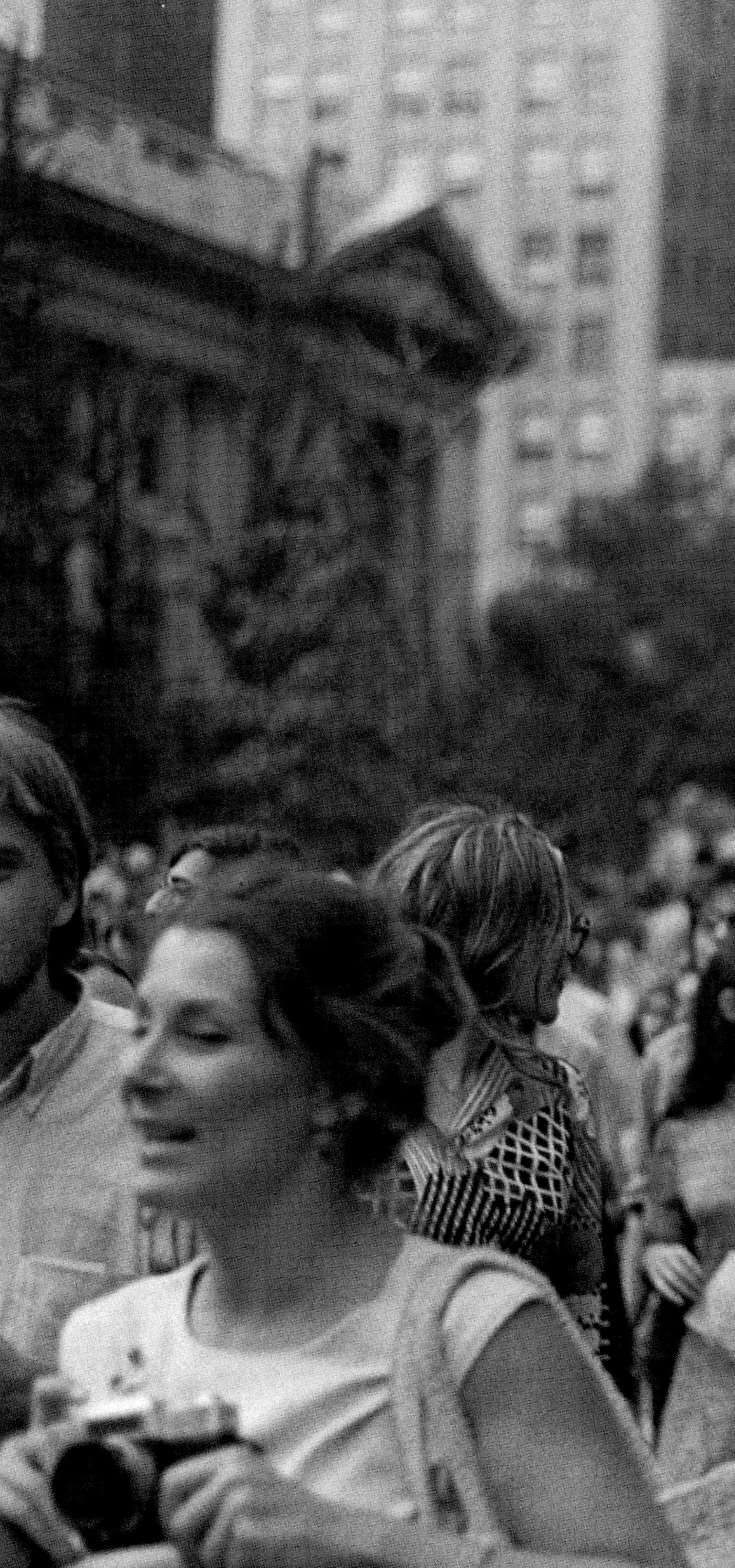

ON THE 26TH OF AUGUST, 1970,
an estimated 50,000 women took to the streets
of New York City in protest, an event referred to
as the Women's Strike for Equality. The marchers had three goals: free abortion on demand,
equal opportunities in the workplace, and free
childcare. *Glamour* reported on the march in
the November 1970 issue—noting the number of "high school feminists sitting beneath
the speaker's platform," and the many mothers who attended with their children. While
Glamour's dispatch highlighted some of the ten-
sions at the march between marchers and the
police, and even internally between different
feminist groups, there was no question that
the issues for which the women were march-
ing were of vital importance—especially the
fight for legal abortions. Passing a law was,
quite literally, a life-saving necessity—it is estimated that during the 1950s and '60s between
200,000 and 1.2 million illegal abortions were
performed each year. And even though, by
1965, the number of deaths attributed to illegal abortions had dropped to below 200, illegal
abortion still accounted for 17% of all deaths in
pregnancy and childbirth that year. The issue
was the lightning rod of a generation—and on
January 22, 1973, the Supreme Court issued a
landmark decision that the 14th Amendment
provided a "right to privacy," which protected a
pregnant woman's right to an abortion. *Glamour*
covered the topic of abortion extensively pre-
and post-*Roe*, and while this decision was over-
turned by the Supreme Court in June 2022,
plunging millions of women back decades, the
magazine continues to call for the right to an
abortion to be enshrined in law.

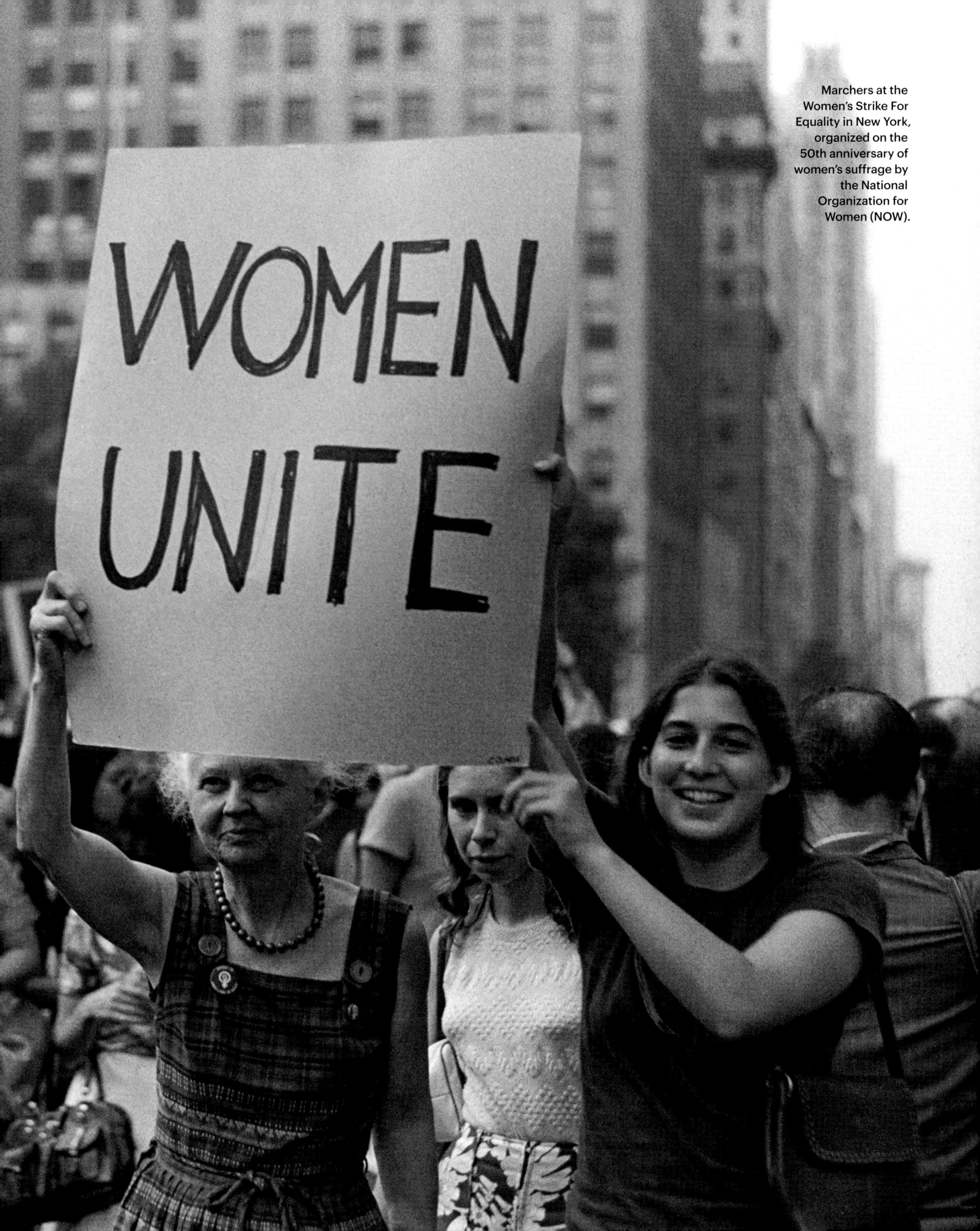

Marchers at the Women's Strike For Equality in New York, organized on the 50th anniversary of women's suffrage by the National Organization for Women (NOW).

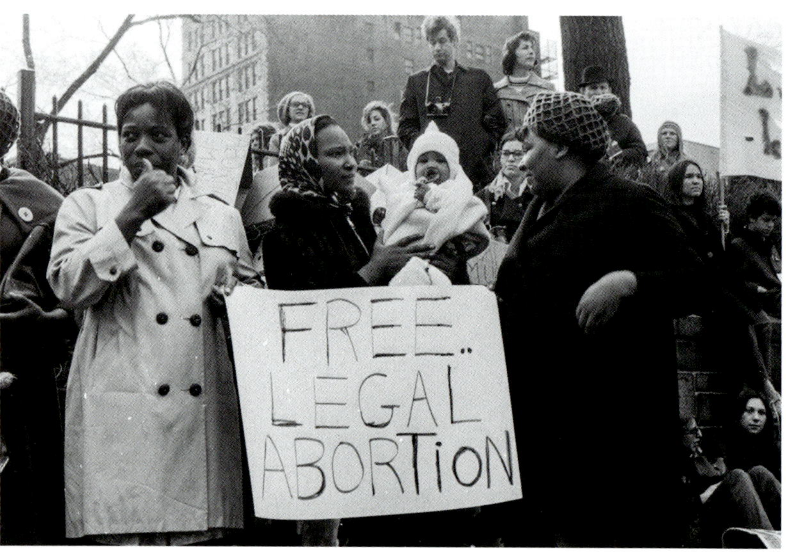

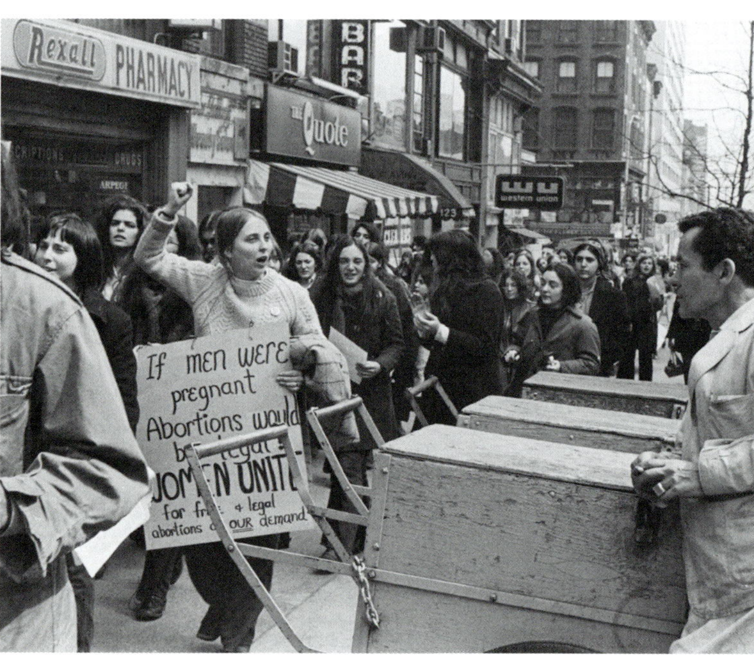

Above and near right, protesters during a mass demonstration against New York State abortion laws, Manhattan, March 28, 1970.

↓

"I work in an abortion clinic," by Susan Paskoski, August 1972.

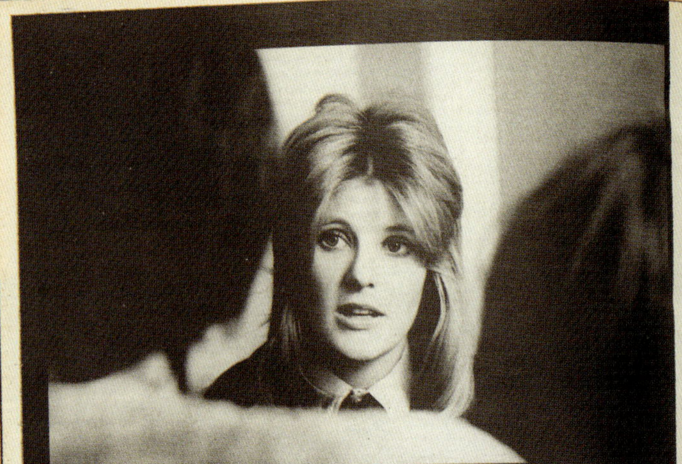

"I work in an abortion clinic"

by Susan Paskoski

February 24, 1971 Today I had a really lucky break: I landed my first social work job. Starting next week, I'll be a counselor at an abortion referral service.

It's a relief after all the months I've spent phoning people at the hospitals and all the social agencies. They always said the same thing: for the kind of work I want to do, they don't hire anybody who doesn't have an M.A. in social work, and of course I don't even have a B.A. yet and won't until June. But I need to work now, both for the money and because I'm tired of school and hungry for the experience.

I got this job in the most unexpected way. I found out that two girls I met last summer when I was doing modeling were working at a referral service. I called one of them and, though she didn't give me much encouragement, I decided I'd take my chances anway, so I just walked in today and asked to talk to the supervisor. I guess he liked me because the next thing I knew he was telling me I could start next week.

It's bound to be a rough schedule with classes a few days a week and work in between; and then there's my *other* job as a live-in babysitter. But I can hardly wait.

March 1 I started work at the referral service today and it was pretty chaotic. It's in an office building like any other: one big room with a sofa for patients to sit on, three desks and a glassed-in office at the back for the supervisor. Everything re-volves around the telephones—they *never* stop ringing. They start at eight in the morning and keep going until eleven at night. I didn't know there were so many women in the country who needed an abortion.

Basically, I will be talking to women on the phone. Today they had me listen to conversations while one of the other counselors did the talking. Then I learned about the filing system and the charts that I have to fill out during phone calls. The questions on the charts are fairly straightforward: name, address, medical information, last menstrual period, etc. But it's difficult sometimes to get the woman started on the questions *she* wants to ask *you*. Often, the counselor will pick up the phone and the person on the other end will mumble, "Uh, well, um, I'd like some, uh. . ." Women just don't know how to ask about abortion.

It's not at all like calling up to find out what to do about a broken leg. So you have to draw the woman out—before you can answer her questions you have to guess what they are. Most of the patients are concerned primarily about the pain involved: they're anxious about the procedure, what it's like, and whether it will hurt. Some of them actually seem reluctant to believe it's so simple. The counselor tells them that the suctioning or removal of the embryonic tissue from the uterus takes just five minutes and that the whole business is over in three or four hours, and it's as though they can't believe their ears. Some of them also want

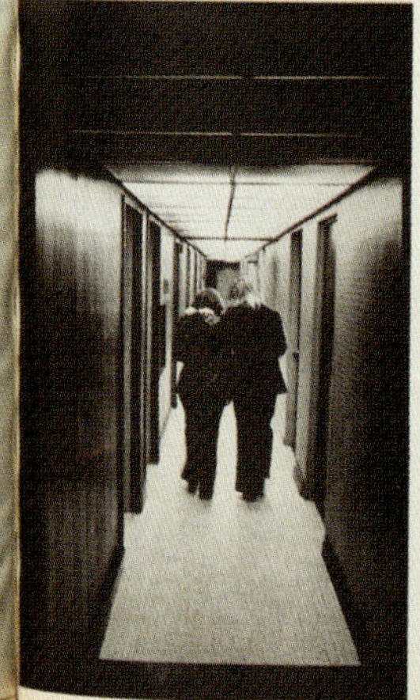

to be reassured that it's legal—I suppose, because it wasn't until 1970. That's why a referral service needs phone counselors who sound very confident and positive—and who sound young, too, like someone with whom the caller can identify. Or so I was told.

After each phone call we make an appointment for the patient at a clinic or hospital. When the day comes she either goes directly there or comes to our office. She stays with us just fifteen or twenty minutes, pays the $75 fee for the referral and then is taken to the clinic in a station wagon or limousine.

The patients I saw at the office today seemed really terribly distressed. One woman broke down and cried, and then apologized for crying; then the others who were there all looked as if they'd like to break down too. I felt like saying, "Please don't stop; go ahead and cry if it will help."

March 2 My second day on the job. Again I listened in on phone calls and learned as much as I could.

I've been thinking about it and I don't really like the fact that the women have to pay a fee for the referral. But on the other hand, we're doing something for them that needs doing. Abortion is still new and a lot of people don't know where to go—the hospitals and clinics aren't allowed to advertise. We, as a referral service, do advertise, and when women call us, we make the arrangements. And in some cases the reassurance we supply over the phone and in the office is obviously important, especially for the out-of-town girls who come in alone (Continued on page 265)

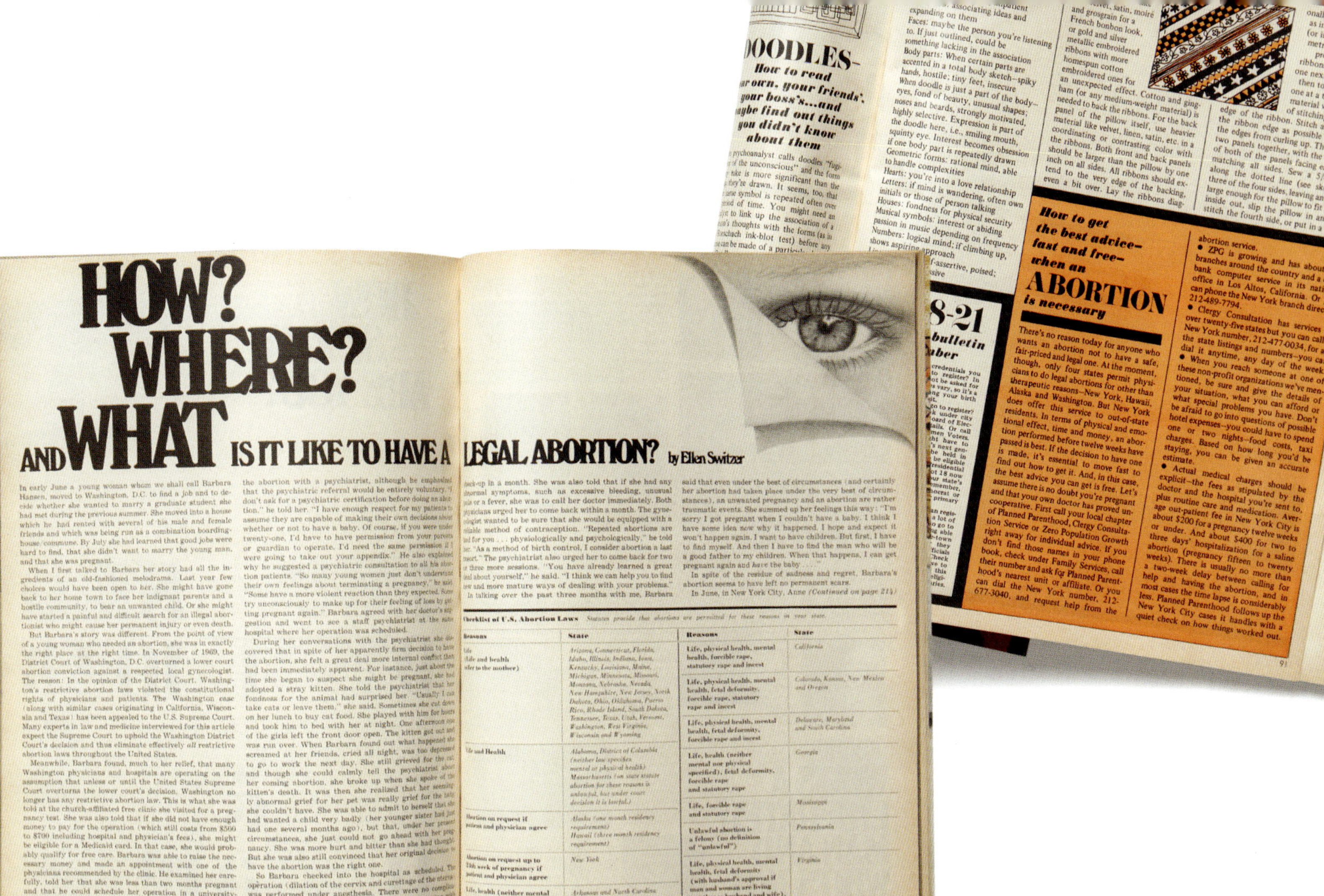

"How? Where? And What Is It
Like to Have a Legal
Abortion?" by Ellen Switzer.

Practical advice for
Glamour readers,
September 1971.

Roe v. Wade

***GLAMOUR* TOOK ITS** responsibility to its readers extremely seriously, both before and after the Supreme Court ruling. Women who needed an abortion had to know where and how to get one. In an article from September 1970 called "How? Where? And What Is It Like to Have a Legal Abortion?" women were given a step-by-step guide for what to expect, and how and where to access a termination in states where abortion was already legalized—as well as following the moving story of a young woman called Barbara who had the procedure. "How to get the best advice—fast and free—when an abortion is necessary" offered similar support. *Glamour* also reported the real-life stories of women working in abortion clinics, and, in the wake of *Roe*, the new abortion methods available to women. This was service journalism at its most courageous: utterly necessary and free of judgment—meeting the moment with stories that not only honored women, but aided them.

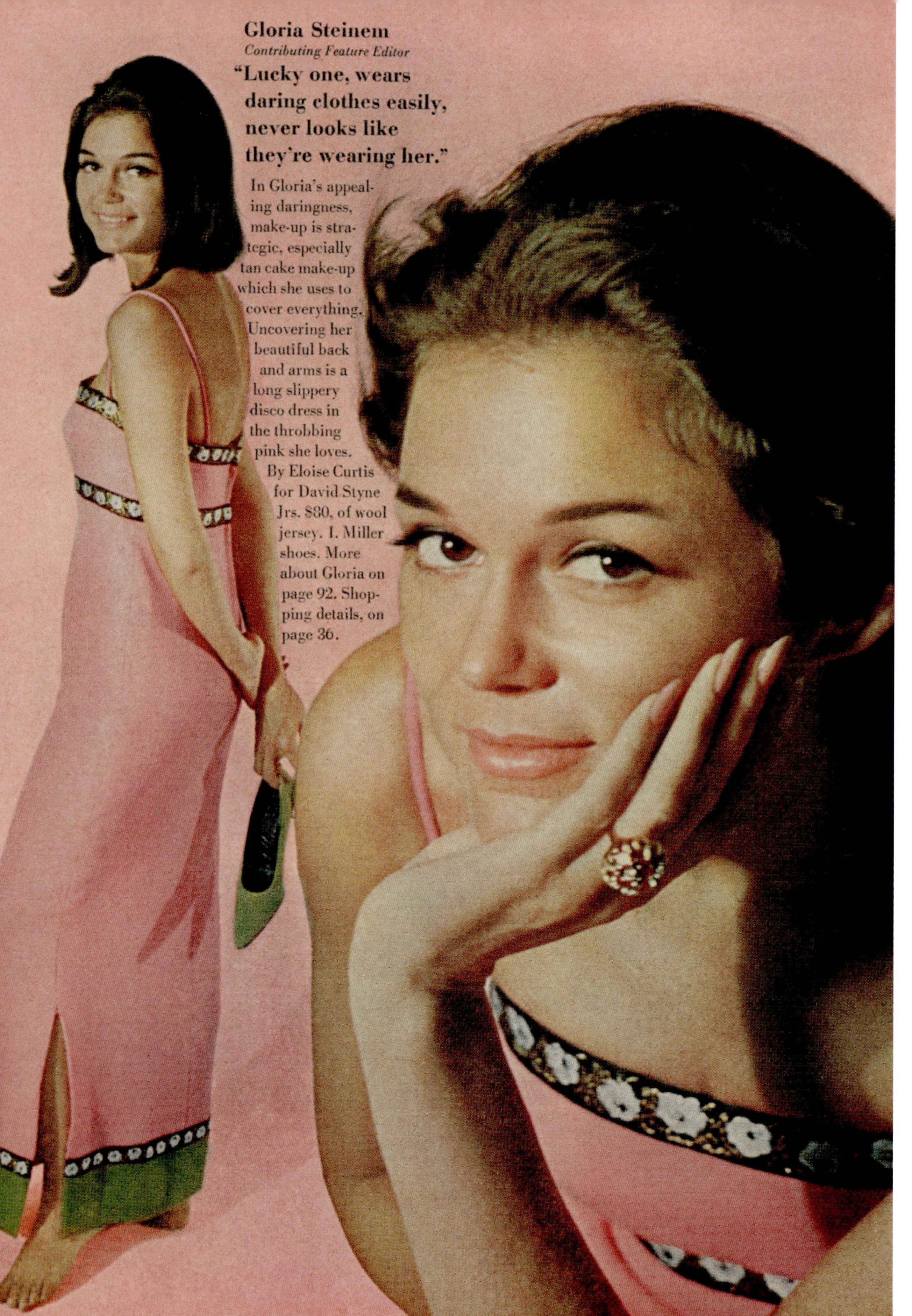

A look at Steinem's style. *Photographed by William Connors, December 1964.*

The Gloria Days

"New York's newest young wit," Gloria Steinem was one of *Glamour*'s most important contributing editors during this era.

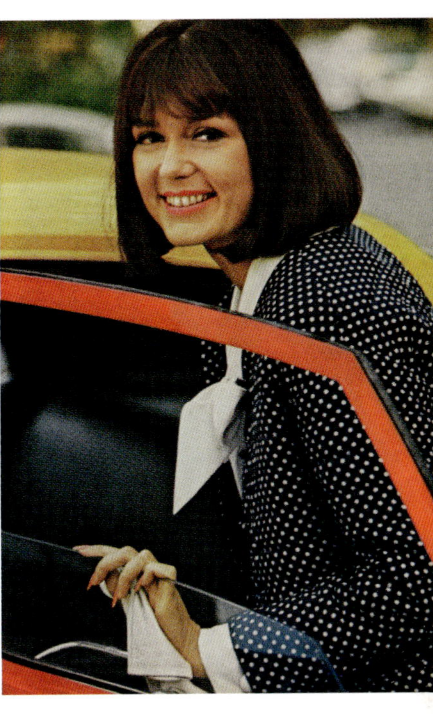

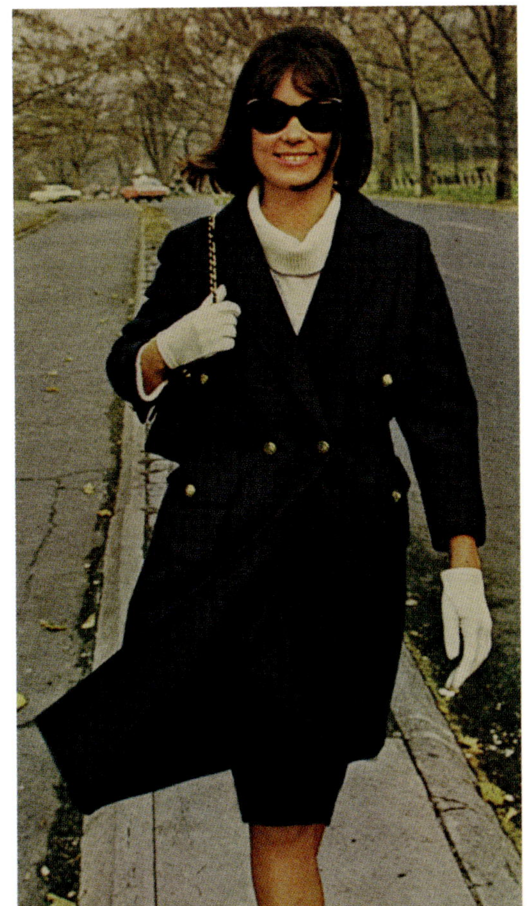

Left and top, Steinem. *Photographed by Frances McLaughlin-Gill, February 1964*

"GLORIA STEINEM SIGNS HER OWN LOOKS—AS WELL as her checks." So began the introduction to a fashion photo shoot starring "New York's newest young wit," writer Gloria Steinem, in the February 1964 issue of *Glamour*. "She is one of the bold spirits, with a sense of intrigue and humor about the way she looks and lives." At the time, Steinem had recently found notoriety having gone undercover as a Playboy Bunny for *SHOW* magazine—an article that exposed harassment and control over women's bodies in the nightclubs—but in its wake she expressed dismay over her own sexualization. As a contributing editor for *Glamour*, lauded for her dress sense, she found her niche as a style and cultural commentator. In March 1964, she reported from the chair of New York's hottest new hair sensation, Vidal Sassoon, and in October 1964 she penned an amusing piece on the "The Death of Cool and the Birth of Beyond-Cool." Her work was fun, frivolous, and witty—covering dating, single life, and more—but a different Gloria Steinem was itching to break free. By late 1964 she had dipped her toe into political coverage for *Glamour*. That was, of course, just the beginning.

In January 1965, Steinem penned a rallying op-ed called "Put Yourself First," planting the seeds of her desire to reshape the narrative of a generation. "If we pay for denying our own best interests in no other coin," she cried out, "we pay in wasted time. And time is all there is." Steinem seized hers: Her writing became bolder, and she became more prolific. Alongside her work for *Glamour*, she started ➡

writing for *New York* magazine, and by 1969 she had become a national sensation—in no small part thanks to the publication of her seminal piece "After Black Power, Women's Liberation." She was also fast establishing herself as the leader of the second-wave feminist movement. She wrote about abortion (she herself had one at the age of 22, when they were still illegal) and campaigned for women's unfettered access to terminations. And in 1972 she founded the feminist-themed *Ms.* magazine. As of 2024, she is the author of eight books.

Glamour's readers were lucky enough to read her work in the publication until 1970, when she departed as a contributing editor. But her ties to the magazine lasted. In 2011 she was awarded a lifetime achievement award at the *Glamour* Women of the Year Awards (which were established in 1990—more of which on page 214), and her importance to women remains colossal.

"

If we pay for denying our own best interests in no other coin, we pay in wasted time. And time is all there is.

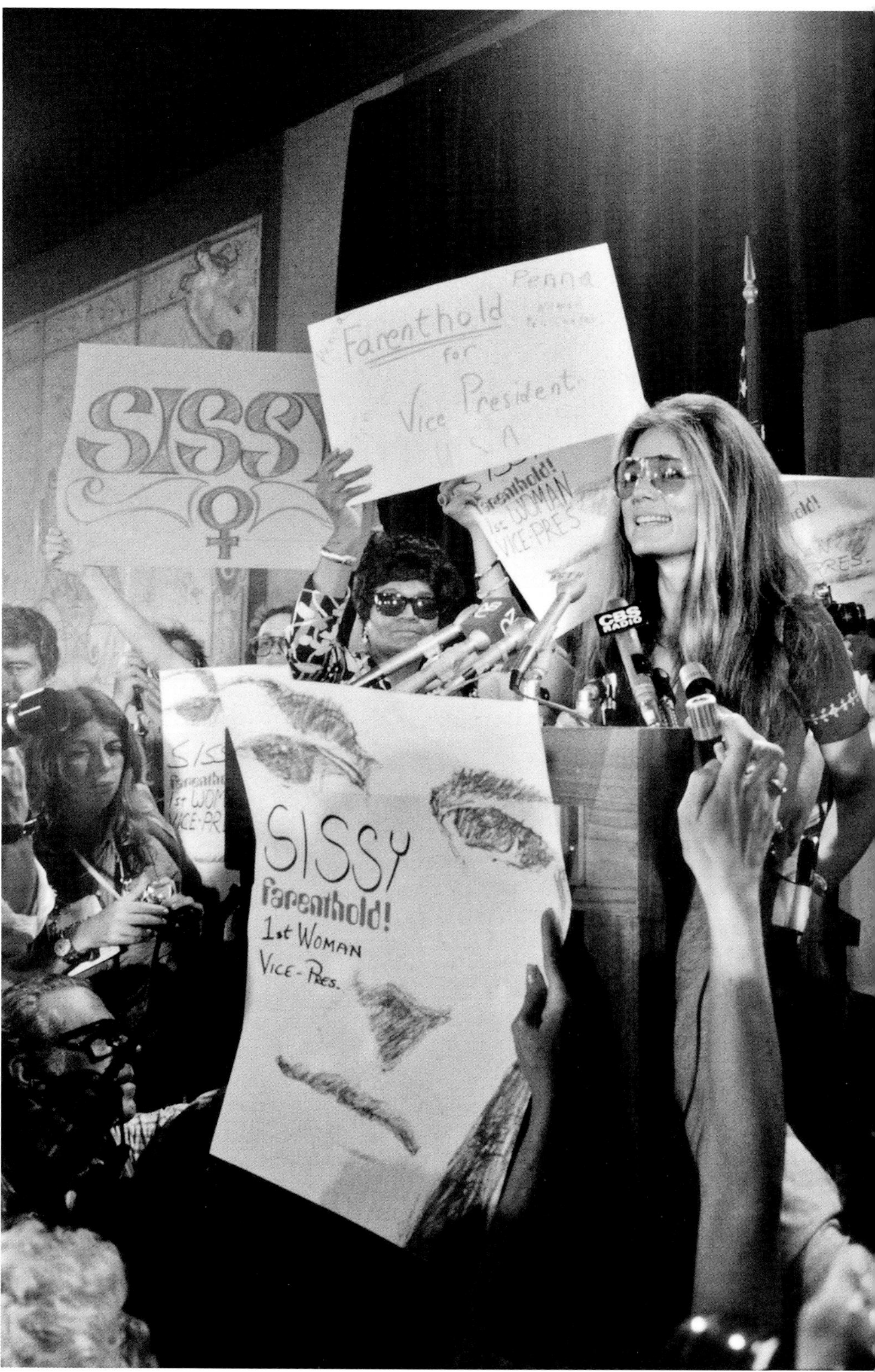

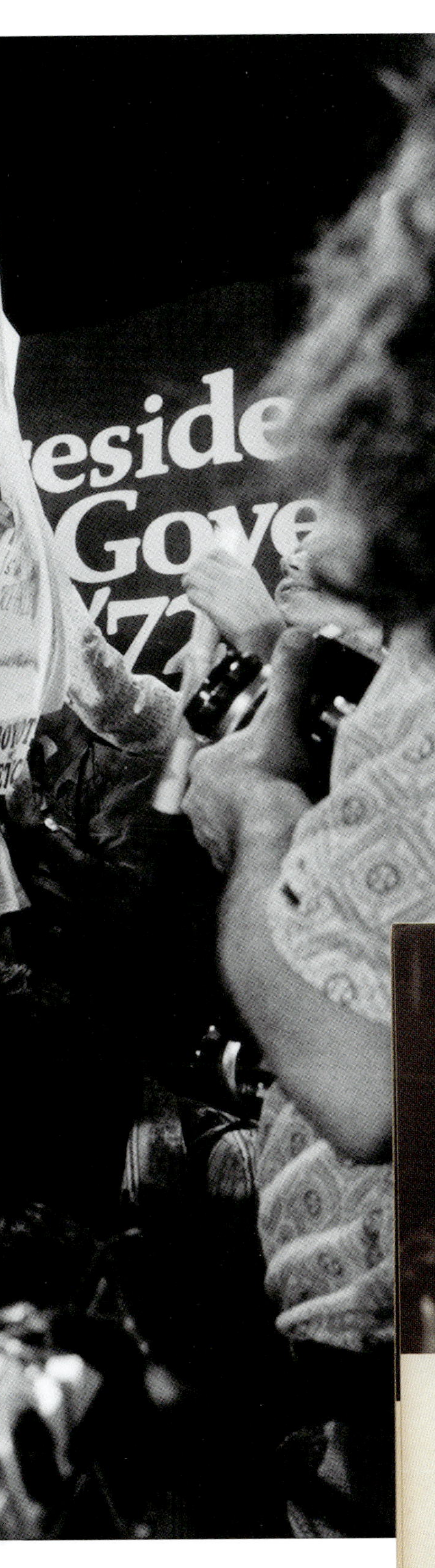

Left, Gloria Steinem at the podium during a 1972 rally for Frances "Sissy" Farenthold for vice president. Top right, "College and What I Learned There," August 1964. Bottom right, "It's a Young Man's Game," August 1965.

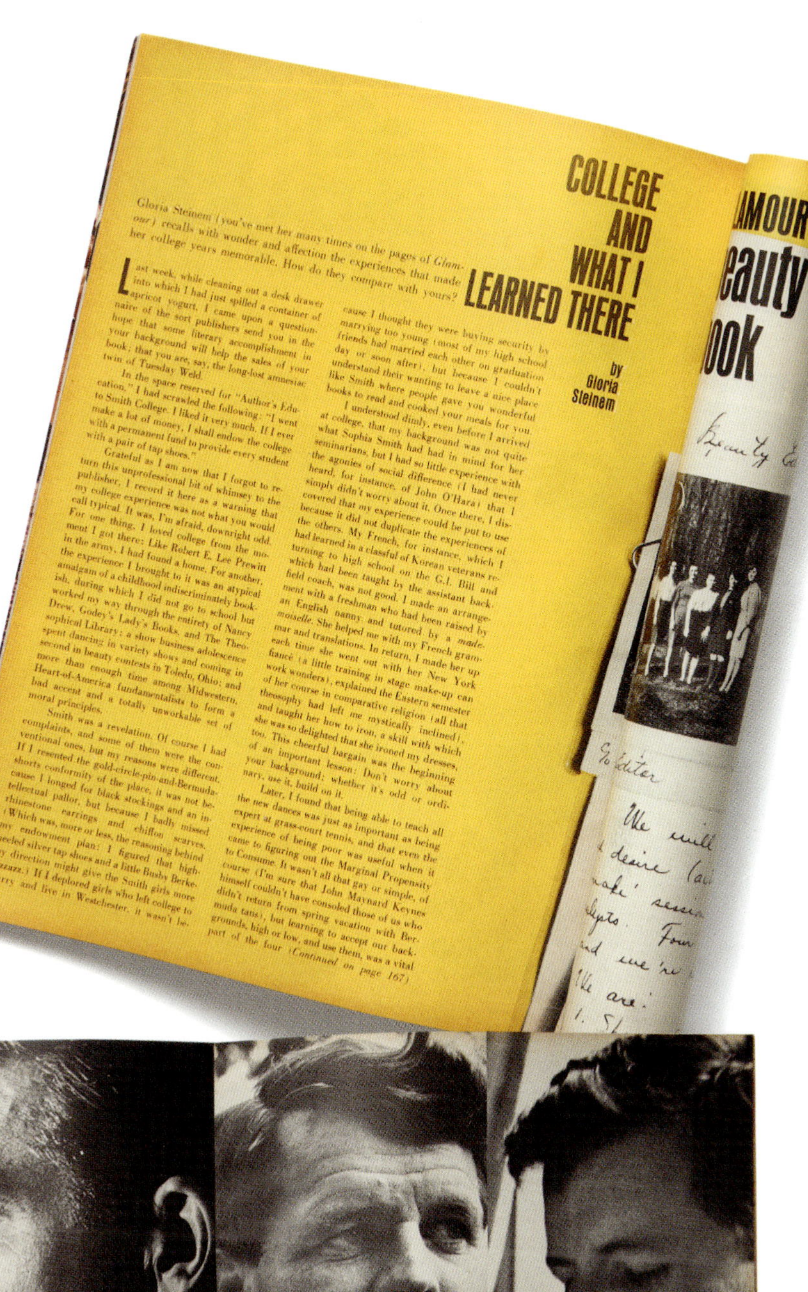

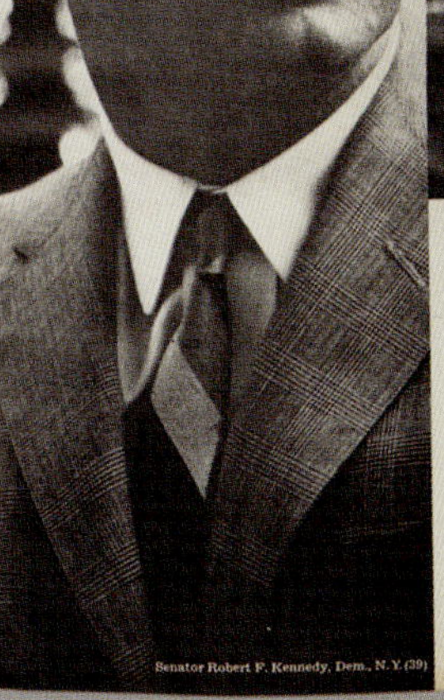

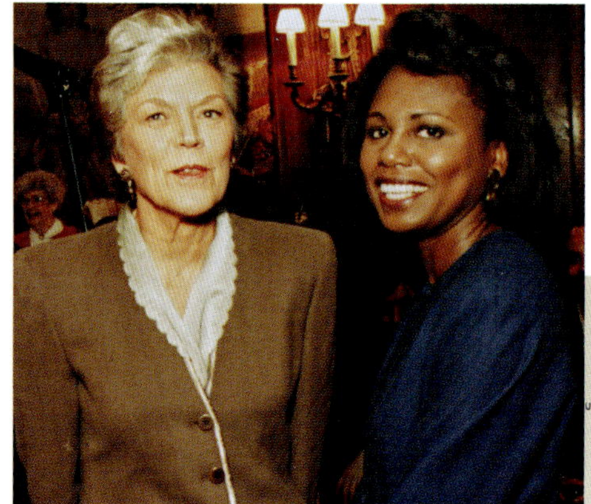

Ruth Whitney

The fearless women's advocate was editor in chief of *Glamour* for 31 years.

WHEN RUTH WHITNEY BECAME editor in chief of *Glamour* in 1967 it was, in her words, "a little white gloves" magazine written for women who "lived, at least on the surface, 'little white glove' lives." But Whitney had a vision that challenged that notion while distinguishing *Glamour* from its competitors: a magazine that actually reflected the contemporary American woman and the issues she faced, with an innovative mix of style, service, and substance.

She changed the annual Best-Dressed College Girls competition into one that selected on the basis of achievement, College Women of the Year (more on that on page 108). She cast models who "look like real people." She greenlit features on interracial dating, women's liberation, abortion, and equal pay, many of which you'll see in this chapter, along with the latest fashion and makeup tips. And less than a year into her tenure, *Glamour* became the first fashion magazine to feature a Black woman on its cover, Katiti Kironde.

"That decision announced boldly to readers that this was a whole new magazine," Whitney said in a 1996 speech. "But the best part of that decision was: That issue of *Glamour* sold more copies on the newsstand than any issue in the history of the magazine. It was as if a whole generation of women were waiting for that cover, and no one had dared to do it."

It is no overstatement to say that in her 31-year tenure Whitney redefined how readers, and her staff, would come to think of *Glamour*. Until her retirement in 1998—and truthfully, even after—Whitney encouraged that defiant spirit among her staff, the women they covered, and the readers themselves. The *Glamour* Women of the Year Awards were created in 1990 to honor "doers and darers" in politics, fashion, beauty, grassroots activism, Hollywood, and more. And under Whitney's direction, the magazine won prestigious awards for articles with headlines like, "The Politics of Birth Control," "Wake Up and Vote," and "Where Are the Doctors Who Will Do Abortions?" She kept her finger on the pulse by reading every single reader letter, good and bad, to create the road map that *Glamour* still follows today.

"Ruth wasn't shy about making us think—she was in our face," Katie Couric said at a memorial for Whitney following the legendary editor's death to Lou Gehrig's disease in 1999. "Beneath her classic, conservative beige suits and sensible Ferragamo pumps, was the heart of a rebel who liked to stir things up."

A former editor shared this story with Phil Whitney, Ruth's son: The editor had assigned an investigative article so potentially controversial that a major company was threatening to pull all ads—not just from *Glamour*, but from Condé Nast as a whole. When the editor was called into Whitney's office, she expected to hear that the article was being pulled. Instead, Whitney read the piece, handed it back, and said, "I just wanted to make sure it hadn't gotten watered down during factchecking."

In that 1996 speech, Whitney said she never found her job boring. "The problems of women are always changing. The lives of women are always changing," she said. "Making an impact on those lives, keeping pace with and addressing those problems is what makes editing *Glamour* an endless, everlasting thrill. Reaching 10 million women with the most socially responsible advice we can publish is truly exhilarating. Social responsibility sounds like such a heavy, heavy topic. It is, in fact, an absolutely heady experience. We push our reader. She pushes us. And both of us gain strength in the process."

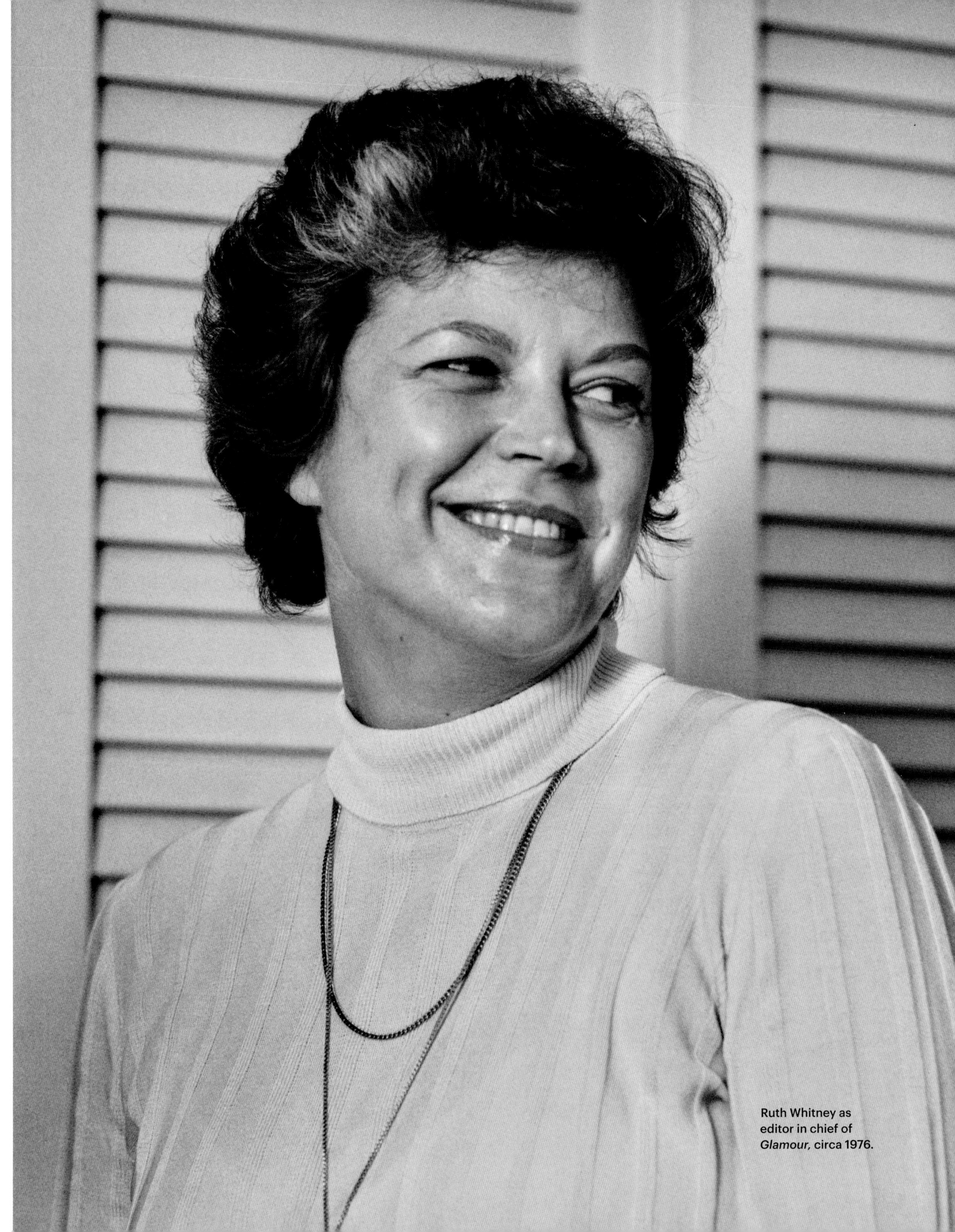

Ruth Whitney as editor in chief of *Glamour,* circa 1976.

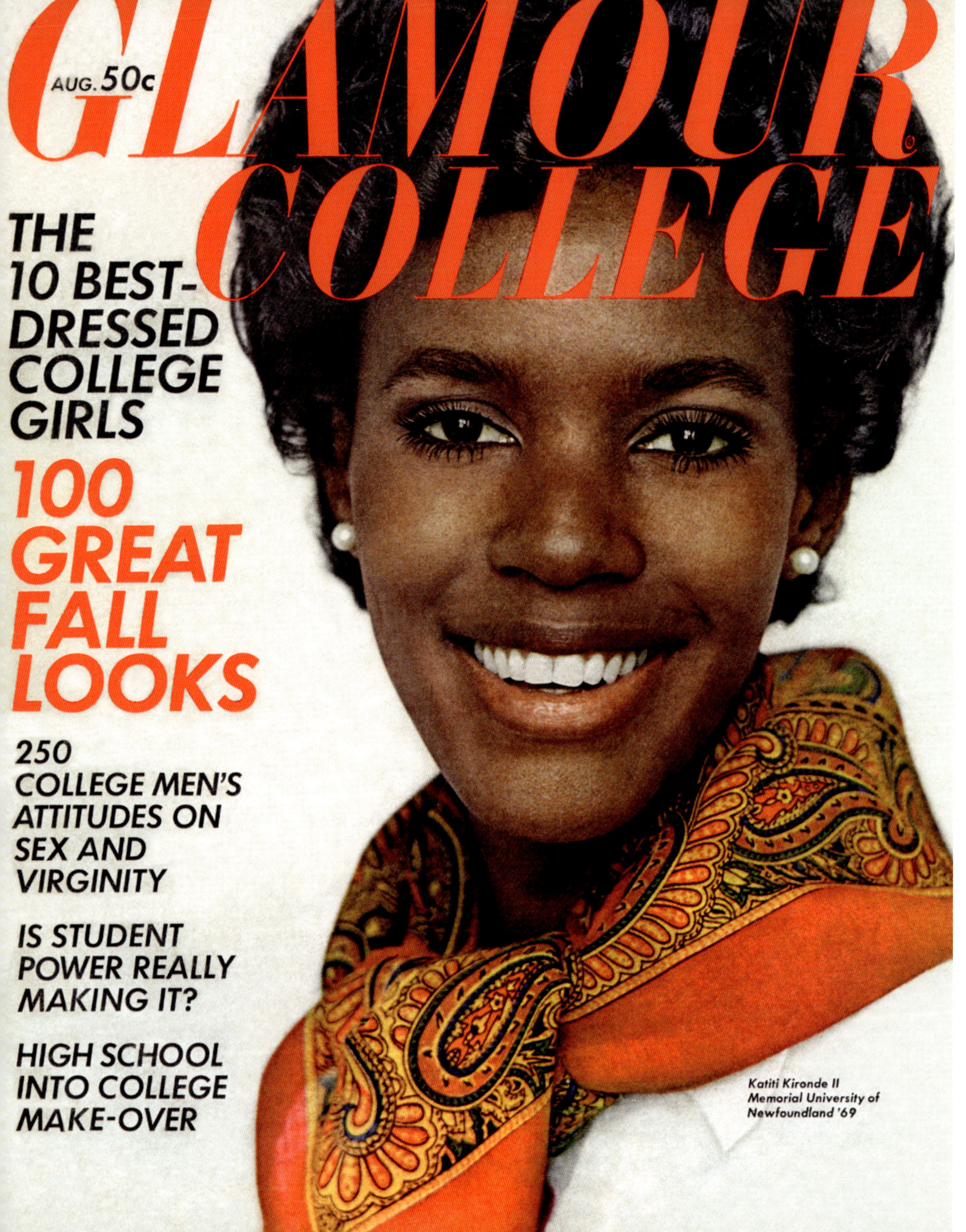

AUG. 50c
GLAMOUR
COLLEGE
THE 10 BEST-DRESSED COLLEGE GIRLS
100 GREAT FALL LOOKS
250 COLLEGE MEN'S ATTITUDES ON SEX AND VIRGINITY
IS STUDENT POWER REALLY MAKING IT?
HIGH SCHOOL INTO COLLEGE MAKE-OVER
Katiti Kironde II
Memorial University of
Newfoundland '69

Katiti Kironde

July 17, 1968

The Editors
Glamour Magazine
420 Lexington Ave.
N.Y. 10017 N.Y.

 I am very pleased to see that _finally_ a magazine has a black face on it's cover. It is about time

 I am black and would like to be a model. I never pursued this thought because there was seldom any encouragement from any magazines. After all, we do wear clothes and we do read your magazine so it is a welcome sight to see the cover of this issue. Maybe in the time to come there can be more black models in the fashion magazines but for now thank you very much.

 Sincerely,

 Cleo Thompson
 New Haven, Conn.

THE YEAR WAS 1968, and Katiti Kironde was a freshman at Memorial University of Newfoundland with a passion for style—and designing and making her own clothes. That year, she applied to *Glamour*'s Best-Dressed College Girls contest and won, earning her a spot on the cover and making history in the process. The August 1968 issue of *Glamour* magazine was the first ever American fashion magazine to feature a Black woman on its cover, and the issue has since sold millions of copies.

"It was such a different way of thinking back then," she told *Glamour* staffer Kateri Benjamin in a 2016 podcast episode. "I had a sense of myself. I was told by people all the time that I was not a bad looking person, and so I just never thought because I was Black I wasn't good looking. But I never saw the representation of my type of looks as celebrated."

The *Glamour* cover changed that—not just for Kironde, but for countless Black readers, many of whom wrote to Glamour to say thank you.

However, looking back, Kironde still felt she represented a more accessible kind of beauty for *Glamour*'s non-Black readers: "I can promise you that if I was a young black woman with a big afro and didn't look how I looked, no matter how good my clothes were they would not have picked me."

"The celebration of Black beauty is something that is very, very new, and has a long way to go, but we have come a long way," she said.

Above, a letter from a *Glamour* reader after Katiti Kironde's cover hit the newsstands, July 1968.

Right, *Glamour*'s 10 Best-Dressed College Girls of 1968, featuring Kironde, far left.
Photographed by William Connors, August 1968.

Left, Kironde on her *Glamour* cover.

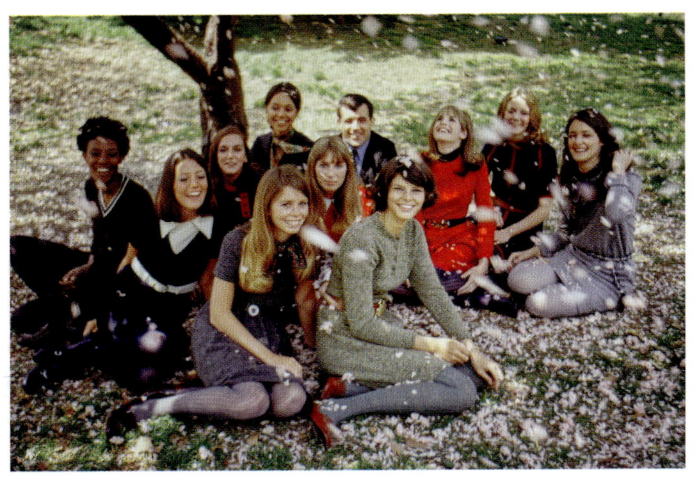

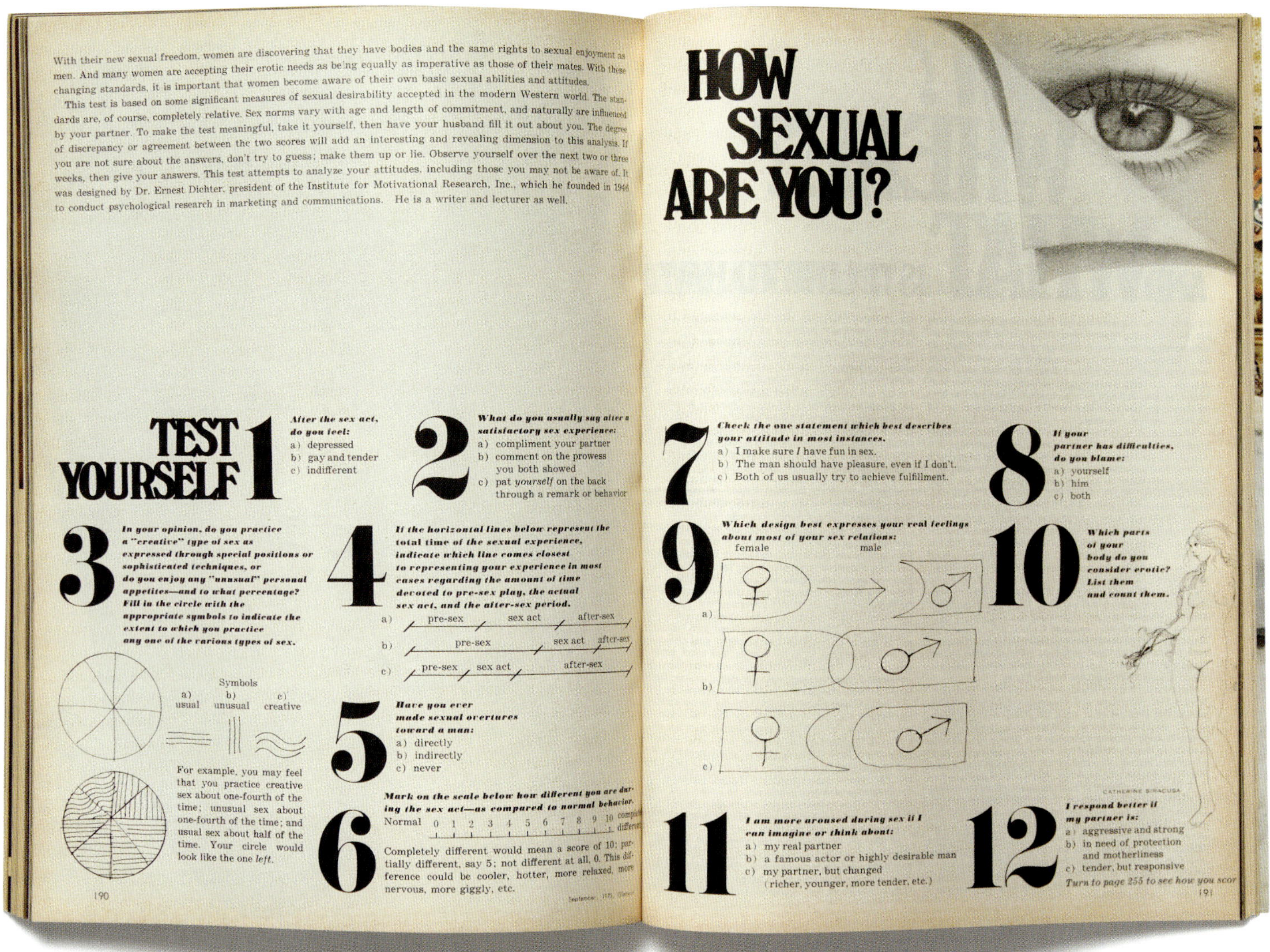

With their new sexual freedom, women are discovering that they have bodies and the same rights to sexual enjoyment as men. And many women are accepting their erotic needs as being equally as imperative as those of their mates. With these changing standards, it is important that women become aware of their own basic sexual abilities and attitudes.

This test is based on some significant measures of sexual desirability accepted in the modern Western world. The standards are, of course, completely relative. Sex norms vary with age and length of commitment, and naturally are influenced by your partner. To make the test meaningful, take it yourself, then have your husband fill it out about you. The degree of discrepancy or agreement between the two scores will add an interesting and revealing dimension to this analysis. If you are not sure about the answers, don't try to guess; make them up or lie. Observe yourself over the next two or three weeks, then give your answers. This test attempts to analyze your attitudes, including those you may not be aware of. It was designed by Dr. Ernest Dichter, president of the Institute for Motivational Research, Inc., which he founded in 1946 to conduct psychological research in marketing and communications. He is a writer and lecturer as well.

HOW SEXUAL ARE YOU?

TEST YOURSELF

1 After the sex act, do you feel:
a) depressed
b) gay and tender
c) indifferent

2 What do you usually say after a satisfactory sex experience:
a) compliment your partner
b) comment on the prowess you both showed
c) pat *yourself* on the back through a remark or behavior

3 In your opinion, do you practice a "creative" type of sex as expressed through special positions or sophisticated techniques, or do you enjoy any "unusual" personal appetites—and to what percentage? Fill in the circle with the appropriate symbols to indicate the extent to which you practice any one of the various types of sex.

Symbols: a) usual b) unusual c) creative

For example, you may feel that you practice creative sex about one-fourth of the time; unusual sex about one-fourth of the time; and usual sex about half of the time. Your circle would look like the one *left*.

4 If the horizontal lines below represent the total time of the sexual experience, indicate which line comes closest to representing your experience in most cases regarding the amount of time devoted to pre-sex play, the actual sex act, and the after-sex period.
a) pre-sex | sex act | after-sex
b) pre-sex | sex act | after-sex
c) pre-sex | sex act | after-sex

5 Have you ever made sexual overtures toward a man:
a) directly
b) indirectly
c) never

6 Mark on the scale below how different you are during the sex act—as compared to normal behavior.
Normal 0 1 2 3 4 5 6 7 8 9 10 completely different
Completely different would mean a score of 10; partially different, say 5; not different at all, 0. This difference could be cooler, hotter, more relaxed, more nervous, more giggly, etc.

7 Check the one statement which best describes your attitude in most instances.
a) I make sure *I* have fun in sex.
b) The man should have pleasure, even if I don't.
c) Both of us usually try to achieve fulfillment.

8 If your partner has difficulties, do you blame:
a) yourself
b) him
c) both

9 Which design best expresses your real feelings about most of your sex relations:
female / male
a)
b)
c)

10 Which parts of your body do you consider erotic? List them and count them.

11 I am more aroused during sex if I can imagine or think about:
a) my real partner
b) a famous actor or highly desirable man
c) my partner, but changed (richer, younger, more tender, etc.)

12 I respond better if my partner is:
a) aggressive and strong
b) in need of protection and motherliness
c) tender, but responsive
Turn to page 255 to see how you score

190   191

> Until now, women have been inhibited from 'looking.' When they claim that they are not aroused by the sight of the genitals or the sexual act, they do not realize that this is because they are victims of a culture that has not allowed them to look.

"THE NEW SEXUAL FREEDOM FOR WOMEN" BY PHYLLIS STARR, MAY 1970

"WHERE THE NEW SEXUAL FREEDOM really is, is in the openness about sex that now exists in places where it has not before—in churches, in legislatures, in family magazines, in films, on TV, in schools." So opened the piece "The New Sexual Freedom For Women," by Phyllis Starr in the May 1970 issue of *Glamour*. "There is a new dimension for women in not seeing themselves as passively programmed objects in the sexual act," the writer continued, "But as enthusiastic, contributing partners, with intense desires and capacities of their own for sexual fulfillment beyond simply orgasm—itself an achievement that was hardly mentionable for them before World War II." This was the perfect articulation of the new frontier that awaited women—acknowledgment, finally, as sexual beings, and the chance to explore pleasure on their own terms. *Glamour* not only reported on this societal shift, it provided service—with articles that covered topics such as which birth control is best, alternatives to the pill, and how to navigate the new sexual freedoms.

↑ "How Sexual Are You?" September 1970.

→ A striking nude model, poised behind a mesh screen. *Photographed by Rico Puhlmann, June 1976.*

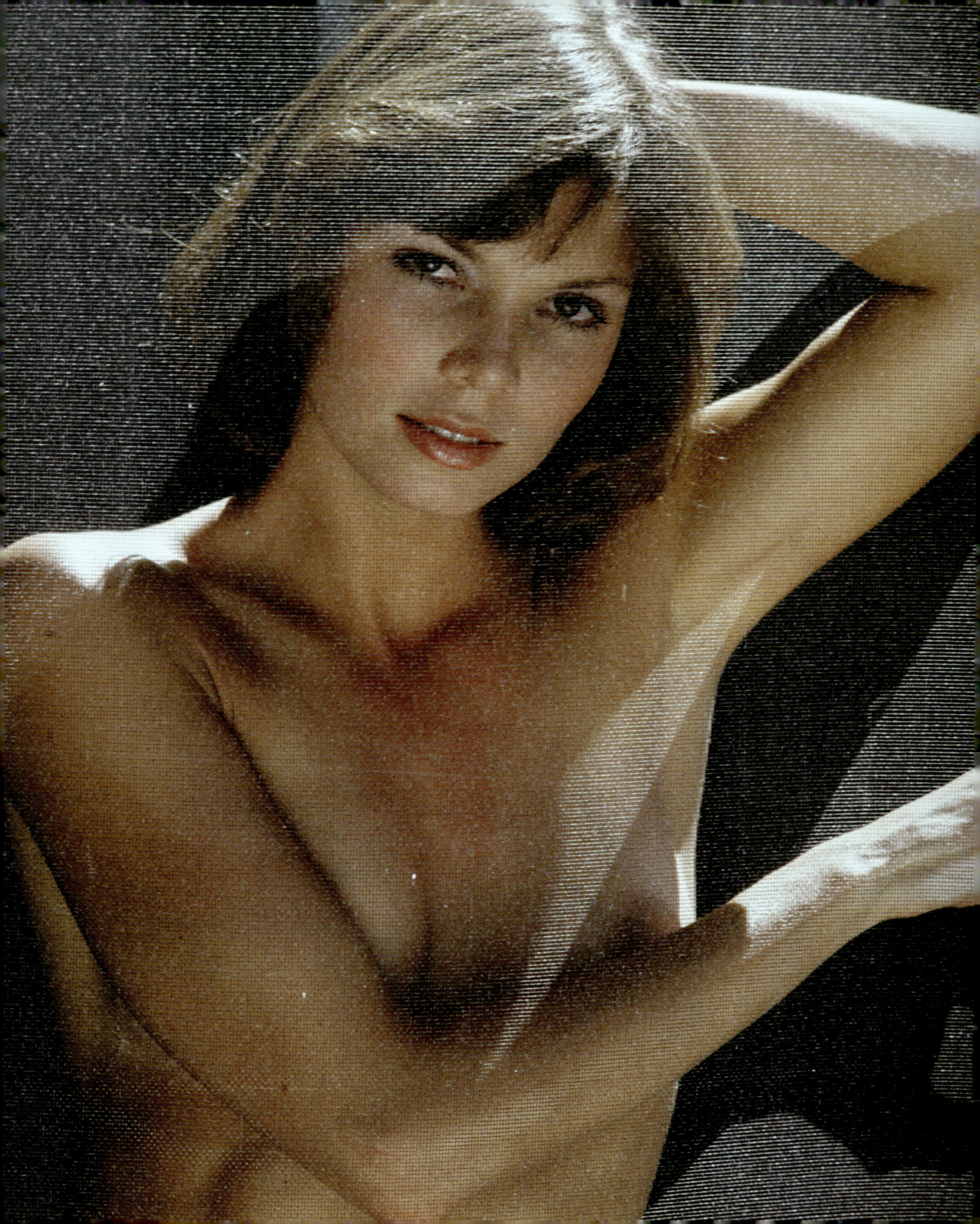

The article I wrote on women that *Playboy* wouldn't publish

In 1969, author Susan Braudy accepted a commission from *Playboy* magazine to write about the women's liberation movement. But the magazine refused to publish the final piece. Braudy's retelling of the incident for *Glamour*'s May 1971 issue, extracted here, is a true must-read.

WHEN MY AGENT TELEPHONED to announce that I would be one of the first women ever to get a writing assignment from *Playboy*, I was wary. It was September 1969. My assignment would be to write an objective article describing the women's liberation movement to *Playboy*'s manly readers.

Jim Goode, who was then *Playboy*'s articles editor, telephoned me twice and speaking more slowly that I would have thought the human voice could, explained that *Playboy* wanted a fair, objective account of the entire spectrum of the women's liberation movement. "These women have important things to say," Goode said. "Write anything you like, and be fair," he finished, still sounding like a 45 rpm record playing at 33. His letter arrived a few days later. In it he repeated that he wanted a fair article, and mysteriously added, "in a tone that is amused, if the author is amused, but never snide." This remark puzzled me. I reread it anxiously several times with the conviction, I suppose, that if I could understand it, I would know if I could win out—keep my integrity and write an article which would surely help my career.

After I started the assignment, I vowed to bring enlightenment to readers. I would write such a poignant piece that the *Playboy* editors would be convinced of the moral and economic imperative of renaming their magazine *Play-People*. Eureka, they would shout. How objective! How fair! How unsnide! How liberated we all are together!

My first women's liberation meeting became the lede of my article. The meeting took place on Manhattan's Upper West Side. In the apartment sat seven strange women about my age talking intimately and painfully, one after another, about personal experiences I never expected I'd hear another human being discuss, let alone another woman.

I had not yet learned how moving it could be to attend a consciousness-raising session like this one, and discover how monotonously similar everybody's sad tales were and how traceable they were to their roles as women.

I didn't fall asleep very easily that night or many nights after. I went to meeting after meeting and heard women talk passionately or woodenly about their "women's rage." They hurled questions at each other about their life's roles. Were they to do women's housework—the sort that most men considered too demeaning to do themselves? Should women abandon their "home" jobs and compete for power in a man's world they never made, fighting for power and money and obeying rules and laws, like the abortion laws, that they never made?

What about the double standard? Were women now as free to enjoy sex as men are, or did the sexual revolution still favor men who now cowed women even more with the new notion that if they didn't put out fast, some other more sexually liberated women would?

Early in my researches I had interviewed a radical leader of the movement who predicted calmly that I would be squeezed out in the conflict between *Playboy* and the feminist movement. She explained that privileged women are only allowed so much power by men in the world of men. And she also said that, though her manner belied the harshness of her words, that since I was taking advantage of the feminist movement to further my ambitions, I should expect pity but little sympathy from her when I lost out.

A few weeks after I mailed my "objective, fair" article to *Playboy* I got a mysterious and anxious call from my sepulchrally-toned editor. It seems a woman had called and asked him who the woman was who had written the piece for them. He'd given her my name. Meanwhile Jim Goode announced he was pleased with the article. "You followed instructions." The woman caller turned out to be a freelance writer, Sandy North, who called because she was writing an article for *The Atlantic* on troubles women had covering women's liberation from both male editors and movement women. When she finally called me I was smug. Of course, I told her, I was having no trouble at all from my male editors at *Playboy*.

In retrospect, I wonder about the error in judgment I made, to believe that *Playboy* would run a fair article about women's liberation. But I also wonder what the editors at *Playboy* like Jim Goode think of the error in judgment they made. Why did they think they could run an article that would be fair to women's liberation?

Hugh Hefner—editor and publisher—admitted on the Dick Cavett show, that *Playboy* didn't try to present a three-dimensional view of the women spread out on his pages and picture and story. Why? Because the magazine is written for men, not for women.

But why can't a magazine written to titillate men present a full picture of real women to those big brave men? Why can't it describe a real woman with women's jokes, insights, smells and love—in short, her threateningly human characteristics? Is the *Playboy* male so weak, so ultimately unable to cope with reality and real women that the fantasy creature of his glossy *Playboy*-inspired reveries must be mechanized, passive, manipulatable and controllable? I was soon to find out.

A few weeks after the supposed acceptance of the article I found myself in Chicago doing another article for another magazine and decided to give Playboy a hello call. When I first arrived at Playboy I spoke to several secretaries. One secretary told me that she didn't think my article would ever see print. When I nervously questioned her, she answered vaguely, "Oh, I just don't trust people around here when it comes to women."

[At] *Playboy*'s posh offices I met Nat Lehrman, *Playboy*'s sex expert, as it were. Lehrman had to approve any article that had anything to do with the *Playboy* philosophy, that is, sex. He was, I suppose, *Playboy*'s sex censor.

Lehrman had read over my article, and now there were, you see, snags. Lehrman showed me his early corrections apologetically. "It might have been easy," he said nervously. But the corrections were now obsolete. A memo had come from on high. Hefner had gotten wind that an objective article was in the works and he was mad. Hefner's memo read in part, "These chicks are our natural enemy… It is time to do battle with them… What I want is a devastating piece that takes the militant feminists apart."

I was a victim if I ever saw one. Lehrman decided that big changes were in order. And most annoying, he decided that he could argue me into making the changes in my article which would please Hefner. Lehrman asked me to change my travel plans and spend the night in Chicago while we puzzled out a compromise. I called my husband and told him that I was not going to be home. Jim Goode checked me into the Knickerbocker Hotel. I took two tranquilizers and went to sleep.

The next morning I argued about my article with a young Englishman named Henry Fenwick. His job was to pinch my prose into a neutral shape that *Playboy* could accept. My perceptions, my analyses and all the things I learned about myself and other women while writing the piece were verboten. Finally, I asked Fenwick to guarantee that if I agreed to his changes, *Playboy* would make no further changes. "No." Meanwhile, Nat Lehrman had contacted Morton Hunt, author of *Woman: Her Infinite Variety*, and Hunt agreed to do the piece reflecting *Playboy*'s position on sex roles in this country—a piece which Lehrman said would be separate from mine. This depressed me more than it should have. Fenwick left the office at 7:30pm. My uneasiness grew as I wandered with notepad and pencil through Lehrman's empty office. Then I called the airport and fled.

Lehrman called me the next day to ask if I'd decided to rewrite the article. I told him I wouldn't make the corrections. My article would not run in *Playboy*. "Up Against The Wall, Male Chauvinist Pig," written by Morton Hunt, appeared in *Playboy* during the spring. He decreed that woman's place is in the home if she has children and that man is "boss" because you need a boss to run things. He concluded by grandly relegating the women's lib movement to "the discard pile of history." *Newsweek* called Hunt's piece "rambling."

I was intensely relieved that I was not associated with it. Suppose my article had gone through and they had slapped a title like that on it. That title would have cast a pall over the most radical feminist polemic. Then I laughed. The title was also the kind of invective I was much too "ladylike" to hurl at my friends at *Playboy*. But I would have liked to have had the wit to have said, "Up Against The Centerfold…"

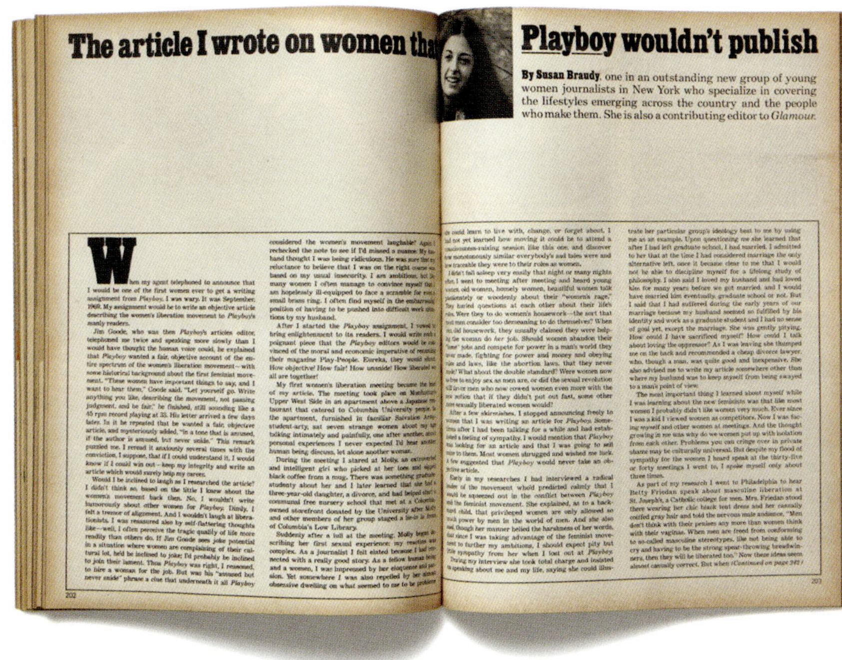

The original article as it appeared in the May 1971 issue.

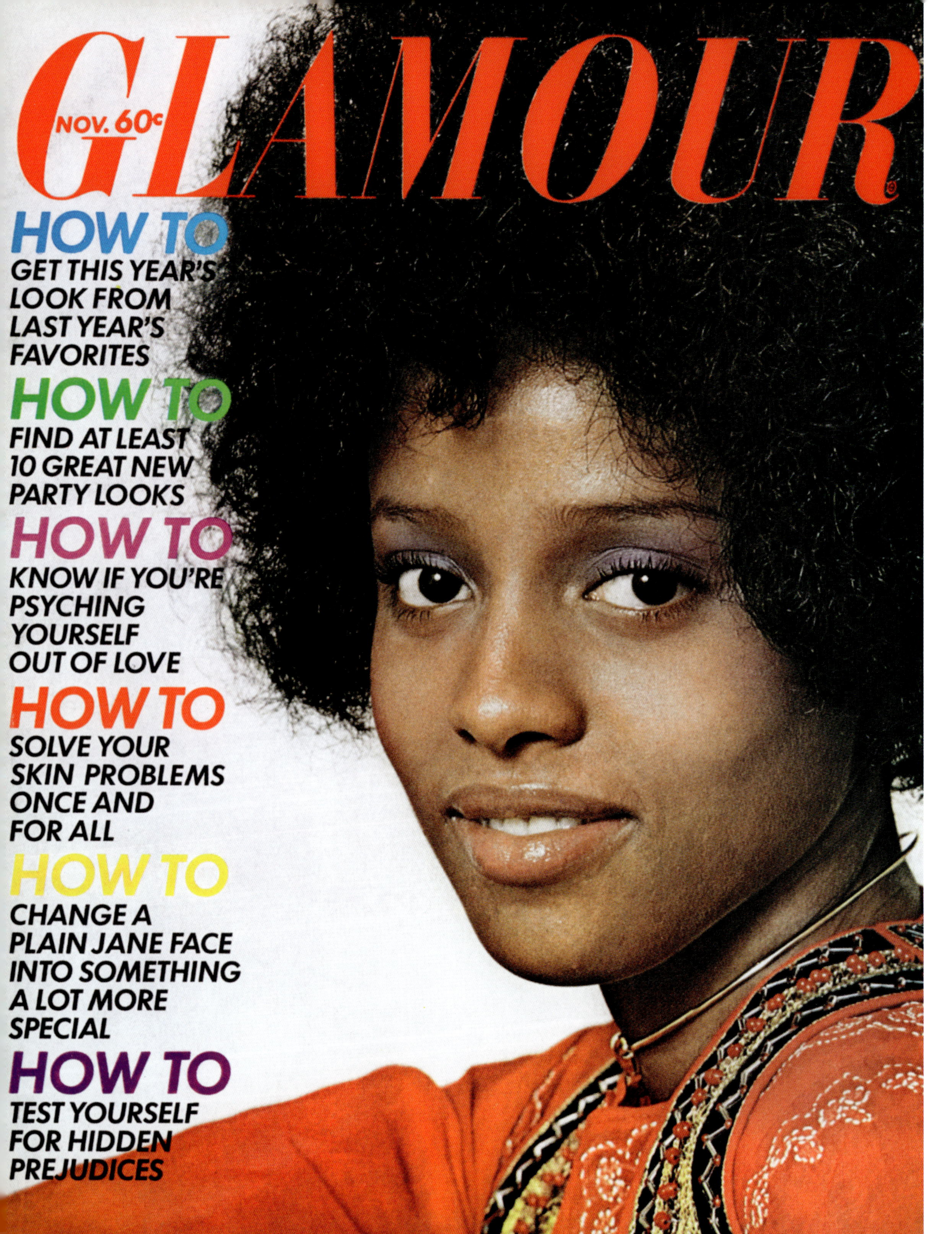

NOV. 60¢
GLAMOUR

HOW TO
GET THIS YEAR'S LOOK FROM LAST YEAR'S FAVORITES

HOW TO
FIND AT LEAST 10 GREAT NEW PARTY LOOKS

HOW TO
KNOW IF YOU'RE PSYCHING YOURSELF OUT OF LOVE

HOW TO
SOLVE YOUR SKIN PROBLEMS ONCE AND FOR ALL

HOW TO
CHANGE A PLAIN JANE FACE INTO SOMETHING A LOT MORE SPECIAL

HOW TO
TEST YOURSELF FOR HIDDEN PREJUDICES

Giving Voice to Black Women

THE EXPLORATION OF BLACK WOMEN'S experiences in *Glamour* began in January 1965 with Marilyn Mercer's article, "The Young American Negro Woman." This pivotal piece signaled the beginning of a new era in the magazine, and coincided with the enactment of the landmark Civil Rights Act of 1964—which, for the first time, prohibited segregation in public places and employment discrimination based on race, color, religion, sex, or national origin.

Against this new, rapidly evolving landscape, Mercer's words were deeply resonant: "This year more than last year, and next year more than this year, in many parts of the country, young white women and young Negro women will find themselves side by side in classrooms, offices, and community work." The sentiment expressed by the white girl, "I want to be friends, but I don't know how," underscored the need to foster connections across racial lines. Simultaneously, the Black girl's query, "Does she really—or does she think she has to?" delved into the challenges faced by two historically segregated groups.

Mercer tried to answer the latter question in her May 1969 piece titled "How It Feels to Be a Black Girl Now." In the article, a woman shared a disheartening experience: "I heard a man say, 'Well, that fills our quota for this month.' I know they hired me just because I'm black…. No matter how hard I work, they resent that." Despite the writer challenging monolithic portrayals of Black society and showcasing the diverse roles of Black women as students, office workers, professionals, or young mothers, it's important to recognize that during this period at *Glamour*, the experiences of Black women were portrayed through the lens of white women. While the intentions may have been genuine, the potential for oversights, or the unintentional reinforcement of stereotypes, should not be overlooked.

Diane Washington covers *Glamour*, November 1970.

The November 1970 issue, featuring the model Diane Washington with an afro on the cover, marked a turning point. One of the cover lines overlaid on Washington's image declared, "How to Test Yourself for Hidden Prejudices"—a notable shift in the magazine's approach to addressing racial issues. The accompanying inside story urged *Glamour*'s readers with a challenge: "You think you're not prejudiced? Test yourself and see." The quiz aimed to "reveal your real—but often subtle—prejudices, as well as some of which you may be totally unaware."

While the article omitted any mention of the deep schisms caused by slavery, segregation, and even the Civil Rights Act of 1964 banning segregation, it marked the beginning of a decade where *Glamour* centered the concerns of Black communities; celebrated Black experiences, style, and beauty; and finally gave opportunities to Black writers. In the subsequent December issue, young Black writer Adrianne L. Carter lamented how "white America turns its back on black problems," especially those related to pollution. In the magazine's monthly Protest column, she wrote, "Pollution is nothing new to blacks… But we called it other names, like malnutrition, rat and roach infestation, disease and filth. Ghetto pollution has been killing for a much longer time than its newfound companions." These conversations were not only urgent and vital but, importantly, firmly presented in front of *Glamour*'s traditionally white audience.

A March 1972 editorial highlighted two new books aimed at improving dialogue between white and Black people. Additionally, a December 1975 article by writer Valerie J. Harris noted that the 1970s version of feminism was deeply white-centric: "If the idea that one's job must be fulfilling and meaningful is a feminist view at all, it is a pampered, white, middle-class view that only serves to further alienate most black women—women who for generations have worked and raised children simultaneously." Harris's incisive critique underscored the magazine's evolving commitment to challenging societal norms.

In tracing *Glamour*'s evolution through the exploration of Black women's experiences, we witness a journey marked by progress while acknowledging challenges and limitations. From the magazine's early endeavors in the '60s to pivotal moments in the '70s, *Glamour* grappled with the complexities of race and identity, demonstrating an enduring commitment to amplifying Black voices and recognizing its responsibility to give voice to the marginalized.

↓

"The Young American Negro Woman" by Marilyn Mercer, January 1965.

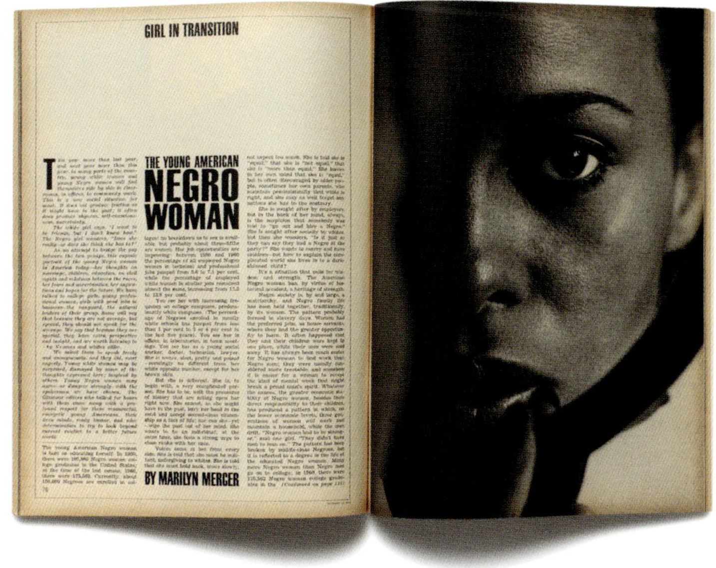

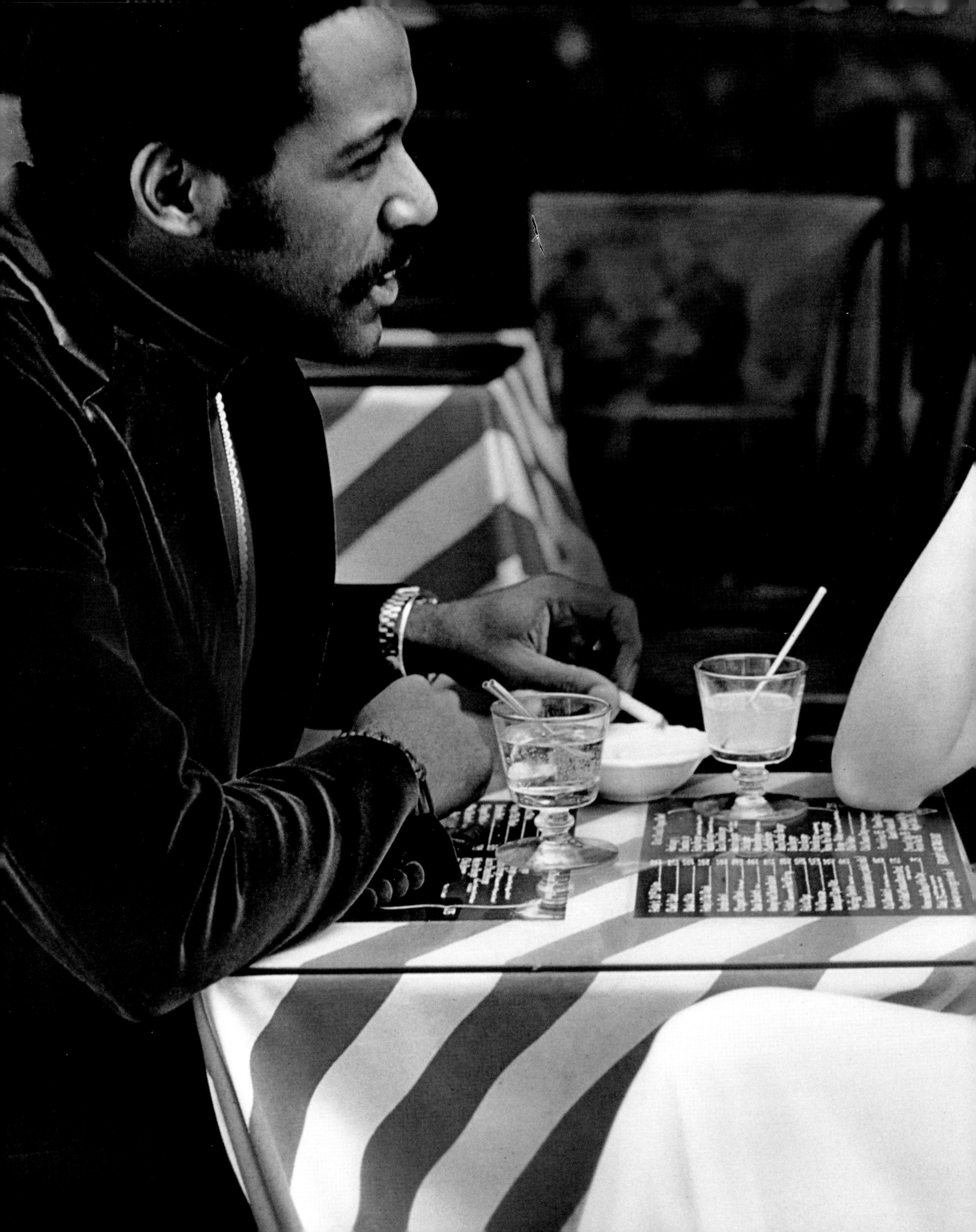

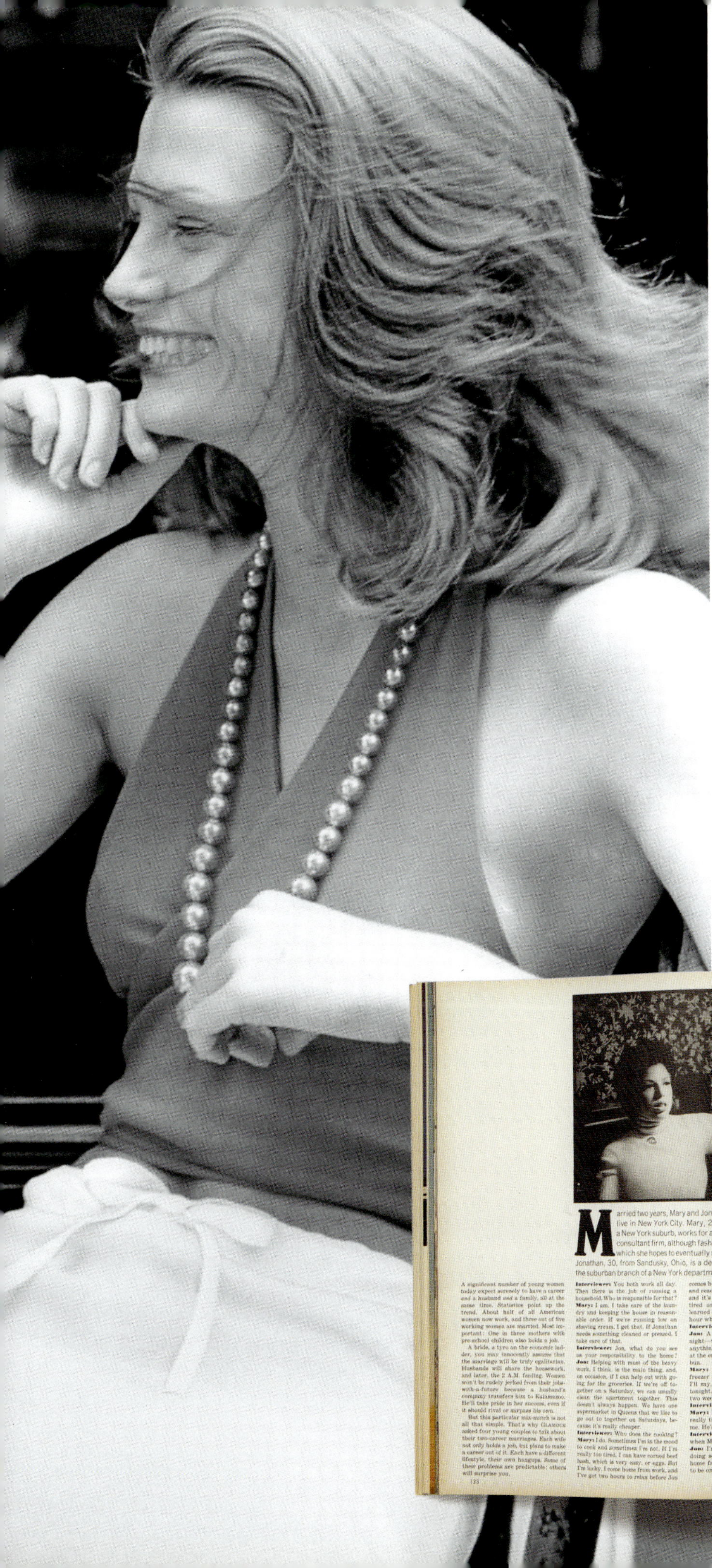

APPROXIMATELY HALF OF ALL marriages in America ended in divorce in the 1970s, but this wasn't seen as a hindrance in the pages of *Glamour*. In the newly liberated world in which *Glamour*'s readers now lived, divorce could be an advantage. In an article about second marriages, the writer Mim Randolph Edmonds observed, "Carol and Peter were right for each other. But it's possible they wouldn't have been if they hadn't been married before." And it wasn't just about the benefits of divorce. *Glamour* wanted to help women have good ones: "Being greatly devoted to the perfect marriage, we are also, of course, greatly devoted to the perfect divorce," a 1973 article began, coming deliciously full circle from 1961's "perfect wife" guide. The magazine's approach to marriage itself changed, too: acknowledging that women's expectations were now similar to men's in wishing to "have a career and a husband and a family, all at the same time." This was explored in an article about couples in "two-career marriages." *Glamour's* new world was a place for women to carve out the relationships they wanted, not the ones they were expected to have.

Left, *Shaft* actor Richard Roundtree with a model for a fashion spread. *Photographed by Rico Puhlmann, January 1973.* Below, the article on two-career marriages from the February 1971 issue, featuring Pulitzer Prize–nominated writer Susan Braudy and her husband, Leo.

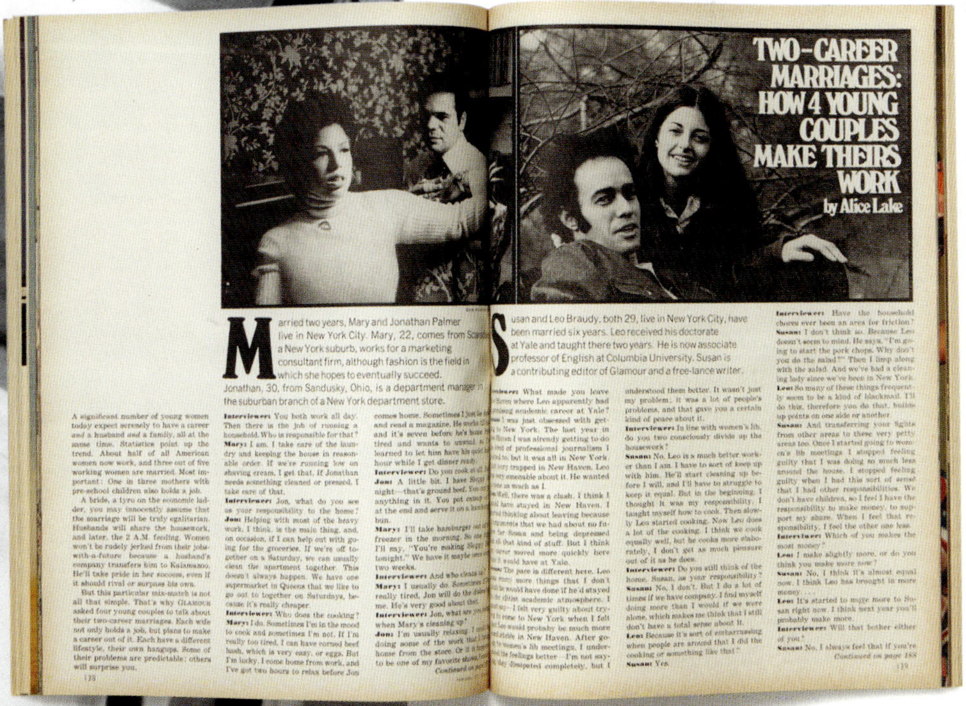

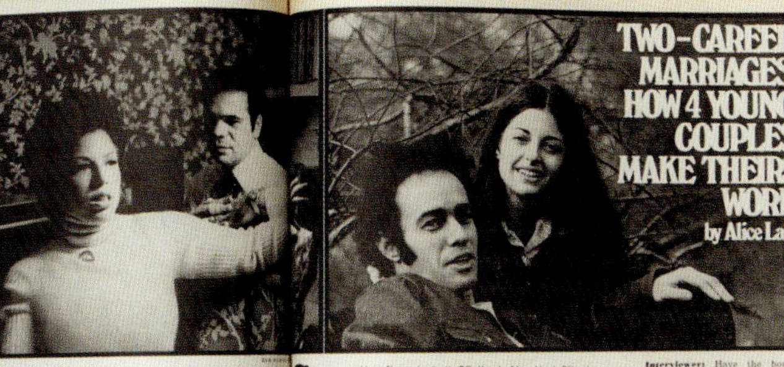

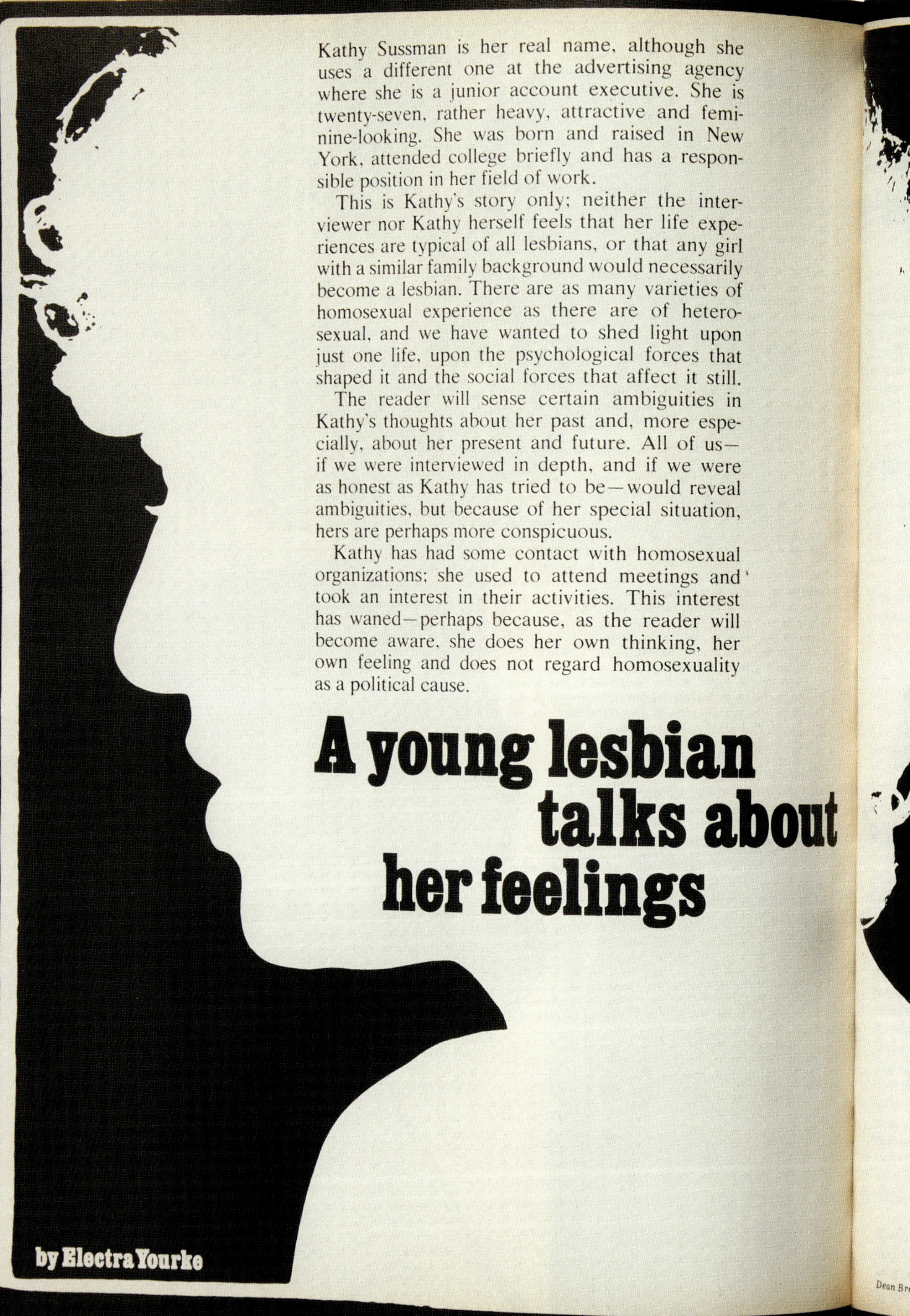

Kathy Sussman is her real name, although she uses a different one at the advertising agency where she is a junior account executive. She is twenty-seven, rather heavy, attractive and feminine-looking. She was born and raised in New York, attended college briefly and has a responsible position in her field of work.

This is Kathy's story only; neither the interviewer nor Kathy herself feels that her life experiences are typical of all lesbians, or that any girl with a similar family background would necessarily become a lesbian. There are as many varieties of homosexual experience as there are of heterosexual, and we have wanted to shed light upon just one life, upon the psychological forces that shaped it and the social forces that affect it still.

The reader will sense certain ambiguities in Kathy's thoughts about her past and, more especially, about her present and future. All of us— if we were interviewed in depth, and if we were as honest as Kathy has tried to be—would reveal ambiguities, but because of her special situation, hers are perhaps more conspicuous.

Kathy has had some contact with homosexual organizations; she used to attend meetings and took an interest in their activities. This interest has waned—perhaps because, as the reader will become aware, she does her own thinking, her own feeling and does not regard homosexuality as a political cause.

A young lesbian talks about her feelings

There are different kinds of lesbians. I am a *woman,* but there are those who want to become men; they feel like a man trapped in a woman's body. When you see them walking down the street, you say, "There's a real butch." Life is hard for them, a constant conflict.

I went through that kind of stage, just to torment my mother. I had my hair all slicked back and no eyelashes. Now, I wouldn't be caught dead in the street in a downpour without eyelashes.

For some people homosexuality is a phase, and if they have the right influences, the right help, they can get away from it. You can't say "do" or "don't" to another person. No one decides, "I am going to become a homosexual." It is a psychological and not a physiological state, in most cases. I know a lot of people who had very difficult, traumatic childhoods which shaped them.

And then there are women who have been married, had children and decided all of a sudden to run away with another woman. Especially if their husbands were running around with another woman, or were violent, or if they were abrupt, ineffective, or insensitive lovers, these women feel such a rejection that they will never again have anything to do with a man.

Once I thought I had recruited a girl into lesbianism and I felt guilty about it for years, until I found out that she had wanted me to think she was innocent, but she was really not. Another time, I went to a resort and met a woman—she had several children and she said she had never done anything like that before, but it wasn't true and I was annoyed that she was lying.

I don't want to initiate people; I don't want to be responsible. Most people don't adjust to homosexuality too well. I used to feel a certain *esprit de corps* with gay guys, but I don't anymore. Some gay men look down on the frivolous type of male homosexual, and there are some gay women who are offended by butch lesbians, because they give all of us a bad name. We're not like that.

I have developed a bad ulcer in the past year—a good percentage of the lesbians you will meet have ulcers. Society is against you, your family is, too. Perhaps *you* are.

As a child, I was always boy-crazy, but I always admired beautiful women. When I was in junior high school, I had a girlfriend who lived across the street. She was masculine-looking and everyone called her a tomboy. I felt sorry for her and said I would be her friend because no one else would, but now I'm not sure that was my only motive.

Later, I remember kids talking about a very boyish-looking girl in school and that she had a girlfriend, but I had no conception of what they were talking about, except that it seemed very exciting—whatever it was.

When I was twenty-one or -two, I went to a gay bar with some friends. There were men and women and mixed dancing. There was a lesbian sitting with a gay man and she invited us all to her table. After a while, she asked me to dance. I accepted, mostly out of curiosity. I had never had any feelings like that before—but something was there and we saw each other again. My mother suspected and told my father. I came home one morning and my father said to the maid, "Don't let her in." There were neighbors in the hall waiting for the elevator and he said, in front of them, "Go back to your dyke lover."

I continued to live with my family for a while, but it was obvious that we were destroying each other. I think that if my father had been a little understanding then, if he had really cared, I would have given these events more thought. But he didn't, so I just did exactly what he told me.

After my first encounter with this girl, I thought, "Oh, my God, I'm *queer!*" Later, after my parents split up, my mother had a lot of boyfriends and she used to tell me about them in some detail. I made little comparisons about my own activities along those lines and I didn't come out too well. I had never really responded to any man.

After I realized I had felt something for a girl, after the first embrace, I was very comfortable. I felt this was fine, this was where I belonged, except that there was so much hassling from my family. Without that pressure from them, I probably would have gotten tired of the experimentation and sought out a man again. When you're a kid and you've just discovered something that is a forbidden fruit, it's a temptation, and at that time I couldn't see the forest for the trees.

Then I met another woman in one of the bars (Continued on page 144)

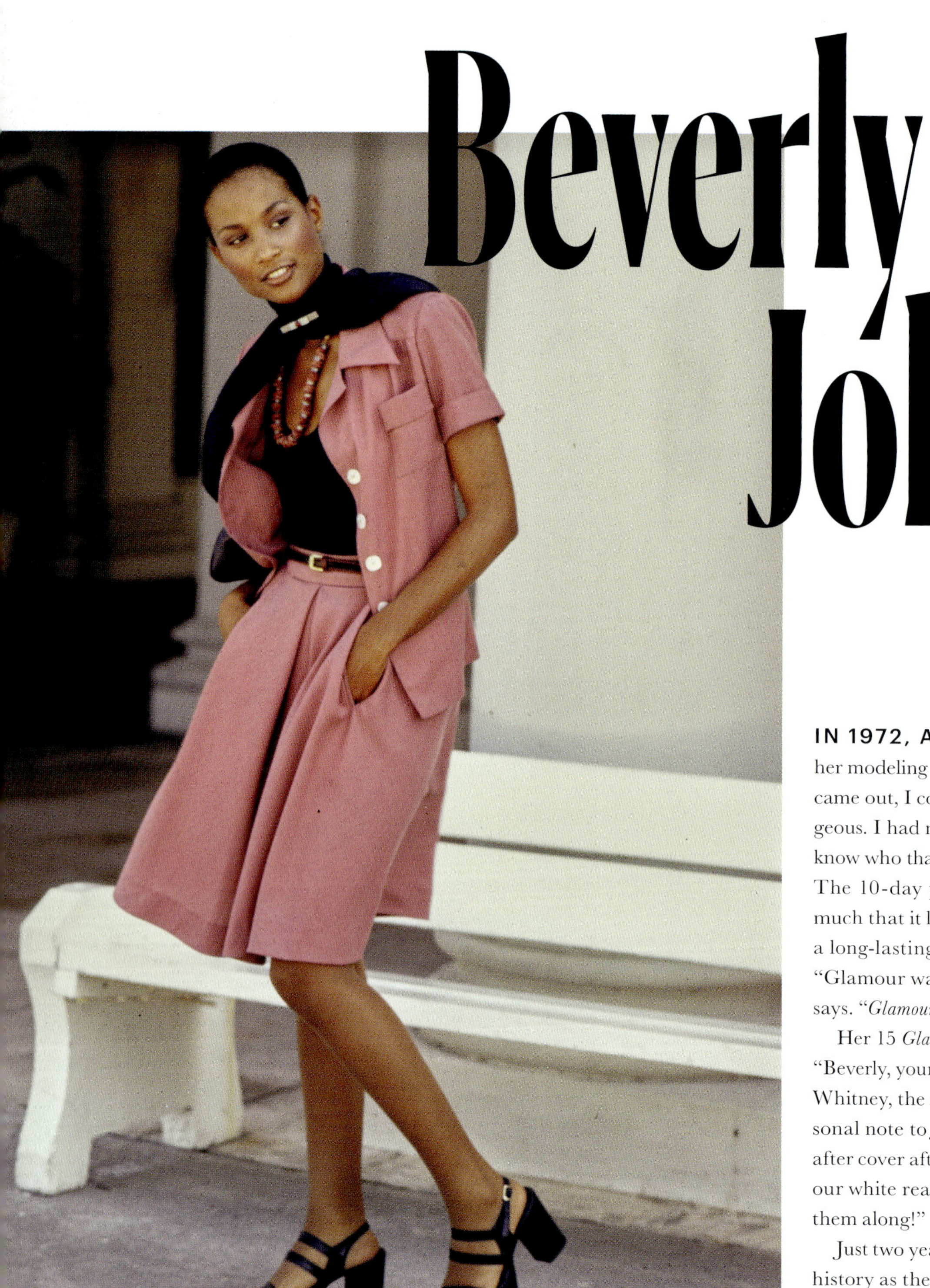

Beverly Johnson

IN 1972, A THEN 20-YEAR-OLD Beverly Johnson made her modeling debut in *Glamour*'s March issue. "When the magazine came out, I could not believe it," she says. "The pictures were gorgeous. I had no idea I was gorgeous…. I was blown away. I didn't know who that was." The world wanted to know who she was too: The 10-day photo shoot and cover resonated with readers so much that it launched her career and became the foundation for a long-lasting partnership between Johnson and the magazine. "Glamour was where I was born and where I grew up," Johnson says. "*Glamour* made me who I am."

Her 15 *Glamour* covers did more than just show the latest styles. "Beverly, your covers always meant something special to me," Ruth Whitney, the magazine's editor in chief at the time, wrote in a personal note to Johnson upon her retirement. "Your face on cover after cover after cover really did finally change the way our white readers thought of Black [women]. Thanks for helping them along!"

Just two years after her debut in *Glamour*, in 1974, Johnson made history as the first Black model to appear on the cover of *Vogue* in the publication's then 82-year history. Here, she looks back on the photo shoot that started it all. ➡

↑

This is one of Johnson's favorite images, captured at the Breakers Hotel in Palm Beach, Florida. *Photographed by Mike Reinhardt, March 1974.*

→

Johnson in profile. *Photographed by Mike Reinhardt, October 1971.*

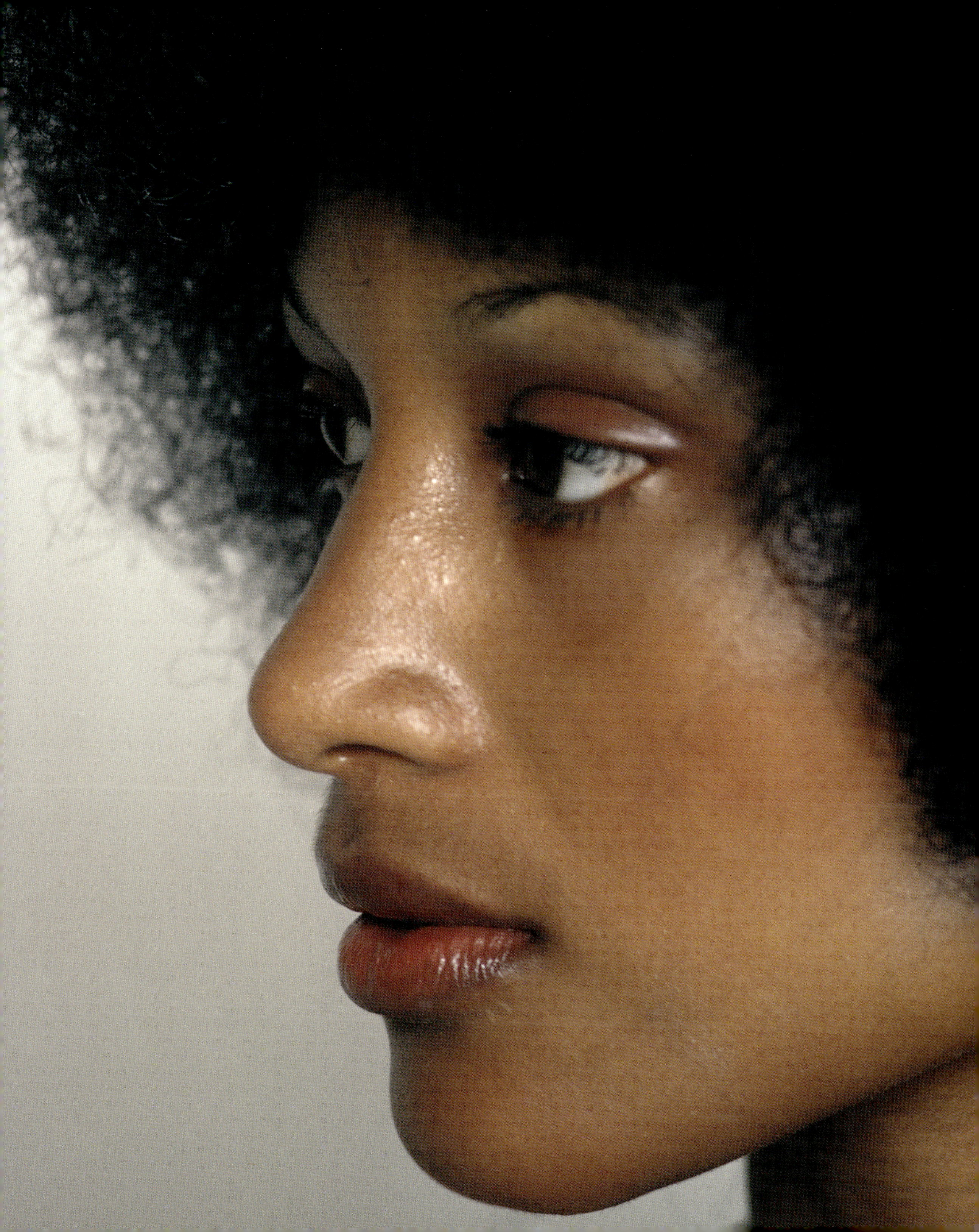

" My whole life and career started with *Glamour* magazine. Before she retired, Ruth Whitney put a book together with all my covers in it. She inscribed, and I will ad-lib here, 'I want to thank you because cover after cover after cover after cover really did bring our white readers around.' I'm not sentimental. I don't have my *Vogue* cover. I don't have the magazines I've been in. But I kept that book, because it meant so much to me. Ruth Whitney was, for me, an icon and a mentor. Someone who was one of my guardian angels, actually.

Glamour used to mail out questionnaires and ask, 'Would you like to live next door to her? Would you like to be her friend?' And the white southerners said, 'I would like to be her.'

I had to convince my parents to let me go to New York to model—my mother went against my father's wishes and took me. We called a contact that my former manager at a clothing store had given me, and she called Glamour. That's how I got the appointment. My mom and I sat in the lobby all day. At one point they had me take a typing test, because even if I didn't become a model I could still do that as a part-time job. I went in there and typed 'the brown cow' or whatever, and they said, 'Nope, you can't type.'

Eventually, at like 5:30 p.m., editorial director Alex Liberman came out and took me back for my casting. After that a woman told my mother, 'We want to take your daughter on a 10-day trip for *Glamour* magazine to Fire Island.' And that's how it started. I looked at my mother and said, 'I told you so.' I was naive and heady. My brothers and sisters said, 'They chose you? Did you tell them you have better-looking siblings at home?' But I was over the moon.

I remember the shoot in Fire Island like it was yesterday. And when the magazine came out, I could not believe it. The pictures were gorgeous. I had no idea I was gorgeous.

I was studying criminal justice at Northeastern at the time because I wanted to be a lawyer, but I got the check from Glamour for $300, and I nearly fainted. My father made $100 a week, so $300 was like $300 million to me. I took the magazine and the check to my dean and said, 'Something has happened.' I was supposed to work at a precinct for my work semester, but I asked him, 'Can I model instead?' He said, 'Go ahead.' Eventually, my interest in becoming a lawyer just kind of petered out. One night I was on the train and saw my professor and thought, 'Oh man, I haven't been there in I don't know how long.' I realized I had to make a decision.

Eileen Ford, the co-founder of Ford Models, had told me, '99.9% of the models leave the business broke. Don't be one of them.' I took that to heart. A model's career then was four, five years tops. So I went into it thinking about what I was going to do after modeling.

I'm very proud of myself. Sometimes I have to have a talk with myself and say, 'Remember who you are, Beverly.' And I call Glamour my home because that's where I was on Thanksgiving, through Christmas, through New Year's. We were always on trips, and they became my family. They treated me so well. Glamour was where I was born and where I grew up. And besides that, it was a great magazine. They were really in touch with what was going on. *Glamour* made me who I am. →

Beverly Johnson.
*Photographed by
Mike Reinhardt,
December 1972.*

<hr>

ICONIC COVERS

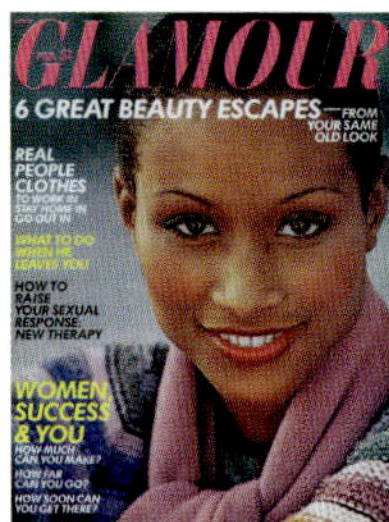

February 1975

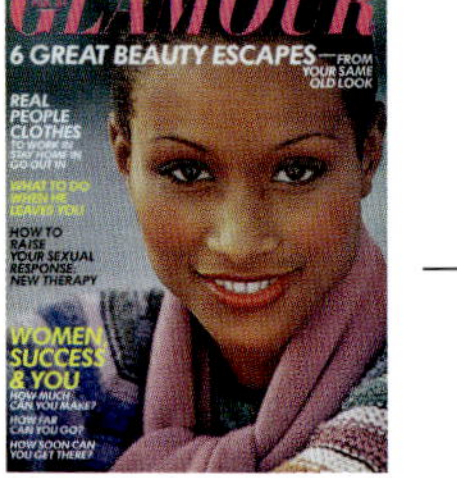

December 1976

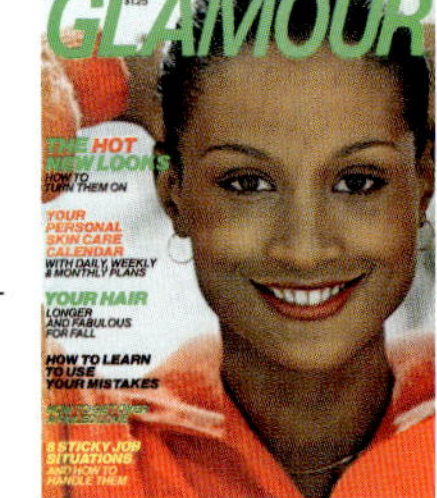

October 1977

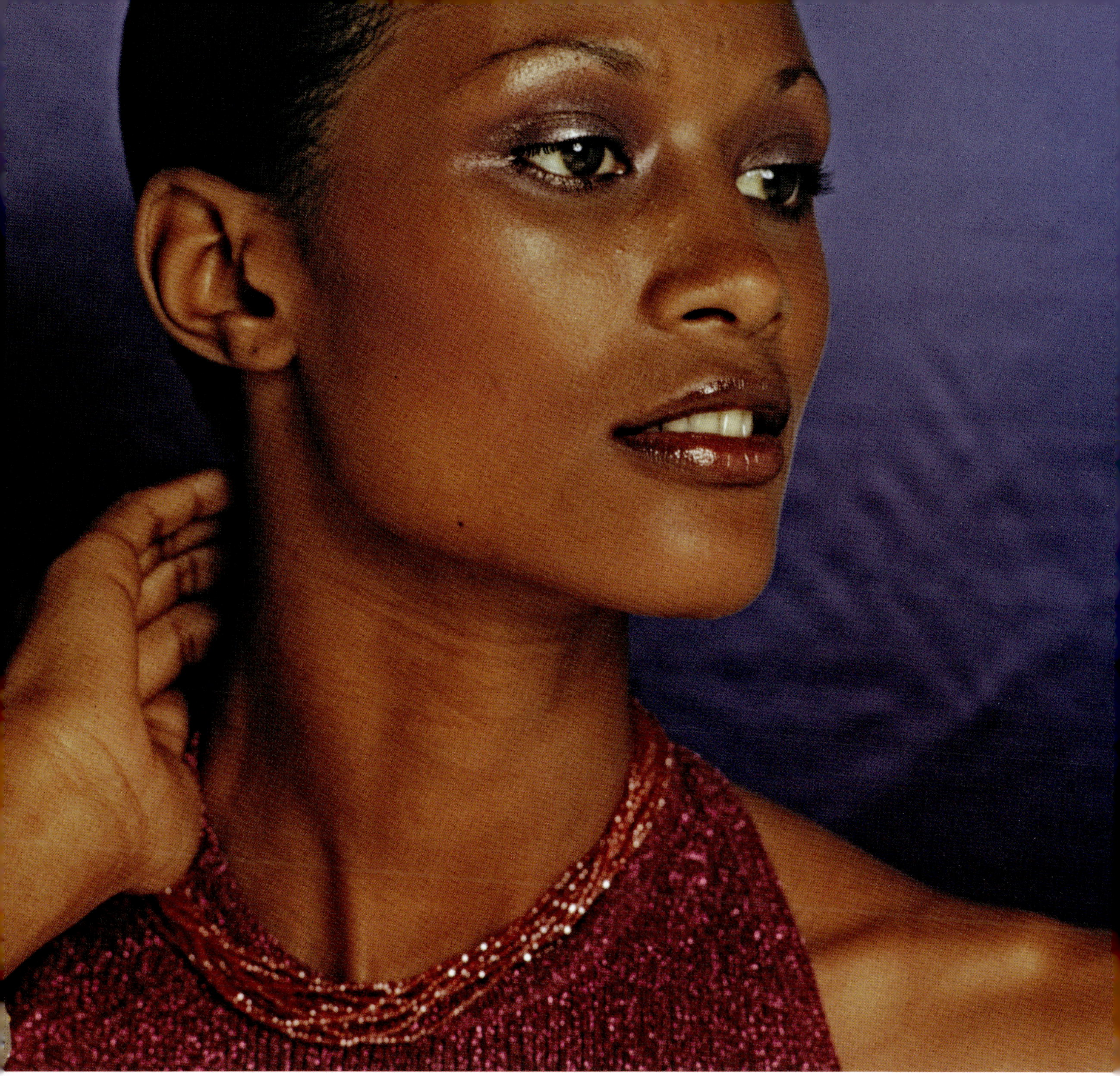

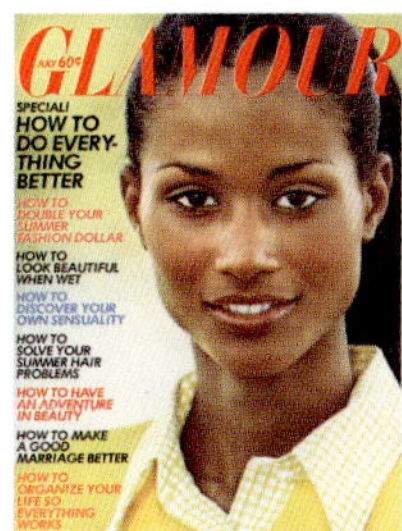

July 1972

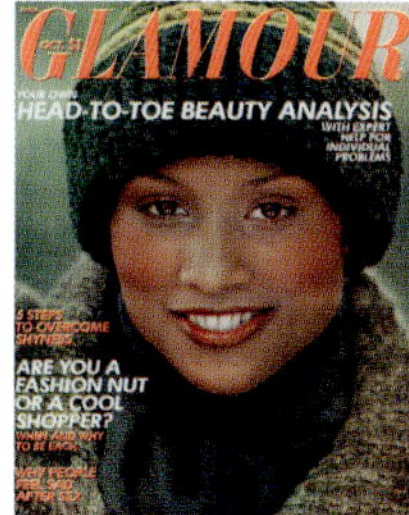

October 1975

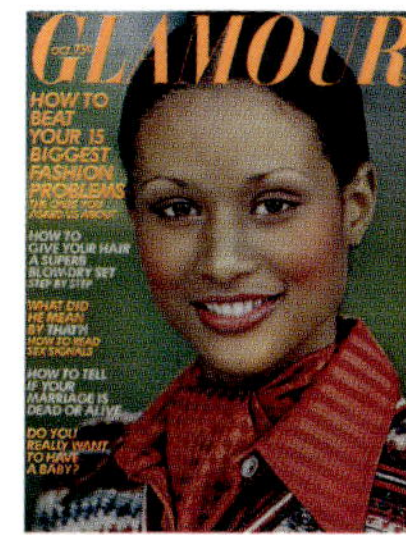

October 1973

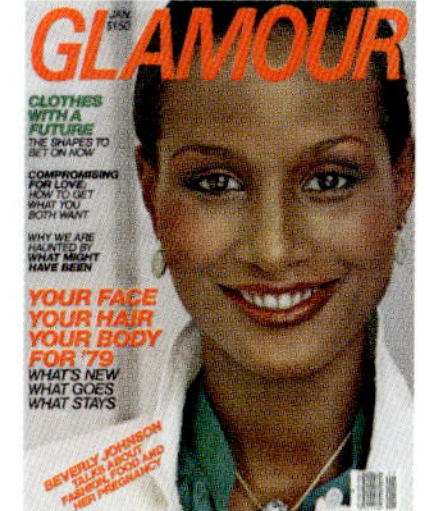

January 1979

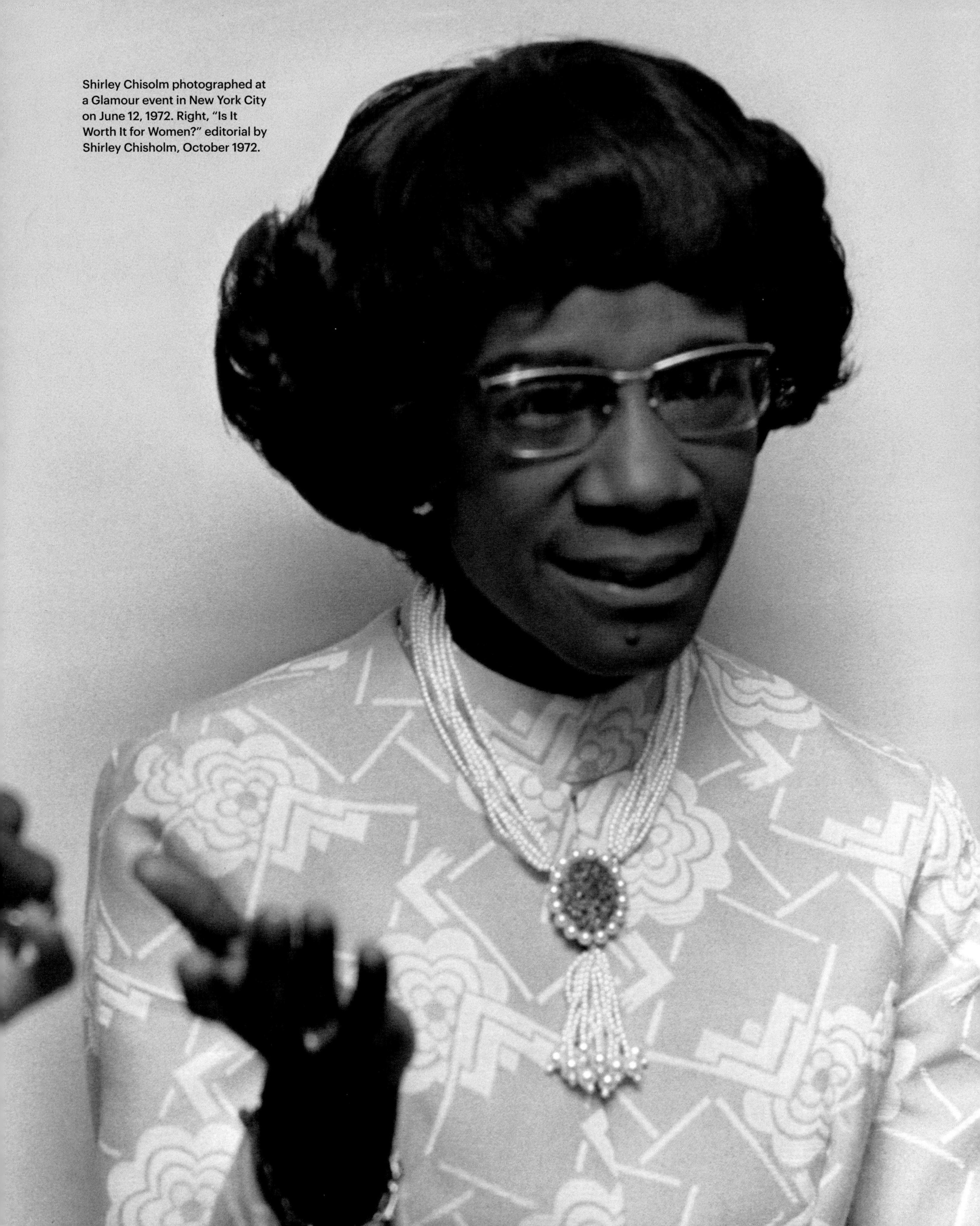

Shirley Chisolm photographed at a Glamour event in New York City on June 12, 1972. Right, "Is It Worth It for Women?" editorial by Shirley Chisholm, October 1972.

Is it WORTH IT for women?

BY SHIRLEY CHISHOLM

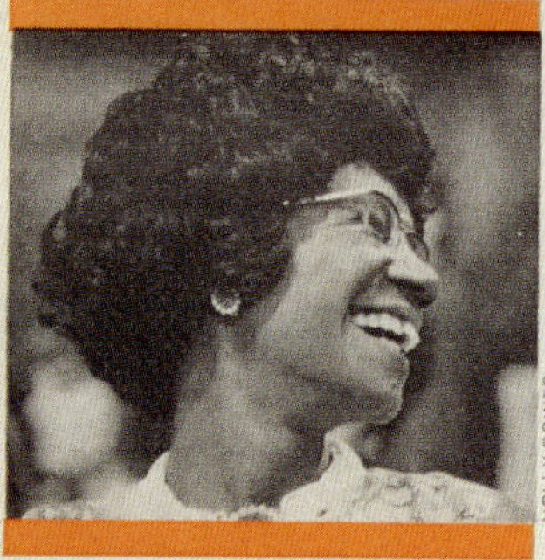

We have waited on the gentlemen for so long in this country. But the gentlemen are hooked into many things that have nothing to do with human values. The women are going to have to take up the issues of man's humanity to man.

I am a black person. And I am a woman. I belong to two segments of society which have never been given any importance in the decision-making process in government.

In the beginning of the campaign many people laughed at me for seeking the nomination for the Presidency, particularly the gentlemen. They thought I was half crazy. But despite the tremendous expenditure of time and energy, it was certainly worth it.

I have blazed a trail, and that was my intention. I was, am, and always will be, a catalyst for change. And as more and more women begin to participate in the political process, we will see the visible effect of that change.

Women participated in the Democratic convention in a way that has *never* been seen before in this country. Had there been few women at the con-

vention, there is no doubt that the issues of Vietnam, abortion and minimum income would have been given only cursory attention. Women, perhaps by virtue of their prescribed role in our society, by virtue of the fact that they are much more closely attached to children and to the social relationships in the family, tend to have more perseverance, more tolerance, more concern for the problems of humanity.

It is true that the abortion plank, for example, was voted down. But the issue had to be raised. As long as you have a civilized society, you're going to have abortions. Why not make them available and acceptable to all people and stop the butchering of poor women who can only afford to go to quacks? It takes women to talk about an issue like this because they're closer to it, they have the experience of it.

From the standpoint of a politician, I knew the plank would be voted down. It is too controversial, too hot to handle, and if you are going to be President of this country, you cannot alienate so many segments of the population. And many of the women were bitter about this and other matters—they felt they had been sold out when they learned of machinations at the convention by the staff of a candidate who was sympathetic to their causes. But I think they learned a valuable lesson: that politics is the art of compromise. Living is the art of compromise.

Despite the necessity for compromise, women can bring a sorely needed morality to politics. If a woman is strong enough, she will determine for herself at what level she is going to compromise, and not permit herself to be the tool of others, to be manipulated like so many politicians in this country who are like

puppets on a string. Every day in Congress I see politicians who may as well not have a brain; they do not operate on the basis of ability and principle, but let themselves be used by bosses and country leaders.

Yes, women will have to learn that sometimes we have to make decisions that we don't exactly like. But this is the real world, and a woman who enters the political arena must be very strong and have confidence in herself so that she can make decisions on the basis of her *own* judgment and is prepared to live with them.

No matter who is elected President (and I personally believe that Senator McGovern is a fine and decent man, with real sympathy for the issues women are concerned with), nothing will stop the women's movement in America. It cannot be stopped. As I traveled around the country, speaking to all kinds of women's groups, from rural housewives to urban radicals, I have seen that *all* women are beginning to realize that they have dimensions no one has thus far taken into consideration.

As they realize their power, I am convinced women will be a great force for change. They will begin to shake up some of the old traditions which no longer hold the answers to the problems that confront us.

But when they begin to move, when they begin to beg, when they begin to plead for this country, they will be labeled everything but children of God. They have to determine whether or not they have the strength and the stamina to take the humiliations and defeats that will surely come from time to time. And I believe that they have courage, commitment, concern and compassion. And they will do it.

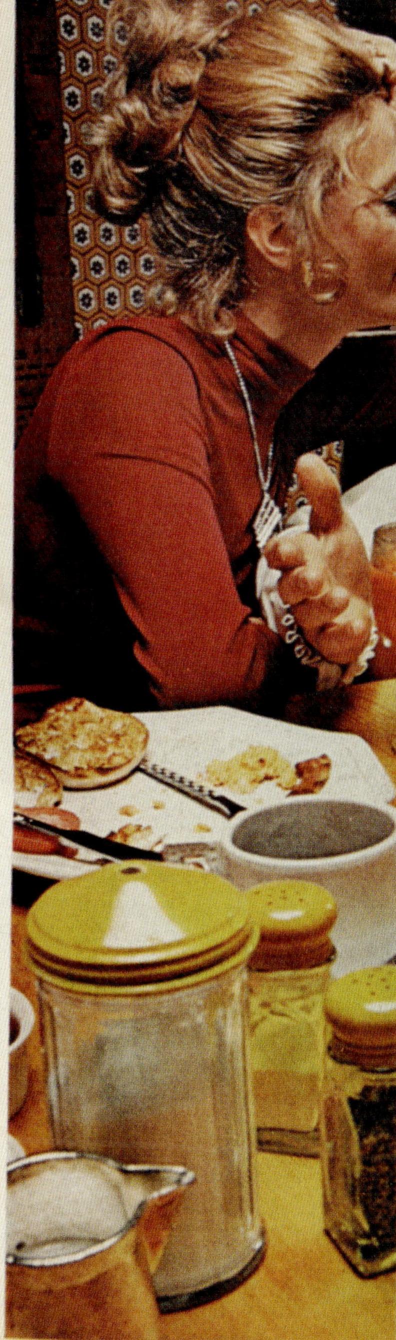

IN 1968, SHIRLEY CHISHOLM became the first Black woman elected to Congress, and represented New York's 12th Congressional District for seven terms from 1969 to 1983. In 1972, she became the first Black candidate to seek the nomination for President of the United States from one of the two major political parties, and the first woman to seek it from the Democratic party. But she faced extraordinary discrimination: She was blocked from taking part in televised debates, and only after taking legal action was she permitted to make one speech. Chisholm passed away in 2005, but President Obama posthumously awarded her the Presidential Medal of Freedom in 2015 for her extraordinary contribution to politics and unwavering commitment to justice. In the powerful editorial above from October 1972, Chisholm recounts the experience of her presidential run.

Models on the cover of *Glamour* (and other women's magazines) were nothing new. But models as superstars, with national fame and acclaim? That was born in this era. Here are some of *Glamour*'s most significant cover stars.

Top left, Mia Farrow the same year she starred in *Rosemary's Baby,* October 1968.

Top right, Beverly Johnson on the first of her 15 *Glamour* covers, March 1972.

Bottom left, Cybill Shepherd—who appeared on 17 *Glamour* covers— the same year that film director Peter Bogdanovich spotted her and cast her in the *The Last Picture Show,* April 1970.

Bottom right, supermodel Patti Hansen, who appeared in *Glamour* regularly throughout the '70s, November 1973.

Opposite, Cheryl Tiegs on one of her 24 *Glamour* covers, February 1972.

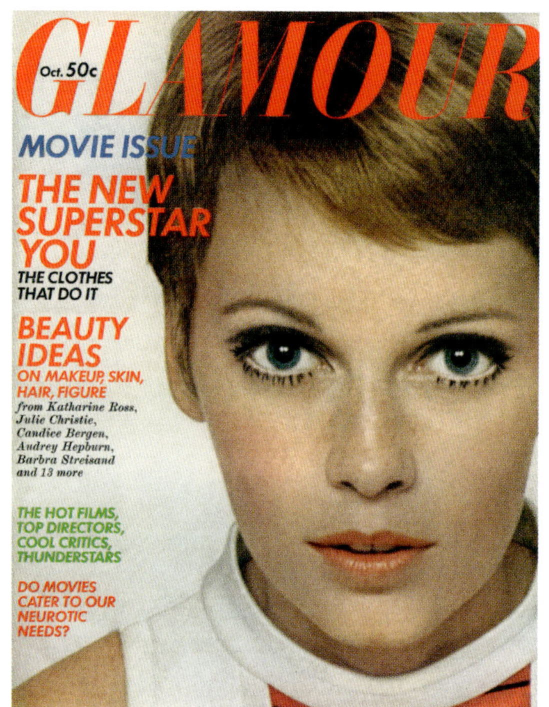

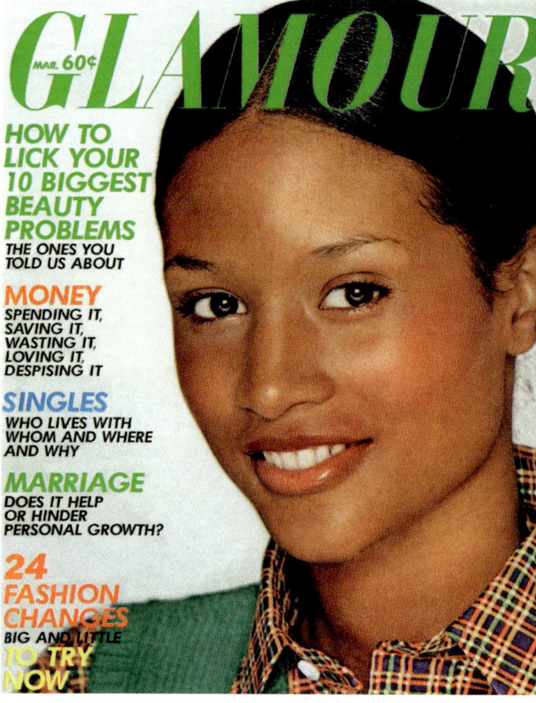

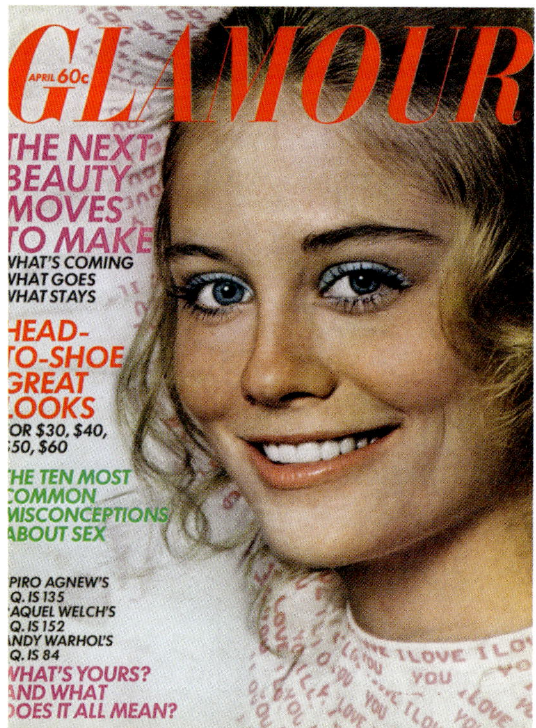

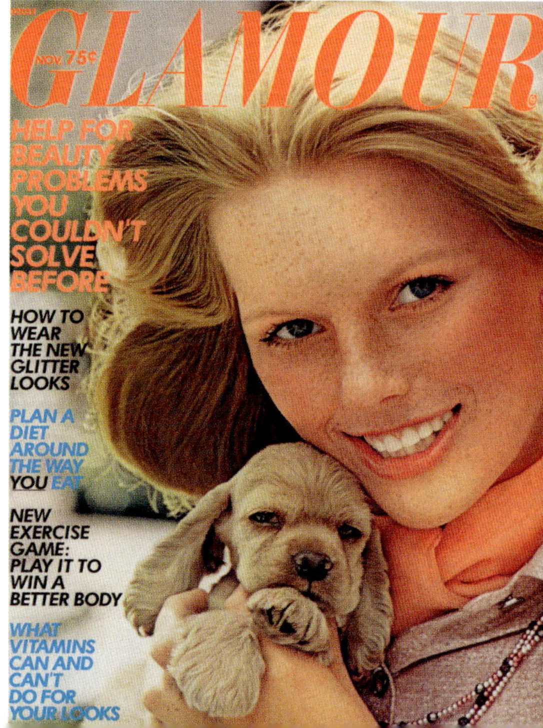

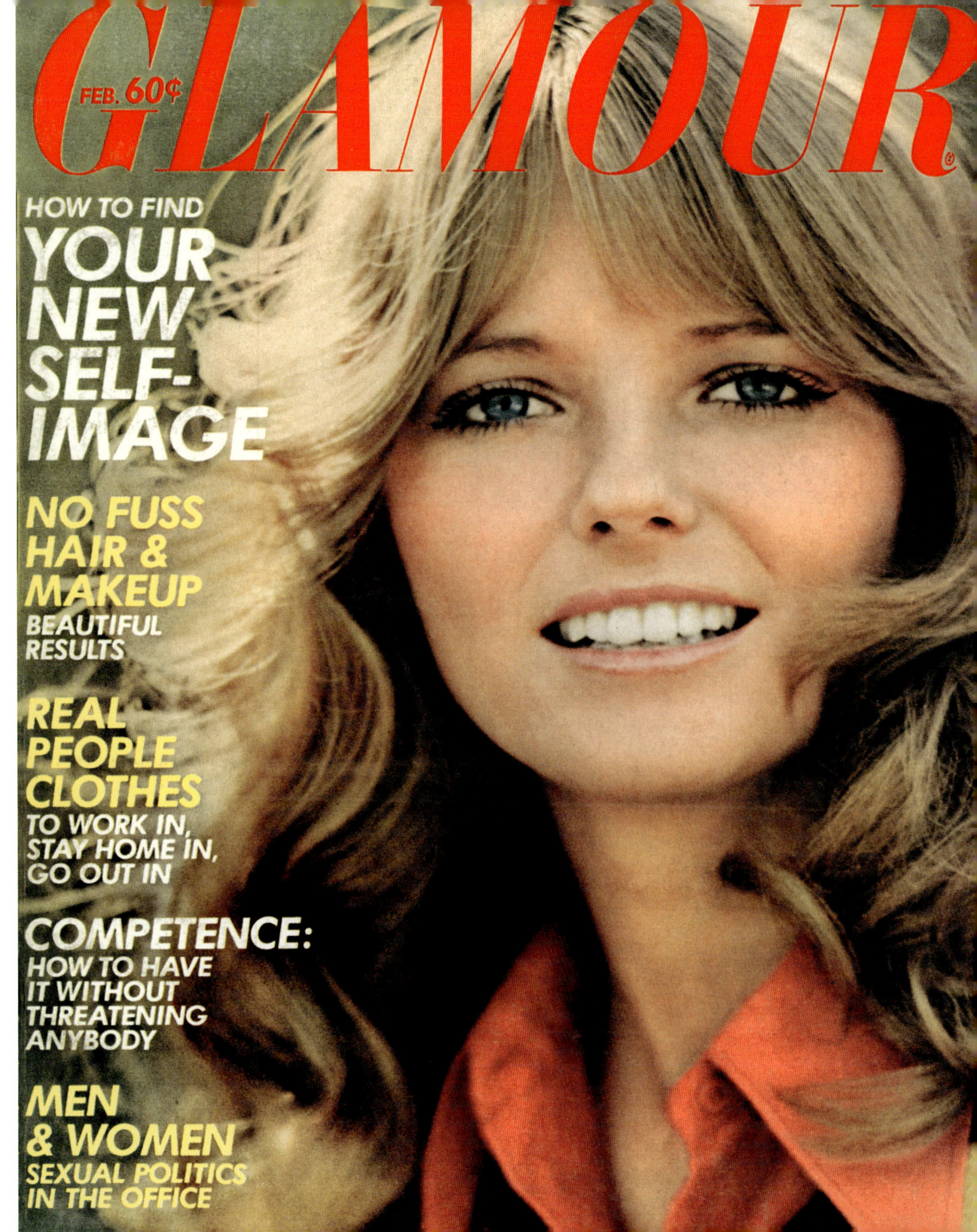

GLAMOUR
FEB. 60¢
HOW TO FIND
YOUR NEW SELF-IMAGE
NO FUSS HAIR & MAKEUP
BEAUTIFUL RESULTS
REAL PEOPLE CLOTHES
TO WORK IN, STAY HOME IN, GO OUT IN
COMPETENCE:
HOW TO HAVE IT WITHOUT THREATENING ANYBODY
MEN & WOMEN
SEXUAL POLITICS IN THE OFFICE

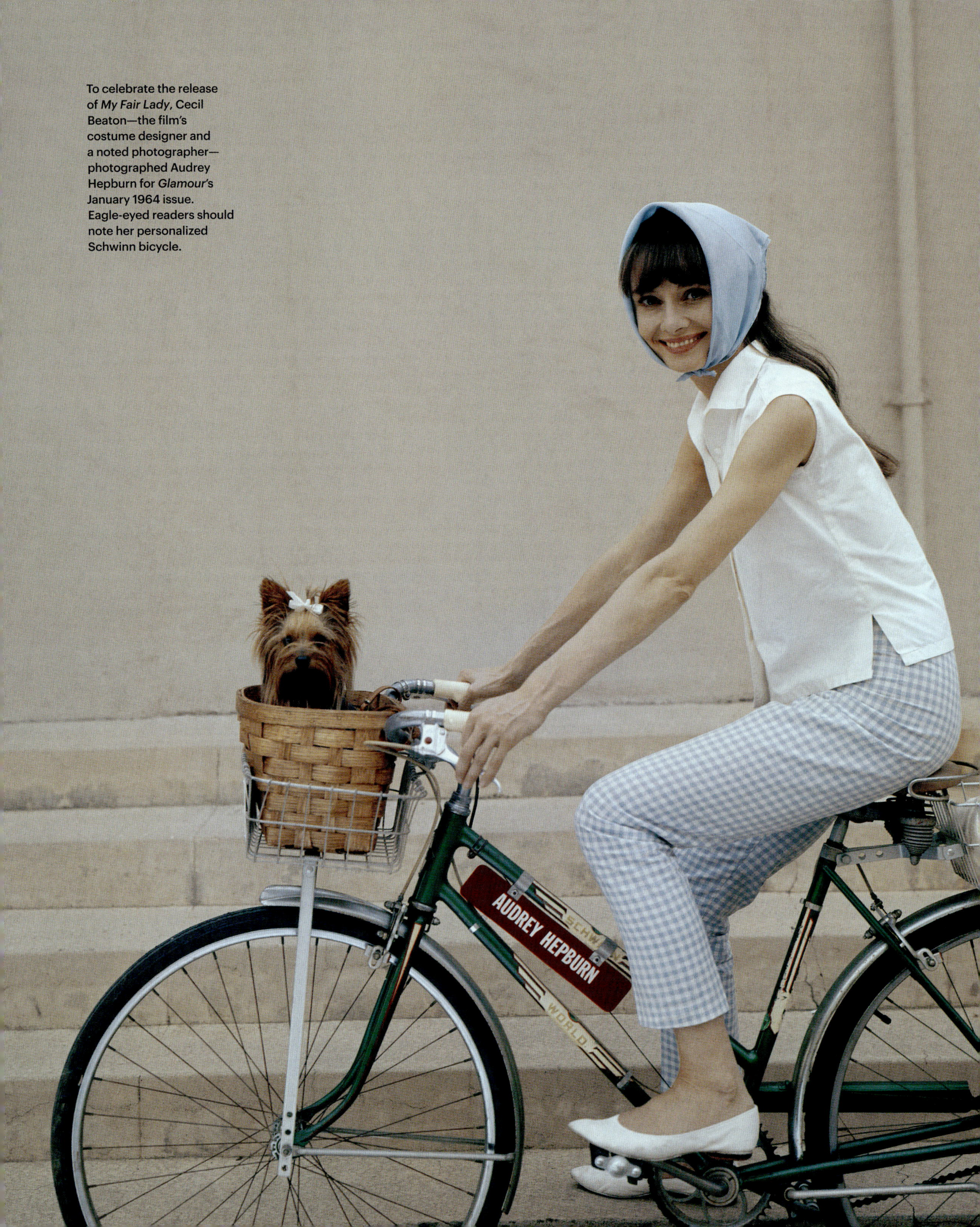

To celebrate the release of *My Fair Lady*, Cecil Beaton—the film's costume designer and a noted photographer—photographed Audrey Hepburn for *Glamour*'s January 1964 issue. Eagle-eyed readers should note her personalized Schwinn bicycle.

While supermodels like Beverly Johnson graced the cover of *Glamour* in this era, some of the world's most important and influential actors, singers, and artists were photographed for the inside of the magazine, too. Here are some of the most iconic.

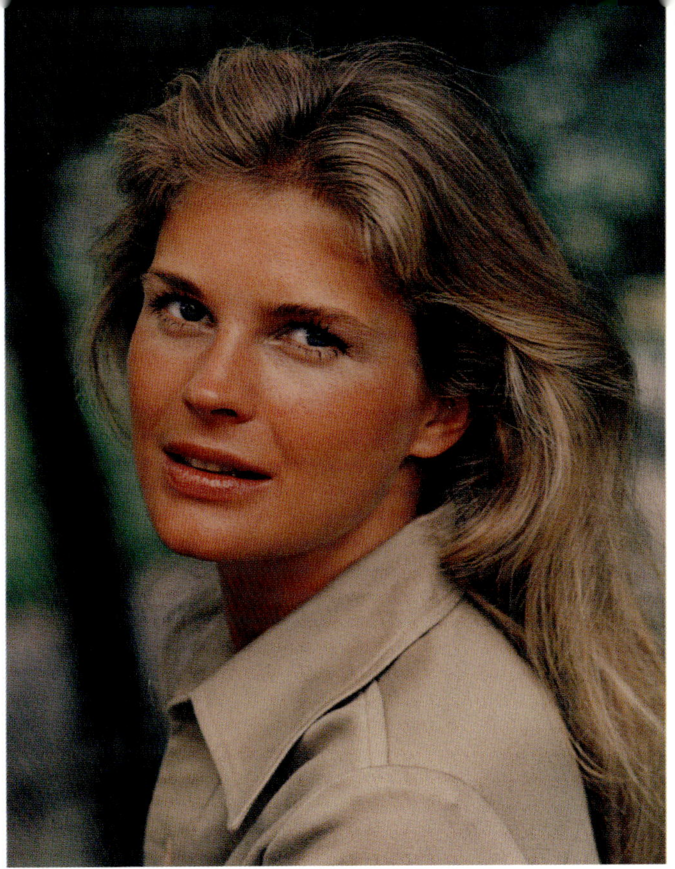

Candice Bergen had just starred in the Mike Nichols film *Carnal Knowledge* when she appeared in *Glamour* celebrating her natural beauty. "She hates to take the time even for mascara," the magazine reported. Her big beauty tip to readers? "A professional cleansing treatment including face steaming" for her skin. *Photographed by William Connors, November 1971.*

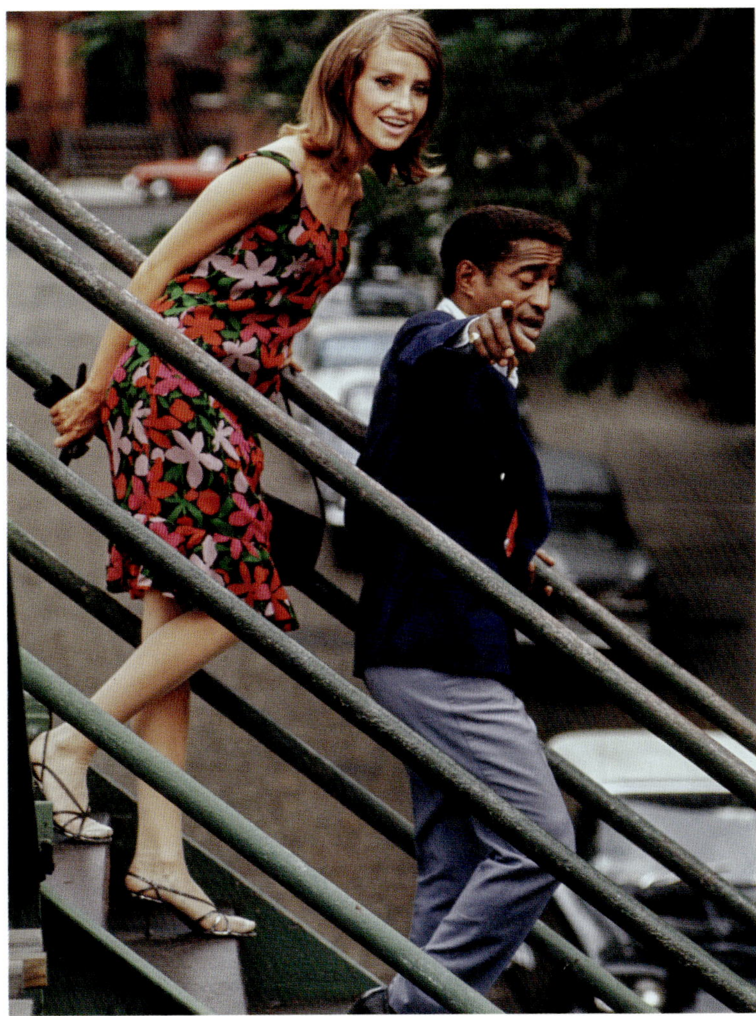

"Broadway's 'Golden Boy' is the golden boy of the entertainment world, too," raved the magazine about **Sammy Davis Jr.** *Photographed by Jerry Schatzberg, November 1964.*

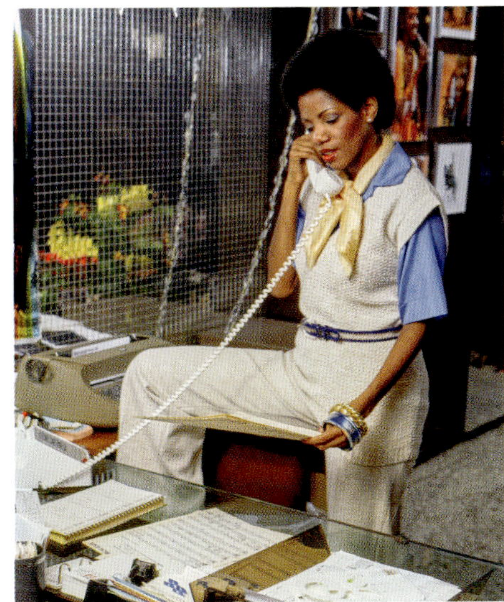

Singer Melba Moore at the Hit Factory recording studio in New York City. *Photographed by William Connors, April 1977.*

OUT ON YOUR OWN

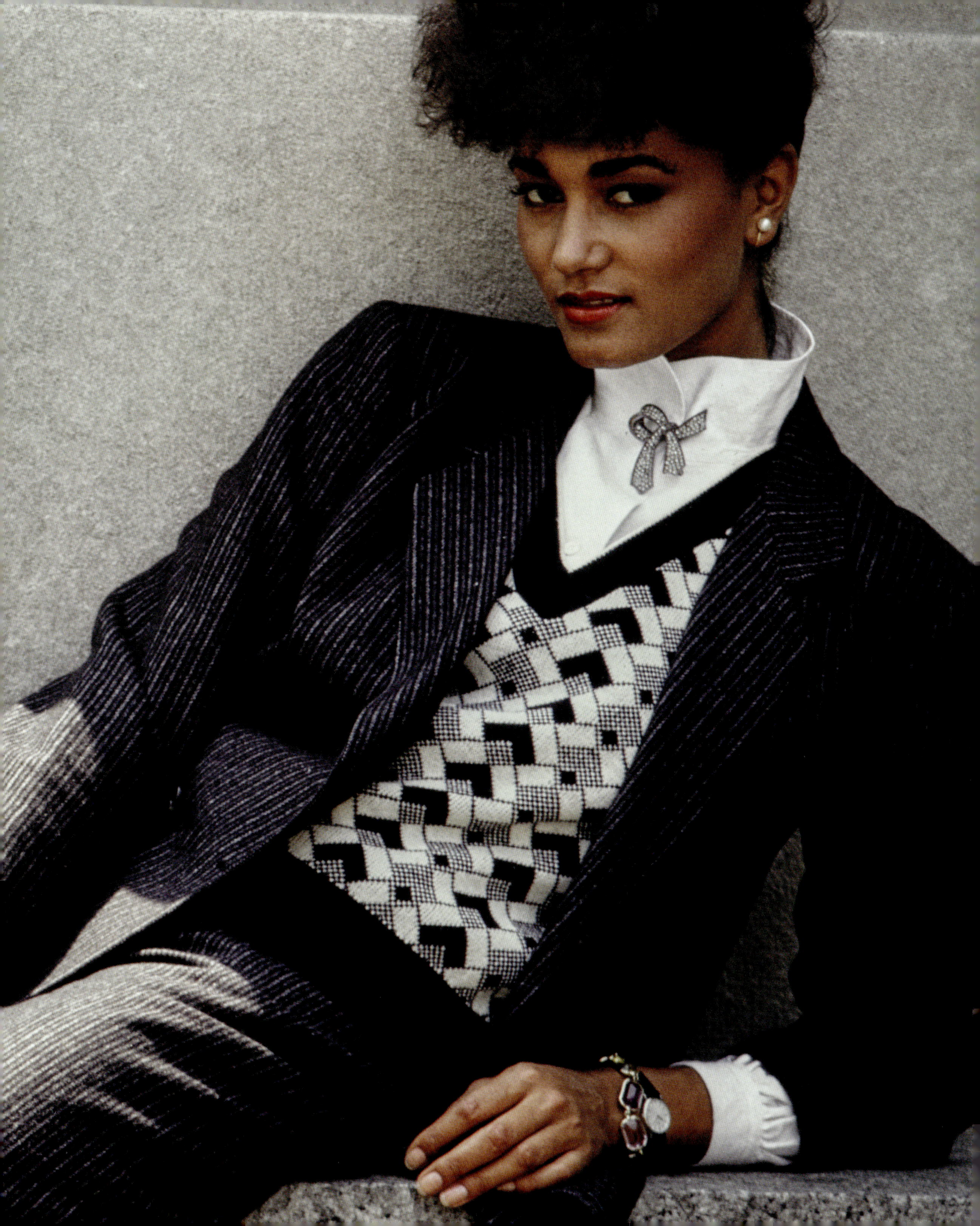

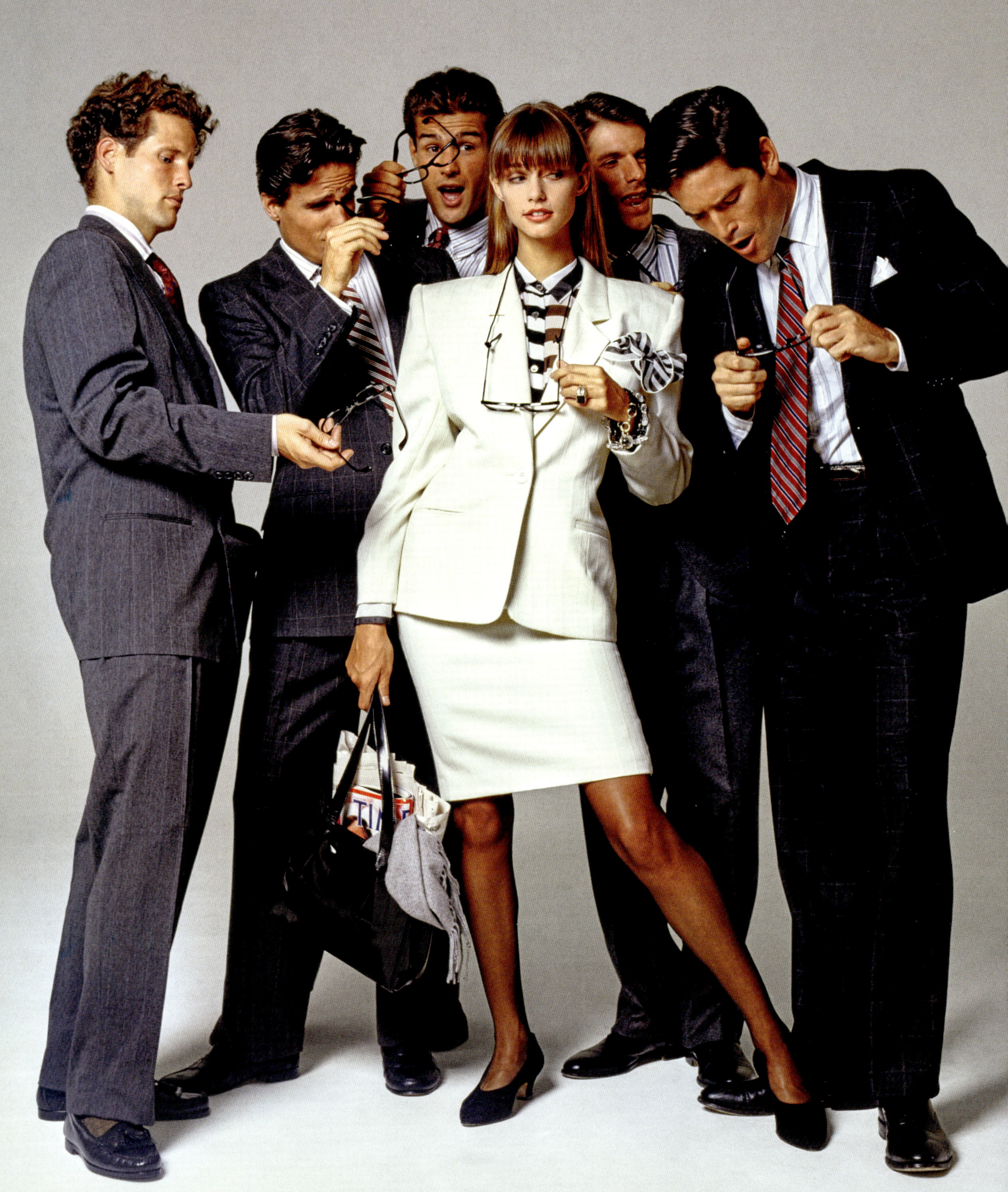

Glamour leaped into the 1980s with a fierce new attitude. Women now controlled their reproductive rights, after the decision in *Roe v. Wade.*

WITH THE PASSAGE OF THE EQUAL CREDIT OPPORTUNITY ACT of 1974, which prohibited lending discrimination based on sex or marital status, they controlled their financial rights, too. Finally, women could get their own credit cards and mortgages. This was the moment for *Glamour*'s readers to strike out on their own and discover independence like they'd never known before. The magazine published articles about women becoming single mothers—or choosing not to have children at all—buying their own houses, maintaining their own cars, getting more out of their romantic and sexual relationships—in short, about women taking full control of their lives, with or without a partner. *Glamour* celebrated women's growing success in the workplace in the annual Outstanding Young Working Women competition, and in 1990 launched the now iconic Women of the Year Awards. It was a time of extraordinary promise, but also extraordinary reckoning. As women's power and influence grew, so did the urgent need to address some of the greatest injustices women experienced—in particular sexual harassment, assault, and rape, which for too long had gone unchecked and unprosecuted. For women to be able to live life fully and freely, these issues needed to be faced down, and *Glamour* led the way with powerful and uncompromising storytelling.

←

Model Roberta Chirko wears a white Norma Kamali skirt suit, surrounded by men in suits and ties. *Photographed by Alex Chatelain, December 1988.* **Previous page, a model reclines in a pinstripe Esprit blazer and pants.** *Photographed by George Barkentin, September 1982.*

THE START OF THE DECADE SAW *GLAMOUR* SPOTLIGHTING WOMEN forging their own paths, whether demonstrating how to make life decisions solo or "How to travel alone—and like it." *Glamour* had introduced "On Your Own," a monthly column "reflecting your growing independence," and, as the '80s and '90s progressed, this commitment to supporting women's self-reliance really came into its own. A 1980 article, "A Mortgage Without a Man," detailed the importance of the Equal Credit Opportunity Act, noting that "by the end of this year single women will have bought ten percent of the homes sold, compared with six percent in 1976," and that by 1984 women would head over a quarter of US households. This was a stunning shift that reflected women's changing roles and the freedom to no longer conform to societal rules. One example of this was the growing community of solo parents. In November 1982, a writer by the name of Linda Lee chronicled her decision to have a baby out of wedlock, with a married man who would not play a part in her child's upbringing. It was powerful, but at the time still provocative—a 1983 article in response argued against women having children outside of a partnership. But by the mid 1990s, *Glamour* had declared it "the decade of the single mother," noting in a 1997 article that "Almost one third of all births in the United States are to unmarried women, nearly twice as many as 20 years ago." Women were truly, in every sense, free to go it alone.

→

Shot for *Glamour*'s What They're Wearing style column, a woman on the street wears an "Outta My Way" graphic tee. *Photographed by Susan Kaufman, April 1990.*

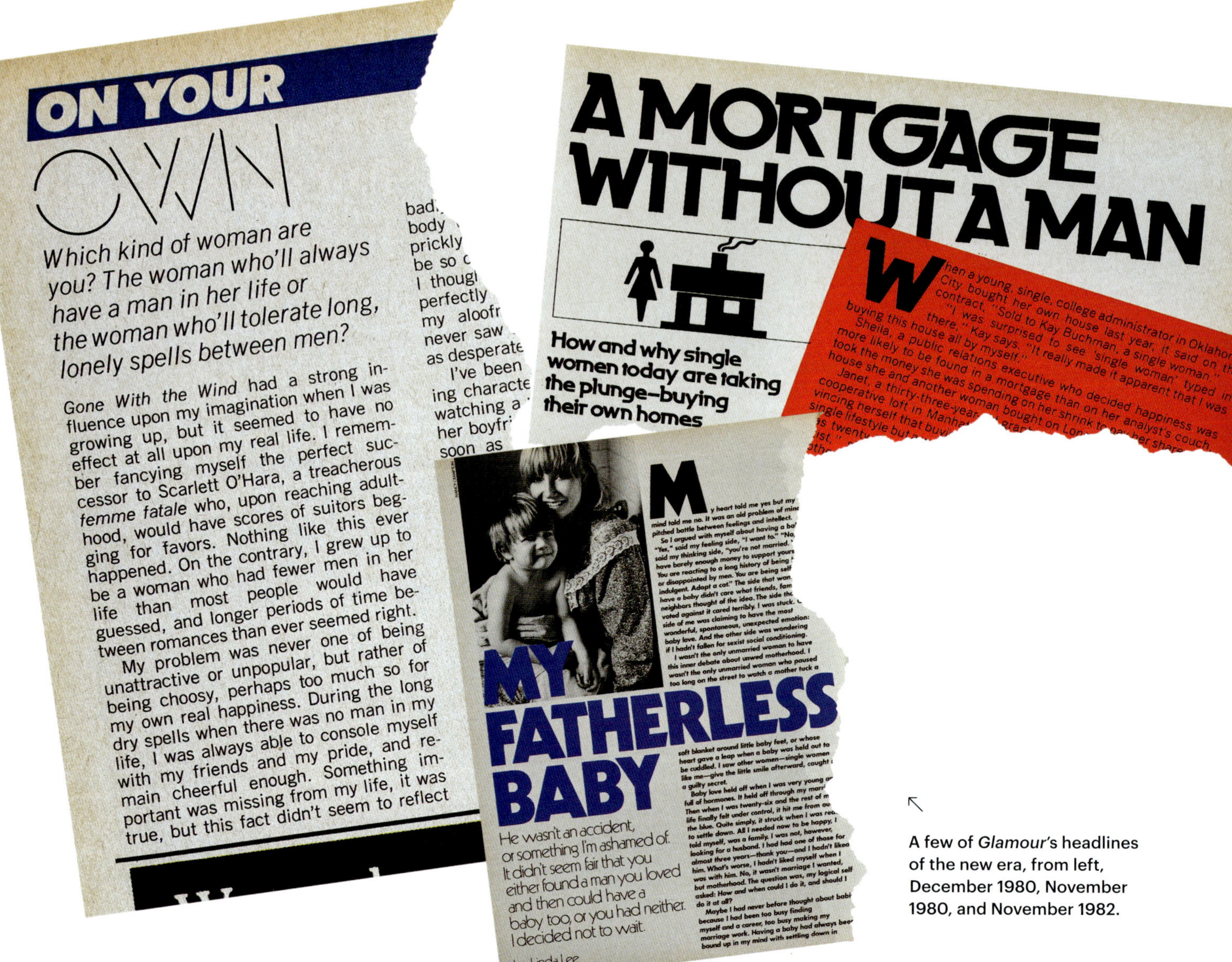

↖

A few of *Glamour*'s headlines of the new era, from left, December 1980, November 1980, and November 1982.

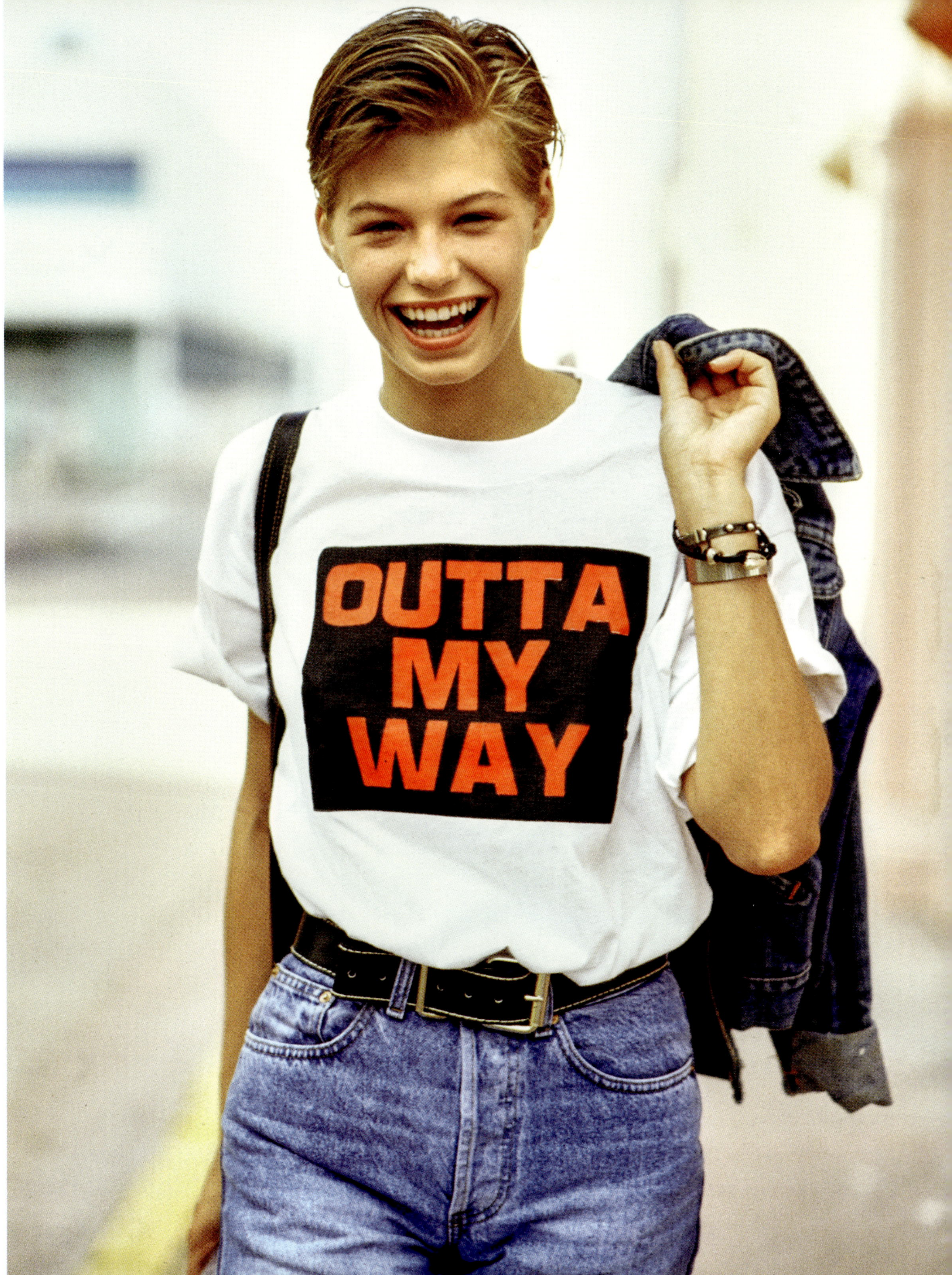
OUTTA
MY
WAY

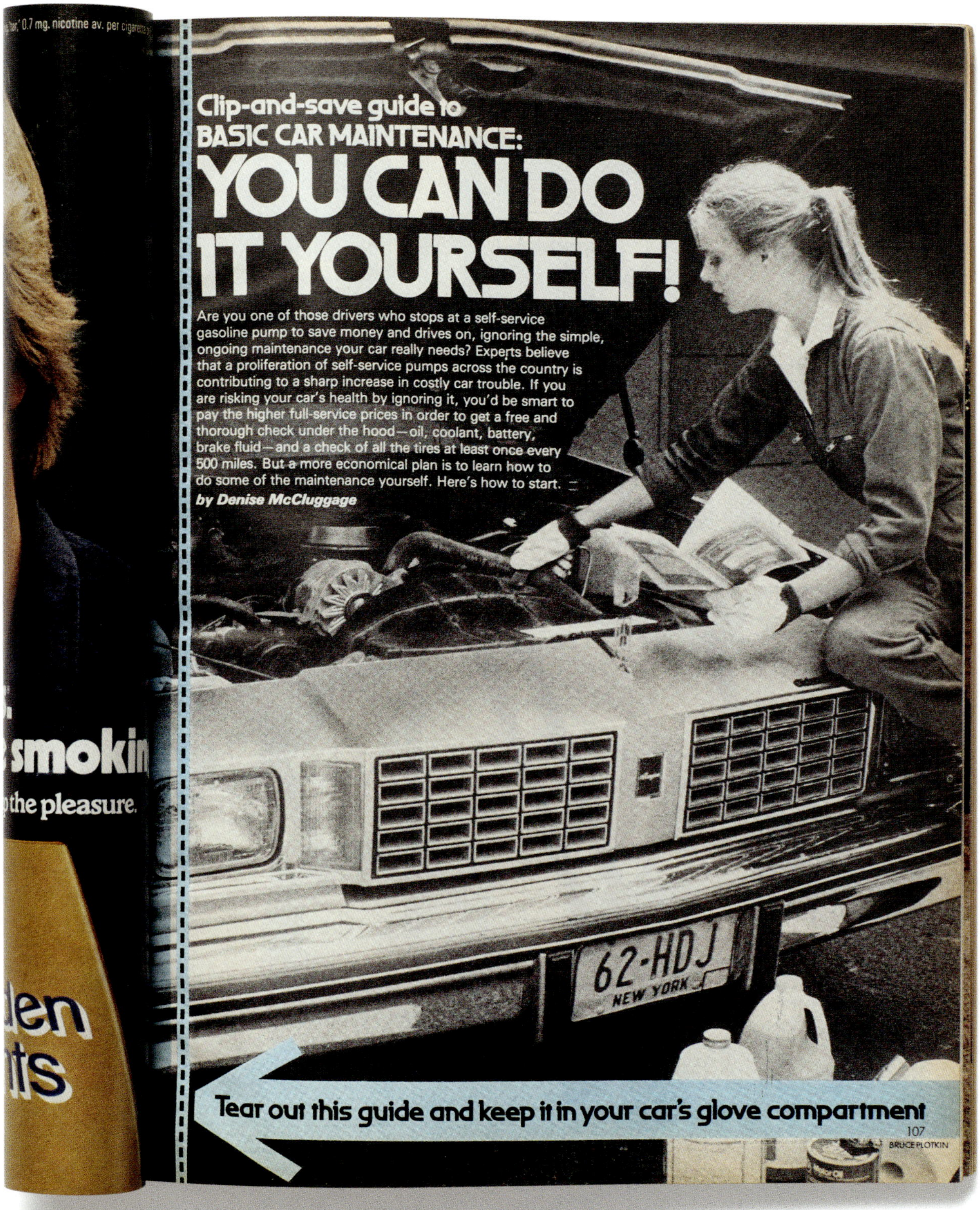

Clip-and-save guide to
BASIC CAR MAINTENANCE:
YOU CAN DO IT YOURSELF!

Are you one of those drivers who stops at a self-service gasoline pump to save money and drives on, ignoring the simple, ongoing maintenance your car really needs? Experts believe that a proliferation of self-service pumps across the country is contributing to a sharp increase in costly car trouble. If you are risking your car's health by ignoring it, you'd be smart to pay the higher full-service prices in order to get a free and thorough check under the hood—oil, coolant, battery, brake fluid—and a check of all the tires at least once every 500 miles. But a more economical plan is to learn how to do some of the maintenance yourself. Here's how to start. —
by Denise McCluggage

THE VERY SAME WOMAN who could now buy her own house, have her own credit card, travel alone, and raise a family on her own, should, of course, be able to buy and maintain her own car. This was a topic that *Glamour* took seriously. One of the more unusual footnotes in the magazine's history is the monthly car column that ran during the late 1970s and '80s. A survey published by Condé Nast (*Glamour*'s publisher) in 1986 found that 40 percent of new car purchases the year before had been by women—a 14 percent increase from 1980. *Glamour* made sure everything women needed to know was in the pages of the magazine—from buyer's guides to how to perform car maintenance alone.

↑

Tips from *Glamour*'s "Clip-and-save guide to Basic Car Maintenance," November 1980.

CAR BUYER'S GUIDE

The facts of OPEC have modified the images of success, luxury and high performance that were so typical of American cars in the '70s. The three cars below, test-driven by Denise McCluggage, Glamour's automotive consultant and author of Are You A Woman Driver?, are entering the '80s in a modified form with smaller appetites at the gas pump but with spirits undampened.

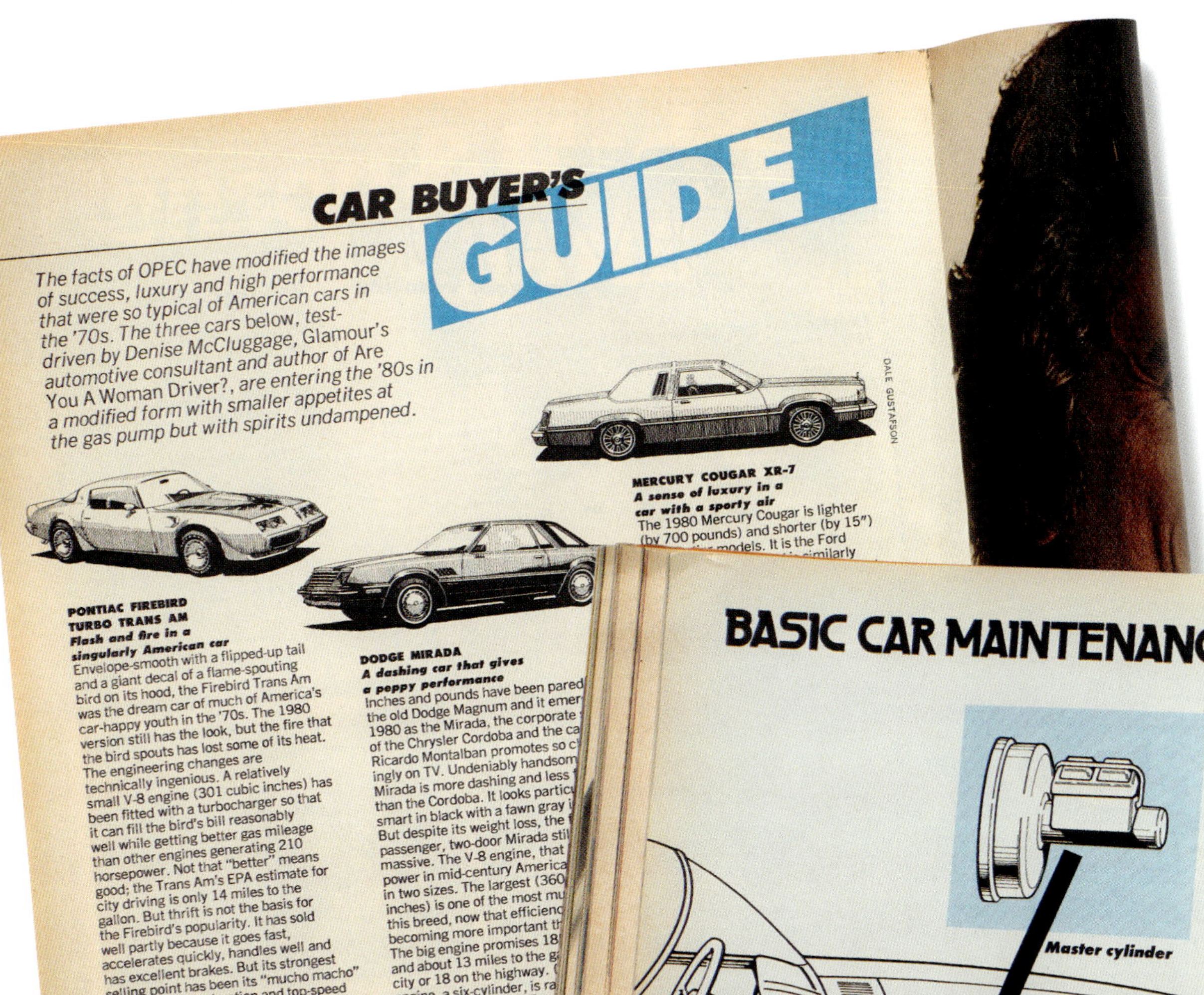

MERCURY COUGAR XR-7
A sense of luxury in a car with a sporty air
The 1980 Mercury Cougar is lighter (by 700 pounds) and shorter (by 15") ... models. It is the Ford ... similarly

PONTIAC FIREBIRD TURBO TRANS AM
Flash and fire in a singularly American car
Envelope-smooth with a flipped-up tail and a giant decal of a flame-spouting bird on its hood, the Firebird Trans Am was the dream car of much of America's car-happy youth in the '70s. The 1980 version still has the look, but the fire that the bird spouts has lost some of its heat. The engineering changes are technically ingenious. A relatively small V-8 engine (301 cubic inches) has been fitted with a turbocharger so that it can fill the bird's bill reasonably well while getting better gas mileage than other engines generating 210 horsepower. Not that "better" means good; the Trans Am's EPA estimate for city driving is only 14 miles to the gallon. But thrift is not the basis for the Firebird's popularity. It has sold well partly because it goes fast, accelerates quickly, handles well and has excellent brakes. But its strongest selling point has been its "mucho macho" image. Now acceleration and top-speed are down a little, so it remains to be seen whether or not these 1980 changes will dull the Firebird's image. The turbocharger is an excellent one but is relatively quiet with no telltale whistle (or sudden surge of power) to announce its presence. This low profile might be a drawback to an image-conscious Firebird fan. And the Turbo Trans Am comes only with an automatic transmission (the V-6 Firebird has a three-speed manual). Going to automatic was the only way the Turbo V-8 could pass government emission standards. Even at that, it fails California's more stringent rules and will not be sold in that state. The Firebird is singularly American, representing all the flash and fire that has made "Detroit iron" so special.

- Length: 196.8" Width: 73" Height: 49.3" Wheelbase: 108.2"
- *Gas mileage: 16 mpg
- **Price: $7,305 to $11,000

DODGE MIRADA
A dashing car that gives a peppy performance
Inches and pounds have been pared ... the old Dodge Magnum and it emer... 1980 as the Mirada, the corporate ... of the Chrysler Cordoba and the ca... Ricardo Montalban promotes so c... ingly on TV. Undeniably handsom... Mirada is more dashing and less ... than the Cordoba. It looks partic... smart in black with a fawn gray ... But despite its weight loss, the ... passenger, two-door Mirada stil... massive. The V-8 engine, that ... power in mid-century America ... in two sizes. The largest (360... inches) is one of the most mu... this breed, now that efficienc... becoming more important th... The big engine promises 18... and about 13 miles to the g... city or 18 on the highway. ... engine, a six-cylinder, is ra... and 25 respectively.) To n... option on the Mirada is th... Sport Handling package t... suspension and makes th... more precisely. Unless y... floating softness of the ... suspension, you should ... I like what Dodge has d... three-speed automatic ... changing its ratios to ... performance at lower ... look great but are too ... not supportive enou... But then, that's look... from a driver's view ... of its stock-car-rac... the Mirada was rea... more of a passeng...

- Length: 209.5... Height: 53.1" Wh...
- *Gas mileage: 1...
- **Price: $6,668...

↑ Car reviews from *Glamour*'s automotive consultant, Denise McCluggage, May 1980.

BASIC CAR MAINTENANCE

GETTING T... YOUR CAR
If you learn be... owner's manu... car's oil dipstic... tery. If you lea... onstration, ma... out of your car... check your oil, b... tions: "Where w... let excess air ou... much?" Even th... this service, be p... stations dropped... when the gas li... streets and have ... Your next stop is ... hardware store wh... items: a tire pressu... oilcan spout so you... (buying oil off the ... buying it at a gas st...
Choose the type ... looks like a pencil... into your purse or ... less vulnerable to d... dial type. The two it... from $5 to $10.
Finally, buy some p... the car. You'll need ti... windows and headlig... your oil dipstick.

SELF-SERVICE, S...
● Getting gas. First, c... serves the kind of g... unleaded, regular or p... sure, check the sticke... your car to see if it or... and check your manua... Turn off your engine... cigarettes—gas fumes ... twist off your gas cap ar...

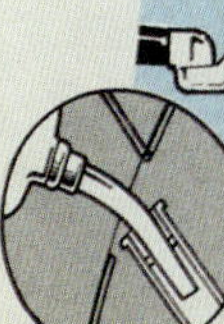

Outstanding Young Working Women

FROM 1975 TO 1990 *GLAMOUR* HONORED THE ACCOMPLISHMENTS of women in the workplace with its groundbreaking annual Outstanding Young Working Women Awards—how the magazine "for the girl with a job" had grown! The awards chronicled success stories, how women had achieved their careers, and what they spent their money on, as well as some of the compromises along the way—"Sleeping with my work instead of a man," having to "act like one of the boys," and postponing marriage and children. But this competition ended up becoming a marker of perhaps the greatest achievement of them all. So commonplace had outstanding working women become that after 15 years, the editors of the magazine decided they had outgrown the need for a competition. The opening words to the final celebration of outstanding working women acknowledged this: "In some ways, the history of *Glamour*'s competition has been the history of women at work—more and more women entering traditionally all-male fields. We decided to end the contest because there are not ten but ten thousand outstanding working women and their number increases daily. A woman seeking a role model needn't look in a magazine; she can just look down a hall." But the end of Outstanding Young Working Women was really just the beginning of another hugely significant chapter in the magazine's history. Just a few months later, the *Glamour* Women of the Year Awards were launched (see page 214). This time, it honored women—from celebrities to activists to business leaders—whose work accomplishments were so mighty they weren't just reshaping their fields, but the world.

Pictured, the winners of *Glamour*'s final Outstanding Young Working Women competition, March 1990.

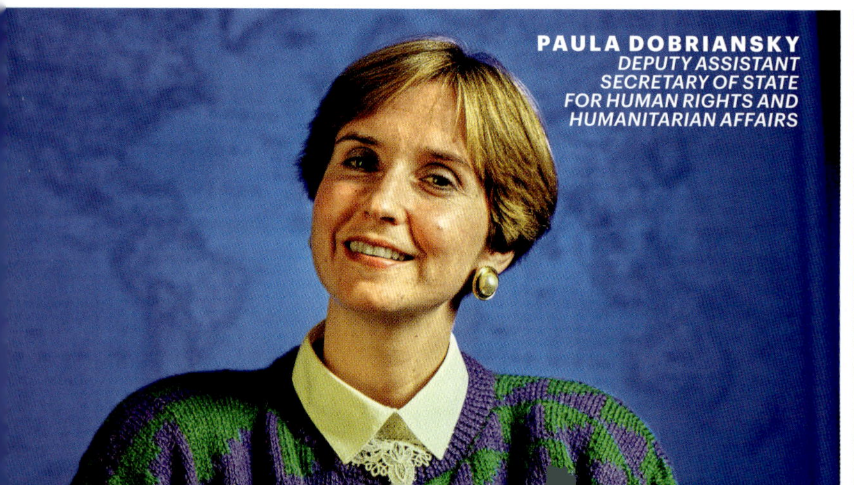

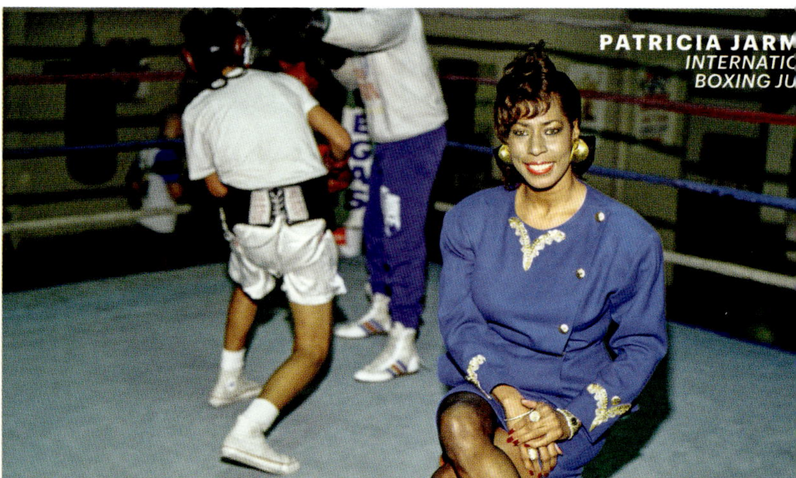

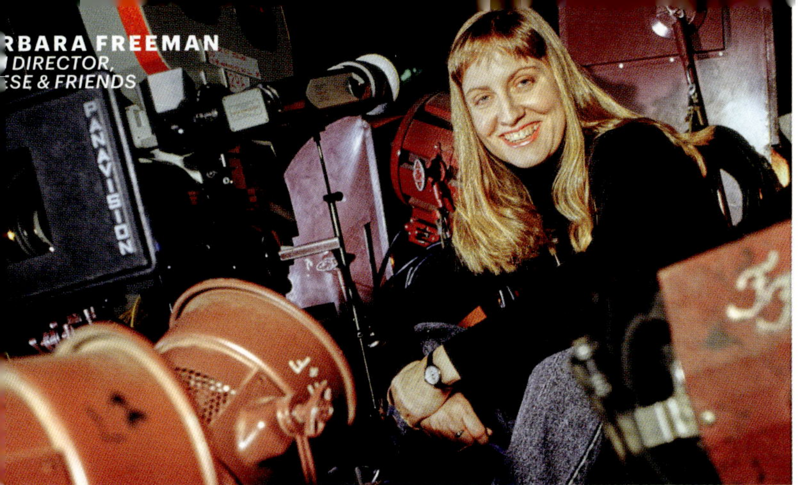

RBARA FREEMAN
DIRECTOR,
SE & FRIENDS

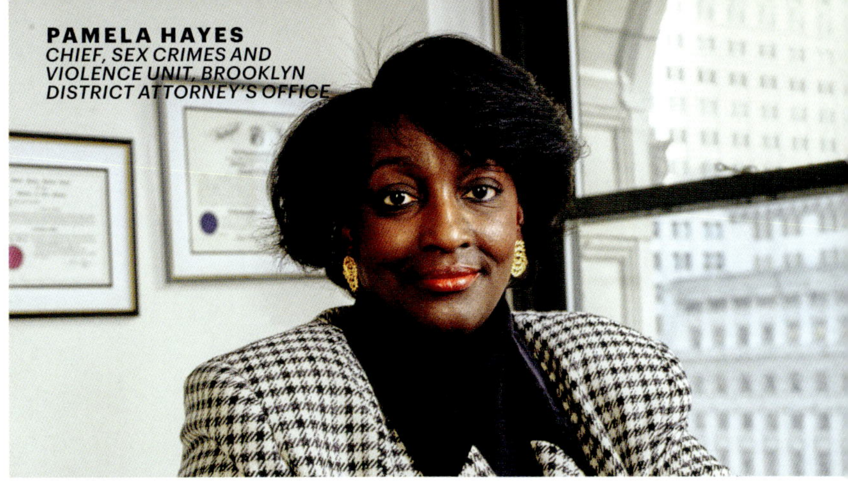

PAMELA HAYES
CHIEF, SEX CRIMES AND
VIOLENCE UNIT, BROOKLYN
DISTRICT ATTORNEY'S OFFICE

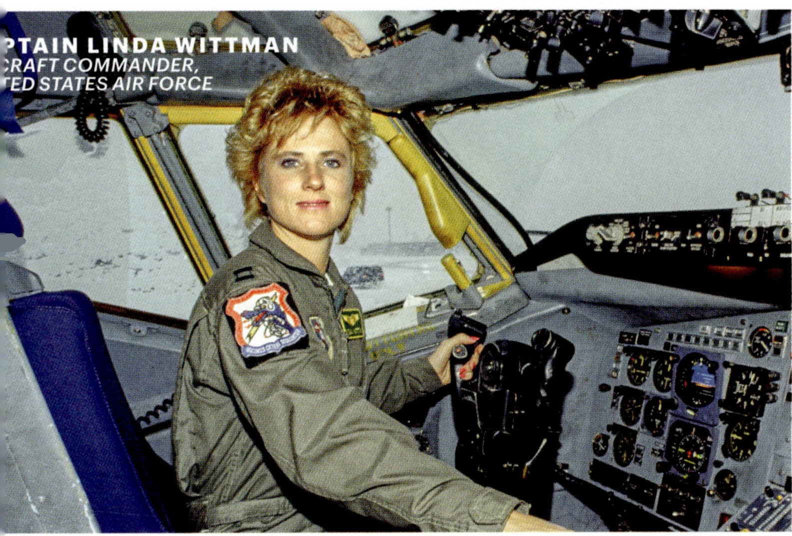

PTAIN LINDA WITTMAN
CRAFT COMMANDER,
TED STATES AIR FORCE

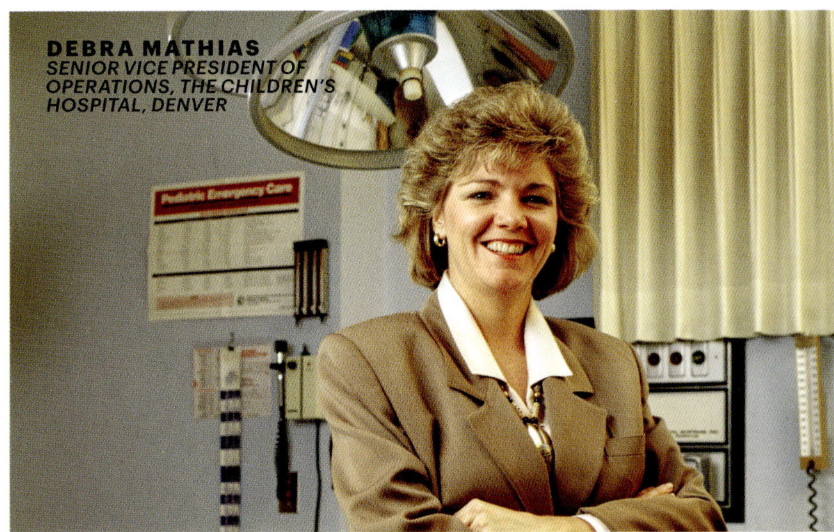

DEBRA MATHIAS
SENIOR VICE PRESIDENT OF
OPERATIONS, THE CHILDREN'S
HOSPITAL, DENVER

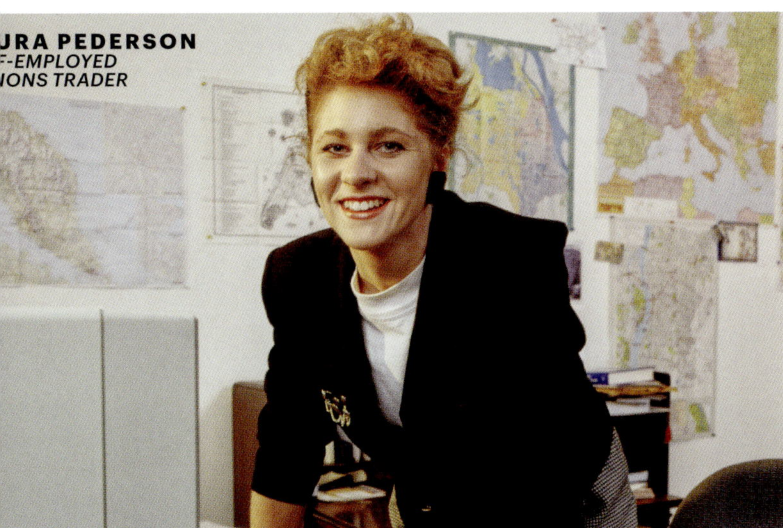

URA PEDERSON
F-EMPLOYED
IONS TRADER

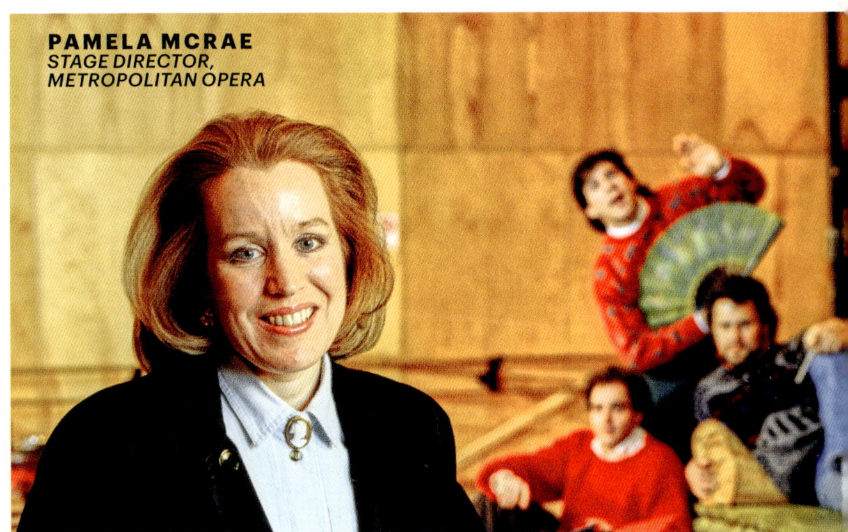

PAMELA MCRAE
STAGE DIRECTOR,
METROPOLITAN OPERA

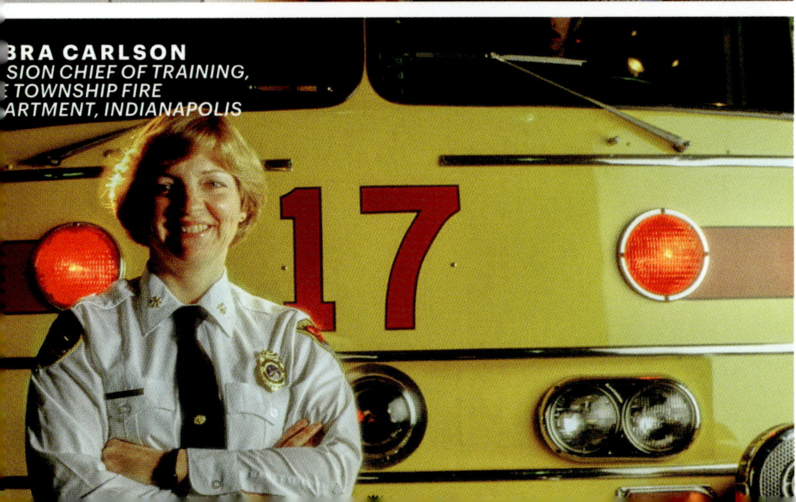

BRA CARLSON
SION CHIEF OF TRAINING,
E TOWNSHIP FIRE
ARTMENT, INDIANAPOLIS

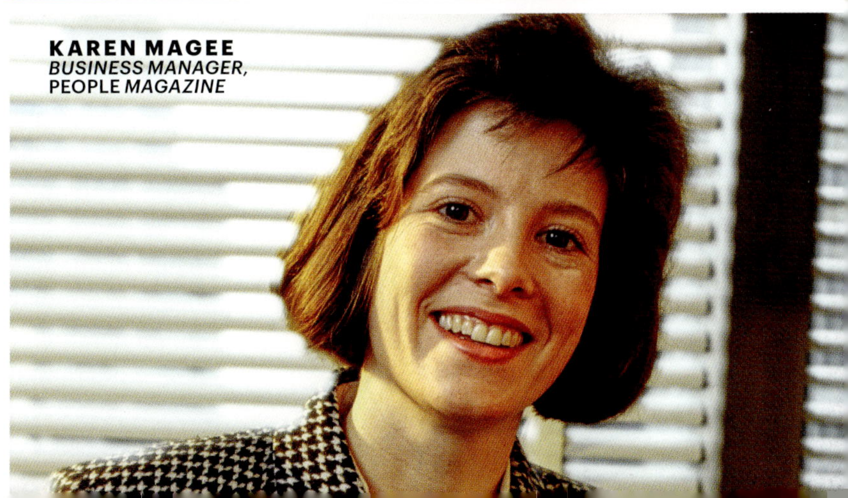

KAREN MAGEE
BUSINESS MANAGER,
PEOPLE MAGAZINE

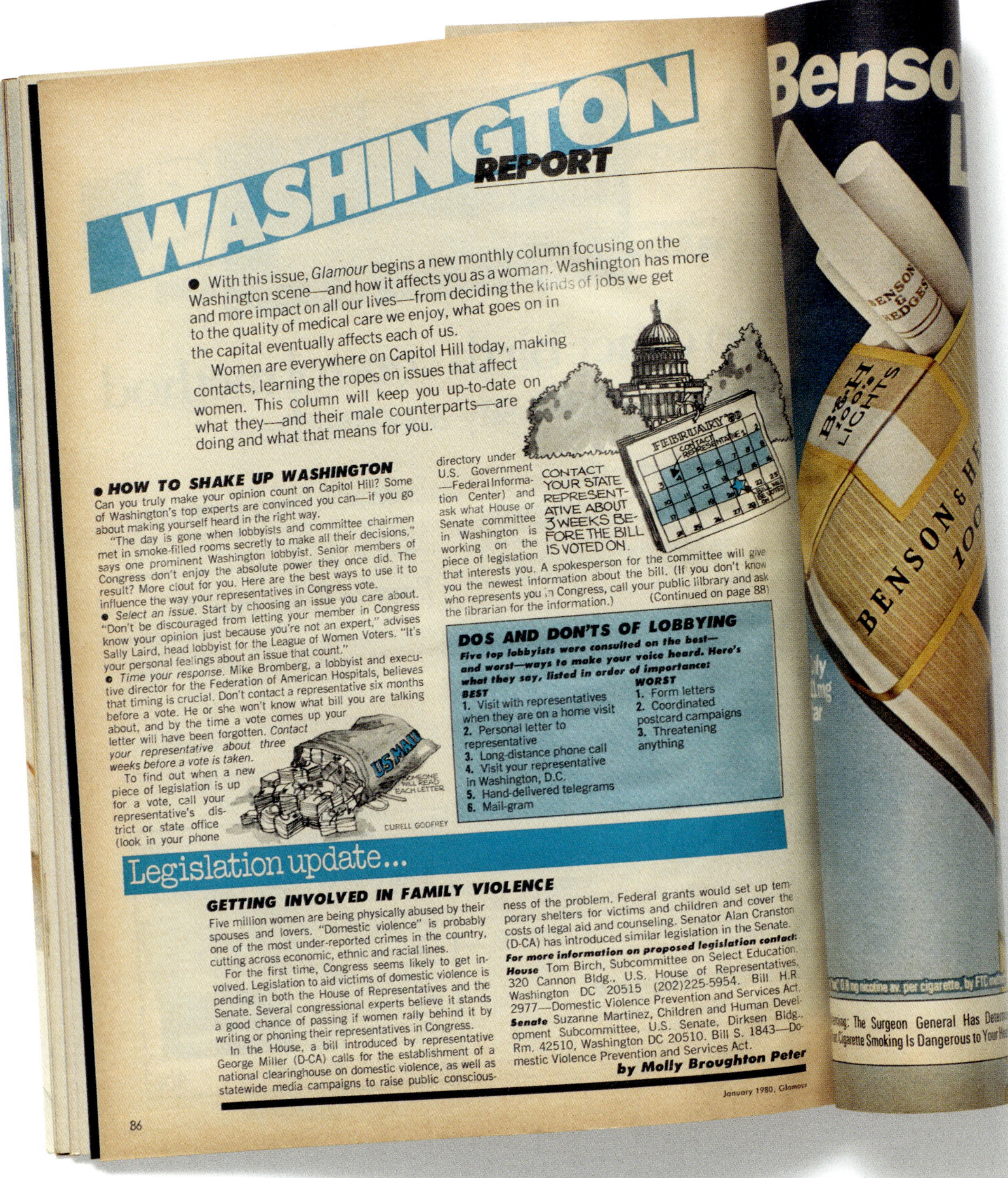

WASHINGTON REPORT

● With this issue, *Glamour* begins a new monthly column focusing on the Washington scene—and how it affects you as a woman. Washington has more and more impact on all our lives—from deciding the kinds of jobs we get to the quality of medical care we enjoy, what goes on in the capital eventually affects each of us.

Women are everywhere on Capitol Hill today, making contacts, learning the ropes on issues that affect women. This column will keep you up-to-date on what they—and their male counterparts—are doing and what that means for you.

● HOW TO SHAKE UP WASHINGTON

Can you truly make your opinion count on Capitol Hill? Some of Washington's top experts are convinced you can—if you go about making yourself heard in the right way.

"The day is gone when lobbyists and committee chairmen met in smoke-filled rooms secretly to make all their decisions," says one prominent Washington lobbyist. Senior members of Congress don't enjoy the absolute power they once did. The result? More clout for you. Here are the best ways to use it to influence the way your representatives in Congress vote.

● *Select an issue.* Start by choosing an issue you care about. "Don't be discouraged from letting your member in Congress know your opinion just because you're not an expert," advises Sally Laird, head lobbyist for the League of Women Voters. "It's your personal feelings about an issue that count."

● *Time your response.* Mike Bromberg, a lobbyist and executive director for the Federation of American Hospitals, believes that timing is crucial. Don't contact a representative six months before a vote. He or she won't know what bill you are talking about, and by the time a vote comes up your letter will have been forgotten. *Contact your representative about three weeks before a vote is taken.*

To find out when a new piece of legislation is up for a vote, call your representative's district or state office (look in your phone directory under U.S. Government —Federal Information Center) and ask what House or Senate committee in Washington is working on the piece of legislation that interests you. A spokesperson for the committee will give you the newest information about the bill. (If you don't know who represents you in Congress, call your public library and ask the librarian for the information.)

(Continued on page 88)

DOS AND DON'TS OF LOBBYING

Five top lobbyists were consulted on the best— and worst—ways to make your voice heard. Here's what they say, listed in order of importance:

BEST
1. Visit with representatives when they are on a home visit
2. Personal letter to representative
3. Long-distance phone call
4. Visit your representative in Washington, D.C.
5. Hand-delivered telegrams
6. Mail-gram

WORST
1. Form letters
2. Coordinated postcard campaigns
3. Threatening anything

Legislation update...

GETTING INVOLVED IN FAMILY VIOLENCE

Five million women are being physically abused by their spouses and lovers. "Domestic violence" is probably one of the most under-reported crimes in the country, cutting across economic, ethnic and racial lines.

For the first time, Congress seems likely to get involved. Legislation to aid victims of domestic violence is pending in both the House of Representatives and the Senate. Several congressional experts believe it stands a good chance of passing if women rally behind it by writing or phoning their representatives in Congress.

In the House, a bill introduced by representative George Miller (D-CA) calls for the establishment of a national clearinghouse on domestic violence, as well as statewide media campaigns to raise public consciousness of the problem. Federal grants would set up temporary shelters for victims and children and cover the costs of legal aid and counseling. Senator Alan Cranston (D-CA) has introduced similar legislation in the Senate.

For more information on proposed legislation contact: **House** Tom Birch, Subcommittee on Select Education, 320 Cannon Bldg., U.S. House of Representatives, Washington DC 20515 (202)225-5954. Bill H.R. 2977—Domestic Violence Prevention and Services Act. **Senate** Suzanne Martinez, Children and Human Development Subcommittee, U.S. Senate, Dirksen Bldg., Rm. 42510, Washington DC 20510. Bill S. 1843—Domestic Violence Prevention and Services Act.

by Molly Broughton Peter

January 1980, Glamour

86

AS WOMEN'S STATURE GREW, it was essential that *Glamour* track the progress of women's rights on Capitol Hill—from the continued fight for the Equal Rights Act (ERA), to the need for more women in Congress (in 1981 *Glamour* noted there were just 21 women to 514 men), the protection of abortion rights, and the then fledgling Family and Medical Leave Act, first reported on in *Glamour* in 1987. The focus on politics was there from the very first issue of the new decade in January 1980, with a new monthly column called Washington Report, alogside a wider focus on politics. *Glamour* set out to hold those in power to account and chronicle progress where it was made. Notably, 5,000 readers wrote letters (via *Glamour*) in May 1981 to the newly elected president, Ronald Reagan, to share what they saw as critical issues for his presidency—the top five were the ERA; legal, safe abortions; married couples tax; key women's appointments; and equal pay for equal work. And in 1995, the writer Susan Estrich espoused the history-making role of Hillary Rodham Clinton, the White House "wife" who rewrote the rules—and of course, paved the way for her own impactful political career.

↑
Glamour's first Washington Report column, January 1980.

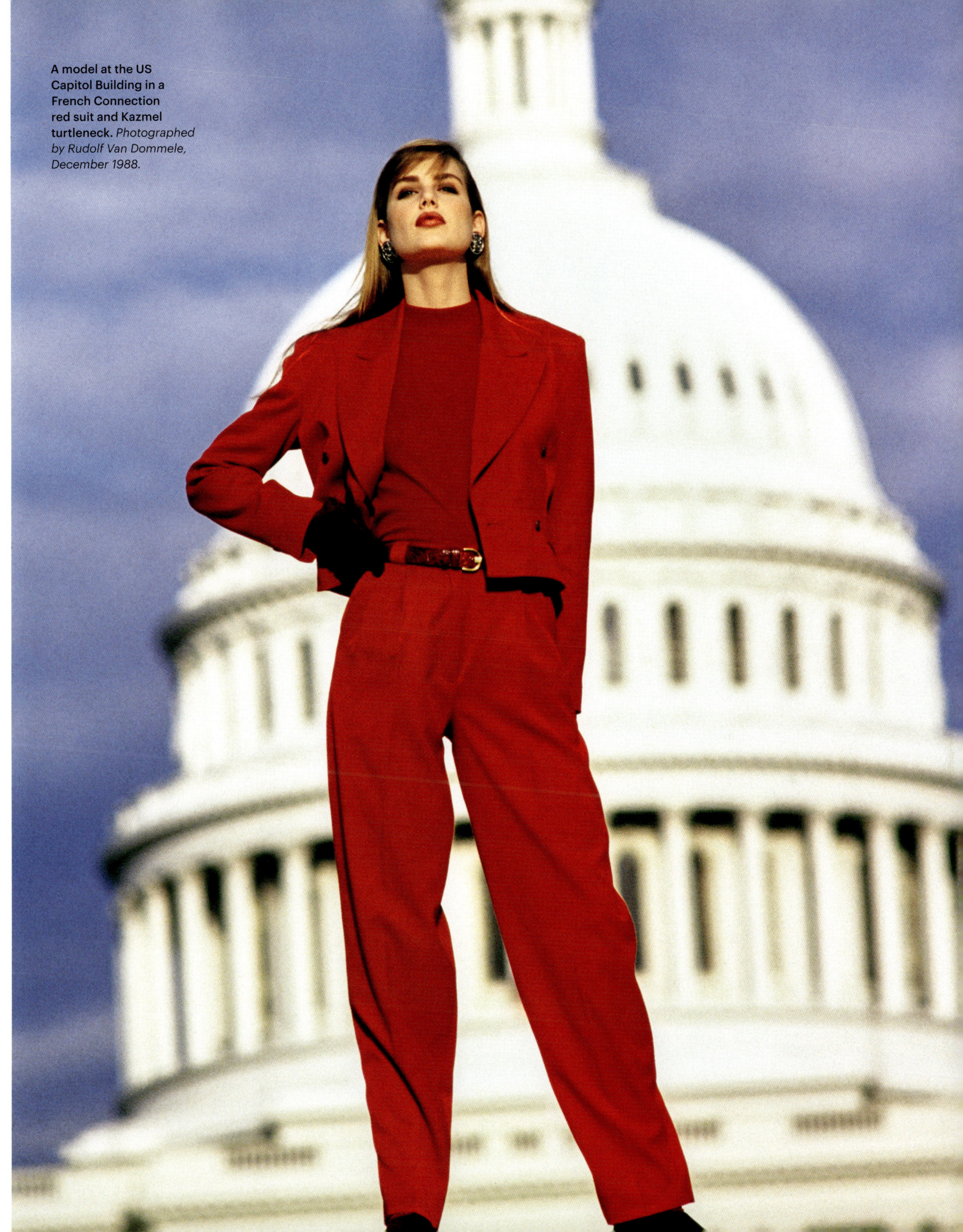

A model at the US Capitol Building in a French Connection red suit and Kazmel turtleneck. *Photographed by Rudolf Van Dommele, December 1988.*

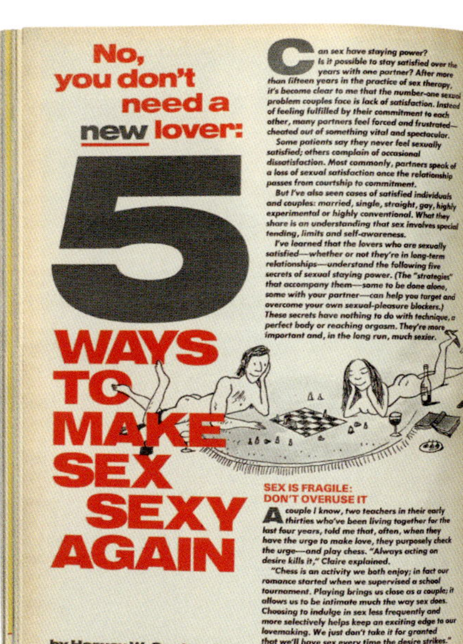

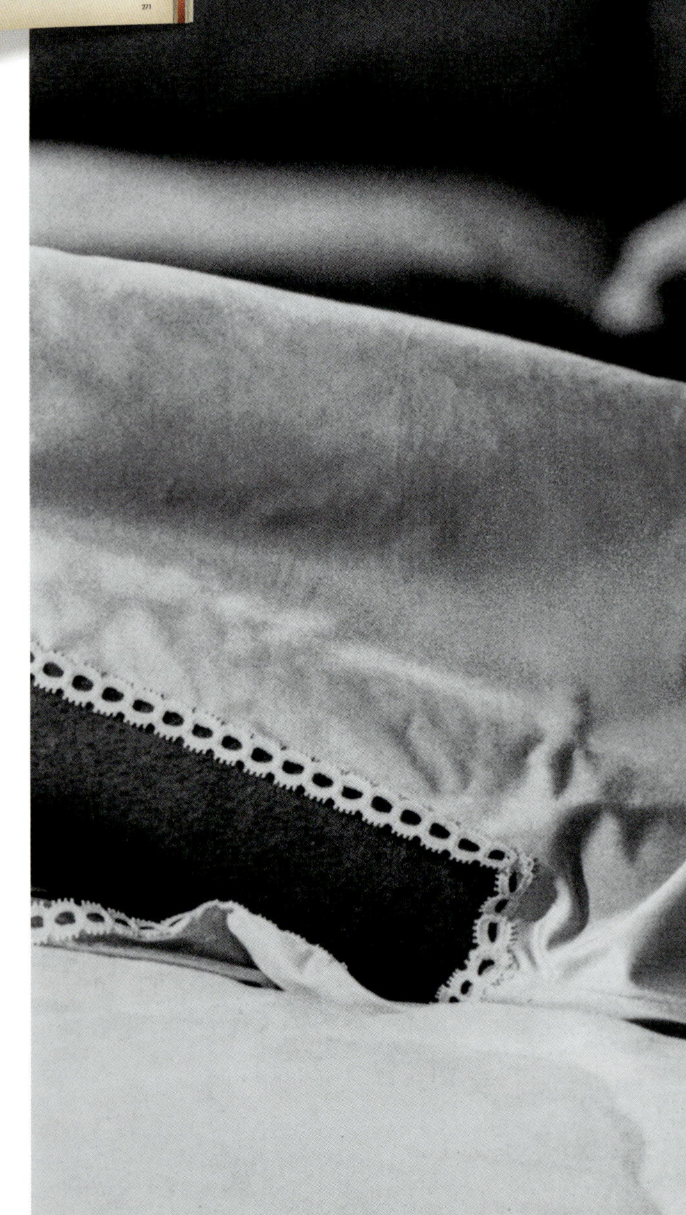

RAUNCHY WAS THE WORD

Ruth Whitney used to describe her monthly cover line meetings with *Glamour* editors and writers, and sex certainly played a big part in the magazine in this era: how to have it after a baby, "sexy body-zones," understanding your orgasm style, how to sexually sync with your partner, becoming a sexually confident woman. It was rarely, if ever, about how to get sex right to please a man, but how women could learn to satisfy themselves, although one sex and health column amusingly explored whether women could ever become dependent on vibrators.

↑

A sex advice article from October 1986.

The enormous impact of the HIV/AIDS epidemic, which was ignored by those in power for far too long and affected everyone, but especially ravaged the LGBTQ+ community, was also felt. In 1987, *Glamour* published its fifth annual Women's Views Survey, and more women than ever cited AIDS as one of their biggest health concerns. As Whitney herself observed, "AIDS has cast a long, long shadow over their personal lives, not just altering their sexual habits but effecting deep shifts even in basic life goals." That same year, 71 percent of women across America told *Glamour* they had become more cautious about sex because of AIDS, 22 percent shared that they had become monogamous, and 11 percent of single women said they had become celibate—a stark contrast to the free love era of the '70s. "Monogamy and celibacy are two of the life-shaping results of the AIDS crisis," Whitney said.

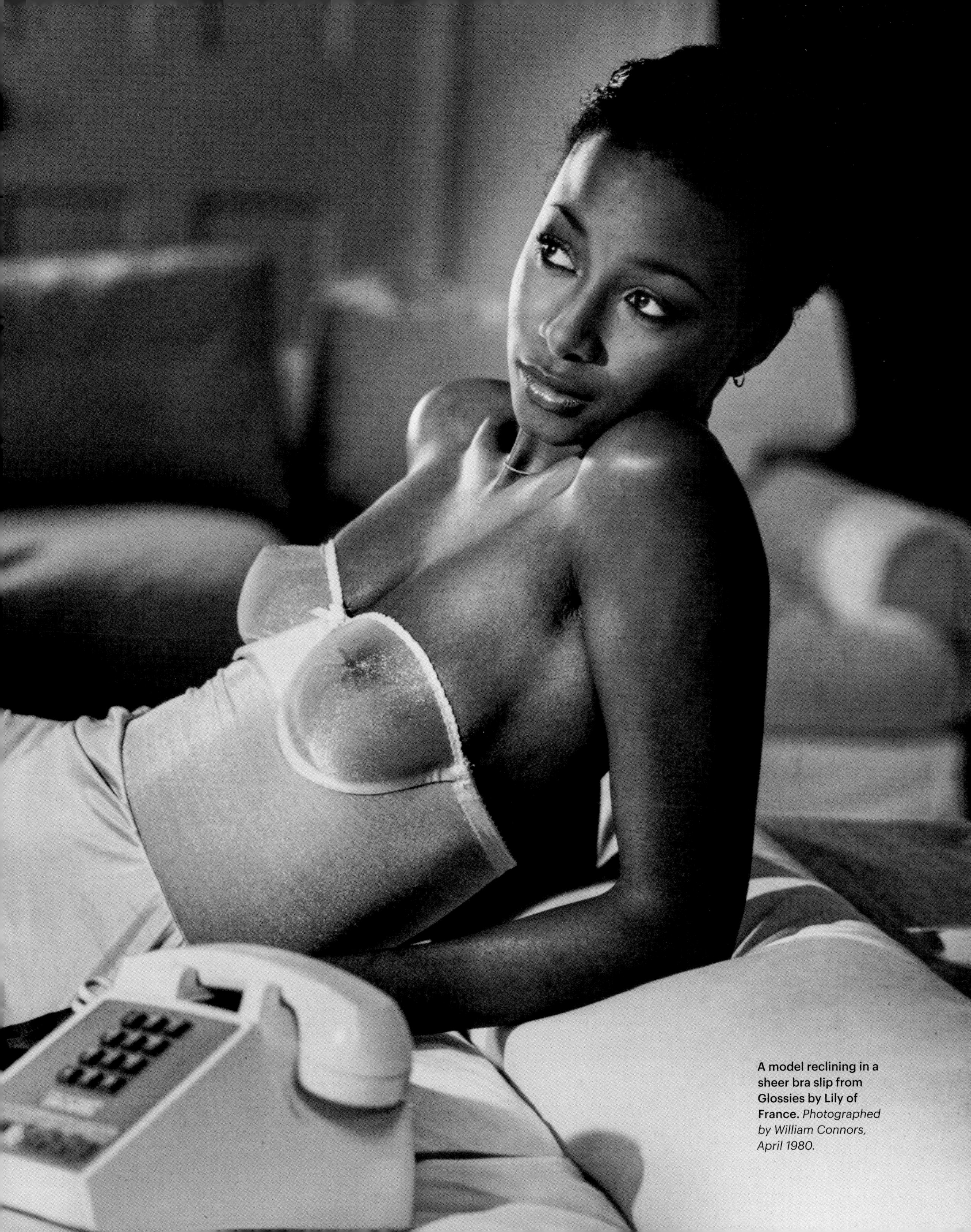

A model reclining in a sheer bra slip from Glossies by Lily of France. *Photographed by William Connors, April 1980.*

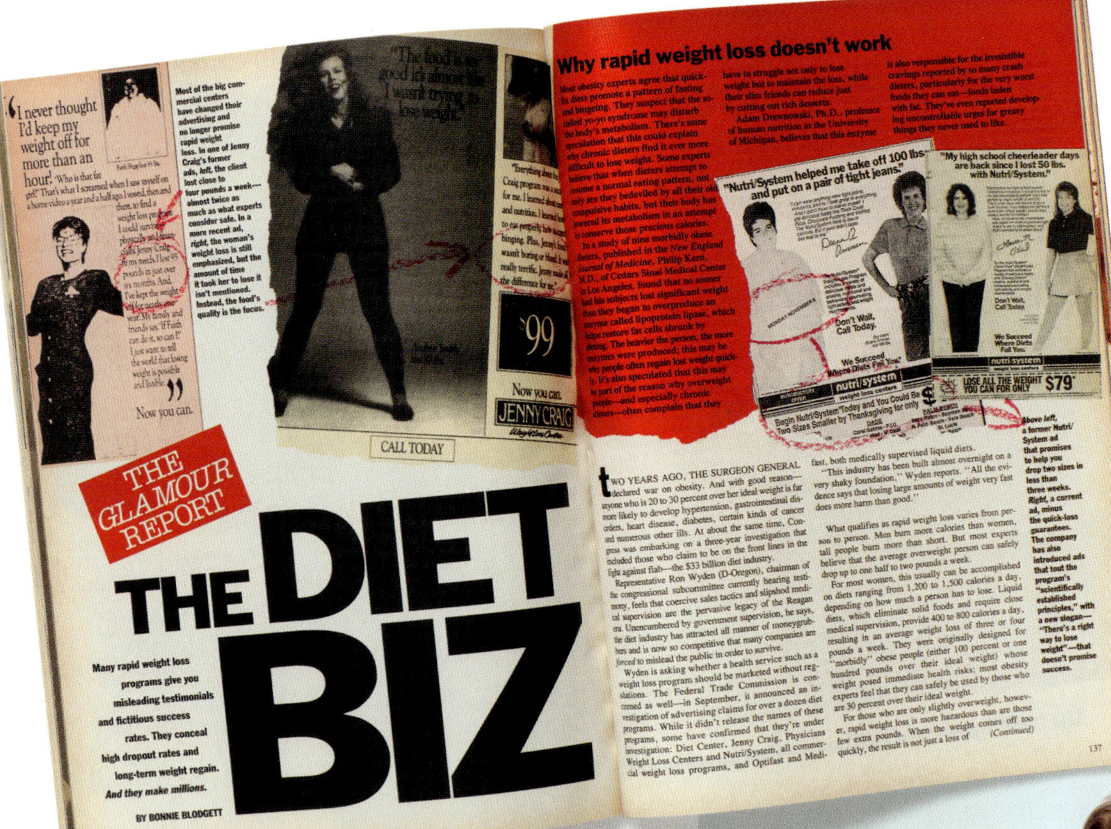

→ Niki Taylor shares a cover with *Glamour*'s "10 steps to a better body," May 1990.

THIN WAS STILL PRIZED IN THIS ERA, and diet culture still ruled. Issue after issue was packed with articles about readers' weight loss journeys, diets to follow, and how to get "10 lbs. thinner!" Multiple *Glamour* covers advertised pull-out diet and exercise supplements and posters, and in the early 1980s, ads for diet pills even graced the magazine's pages (though two of the pills were withdrawn by the FDA for containing too much phenylpropanolamine, a drug with dangerous side effects). But there was a growing unease about the diet industry as a whole. A 1991 investigative report into the misleading claims of weight-loss companies, which were making hundreds of millions of dollars from dieters, certainly challenged the accepted narrative. But the magazine was still a long way from abandoning weight loss in favor of body inclusivity and the celebration of all women's bodies—something that only finally began in the late 2000s (see pages 266 and 302).

↑ A January 1991 article on the fallacy of rapid weight loss.

→ Model Kim Alexis weighs herself on a New York City terrace. *Photographed by Alex Chatelain, October 1982.*

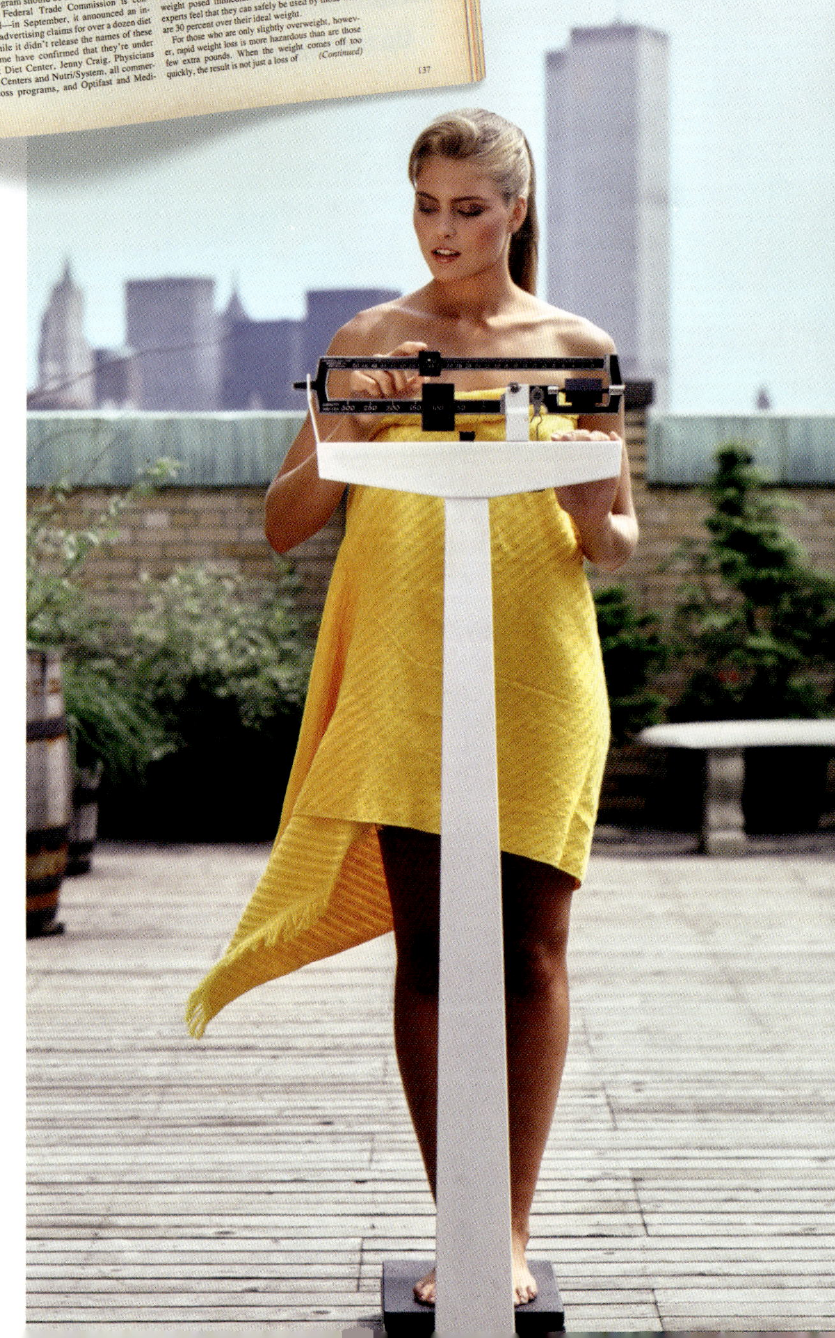

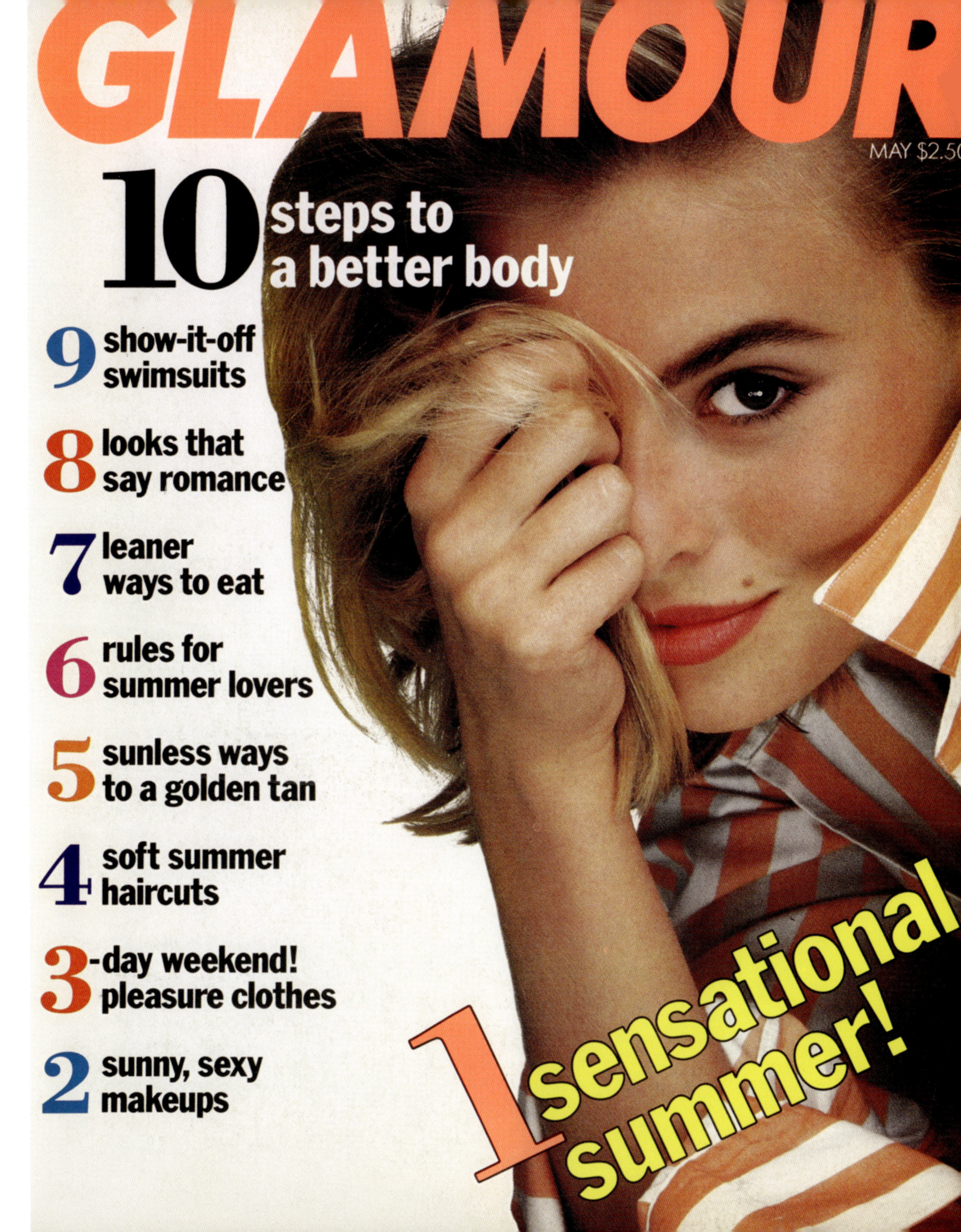

GLAMOUR
MAY $2.50
10 steps to a better body
9 show-it-off swimsuits
8 looks that say romance
7 leaner ways to eat
6 rules for summer lovers
5 sunless ways to a golden tan
4 soft summer haircuts
3 -day weekend! pleasure clothes
2 sunny, sexy makeups
1 sensational summer!

WHAT THE STARS EAT IN BED

Is your bedroom a "living" room? Do you use it for watching TV, diving into a novel or working on that take-home-from-the-office assignment? Then you probably eat there, too. Whether it's just a late-night nosh or a more substantial feast, you're not alone. Even famous people eat in bed . . . and love it. We asked some of our favorites to reveal their secret snacks and the recipes, so you can try them, too. Here's what they told us:

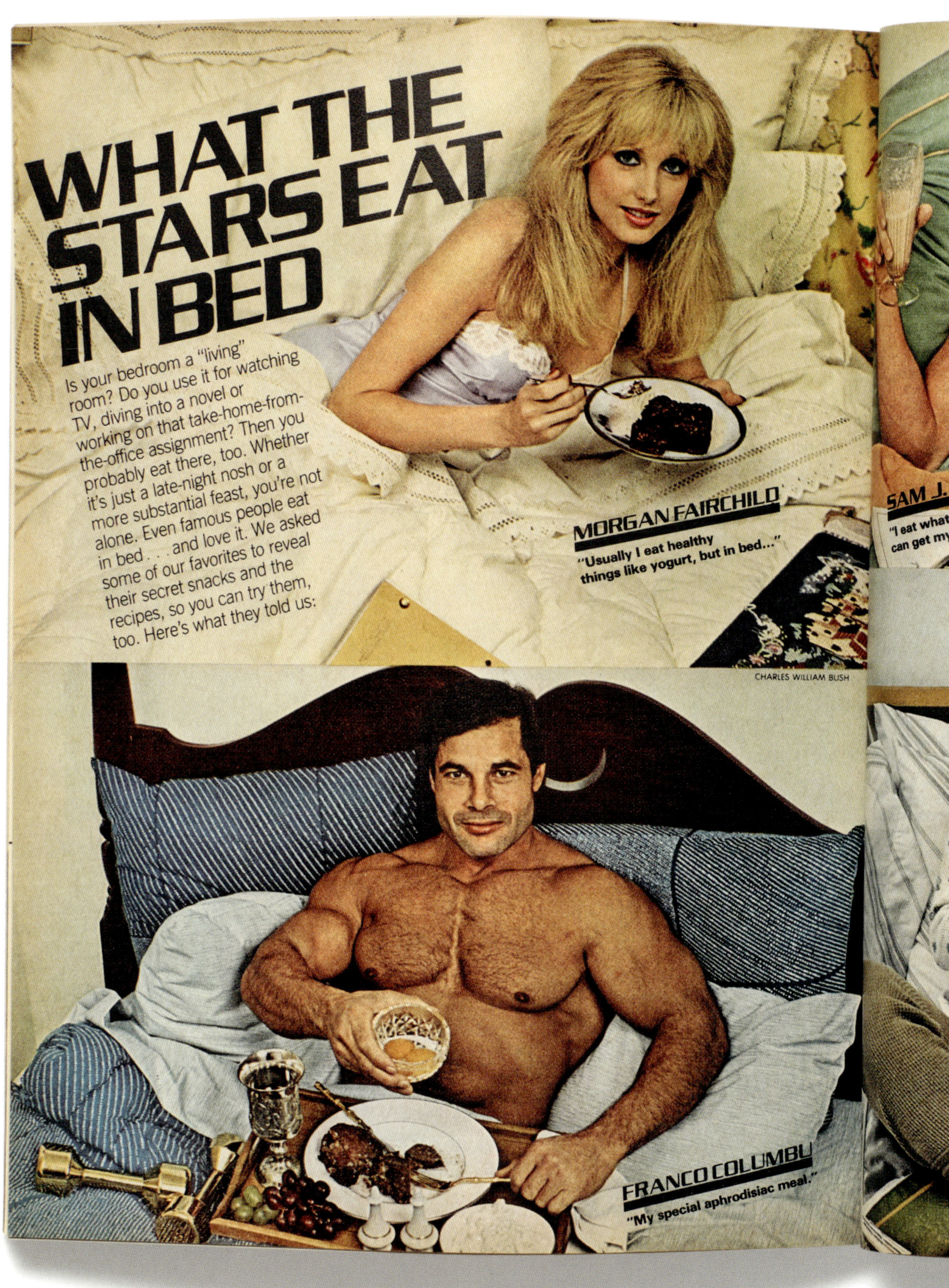

MORGAN FAIRCHILD

"Usually I eat healthy things like yogurt, but in bed..."

FRANCO COLUMBU

"My special aphrodisiac meal."

SAM J.

"I eat whatev can get my h

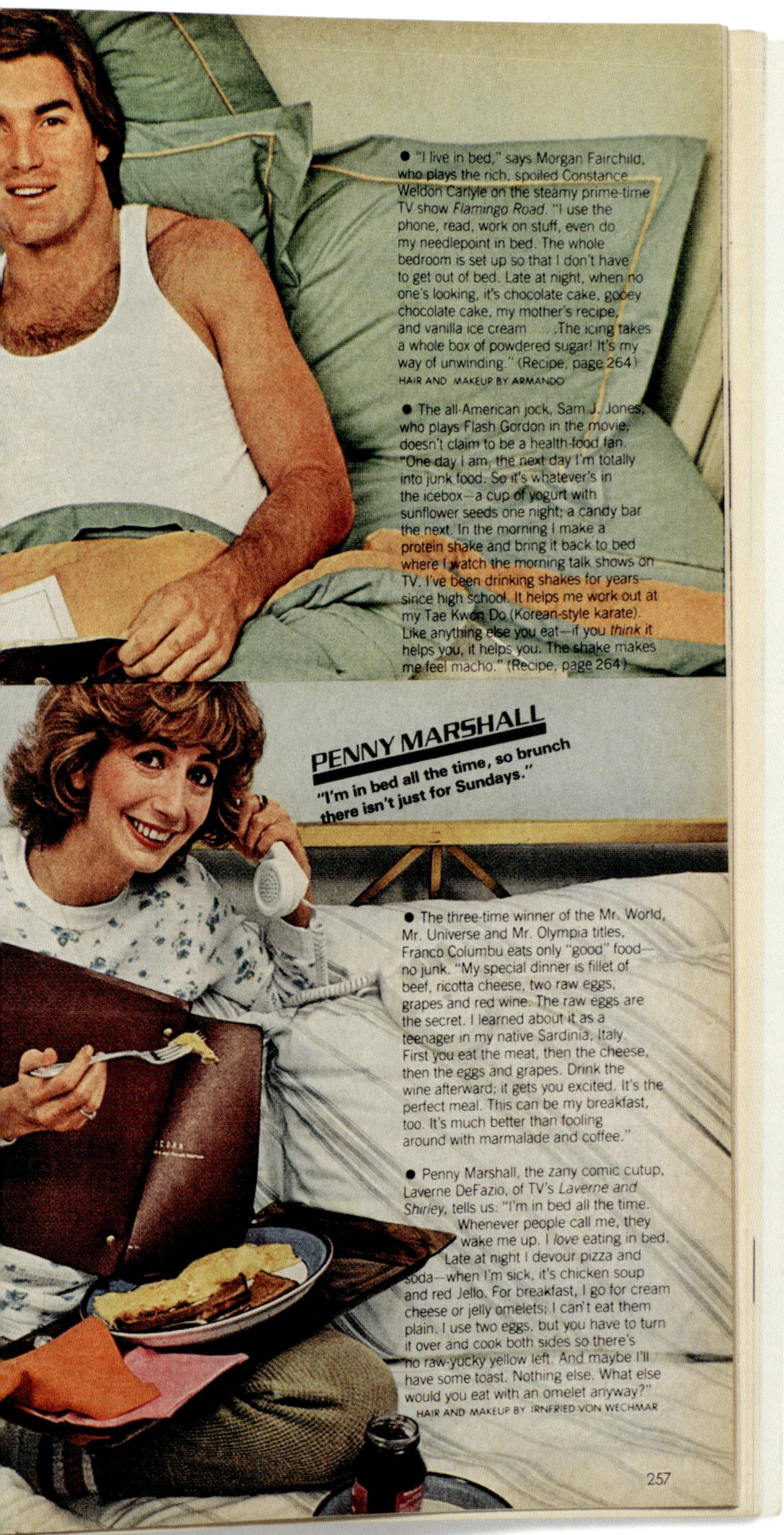

1981

YES, *GLAMOUR* OFTEN TACKLED hard-hitting subjects. But sometimes readers just wanted to open the pages of the magazine and know that stars of big and small screens were just like them. While celebrities didn't feature regularly in the magazine, this leftfield feature "What the Stars Eat in Bed" was deliciously surreal, and a moment in history too brilliant to keep hidden in the archives. We reprint it here for you to enjoy.

THIS WAS THE ERA OF THE BEFORE AND AFTER. In the 1940s, early issues of *Glamour* had toyed with fashion and beauty makeovers—the magazine's staff were usually the guinea pigs—but it was in the '80s and '90s that they burst onto its pages in a significant way. This time it was *Glamour*'s readers who were transformed month after month. The magazine's staff made over mothers and daughters, nurses, television anchors, and swim teams. They traveled to different states to make over working women. They revisited makeover subjects to see how the style and beauty overhauls had lasted (not all had approved of them for the long term.) The makeovers were fun and glamorous and engaged *Glamour*'s countrywide audience, but to dismiss them as simply superficial would be wrong. In a 1992 speech, *Glamour*'s then editor in chief Ruth Whitney noted, "During my 25 years at *Glamour*, the lives of women have been transformed, as sexual objects and as sexual beings, as wives and mothers, as students and teachers, as workers and as professionals." It's perhaps no wonder that the lure of a makeover, to meet this new moment with a new self, inside and out, was hard to resist for *Glamour*'s staff and readers alike.

↓

Glamour gives Laurie Leipham a new look in its Please Make Me Over! column, May 1980.

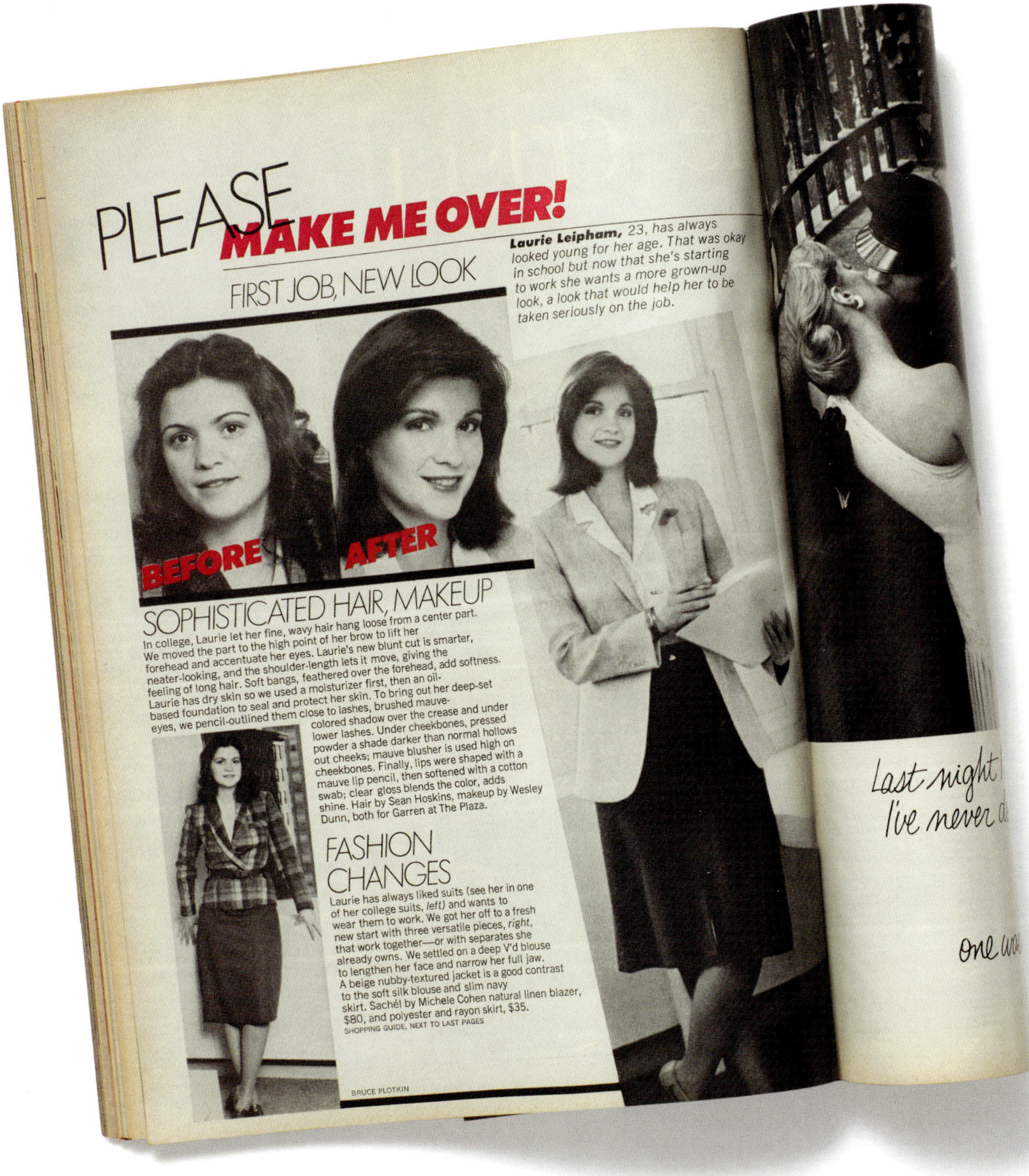

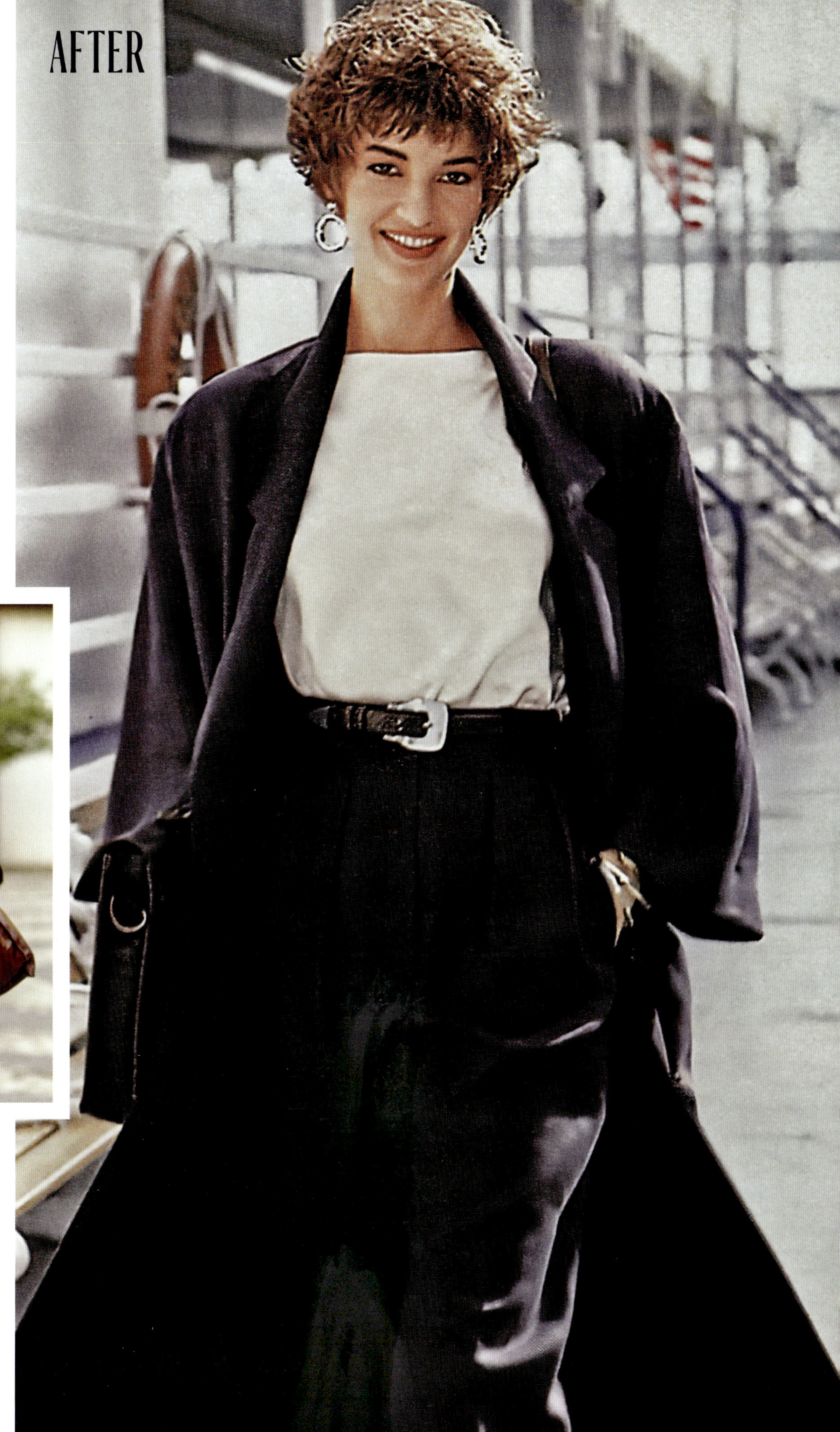

↑

Melissa Fryauf, a PR officer for the mayor of New Orleans, gets an '80s-style upgrade, courtesy of *Glamour. Photographed by Jan Francis, February 1986.*

THE FASHION OF THIS ERA was a riot of color and bold suiting, mixed in with a smattering of the biggest names to come—think Naomi Campbell and Claudia Schiffer. These iconic shots perfectly capture the mood, and the style, of the time.

Model Sandra Zatezalo, wearing a Patrick Kelly dress with pink bows and James Arpad earrings, embraces a male model. *Photographed by Paul Lange, December 1988.*

A model, beside male model Bill Skinner, on the street wearing a floral print Tracy Reese for Magaschoni skirt suit with a Marvella faux-pearl necklace and a Fendi case. *Photographed by J.R. Duran, February 1991.*

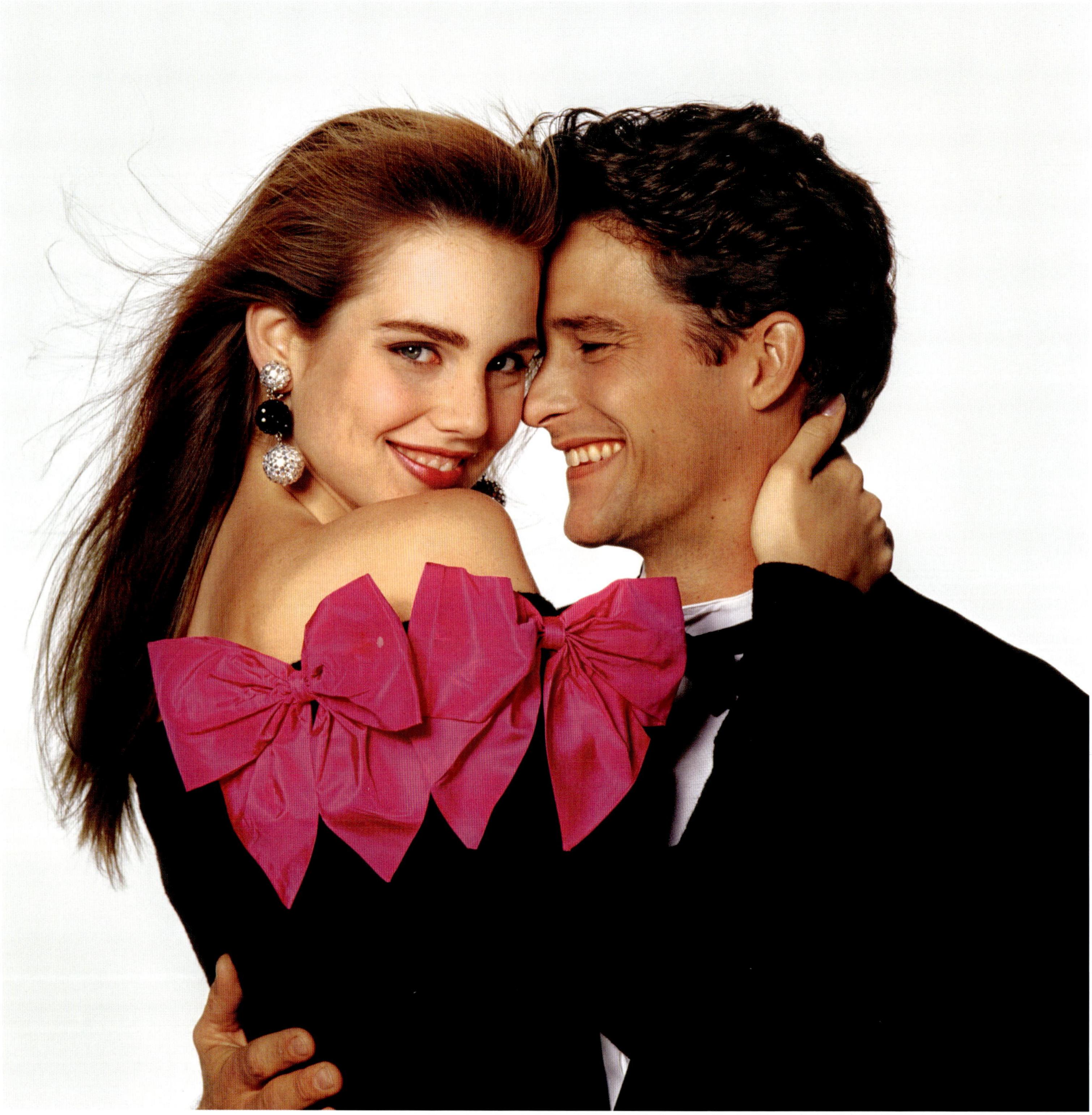

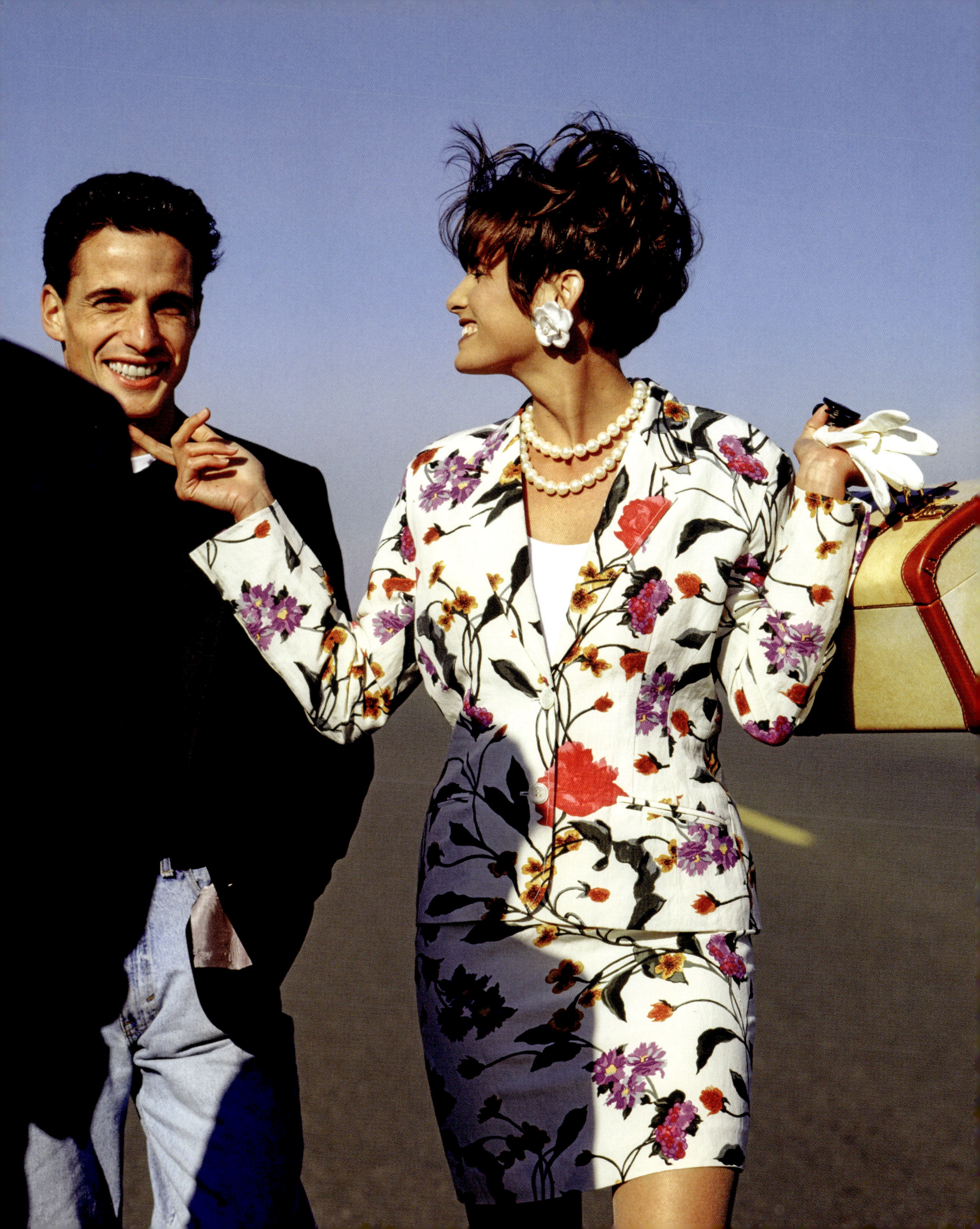

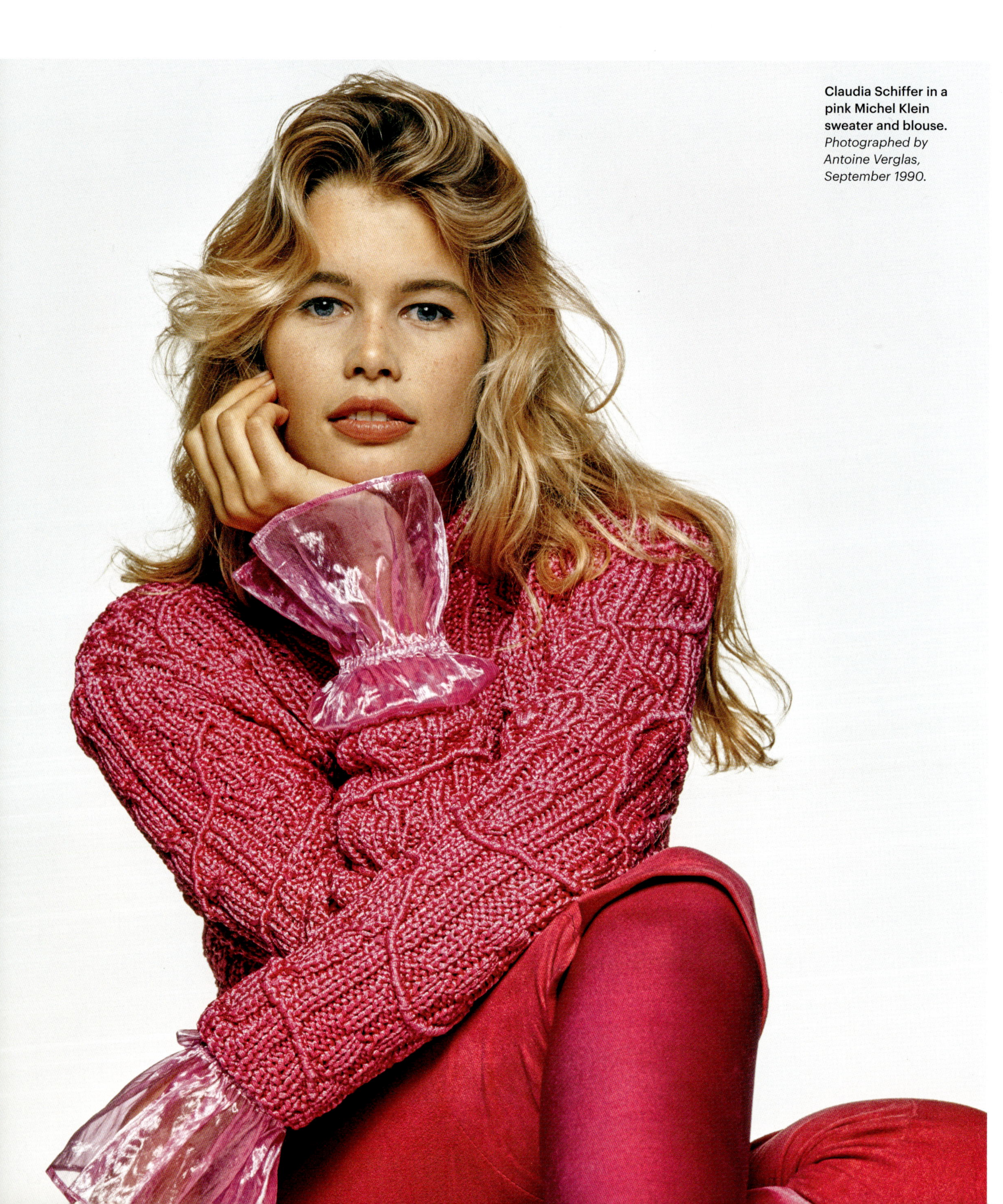

Claudia Schiffer in a pink Michel Klein sweater and blouse. *Photographed by Antoine Verglas, September 1990.*

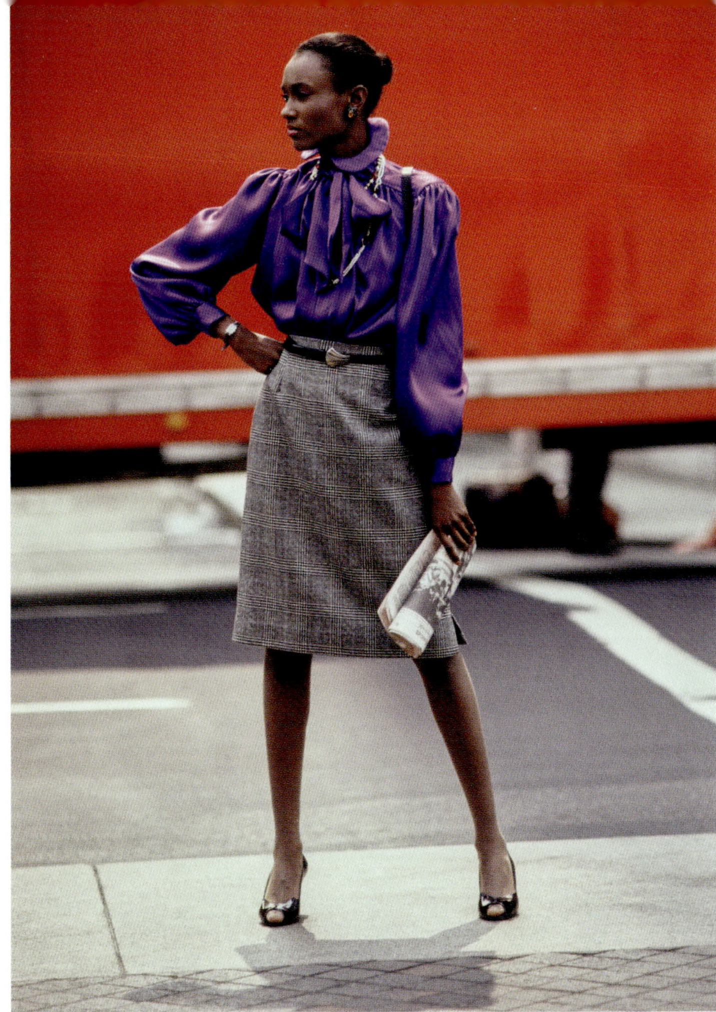

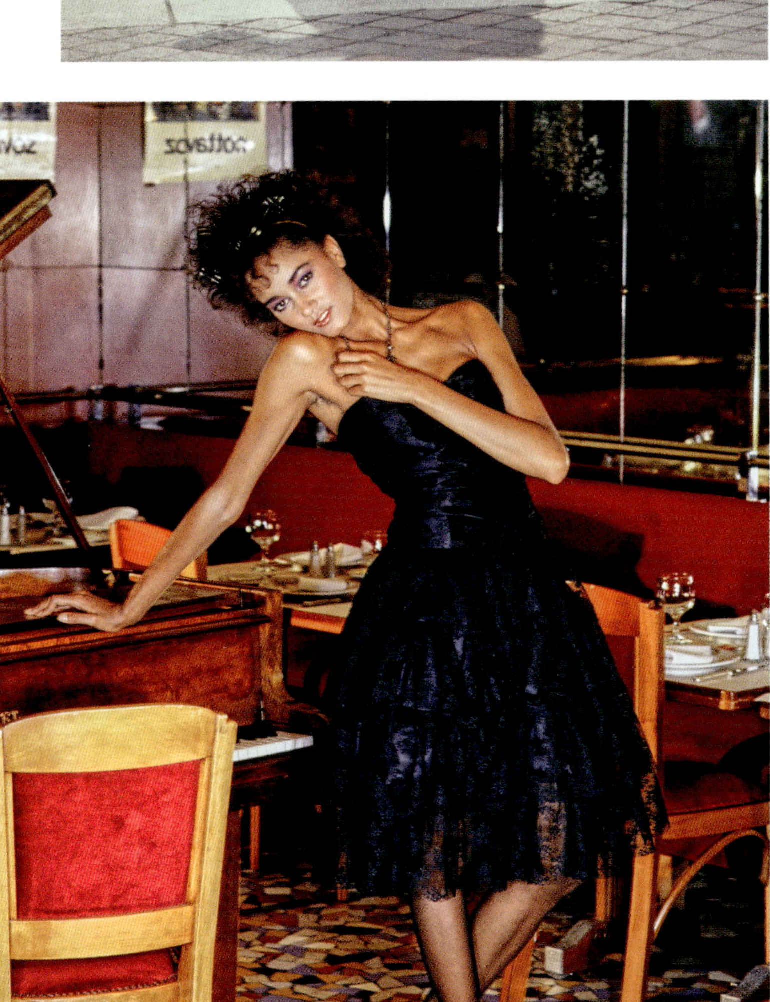

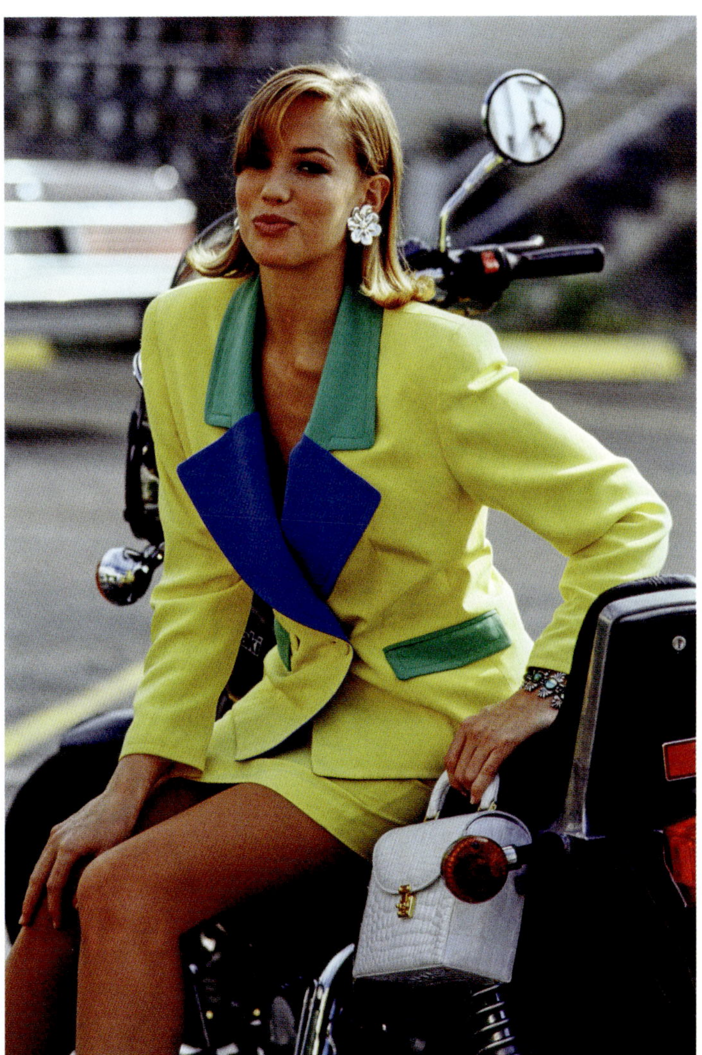

Model Aria, of Zoli models, wearing a purple silk Helene Sidel blouse with a gray plaid Jones New York skirt. *Photographed by George Barkentin, September 1982.*

Model Julie Wolfe at New York's La Coupole restaurant wearing a black lace party dress with a bustier top by Marlene Stewart for COVERS. *Photographed by Claude Mougin, September 1982.*

A model sits on a motorcycle wearing a bold yellow Randy Kemper suit with a Lana of London bag. *Photographed by J.R. Duran, March 1991.*

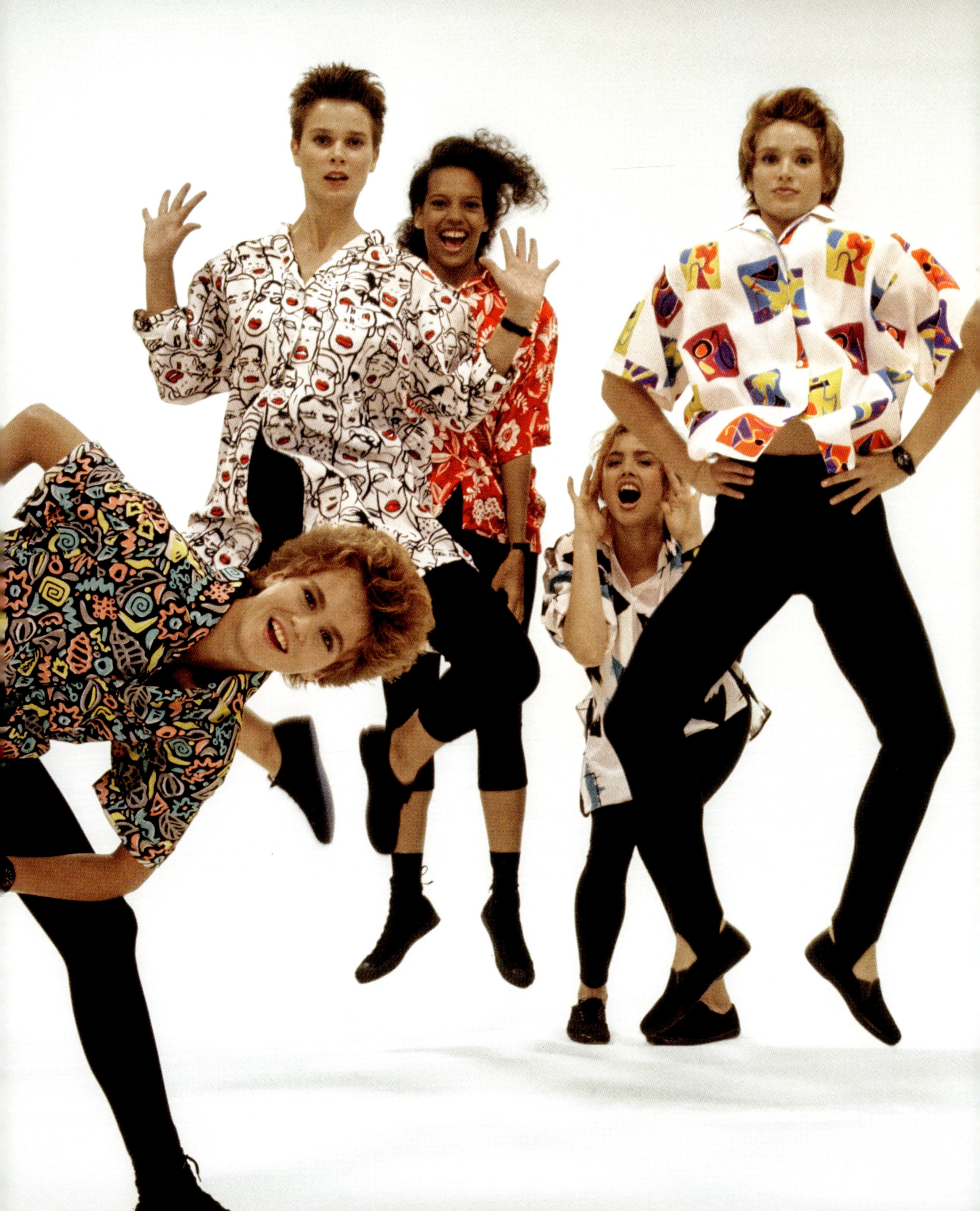

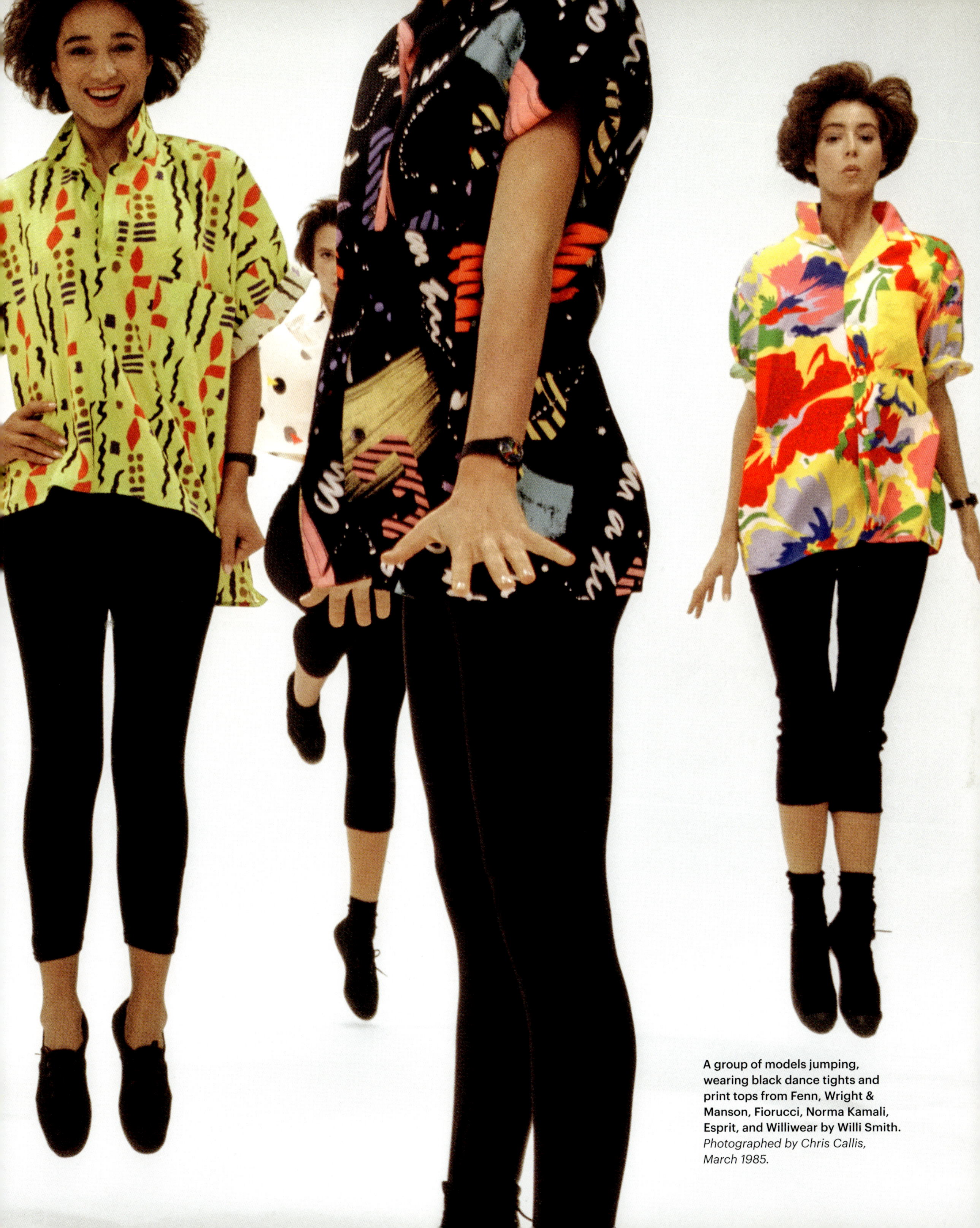

A group of models jumping, wearing black dance tights and print tops from Fenn, Wright & Manson, Fiorucci, Norma Kamali, Esprit, and Williwear by Willi Smith. *Photographed by Chris Callis, March 1985.*

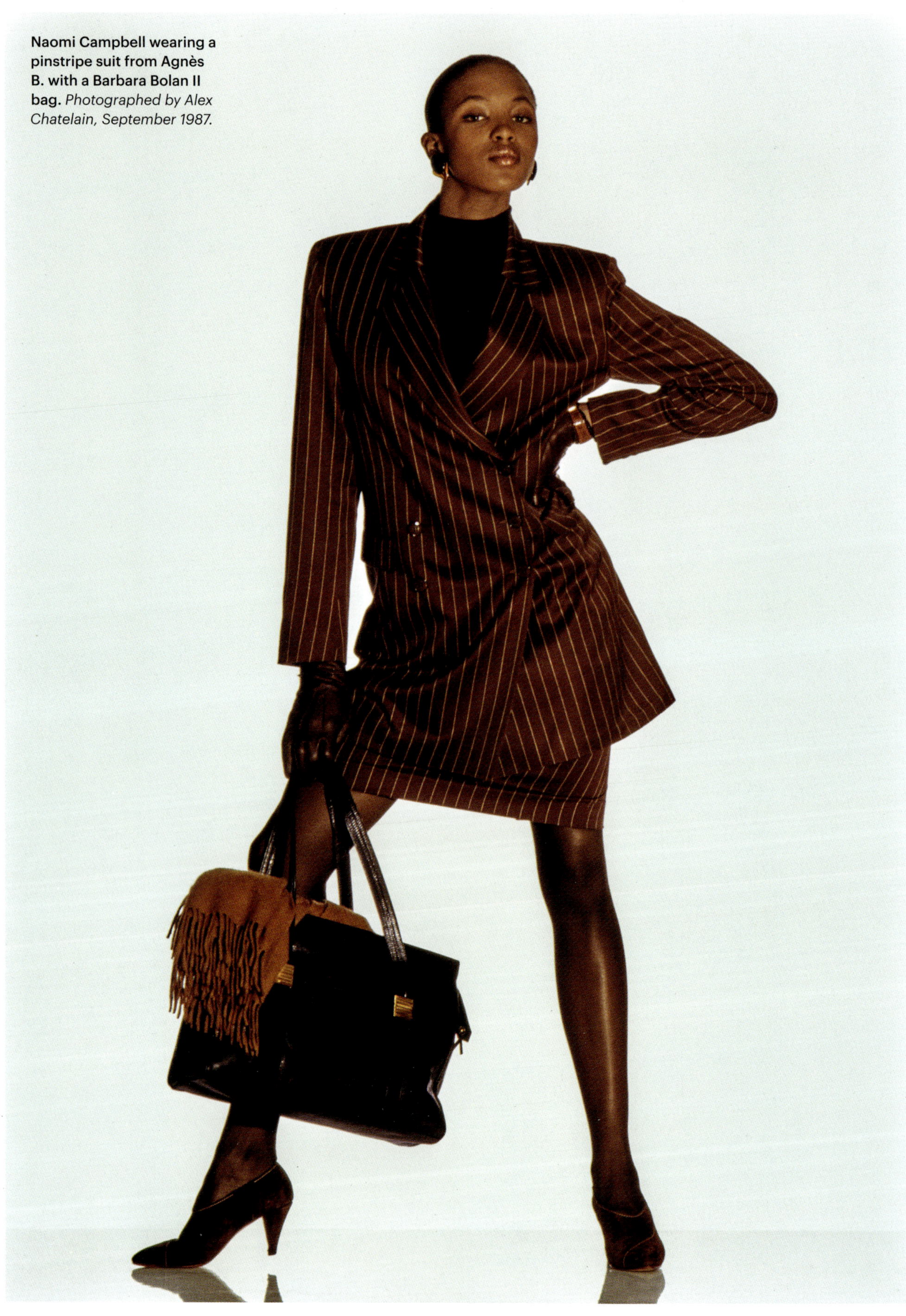

Naomi Campbell wearing a pinstripe suit from Agnès B. with a Barbara Bolan II bag. *Photographed by Alex Chatelain, September 1987.*

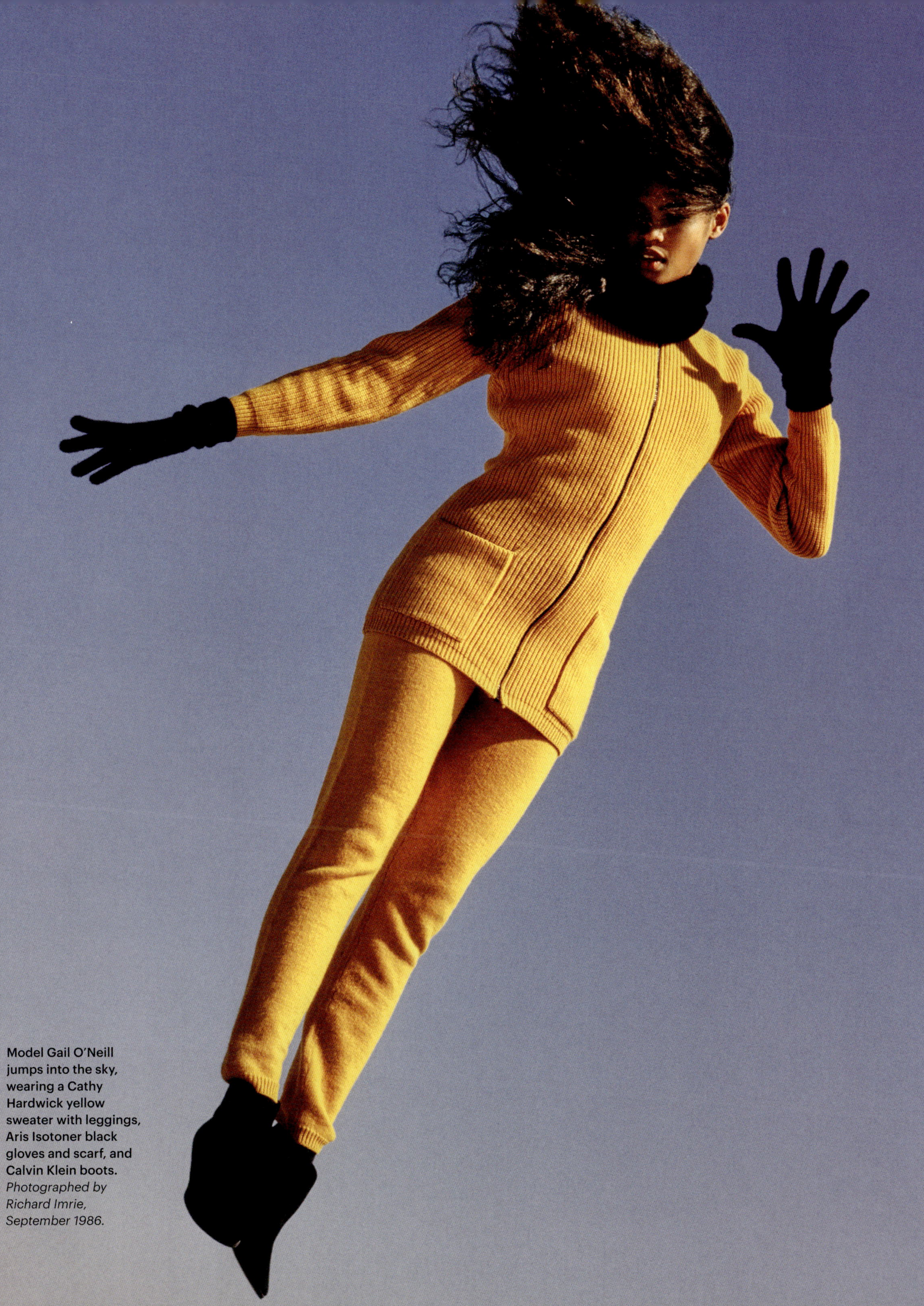

Model Gail O'Neill jumps into the sky, wearing a Cathy Hardwick yellow sweater with leggings, Aris Isotoner black gloves and scarf, and Calvin Klein boots. *Photographed by Richard Imrie, September 1986.*

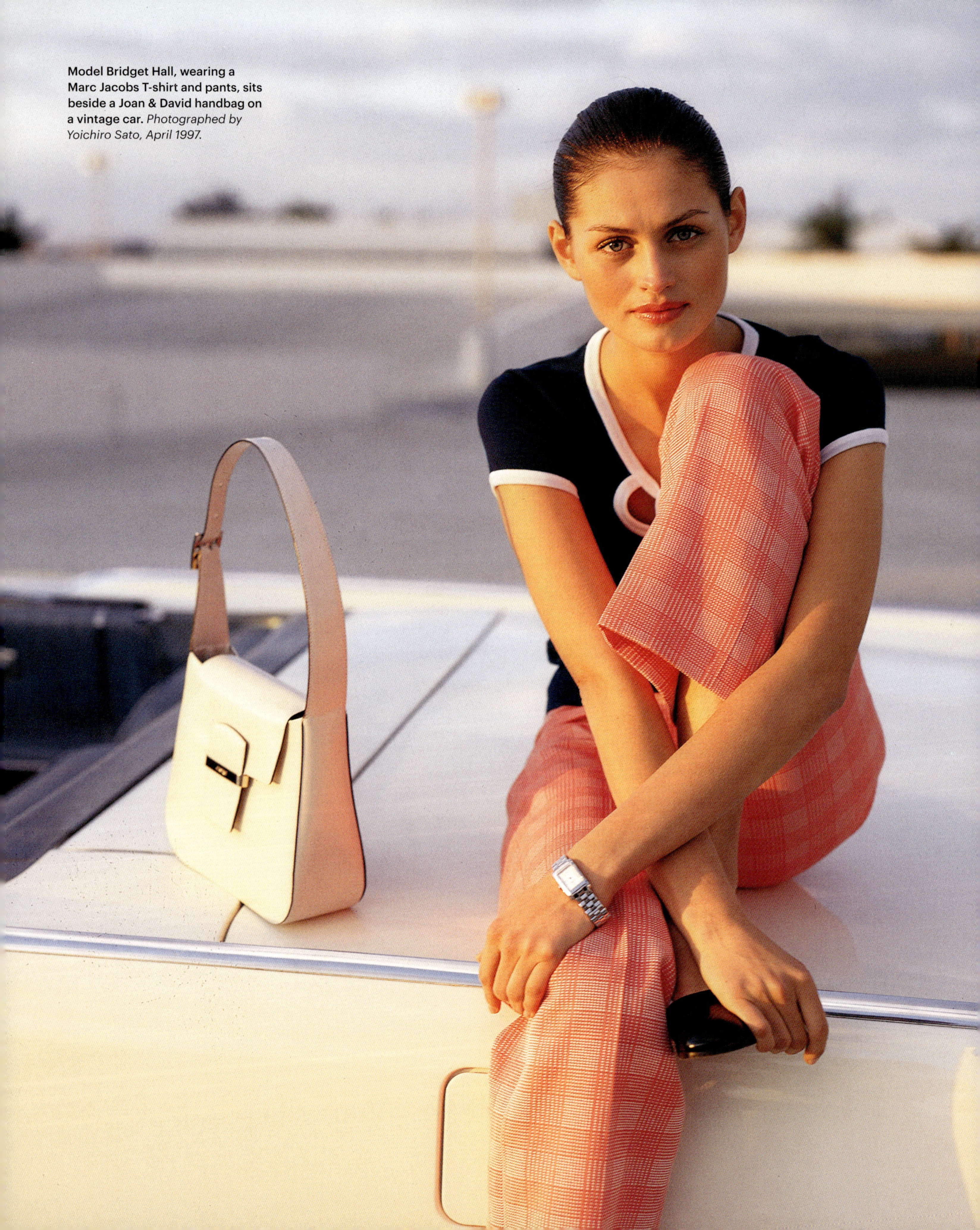

Model Bridget Hall, wearing a Marc Jacobs T-shirt and pants, sits beside a Joan & David handbag on a vintage car. *Photographed by Yoichiro Sato, April 1997.*

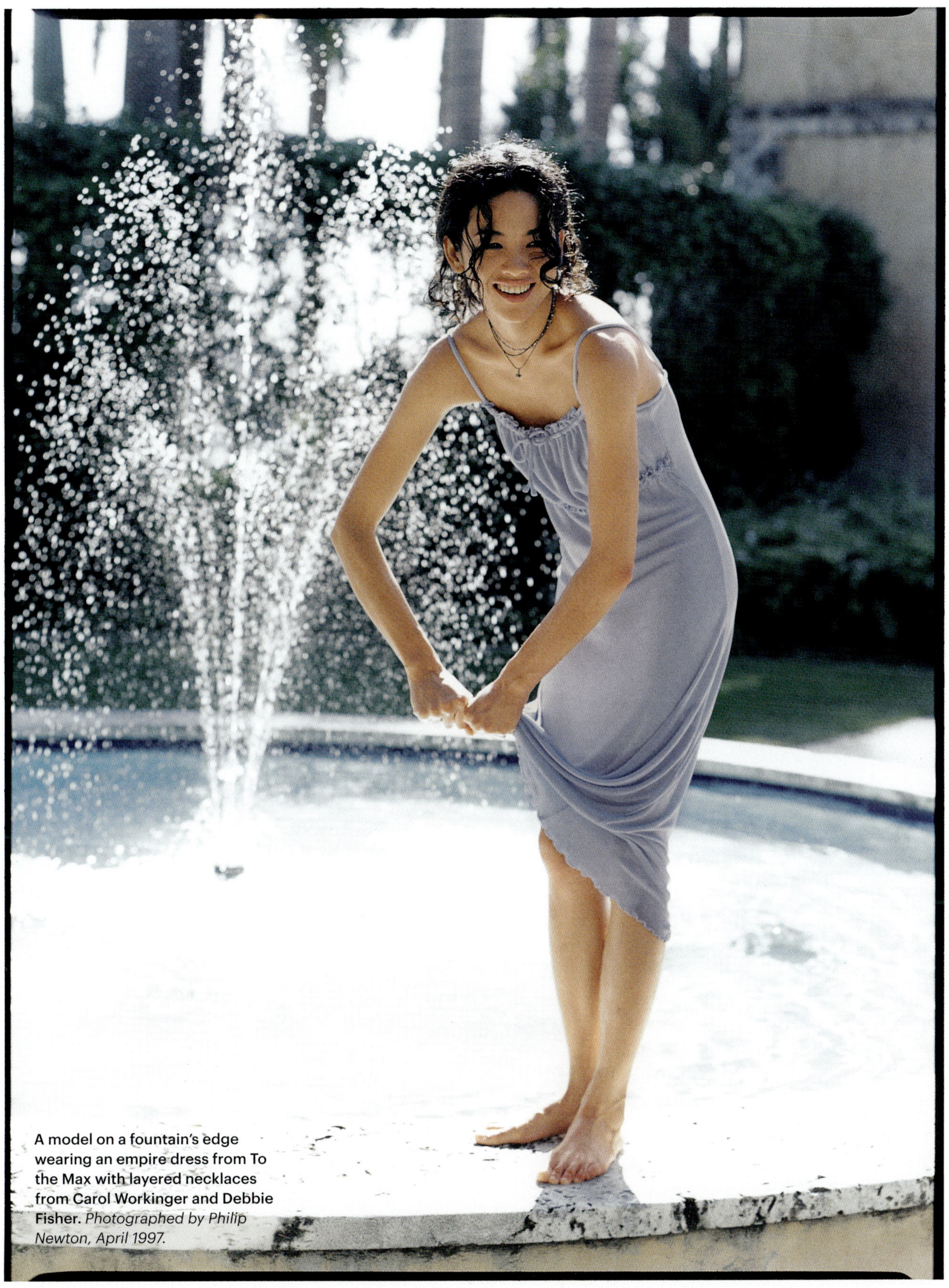

A model on a fountain's edge wearing an empire dress from To the Max with layered necklaces from Carol Workinger and Debbie Fisher. *Photographed by Philip Newton, April 1997.*

" In more than half the United States marital rape is not a crime, no matter how brutal the assault—because a married woman is considered the 'property' of her husband. It is not a crime to misuse one's own property. Moreover, according to these laws, a wife has no sexual rights—her husband is entitled to have sex with her whenever he wants.

" Word-processing machines look like typewriters hooked into TV screens, and all you do to operate one is type in the text. What you've typed appears on the TV screen. Then comes the great part: You can correct errors, change paragraphs around, add words and sentences, remove sections— all by moving a marker.

"SEX, MONEY, FOOD—WHAT WILL COMPUTERS INFLUENCE NEXT?" BY CHRISTINE BEGOLE, MAY 1983

" DON WOULD SPEND WEEKENDS, AND A NIGHT OR TWO DURING THE WEEK, AT HER PLACE. SHE RARELY STAYED AT HIS. AND ALTHOUGH DON HAPPILY ASSUMED DOMESTIC TASKS—LIKE DOING DISHES WITHOUT BEING ASKED—HELEN WOULD NEVER GIVE HIM A KEY. SHE MADE SURE HE KNEW HER PLACE DID NOT BELONG TO HIM.

"LIVING TOGETHER, BUT NOT" BY MARCIA STAMELL, NOVEMBER 1983

" IF WOMEN'S STATUS HAS NEVER BEEN HIGHER, WHY IS THEIR EMOTIONAL STATE SO LOW? IF AMERICAN WOMEN ARE SO EQUAL, WHY DO THEY REPRESENT TWO THIRDS OF ALL POOR ADULTS? WHY DOES THE AVERAGE WORKING WOMAN'S SALARY STILL LAG NEARLY AS FAR BEHIND THE AVERAGE MAN'S AS IT DID TWENTY YEARS AGO?

"BACKLASH" BY SUSAN FALUDI, OCTOBER 1991

" Most married women fret about a tardy husband; young black women like myself worry more. For most people in New York—truth be told—the urban bogeyman is a young black man in sneakers. But we live in Central Harlem, where every young man is black and wears sneakers…. I fear white men in police uniforms; white teenagers driving by in a car with Jersey plates; thin, panicky, middle-aged white men on the subway. Most of all, I fear that their path and my husband's path will cross one night as he makes his way home.

"IT'S TEN O'CLOCK AND I WORRY ABOUT WHERE MY HUSBAND IS" BY ROSEMARY L. BRAY, APRIL 1990

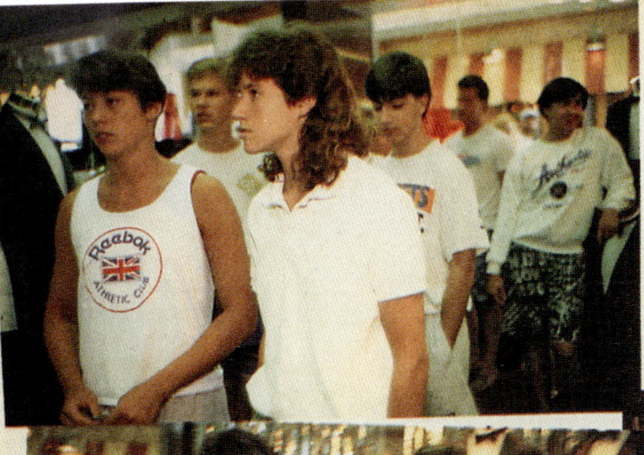

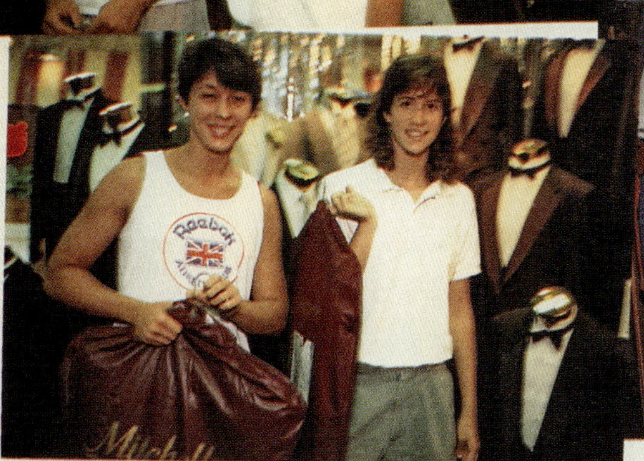

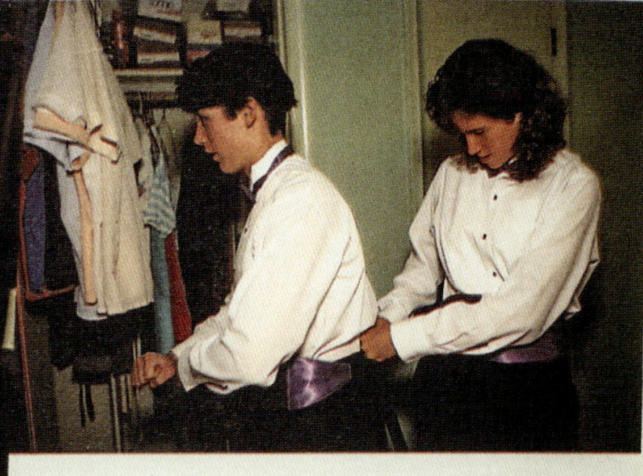

not just another **prom** *night*

SEVENTEEN-YEAR-OLD HEIDI LEITER scrutinizes herself in the mirror on the back of the closet door, one minute pleased with her appearance, the next minute totally discontent. She's so nervous about attending Osbourn High School's senior prom tonight that she hasn't been able to eat. "I feel like I'm getting ready to play the biggest district-tournament game *of my life*," she says.

"*I feel like I'm drunk or something, in these shoes!*" says her 20-year-old friend Missy Peters, walking unsteadily around the bedroom in the two-inch-high pumps she borrowed.

"Missy in heels," says Candi Schleig, a friend who has come to watch the preparations. "I never thought I'd see the day."

"You guys look great," another friend, Tammy Stephens, says supportively.

By Amy Cunningham

"Where's Dad?" Missy asks, brightening, ready for pictures. "He's sort of hiding," says her mother, Mary Ellen, monitoring the scene from the edge of the door frame.

"Well, tell him he better come up here!"

It could be mistaken for a timeless Norman Rockwell sketch of small-town American life. But today this two-story house in Manassas, Virginia, is the set for something quite unlike your standard-issue prom night.

Heidi and Missy are a lesbian couple, attending tonight's prom as each other's date. And instead of chiffon or taffeta, their outfits will *(Continued)*

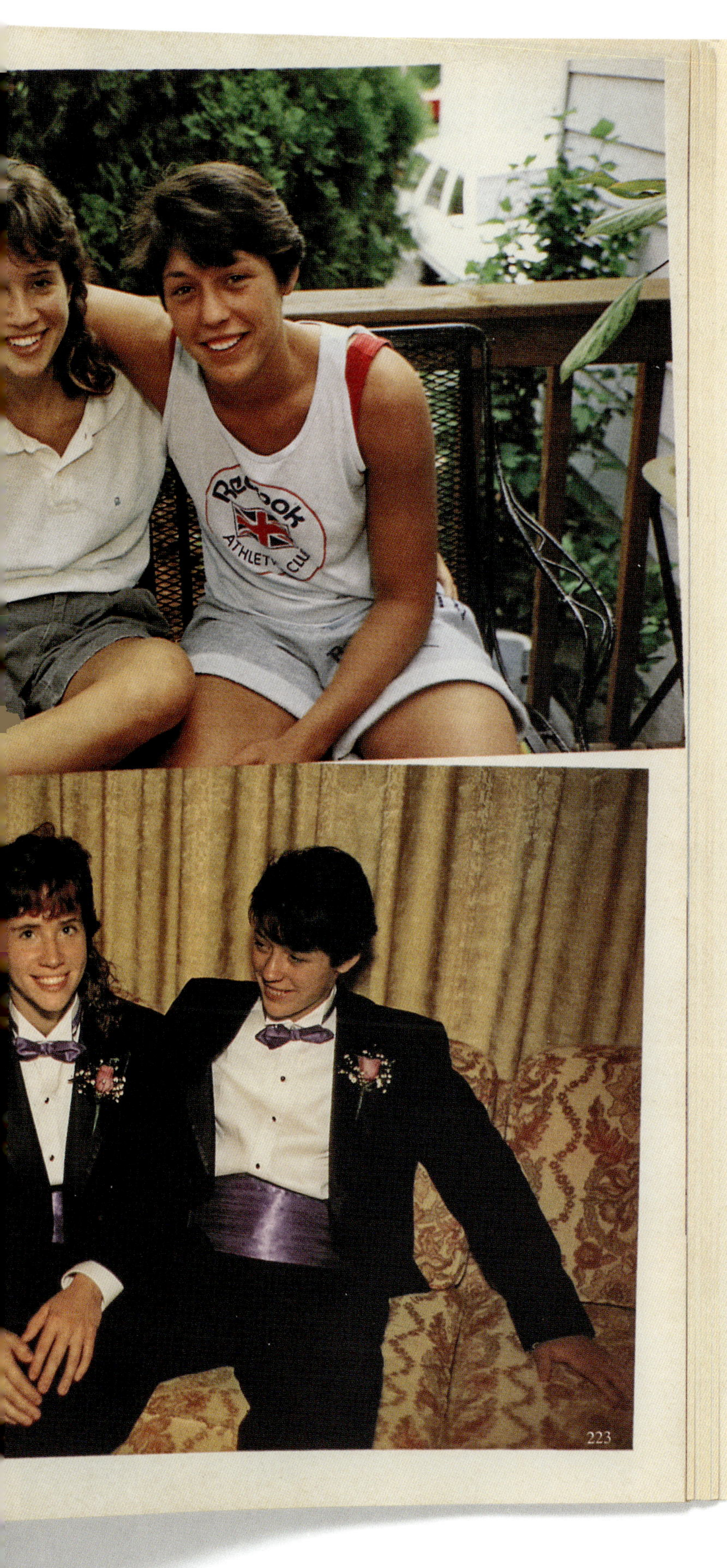

1992

LESBIANISM WASN'T A TOPIC

often explored in the pages of *Glamour*. It had been touched on in the 1970s, and was barely found in the 1980s, but by the 1990s the magazine had begun to explore relationships that weren't just heteronormative. In December 1998, a joyful article celebrating the coming out of a young, high-flying Manhattan executive demonstrated that *Glamour* was embracing a more inclusive approach in its relationship coverage. But perhaps the most notable piece was from June 1992, when the magazine followed a high school lesbian couple from Virginia heading off to prom together—and how their community of friends, family and fellow high school students had embraced them without prejudice.

←

Heidi Leiter and her girlfriend, Missy Peters, on the day of Heidi's prom in Manassas, Virginia. *Photographed by Nan Goldin, June 1992.*

Driving Forward on Race

IN JANUARY OF 1990, *Glamour* asked readers to answer a provocative survey: "Are Americans becoming more racist?" It came on the heels of disturbing incidents that shook the nation's conscience: A young Asian American killed by two white men. And just weeks later, the fatal shooting of an 18-year-old Black man by a group of white youths in New York. The survey's findings, unveiled in March 1990, painted a sobering picture: Sixty-one percent of respondents reported an increase in racial incidents within their communities, while a significant portion remained skeptical about progress toward integration. Shockingly, over half believed that racism had surged over the past decade.

The following month, the magazine published a piece by Rosemary L. Bray—detailing her fears that her husband would one day fall victim to the racism of white police officers and lose his life—that would go on to shape the next year's worth of coverage and discourse.

Bray's essay ignited a firestorm of reactions, ranging from accusations of racism to poignant reflections on societal divides. One comment read, "Shame on you, *Glamour*, for publishing such a racist article. Has the American government raised the quota for black staffers again?" Such was the response that Bray penned a follow-up article in August 1990, asking, "Do white people fear blacks unreasonably—so much so that innocent black men are often victimized, even killed, by fearful, panicky whites?" Addressing the backlash, she wrote, "I was depressed by the letters in the way that writers are when they have tried to say something and failed to communicate it." But she also pointed out that in the period of time she had been writing this article, another young Black man, Phillip Pannell, had lost his life in a racial attack.

"I didn't fan the flames of racial discord when I wrote this piece," she continued. "They were already burning bright, and black people are typically the ones close enough to feel the heat."

Once again, her article received an overwhelming response, more letters, in fact, than any *Glamour* article published in that year. But this time, some white readers expressed gratitude for the opportunity to confront their own biases and see the world through a different lens. One wrote to *Glamour*, "THANK YOU SO MUCH FOR Rosemary Bray's article. We all like to think that because we have a black friend or coworker we're free from racism. Never have I read anything that opened my eyes so much to my own prejudices."

As the decade progressed, *Glamour* remained at the forefront of the conversation on race. In March 1992, Martha Southgate's article "Women of color: on the front lines of a changing workplace" shed light on the internal biases prevalent in corporate settings. Additionally, the magazine highlighted significant milestones, such as Julie Dash's groundbreaking film *Daughters of the Dust*, marking a shift toward greater representation of Black women among filmmakers. In another side of Hollywood, *Glamour*'s June 1995 issue addressed the industry's historic lack of opportunities for ➡

Rosemary L. Bray's article in *Glamour*'s April 1990 issue.

BY ROSEMARY L. BRAY

It's ten o'clock, and I worry about where my husband is

He phoned more than an hour ago, to say he was on his way home. But I have yet to hear the scrape of the iron gate, the rattling keys, so I worry.

Most married women fret about a tardy husband; young black women like myself worry more. For most people in New York—truth be told—the urban bogeyman is a young black man in sneakers. But we live in Central Harlem, where every young man is black and wears sneakers, so we learn to look into the eyes of young males and discern the difference between youthful bravado and the true dangers of the streets. No, I have other fears. I fear white men in police uniforms; white teenagers driving by in a car with Jersey plates; thin, panicky, middle-aged white men on the subway. Most of all, I fear that their path and my husband's path will cross one night as he makes his way home.

Bob is tall—5'10" or so, dark, with thick hair and wire-rimmed glasses. He carries a knapsack stuffed with work from the office, old crossword puzzles, Philip Glass tapes, *Ebony Man* and *People* magazines. When it rains, he carries his good shoes in the bag and wears his Reebok sneakers. He cracks his knuckles a lot, and wears a peculiar grimace when his mind is elsewhere. He looks dear and gentle to me—but then, I have looked into those eyes for a long time.

I worry that some white person will see that grim, focused look of concentration and see the intent to victimize. I fear that some white person will look at him and see only his or her nightmare—another black man in sneakers. In fact, my husband *is* another black man in sneakers. He's also a writer, an amateur cyclist, a lousy basketball player, his parents' son, my life's companion. When I put aside the book I'm reading to peek out the window, the visions in my head are those of blind white panic at my husband's black presence, visions of a flashing gun, a gleaming knife: I see myself a sudden, horrified widow at thirty-four.

Once upon a time, I was vaguely ashamed of my paranoia about his safety in the world outside our home. After all, he is a grown man. But he is a grown black man on the streets alone, a menace to white New Yorkers—even the nice, sympathetic, liberal ones who smile at us when we're together. And I am reminded, over and over, how dangerous white people still can be, how their fears are a hazard to our health. When white people are ruled by their fear of everything black, every black woman is an addict, a whore; every black man is a rapist—even a murderer.

Charles Stuart understood this fear well enough to manipulate an entire nation. When he said a black man in Boston's Mission Hill district put a bullet through the head of his pregnant wife, who could doubt him? So a city's police force moved through the neighborhood, stopping and strip-searching black men at random, looking for the apocryphal black savage who, it turned out, existed only in Boston's collective imagination. Yet an innocent African-American man, William Bennett, was paraded before the nation for weeks, until Stuart's brother had an attack of conscience and went to the police.

The Stuart case was shameful, but it could have been worse—after all, William Bennett is still alive. When whites' fear of black people is allowed its freest reign, black people can die.

Wasn't Michael Griffith a bum out to make trouble when a teenage posse in Howard Beach chased him onto the Shore Parkway into the path of a car? Wasn't Yusef Hawkins a thug coming to beat up a white man in Bensonhurst when he was surrounded by a gang of teenagers and shot? It doesn't seem to matter that Michael Griffith was a construction worker, that Yusef Hawkins was a student looking for a used car. Someone looked at those two men and saw danger, and so they are dead. And the women who waited for them—who peeked out the front windows and listened for footsteps on the stairs—waited in vain.

So when it's ten o'clock and he's not home yet, my thoughts can't help but wander to other black men—husbands, fathers, sons, brothers—who never do make it home, and to other black women whose fingers no longer rest at a curtain's edge. Even after I hear the scrape of our iron gate, the key in the lock, even after I hear that old knapsack hit the floor of the downstairs hallway and Bob's voice calling to me, my thoughts return to them.

Rosemary L. Bray is an editor at The New York Times Book Review.

↑

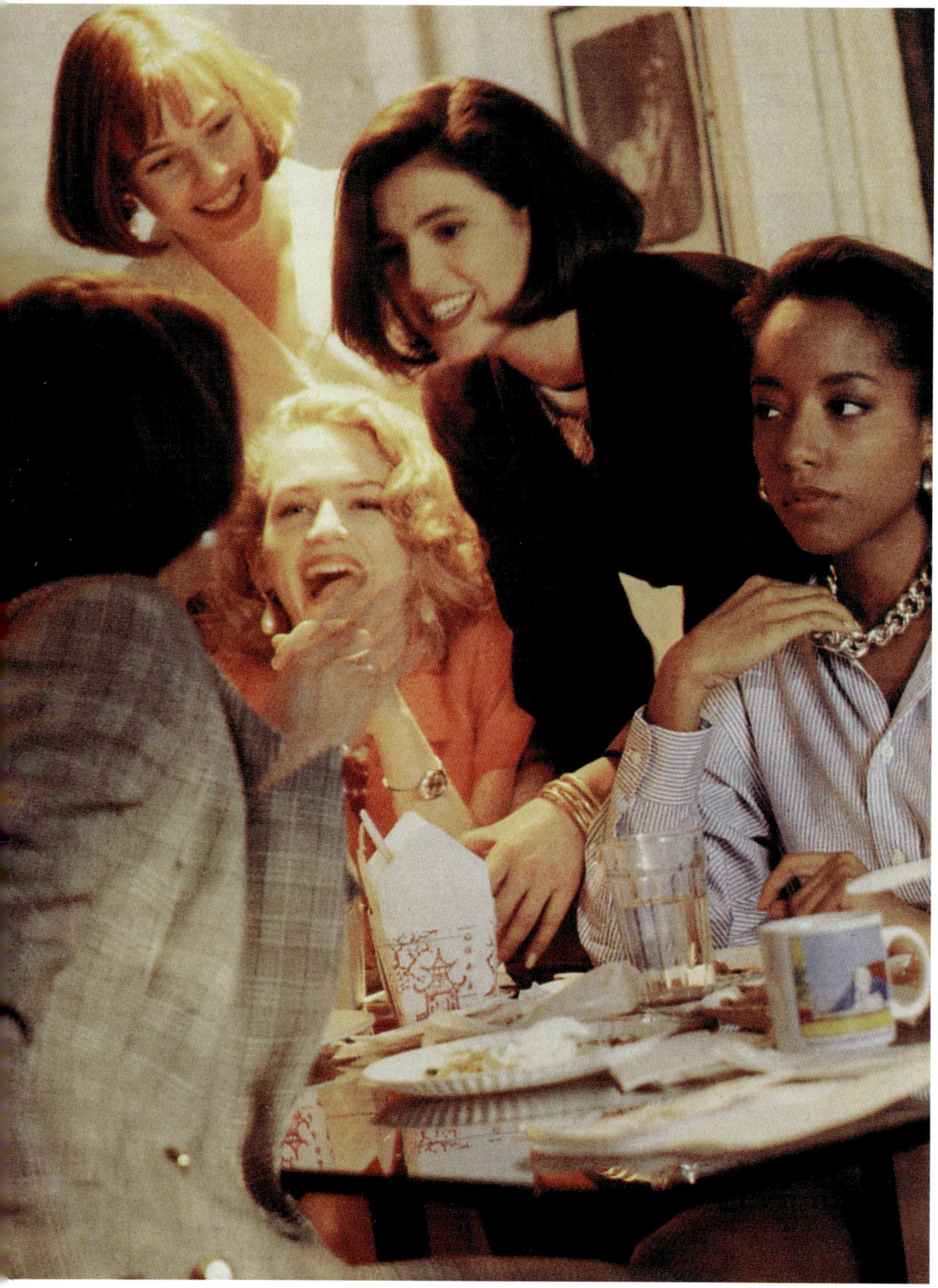

A photo taken to illustrate *Glamour*'s article "Women of color: on the front lines of a changing workplace." *Photographed by Chris Sanders, March 1992.*

actresses of color. While acknowledging progress with rising stars like Angela Bassett, Halle Berry, Whitney Houston, and Jada Pinkett, and supermodels like Tyra Banks and Naomi Campbell, the magazine underscored ongoing challenges in achieving true diversity onscreen.

These were just a handful of the topics that *Glamour* covered—others included the women coming together to rebuild Los Angeles in the aftermath of the 1992 riots, the childhood experiences of racism for women of color, "The Racism of Well-Meaning White People," and a thought-provoking piece by Veronica Chambers about the unique burden placed on Black women to prioritize racial solidarity, even at the expense of addressing their own experiences of sexism within their community.

As the 1990s came to an end, *Glamour*'s race coverage encapsulated the decade's shifting dialogues, amplified diverse voices, and urged readers to confront uncomfortable realities and scrutinize their own prejudices. Yet, amid its strides, *Glamour* faced a glaring gap in representation. The staff of the magazine was still overwhelmingly white, and for all the important dialogue these articles sparked, there was still much progress to be made.

→

A selection of *Glamour* pieces dealing with race and racism in the 1990s.

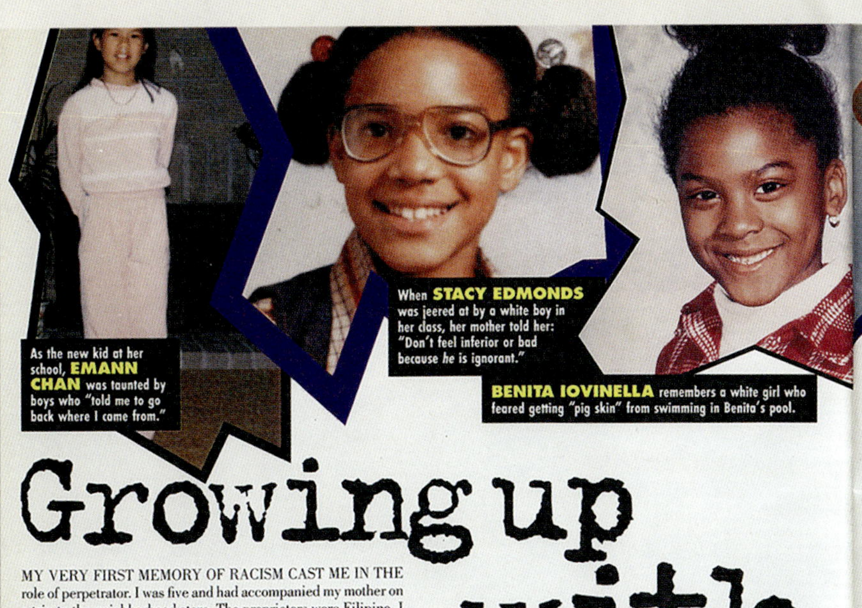

As the new kid at her school, **EMANN CHAN** was taunted by boys who "told me to go back where I came from."

When **STACY EDMONDS** was jeered at by a white boy in her class, her mother told her: "Don't feel inferior or bad because he is ignorant."

BENITA IOVINELLA remembers a white girl who feared getting "pig skin" from swimming in Benita's pool.

One childhood friend told **RENAE MOORE:** "You're black, and my parents don't want you over at our house."

DEBBIE COATS tells her biracial daughter "to let the kids who are bothering her know that she is still a very nice person."

Growing up with racism

MY VERY FIRST MEMORY OF RACISM CAST ME IN THE role of perpetrator. I was five and had accompanied my mother on a trip to the neighborhood store. The proprietors were Filipino. I know that now, but I didn't then. What I knew at age five was that the couple behind the counter had straight hair and slanted eyes—not white people, but not black like me either. I liked the couple; they always smiled at Mama and me and gave me a piece of penny candy. But they were different, and this time I thought I knew why.

"Mama, they're Japs," I … childish … hear …

safely raising their own children in a prejudice-laden world. Hundreds of women responded, not with casual notes or brief messages but with poems and short stories, handwritten letters three and four pages long, faxes from their offices sent during lunch breaks. In asking readers to recall the searing experience of learning how it feels to be hated for who you are, *Glamour* clearly opened old wounds. Women of African American descent wrote of insults endured 20 years earlier—and still remembered in every detail. Women who are Native American wrote of feeling nearly invisible in the nation's loaded debate about ethnicity. Women of Asian and Hispanic descent wrote, sometimes in res-

there are people who do not deserve the same life as her own; she will forever be looking over her shoulder, tracking the path of the encroaching other, feeling under siege. If bigots are lucky, they … words ha…

ignation, sometimes in bitterness, about their hostile encounters with other people of color as well as with whites. Biracial and multiracial women spoke of the loneliness that comes with belonging to no particular group … confusion that comes with belonging to several. … tigate *Glamour* for not … ence …

up against a boy in the hallway … he yelled, 'Oh no, a nigger tou… me.' Then everyone within ea… started laughing...."

Renae C. Moore, 26, now of L… ville, Colorado, recalled that durin… Chicago childhood her friends' pa… had been confused to discover tha… mother was white and her father b… "I can remember when another … friend and I had to drink from hos… some people's backyards on hot days, while the white chi… would drink comfortably inside one of their homes. We we… allowed in.

"One summ… s a big backyard party at the h… e. All of the children on the…

You gotta be cool, you gotta be strong, you gotta be wiser…

If you think white actresses have trouble finding roles, try being one of the dazzling pack of talent pushing Hollywood to go color-blind

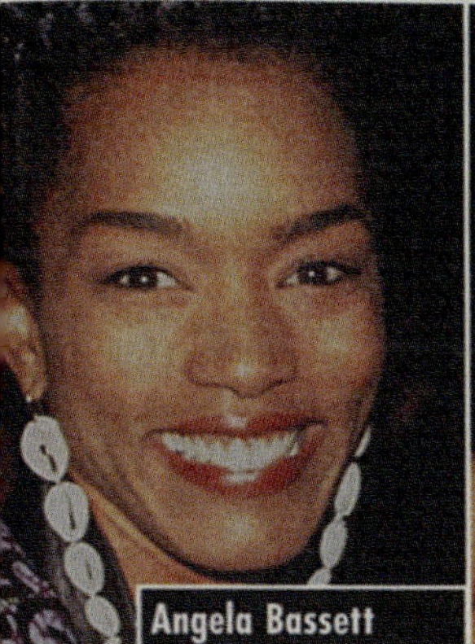

Angela Bassett

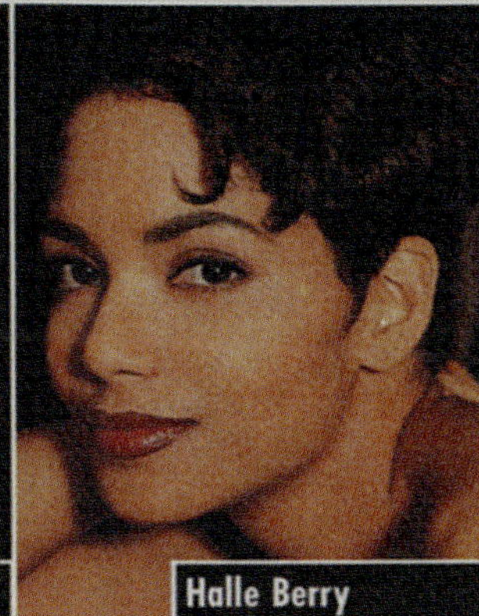

Halle Berry

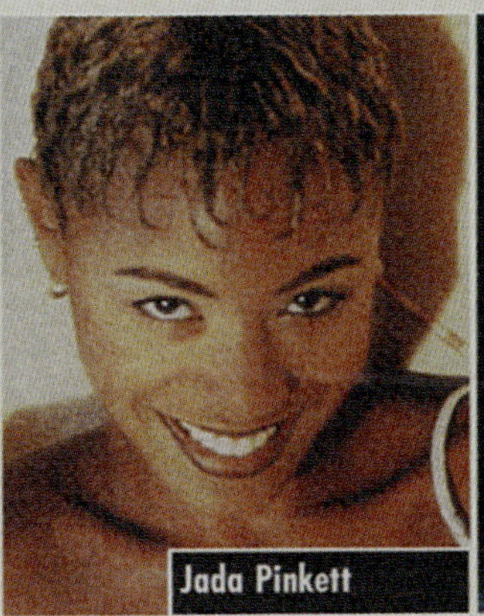

Jada Pinkett

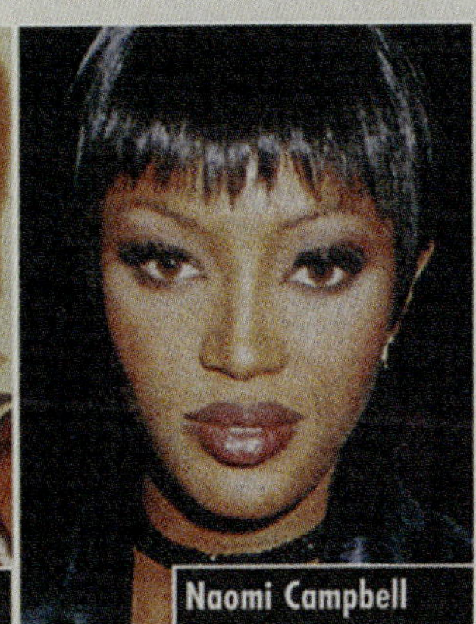

Naomi Campbell

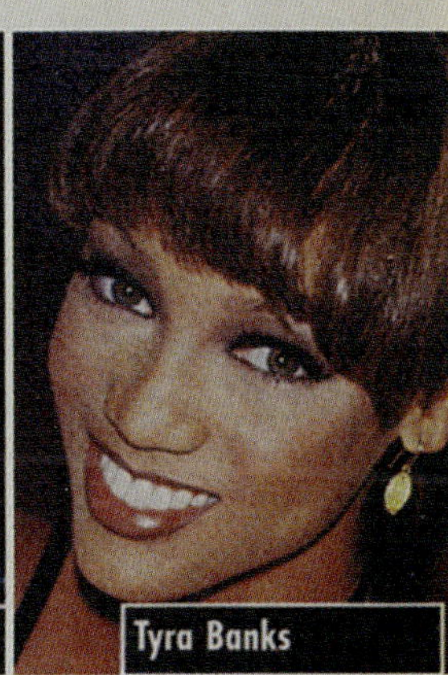

Tyra Banks

Is the war on drugs racist?

A WHITE MAN BUYS THREE grams of cocaine at a party. A black man buys three grams of crack on the street. Both get caught—but the cocaine user gets put on probation… ent," says Richard Wintory, director of the National Drug Prosecution Center. "Crack is cheaper, and—since it's smoked rather than snorted—gets a person high faster. If someone has three grams of pow-

A teenager fights anti-Semitism

Residents of Wellesley, Massachusetts, woke up to an ugly surpri[se] last October. During the night—the eve of Yom Kippur, the ho[liest]

No more waiting our turn

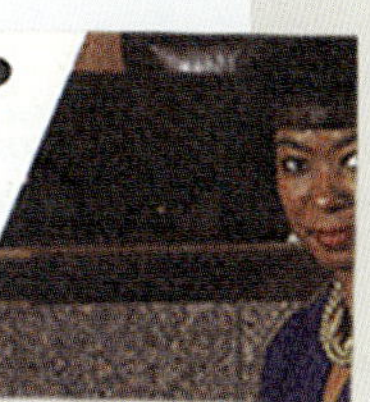

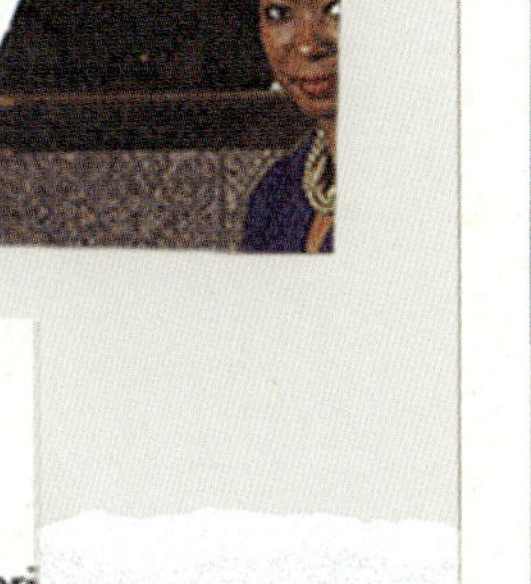

Why should black women swallow their protests in the name of racial unity?

women on either side of us glanced over— then quickly looked away. "I completely understand you," Roger said. "But you have to be careful how you say things. You don't want people to think that you're not pro-black."

I wanted to laugh, but I also wanted to cry. Not pro-black? I wake up black every day. But I also wake up female every day, and I, like many black women before me, am fed up with taking sides against myself. In the 1950s, when the black community began agitating in earnest for civil rights,

BY LE ANNE SCHREIBER

campus rape

Welcome to the "honeymoon period," "blackout sex" and other dangers of college life

This month the class of

1994 will arrive on college campuses across the country. The traditional rites of welcome will no doubt include a chancellor's address in which the new students are told that one out of four of them will not graduate or one out of twenty will go on to receive Ph.D.'s or one out of fifty is bound for fame and glory. The figures will vary from campus to campus but the message of possibility remains the same. What the students will not be told is that another statistic, this one virtually unvarying from campus to campus, will cast a shadow over their college years.

At schools large and small, urban and rural, Midwestern and Ivy League, one out of seven female students is a victim of rape. By their own admission, one out of twelve male students commits or attempts rape, usually more than once. The problem of sexual assault on college campuses is national, widespread and unabated, and yet, despite the evidence, it is largely unaddressed by students, their parents or college administrators. Because the vast majority of these rapes go unreported except on the blanks of anonymous questionnaires, it is all too easy for college administrators to believe that it isn't happening in *their* quads, in *their* dorms, on *their* fraternity row.

In the rare case of a reported rape on campus, the temptation is to treat it as an isolated event, shocking, frightening and aberrant. That was the response of both students and officials one year ago at Syracuse University, a large private school located in central New York State, when an eighteen-year-old student reported that she had been raped near the chancellor's home during the first week of classes.

The following week, when another eighteen-year-old student reported that she had been raped in her dorm room by two young men who had escorted her home from a nearby bar, the temper of the campus began to change. Two hundred placard-carrying students marched to the administration building to demand that something be done. Seeing a public relations disaster in the making, Chancellor Melvin Eggers responded later that afternoon by appointing a task force to study the issue and report back to him within thirty days. During the month it took the university task force to do its work, four more rapes were reported.

The impact of six reported rapes in five weeks *(Continued)*

Was it rape?

The annual National Crime Survey indicates that for every reported rape, there are three to ten unreported ones. But there is reason to believe that the estimate of underreporting is itself an underestimation, particularly in cases of date and acquaintance rape. The myth of the rapist as psychopathic stranger is so firmly rooted that victims of rape by an acquaintance often do not realize the word "rape" applies to their experience, and so do not respond accurately to questions about the crime.

Researchers have tried to overcome the inadequacies of government figures on rape by devising survey questions about specific sexual experiences that meet the prevailing legal definition of rape without using the word rape. The largest such study ever undertaken was organized by clinical psychologist Mary P. Koss, Ph.D., now a professor at the University of Arizona Medical School. The subjects of her 1984 to 1985 survey, conducted with the help of the *Ms.* Foundation and the National Institute of Mental Health, were 6,159 male and female undergraduates at thirty-two American colleges.

Fifteen percent of the female students surveyed by Koss indicated that they had been victims of one or more rapes since the age of fourteen. Another 12 percent said they had been victims of one or more attempted rapes.

Even more disturbing were the answers female students gave to questions about their sexual experience in the previous six months. According to the narrow definition of rape— penetration against consent use of force or the threat o harm—thirty-eight women pe sand indicated they had been the previous six months. If one broader definition of rape that oral, anal or vaginal pene against consent through use of threat of bodily harm, or intent capacitation of the victim by al drugs—the rate jumps to eigh rape victims per thousand, o twelve female students, ove

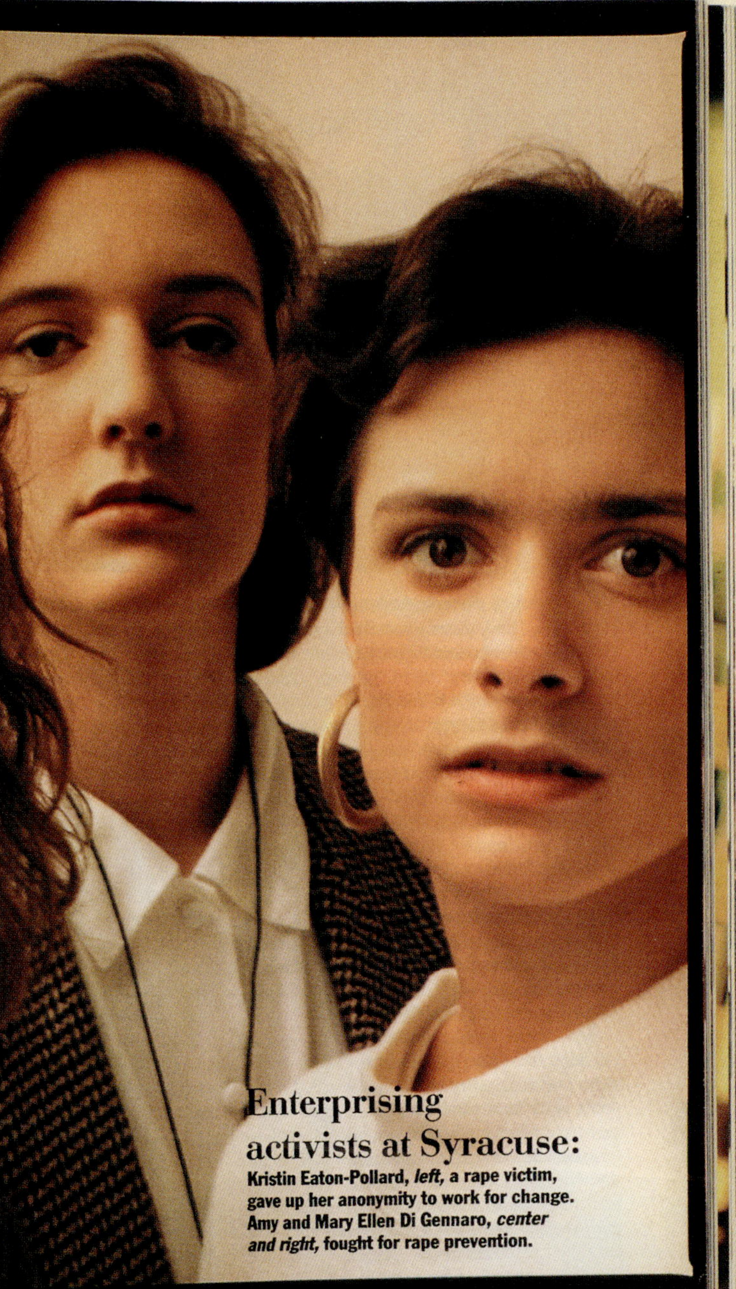

...eriod. Yet only 27 percent of ...s used the term rape. Perhaps ...st result of the survey is that ...t of the victims expected to be ...ain.

...t of four male students said he ...ged in some form of sexual co-...nd one out of twelve admitted ...ng acts that met legal defini-...rape or attempted rape; only ...ent of these men identified ...gression as rape or attempted ...s important to note that these ...itted to committing such acts more than once in a six-month period.

The fact that men who rape tend to do it repeatedly underscores the importance of reporting sexual assault to campus authorities or rape-crisis centers as well as to the police. Even if a victim decides not to press charges, her report may help past or future victims of the same man who do choose to pursue prosecution.

Additional information on acquaintance rape can be found in *I Never Called It Rape*, by Robin Warshaw (Harper & Row). —L.S.

1990

BEGINNING IN THE EARLY '80S, *Glamour* began to tackle one of the greatest threats women faced—sexual violence. It permeated college campuses, relationships, and even workplaces. Yet the law didn't offer anywhere near enough protection for women. In September 1986, Elizabeth Holtzman, the first woman elected district attorney in New York City, wrote a *Glamour* article titled "The 'Right' to Rape: The male belief that promotes violence against women," calling for sweeping legal reforms. The magazine published moving real-life stories—including in 1981 by writer Carole Thompson about outsmarting her rapist, yet not being believed by the police when she first reported it. As the '90s dawned, *Glamour*'s coverage explored the emerging complexities of rape culture. A September 1990 report, "Campus Rape," exposed the prevalence of sexual assault, with one in seven female students falling victim; a January 1992 article asked the question "Can a whole company be guilty of sexual harassment?" after three employees launched a class action lawsuit on behalf of all female workers at a Minnesota mining company; and piece after piece examined rape in relationships and acquaintanceships. *Glamour*'s coverage, spanning two transformative decades, served as a beacon for advocacy and awareness against sexual violence. While progress was made, the magazine's legacy underscored the ongoing need for societal shifts and support for survivors during that time.

←

Three advocates for change in rape prevention. *Photographed by Frank W. Ockenfels III, September 1990.*

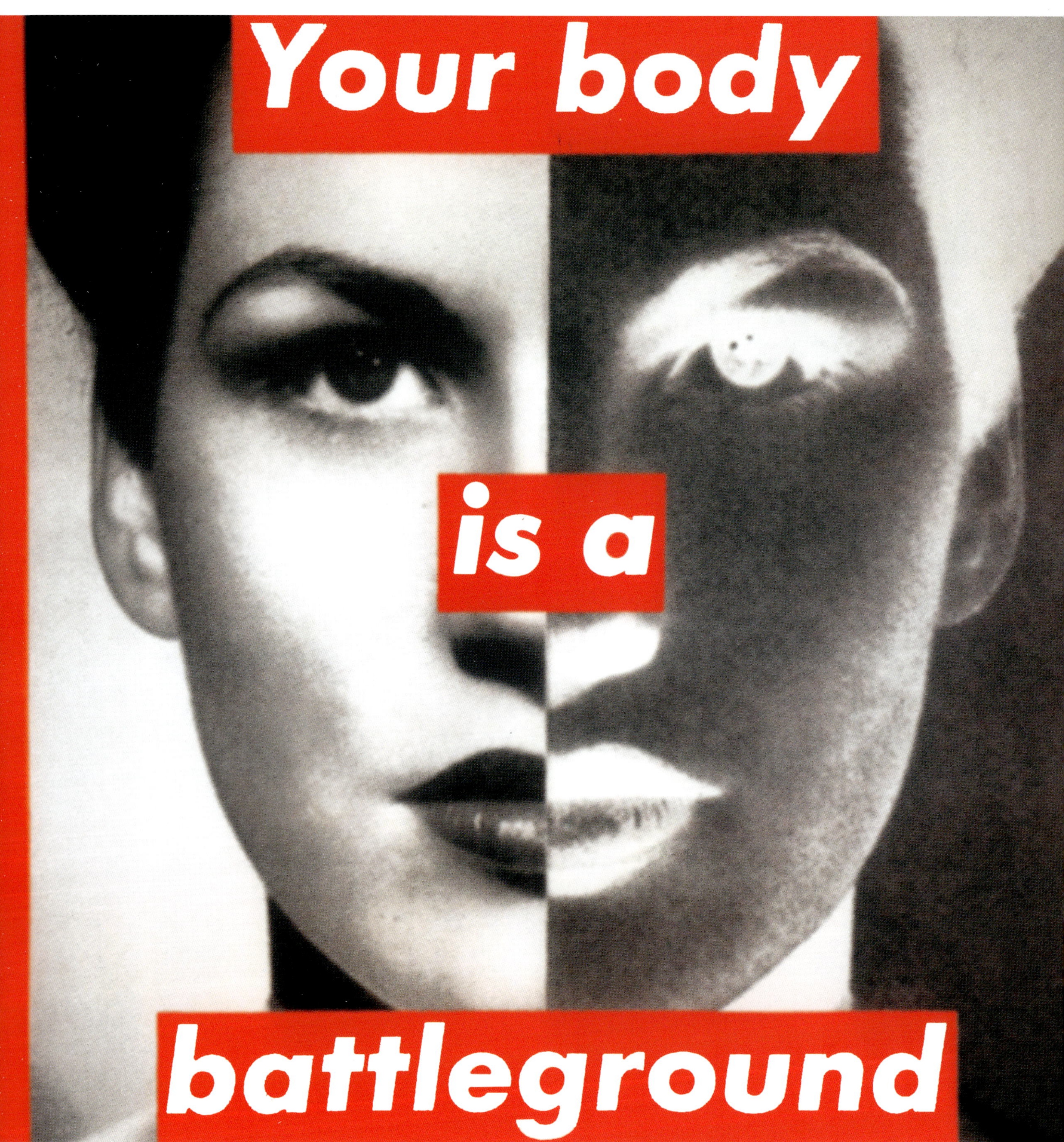

↑

Barbara Kruger, *Untitled (Your body is a battleground)*, 1989.
Courtesy of the artist, The Broad Art Foundation, and Sprüth Magers.

IT QUICKLY BECAME CLEAR that despite the Supreme Court ruling on *Roe v. Wade*, women's right to an abortion was not safe. In 1981, *Glamour* reported that three days after President Ronald Reagan took office, "he became the first President to meet in the Oval Office with groups that are working to make abortion illegal." And there were two bills and 17 constitutional amendments filed in the then current session of Congress to make it illegal. *Glamour* was, and remains, staunchly pro-choice and did not let up on coverage. While there were many pieces on the topic published over the course of these two decades (as well as those examining the impact of the pro-life movement on the availability of contraception), three in particular stand out: "Teenage and Pregnant" (March 1991) and "Where Are the Doctors Who Will Do Abortions?" (September 1991), both by Le Anne Schreiber, and "A Town Held Hostage" (December 1991) by Francis Wilkinson. Together, the three articles won the prestigious public interest category at the 1992 National Magazine Awards. Editor in chief Ruth Whitney's words on the articles are worth still heeding today: "Le Anne Schreiber's job was to find real girls, real case histories, and report on real experiences. In the process she learned that it was…sometimes almost impossible for a rural woman to travel the hundreds of miles necessary to reach a doctor who could do the abortion. There were so few doctors available that even though abortion was legal, it was often inaccessible. So when she finished the story in Minnesota, she researched and wrote 'Where are the doctors who will do abortions?' You have heard a lot about the subject since. [And] we clearly took a leadership role and exposed a doctor shortage which poses a real danger to the right to choose."

↓

An article from *Glamour*'s September 1991 issue.

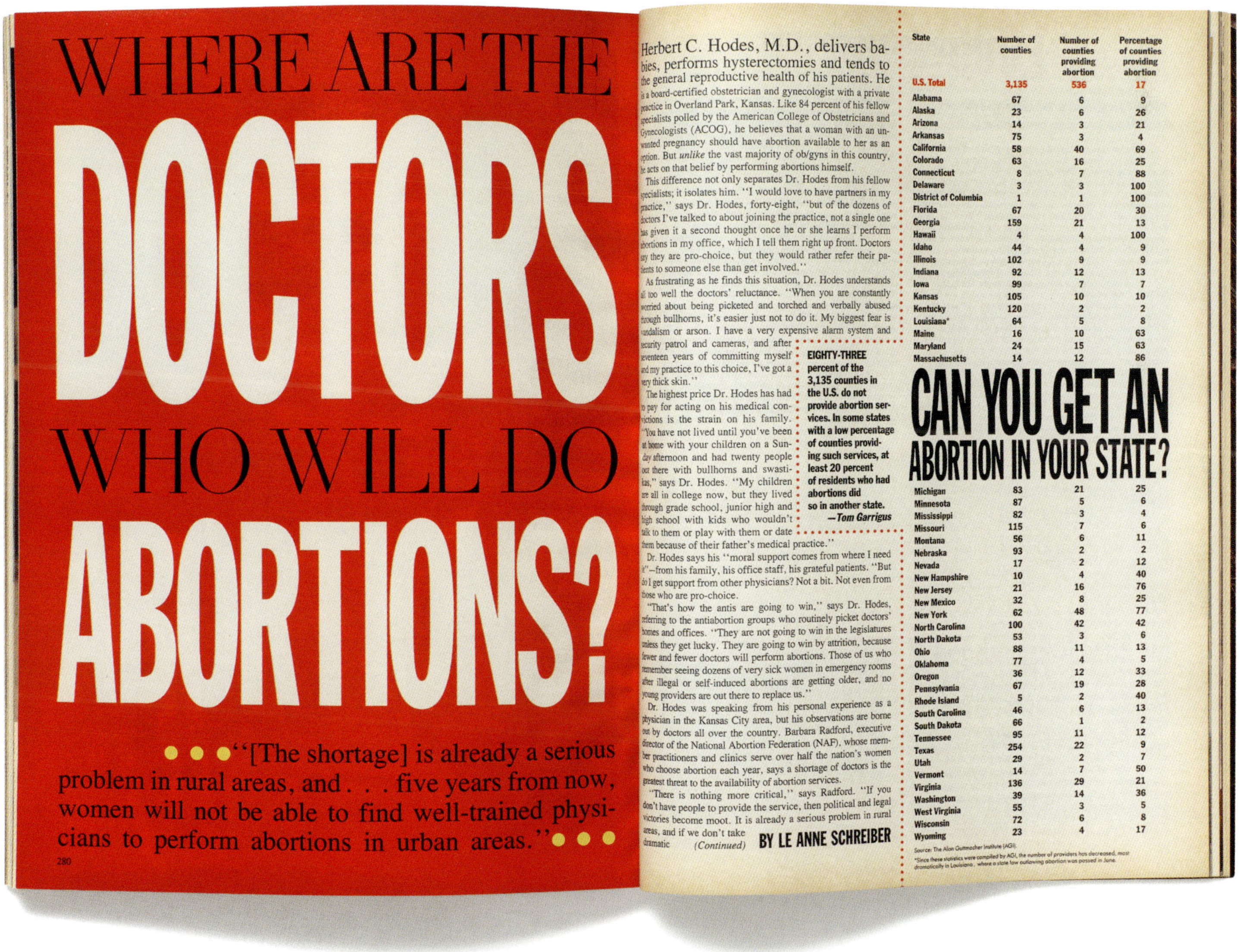

WHERE ARE THE DOCTORS WHO WILL DO ABORTIONS?

●●● "[The shortage] is already a serious problem in rural areas, and . . . five years from now, women will not be able to find well-trained physicians to perform abortions in urban areas." ●●●

Herbert C. Hodes, M.D., delivers babies, performs hysterectomies and tends to the general reproductive health of his patients. He is a board-certified obstetrician and gynecologist with a private practice in Overland Park, Kansas. Like 84 percent of his fellow specialists polled by the American College of Obstetricians and Gynecologists (ACOG), he believes that a woman with an unwanted pregnancy should have abortion available to her as an option. But *unlike* the vast majority of ob/gyns in this country, he acts on that belief by performing abortions himself.

This difference not only separates Dr. Hodes from his fellow specialists; it isolates him. "I would love to have partners in my practice," says Dr. Hodes, forty-eight, "but of the dozens of doctors I've talked to about joining the practice, not a single one has given it a second thought once he or she learns I perform abortions in my office, which I tell them right up front. Doctors say they are pro-choice, but they would rather refer their patients to someone else than get involved."

As frustrating as he finds this situation, Dr. Hodes understands all too well the doctors' reluctance. "When you are constantly worried about being picketed and torched and verbally abused through bullhorns, it's easier just not to do it. My biggest fear is vandalism or arson. I have a very expensive alarm system and security patrol and cameras, and after seventeen years of committing myself and my practice to this choice, I've got a very thick skin."

The highest price Dr. Hodes has had to pay for acting on his medical convictions is the strain on his family. "You have not lived until you've been at home with your children on a Sunday afternoon and had twenty people out there with bullhorns and swastikas," says Dr. Hodes. "My children are all in college now, but they lived through grade school, junior high and high school with kids who wouldn't talk to them or play with them or date them because of their father's medical practice."

Dr. Hodes says his "moral support comes from where I need it"—from his family, his office staff, his grateful patients. "But do I get support from other physicians? Not a bit. Not even from those who are pro-choice.

"That's how the antis are going to win," says Dr. Hodes, referring to the antiabortion groups who routinely picket doctors' homes and offices. "They are not going to win in the legislatures unless they get lucky. They are going to win by attrition, because fewer and fewer doctors will perform abortions. Those of us who remember seeing dozens of very sick women in emergency rooms after illegal or self-induced abortions are getting older, and no young providers are out there to replace us."

Dr. Hodes was speaking from his personal experience as a physician in the Kansas City area, but his observations are borne out by doctors all over the country. Barbara Radford, executive director of the National Abortion Federation (NAF), whose member practitioners and clinics serve over half the nation's women who choose abortion each year, says a shortage of doctors is the greatest threat to the availability of abortion services.

"There is nothing more critical," says Radford. "If you don't have people to provide the service, then political and legal victories become moot. It is already a serious problem in rural areas, and if we don't take dramatic *(Continued)*

EIGHTY-THREE percent of the 3,135 counties in the U.S. do not provide abortion services. In some states with a low percentage of counties providing such services, at least 20 percent of residents who had abortions did so in another state.
—Tom Garrigus

BY LE ANNE SCHREIBER

CAN YOU GET AN ABORTION IN YOUR STATE?

State	Number of counties	Number of counties providing abortion	Percentage of counties providing abortion
U.S. Total	3,135	536	17
Alabama	67	6	9
Alaska	23	6	26
Arizona	14	3	21
Arkansas	75	3	4
California	58	40	69
Colorado	63	16	25
Connecticut	8	7	88
Delaware	3	3	100
District of Columbia	1	1	100
Florida	67	20	30
Georgia	159	21	13
Hawaii	4	4	100
Idaho	44	4	9
Illinois	102	9	9
Indiana	92	12	13
Iowa	99	7	7
Kansas	105	10	10
Kentucky	120	2	2
Louisiana*	64	5	8
Maine	16	10	63
Maryland	24	15	63
Massachusetts	14	12	86
Michigan	83	21	25
Minnesota	87	5	6
Mississippi	82	3	4
Missouri	115	7	6
Montana	56	6	11
Nebraska	93	2	2
Nevada	17	2	12
New Hampshire	10	4	40
New Jersey	21	16	76
New Mexico	32	8	25
New York	62	48	77
North Carolina	100	42	42
North Dakota	53	3	6
Ohio	88	11	13
Oklahoma	77	4	5
Oregon	36	12	33
Pennsylvania	67	19	28
Rhode Island	5	2	40
South Carolina	46	6	13
South Dakota	66	1	2
Tennessee	95	11	12
Texas	254	22	9
Utah	29	2	7
Vermont	14	7	50
Virginia	136	29	21
Washington	39	14	36
West Virginia	55	3	5
Wisconsin	72	6	8
Wyoming	23	4	17

Source: The Alan Guttmacher Institute (AGI).

*Since these statistics were compiled by AGI, the number of providers has decreased, most dramatically in Louisiana, where a state law outlawing abortion was passed in June.

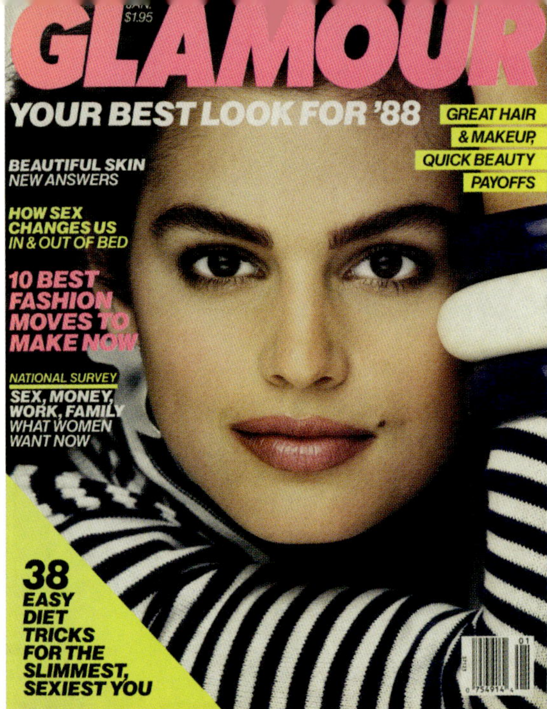

← Cindy Crawford's second of her five *Glamour* covers, shot here at the beginning of the supermodel era, January 1988.

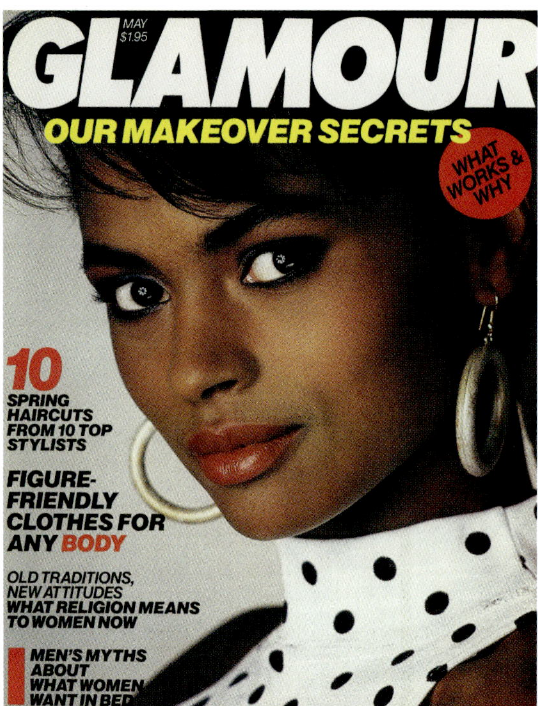

← Karen Alexander, a barrier-breaking model of the '80s and '90s, who in 1988 became one of the first models of color to cover *Sports Illustrated*. May 1986.

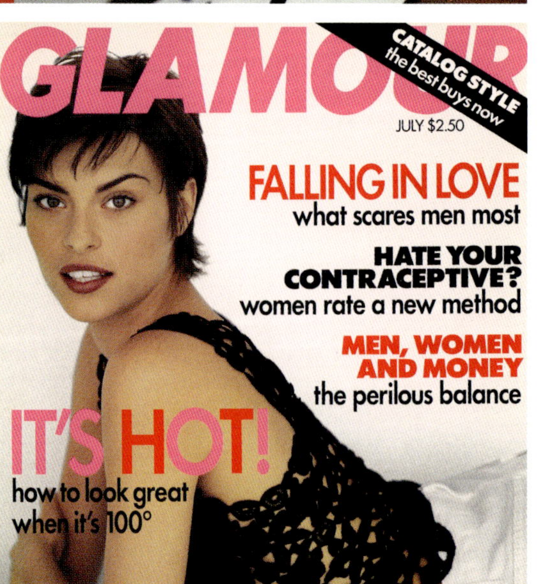

← Magali Amadei would go on to star in *The Wedding Planner* (2001) and *Taxi* (2004). She is seen here on *Glamour*'s July 1994 cover.

→ Naomi Campbell, who graced *Glamour*'s fashion pages in the '80s and '90s, on her first and only cover, February 1991.

"THE COVER MODEL serves as a kind of role model." So wrote *Glamour*'s editor in chief Ruth Whitney in a Howard University Speech in 1989. "When I'm choosing a picture for the cover of *Glamour*, the main thing I look for in the face of any model, any month of the year, is the feeling that she wants to relate to me." This clearly resonates in these iconic and memorable covers.

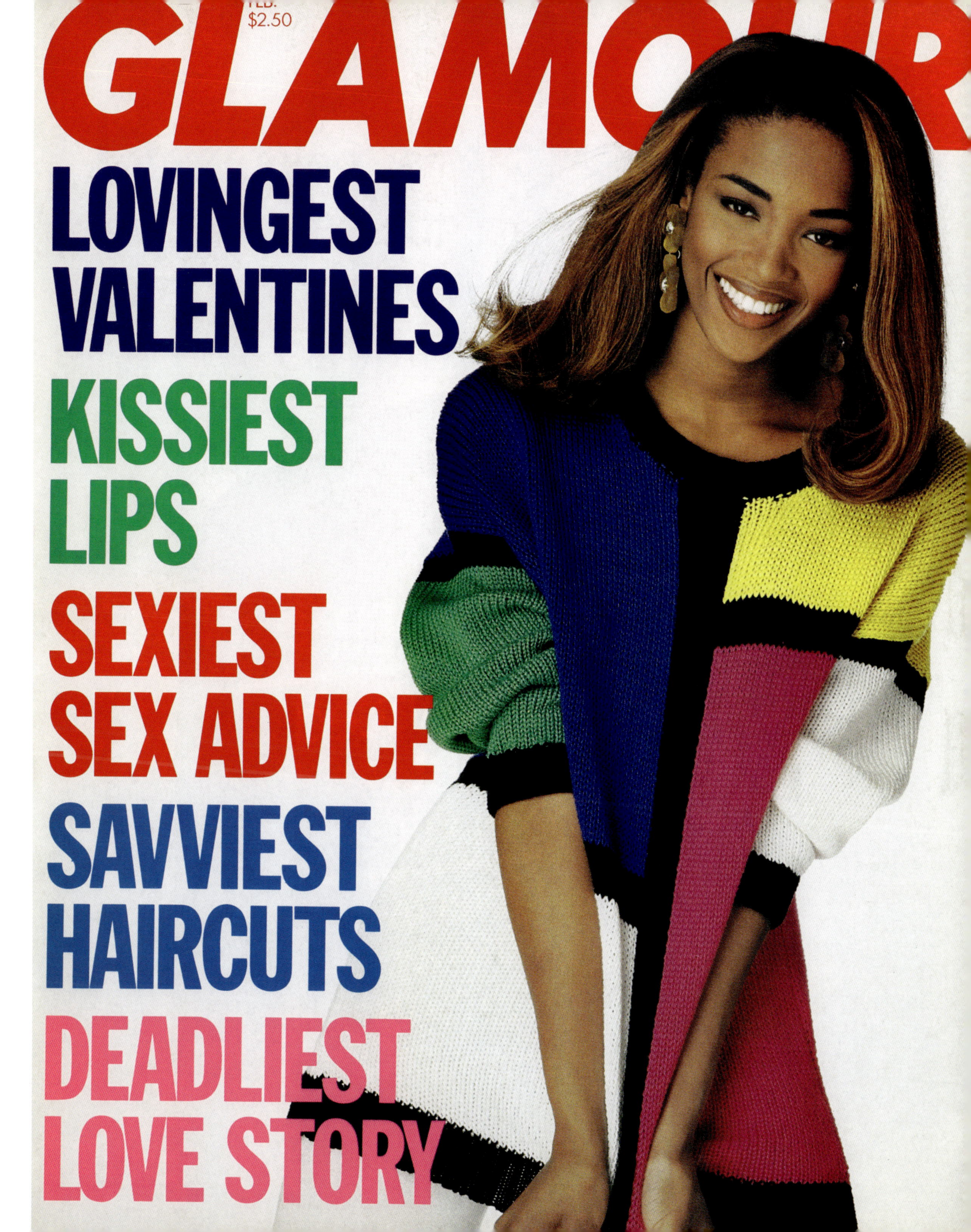

FEB.
$2.50
GLAMOUR
LOVINGEST
VALENTINES
KISSIEST
LIPS
SEXIEST
SEX ADVICE
SAVVIEST
HAIRCUTS
DEADLIEST
LOVE STORY

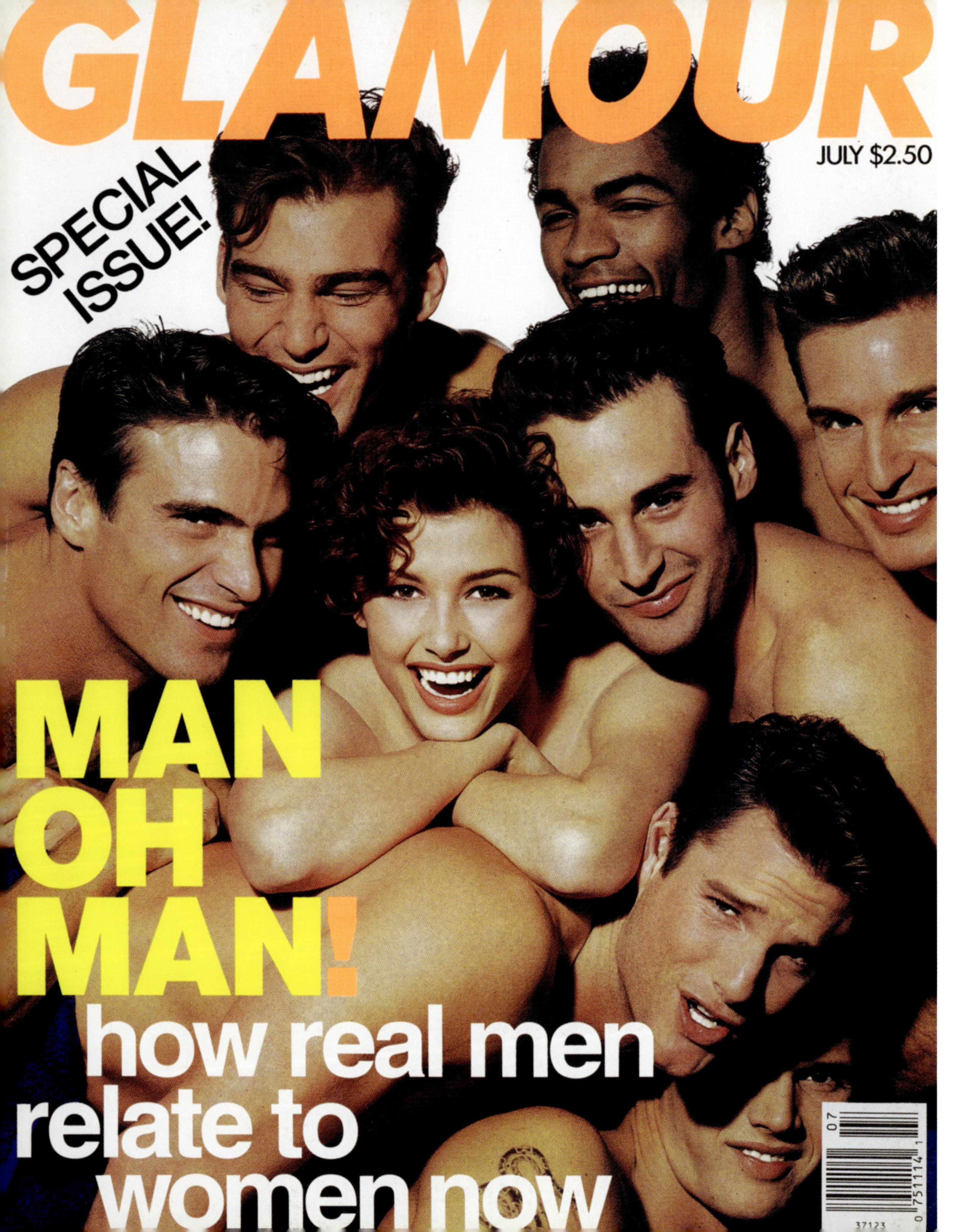

GLAMOUR
JULY $2.50
SPECIAL ISSUE!
MAN OH MAN!
how real men relate to women now
07
37123
0 75111 4 1

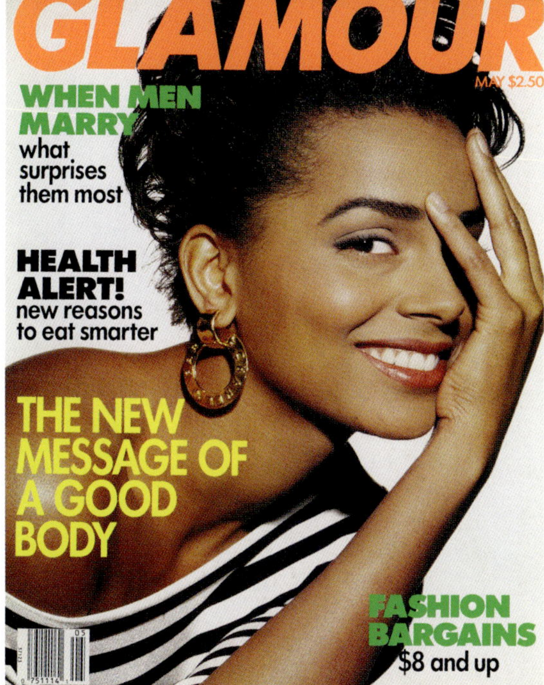

→

Dutch model Louise Vyent on her ninth of 10 *Glamour* covers (her first was in 1986), May 1992.

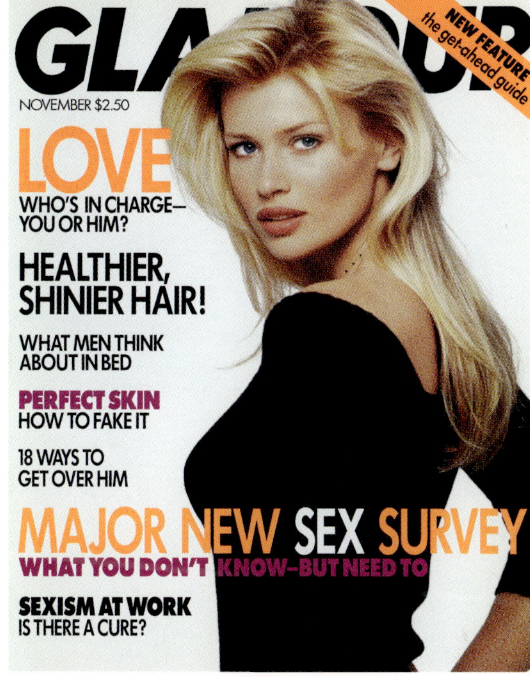

→

Daniela Peštovà, one of the earliest Victoria's Secret Angels and a repeat on the cover of *Sports Illustrated*'s Swimsuit Issue, also went on to have 11 *Glamour* covers, including this one, November 1995.

→

Four of *Glamour*'s most prolific cover models united for the magazine's 50th anniversary. Clockwise from top left, Christie Brinkley, Beverly Johnson, Kim Alexis, and Cheryl Tiegs, April 1989.

←

Bridget Moynahan surrounded by seven shirtless men, for an issue focused on the state of relations between men and women, July 1992.

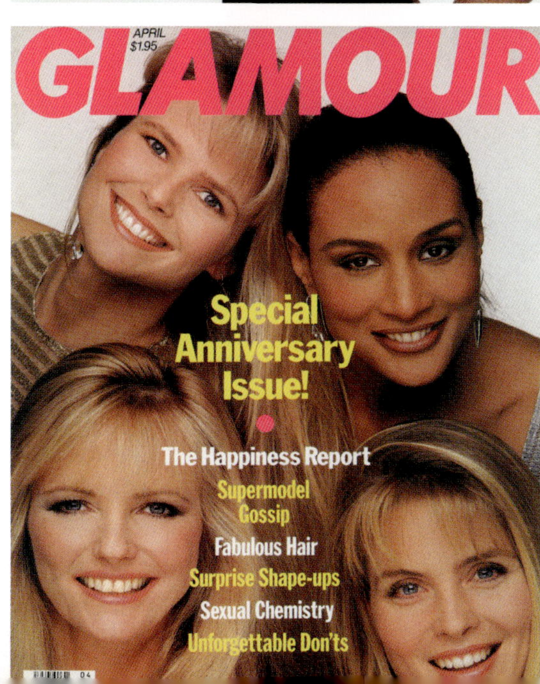

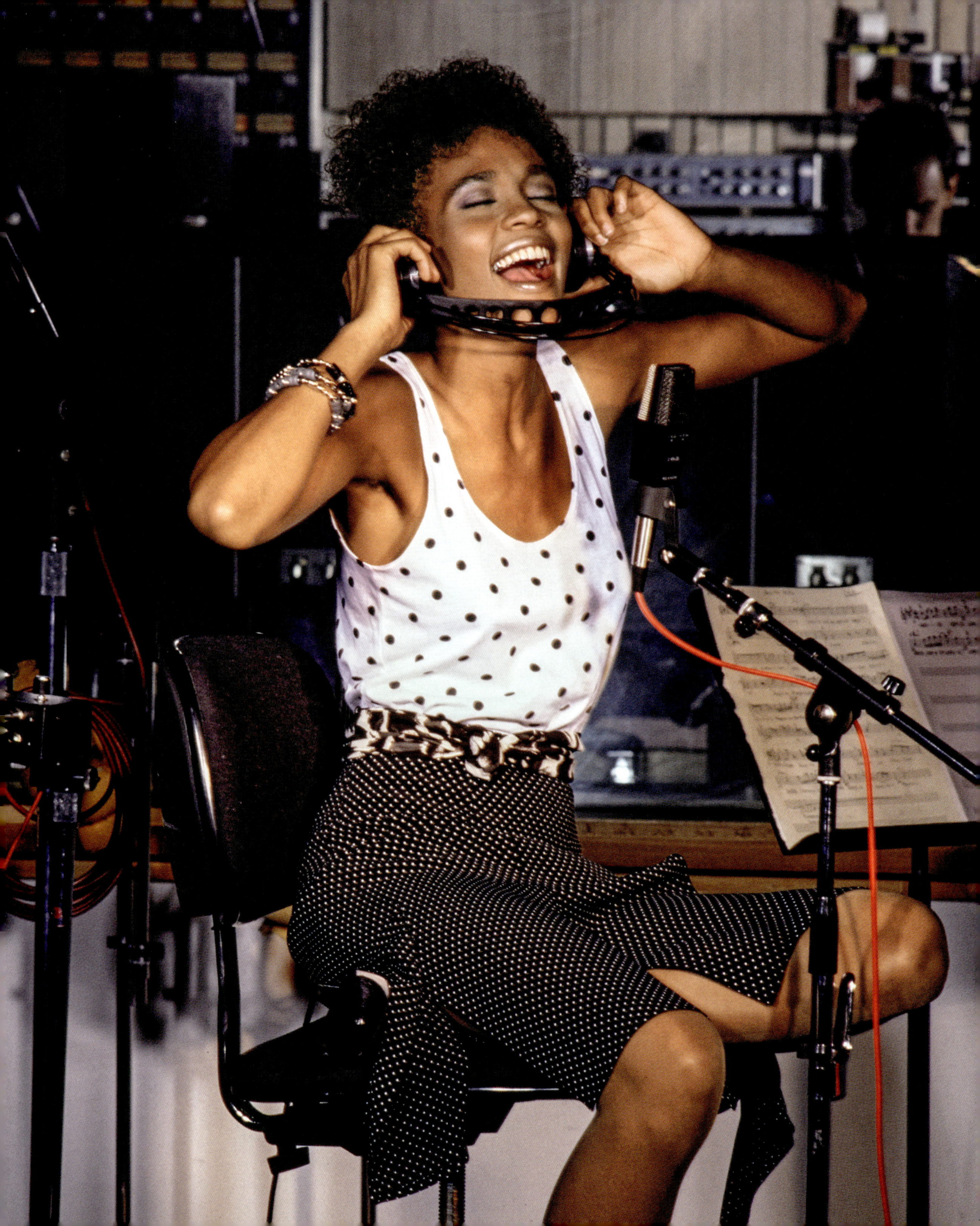

1998

CELEBRITIES MADE A RESURGENCE in *Glamour* during this era. A monthly "People" section during the '80s reported on the lives and relationships of actors, musicians, and models, as well as noting the big new films. And rising stars, such as Diane Lane and Whitney Houston, were occasionally (and notably) photographed and interviewed. But within the wider magazine, it was more often about what stories the big films and television shows were telling—and how they either impacted or reflected readers' lives. Culture evolves, of course, and so did *Glamour*. The launch of *Friends* (in 1994) and *Sex and the City* (1998) made global superstars of the casts and sparked new conversations around the importance of friendships and the power of sex. Most significantly, viewers saw themselves in the characters. They now reflected, as Ruth Whitney once noted about her model cover stars, "the aspirations of the women who buy that magazine." *Glamour* understood this, and by 1998 had begun to feature actors more prominently—within and on the cover, paving the way for a new decade and, ultimately, the celebrity revolution of the 2000s.

←

Singer and former teen model Whitney Houston, then 20, in the recording studio, before the release of her debut album, *Whitney Houston*. *Photographed by Claude Mougin, January 1984.*

Drew Barrymore. *Photographed by Tiziano Magni, April 1994.*

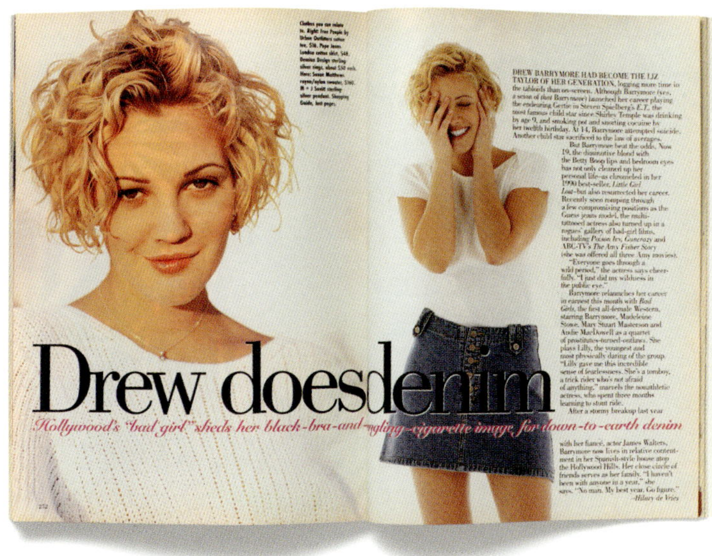

Halle Berry. *Photographed by Calliope, February 1993.*

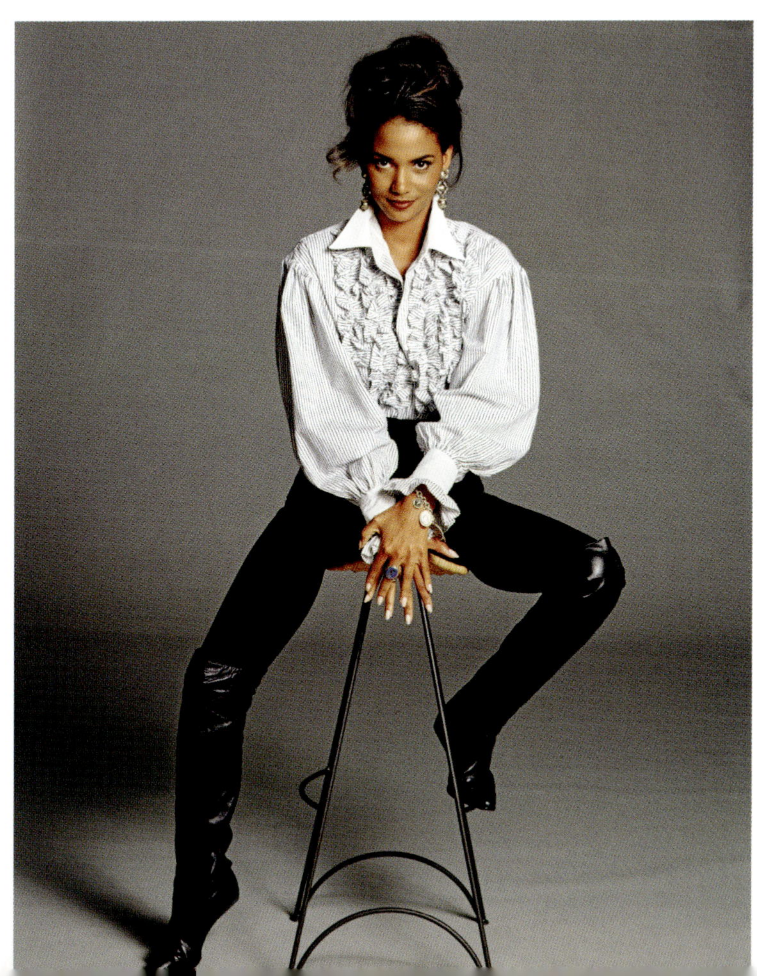

IN DECEMBER 1990, *GLAMOUR* LAUNCHED ITS INAUGURAL Women of the Year Awards, honoring "ten women who lit up the year with their daring, enterprise and vision," women who, as the magazine noted, "took charge, spoke out, risked their lives.... Made us proud to be women." Included in that first class were Marian Wright Edelman, founder of Children's Defense Fund; the late Elizabeth Glaser, wife of *Starsky & Hutch* actor Paul Michael Glaser and founder of the Elizabeth Glaser Pediatric AIDS Foundation (which she set up after contracting HIV during a blood transfusion during childbirth); and Madonna, who 35 years later remains as culture-defining and influential as ever. The first Women of the Year Awards, which were celebrated at New York's famous Rainbow Room, laid the foundation for a franchise that has come to define *Glamour* ever since. The winners serve as a living embodiment of the evolution of women's power, from trailblazers like Michelle Obama and Gloria Steinem, to the cofounders of Black Lives Matter, Nobel Peace Prize winner Malala Yousafzai, and the female first responders who were on the scene at 9/11. Here's a timeline of the indelible moments and remarkable winners.

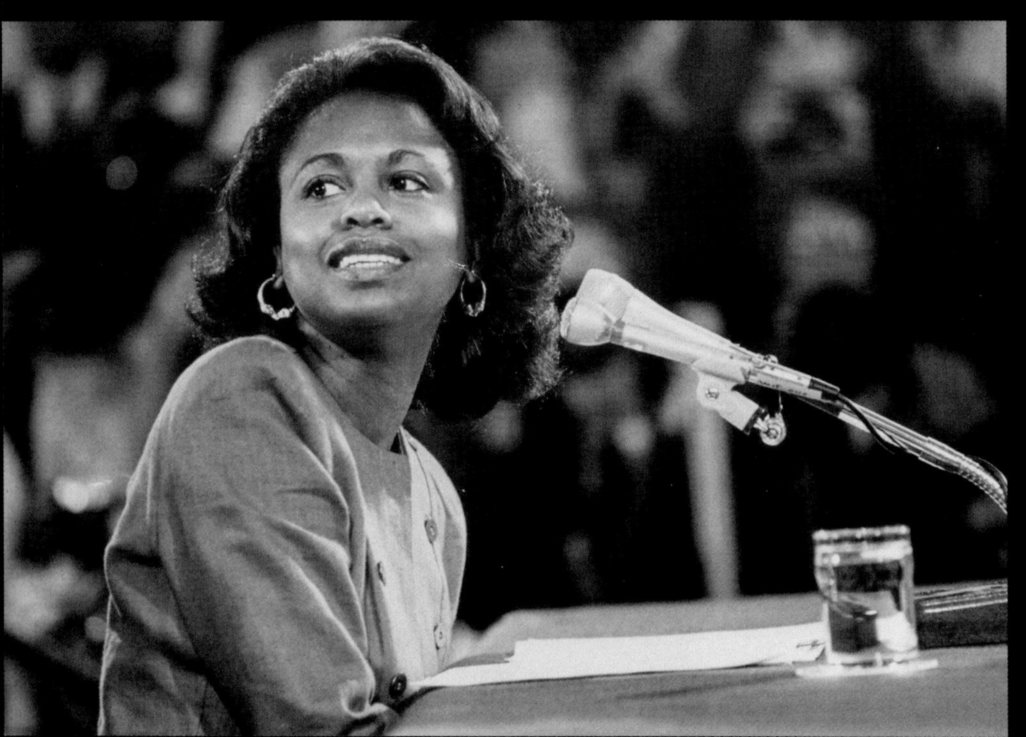

1991

ANITA HILL was honored just two months after she testified in front of an all-male Senate Judiciary Committee about the sexual harassment she experienced from Supreme Court nominee Clarence Thomas.

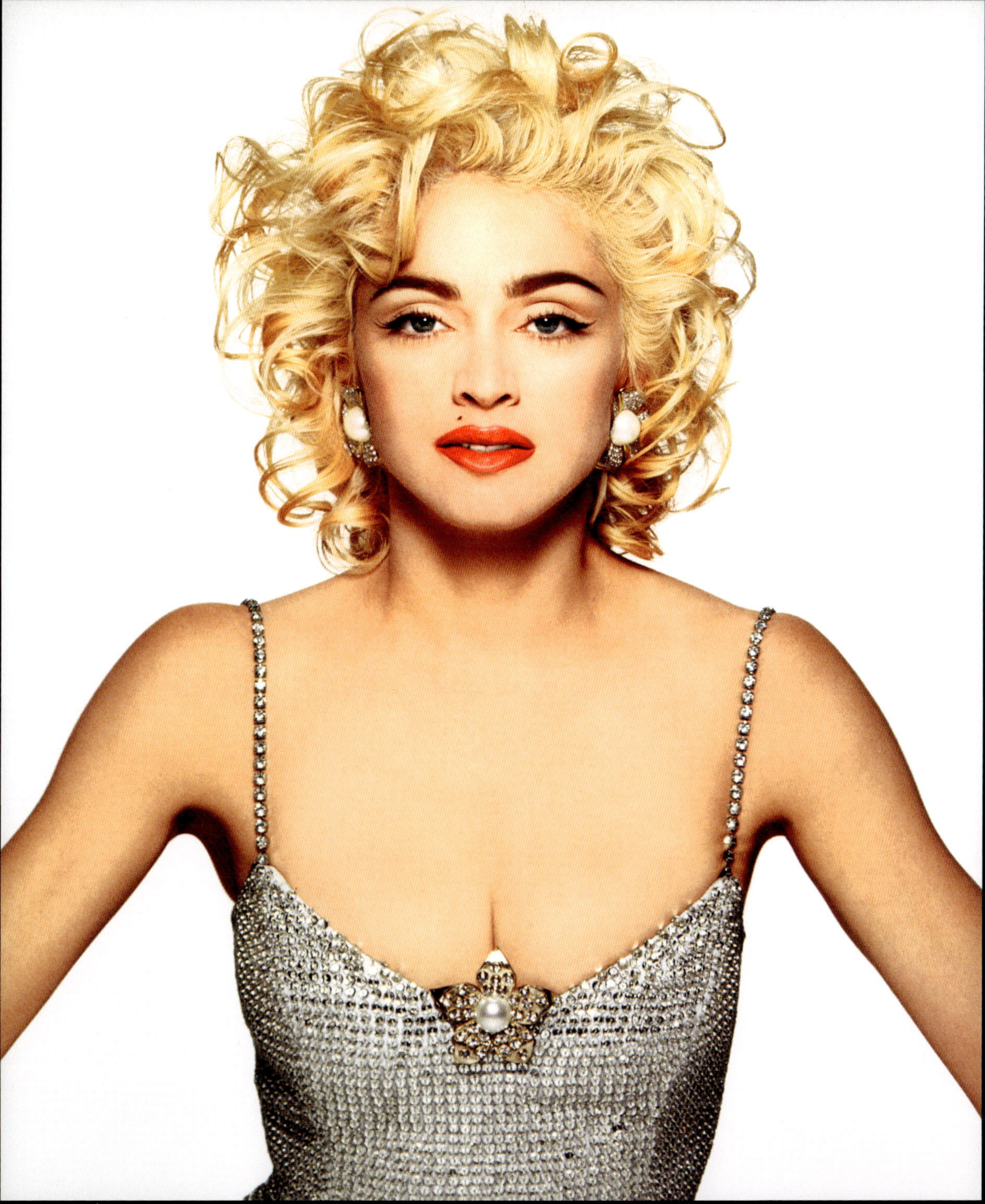

MADONNA, following the success of her pop anthem "Like a Prayer," was selected to be the magazine's first WOTY cover star. *Photographed by Patrick Demarchelier, December 1990.*

HILLARY CLINTON received the first of her two WOTY awards in November 1992. She was honored again in 2008 for her Democratic Party presidential primary campaign.

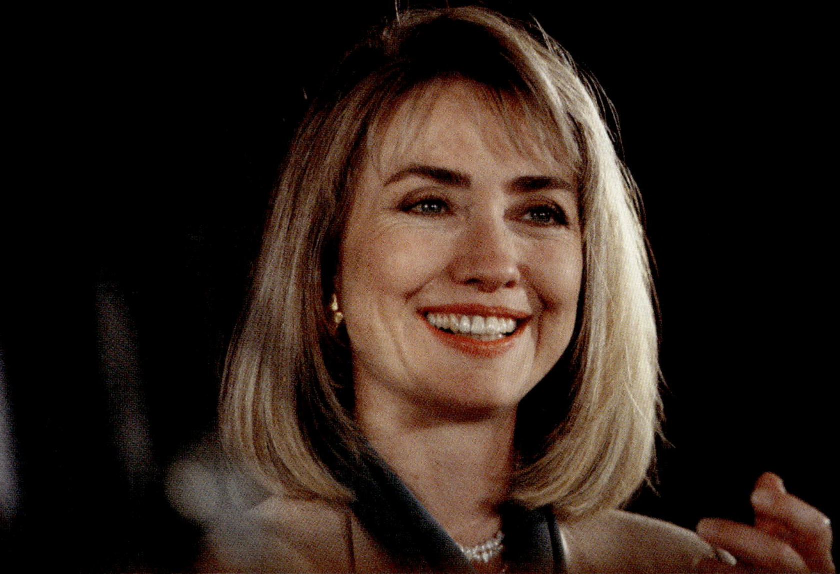

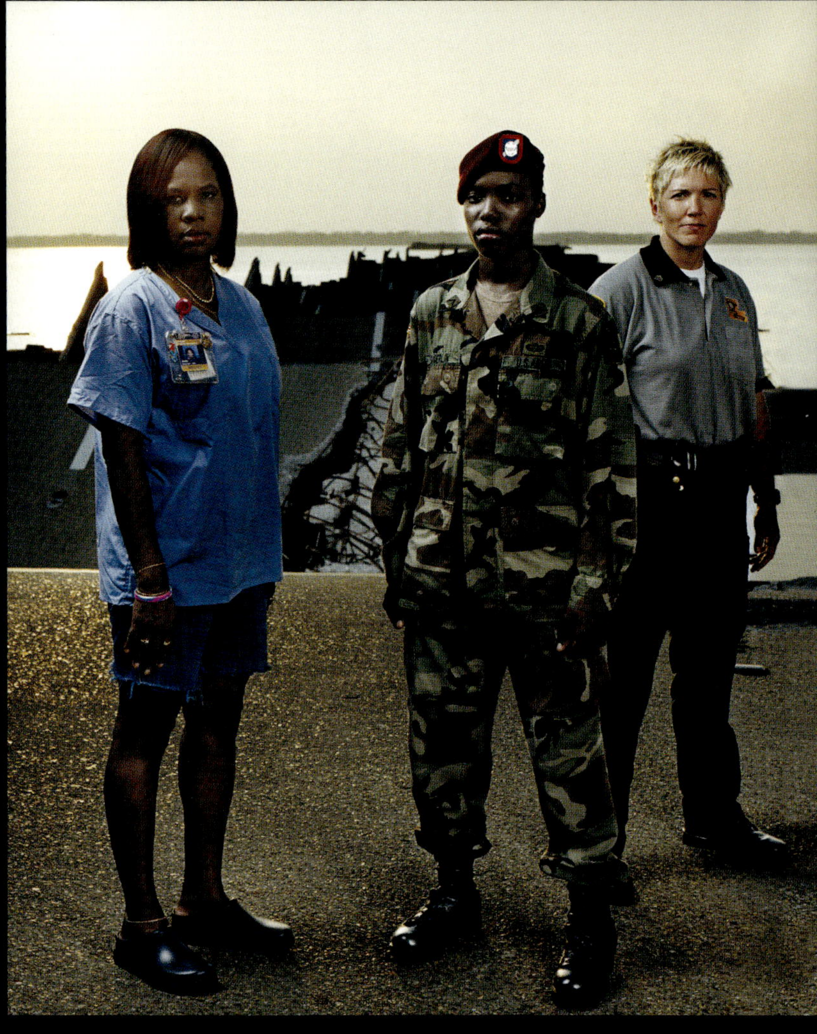

YAMILY BASS-CHOATE, RACHEL ZECHENELLY, YAKIMA SANDERLIN, **JULIE NEWMAN,** and **SARA FAULKNER** were honored for heroism during Hurricane Katrina. *Photographed by Norman Jean Roy, December 2005.*

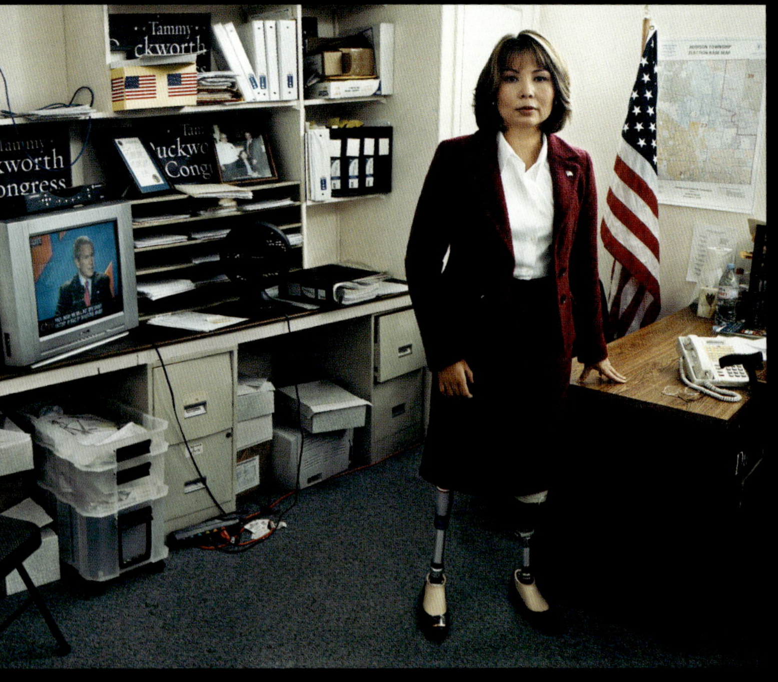

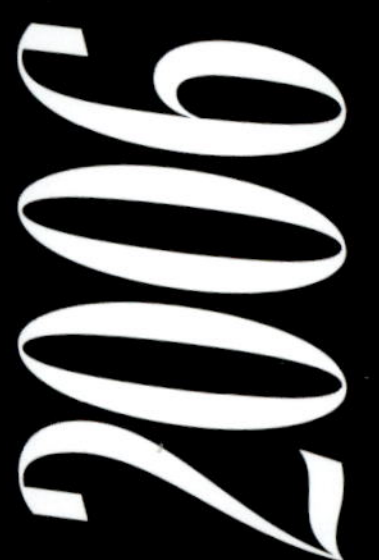

2006

Now a senator, **TAMMY DUCKWORTH** was running for Congress when she was honored as a Woman of the Year. *Glamour* recognized the double amputee for her commitment to justice and abortion rights. "I wasn't going to let some guy with a rocket launcher ruin my life," she said at the time. *Photographed by Norman Jean Roy, December 2006.*

QUEEN LATIFAH rose to fame at 19 with the release of her album *All Hail the Queen*, but she was already Hollywood royalty when she was honored by *Glamour* as a Woman of the Year in 2006, the same year she starred in *Last Holiday* and *Stranger Than Fiction* and landed a star on the Hollywood Walk of Fame. *Photographed by Norman Jean Roy, December 2006.*

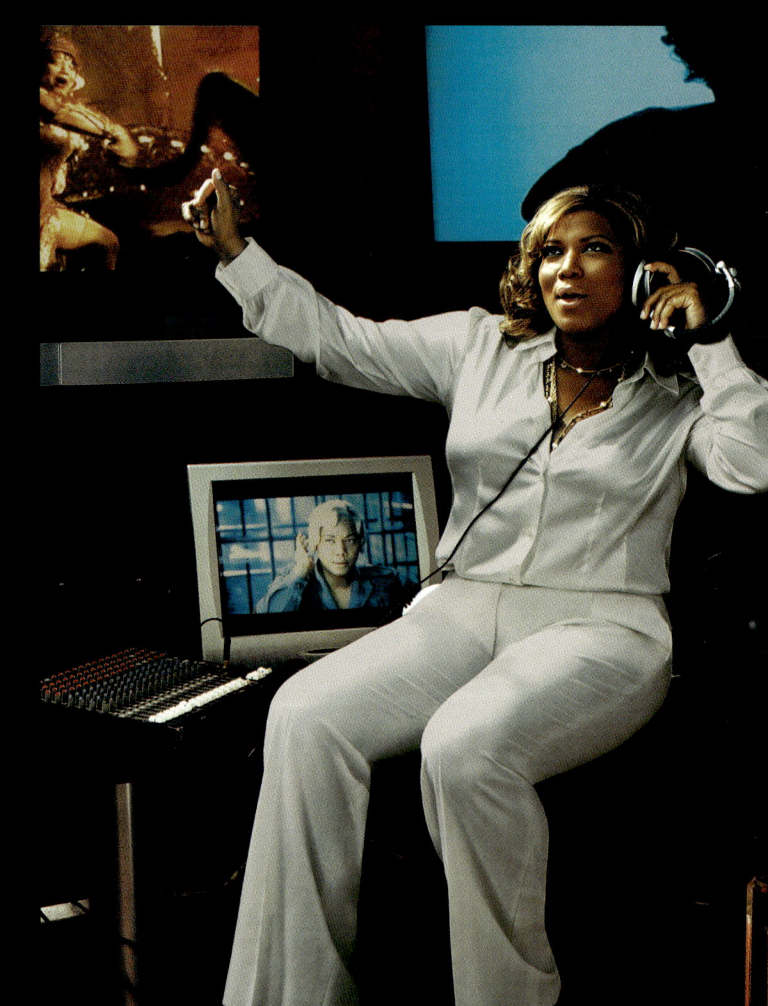

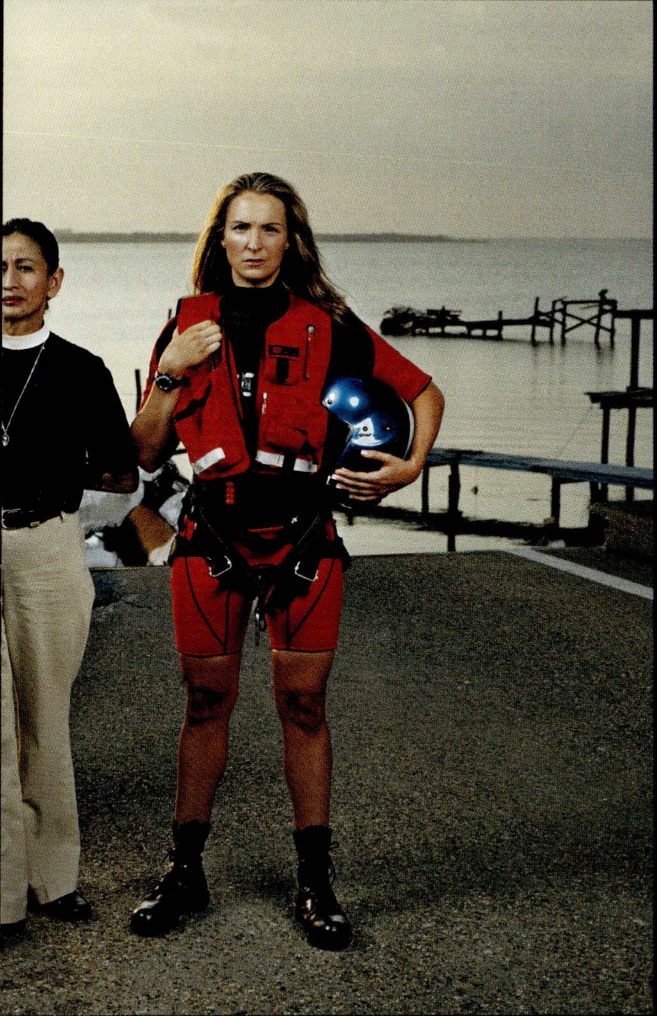

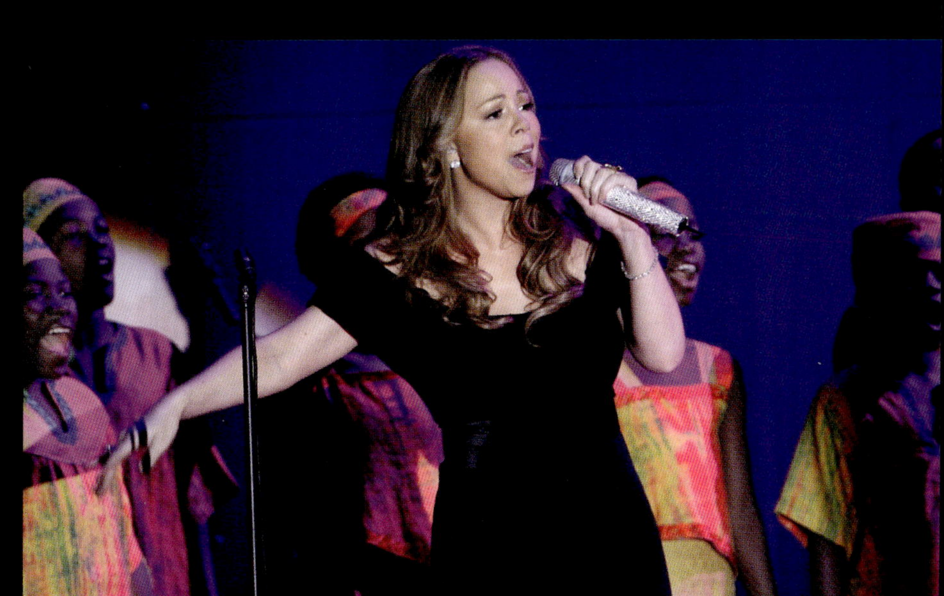

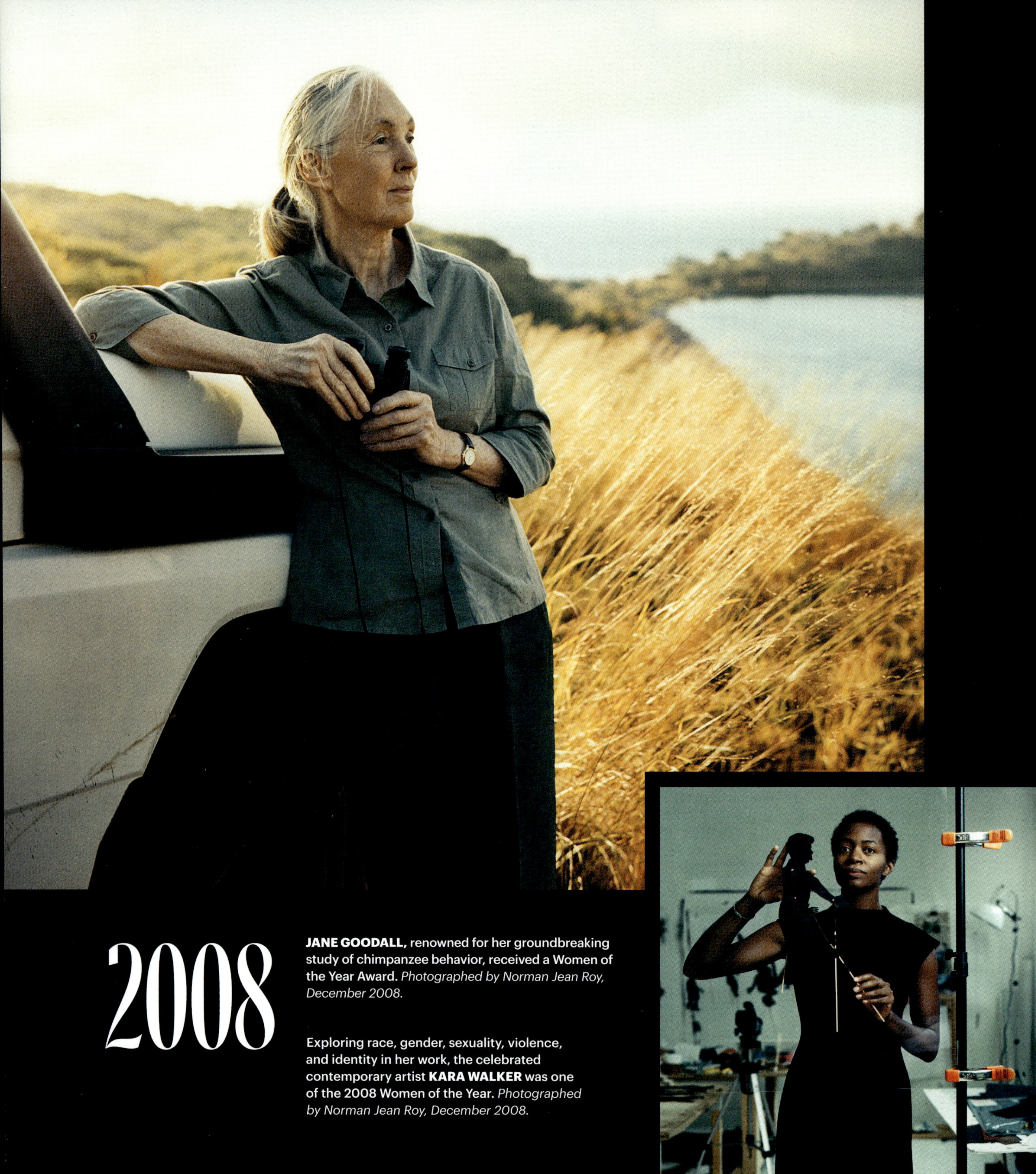

2008

JANE GOODALL, renowned for her groundbreaking study of chimpanzee behavior, received a Women of the Year Award. *Photographed by Norman Jean Roy, December 2008.*

Exploring race, gender, sexuality, violence, and identity in her work, the celebrated contemporary artist **KARA WALKER** was one of the 2008 Women of the Year. *Photographed by Norman Jean Roy, December 2008.*

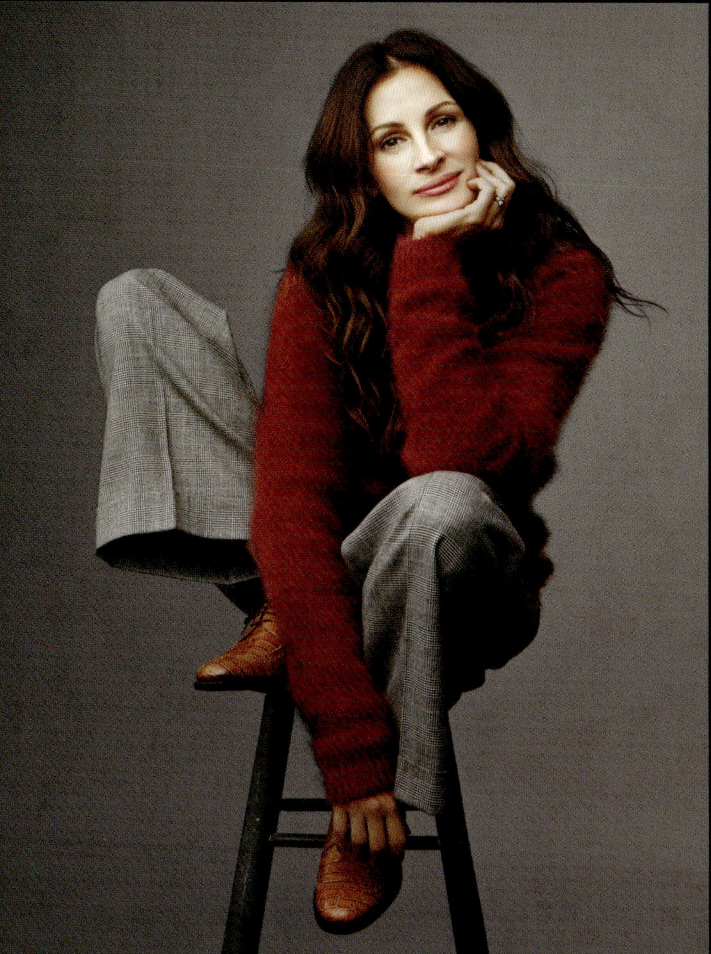

JULIA ROBERTS, honored for her trailblazing Hollywood career and commitment to philanthropy, was presented with a 2010 Women of the Year Award by Oprah Winfrey. *Photographed by Martin Schoeller, December 2010.*

DR. HAWA ABDI and her daughters, **DR. DEQO MOHAMED** and **DR. AMINA MOHAMED,** earned the title "The Saints of Somalia" for their unwavering commitment to serving Somali refugees. *Photographed by Martin Schoeller, December 2010.*

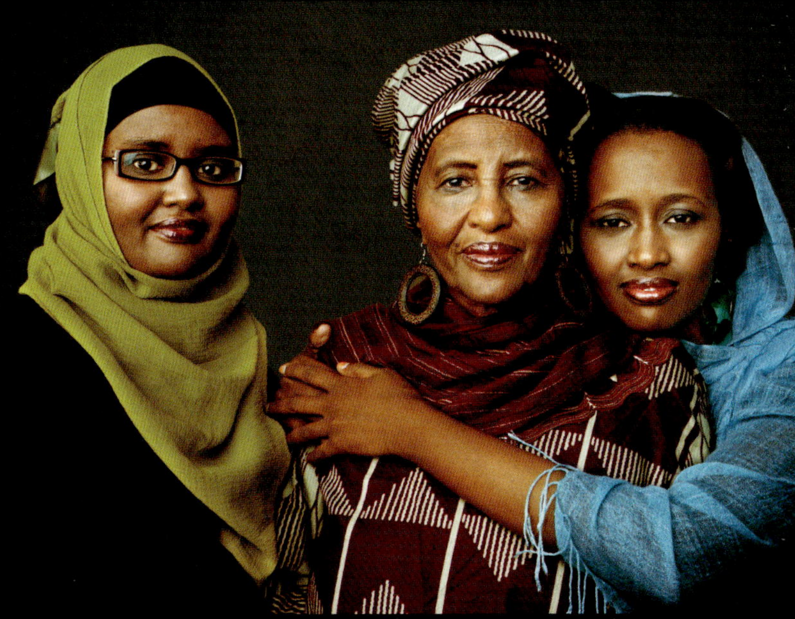

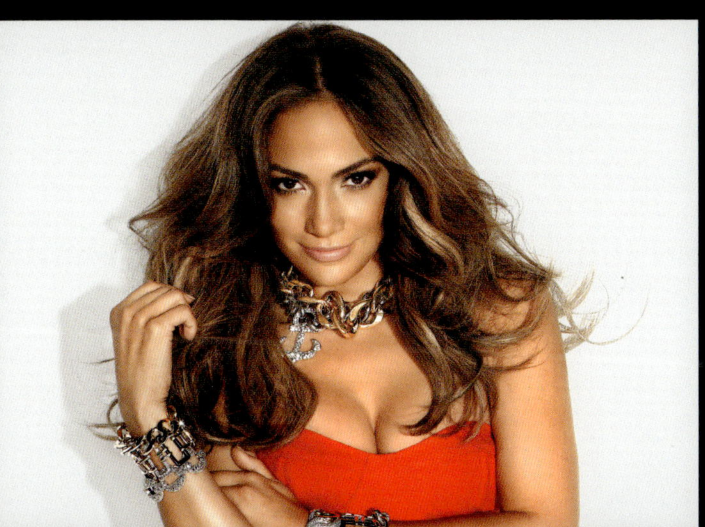

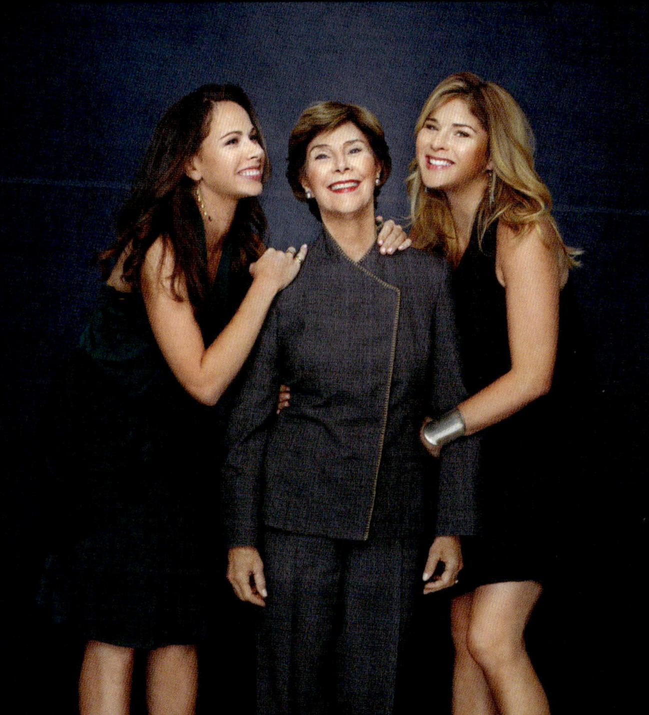

JENNIFER LOPEZ, a Woman of the Year in 1999 and 2011, was celebrated for her extraordinary contribution to today's culture—as a performer, songwriter, and actor. *Photographed by Matthias Vriens, December 2011.*

LAURA BUSH and her daughters, **JENNA** and **BARBARA,** were presented with the Generations Award by former secretary of state Condoleezza Rice. *Photographed by Martin Schoeller, December 2011.*

2012

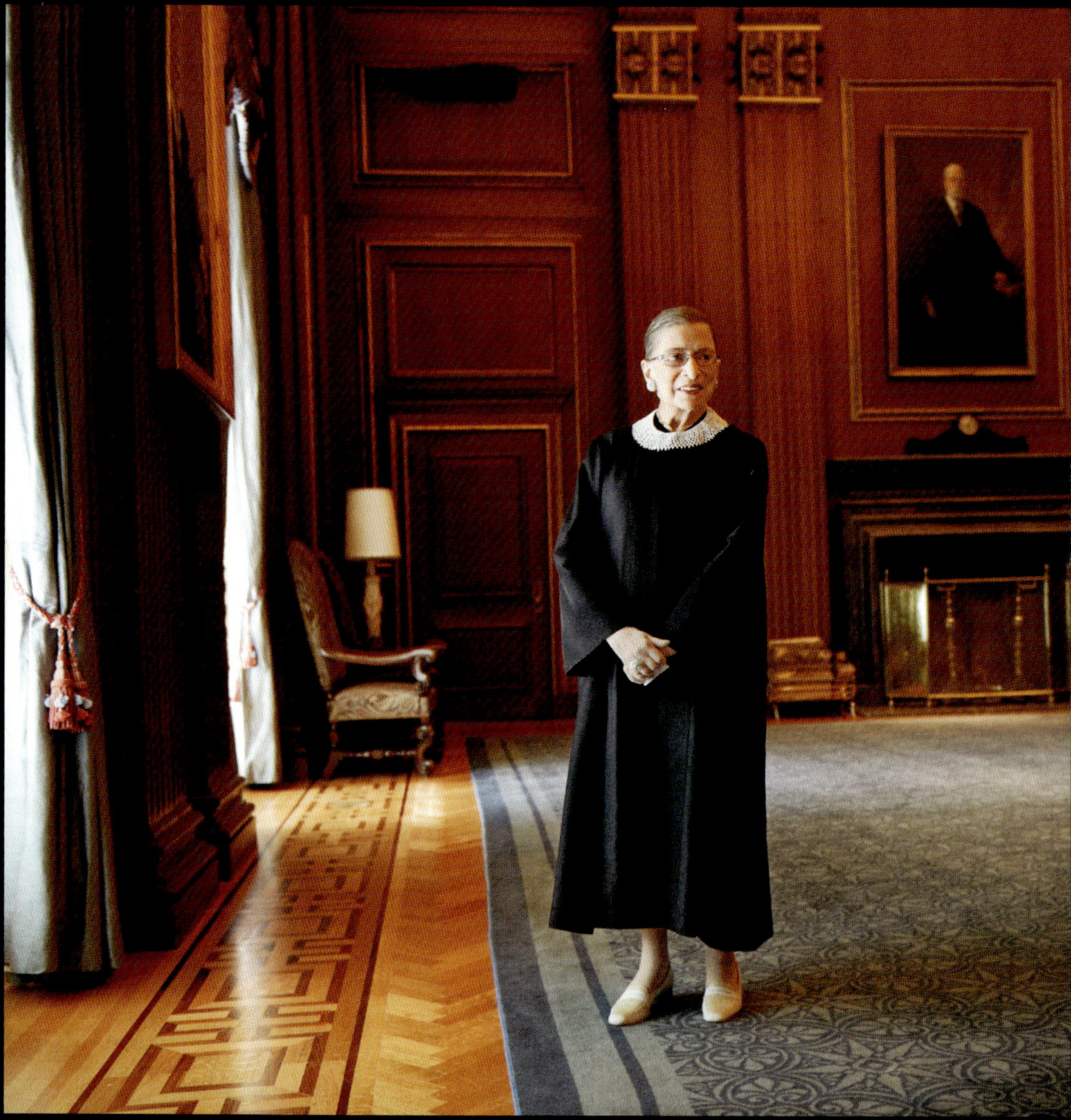

RUTH BADER GINSBURG was honored with a lifetime achievement award for her dedication to passionately defending the rights of all people, especially the underserved. *Photographed by Lynsey Addario, December 2012.*

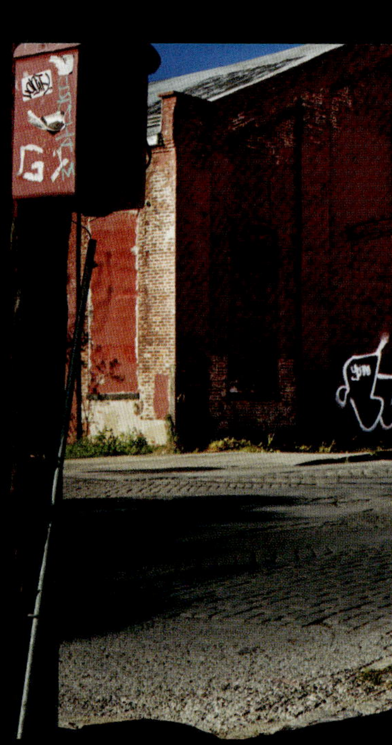

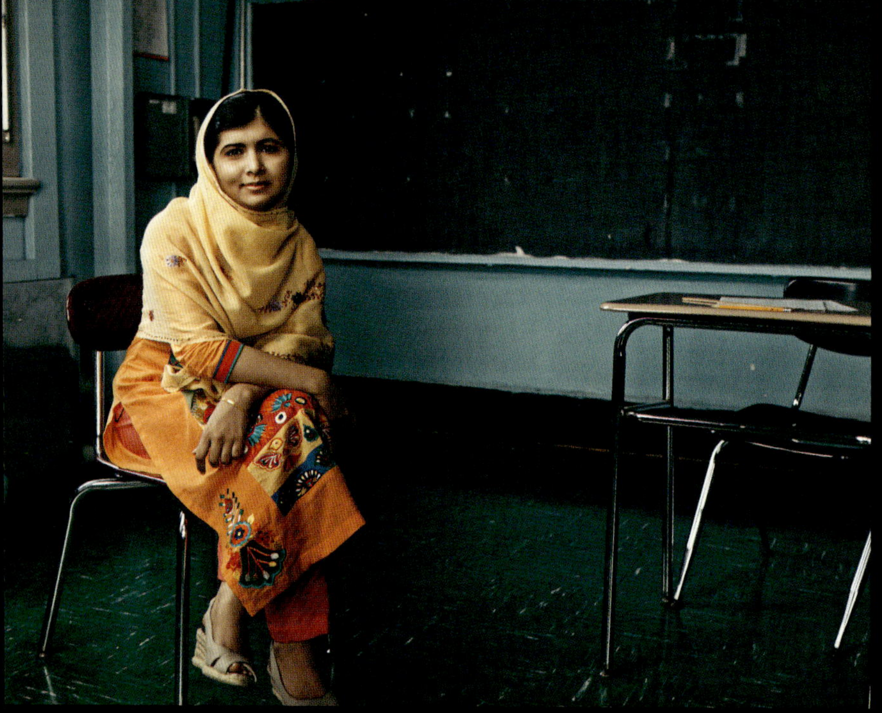

2013

MALALA YOUSAFZAI was honored for her remarkable courage and education advocacy. As Ban Ki-moon, secretary-general of the United Nations, said, "By targeting her, extremists showed what they feared most: a girl with a book. Malala embodies the power of education to build peace. She is truly a role model for the world." *Photographed by Norman Jean Roy, December 2013.*

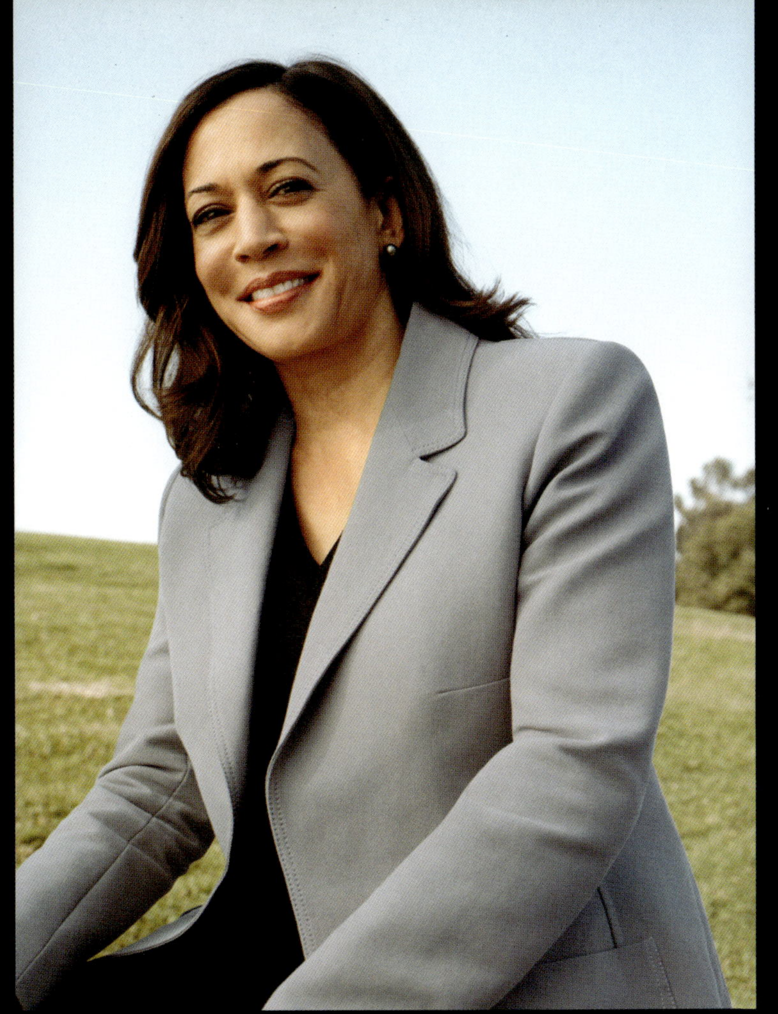

2018

KAMALA HARRIS emphasized the importance of speaking truth to power when she took to the stage as a recipient of the 2018 Women of the Year Award.

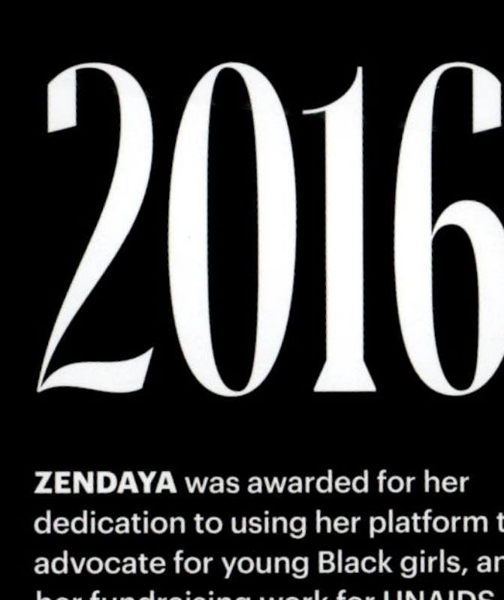

2016

ZENDAYA was awarded for her dedication to using her platform to advocate for young Black girls, and her fundraising work for UNAIDS. *Photographed by Victor Demarchelier, December 2016.*

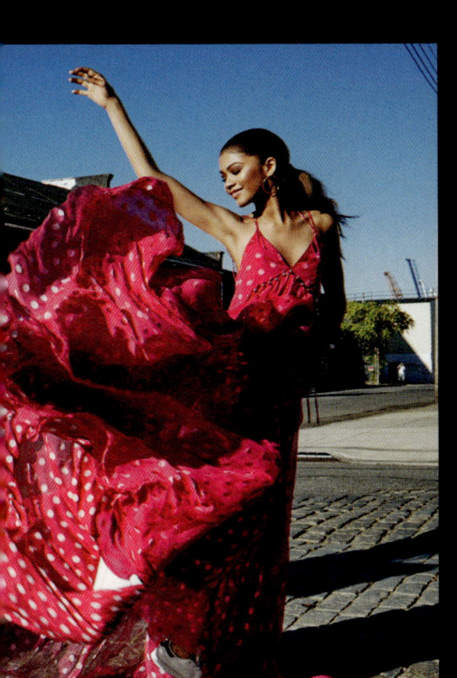

2015

CAITLYN JENNER was honored by Judith Light at the Women of the Year Awards, receiving an award as a tribute to her work raising awareness of transgender issues. She was the second transgender woman to receive a Women of the Year Award. Actor Laverne Cox was honored in 2014, and in 2023 model and author Geena Rocero was recognized for her contributions to the community. *Photographed by Ben Hassett, December 2015.*

2020

VERONICA HENRY, NAVDEEP KAUR, RN, MEIDA SANCHEZ, and **JASMIN MOSHIRPUR, MD,** were honored for their dedication to protecting life, displayed in their heroic efforts at New York's Elmhurst Hospital as COVID-19 spread across the United States. *Photographed by Shaniqwa Jarvis, October 2020.*

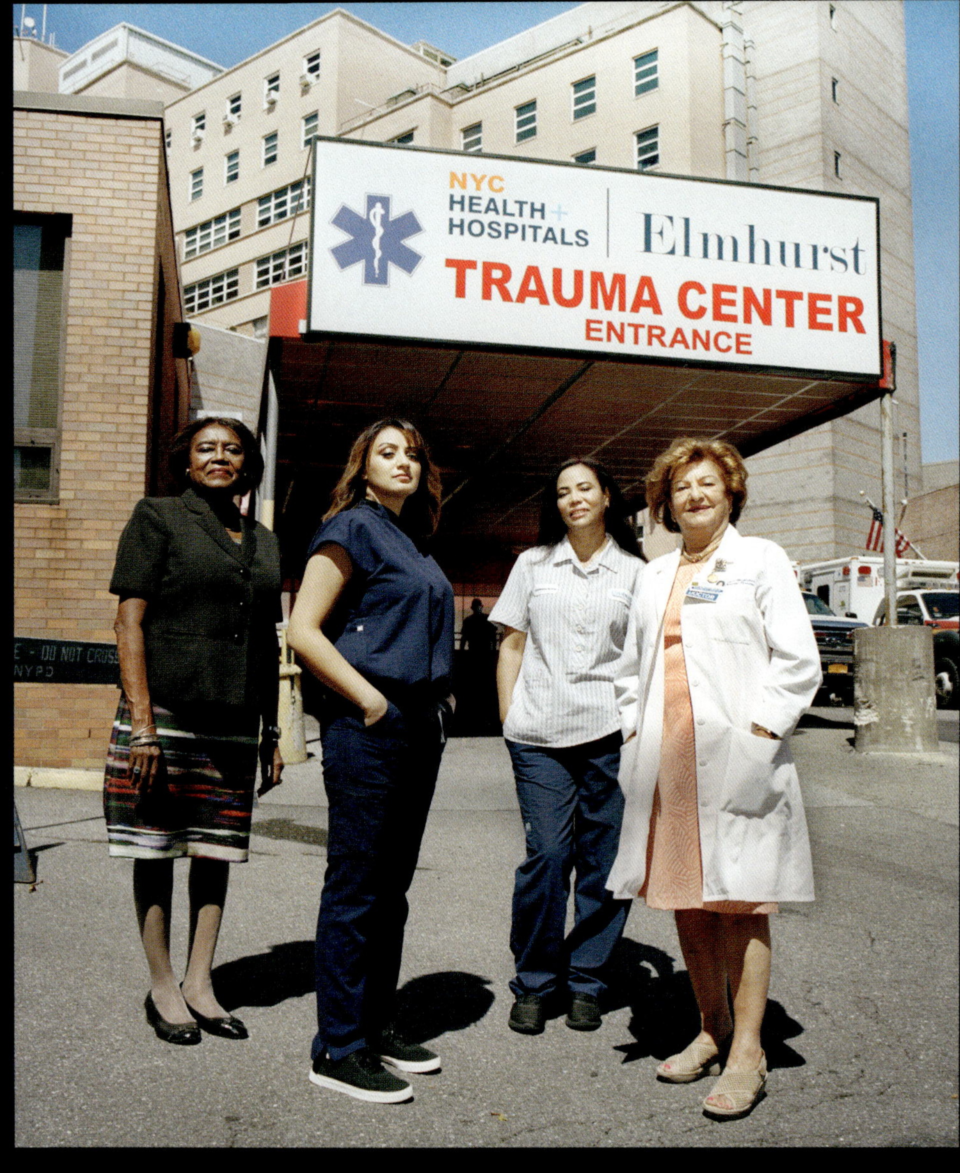

2021

MARISKA HARGITAY received a *Glamour* Woman of the Year Award. Her former *Law & Order: Special Victims Unit* co-star, Christopher Meloni, had the honor of presenting the award to her. *Photographed by Victoria Will, November 2021.*

YIN CHANG and **MOONLYNN TSAI** fought back against soaring anti-Asian hate during the pandemic by feeding the community through their initiative, Heart of Dinner, earning them the award in 2021. *Photographed by Michelle Watt, November 2021.*

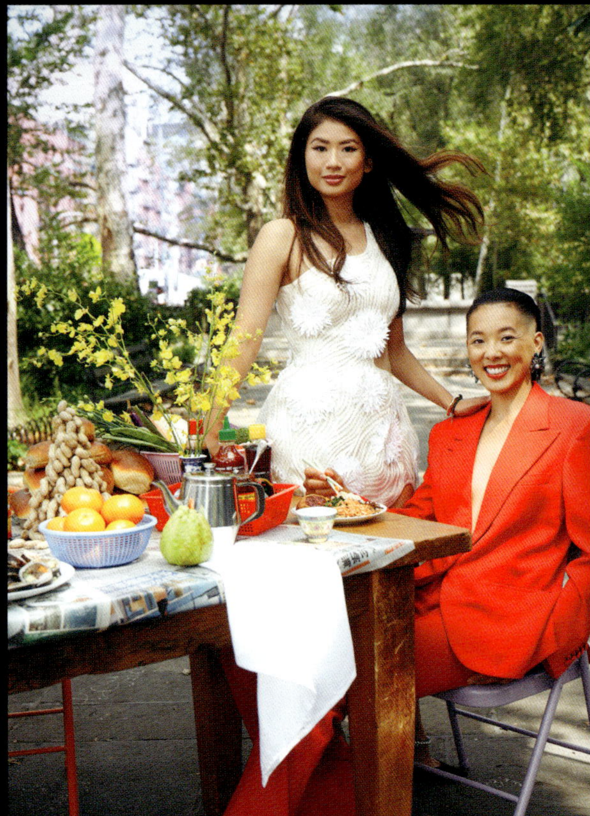

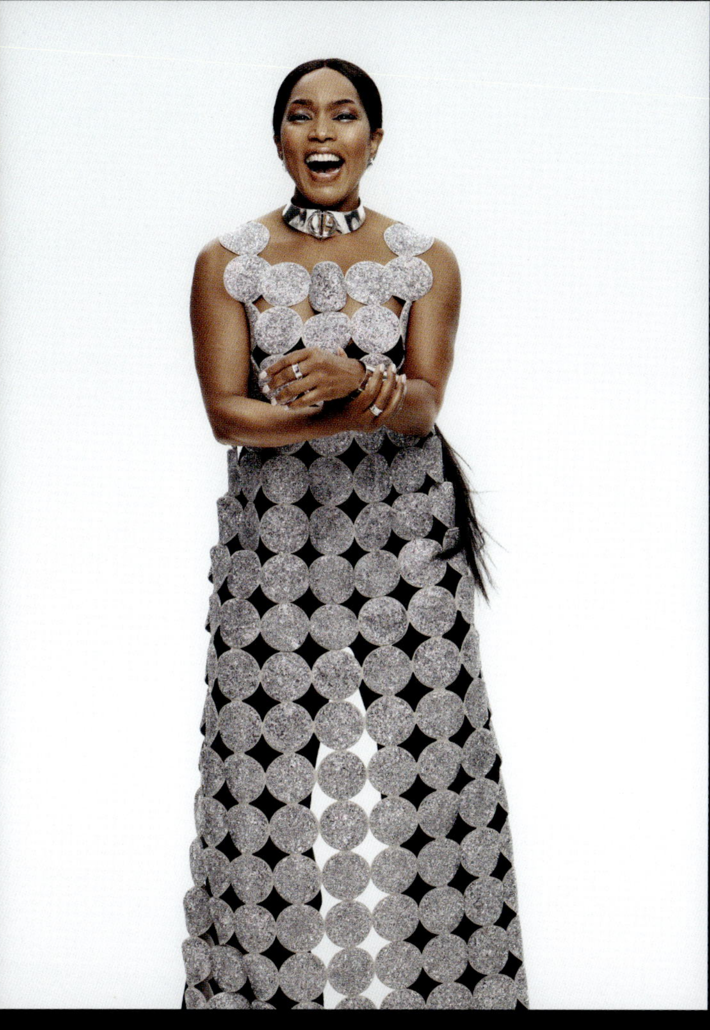

ANGELA BASSETT received a lifetime achievement award for her outstanding contributions to stage and screen. "I encourage you, in the words of my character Queen Ramonda, to always show them who you are," she said at the awards. *Photographed by Lauren Dukoff, October 2022.*

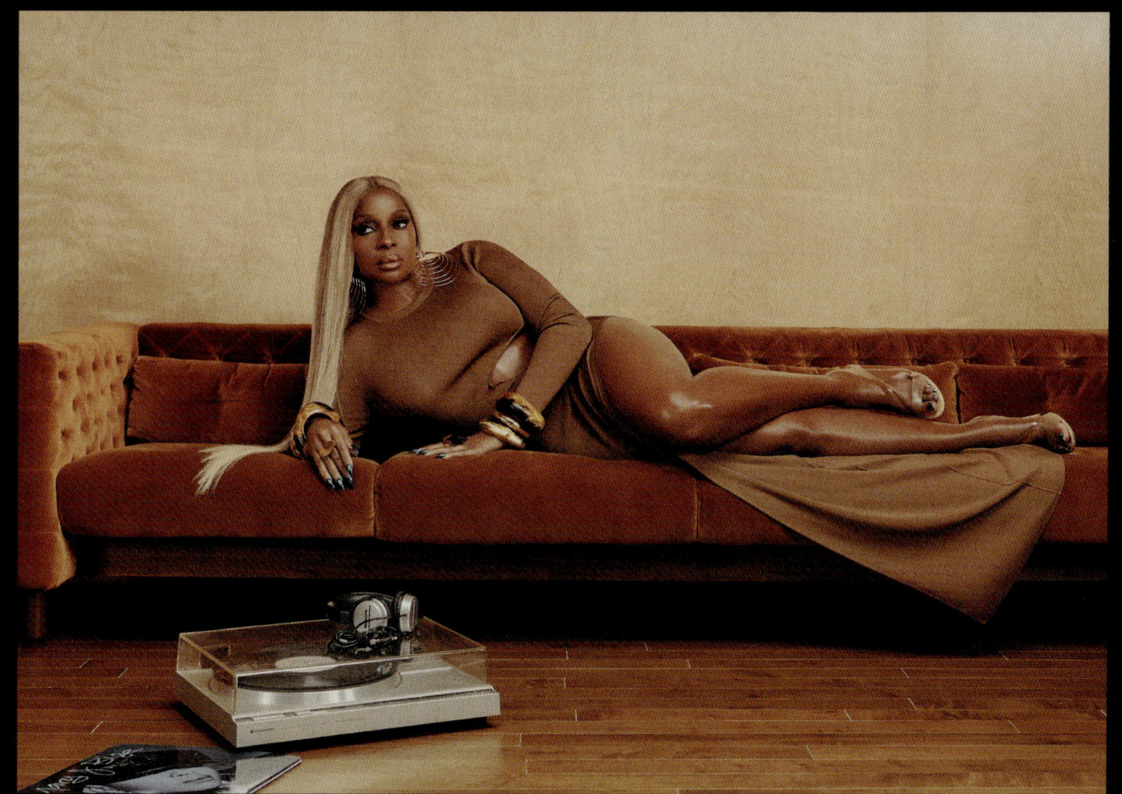

MARY J. BLIGE, the Queen of Hip-Hop Soul, received the award for transforming her pain into an era-defining sound. At *Glamour's* Women of the Year Awards, she was moved to tears by a special performance of her hits by the Sing Harlem Choir. *Photographed by Adrienne Raquel, November 2023.*

Iconic WOTY Covers

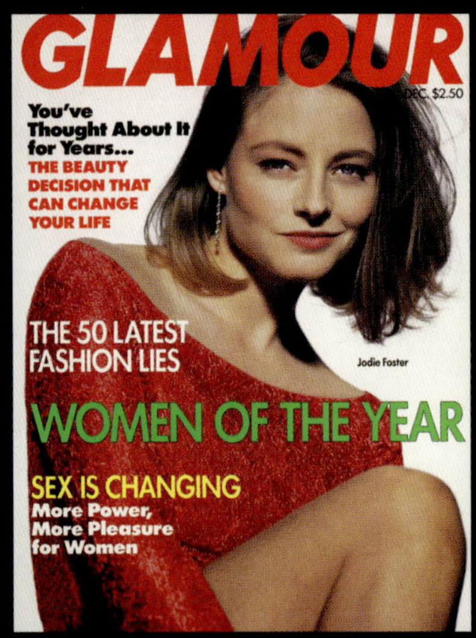

JODIE FOSTER, December 1991

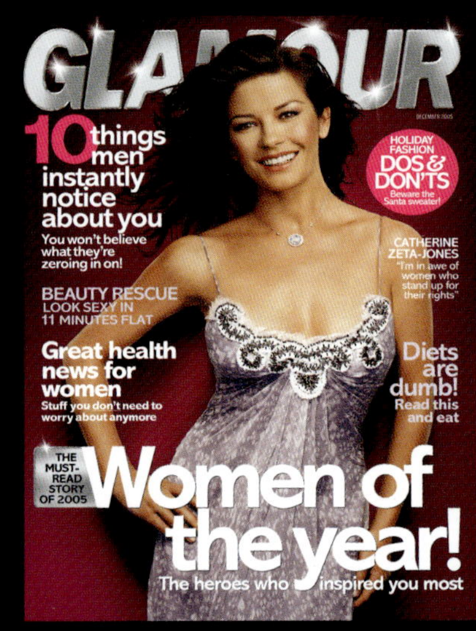

BRITNEY SPEARS, December 2003

CATHERINE ZETA-JONES, December 2005

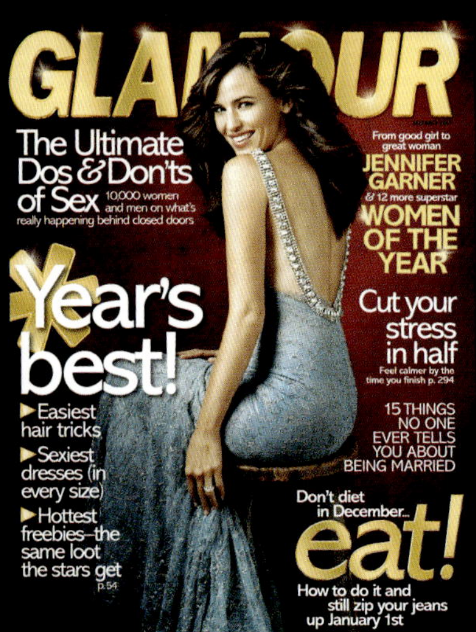

JENNIFER GARNER, December 2007

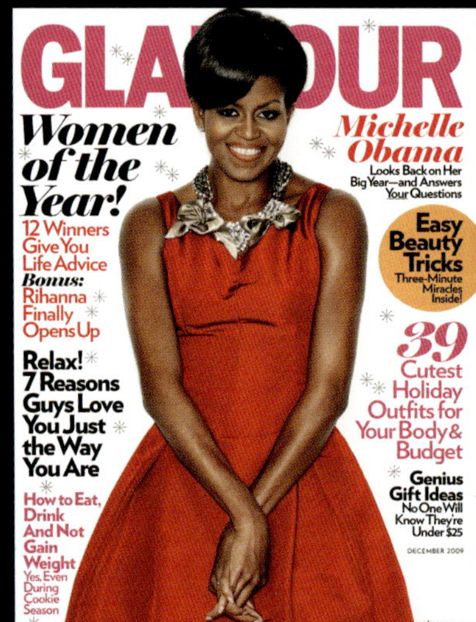

MICHELLE OBAMA, December 2009

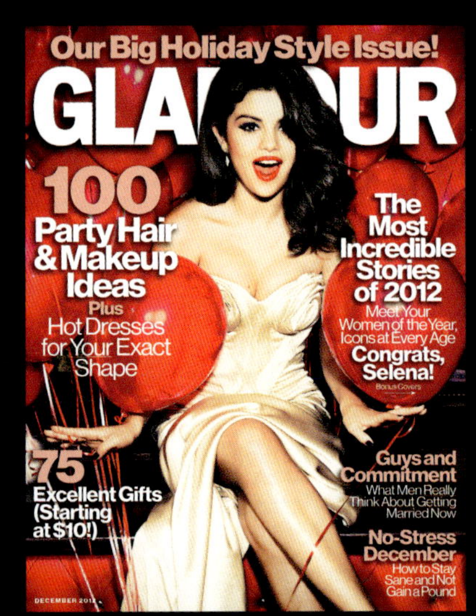

SELENA GOMEZ, December 2012

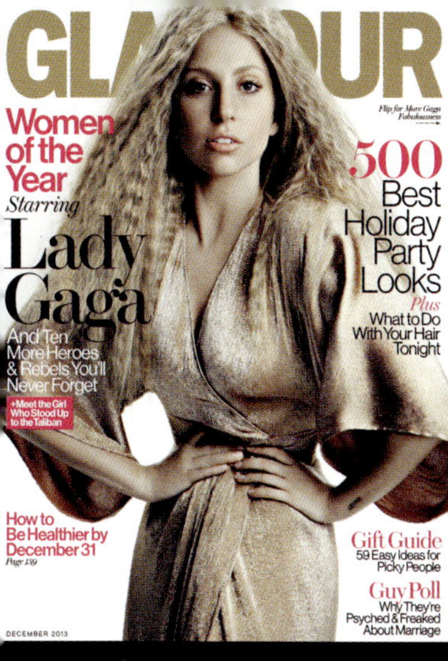

LADY GAGA, December 2013

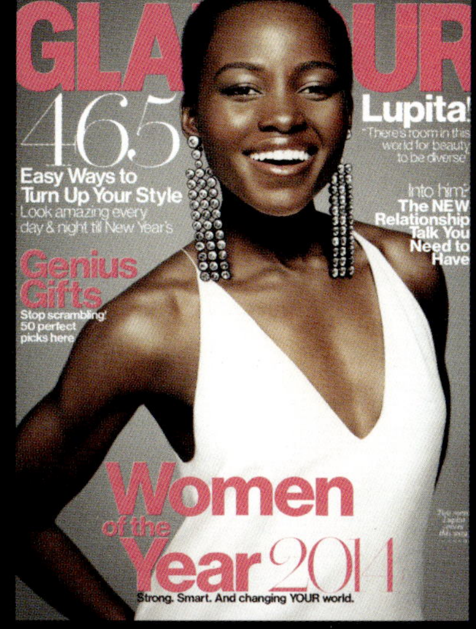

LUPITA NYONG'O, December 2014

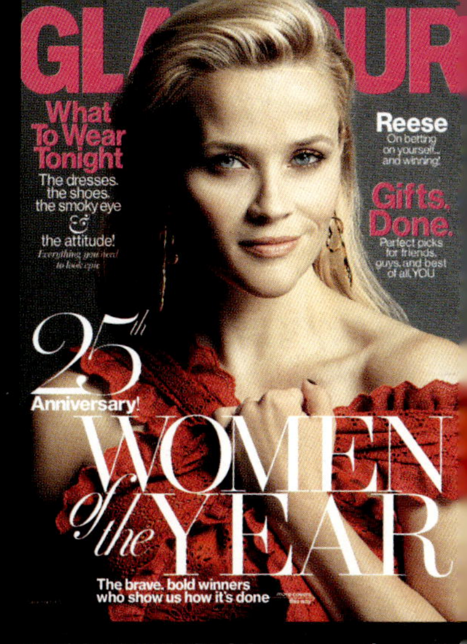

REESE WITHERSPOON, December 2015

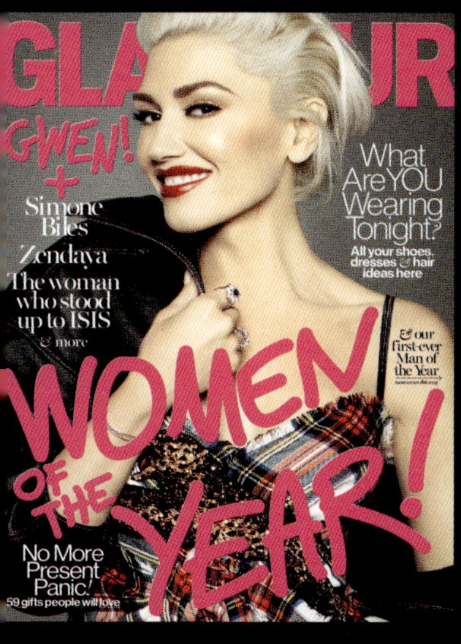

GWEN STEFANI, December 2016

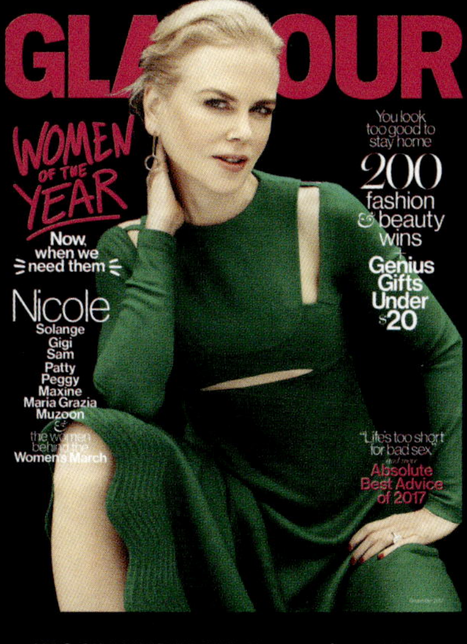

NICOLE KIDMAN, December 2017

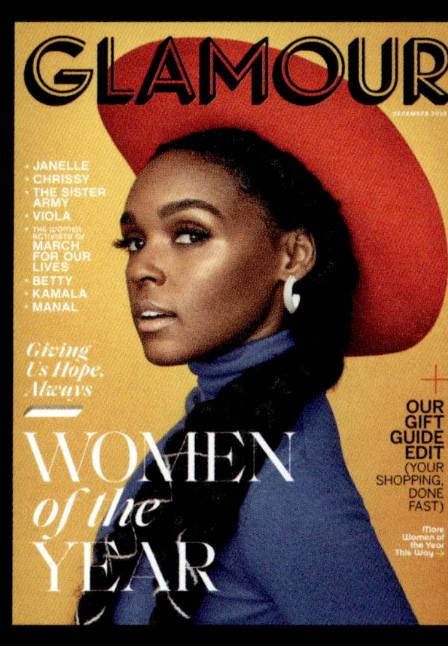

JANELLE MONAE, December 2018

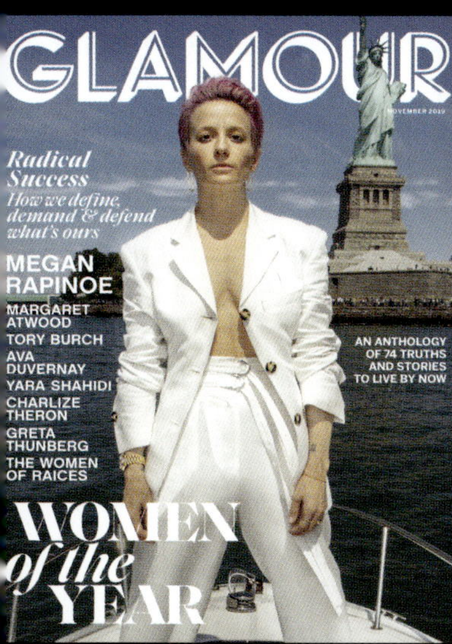

MEGAN RAPINOE, November 2019

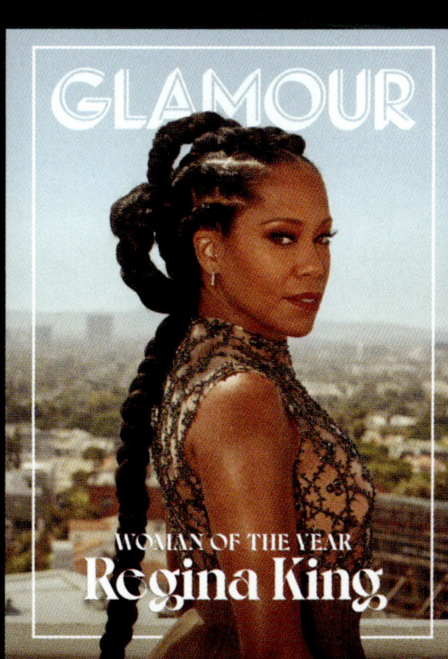

REGINA KING, November 2020

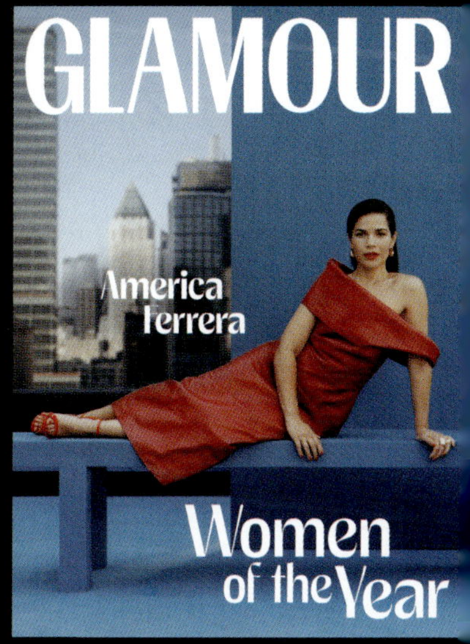

AMERICA FERRERA, November 2023

ALL ABOUT YOU

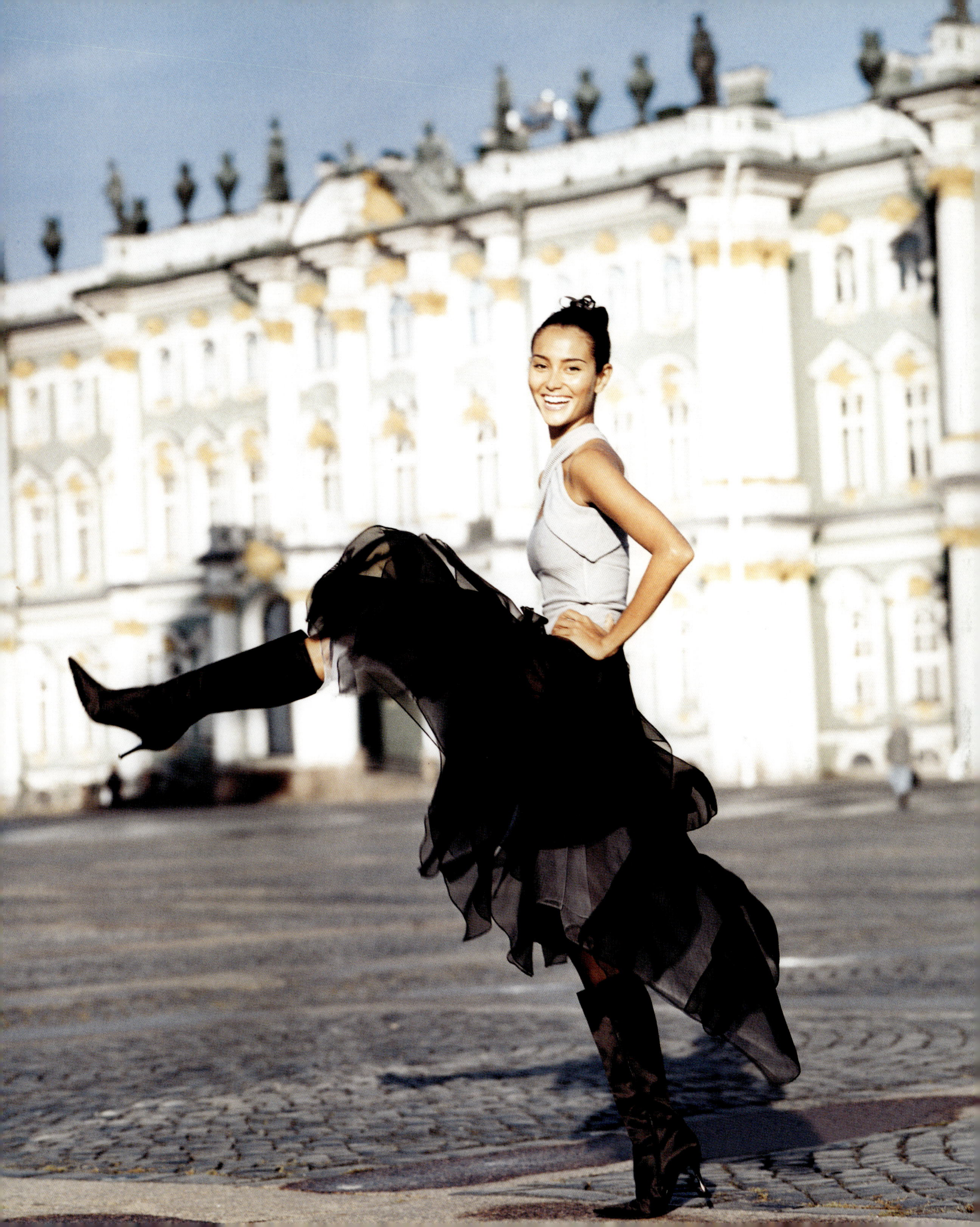

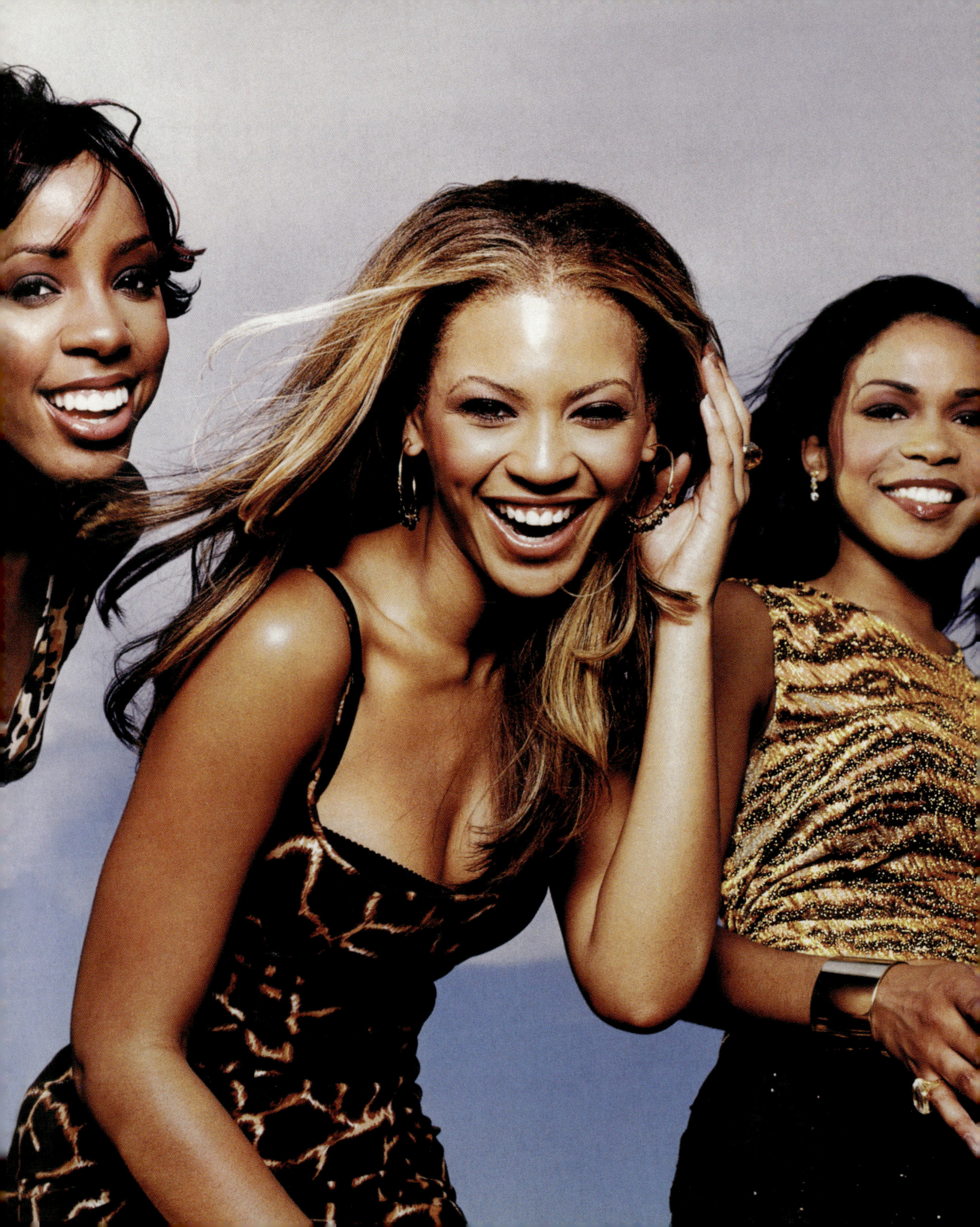

The shoes on my feet (I bought 'em)
The clothes I'm wearing (I bought 'em)
The rock I'm rocking (I bought it)
'Cause I depend on me

VERY LITTLE COULD SUM UP THE ESSENCE of the late '90s and early 2000s better than these lyrics from Destiny's Child's "Independent Women Part I." Released in August 2000, it topped the US *Billboard* Hot 100 for 11 consecutive weeks. The world wasn't perfect—a woman had never been president, women and men weren't paid equally (both still true)—but the message coming from so many corners was that women could do it all, and have it all. This same message was echoed all over the pages of *Glamour*. Whether it was by spotlighting female politicians (following Hillary Clinton's first run for president in 2008) or the female heroes of each month (Grand Slam tennis champions conquering cancer, actor Mariska Hargitay's advocacy for sexual assault survivors, a Paraguayan journalist risking her life to expose corruption in her country), *Glamour* told readers: Women are survivors, fighters, leaders, and winners. Even the so-called "fun" sections had a purpose—how to have better sex, better finances, better mental health, and how to dress for yourself and no one else. It really was, as one of the magazine's brand new sections declared, All About You.

But while women forged ahead in so many ways, the turn of the century was also marked by world-altering events—in particular, 9/11 and the wars in Iraq and Afghanistan—and two history-making US presidents: George W. Bush and Barack Obama.

Glamour was there on the front lines: reporting from New York during 9/11, featuring dispatches from women soldiers in battle, and sitting down with the presidents, their wives, and their opposition, to understand what the future held, not just for its readers, but for all women.

Some dismissed the glossy package of fashion, beauty, politics, and culture found in so many women's magazines as superficial, or pop feminism. But that would be a grave misjudgment. *Glamour*, like so many of its counterparts, was a magazine that reflected all parts of the lives of its readers—without judgment, and with the advancement of women at its heart.

←

The members of Destiny's Child—Beyoncé Knowles, Kelly Rowland, and Michelle Williams—first appeared in *Glamour*'s December 2000 issue, shortly after the release of "Independent Women Part I." The magazine noted they were on the brink of "Supremes style stardom." *Photographed by Riccardo Tinelli, December 2000.*

Previous page, a model high kicks in the plaza outside Catherine Palace, St. Petersburg, Russia, wearing a halter and skirt by Giorgio Armani with boots by Via Spiga. *Photographed by Arthur Elgort, December 2001.*

The Celebrity Revolution

For decades, celebrities had featured inside the pages of *Glamour*. But not since the long-abandoned *Glamour of Hollywood* years had they starred consistently on the cover. That all changed in 1998 under the direction of a new editor in chief, Bonnie Fuller, who helmed the magazine until 2001. *Glamour* embraced this new world with fervor—and never looked back. The first tranche of Hollywood celebrity covers from late 1998 and early 1999 included Salma Hayek, Halle Berry, Courtney Cox, Mariah Carey, and Catherine Zeta-Jones. By the close of the decade, nearly every major music star or Hollywood actor of the moment (many of them Oscar winners) had featured on *Glamour*'s cover: Jennifer Lopez, Taylor Swift, Beyoncé, Britney Spears, Nicole Kidman, and Julia Roberts, to name a few.

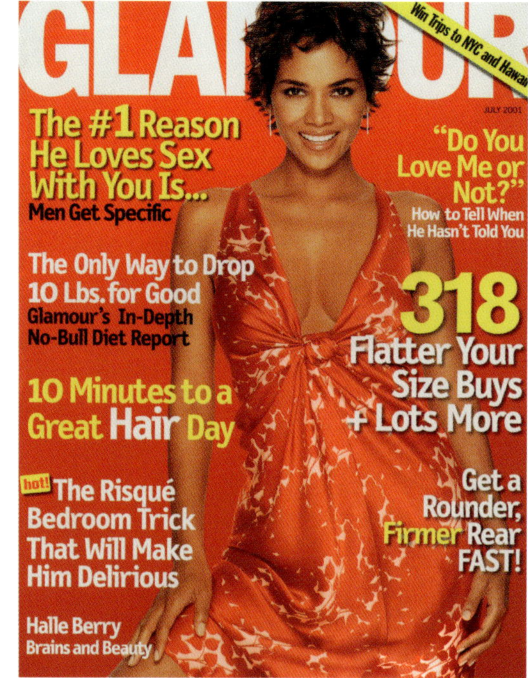

←

Halle Berry appeared on *Glamour*'s cover the same year she won her Oscar, July 2001.

↓

Nicole Kidman was interviewed by Norah Ephron for this cover, August 2005.

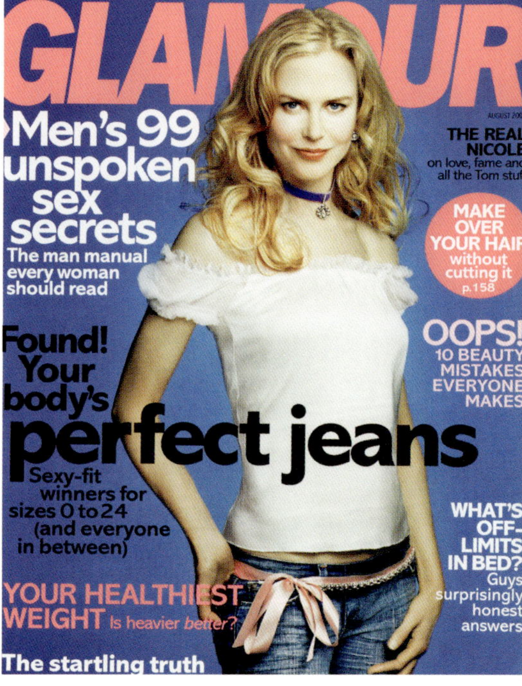

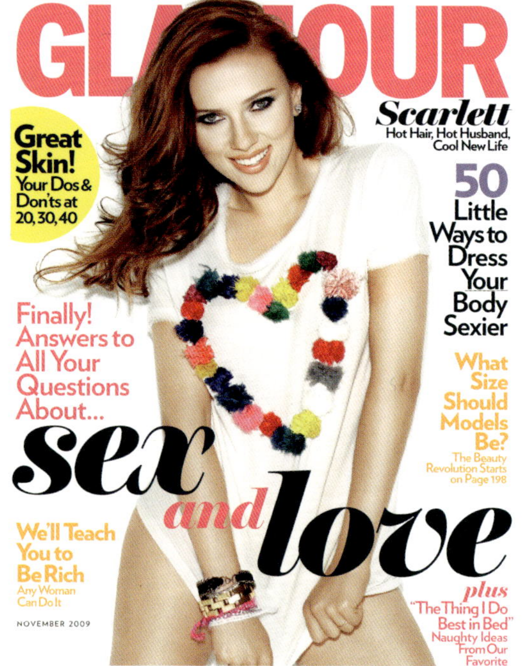

→

Scarlett Johansson makes her debut on the cover of *Glamour*, November 2009.

↓

Mariah Carey appeared on two covers: in 1999 and in November 2007 (pictured here).

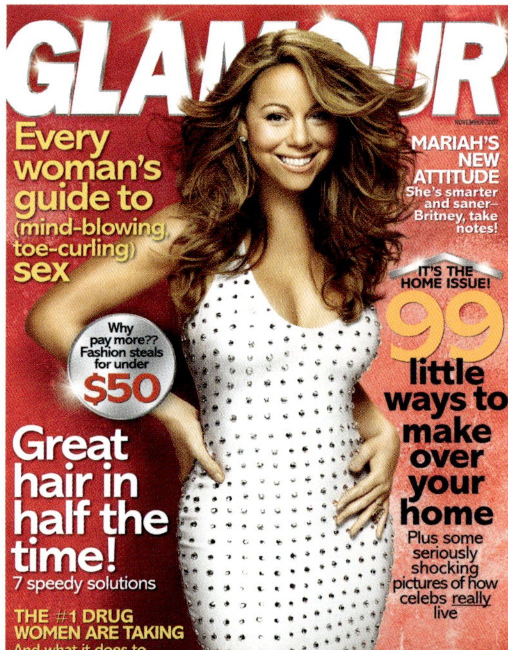

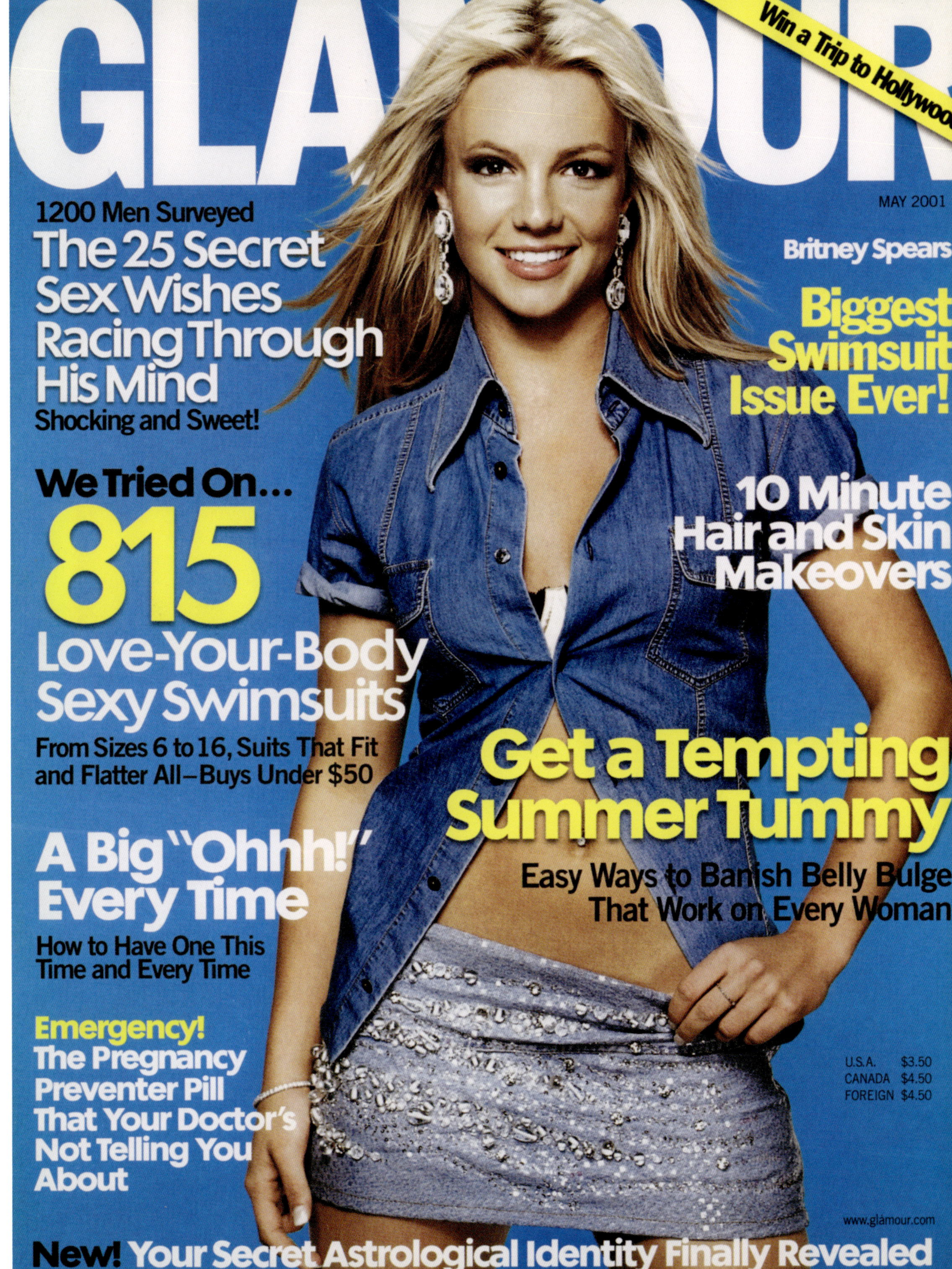

→ In May 2001, a 19-year-old Britney Spears appeared on this, her first *Glamour* cover. In December 2003, she starred on the cover again, this time honored as one of the Women of the Year. Her third cover for the magazine came in January 2009, while under the conservatorship of her father.

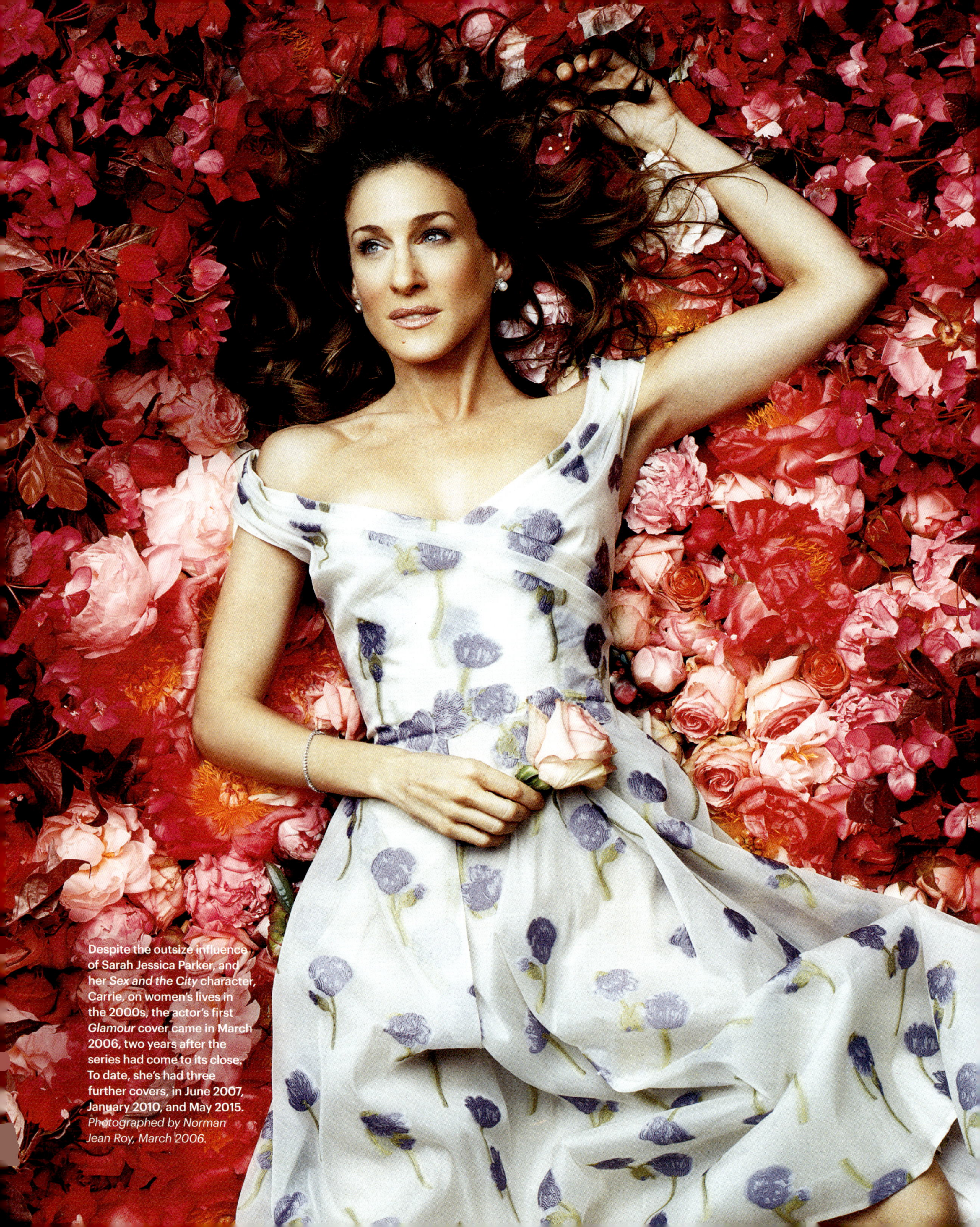

Despite the outsize influence
of Sarah Jessica Parker, and
her *Sex and the City* character,
Carrie, on women's lives in
the 2000s, the actor's first
Glamour cover came in March
2006, two years after the
series had come to its close.
To date, she's had three
further covers, in June 2007,
January 2010, and May 2015.
*Photographed by Norman
Jean Roy, March 2006.*

A fashion shoot with the Queen of Hip-Hop Soul, Mary J. Blige. In October 2023 she was a Women of the Year honoree.
Photographed by Walter Chin, June 2006.

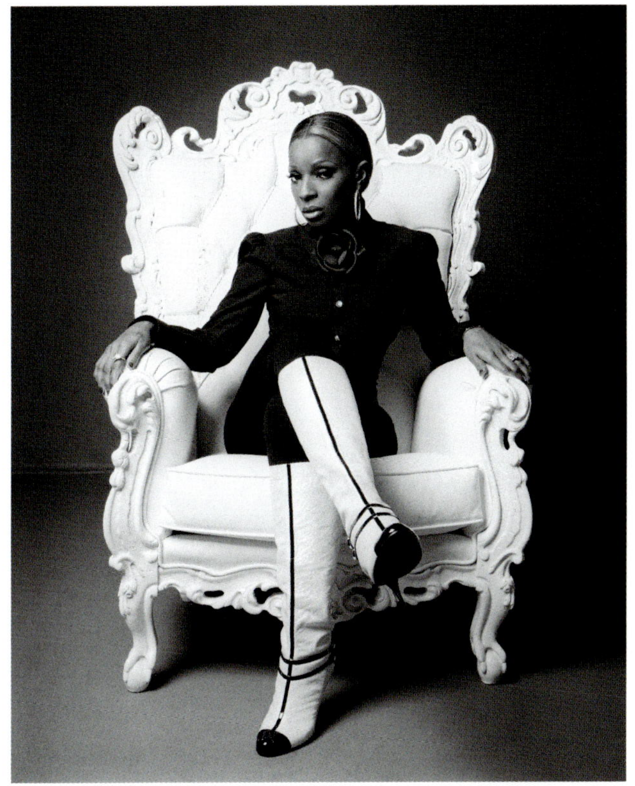

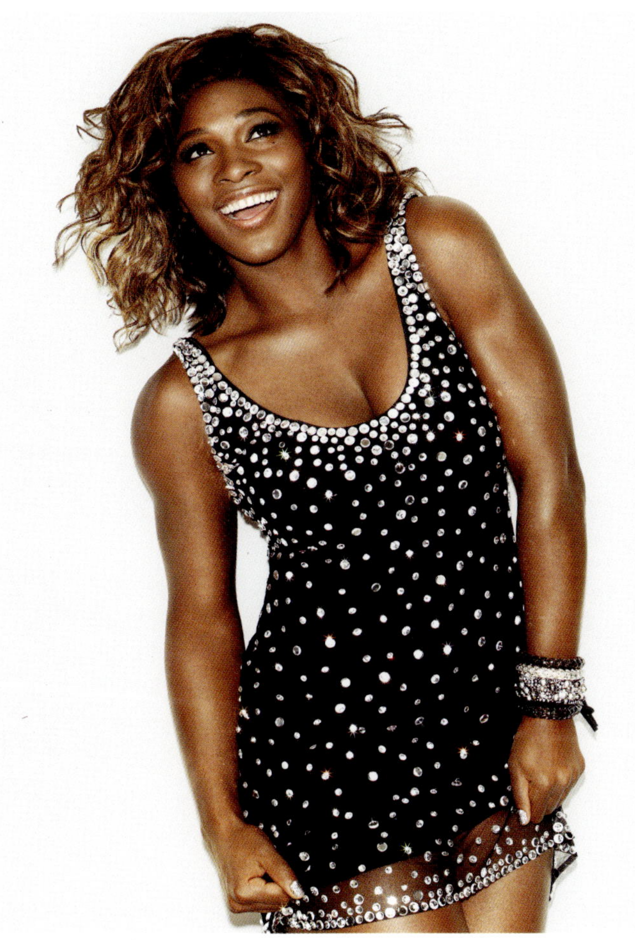

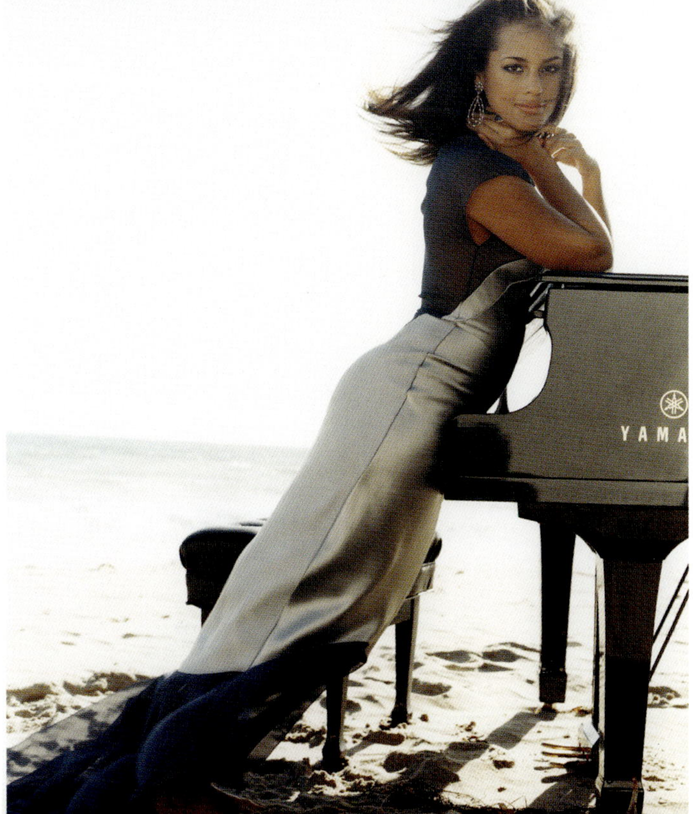

Serena Williams appeared on the cover of *Glamour* in 2009 as a Woman of the Year.
Photographed by Matthias Vriens, December 2009.

Alicia Keys appeared in *Glamour* in 2004, at the end of a year that saw her pick up numerous awards for her second album, *The Diary of Alicia Keys*.
Photographed by Jonathan Skow, December 2004.

Gwen Stefani. *Photographed by Matthias Vriens, October 2009.*

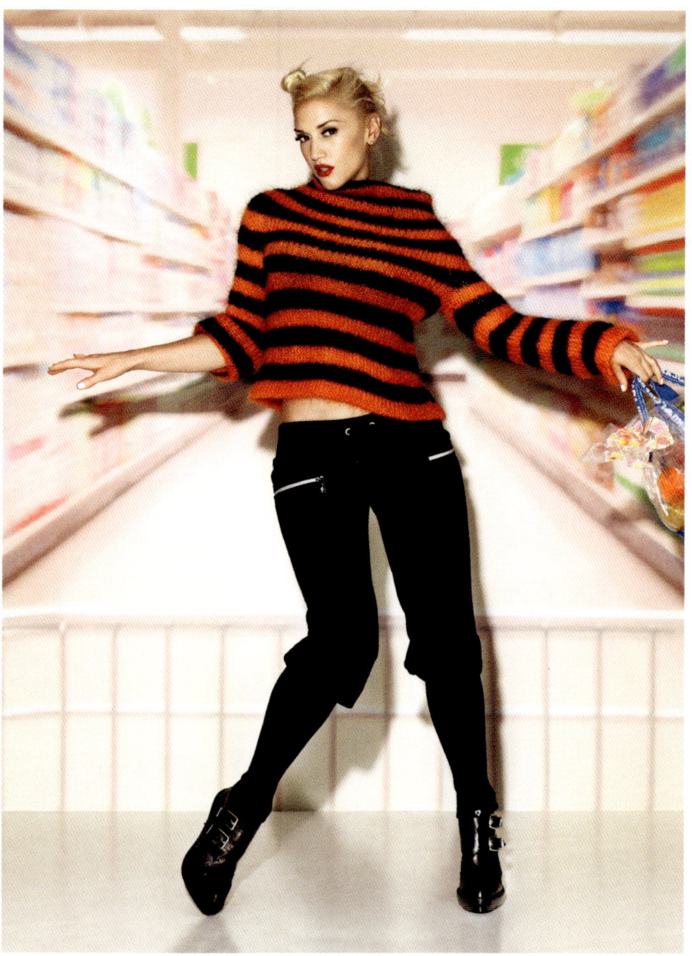

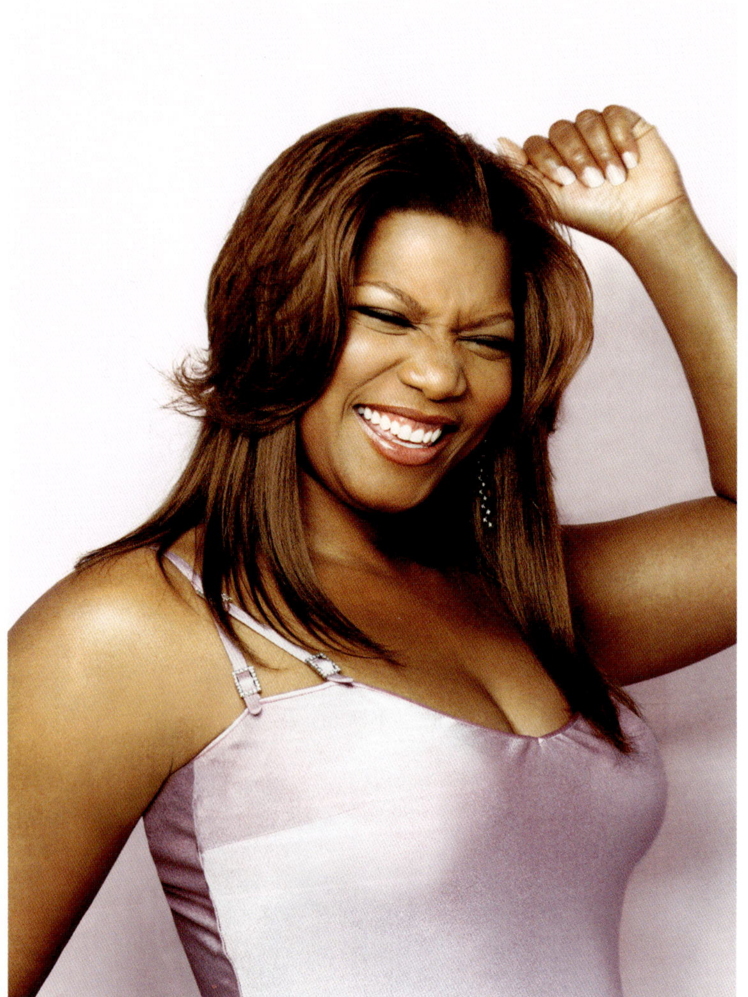

Queen Latifah appeared on two *Glamour* covers, in 2004 and 2007. *This photograph by Wayne Maser was from her cover debut, May 2004.*

Rihanna. *Photographed by Matthias Vriens, December 2009.*

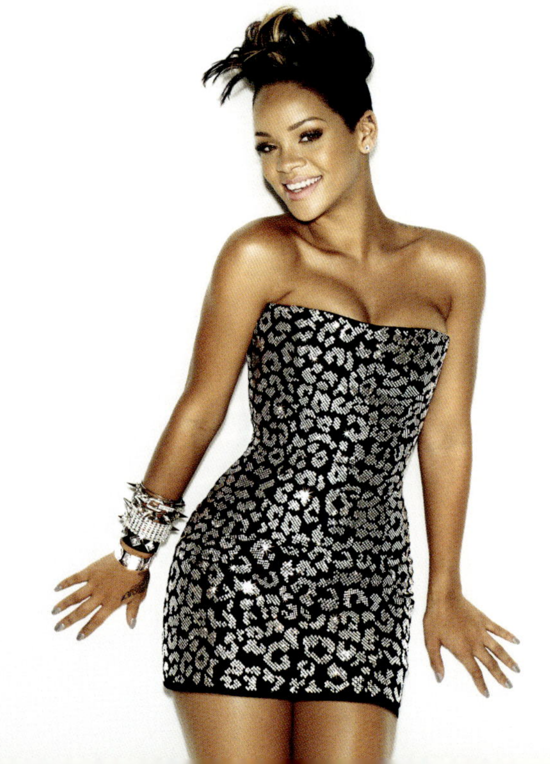

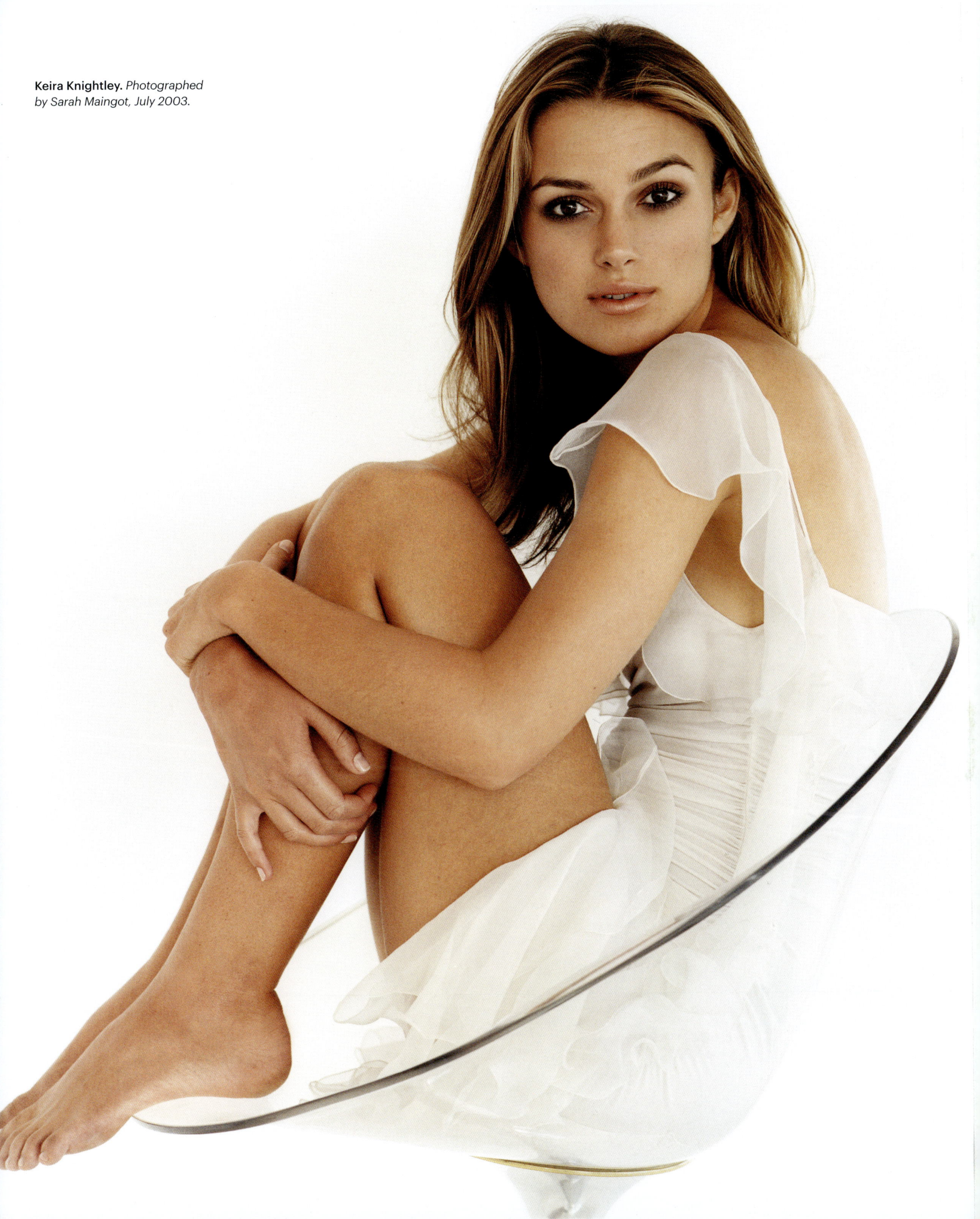

Keira Knightley. *Photographed by Sarah Maingot, July 2003.*

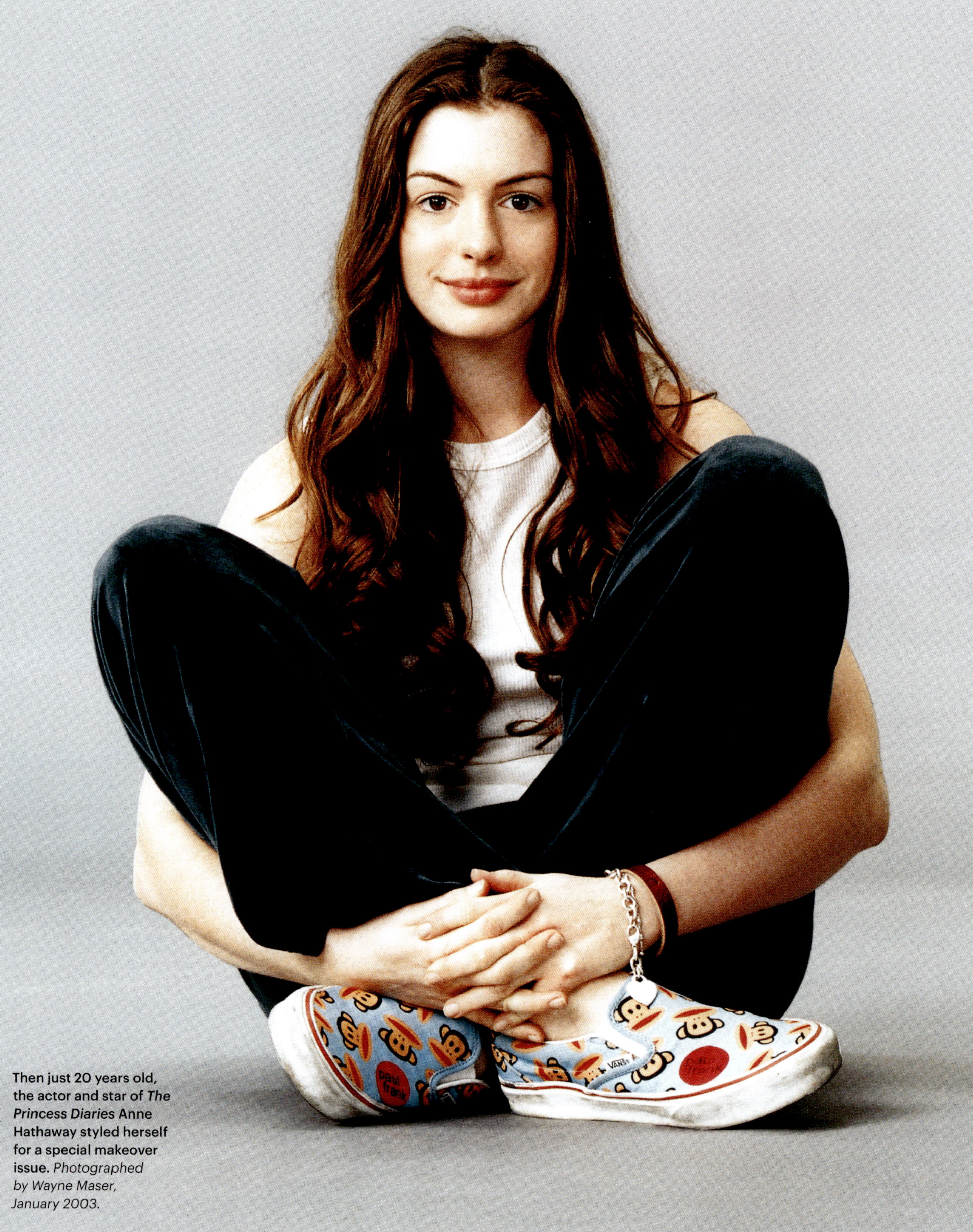

Then just 20 years old, the actor and star of *The Princess Diaries* Anne Hathaway styled herself for a special makeover issue. *Photographed by Wayne Maser, January 2003.*

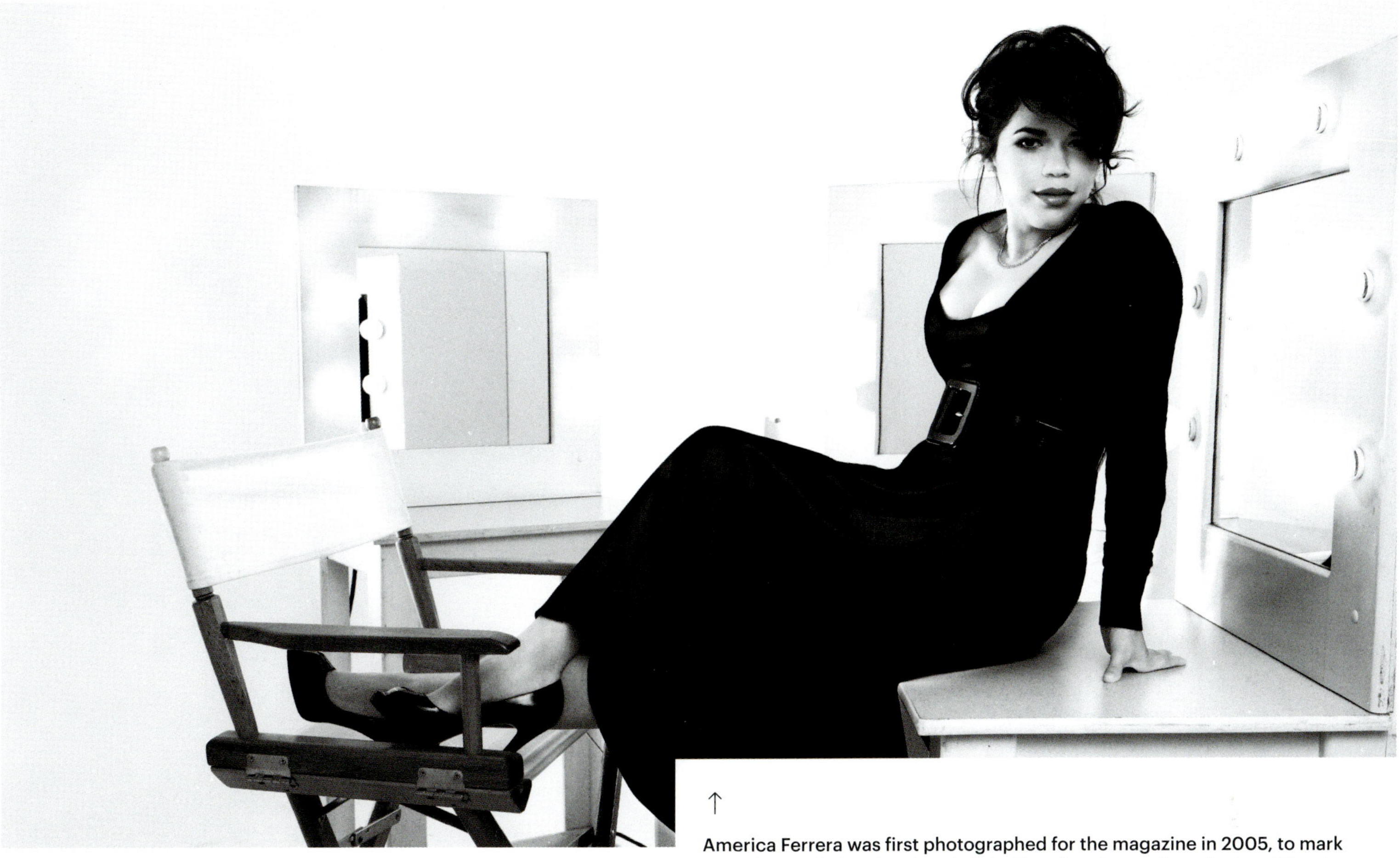

↑

America Ferrera was first photographed for the magazine in 2005, to mark the release of *The Sisterhood of the Traveling Pants*. Here she is celebrating her star turn in *Ugly Betty*. She landed her first cover in October of that year. In 2023, for her many years of activism, she was honored as a *Glamour* Woman of the Year. Hillary and Chelsea Clinton presented the award to her. *Photographed by Mark Abrahams, February 2007.*

Glamour was also passionate about spotlighting stars at the beginning of their careers. Take, for example, Kim Kardashian. In February 2007 a private sex tape she had made was leaked, and her fight to regain the rights to it made as many headlines as the video itself. A few months later, before the now iconic television show *Keeping Up With the Kardashians* had even aired, Kardashian told her story to *Glamour*. Her words bear listening to. "I do want to tell you what it's like to have your most intimate moments scrutinized by thousands; to have your stepfather refuse to speak to you for weeks; to be forced to explain the term "porn star" to your nine-year-old sister…. When my mom hired lawyers, I had to rehash every detail of what I'd done on the tape so they would know what they were dealing with. Imagine describing any part of your sex life to your mom. Now imagine doing that in front of a team of attorneys…. Now that some time has passed, I'm able to see the lessons in all of this: Be careful who you trust. Stick up for yourself…. I came to a large settlement with the company distributing the tape. Would I erase the tape if I could? Of course. Would I change what's happened since it came out? Actually, I wouldn't. My 20-year-old brother has become more sensitive to women's feelings from watching me go through this. My younger sisters have learned the importance of dignity and self-respect. And, most important, I have too."

←

Kim Kardashian's piece in *Glamour* from August 2007.

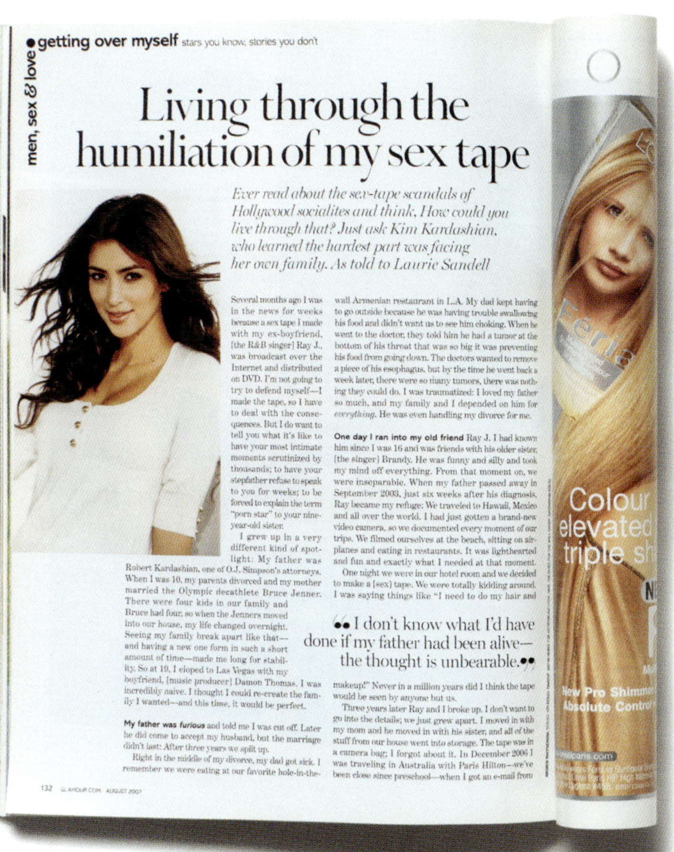

Living through the humiliation of my sex tape

Ever read about the sex-tape scandals of Hollywood socialites and think, How could you live through that? Just ask Kim Kardashian, who learned the hardest part was facing her own family. As told to Laurie Sandell

Several months ago I was in the news for weeks because a sex tape I made with my ex-boyfriend, [the R&B singer] Ray J., was broadcast over the Internet and distributed on DVD. I'm not going to try to defend myself—I made the tape, so I have to deal with the consequences. But I do want to tell you what it's like to have your most intimate moments scrutinized by thousands; to have your stepfather refuse to speak to you for weeks; to be forced to explain the term "porn star" to your nine-year-old sister.

I grew up in a very different kind of spotlight: My father was Robert Kardashian, one of O.J. Simpson's attorneys. When I was 10, my parents divorced and my mother married the Olympic decathlete Bruce Jenner. There were four kids in our family and Bruce had four, so when the Jenners moved into our house, my life changed overnight. Seeing my family break apart like that—and having a new one form in such a short amount of time—made me long for stability. So at 19, I eloped to Las Vegas with my boyfriend, [music producer] Damon Thomas. I was incredibly naive. I thought I could re-create the family I wanted—and this time, it would be perfect.

My father was *furious* and told me I was cut off. Later he did come to accept my husband, but the marriage didn't last: After three years we split up.

Right in the middle of my divorce, my dad got sick. I remember we were eating at our favorite hole-in-the-wall Armenian restaurant in L.A. My dad kept having to go outside because he was having trouble swallowing his food and didn't want us to see him choking. When he went to the doctor, they told him he had a tumor at the bottom of his throat that was so big it was preventing his food from going down. The doctors wanted to remove a piece of his esophagus, but by the time he went back a week later, there were so many tumors, there was nothing they could do. I was traumatized: I loved my father so much, and my family and I depended on him for *everything*. He was even handling my divorce for me.

One day I ran into my old friend Ray J. I had known him since I was 16 and was friends with his older sister, [the singer] Brandy. He was funny and silly and took my mind off everything. From that moment on, we were inseparable. When my father passed away in September 2003, just six weeks after his diagnosis, Ray became my refuge: We traveled to Hawaii, Mexico and all over the world. I had just gotten a brand-new video camera, so we documented every moment of our trips. We filmed ourselves at the beach, sitting on airplanes and eating in restaurants. It was lighthearted and fun and exactly what I needed at that moment.

One night we were in our hotel room and we decided to make a [sex] tape. We were totally kidding around. I was saying things like "I need to do my hair and makeup!" Never in a million years did I think the tape would be seen by anyone but us.

Three years later Ray and I broke up. I don't want to go into the details; we just grew apart. I moved in with my mom and he moved in with his sister, and all of the stuff from our house went into storage. The tape was in a camera bag; I forgot about it. In December 2006 I was traveling in Australia with Paris Hilton—we've been close since preschool—when I got an e-mail from

⟪ I don't know what I'd have done if my father had been alive— the thought is unbearable. ⟫

GEORGE W. BUSH

WHO IS THE REAL MAN IN THIS PICTURE?

FROM WHERE I WAS STANDING—high on a hotel balcony in New York City, watching George W. Bush twirl through a $1,000-a-plate fund-raising luncheon last March—it was clear why he inspires such feverish admiration among his core followers. Circling from table to table, grasping an endless offering of hands, Bush seemed actually to *delight* in this election-year ritual. The Texas governor kind of *twin-kled*. New York governor George Pataki and mayor Rudy Giuliani were making their own circles through the room, and neither showed Bush's nimbleness for the stump.

In person, Bush has a sort of star quality. People want to touch him—even his harshest critics. Molly Ivins, the acid-tongued political commentator whose *Fort-Worth Star-Telegram* column is syndicated nationally, has begrudgingly conceded that he's "a pretty nice guy—I really think you would have to work hard to dislike the man." The audience adored his mixture of frat-house humor and old-fashioned goofiness (his opening line: "When I told my wife, Laura, I was going to come to New York, she said, 'Don't try being charming, witty and debonair—*just be yourself!*'"). They couldn't have been more charmed if he had passed out their share of the government surplus (his key campaign promise) right then and there.

✓ NIGHTMARE AT 20,000 FEET

That's why I was so startled when 90 minutes later, on the Bush campaign plane, I found myself in the middle of a fight. I realized it with a buzzing terror not five minutes into a long-planned *Glamour* interview, the purpose of which was to flesh out Bush's thoughts on "women's issues." The mood of the man *New York Times* columnist Maureen Dowd calls "tetchy" turned astonishingly volcanic.

There had been early warning signs. For one thing, he barely glanced in my direction when we were introduced. And everything about the governor's body language at our meeting was chilly. He was slumped so low in his seat, in the first row of first class, that the man's bottom half was actually hanging off the cushion and his chin was pinned flat against his chest. To keep from pouring right into the aisle, he had planted his shoes (tasseled loafers) square on the carpeted wall in front of him. One sock was slightly twisted, like his mood. It was a *Malcolm in the Middle* pose, all knees and elbows.

After our interview, there would be speculation among the press corps about why this was. His trusted communications director, the Texas amazon Karen Hughes, had made us 20 minutes late for our

Is this upstanding husband and father who espouses "compassionate conservatism" the perfect pick for American women weary of Monica-gate morality? Or does the Texas governor, who supports the Republican platform's ban on abortion—even if the mother's life is in danger—require far deeper scrutiny? <u>Glamour's</u> national affairs editor, DAVID FRANCE, hit the campaign trail to find out more about the man who could be your next president.

PHOTOGRAPHS BY RONNIE ANDREN

departure from Newark, and the governor hates to be tardy. Or perhaps he was inconsolable over the tepid reviews of his new school-vouchers plan. ("All these catchphrases are horses that are not going to trot anymore," one principal he visited in Little Rock, Arkansas, told reporters.) Or maybe it was because of that morning's awful twister, which wreaked $450 million worth of damage in Fort Worth, Texas.

But whatever the explanation, if Al Gore is the wooden candidate, George W. Bush is the moody one, a candidate whose ability to shine in a crowd is matched only by his ability to appear churlish on television. News reports frequently mention his off-putting sneer—so much so that the ultraconservative New Hampshire newspaper the *Manchester Leader* labeled him "Gov. Smirk." No matter what they believe politically, Americans take this body-language stuff seriously, and when asked recently for a one-word description of Bush, the presumptive Republican nominee, one third chose something negative, like "cocky," "smug" or "arrogant," according to a recent poll by the nonpartisan Pew Research Center for the People and the Press.

We were playing a game of verbal Rorschach—I was rattling off names and concepts, and he was telling me the first thought that came to his mind. Neither of us was having much fun. Instead of elucidating political insights on, for instance, New Jersey governor Christine Todd Whitman, he was giving me, "Good friend."

No matter. Along like this we were going, for better or worse, screaming our questions and answers over the din of the airplane,

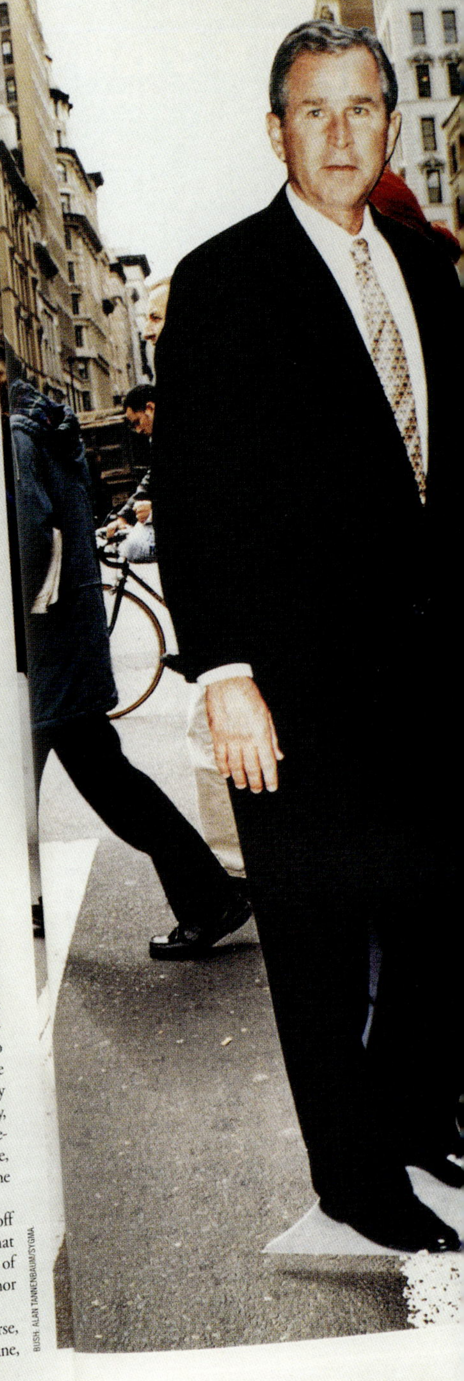

IN JUNE 2000, A HANDFUL OF months before one of the most significant presidential elections in US history, *Glamour*'s reporter David France had been granted an interview with then presidential wannabe George W. Bush on the campaign plane. What happened next made headlines far beyond the magazine. Mid-flight, at 20,000 feet, Bush lost his temper with the reporter, turning "astonishingly volcanic" when he misunderstood a question about the television show *Sex and the City*, and one about the Taliban. The editor in chief at the time, Bonnie Fuller, remains enormously proud that "we were on top of the issue." In a recent interview, she recalled, "The fact that he didn't even know, he wasn't aware of who they were, and then he was the president when 9/11 happened…. It was shocking." Read the extracted piece, above.

'The Taliban,' I repeated. The interval was endless. 'Oh,' he said finally. 'I thought you said some band.'

"GEORGE W. BUSH: WHO IS THE REAL MAN IN THIS PICTURE" BY DAVID FRANCE, JUNE 2000

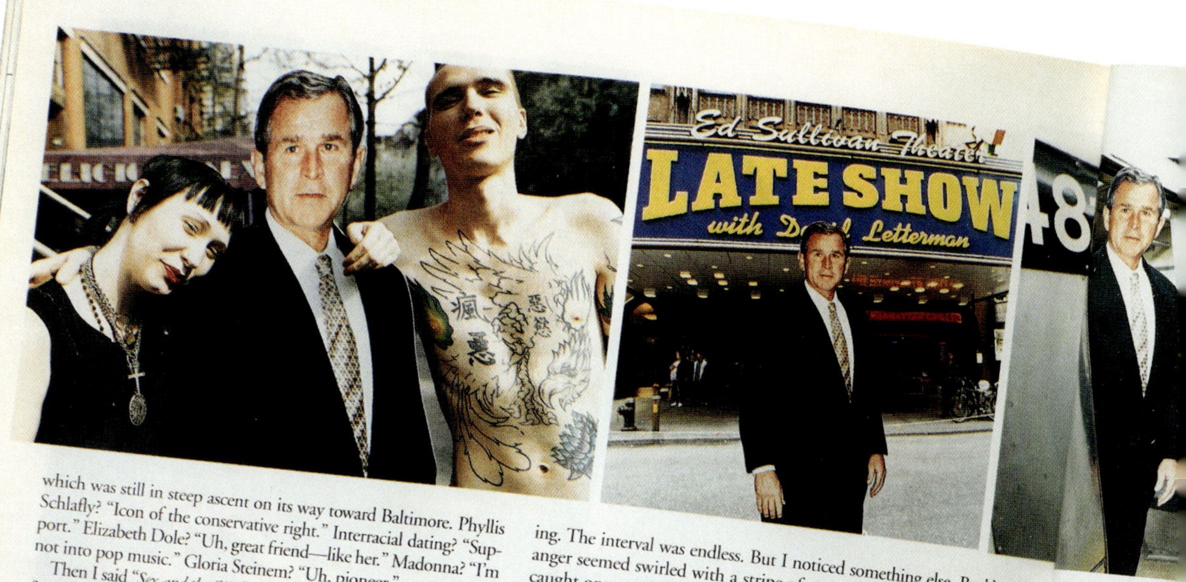

which was still in steep ascent on its way toward Baltimore. Phyllis Schlafly? "Icon of the conservative right." Interracial dating? "Support." Elizabeth Dole? "Uh, great friend—like her." Madonna? "I'm not into pop music." Gloria Steinem? "Uh, pioneer."

Then I said "*Sex and the City*," and our game took a dark turn. The face of the man who would be president blistered in a purple fury. He turned toward me for the first time, only to narrow his dark eyes and glower. He was giving me the politician's equivalent of a pro-wrestling belly-butt! For the life of me, I did not know why he had snapped like this. Had a *Sex and the City* episode been cruel toward him? Had one of his twin 18-year-old daughters been turned down for a part?

"Governor," said media coordinator Gordon Johndroe, "it's an HBO television show." In retrospect, I suppose now that Bush thought I was asking about sexual *activity* in the city, a provocative question for the anti-choice candidate, monogamous since the day "I put my hand on a Bible and said 'till death do us part.'" After all, this is the man who said to me, "I think for every dollar we spend on contraception we ought to spend one on abstinence education as well."

But his harrowing look did not soften. I tried meekly to cut the tension by offering a joke: "You don't have cable in Texas, I guess!"

It was an awful mistake. "What?" he bellowed. He moved his feet from the wall in front of him and tilted at me squarely. "I don't get cable?!" Even the press aide seemed worried for me as he offered his own explanation for his boss' very understandable ignorance of a television program ("We've been on the campaign trail").

Stung by his unexpected anger, I went into full backpedaling retreat. I skimmed through my list and dropped all pop-culture questions of the sort Clinton so good-naturedly fielded on his MTV appearances (who can forget "boxers or briefs?"). I also tossed those I felt had the potential to make the man even angrier, like mentions of homosexuals, whose basic rights—adoption, job protections, spousal benefits—he does not support. I wanted to lob the guy a softball, if only for my own preservation. So I went right to a question in the mainstream of political discourse: the Islamic fundamentalist faction that brutally represses women throughout Afghanistan.

"The Taliban," I said.

Gripping his armrests powerfully, the governor jutted his chin forward and shook his head in a silent, choleric rejection of my query. He was so tightly wound, I thought he might spin right out of first class, taking a few of my internal organs with him.

"The Taliban," I repeated hopefully, much louder this time thanks to my tremor, adding plaintively, "It's a big question for our readers?" If he hadn't heard me the first time, he did now. Still nothing. The interval was endless. But I noticed something else. Bush's anger seemed swirled with a stripe of uncertainty. Perhaps he felt caught once more by a pop quiz he could not answer. It scarcely seemed possible. The Taliban has been on the cover of *Time* magazine, in U.N. resolutions and in constant headlines.

And even if it were true—which it wasn't—that I'd hoped to ambush Bush with some obscurantism, why didn't he just scold me presidentially? He simply could have answered that he believed running for president was too grave an undertaking to be measured by a list of his replies. Why was he instead just sitting there, to borrow from Mark Twain, looking like an envelope without an address on it? If an innocent *Glamour* question freezes him cold, how might he respond later, as president, when a bona fide adversary asks where he's dispatched his troops?

Finally, I slid him a clue: "Because of the repression of women—in Afghanistan?"

"Oh," he said finally. "I thought you said some band. The Taliban in *Afghanistan*! Absolutely. Repressive."

☑ CURIOUS GEORGE

George W. Bush's official Web site—not the several unofficial ones, dedicated repositories of what are now being called Bush-isms, as when he called Greeks "Grecians" or asked in a rhetorical campaign flourish, "Will the highways on the Internet become more few?"—is full of black-and-white pictures dating back 54 years, when Bush was an infant in the arms of his mother, Barbara, and his father, George Herbert Walker Bush, who at the time was still a Yale undergraduate. Over the years, the gallery shows the handsome eldest Bush offspring (three brothers and two sisters followed, but his baby sister Robin died of leukemia when George was just seven) in successive sizes of baseball uniforms. Though he grew up beneath the sturdy awning of his father's political career, which included a posting as ambassador to China, where George W. visited for a summer, his passions leaned more toward baseball than the Beltway. "I never dreamed about being president," the candidate has said. "When I was growing up I wanted to be Willie Mays."

He had little aptitude for school, though he followed in his father's footsteps first at Andover, the old guard's favorite prep school, and then at Yale. But he was clever enough to serve as a fighter pilot in the Texas Air National Guard from 1968 to 1973 (meaning he got a Vietnam deferral) and then to earn a master's in business from Harvard before heading back to Texas to do as his father did: dabble in the oil business. But despite his successes since then—he eve[r] the Texas Ran[gers] governor of T[exas] shocker (he ea[rned] dodging the im[…] women's health[…] columnist Liz S[…] down from back[…] "I don't really [...] Bush found him[…] myself out to be a[…] good common se[nse] Nonetheless, he[…] with presidential d[…] *Talk* magazine rece[…] down and reading[…] or something." He[…]

50th in choice*: In [...] governor, Bush has s[...] sions into law limitin[g] abortion, including a[...] family-planning fund[s] parental-notification [...] tory 48-hour waiting p[...] earning him this low r[...] National Abortion and[...] Rights Action League.

*Most rankings based on 50 st[...]

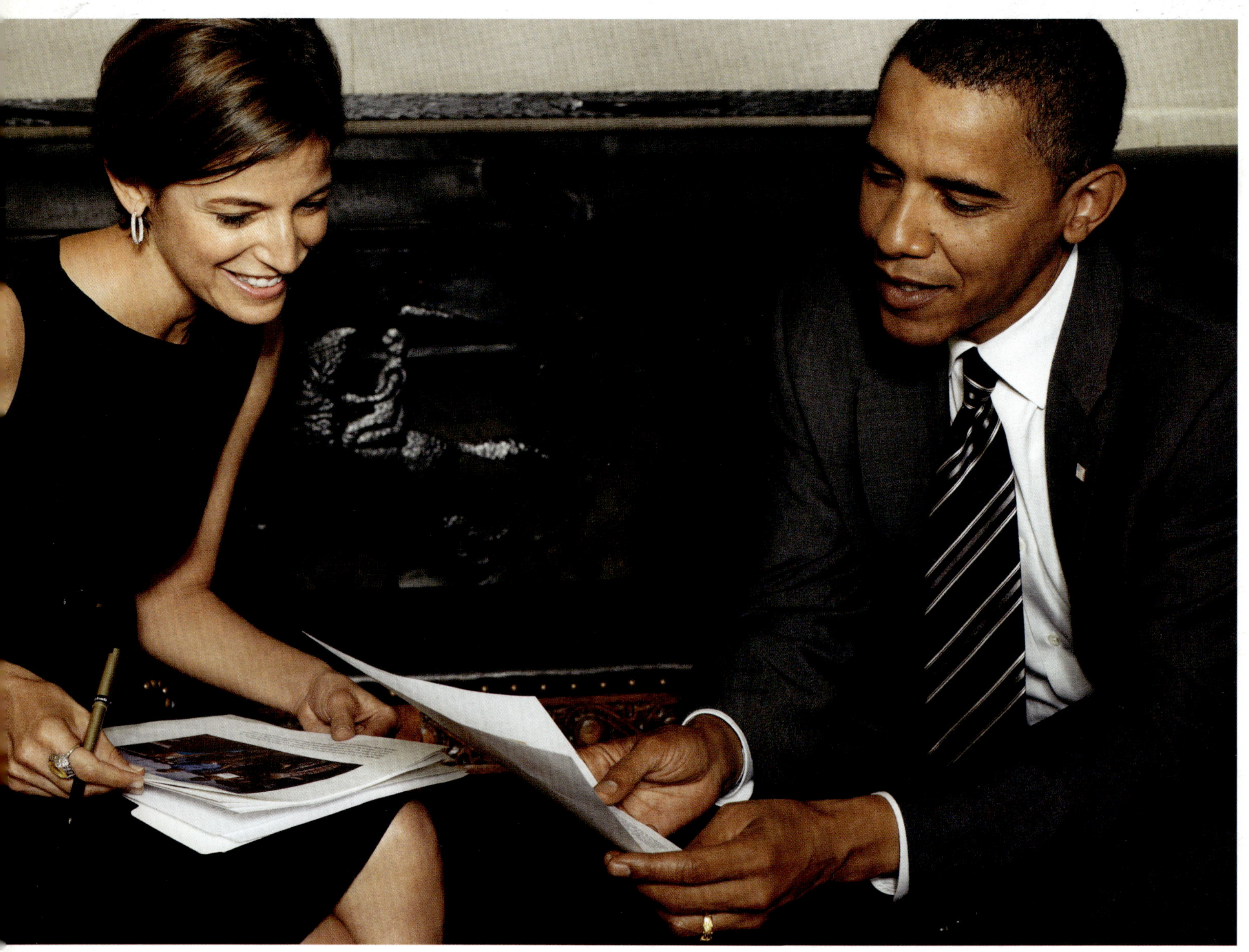

During the course of this era, *Glamour* established itself as an important avenue of political access for its millions of readers, and built on the magazine's rich history covering politicians on the way up (in the early decades, the magazine featured Ronald Reagan, John F. Kennedy, Richard Nixon, and Lyndon B. Johnson, all of whom would go on to hold the country's highest office.) But this decade marked the first time sitting presidents and their first ladies gave interviews to the magazine. *Glamour*'s leader during this momentous period was Cindi Leive, who became editor in chief in 2001 and steered the magazine for 16 years. Between 2001 and 2009 *Glamour* featured interviews with, or pieces from, every Republican and Democratic presidential candidate, including heartfelt letters from President Bush and Senator John Kerry to their daughters, and Leive herself interviewed Senator John McCain, then senator Barack Obama (she interviewed him again in November 2012), and first lady Laura Bush. *Glamour*'s access ensured key issues impacting women—such as affordable healthcare, paid family leave, the protection of abortion rights, and more—were put to the most influential politicians in the country. In 2008, Obama told *Glamour* that his priorities as president would be "Equal pay for equal work, making sure that women with similar qualifications are getting treated similarly in the workplace." He also believed that "the best indicator of whether a country does well is how it treats its girls and its women."

↑

"Senator Obama bounds into a room with limitless energy and a marvelous ability to speak about the issue you care about." This was how Cindi Leive described meeting Obama. *Photographed by Matthias Vriens, October 2008.*

→

In 2003, first lady Laura Bush launched a campaign in *Glamour* to combat heart disease, which at the time claimed the lives of more women than cancer annually. "My husband and I, we're very careful with our health. We go to bed early. In this job, fatigue would be very detrimental!" *Photographed by Firooz Zahedi, October 2003.*

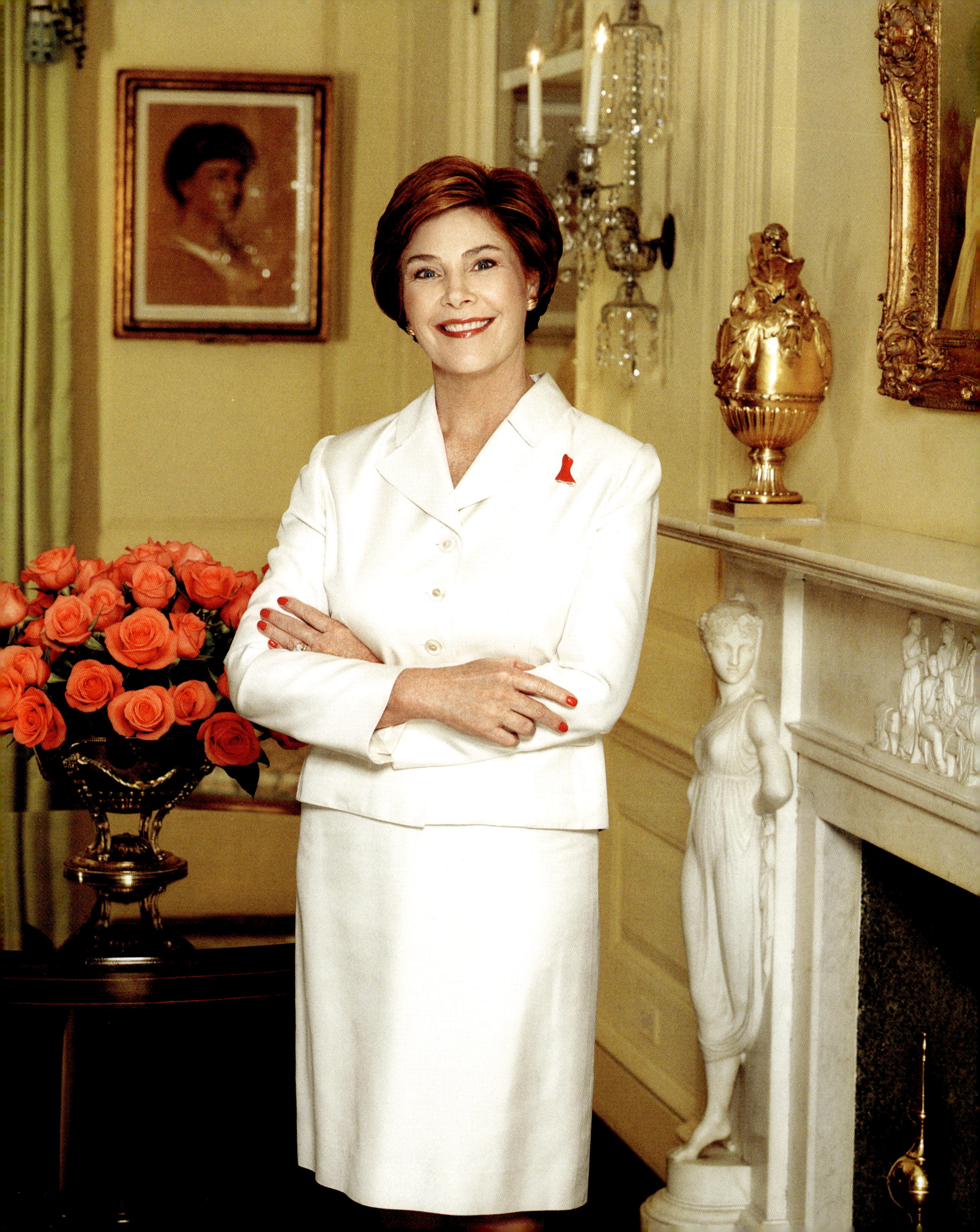

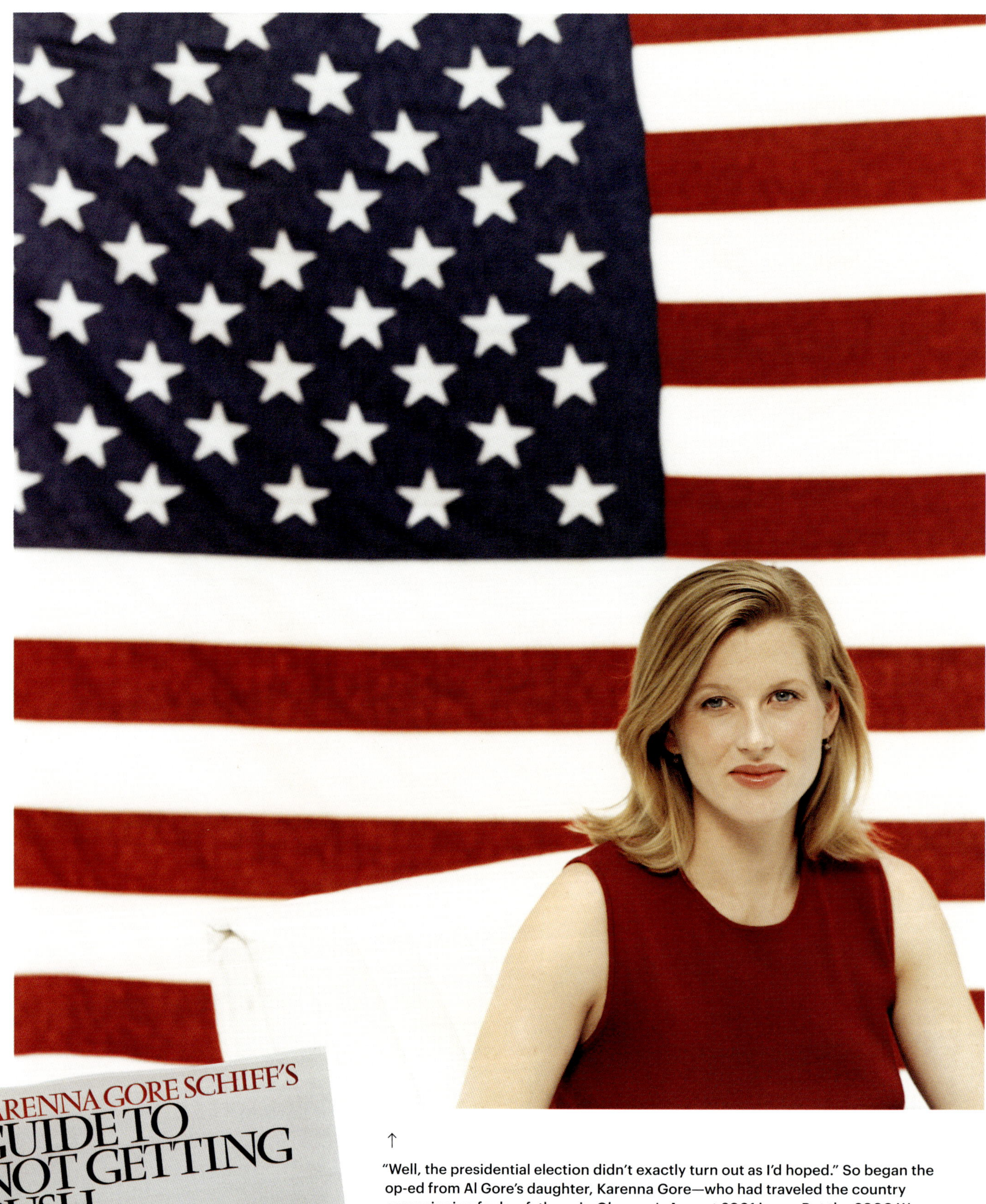

↑

"Well, the presidential election didn't exactly turn out as I'd hoped." So began the op-ed from Al Gore's daughter, Karenna Gore—who had traveled the country campaigning for her father—in *Glamour*'s August 2001 issue. But the 2000 Women of the Year honoree offered a message of hope to the magazine's readers: "We all have at least some power to make a real difference. There's letter writing. Did you know that the correspondence offices in the White House and Congress pay careful attention to how many letters and e-mails they receive on each issue? Most importantly, we must keep tabs on elected representatives and hold them accountable for their actions and promises. If we've learned anything from this crazy election, it's that a handful of votes has an enormous ability to change our national and global destiny." *Photographed by Deborah Jaffe, August 2001.*

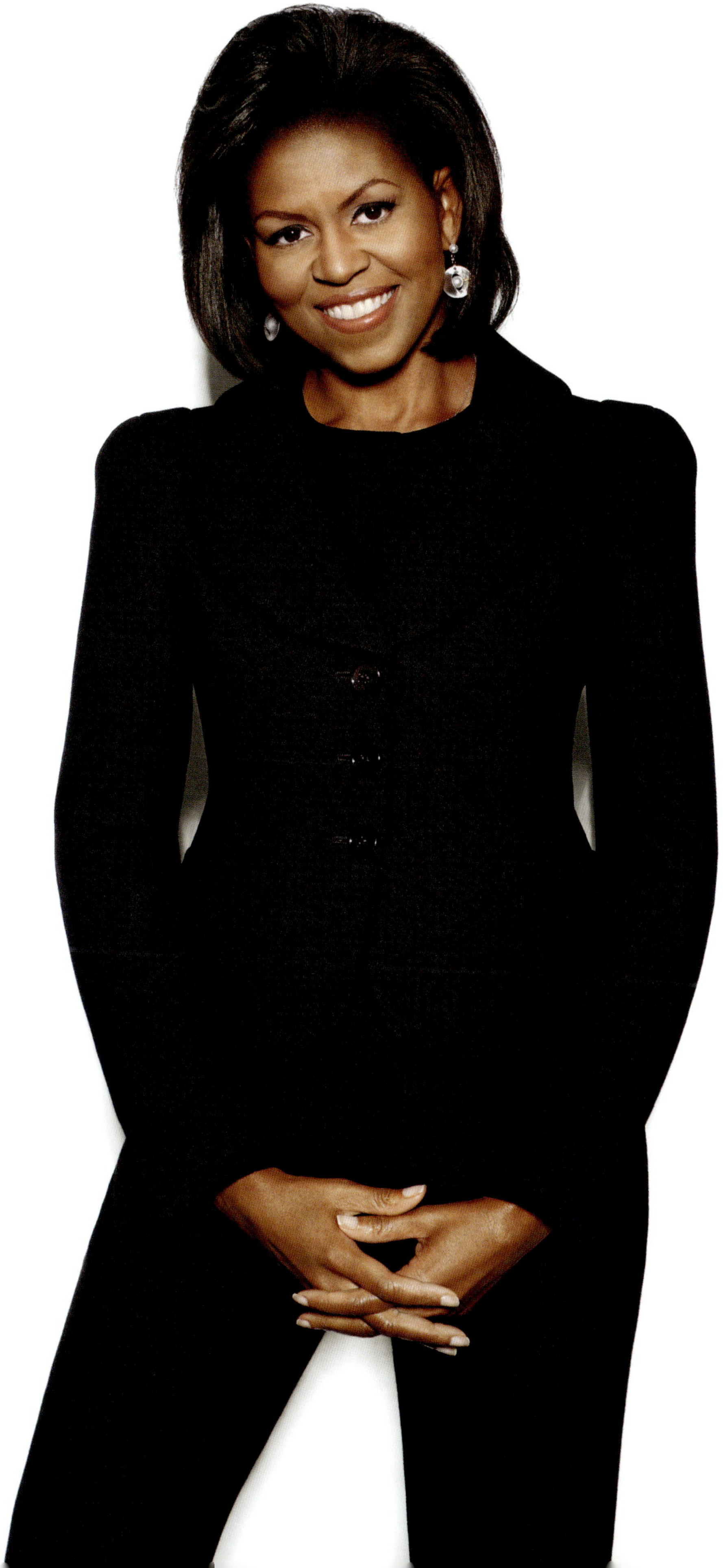

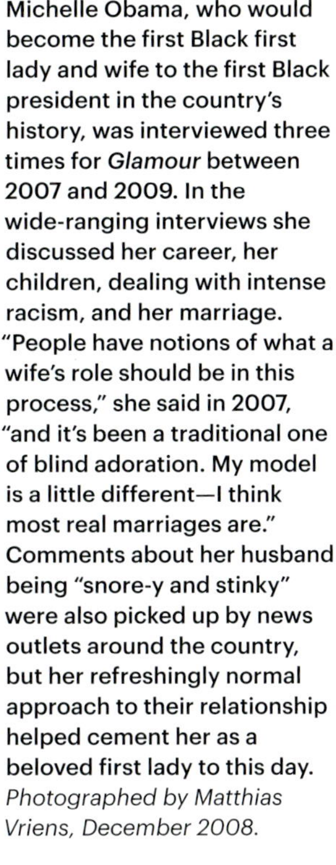

Michelle Obama, who would become the first Black first lady and wife to the first Black president in the country's history, was interviewed three times for *Glamour* between 2007 and 2009. In the wide-ranging interviews she discussed her career, her children, dealing with intense racism, and her marriage. "People have notions of what a wife's role should be in this process," she said in 2007, "and it's been a traditional one of blind adoration. My model is a little different—I think most real marriages are." Comments about her husband being "snore-y and stinky" were also picked up by news outlets around the country, but her refreshingly normal approach to their relationship helped cement her as a beloved first lady to this day. *Photographed by Matthias Vriens, December 2008.*

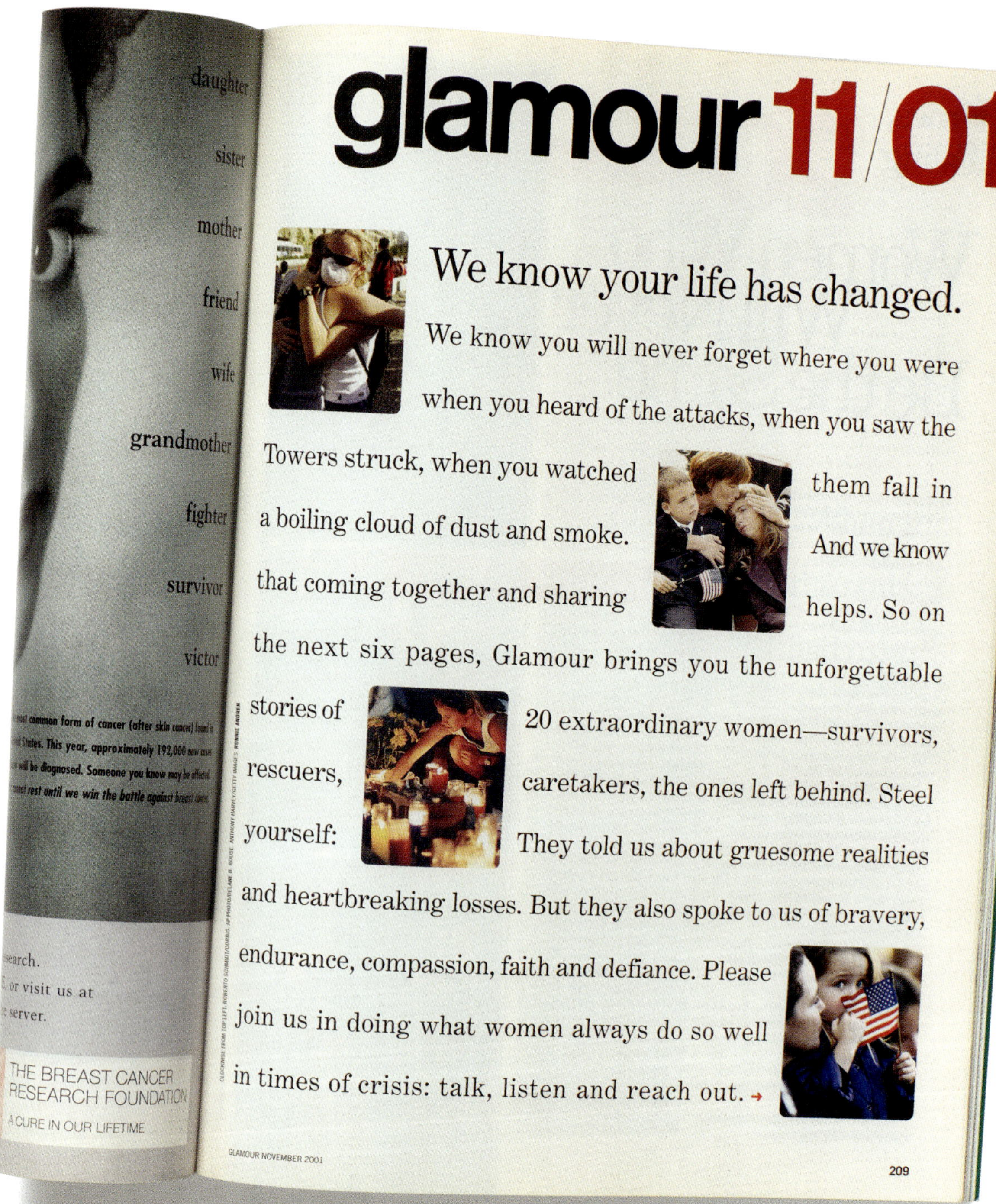

9/11

The devastating attacks of September 11, 2001, unfolded as *Glamour* was going to press with its November issue. Life for people around the world would never be quite the same. Amidst huge grief and collective heartache, a staff of 27 writers, editors, and reporters "rushed in two stories that reflect[ed] the new world Americans inhabit." Above, we reprint the cover page for the issue's special section, and over the following pages, images that appeared in that same issue, which was also Cindi Leive's first as *Glamour*'s editor in chief. The following month, Leive honored EMT Yamel Merino and police officer Moira Smith posthumously at *Glamour*'s Women of the Year Awards: "On September 11, hundreds of firefighters, police officers, and emergency medical technicians raced into the burning towers of the World Trade Center to help others get out. When the buildings collapsed, many of those rescue workers died alongside the people they were trying to save. Only two were women: EMT Yamel Merino and police officer Moira Smith. By honoring them, *Glamour* remembers all of those who died that day in New York City; Arlington, Virginia; and Somerset County, Pennsylvania."

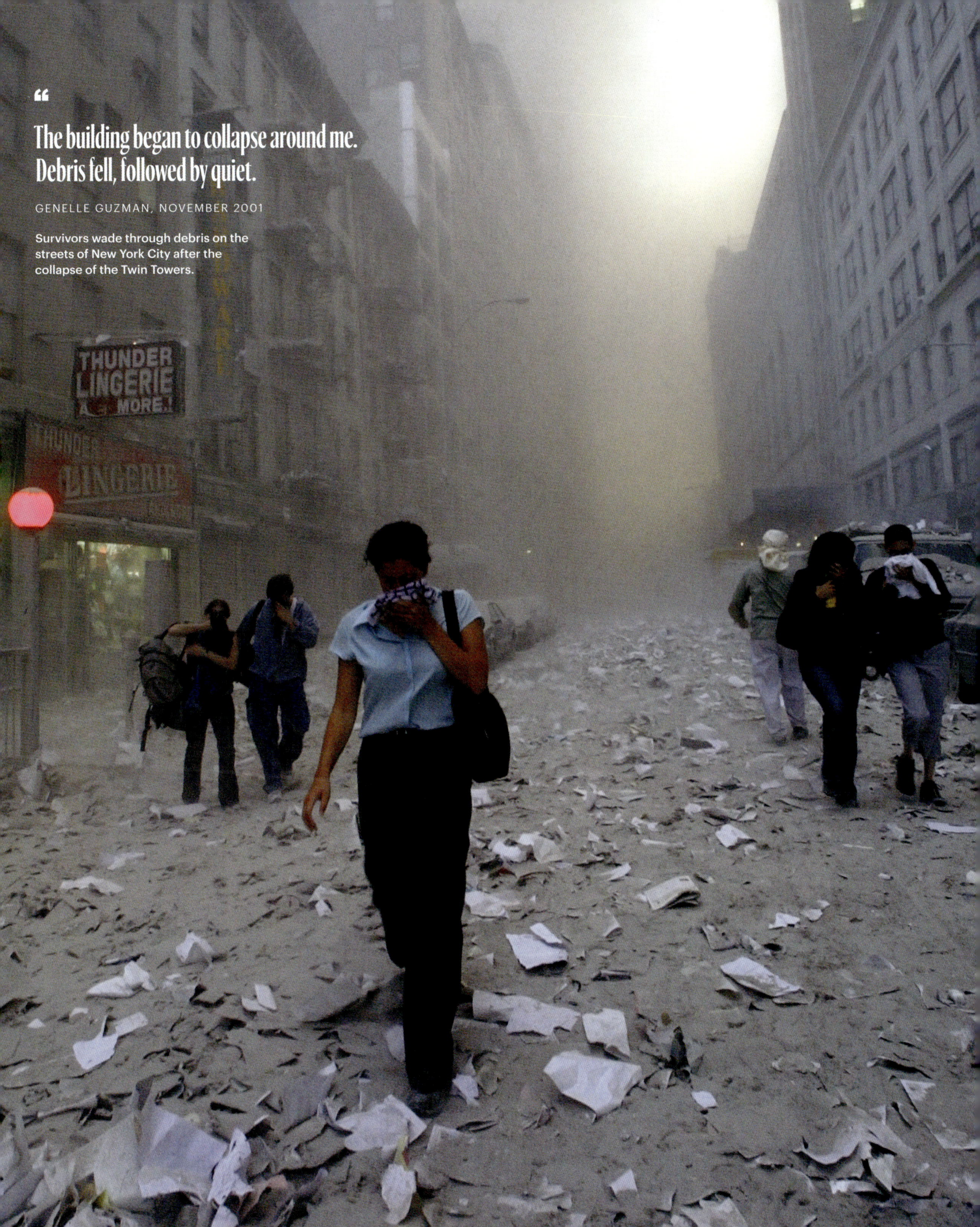

"The building began to collapse around me. Debris fell, followed by quiet.

GENELLE GUZMAN, NOVEMBER 2001

Survivors wade through debris on the streets of New York City after the collapse of the Twin Towers.

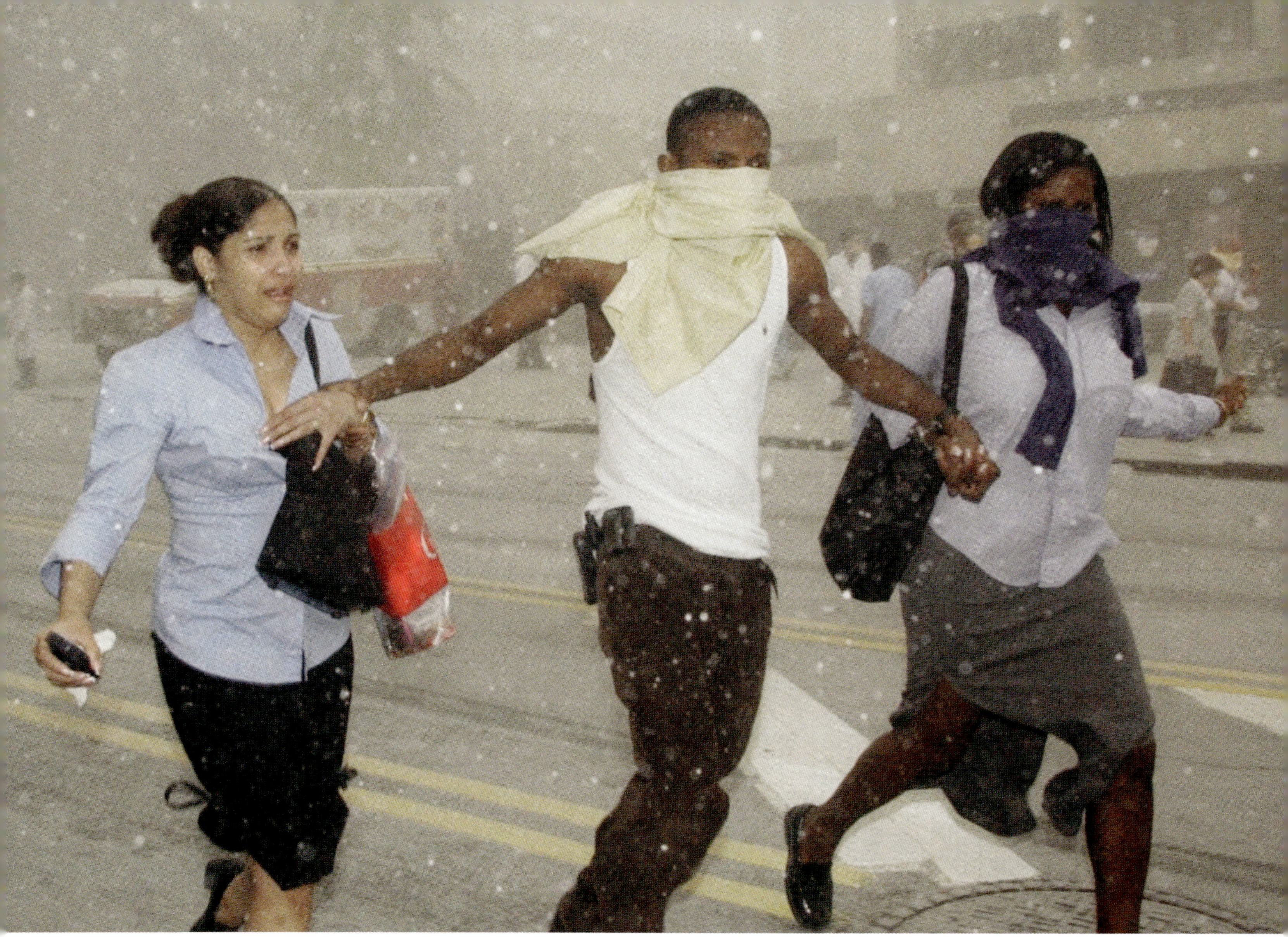

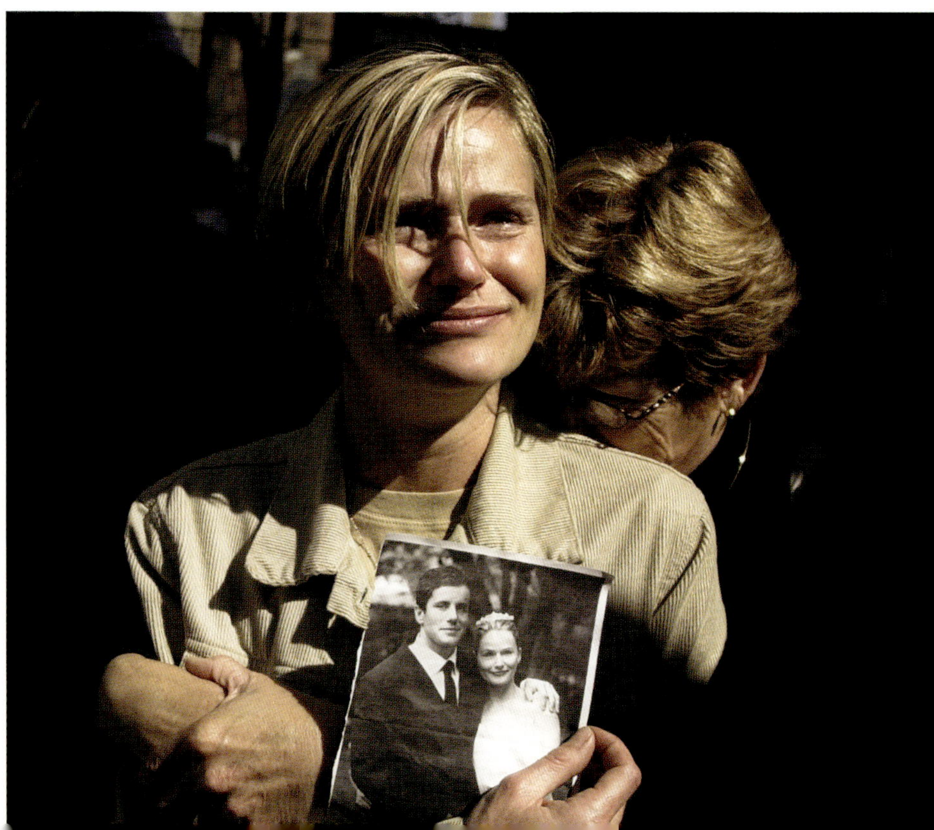

↑

Three people make their way through a cloud of dust in downtown New York.

→

Mary Ortale, who lost her husband Peter in the attacks, holds a photograph of him.

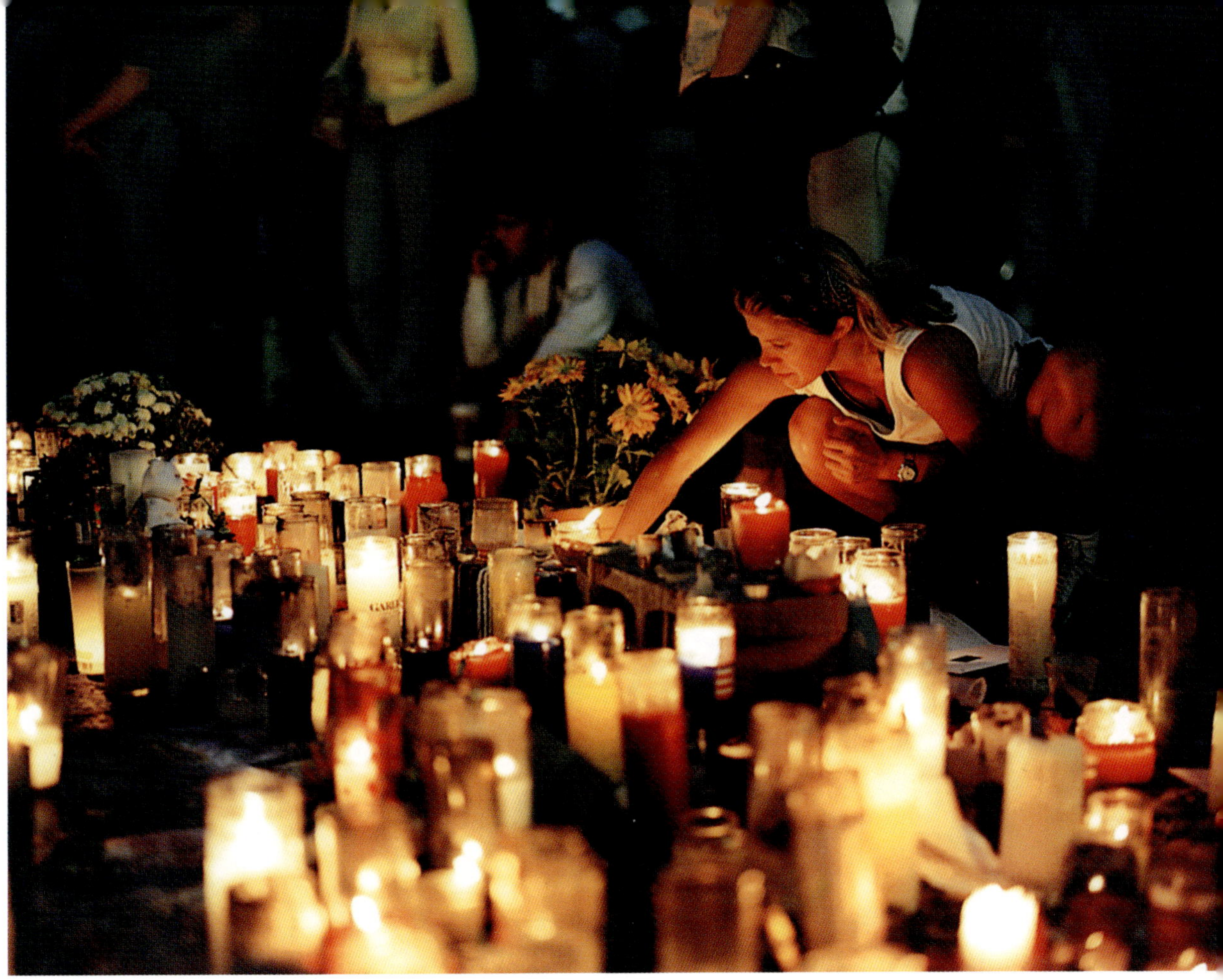

→
New Yorkers come together to mourn,
showing their sympathy and strength.
*Photographed by Ronnie Andren,
November 2001.*

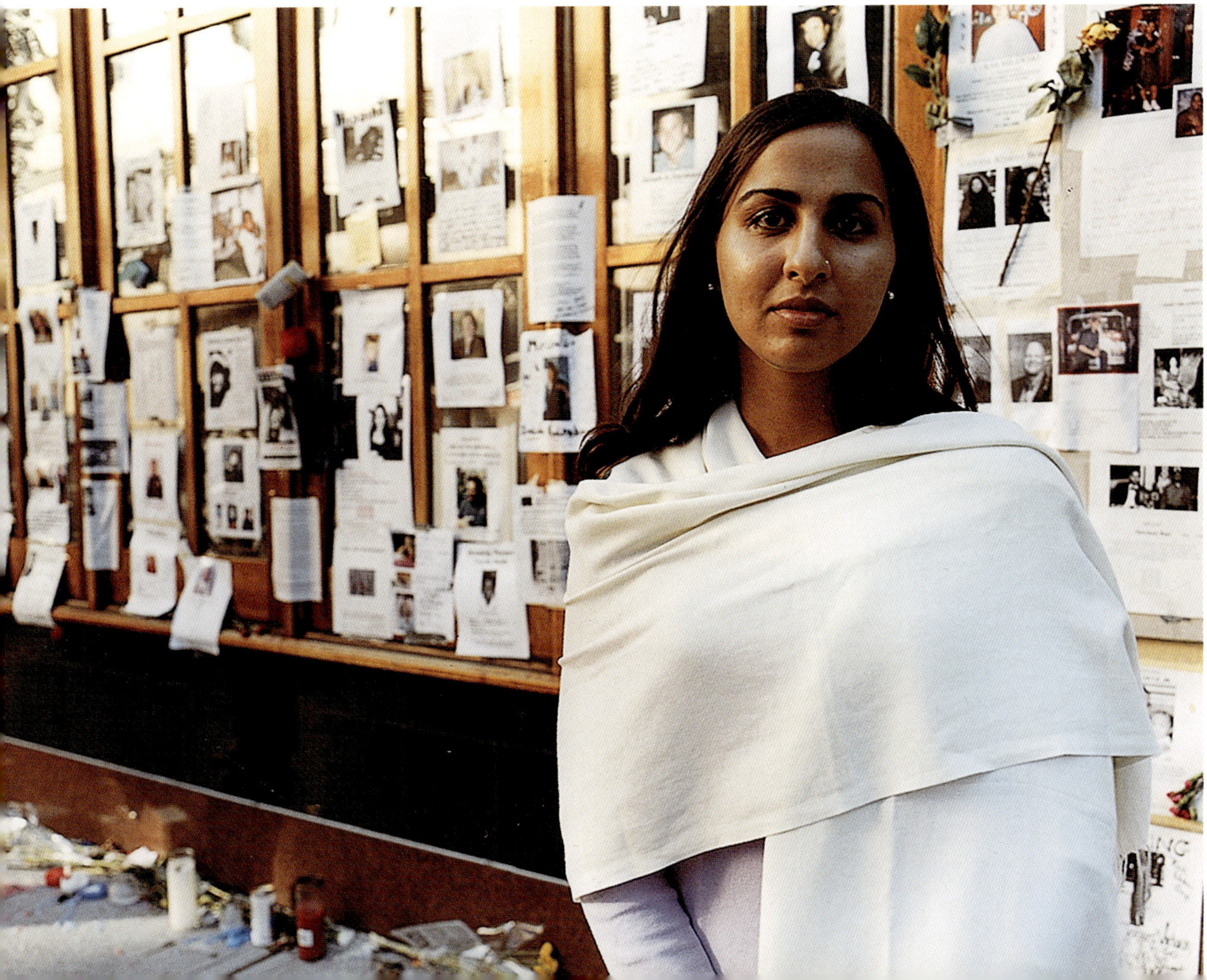

←
Nyla Ibrahim, who
lived in Manhattan,
told *Glamour*, "The
day after the attack,
my husband and I
went to Ground
Zero to volunteer.
I wanted people
to know I was a
Pakistani American—
and a Muslim. I
told them, 'I don't
know if Muslims are
responsible for this,
but I want to tell you
that you've just met
a Muslim, and I'm
standing here
with you.'"

Cindi Leive

In 2001 Cindi Leive was appointed editor in chief of *Glamour*. A relentless champion of women, she won awards for the magazine's work investigating toxic breast implants and partner violence. She expanded *Glamour*'s commitment to body diversity, and ensured that presidents of America paid attention to women voters. Few can say it better than Leive herself, in her 2017 farewell editor's letter, extracted here.

"To me, the real change…is in our attitude as women: our willingness to say how we feel, live how we like, and ask the world to keep up. *Glamour* has always prided itself on taking on a wide range of subjects. Our team has covered the opioid epidemic, racial injustice, the attempts to defeat Planned Parenthood, and yes, the wage gap; while we are sometimes admonished to 'stay in our lane,' our lane is women, so that means both lipstick and legislation are on the table. But some of the work I'm proudest of has started with you, our readers—who have urged us more and more each year to represent women fully and without judgment.

I think if we're going to get anywhere as women, it's on all of us to support one another in real, not-just-a-hashtag ways…. Give compliments publicly. *Take* compliments publicly. Get behind women who speak out about their experiences…. Once you are a boss, wield your honcho powers on behalf of other women, and take a tough look at your own biases. We all have to be leaders. Back in my early days at *Glamour*, on an indelibly sunny September day just weeks into the job, I found myself packed into a conference room with my colleagues, silent with disbelief as we watched the Twin Towers fall on TV. One staffer sat at my feet, and as he began to shake with sobs, I remember rubbing his back feebly, wondering what to do and when someone would show up to help us do it. In that moment I realized, of course, that I was supposed to be that someone, meant to calm and soothe and determine next steps. But what did I know?

I don't know if I did my best that day, though our coverage of the female heroes of 9/11 gave our staff purpose during the dark weeks that followed. But I do know that was the day I began to truly feel like someone responsible for others. We all are, of course. My hopes for the world 16 years from now are simple. That we will have leaders who respect, value, and frequently are women. And that you—all of you—will be able to walk through any front door you want, knowing that inside there's a massive party of other women ready to hand you the champagne and celebrate."

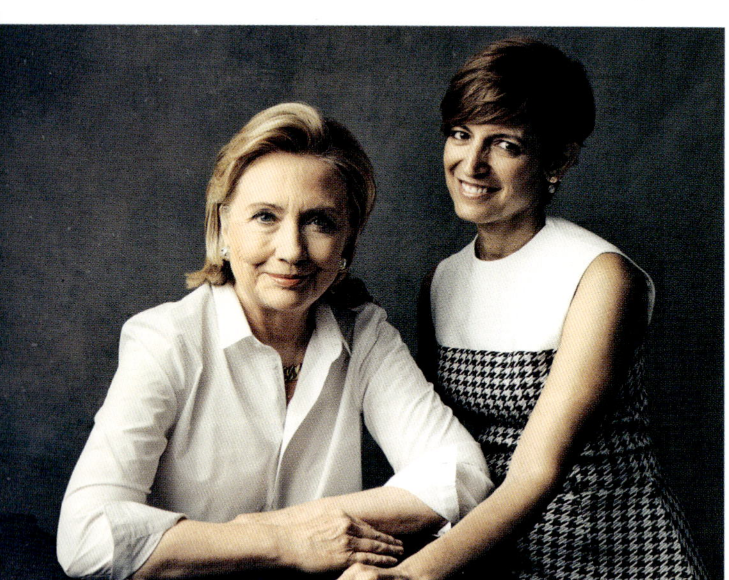

←

Cindi Leive with former secretary of state Hillary Clinton at her *Glamour* cover shoot. *Photographed by Norman Jean Roy, September 2014.*

→

Cindi Leive pictured in her office at Condé Nast. *Photographed by Mark Leibowitz, 2011.*

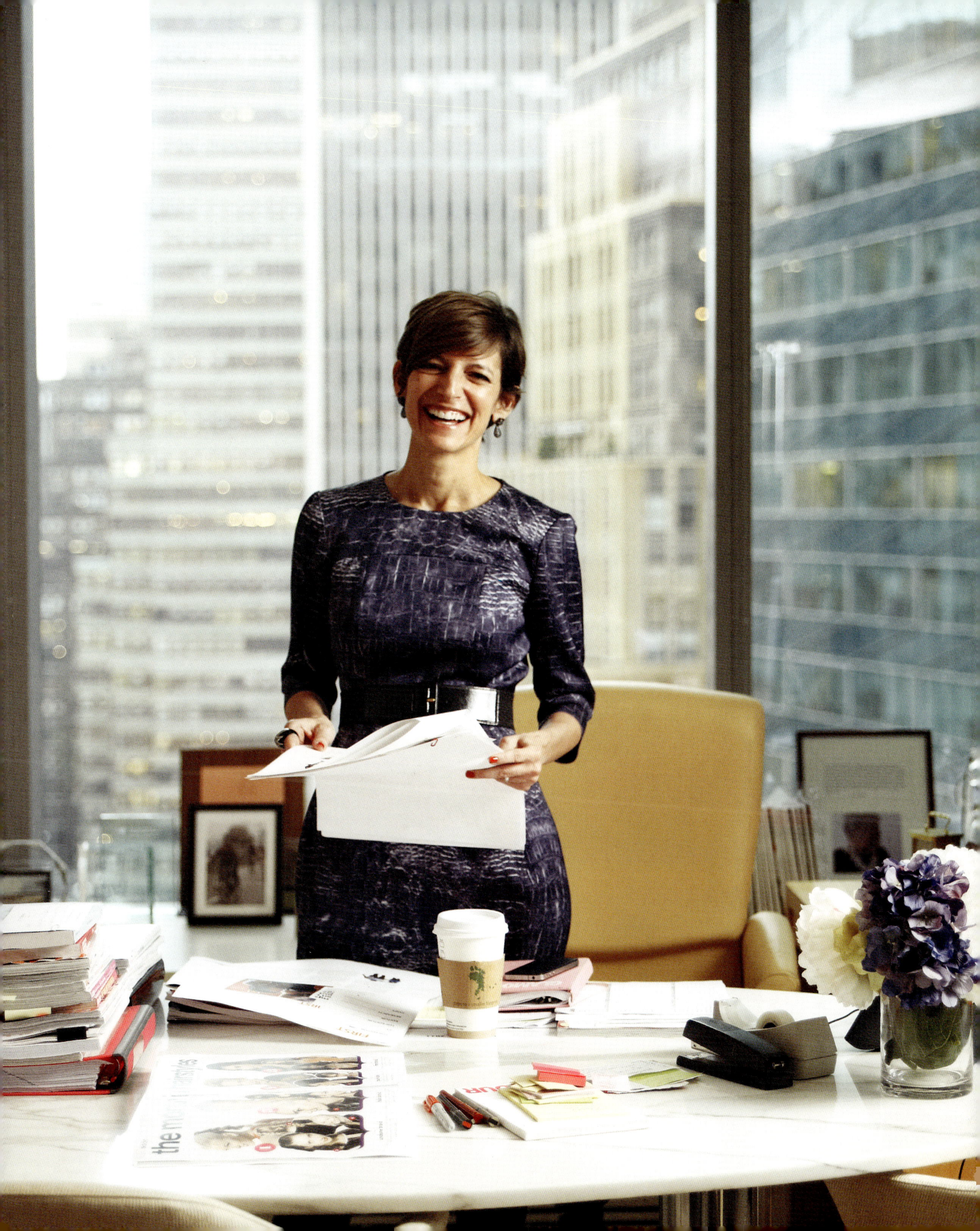

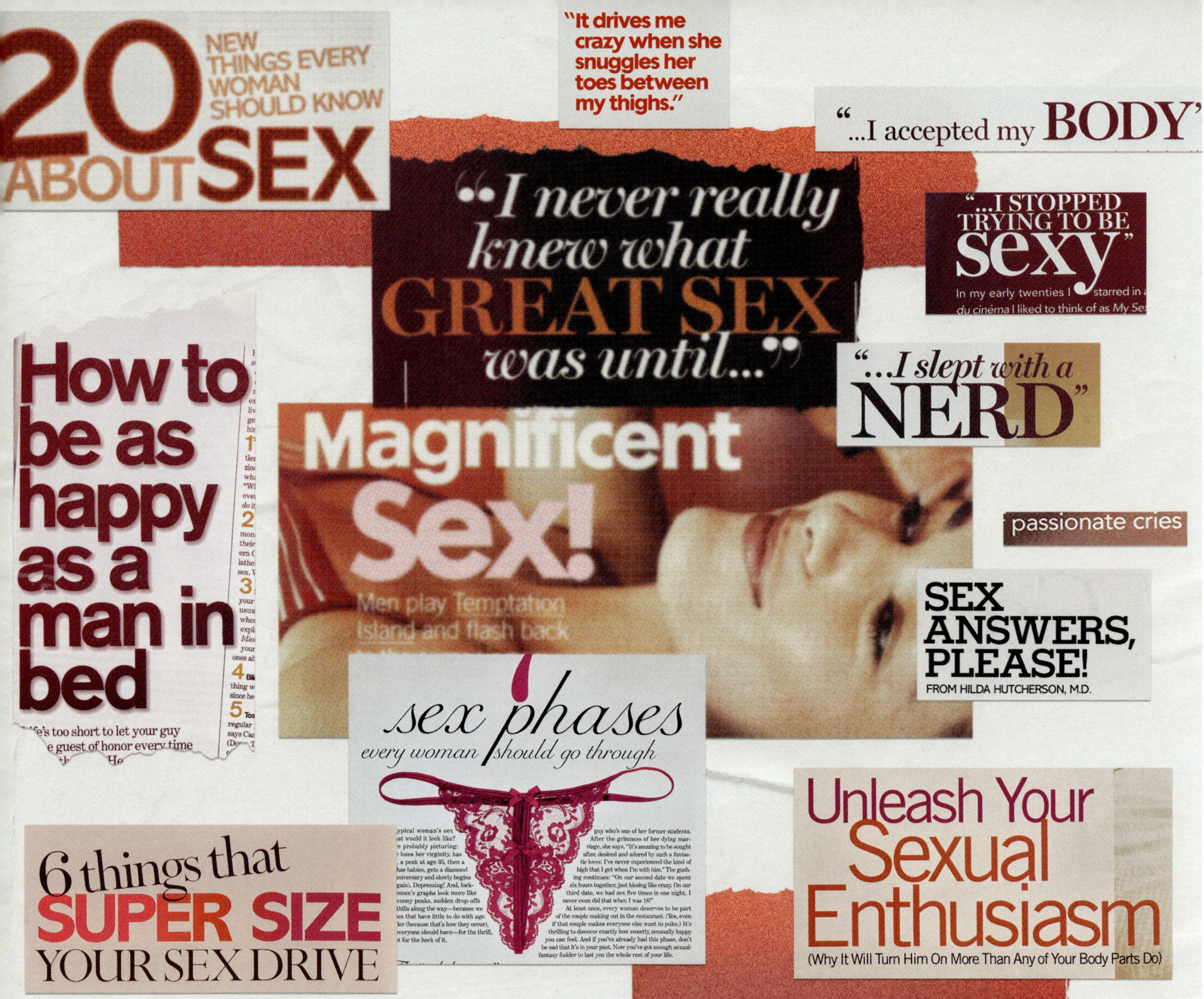

"**EIGHT REASONS TO HAVE SEX…** tonight, tomorrow afternoon, and all weekend!" "Honey, Have We Got Sex Advice for You!" "Hey, Guys, We Wrote You a Sex Manual!"—these are just a sample of the many hundreds of articles *Glamour* published about sex during this era, and these three are even from the same issue. All of which is to say, in the 2000s, *Glamour* didn't just embrace good sex—it sold it, hard.

Sex wasn't new to the pages of the magazine—this was a publication that had seen its readers through the advent of the pill, abortion rights, the free love era of the '70s, and the AIDS epidemic of the '80s and '90s. But the approach that centered and empowered women was new. And it got no small amount of help from *Sex and the City*, a show that followed the lives of four women navigating sex, relationships, careers, and friendship in New York City. The show normalized self-pleasure; opposed "slut-shaming;" and explored voracious sexuality, one-night stands, marriage, infertility, and same-sex relationships. It gave women ownership of sex on a global platform like never before. But women didn't just want to watch it, they wanted to translate its themes of pleasure and power into their own lives. And that's where *Glamour* came in. Whether it was following the stories of real women with "*Sex and the City* Love Lives" or advising women on how to have "Magnificent Sex," this was the era of women's love lives coming out on top.

Oh, another thing: You don't have to go at it forever. In fact, I'd title my sex manual for men *Please Come.*

AMY POEHLER, NOVEMBER 2001

↑
Headlines from *Glamour* **sex articles between 1999 and 2009.**

→
Lovers on the grass. *Photographed by Chris Craymer, May 2009.*

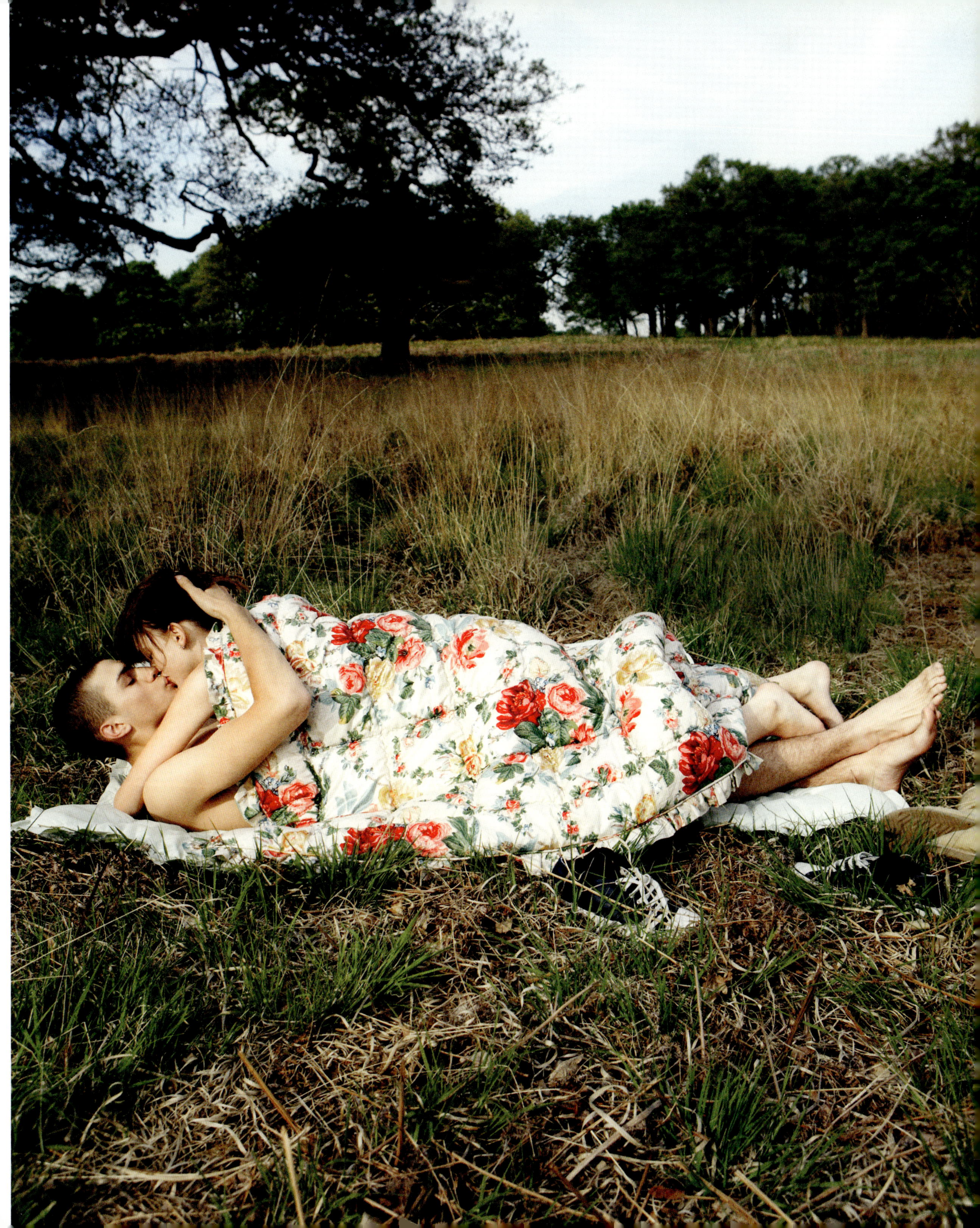

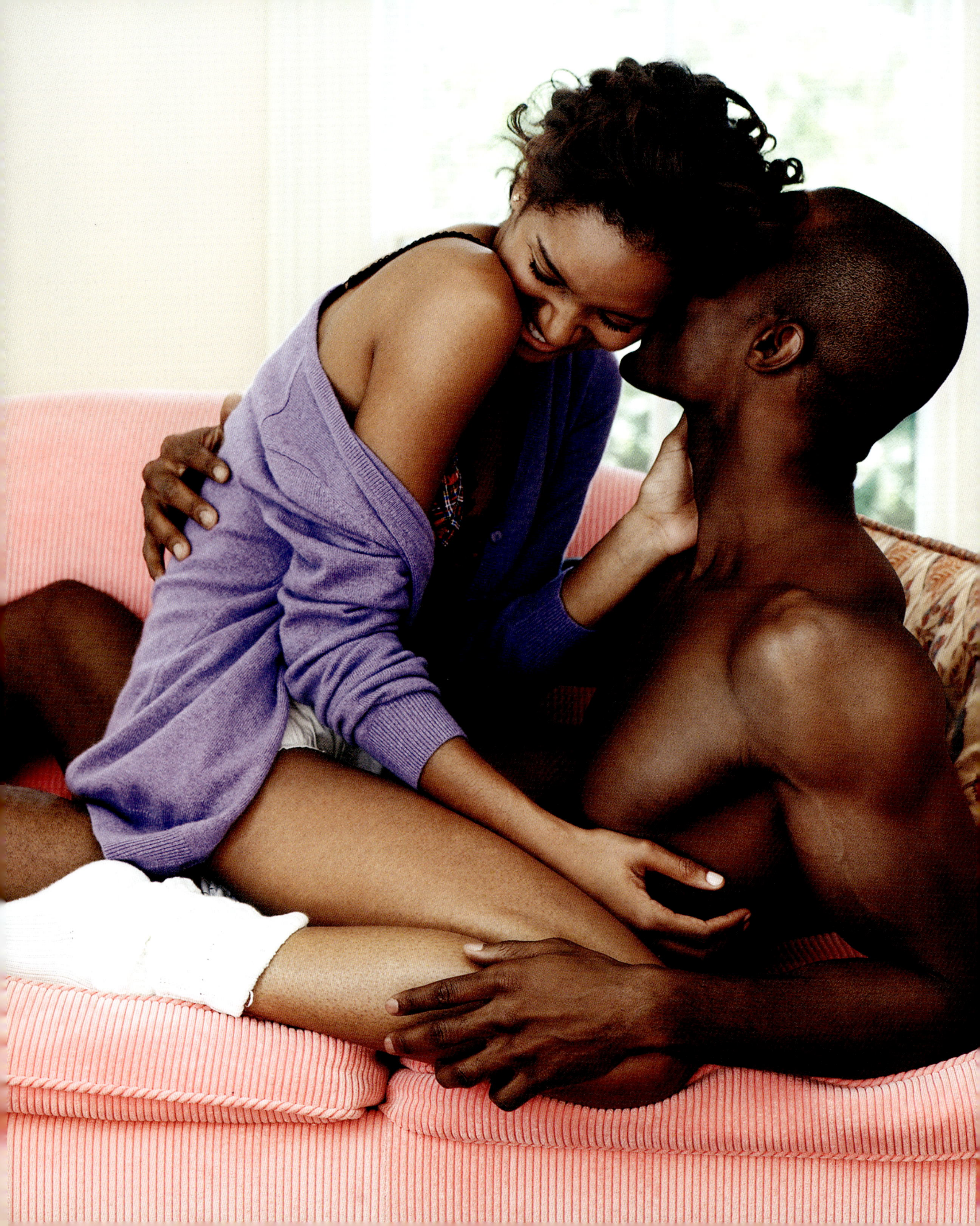

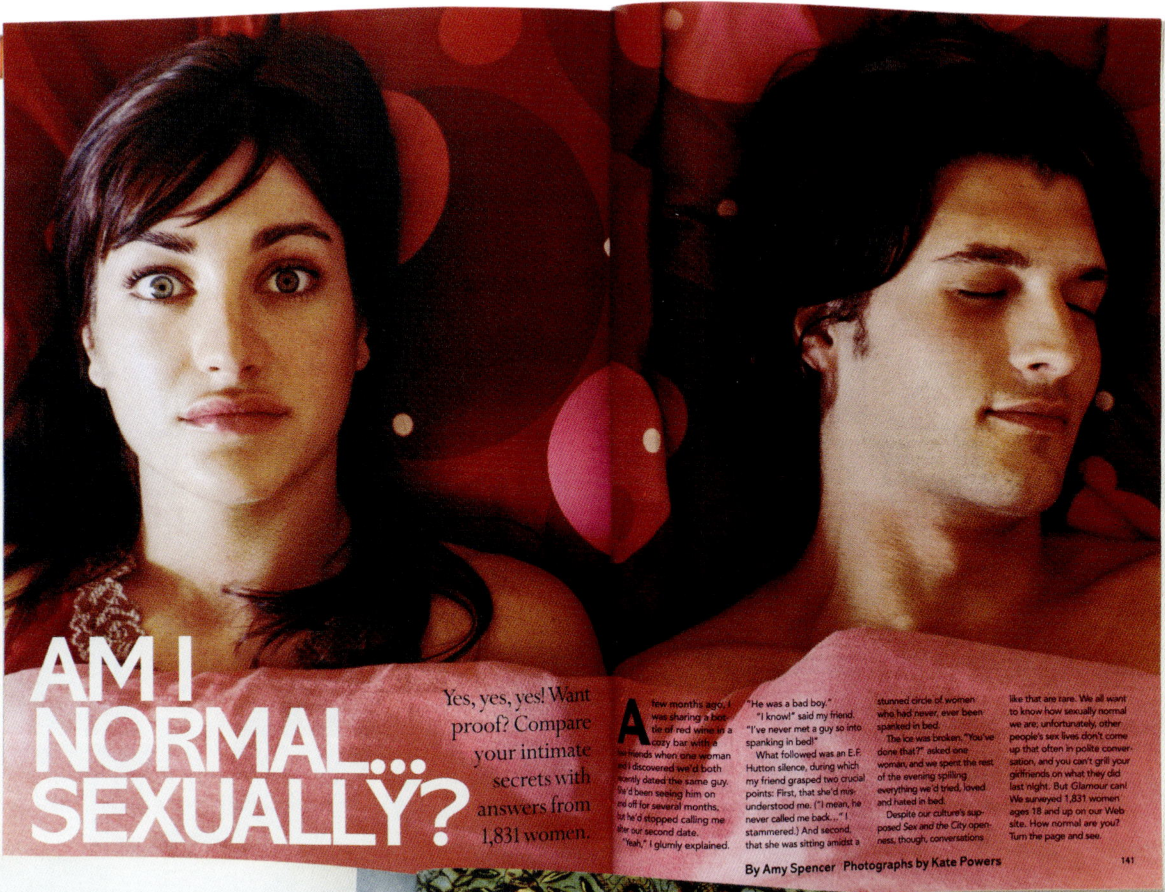

AM I
NORMAL…
SEXUALLŸ?

Yes, yes, yes! Want proof? Compare your intimate secrets with answers from 1,831 women.

A few months ago, I was sharing a bottle of red wine in a cozy bar with a few friends when one woman and I discovered we'd both recently dated the same guy. She'd been seeing him on and off for several months, but he'd stopped calling me after our second date.

"Yeah," I glumly explained. "He was a bad boy."

"I know!" said my friend. "I've never met a guy so into spanking in bed!"

What followed was an E.F. Hutton silence, during which my friend grasped two crucial points: First, that she'd misunderstood me. ("I mean, he never called me back…" I stammered.) And second, that she was sitting amidst a stunned circle of women who had never, ever been spanked in bed.

The ice was broken. "You've done that?" asked one woman, and we spent the rest of the evening spilling everything we'd tried, loved and hated in bed.

Despite our culture's supposed Sex and the City openness, though, conversations like that are rare. We all want to know how sexually normal we are; unfortunately, other people's sex lives don't come up that often in polite conversation, and you can't grill your girlfriends on what they did last night. But Glamour can! We surveyed 1,831 women ages 18 and up on our Web site. How normal are you? Turn the page and see.

By Amy Spencer   Photographs by Kate Powers

141

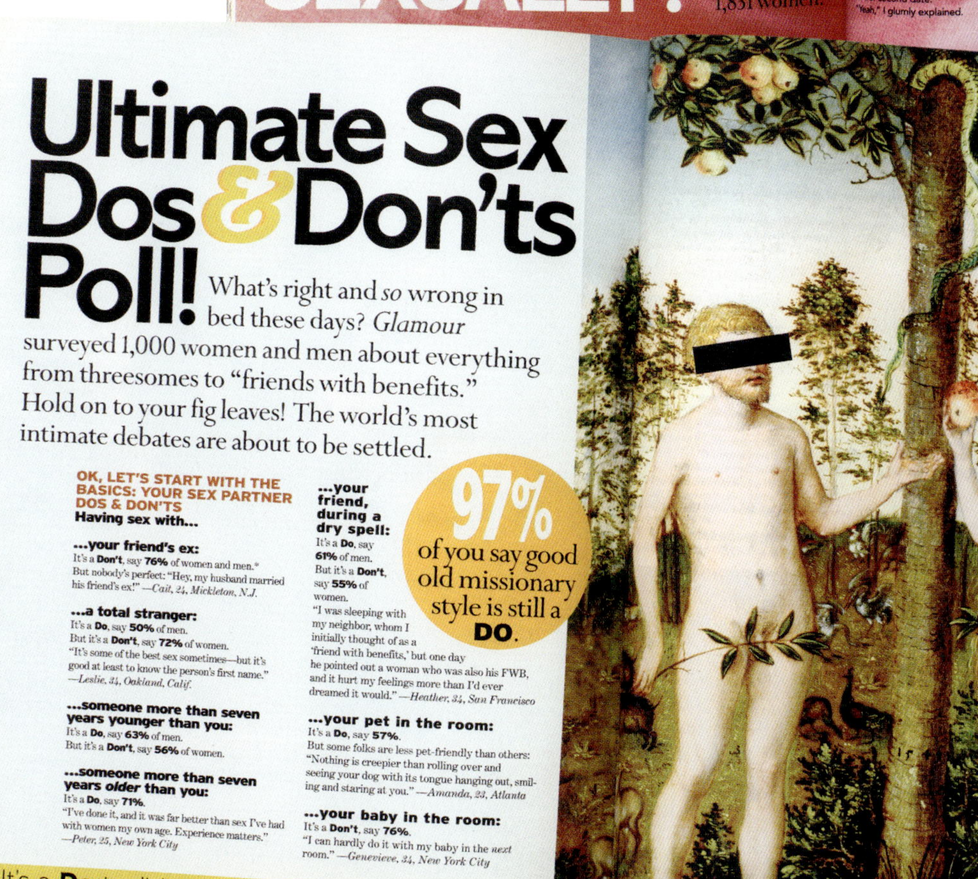

Ultimate Sex Dos & Don'ts Poll!

What's right and so wrong in bed these days? Glamour surveyed 1,000 women and men about everything from threesomes to "friends with benefits." Hold on to your fig leaves! The world's most intimate debates are about to be settled.

OK, LET'S START WITH THE BASICS: YOUR SEX PARTNER DOS & DON'TS
Having sex with…

…your friend's ex:
It's a Don't, say 76% of women and men.* But nobody's perfect: "Hey, my husband married his friend's ex!" —Cait, 24, Mickleton, N.J.

…a total stranger:
It's a Do, say 50% of men. But it's a Don't, say 72% of women. "It's some of the best sex sometimes—but it's good at least to know the person's first name." —Leslie, 34, Oakland, Calif.

…someone more than seven years younger than you:
It's a Do, say 63% of men. But it's a Don't, say 56% of women.

…someone more than seven years older than you:
It's a Do, say 71%. "I've done it, and it was far better than sex I've had with women my own age. Experience matters." —Peter, 25, New York City

…your friend, during a dry spell:
It's a Do, say 61% of men. But it's a Don't, say 55% of women. "I was sleeping with my neighbor, whom I initially thought of as a 'friend with benefits,' but one day he pointed out a woman who was also his FWB, and it hurt my feelings more than I'd ever dreamed it would." —Heather, 34, San Francisco

…your pet in the room:
It's a Do, say 57%. But some folks are less pet-friendly than others: "Nothing is creepier than rolling over and seeing your dog with its tongue hanging out, smiling and staring at you." —Amanda, 23, Atlanta

…your baby in the room:
It's a Don't, say 76%. "I can hardly do it with my baby in the next room." —Genevieve, 34, New York City

97% of you say good old missionary style is still a DO.

It's a Do to dish about sex with your friends, say 70% of women. Men are actually more discreet: 52% say it's a Don't.

*Unless otherwise indicated, women and men responded similarly (they really did). Respondents were both single and married, between the ages of 18 and 40.

Sex on a first date? 58% of men say it's a Do. But 65% of women say it's a Don't.

253

Think outside the Pill!

Could *your* best birth control be something you've never heard of? Here, all the other options doctors should discuss with you but *don't*. By Roxanne Patel. Photographs by Davies+Starr

IT'S THE AD EXECUTIVE'S ALL-TIME FAVORITE LINE: "COME ON IN and try the #1 _________ in America!" That pitch sells SUVs, burgers, romance novels, paper towels—you name it. Turns out it also sells birth control. The Pill is the number-one form of reversible contraception in the United States, used by more than 11.5 million women. Because it's the most popular method, women often assume it's the best for them, and doctors do the same. "Doctors have been prescribing the Pill for 40 years when women come in asking for birth control," says Kirsten Moore, president and CEO of Reproductive Health Technologies Project, a women's health advocacy group. "Every woman knows about it, so doctors don't have a lot of incentive to tell their patients what else is out there. As a result, women may not know if something would be better for them—as might be the case."

Don't get us wrong: The Pill has *many* pluses. Not only is it 92 percent effective in preventing pregnancy with typical use, but it also reduces the risk of endometrial cancers, colon cancer, ovarian cysts and pelvic inflammatory disease; can clear up acne; may lessen menstrual cramps; and, in some cases, eliminates hormone-induced migraines. But like all methods, it also has its minuses: You have to remember to take it every day; some women find it diminishes sex drive; others report feeling bloated or experiencing spotting. And for certain women, the Pill, which contains a combination of the hormones estrogen and progestin to prevent ovulation, is a downright bad idea. Women who are over 35 or who smoke are at greater risk of strokes, heart attacks and blood clots on the Pill; and those who

What are those things? From top, left to right: Depo Provera, mini Pill, Today Sponge, NuvaRing, CycleBeads, Essure, monophasic Pill, Mirena IUD, triphasic Pill, diaphragm, cervical cap, condoms, ParaGard IUD, Seasonale, Ortho Evra Patch, Plan B

360

↗

An article from September 2005 exploring alternative contraception.

→

A January 2002 piece calling for the creation of a male oral contraceptive.

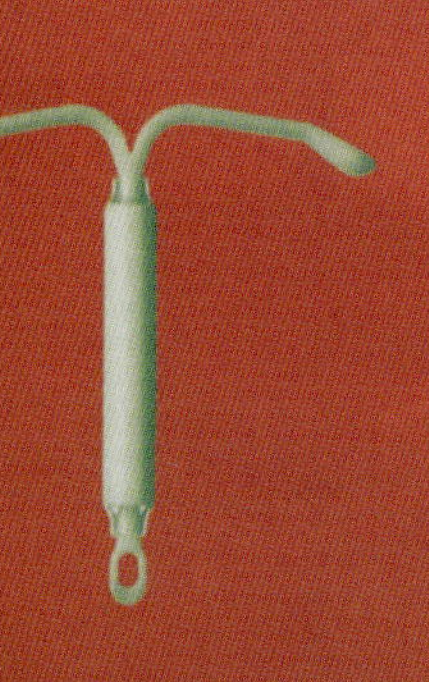

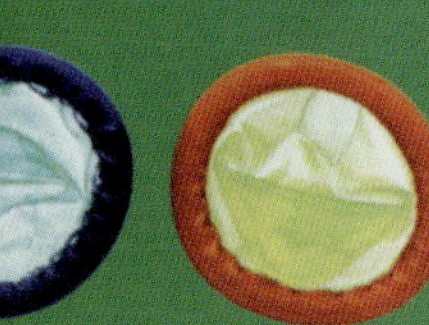

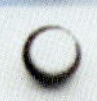

IN JUNE 1960, THE FIRST oral contraceptive was approved by the FDA for sale. By 1965, one in four married American women under 45 had used the pill (single women were not permitted to use it until 1972). By 1984, an estimated 50 million–plus women around the world were taking it, and by 2013, that number had passed 100 million. It was revolutionary, no doubt. But, as many a *Glamour* article explored, it also had drawbacks—women complained of bloating and break-through spotting, there were risks of blood clotting, and it didn't protect against sexually transmitted diseases. The magazine believed their sexually active readers had the right to know the alternatives. This was service journalism for the *Sex and the City* generation. It also posed an important question: In a world where sex was now perceived more equally, why were women solely responsible for contraception?

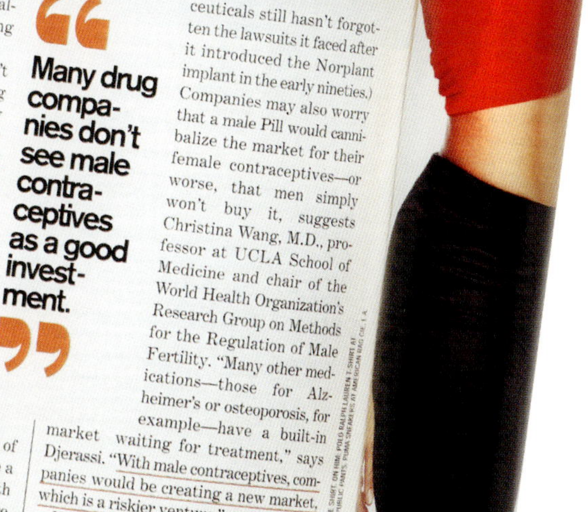

Here's good news for any woman who's ever fumbled with a diaphragm, forgotten to take her Pill or otherwise lamented the shortcomings of birth control: Last year, the Netherlands-based pharmaceutical firm Organon began trials for a contraceptive implant and Pill for men with the hope of bringing one of the products to market, possibly by 2006.

It's a reason for women to stand up and cheer—*and* wonder why it's taken so long. Was this project really so tough? After all, it's been more than 50 years since Carl Djerassi, Ph.D., first produced an oral con-traceptive that later became the Pill, and currently there are more than 40 brands to choose from in the United States. So why do guys still have just one option—the con-dom—other than vasectomy? This is Hor-mones 101, right? Can the science behind male contraceptives be that difficult?

"The science for the male pill is old hat," confirms Djerassi, author of *This Man's Pill* (Oxford University Press). While experts agree it is harder to stop millions of sperm than one monthly egg, a workable blueprint for a male contraceptive has been around since the early nineties. The most likely formula, which served as the framework for Organon's trials, involves using the female hormone progestin to suppress sperm formation, along with testosterone to counterbalance the medicine's dampening effect on the body's own supply.

You might think the drug hasn't found its way from the drawing board to the drugstore due solely to some complicated scientific conundrum. You're wrong. Many pharmaceutical companies simply don't see male contraceptives as a worthwhile investment. "According to my research, none of the world's 10 largest drug firms is actively developing a male contra-ceptive," says Djerassi. "At this point, our focus in the contracep-tive area remains on women," says Kellie McLaughlin, spokeswoman for Ortho-McNeil Pharmaceutical, which makes nine versions of the Pill.

Drug companies argue that the cost of creating any new product is on average a formidable $500 million. And since birth control goes to healthy people, who are generally more annoyed by side effects than the seriously ill, says Djerassi, firms fear litigation. (Wyeth-Ayerst Pharma-ceuticals still hasn't forgot-ten the lawsuits it faced after it introduced the Norplant implant in the early nineties.) Companies may also worry that a male Pill would canni-balize the market for their female contraceptives—or worse, that men simply won't buy it, suggests Christina Wang, M.D., pro-fessor at UCLA School of Medicine and chair of the World Health Organization's Research Group on Methods for the Regulation of Male Fertility. "Many other med-ications—those for Alz-heimer's or osteoporosis, for example—have a built-in market waiting for treatment," says Djerassi. "With male contraceptives, com-panies would be creating a new market, which is a riskier venture."

Wyeth-Ayerst, which markets five ver-sions of the Pill, is currently developing a nonhormonal male contraceptive, but "it's not a super-high (continued on page 159)

 high fashion hit high exposure. With the explosion of celebrity culture and the growth of the internet, audiences were exposed to designer clothing like never before. And while *Glamour*'s more practical shopping guides remained more affordably priced, the ambitious fashion shoots from some of the most notable photographers of the era offered inspiration, if less accessibility.

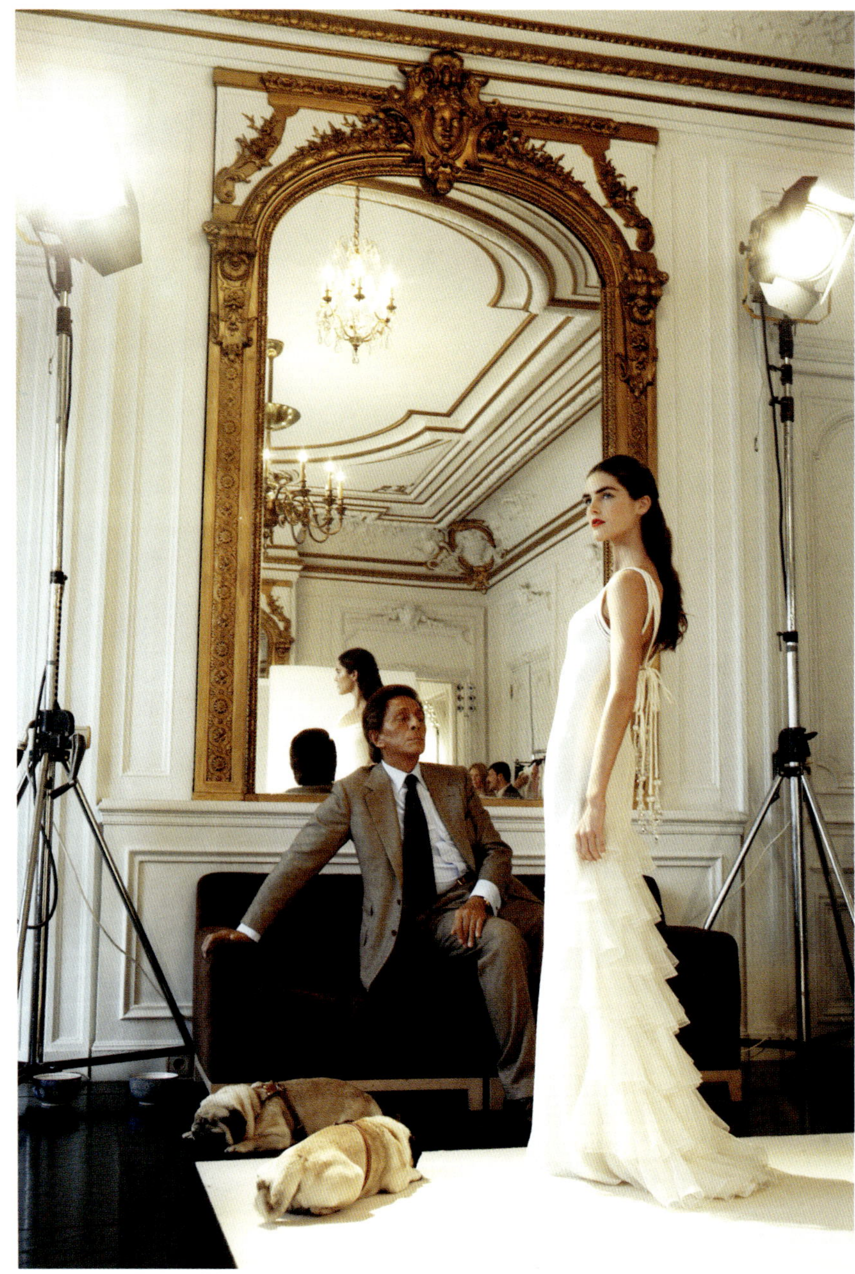

↑

"Underdressing is often more stylish." "Invest in a tailor." These are just two of the pieces of fashion advice the legendary designer Valentino dished up to readers in 2006. Here he is in his Paris studio with model Hilary Rhoda and his pugs Milton and Margot. *Photographed by Patrick Demarchelier, March 2006.*

→

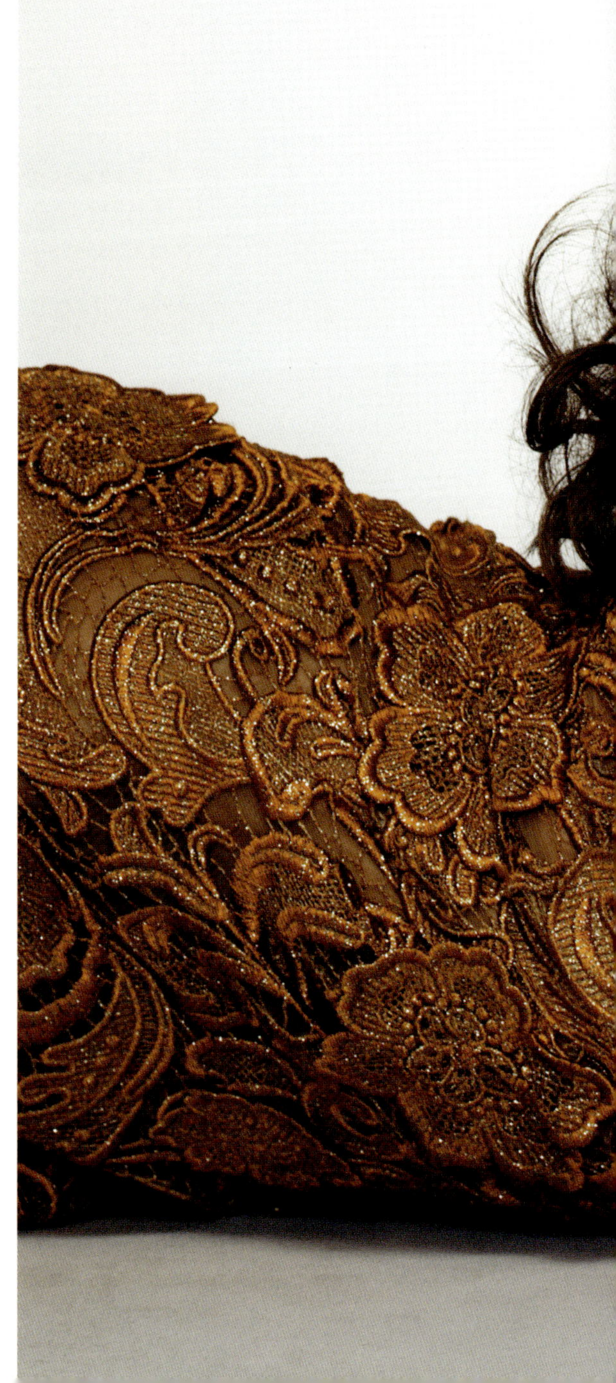

Model Emily DiDonato wearing a lace Prada dress. *Photographed by Matthias Vriens, November 2008.*

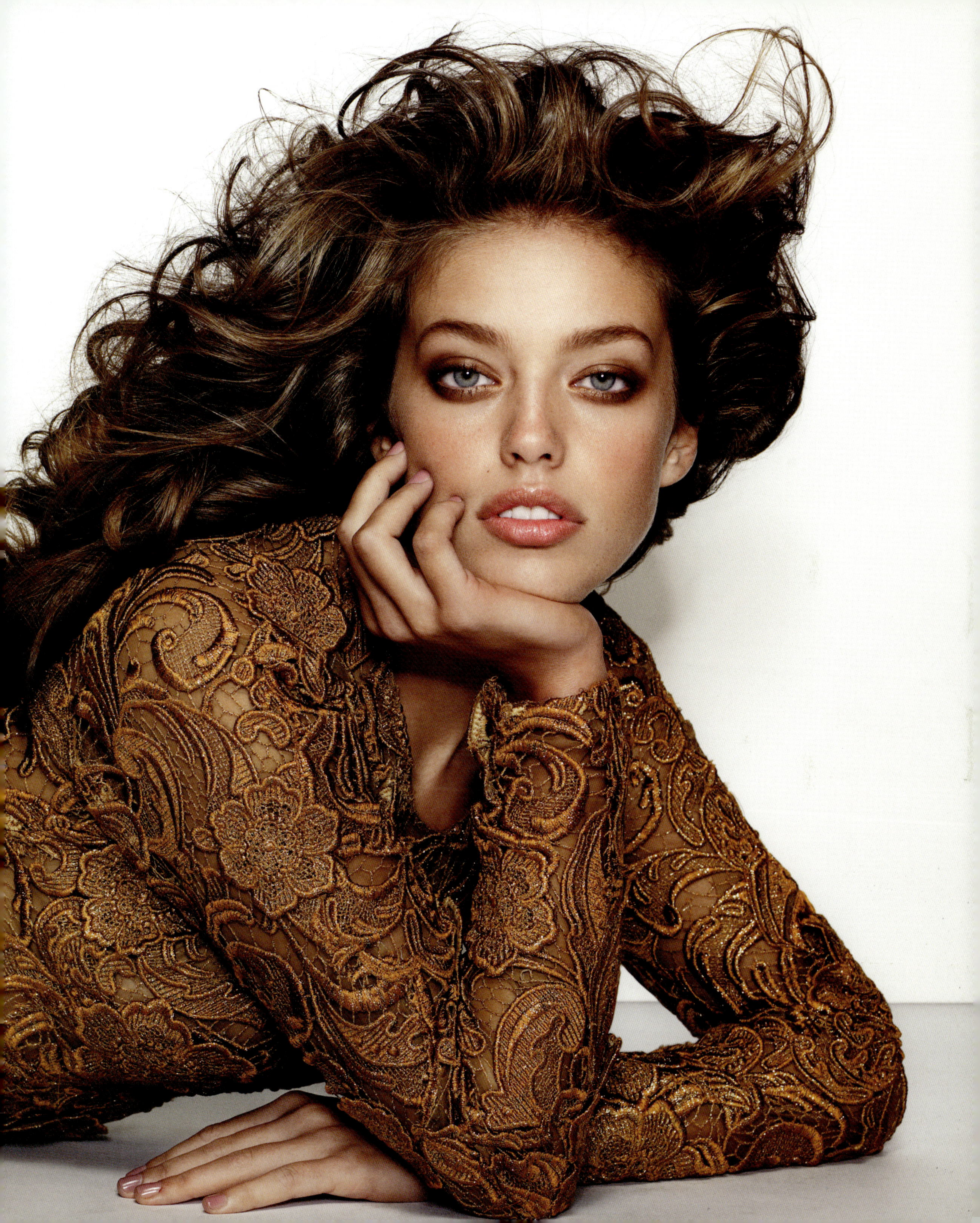

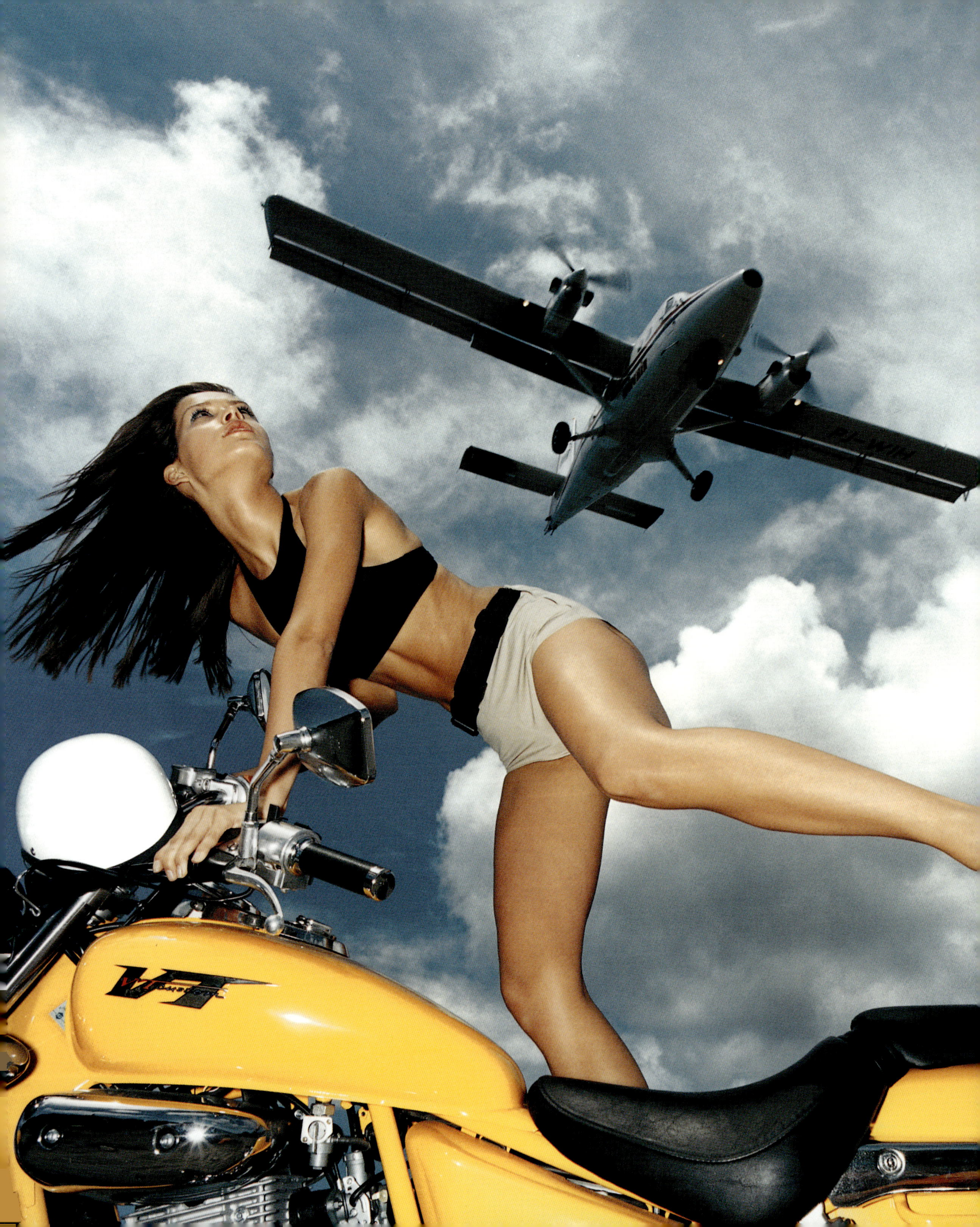

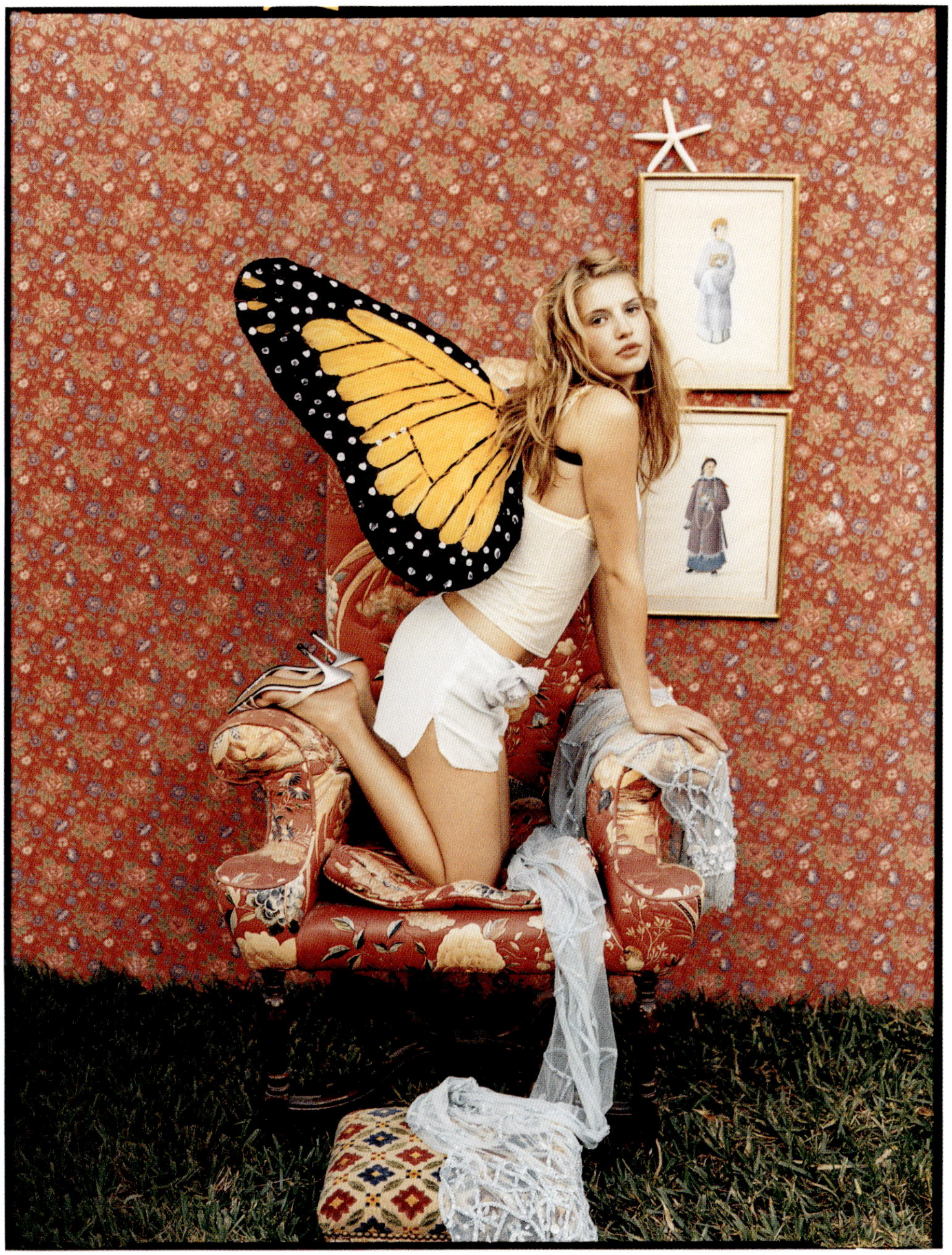

A model wears a black cropped halter top from Norma Kamali with Miu Miu belted shorts and Chanel black sandals. *Photographed by Riccardo Tinelli, July 1999.*

In this "Alice in Underwear" fashion story, a model wears a yellow Swiss dot camisole and bra by Tommy Hilfiger, white shorts by A.F. Vandevorst, Stuart Weitzman sandals, and periwinkle tulle stole by Adrienne Landau. *Photographed by Kim Myers Robertson, February 2002.*

↓

Alexandra and Theodora Richards (daughters of the Rolling Stones' Keith) with their dog Abbey. *Photographed by Pamela Hanson, July 2009.*

→

A classic New York shot. The model wears a jacket and skirt from Donna Karan, a D&G tote, and Prada sandals. *Photographed by Riccardo Tinelli, January 2003.*

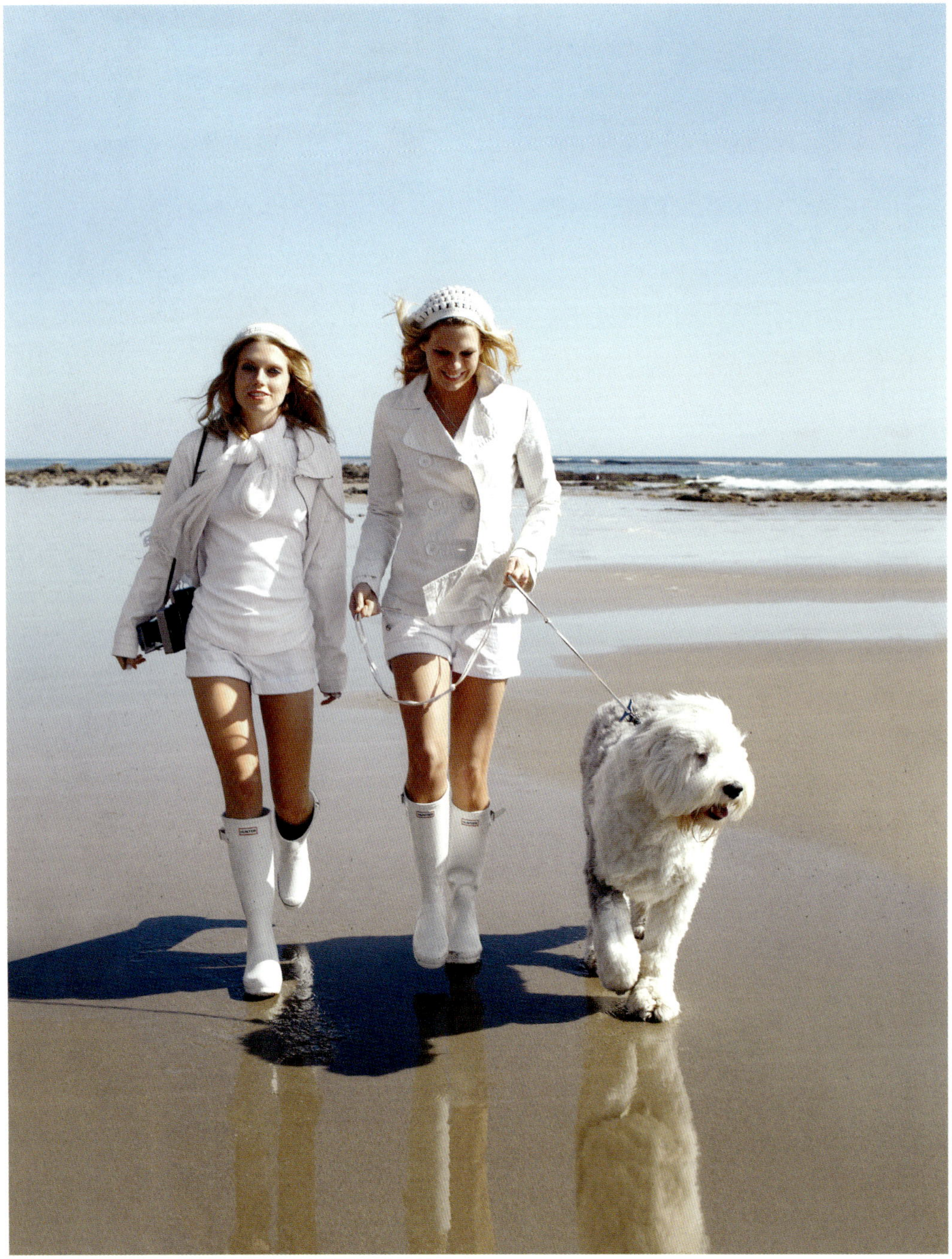

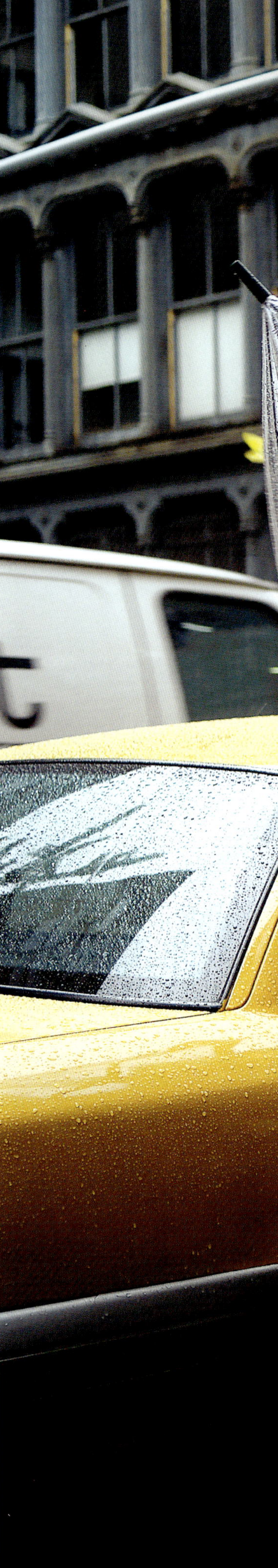

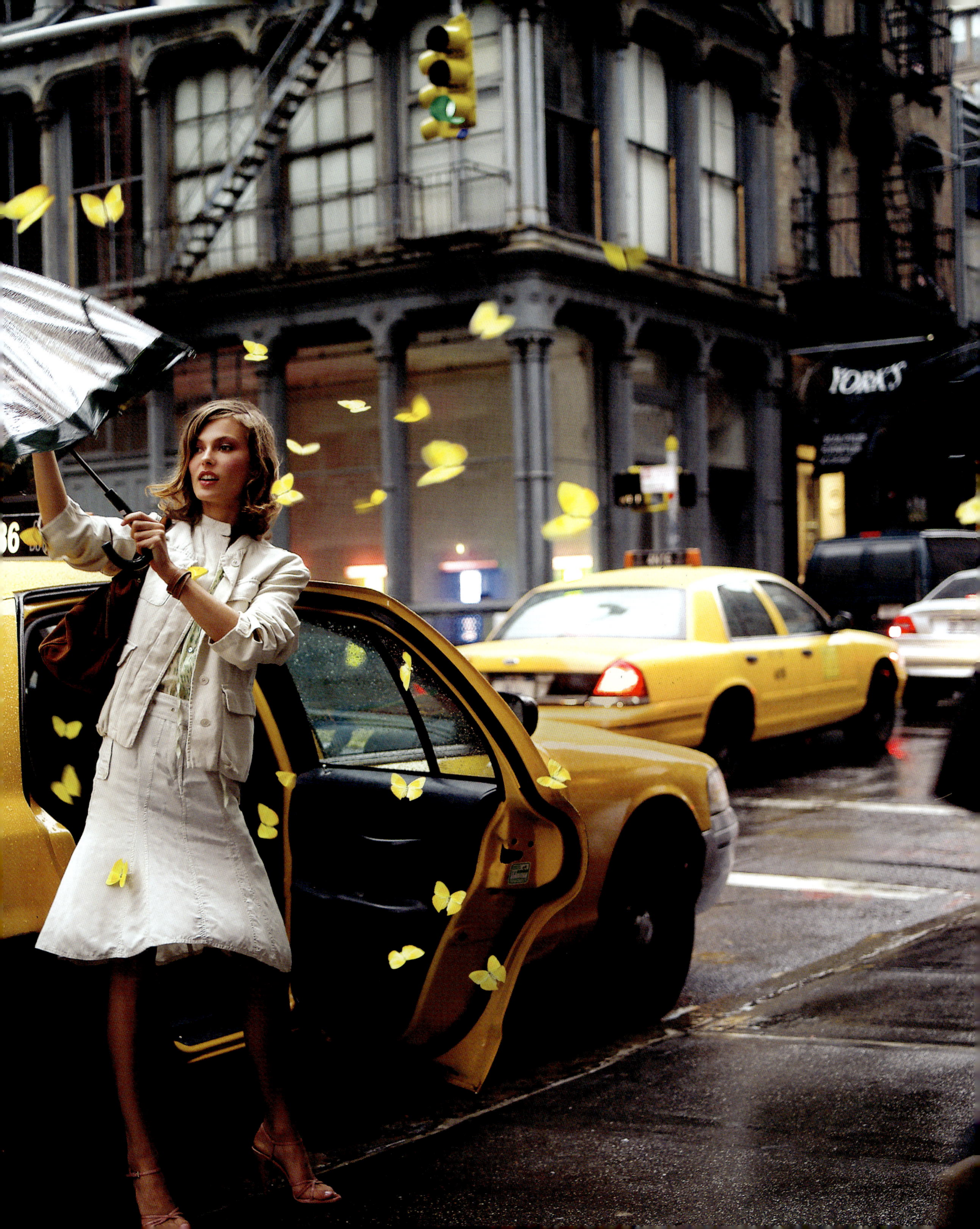

YORK'S

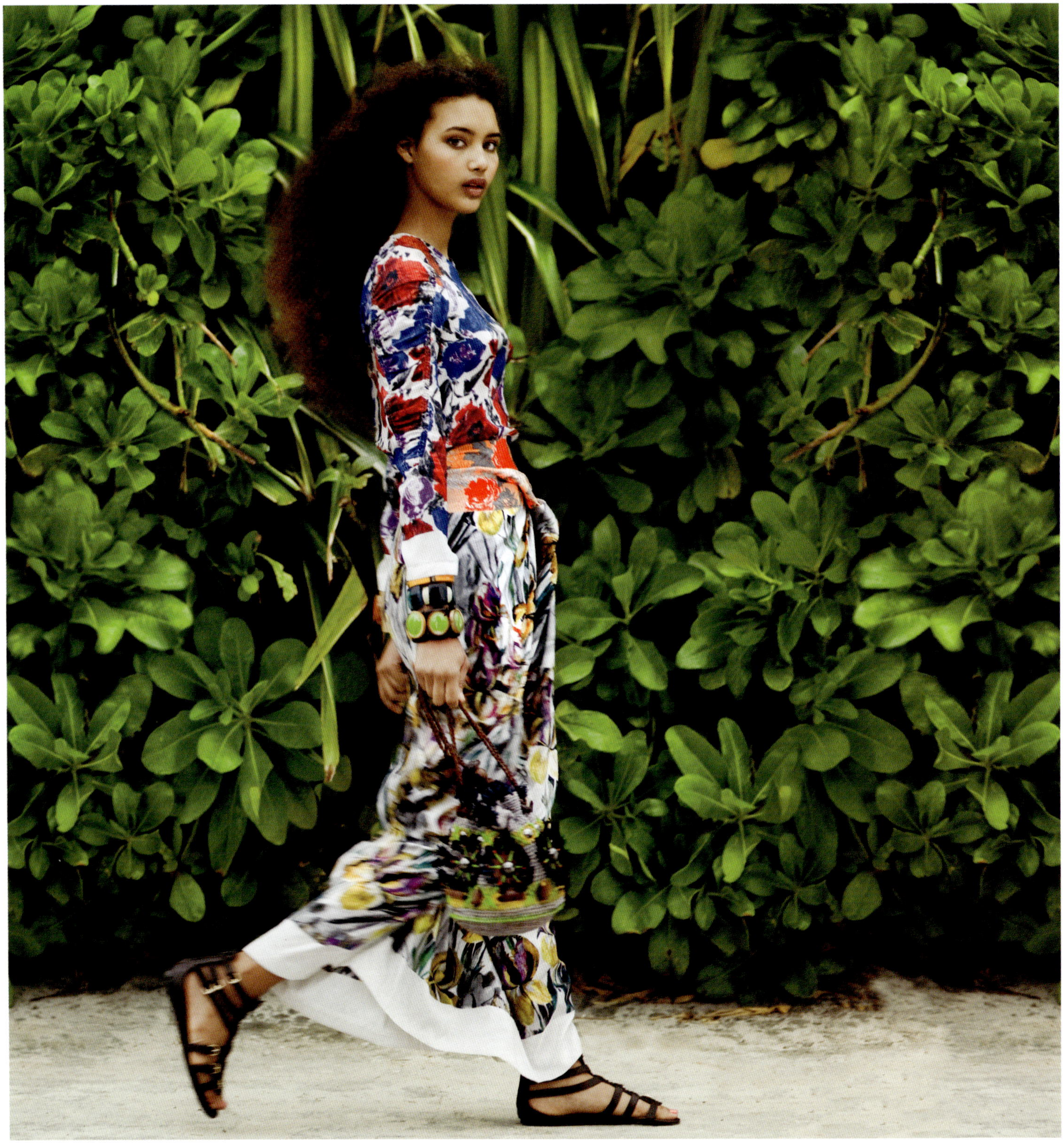

For a fashion story, "The Happiest Clothes on the Planet," a model wears a skirt and top by Dries Van Noten with flat Bakers sandals, and Marni bangles with a Jamin Puech bag. *Photographed by Walter Chin, April 2008.*

→

Supermodel Alek Wek wearing a Roberto Cavalli gown with blue Anthony Nak earrings and pink Badgley Mischka sandals. *Photographed by Robert Erdmann, March 2004.*

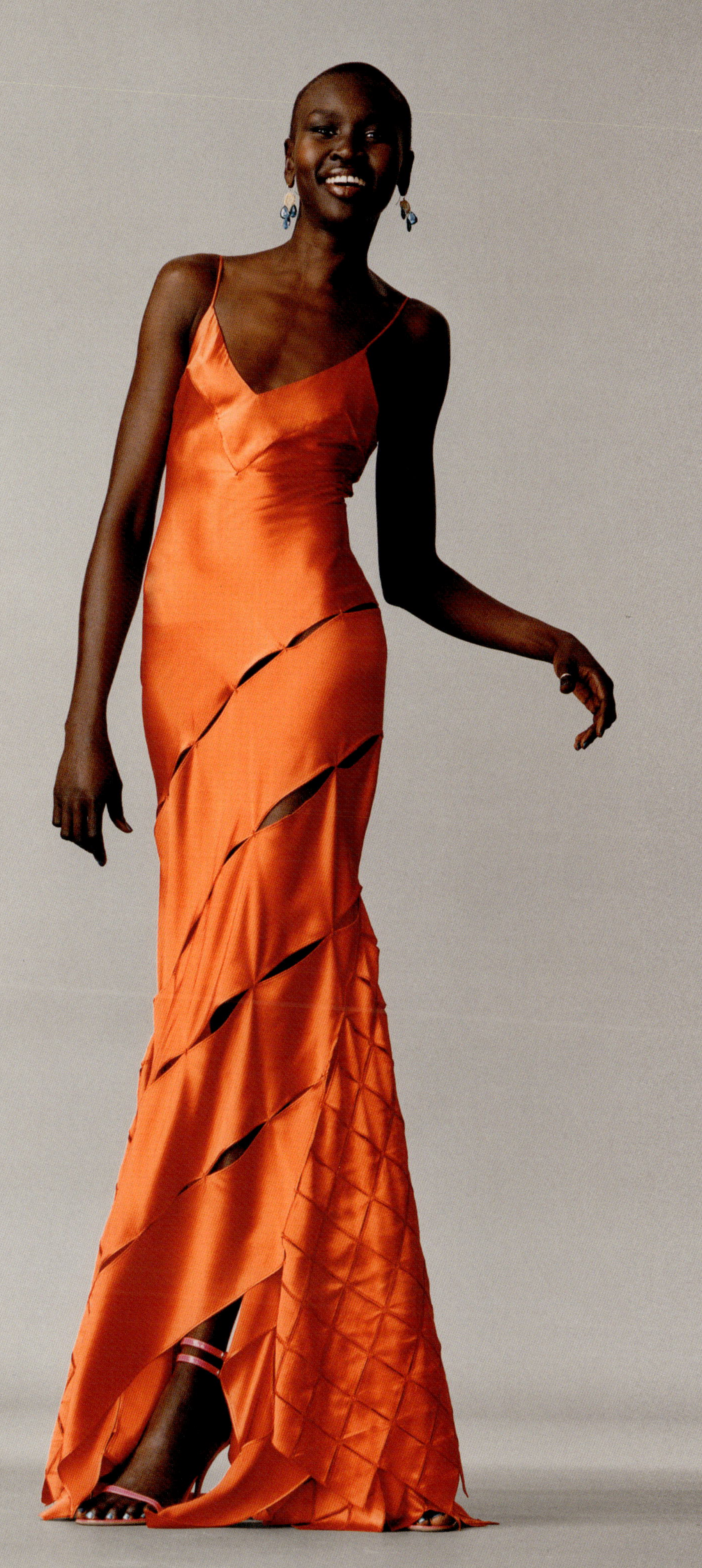

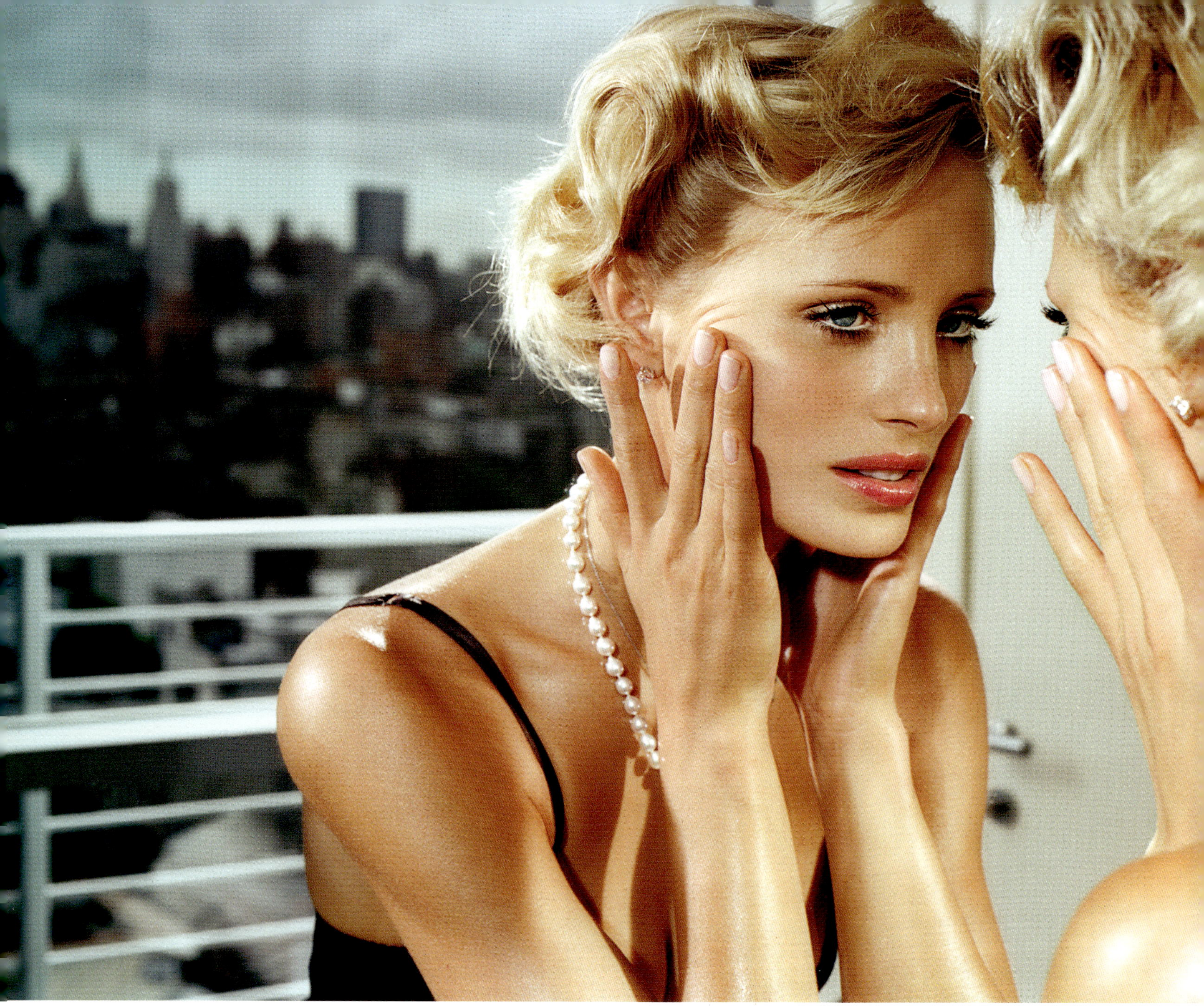

IN 1999, SURGICAL AND NONSURGICAL COSMETIC procedures were on the rise—increasing 66 percent year over year from 1998. By 2009, according to the American Society of Plastic Surgeons, there were 12.5 million cosmetic procedures being performed each year in the country—a rise of 69 percent since the turn of the millennium. All of this should make it no surprise that in almost every single *Glamour* issue from January 2000 on you will find mentions of plastic surgery. Women were getting rhinoplasties, breast augmentations, chemical peels, Botox, tummy tucks, and eyelid surgeries—and *Glamour* set out to report on it. Comedian Kathy Griffin shared her liposuction warning story in the January 2000 issue after a procedure went wrong. Writer Liz Welch investigated the pitfalls of age-defying surgery in the April 2001 issue. Women shared real-life stories of nose jobs they regretted. The magazine largely took a skeptical approach—an article from makeup artist Bobbi Brown in 2006 lamented the rising trend: "Plastic surgery erases the very features that make a woman unique. A strong brow, a bump on the nose, bedroom eyes—these are the things that inspire me," she told *Glamour.* But with the growing trend of women actually going under the knife or the needle, the magazine took its mission to provide service to its readers seriously—offering advice, and not judgment, for readers who wanted to try it. Plastic surgery had changed society, and, whatever your ultimate view, it was here to stay.

↑

A model gazing in the mirror for an article titled "Your looks: Are you obsessed?" *Photographed by Kenneth Willardt, May 2007.*

↗

An article from the September 2004 issue.

→

A January 2004 article by journalist Susan Dominus on the control women were taking over their bodies.

GLAMOUR HIT *THE SWAN* TRYOUTS TO TELL THESE WOMEN:

You don't need plastic surgery. You just need a makeover!

Makeovers by Suze Yalof Schwartz

Why are women lining up to have their unique, beautiful features sliced and diced into Stepford masks on TV shows and in real life? *Glamour* found these six in line at an L.A. casting call for the second season of *The Swan* and offered them an alternative: a no-knife, no-pain, quickie makeover. After all, who ever said extreme surgery is the only way to make the most of your looks? Hello, haircut? Mascara? Jogging? *Confidence?* We don't know if our Swanabees will resort to plastic surgery in the end, but these gorgeous photos send a strong message: Sometimes, the blow-dryer and the makeup brush are mightier than the scalpel.

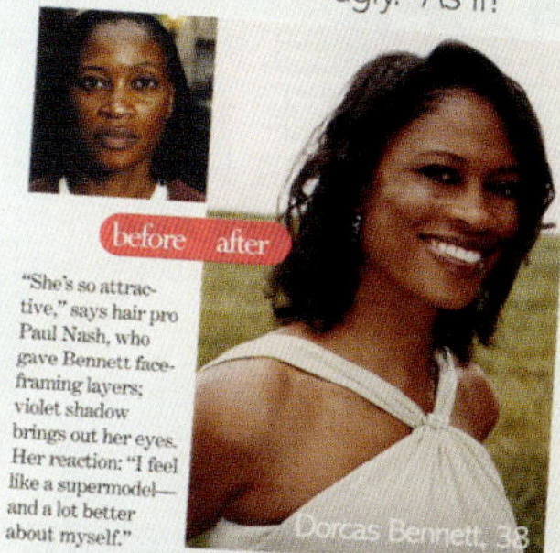

Last season's winner of *The Swan,* the show that gives women head-to-toe surgery

Was she born this way—or just assembled in Taiwan?

Thinks she looks "ugly." As if!

before after

"She's so attractive," says hair pro Paul Nash, who gave Bennett face-framing layers; violet shadow brings out her eyes. Her reaction: "I feel like a supermodel—and a lot better about myself."

Dorcas Bennett, 38

Forget surgery—try a *smile.*

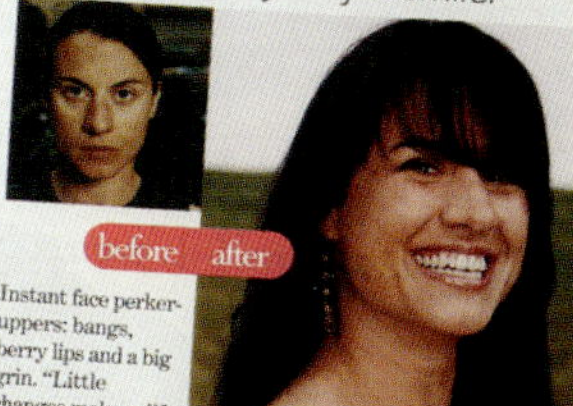

Instant face perker-uppers: bangs, berry lips and a big grin. "Little changes make a difference," agrees Morley. "But I want to be on *The Swan.*" We hope they leave her nose and...

Cheek lipo? Her? Why? *Why?*

before after

Wilcoxon wants slimmer cheeks, but "a little padding is *pretty,*" says Sergio Corvacho, makeup pro. Colorist Hilda Contreras reddened Wilcoxon's hair. "My friends say I look great," she says. "I still want surgery."

Summer Wilcoxon, 23

No, she doesn't need a nose job!

before after

"A bump makes you gorgeously unique," says Nash. Lilac eyeshadow and an edgy bob give Mills even more standout style. "I look like me, not a stranger," she says. "Truthfully, that scared me about *The Swan.*"

Cherie Mills, 32

Wants better skin and bigger boobs.

before after

Our pros say: Cover up acne scars if they bother you (they swiped on a gel bronzer), but don't undersell your natural beauty. Ker listened. "It's...

Nothing's "saggy" about her face.

before after

"Look at her—what does she need?" says Corvacho. A spiky cut and liner play up her features. Says Ballard, "I love the cut. But...

Why **pretty** isn't pretty enough anymore

In our new nip-and-tuck world, young women are remaking everything from their lips to their inner thighs with cosmetic surgery. Even perfectly gorgeous Audrey and Marilyn wouldn't have held up to today's sky-high standards! Glamour investigates the plastic surgery problem—and what it means for you. By Susan Dominus

Once a month, Lee, a 29-year-old banker in Atlanta, gets together with eight of her oldest friends to catch up over a few bottles of red wine. They talk about things women have been bonding over forever, like men, work, sample sales. But lately, a new topic has been headlining the gatherings: their breasts. Specifically, the work they've had done on them. Two of Lee's friends have had cosmetic surgery on theirs, and as for Lee, she just had an augmentation—which her friends were eager to see in close detail. Three glasses of wine into their most recent get-together, off came Lee's top, to cheers all around. "A few of them were like, 'Can we touch 'em?'" says Lee. "I said, 'Sure, what do I care?' I love them."

Lee and her friends aren't wealthy, older ladies who lunch, nor are any of them strippers or even aspiring sitcom stars. They're career women in their twenties and thirties, and they're hardly unique. "I see plenty of young, middle-class women who might decide to have a procedure instead of a vacation," says New York City plastic surgeon Philip Godfrey, M.D., echoing doctors around the country. The number of women getting their physiques cut-and-pasted has surged 128 percent in the past six years, with countless more craving the procedures: A whopping 83 percent of the 7,701 readers who responded to an online *Glamour* poll said they'd like to have work done, with breast enhancement and liposuction topping their lists.

You don't need to have had LASIK surgery to see that plastic surgery has gone mainstream. Safer than ever, it's also cheaper: Breast implants that might have cost $10,000 in 1994 can now be found for half the price. If even that's too much, you could always put yours on layaway (available through some surgeons' offices) or turn directly to lending agencies that target the surgery market—some of which promise revolving credit so you can go ahead with the next procedure while you're still recovering, financially and otherwise, from the first. With costs dropping, so are patients' ages; doctors report that half the women who are getting implants are under 34, as are a third of those getting liposuction.

Some part of me used to feel a little sorry for women who got implants instead of shrugging off their anxieties or pulling on a padded bra like the rest of us—*sheesh,* didn't they have any self-esteem? But lately, when I spot the happy owner of another impressively protruding pair at the gym, I've started to wonder if she might know something I don't about giving your ego a lift. Maybe there's something to all those ads for plastic surgery, the ones that pitch their product as a vehicle of self-expression, even self-love: "Be your best," encourages one Web ad. "After all, you're worth it," assures another (never mind that they haven't met you). It's enough to make those of us still wearing padded bras think. *Sheesh,* where's *my* self-esteem?

Women are buying in and coming out, eager to display the way they've taken control of their bodies. Instead of entering doctors' offices through private doorways, patients talk about their fabulous surgeons over brunch—recommending them as they do hairstylists—or throw themselves parties just to celebrate their recently endowed busts (giving new meaning to the words "hostess with the mostest").

The stigma that used to overshadow plastic surgery is, evidently, history. TV stars, whether anchors or actors, once went to great

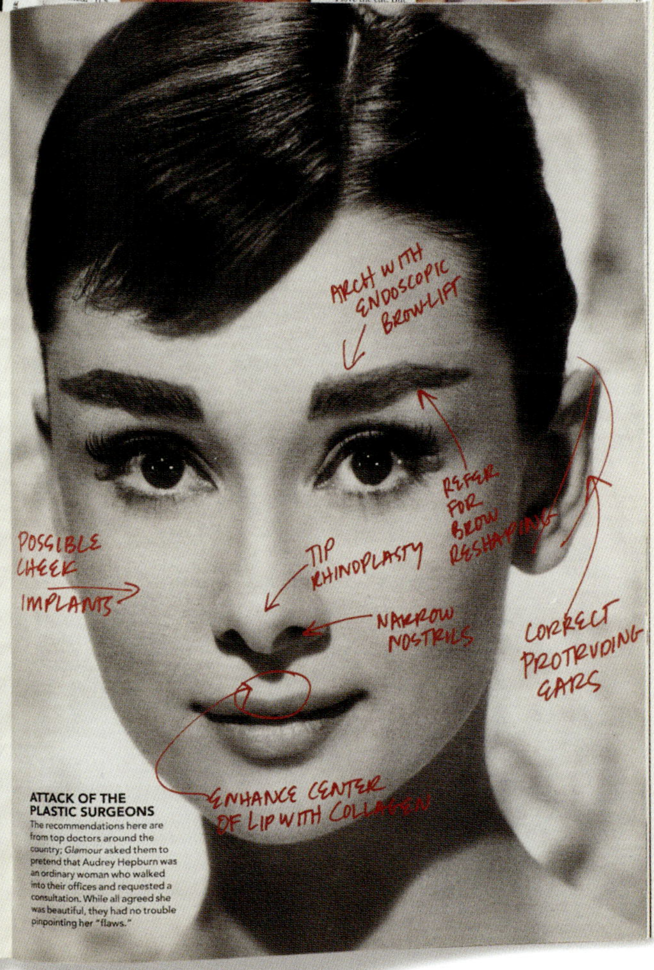

ATTACK OF THE PLASTIC SURGEONS
The recommendations here are from top doctors around the country; Glamour asked them to pretend that Audrey Hepburn was an ordinary woman who walked into their offices and requested a consultation. While all agreed she was beautiful, they had no trouble pinpointing her "flaws."

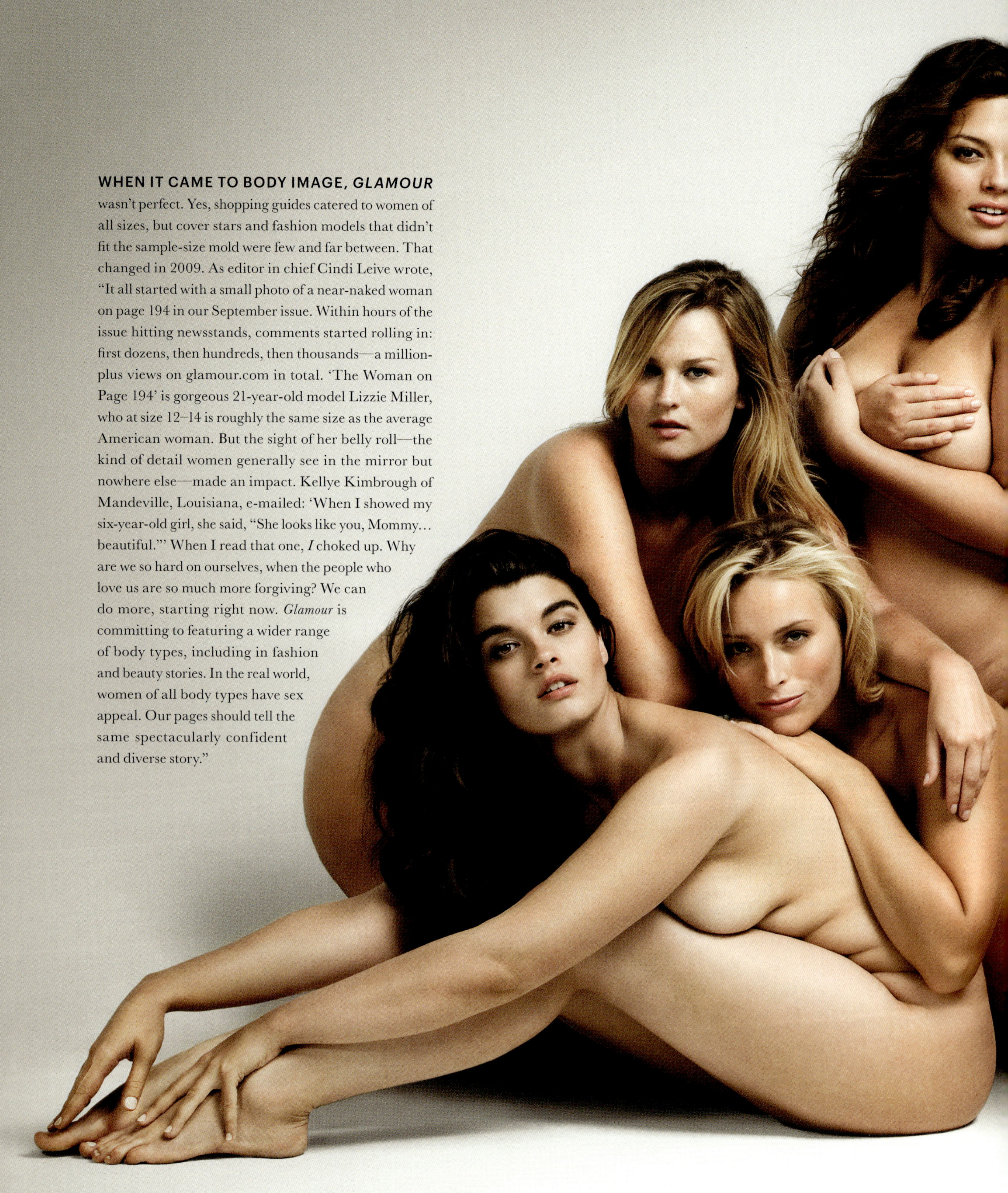

WHEN IT CAME TO BODY IMAGE, *GLAMOUR*
wasn't perfect. Yes, shopping guides catered to women of
all sizes, but cover stars and fashion models that didn't
fit the sample-size mold were few and far between. That
changed in 2009. As editor in chief Cindi Leive wrote,
"It all started with a small photo of a near-naked woman
on page 194 in our September issue. Within hours of the
issue hitting newsstands, comments started rolling in:
first dozens, then hundreds, then thousands—a million-
plus views on glamour.com in total. 'The Woman on
Page 194' is gorgeous 21-year-old model Lizzie Miller,
who at size 12–14 is roughly the same size as the average
American woman. But the sight of her belly roll—the
kind of detail women generally see in the mirror but
nowhere else—made an impact. Kellye Kimbrough of
Mandeville, Louisiana, e-mailed: 'When I showed my
six-year-old girl, she said, "She looks like you, Mommy…
beautiful."' When I read that one, *I* choked up. Why
are we so hard on ourselves, when the people who
love us are so much more forgiving? We can
do more, starting right now. *Glamour* is
committing to featuring a wider range
of body types, including in fashion
and beauty stories. In the real world,
women of all body types have sex
appeal. Our pages should tell the
same spectacularly confident
and diverse story."

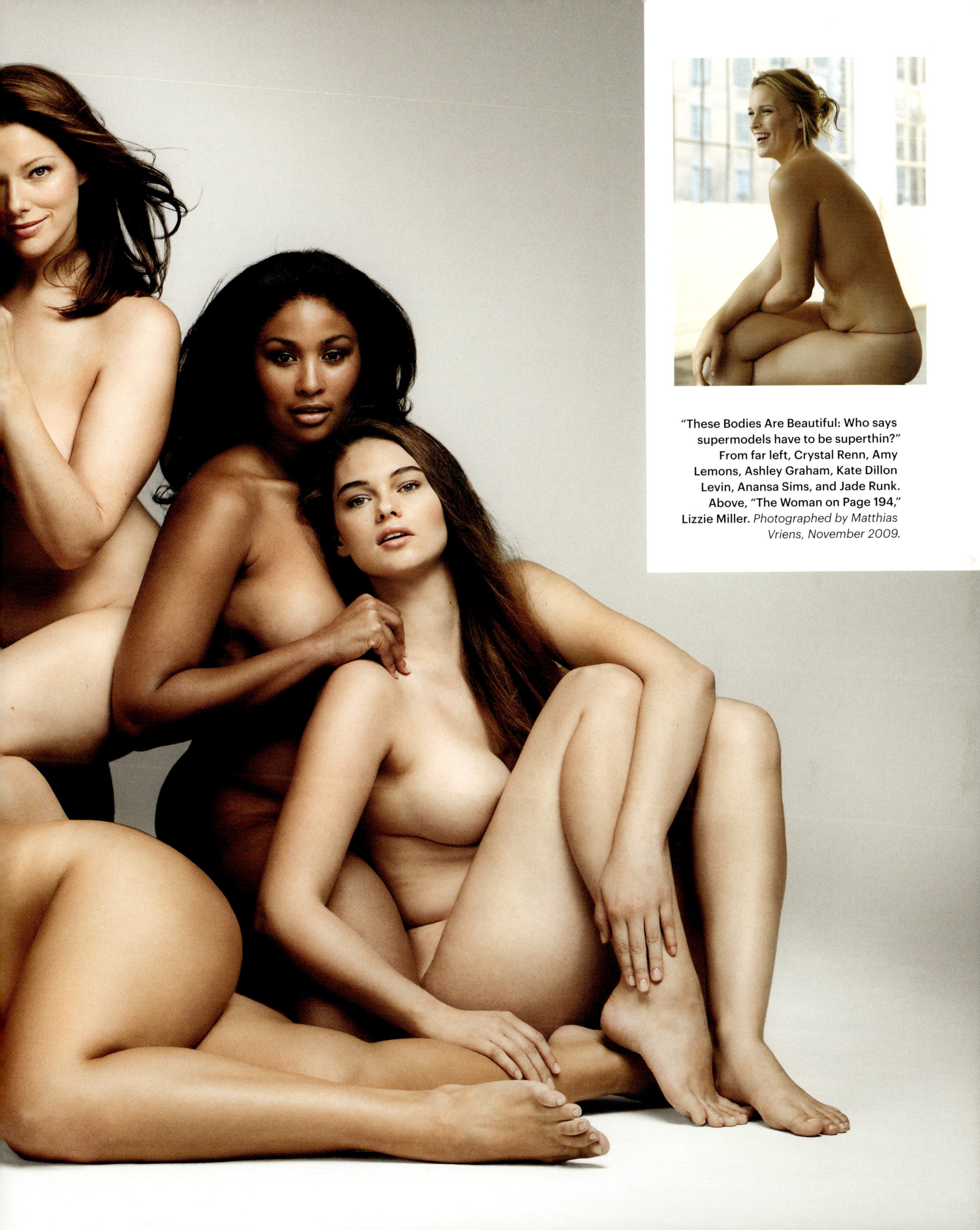

"These Bodies Are Beautiful: Who says supermodels have to be superthin?" From far left, Crystal Renn, Amy Lemons, Ashley Graham, Kate Dillon Levin, Anansa Sims, and Jade Runk. Above, "The Woman on Page 194," Lizzie Miller. *Photographed by Matthias Vriens, November 2009.*

The *Glamour* Girls

In 2004, *Glamour* turned 65, and to celebrate this the magazine looked back at many milestones—Katiti Kironde's historic cover, Gloria Steinem in *Glamour*, a potted history of Jake. They also united some of the magazine's most important cover stars from across the decades in this now iconic photograph, capturing them in "The quintessential all-American look: a white top and jeans." We're proud to reprint it here.
Photographed by Pamela Hansen, April 2004.

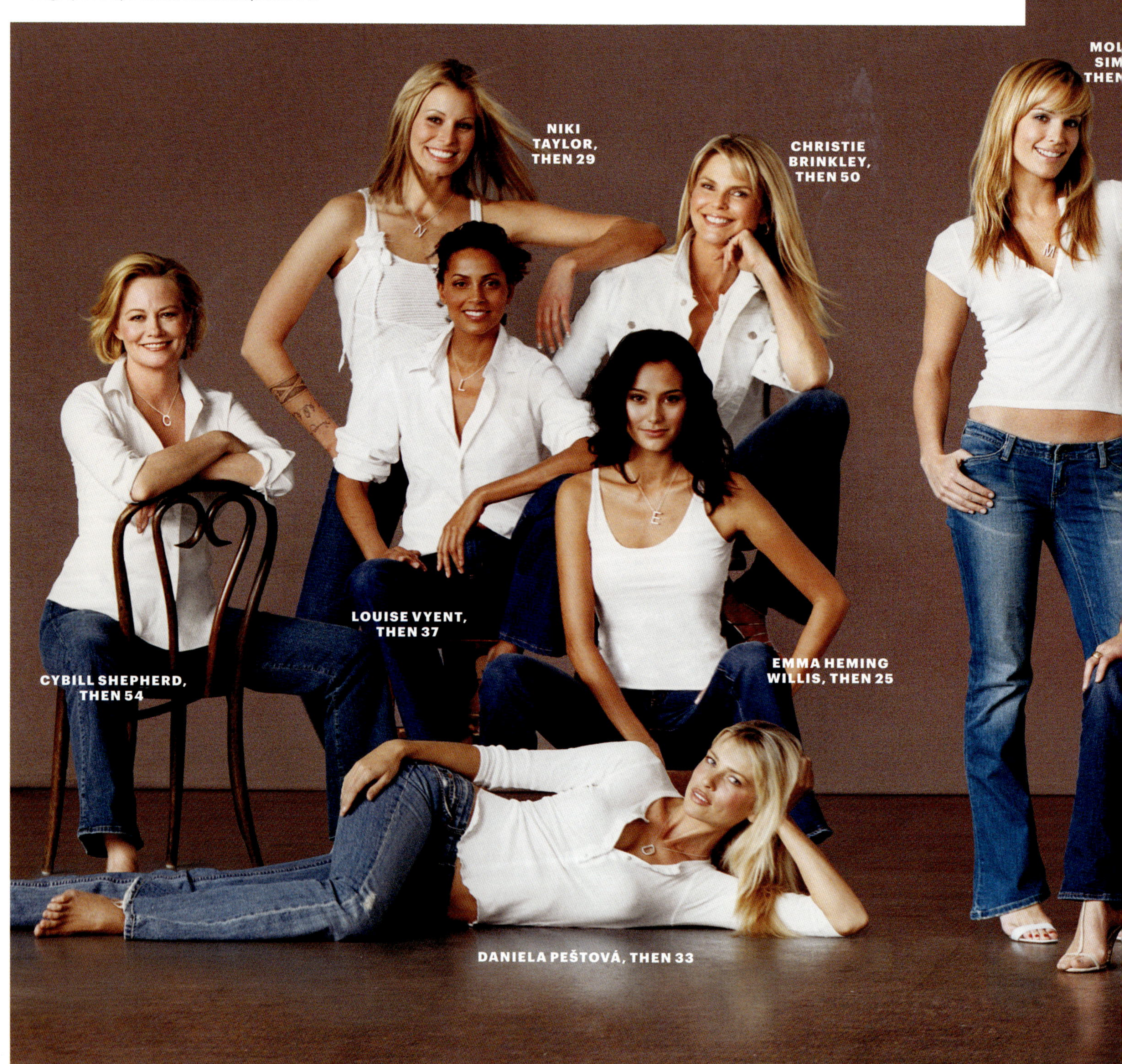

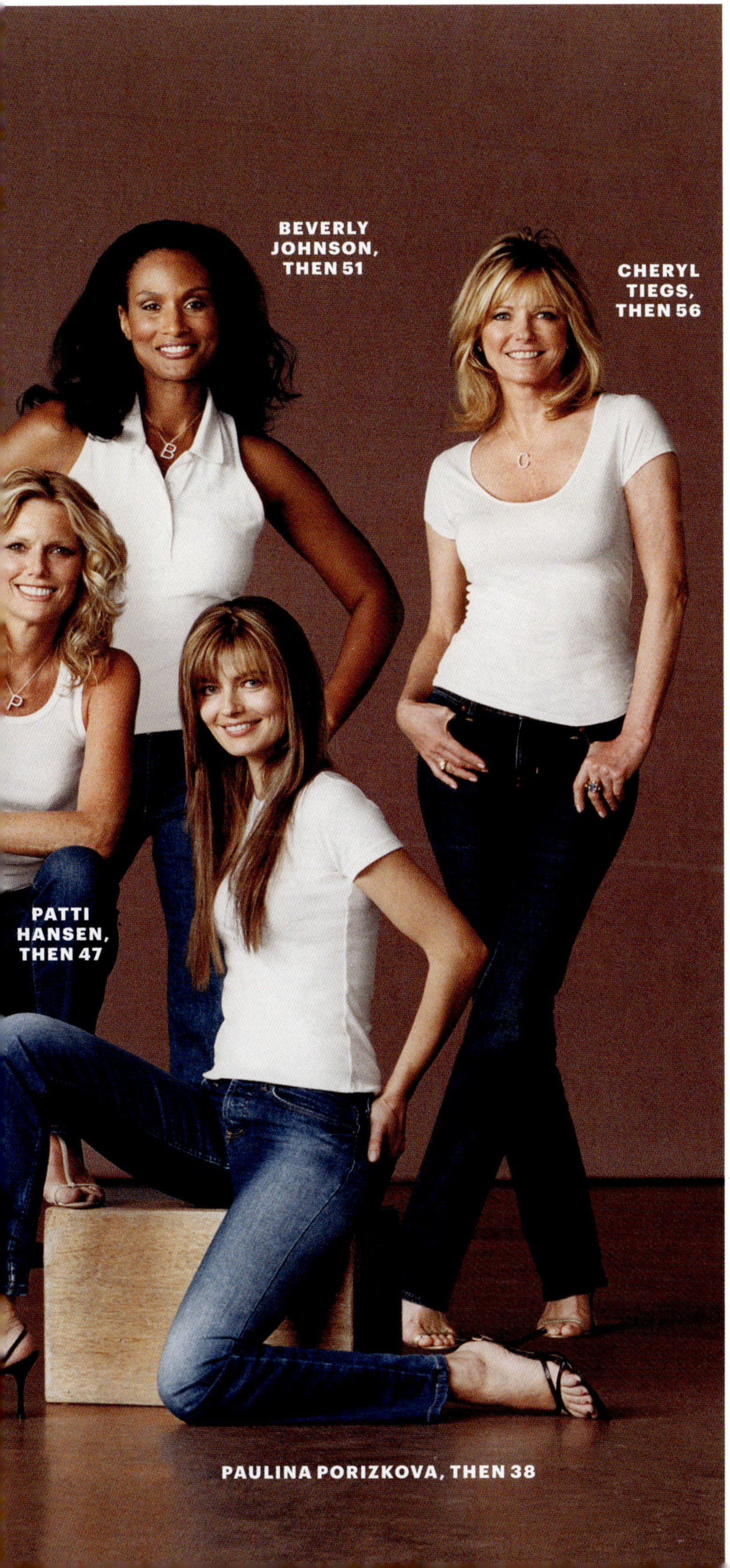

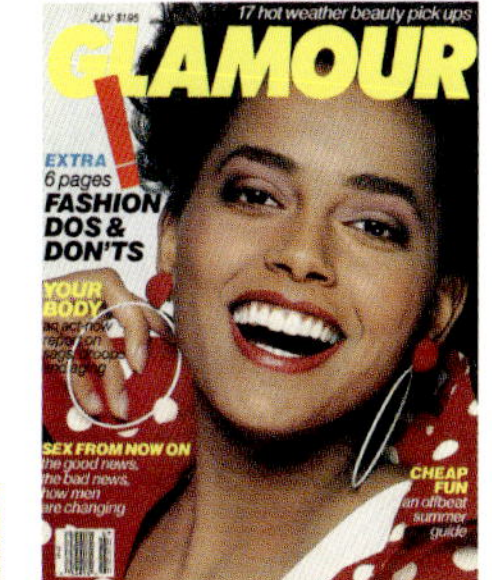

LOUISE VYENT,
JULY 1988.

PATTI HANSEN,
JULY 1973.

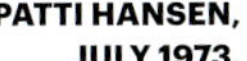

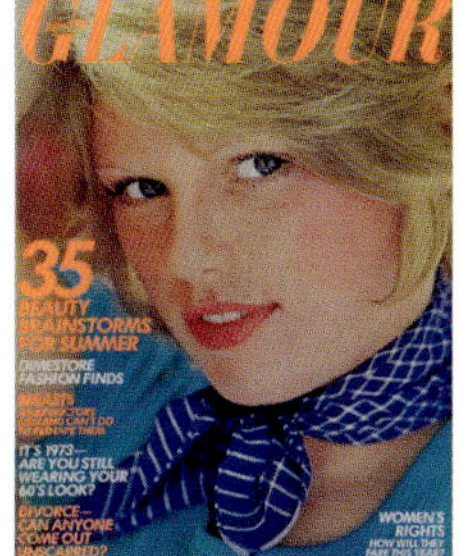

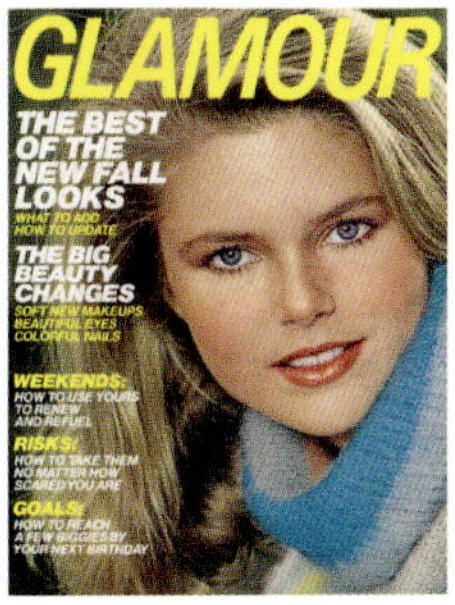

CHRISTIE
BRINKLEY,
SEPTEMBER 1977.

PAULINA
PORIZKOVA,
JANUARY 1992.

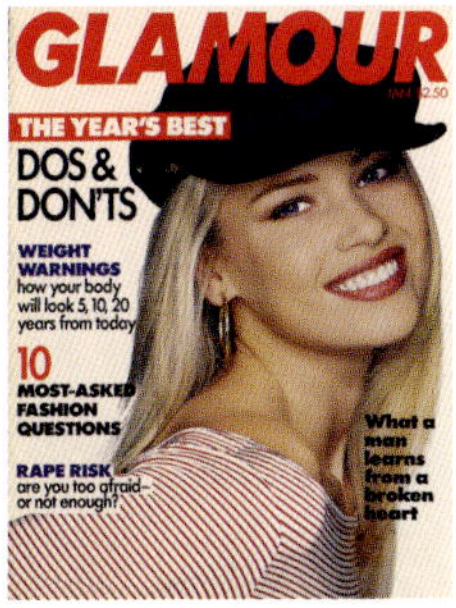

DANIELA
PEŠTOVÁ,
JANUARY 1993.

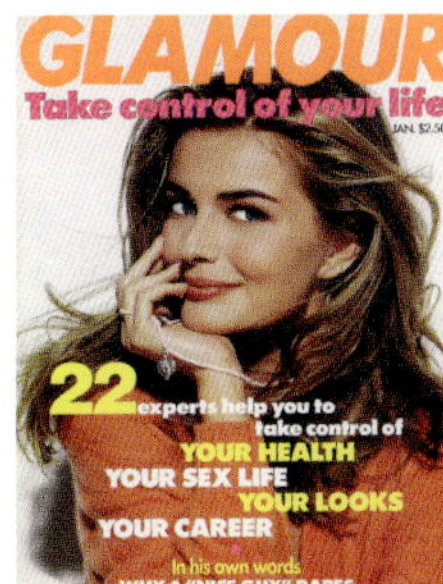

BEVERLY
JOHNSON,
JULY 1972.

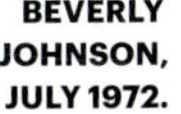

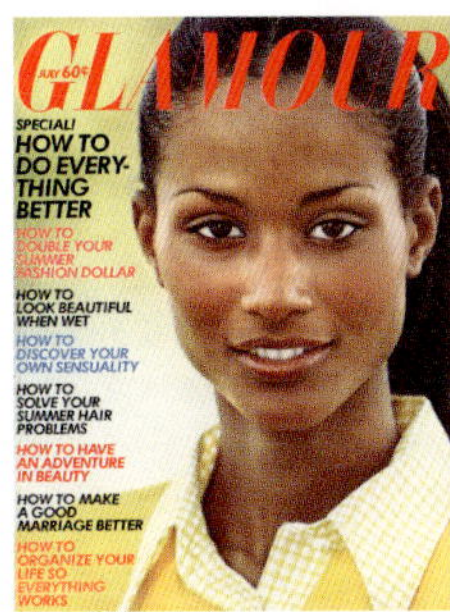

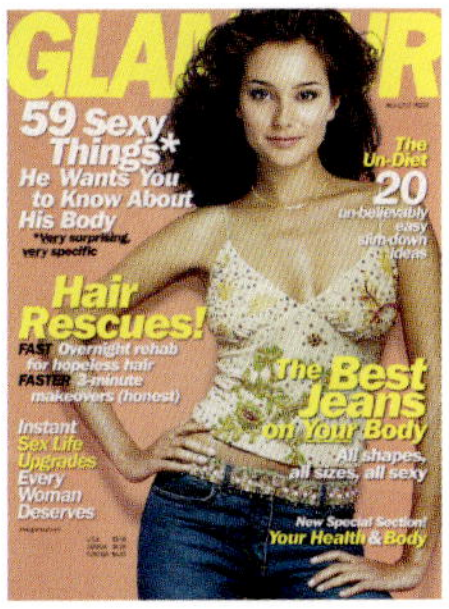

EMMA HEMING
WILLIS, AUGUST
2002.

MOLLY SIMS,
NOVEMBER 2002.

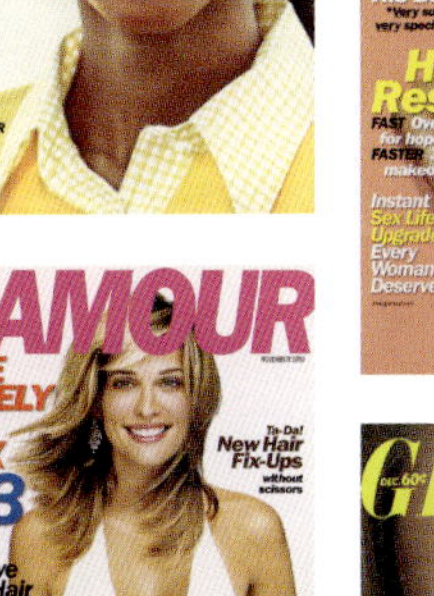

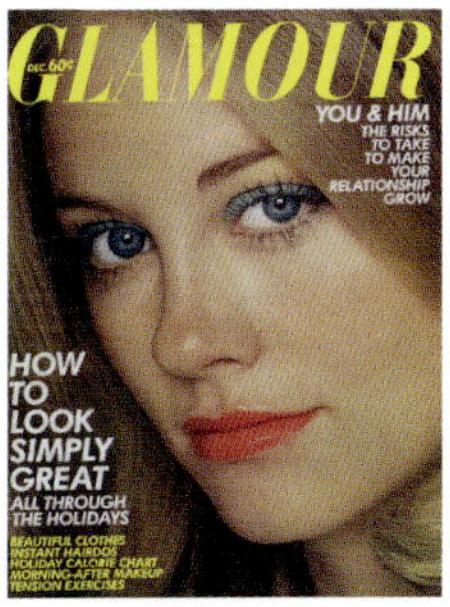

CYBILL
SHEPHERD,
DECEMBER 1971.

CHERYL TIEGS,
OCTOBER 1970.

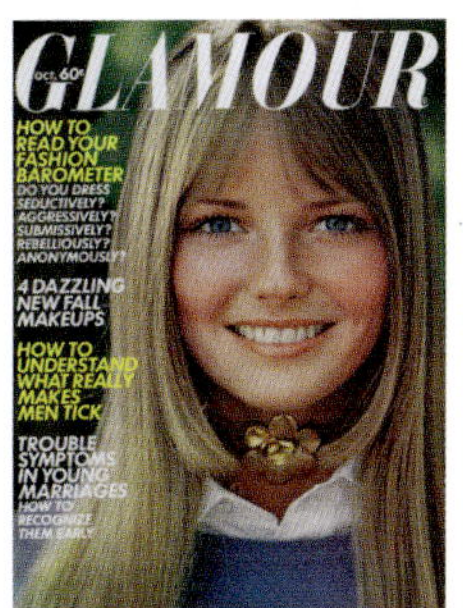

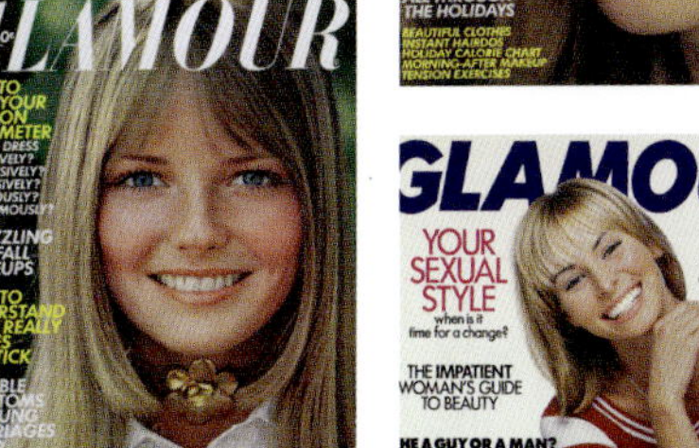

NIKI TAYLOR,
JULY 1996.

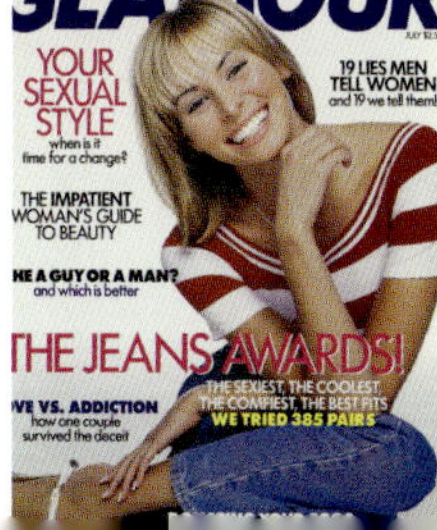

BEVERLY
JOHNSON,
THEN 51

CHERYL TIEGS,
THEN 56

PATTI
HANSEN,
THEN 47

PAULINA PORIZKOVA, THEN 38

Engagement Chicken

ONCE UPON A TIME IN 1982, so it goes, a *Glamour* fashion editor by the name of Kim Bonnell gave a roast chicken recipe to her assistant, Kathy Suder, who made it for her boyfriend, who proposed a month later. The recipe made the rounds, more people's boyfriends proposed, and decades later, *Glamour* dubbed it "Engagement Chicken" and published it without much fanfare in 2004. Who could have known that nearly two decades later, people would still be talking about it? A recipe book inspired by it was published, Martha Stewart cooked it on her television show, and publications speculated that Meghan, the Duchess of Sussex, had cooked Ina Garten's version of it for Prince Harry ahead of their engagement. There was even a whole debate that came and went about whether a women's magazine that stood for empowering women should have even published a recipe that encouraged the old-fashioned idea that women just wanted to get married, and its 21st-century equivalent "Marry Me Chicken" trended on the internet. Like we said, who knew? Either way, we had to mark this deliciously unexpected moment in *Glamour*'s history. And you never know, you might even be inspired to cook it one day.

"

Be skeptical if you must, but this recipe may be charmed.

GLAMOUR EDITORIAL, JANUARY 2004

Opposite, *Glamour*'s famous engagement chicken recipe, from the January 2004 issue. Right, the 2011 cookbook.

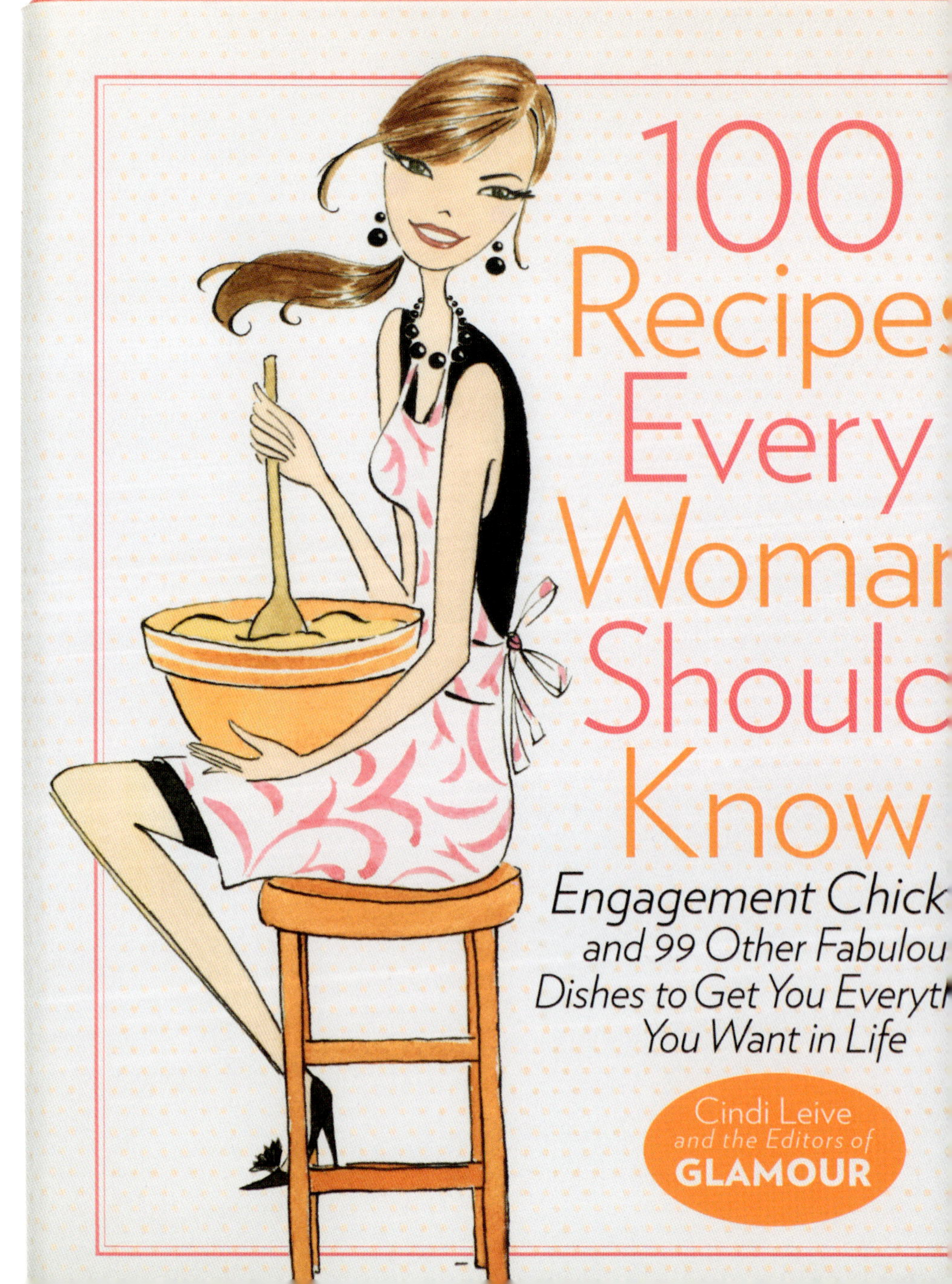

HOW TO…
Make "engagement chicken"

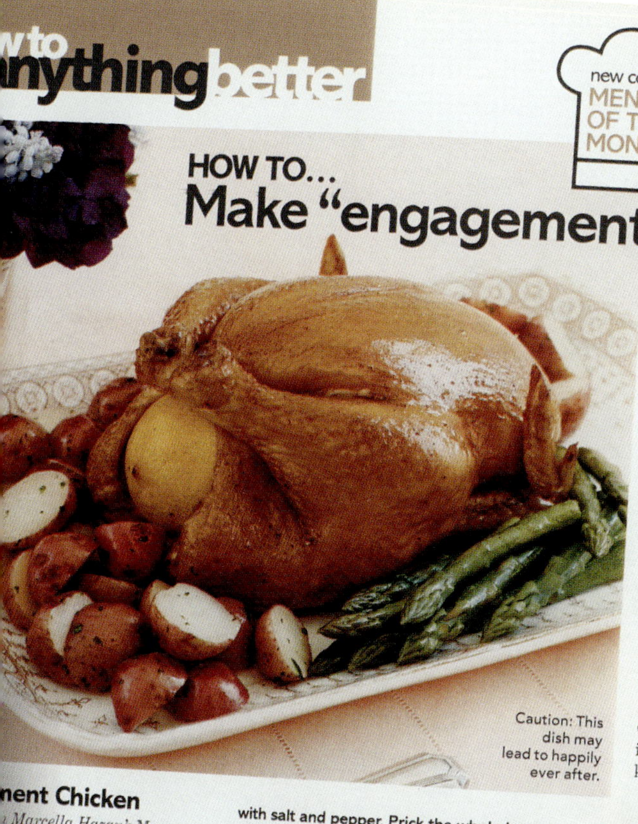

First comes chicken, then comes marriage? Be skeptical if you must, but this recipe may be charmed. It all began 22 years ago, when then–*Glamour* fashion editor Kim Bonnell gave the recipe to her assistant, Kathy Suder, who made the chicken for her boyfriend, who, a month later, asked her to marry him. "It's a meal your wife would make. It got me thinking," says Jon Suder, who now has three children with Kathy. Details of the simple dish passed from assistant to assistant like a culinary chain letter. When Bonnell heard that her recipe had inspired three weddings, she dubbed it Engagement Chicken. Try the recipe, give it to a friend—oh, and let us know when it works!

—TIFFANY BLACKSTONE

Caution: This dish may lead to happily ever after.

...ment Chicken

...1 Marcella Hazan's More ...Cooking)

...icken (approx. 3 lb.)
...emons
...n juice (½ cup)
...sea salt
...ck pepper

...per third of oven and preheat ...chicken inside and out with ...ove the giblets, then let the ...avity down, in a colander until ...temp (about 15 minutes). Pat ...owels. Pour lemon juice all ...(inside and outside). Season with salt and pepper. Prick the whole lemons three times with a fork and place deep inside the cavity. (Tip: If lemons are hard, roll on countertop with your palm to get juices flowing.) Place the bird breast-side down on a rack in a roasting pan, lower heat to 350° and bake uncovered for 15 minutes. Remove from oven and turn it breast-side up (use wooden spoons!); return it to oven for 35 minutes more. Test for doneness—a meat thermometer inserted in the thigh should read 180°, or juices should run clear when chicken is pricked with a fork. Continue baking if necessary. Let chicken cool for a few minutes before carving. Serve with juices.

...ks, it really, really works!

+ =

...oking for ...who you ...to!" says ...e with Jon.

"You'll have a chicken with ultracrisp skin and a subtle lemon flavor. Who can resist that?" says Bonnell.

"Twenty-two years later, Jon still tells the story every time I make it," says Suder.

What do I serve on the side?

Just keep it simple.
Two choices:
● **New Potatoes** Boil until tender, toss with olive oil, sprinkle with fresh chopped parsley.
● **Asparagus** Cut off tough ends, steam until tender and top with a pat of butter.

And for wine?

Leslie Sbrocco, author of *Wine For Women*, suggests these easy-to-find bottles:
● **Gallo of Sonoma Chardonnay** ($10) Smooth with a touch of citrus. "Chardonnay is the little black dress of white wines," says Sbrocco.
● **Louis Jadot Beaujolais-Villages** ($9) Refreshing with a kick of spice. "Light and fruity, like Kool-Aid for adults," says Sbrocco.

...e Palette, a full line of multi-colored ... ...your skin tone. Choose from Bronze... ...drug and discount stores. For a store ...

Powder Palette
Multi-colored face powders

70+
MARRIAGE PROPOSALS,
GLAMOUR 2011

4.9M
RESULTS FOR
"ENGAGEMENT CHICKEN
GLAMOUR" ON GOOGLE

73.6B
VIEWS OF "ENGAGEMENT
CHICKEN" VIDEOS ON
TIKTOK

Sporting Superheroes

Celebrating successful sportswomen has long been a part of *Glamour*'s history. In 1996, the USA Basketball Women's National Team was honored as Women of the Year after they won Olympic gold—and helped secure the future of the Women's National Basketball Association. The US Women's National Soccer Team was honored twice: in 1999 and 2015. And that's not to mention the Women of the Year Awards that went to gymnast Simone Biles, tennis champions and sisters Venus and Serena Williams, and more. So it should come as no surprise that during every Olympics cycle, the women vying for gold were the stars of the issue, as in this shoot from the August 2008 issue that captures the power and strength of sprinters Allyson Felix and Sanya Richards-Ross, as well as soccer stars Leslie Osborne, Heather O'Reilly, Christie Rampone, and Abby Wambach.

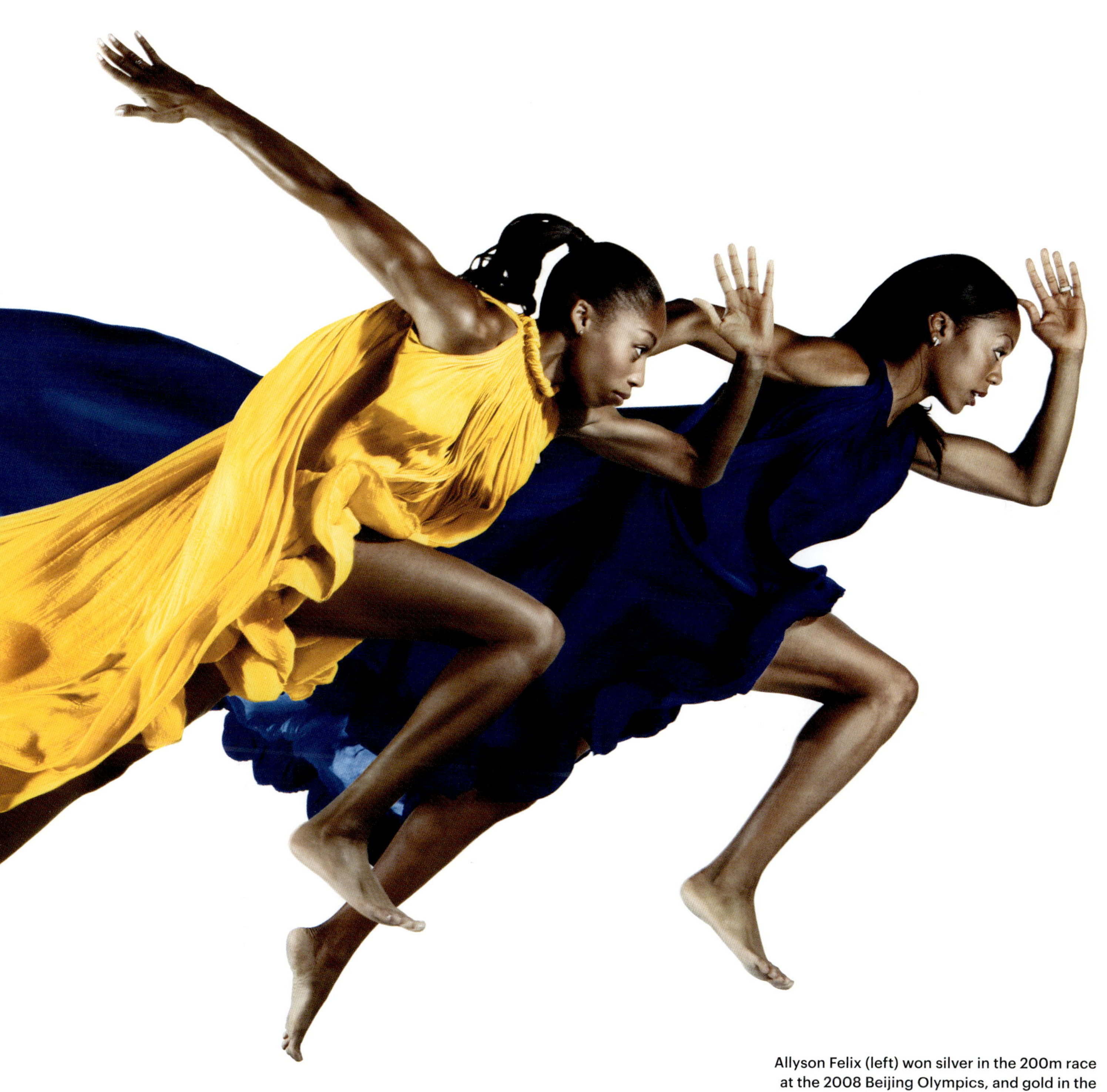

Allyson Felix (left) won silver in the 200m race at the 2008 Beijing Olympics, and gold in the 4x400m relay. Sanya Richards-Ross also won gold in the 4x400m relay, and bronze in the 400m. In 2012, Felix was honored as a *Glamour* Woman of the Year, following her incredible medal haul at the London Olympics that same year. *This page and next photographed by Christopher Griffith, August 2008.*

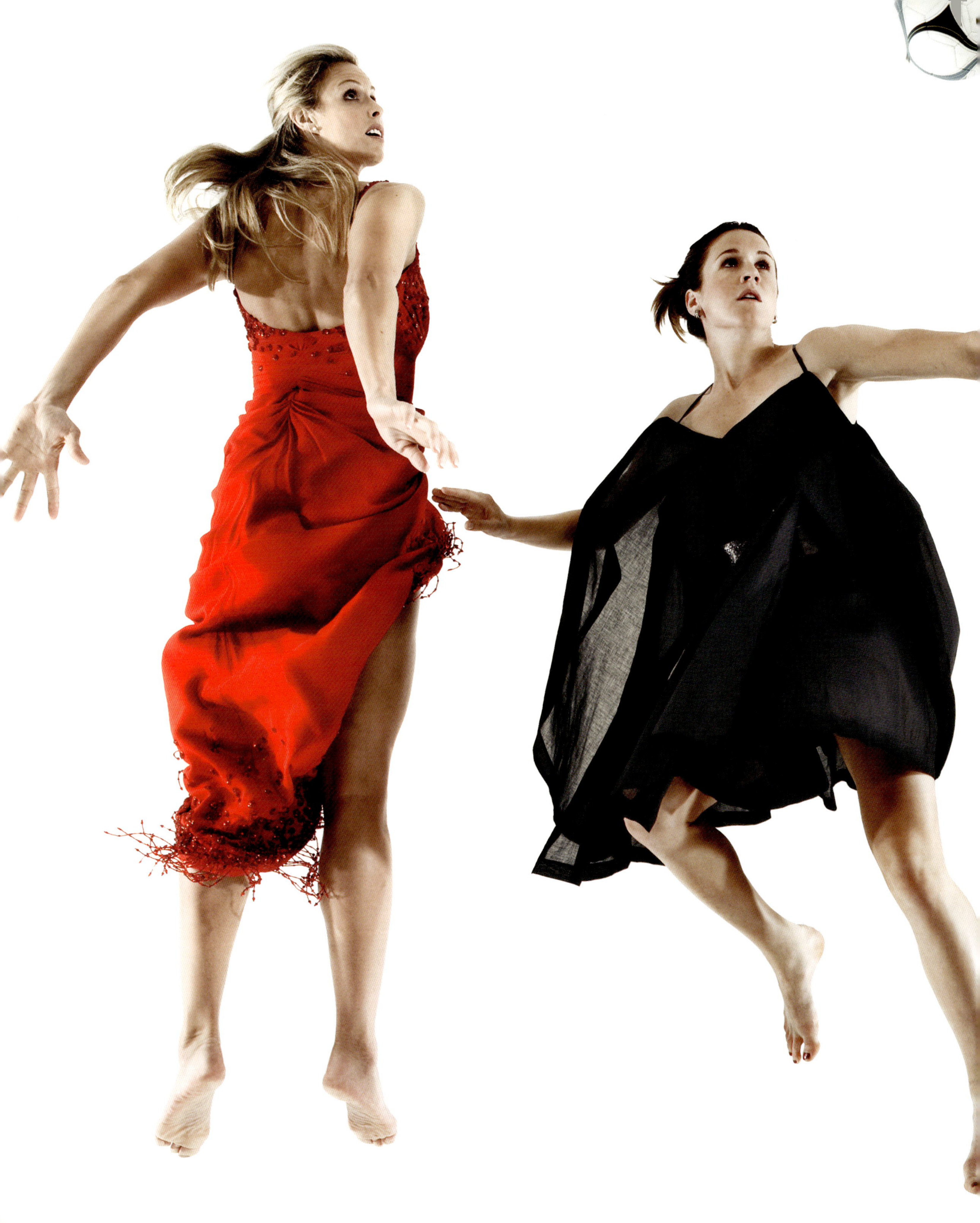

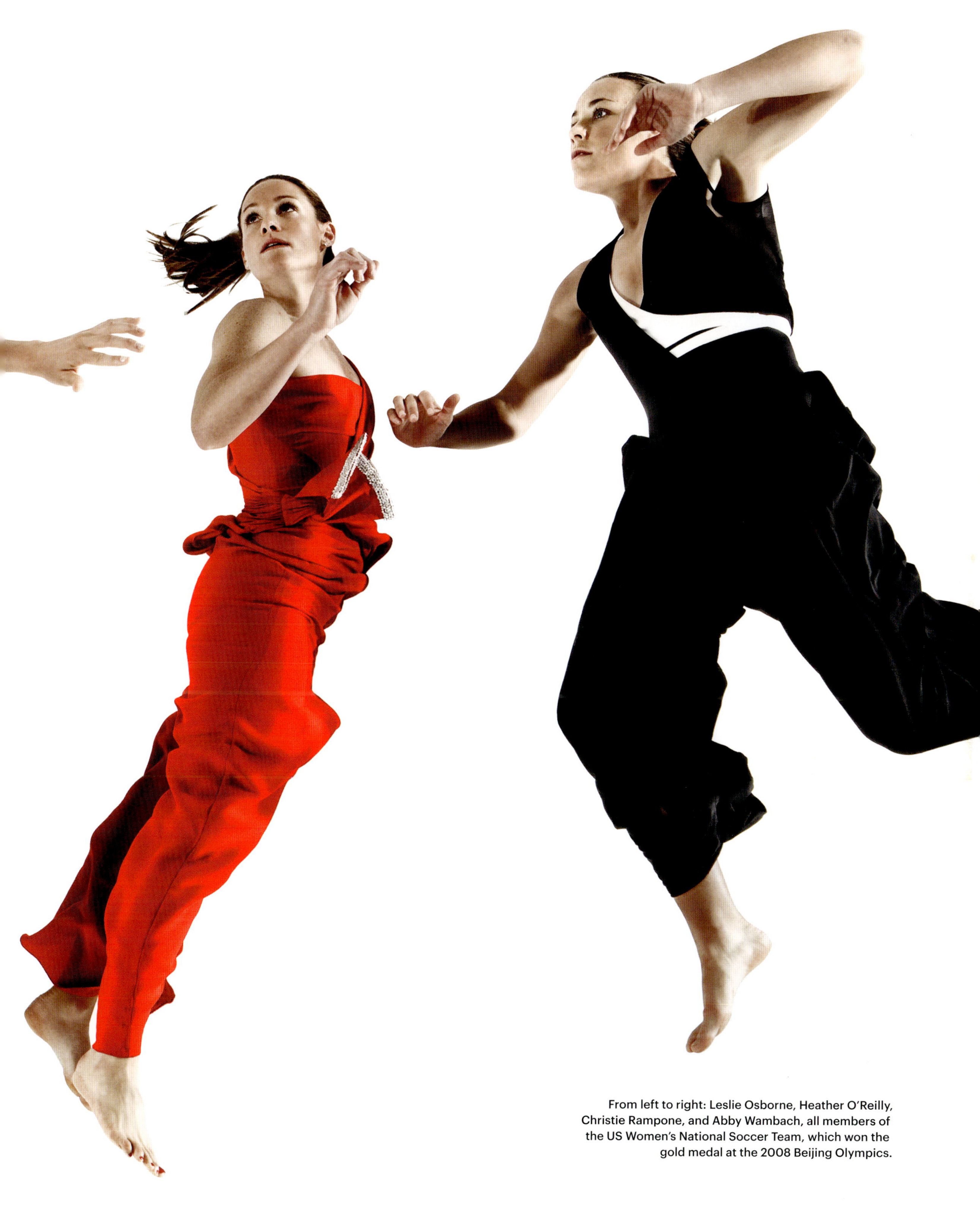

From left to right: Leslie Osborne, Heather O'Reilly, Christie Rampone, and Abby Wambach, all members of the US Women's National Soccer Team, which won the gold medal at the 2008 Beijing Olympics.

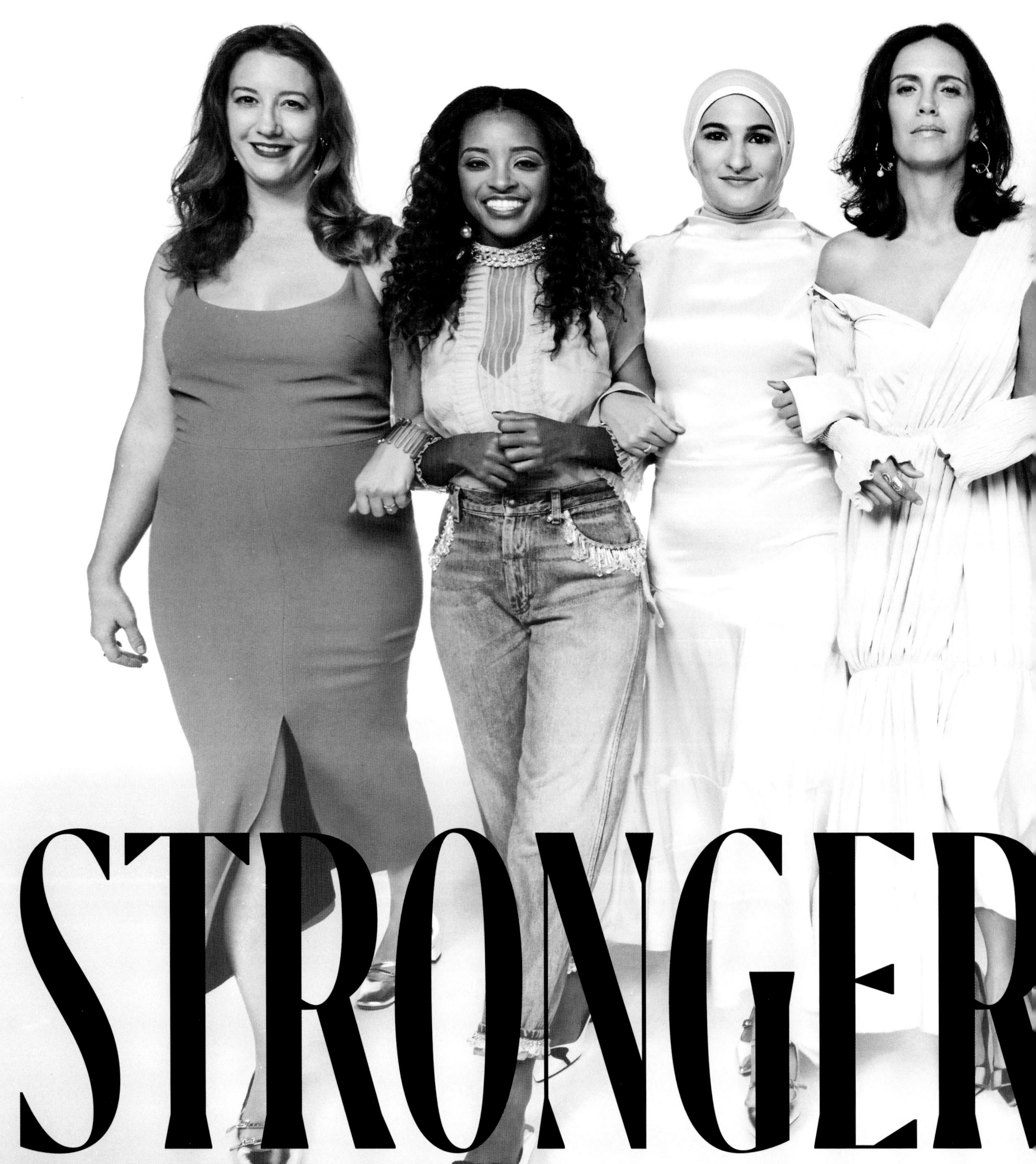

STRONGER

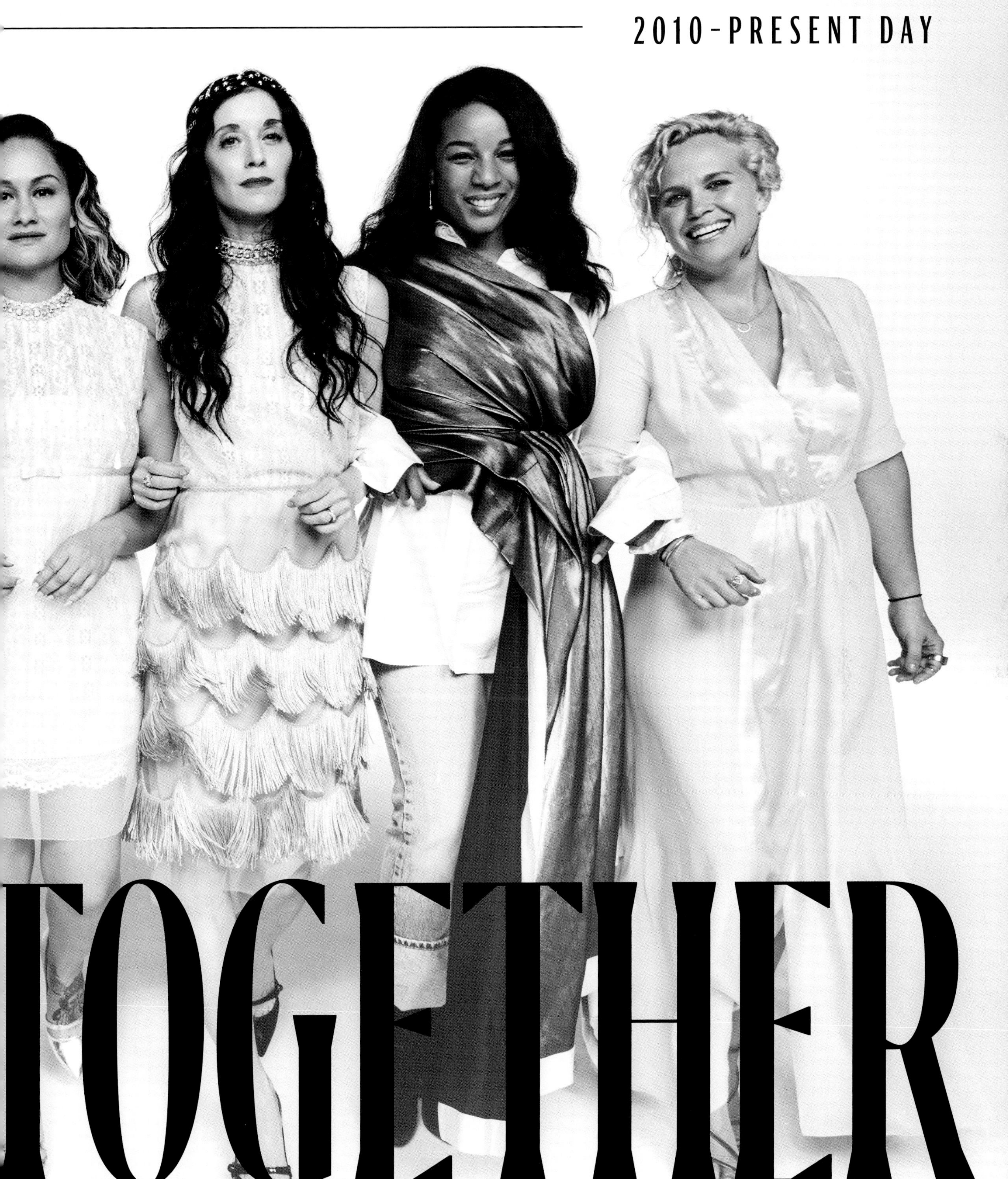

TOGETHER

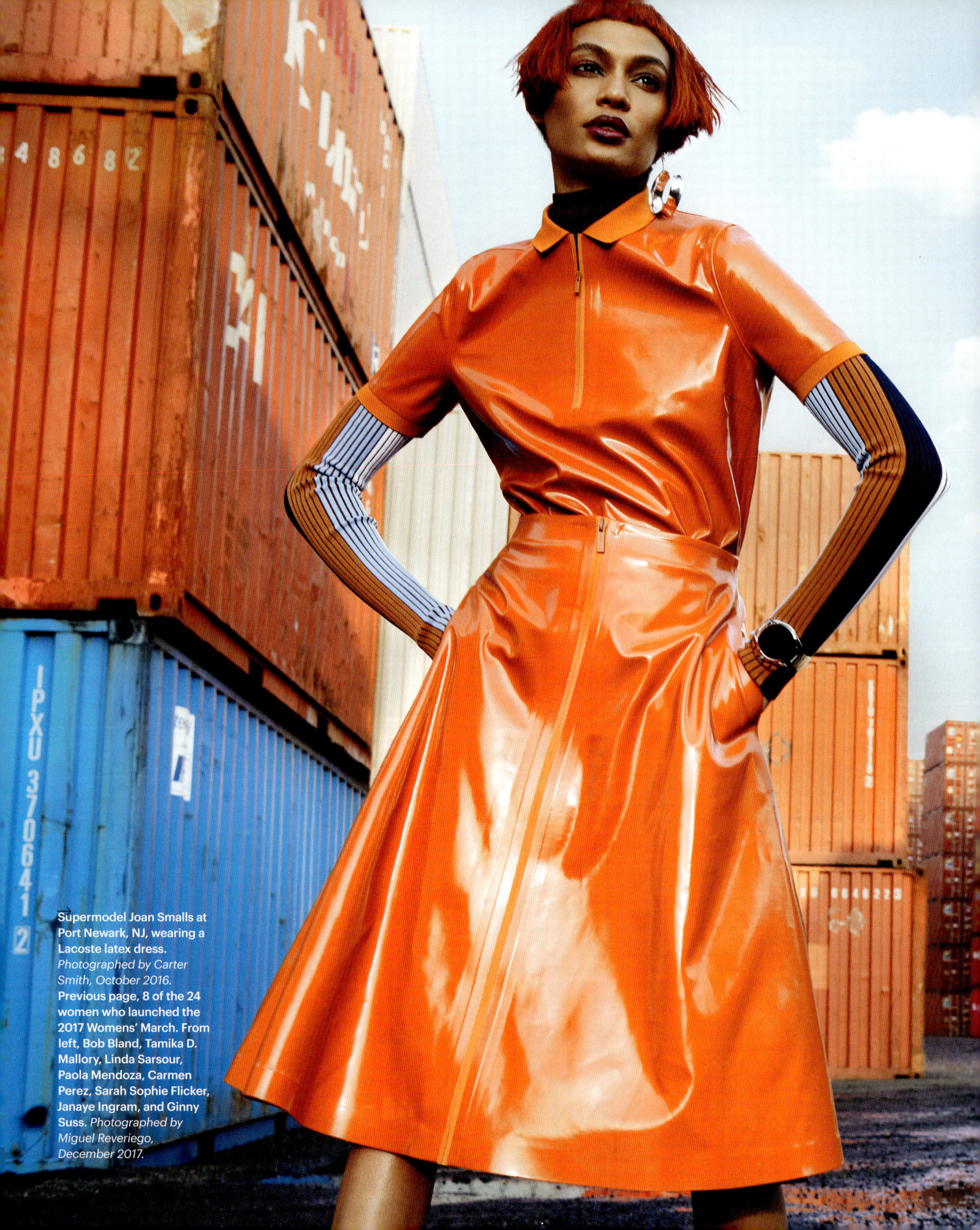

Supermodel Joan Smalls at Port Newark, NJ, wearing a Lacoste latex dress. *Photographed by Carter Smith, October 2016.* Previous page, 8 of the 24 women who launched the 2017 Womens' March. From left, Bob Bland, Tamika D. Mallory, Linda Sarsour, Paola Mendoza, Carmen Perez, Sarah Sophie Flicker, Janaye Ingram, and Ginny Suss. *Photographed by Miguel Reveriego, December 2017.*

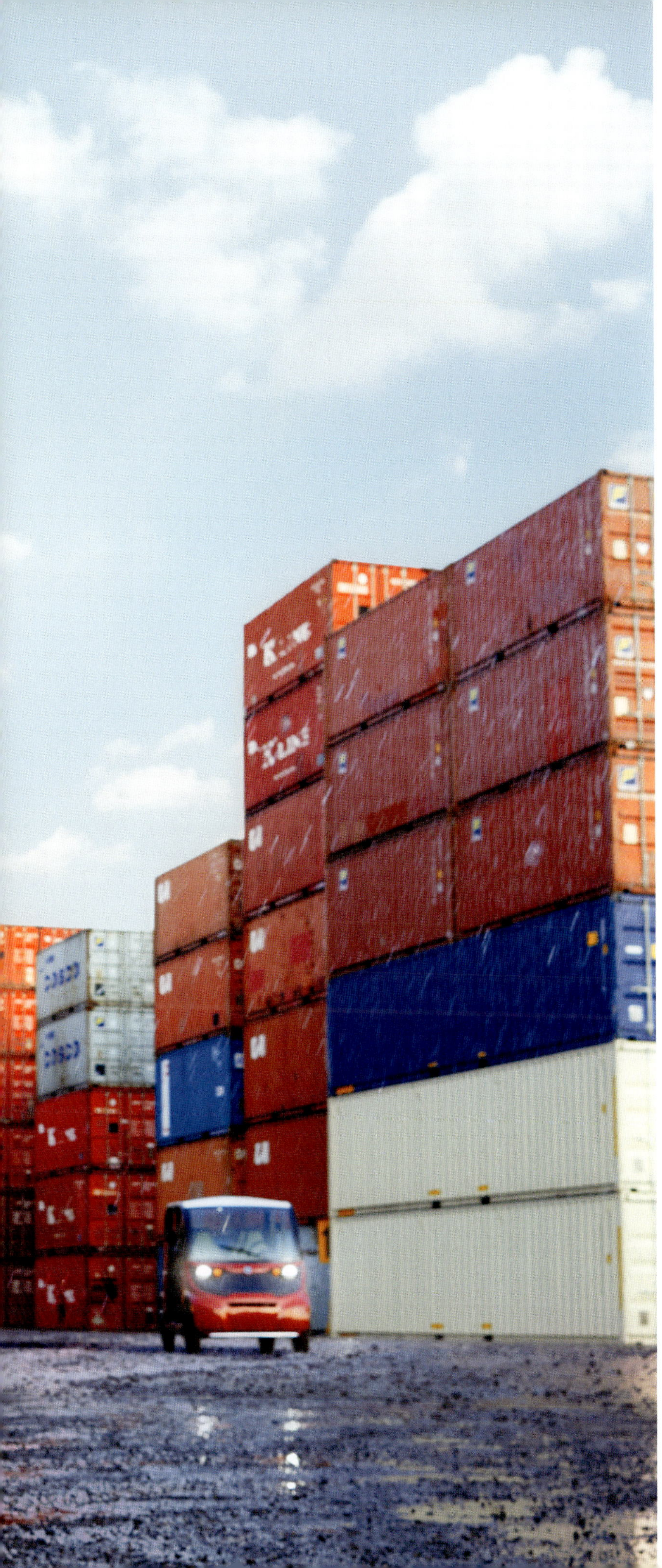

A new decade brought a tidal wave of change in women's lives.

Instagram reshaped the way society interacted with media, and each other. And the rising swell of social movements like #MeToo and Black Lives Matter, both led by women, birthed a new generation of activists. But for all the strides documented by *Glamour* over the previous seven decades, sexism, harassment, and abuse in the workplace and beyond still abounded—an all-too-silent suffering that #MeToo blew the lid off of. Men in some of the most powerful positions were held to account—and in some instances jailed for criminal actions—by women, some of whom shared their stories with *Glamour*. Deep-rooted institutional racism was also being confronted in the wake of numerous killings of Black people by police. The founders of Black Lives Matter, Patrisse Cullors, Alicia Garza, and Ayọ (formerly known as Opal) Tometi, were honored by *Glamour* in 2016 as Women of the Year. Their work would take on even greater prominence in 2020 after the murder of George Floyd in Minneapolis, as protests swept the country, urging Americans to confront institutional racism. These movements signaled a breaking apart of the old and a moment of women recognizing the strength of their collective power.

The power and intensity of women's voices was made possible by the ever expanding reach of the internet and social media, and their hold on our lives—an evolution that also reshaped the magazine. In January 2019, under new editor in chief Samantha Barry, *Glamour* published its final monthly print issue and embarked on a new journey beyond the printed page—telling stories in new and interactive formats and continuing, as always, to celebrate women's diverse interests in news, politics, beauty, entertainment, and style. But this time, with even more ways to reach the audience.

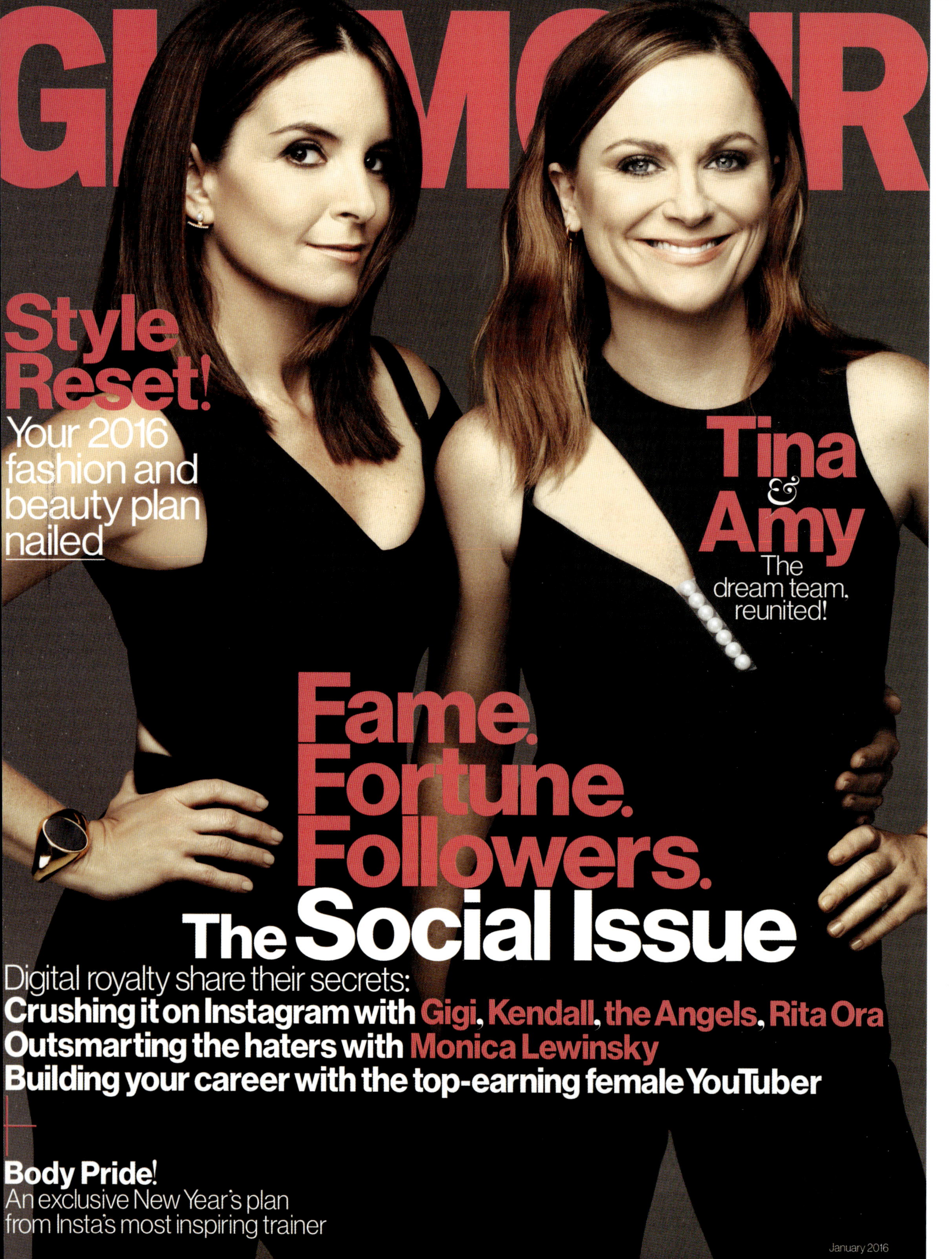

GLAMOUR
Style Reset!
Your 2016 fashion and beauty plan nailed
Tina & Amy
The dream team, reunited!
Fame.
Fortune.
Followers.
The Social Issue
Digital royalty share their secrets:
Crushing it on Instagram with Gigi, Kendall, the Angels, Rita Ora
Outsmarting the haters with Monica Lewinsky
Building your career with the top-earning female YouTuber
Body Pride!
An exclusive New Year's plan from Insta's most inspiring trainer
January 2016

The Social Influence

SOCIAL MEDIA WASN'T NEW IN THIS ERA—MYSPACE LAUNCHED IN 2003, FACEBOOK in 2004, YouTube in 2005, Twitter in 2006, and Instagram in 2010. But by the 2010s, it had become ubiquitous—in 2012 Facebook had a billion users. Instagram also became one of the largest social networks—it too now has over one billion users. People could share their lives as they wished to be seen, and access news, sports, style, and beauty advice like never before. In *Glamour*'s September 2011 issue, a then 23-year-old Rihanna told the magazine why she had joined Twitter—which by then had over 100 million active accounts: "It was easy for my fans to believe everything else they were hearing about me because they weren't really hearing much from *me*. Now they don't believe rumors anymore." Today, Rihanna is one of the most followed people in the world.

The internet and social media offered new possibilities, and both would ultimately reshape the traditional print media landscape. Magazines needed to embrace the breakout social media stars and create their own social media presences. At the same time, editors had to navigate creating relevant monthly content in a world where news, politics, and fashion moved on in a matter of hours. While this would ultimately prompt *Glamour* to become a fully digital publication, in the early part of the 2010s the magazine shifted to featuring fashion bloggers—now better known as content creators—as never before, hiring a digital team to run the daily content on Glamour.com, and keeping up (in print and online) with the always-on new normal. In fact, *Glamour*'s January 2016 Social Issue was fully dedicated to navigating life online. By 2019, *Glamour* had left print behind, coming to meet their readers where they were—which was, mostly, with a smartphone in the palm of their hands. Nevertheless, parts of the magazine's DNA—like great covers and gripping storytelling—remained the same.

↓

Blogger Tavi Gevinson at 13. *Photographed by Williams + Hirakawa, March 2011.*

←

Tina Fey and Amy Poehler, January 2016.

→

Blogger Tamu McPherson. *Photographed by Patrick Demarchelier, August 2010.*

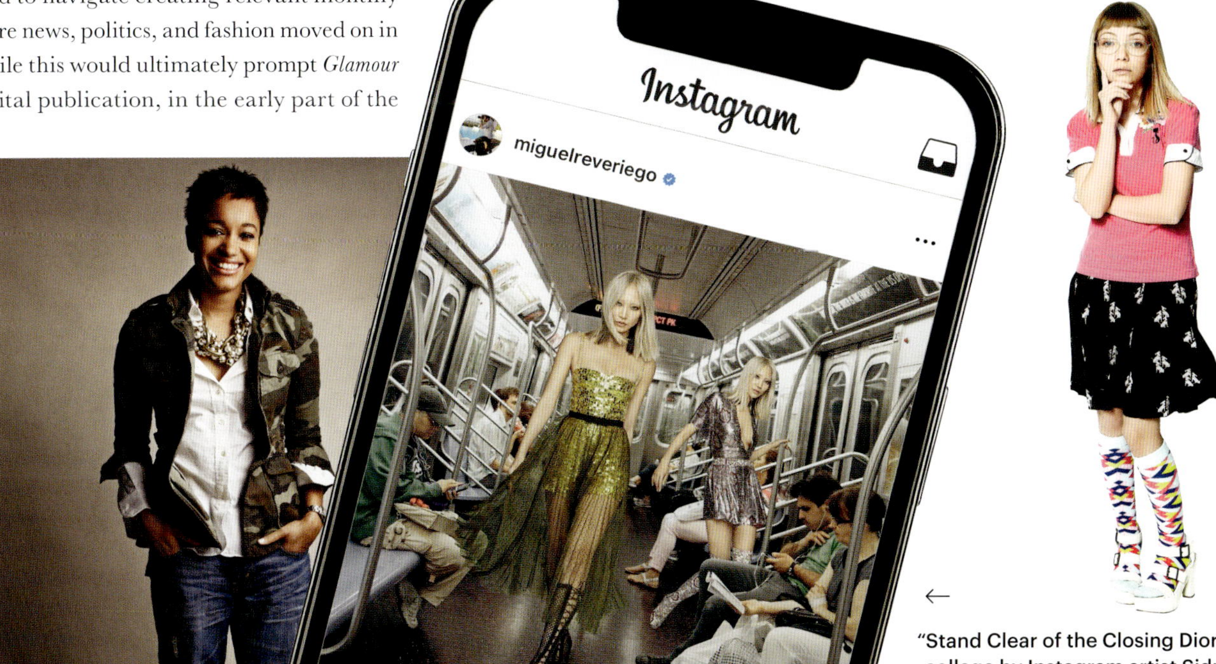

←

"Stand Clear of the Closing Dior," a collage by Instagram artist Sidney Prawatyotin featuring model Soo Joo Park. *Photographed by Miguel Reveriego, March 2018.*

↘ →

The May 2015 cover featuring Michelle Obama, Sarah Jessica Parker, and Kerry Washington was the second time the first lady had been a *Glamour* cover star. The three women had joined forces to support military families.

The television show *Girls*, which ran for six seasons from 2012 to 2017, became a cult hit and supercharged the careers of the cast. This February 2017 cover featuring the four main actors, (from left) Allison Williams, Zosia Mamet, Lena Dunham, and Jemima Kirke, celebrated the launch of the final season.

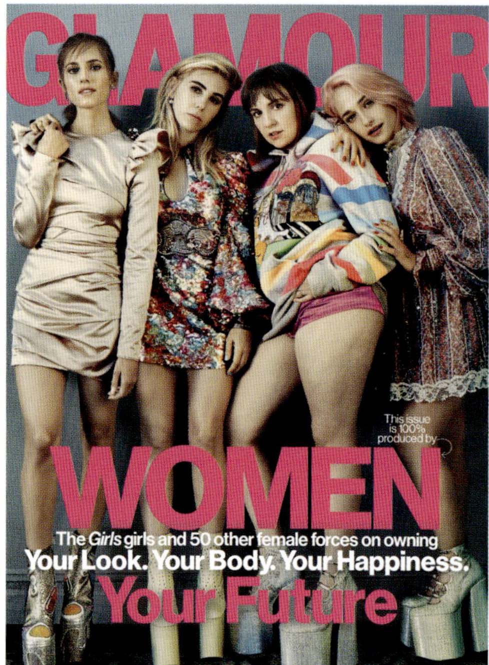

→

In December 2016, Ashley Graham was honored as one of *Glamour*'s Women of the Year. She is pictured here on her third cover, July 2017.

↘

Serena Williams on the cover of *Glamour*'s Women Are Strong as Hell issue in July 2016— her second cover for the magazine (her first was as a Women of the Year honoree in December 2009).

↘

Marking the release of the long-anticipated *Fifty Shades of Grey* movie, the film's stars Dakota Johnson and Jamie Dornan appeared on the March 2015 cover, in both the US and UK.

Opposite, in her November 2013 cover interview, Rihanna told *Glamour*: "I had to regain my fearlessness because it did go away for a little bit."

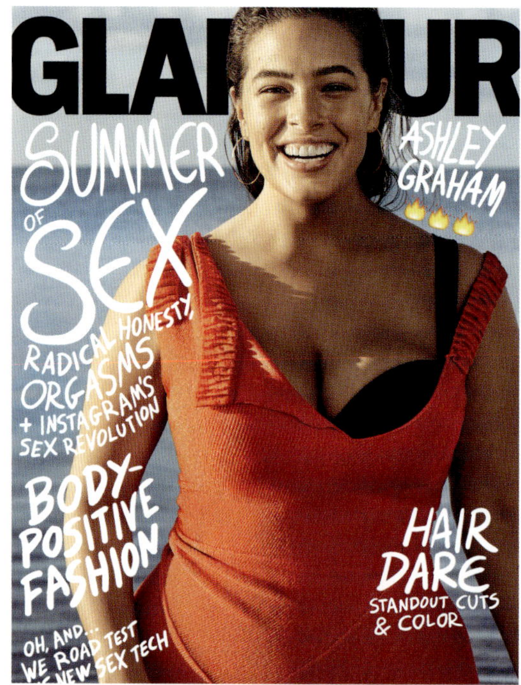

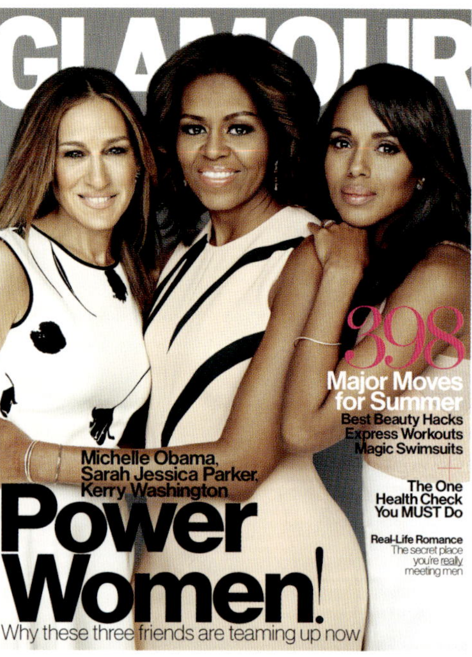

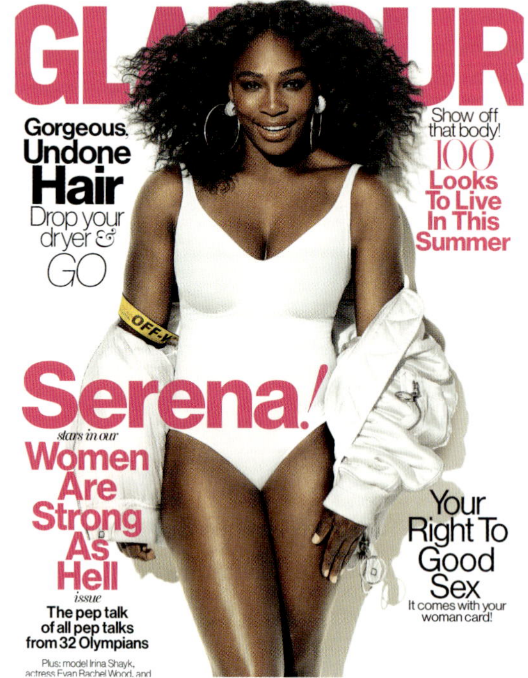

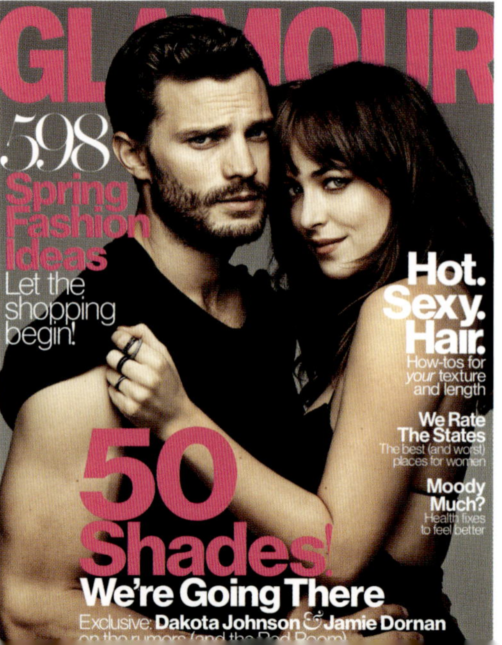

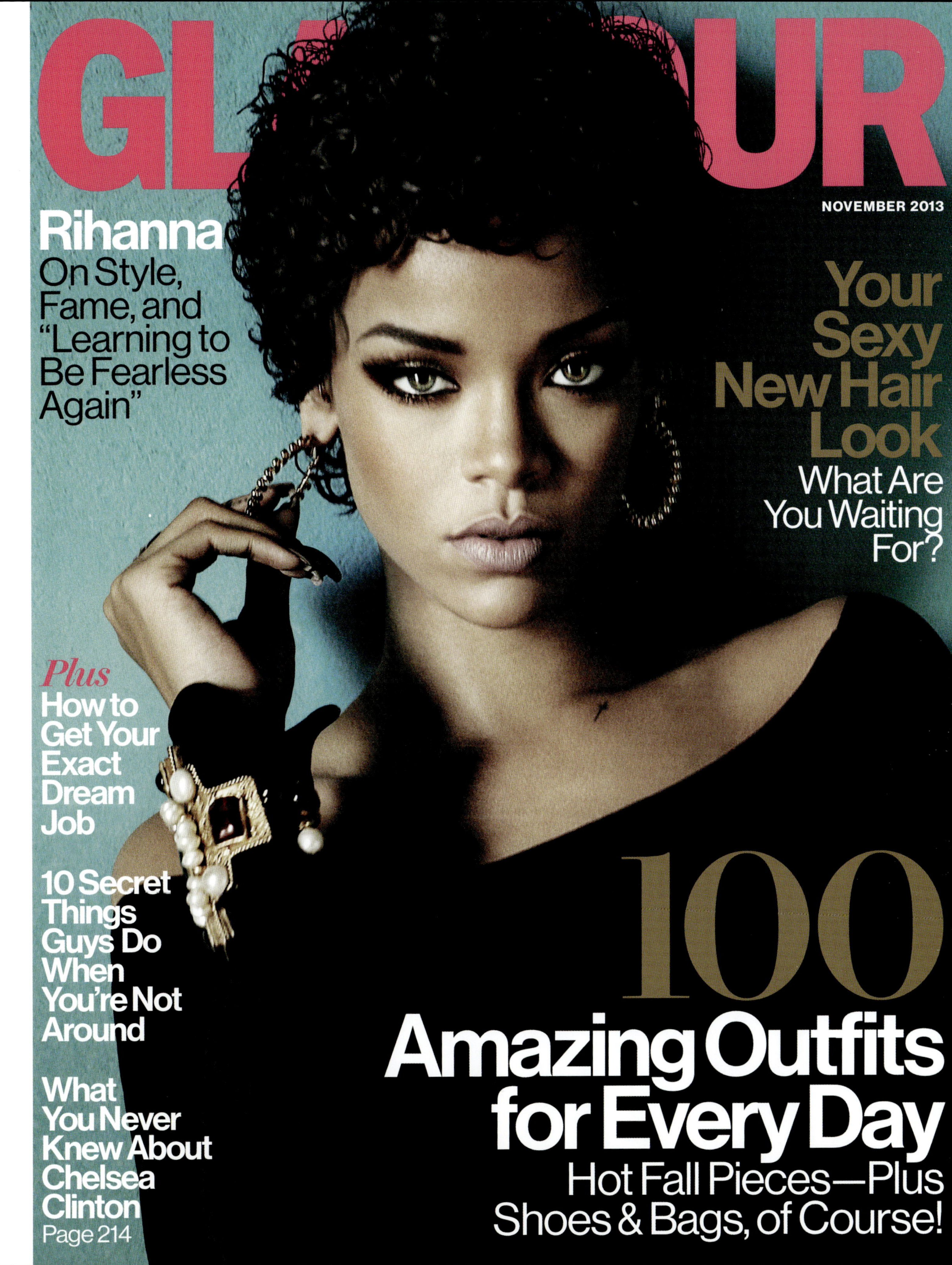

GLAMOUR
NOVEMBER 2013
Rihanna
On Style, Fame, and "Learning to Be Fearless Again"
Your Sexy New Hair Look
What Are You Waiting For?
Plus
How to Get Your Exact Dream Job
10 Secret Things Guys Do When You're Not Around
What You Never Knew About Chelsea Clinton
Page 214
100
Amazing Outfits for Every Day
Hot Fall Pieces—Plus Shoes & Bags, of Course!

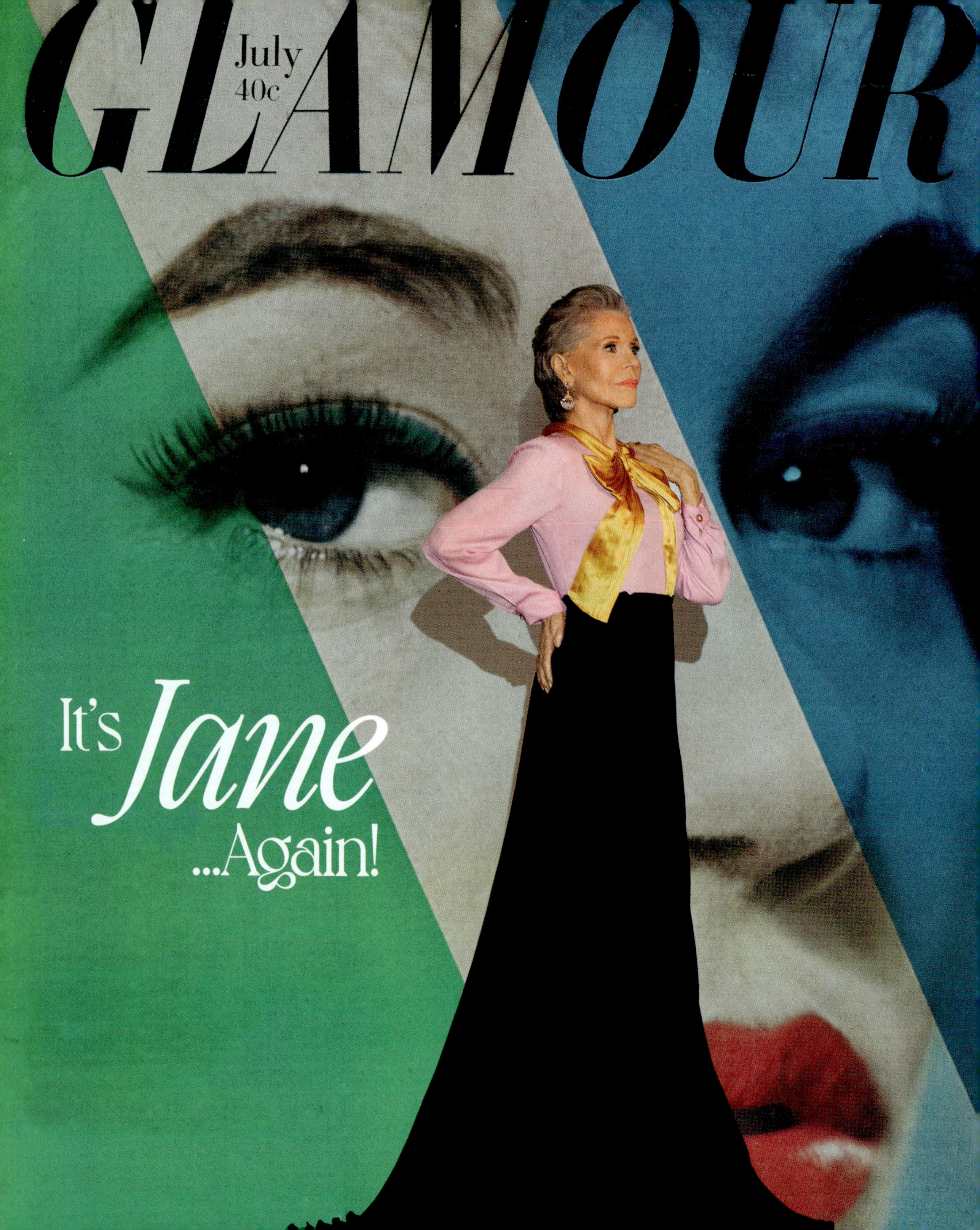
GLAMOUR
JULY
40c
It's Jane ...Again!

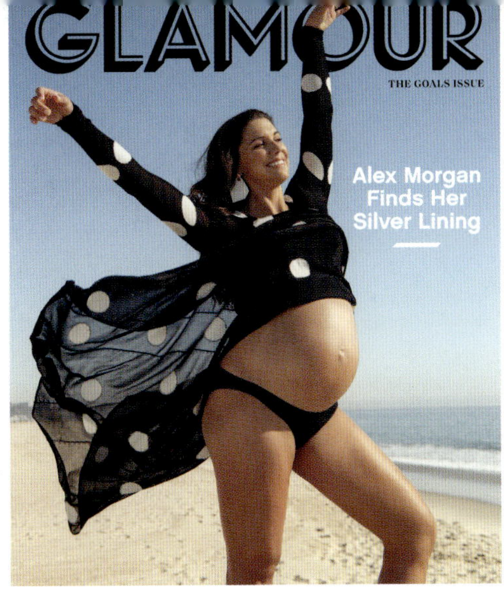

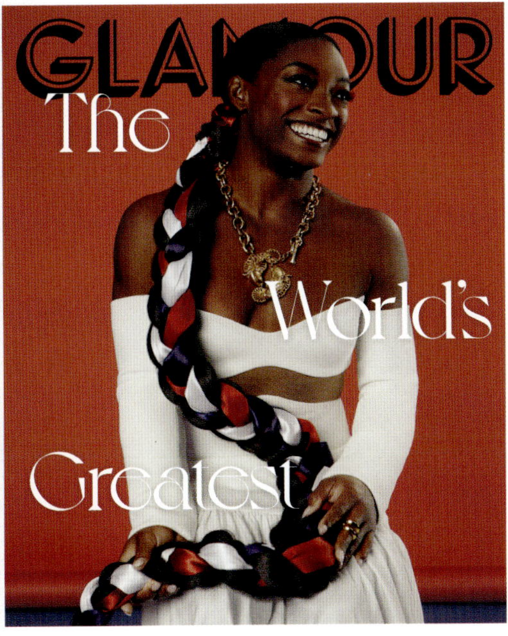

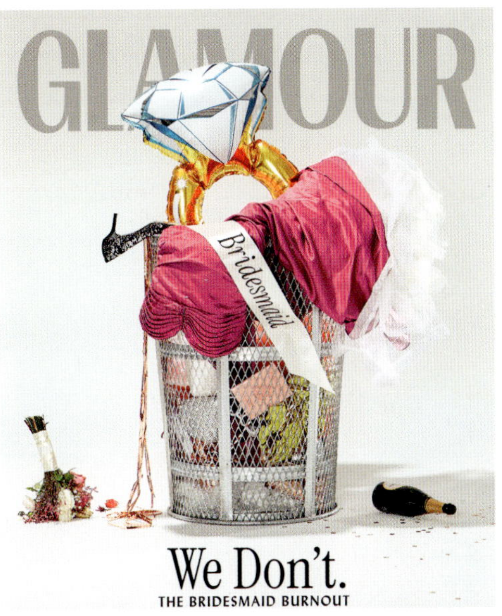

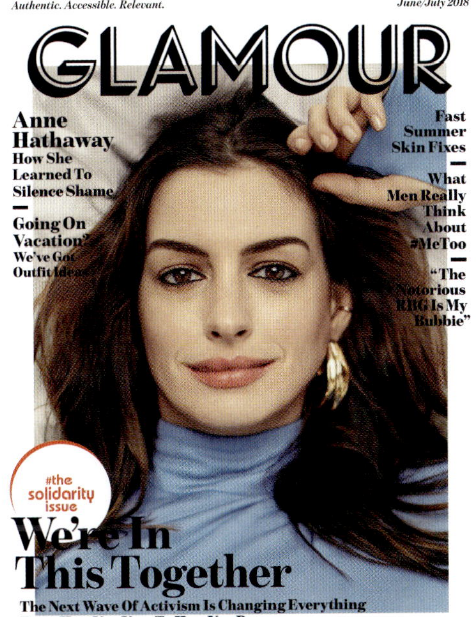

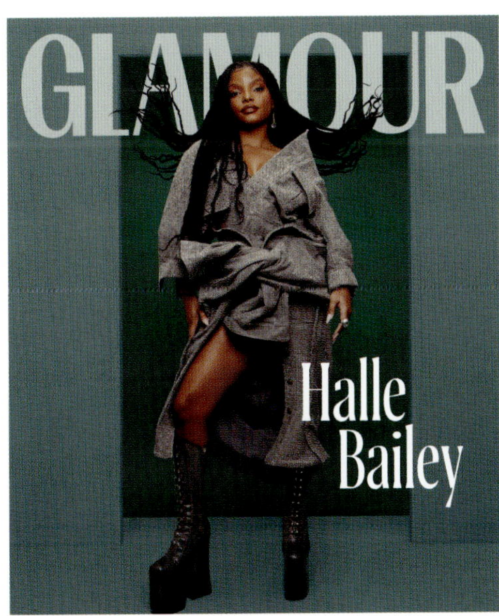

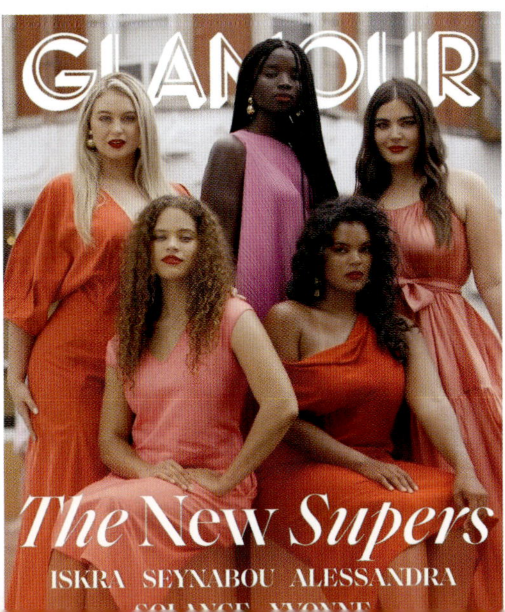

Opposite, Jane Fonda is photographed for her second ever *Glamour* cover in front of her first from 1959 (see page 105), May 2022.

←

Ahead of the 2020 Olympics (that actually took place in 2021 because of the pandemic), Simone Biles—one of the greatest gymnasts of all time—made her *Glamour* cover debut, June 2021.

↖

World Cup soccer star Alex Morgan became the first visibly pregnant woman to feature on the cover of US *Glamour*, March 2020.

←

The September 2023 cover was a departure from *Glamour*'s usual celebrity focus—calling time on the ruinously expensive bridesmaid industry, and going viral in the process.

←

The digital-first era welcomed more creativity to *Glamour*, with motion covers and topic-led issues. Here is Anne Hathaway's June/July 2018 cover.

←

Halle Bailey, star of the 2023 remake of *The Little Mermaid*, covered four global issues of *Glamour* in May 2023.

↙

In August 2019, *Glamour* unveiled a cover celebrating the supermodels for a new age—who were also champions of body positivity and runway and curve campaign stars.

DOS *and* DON'TS

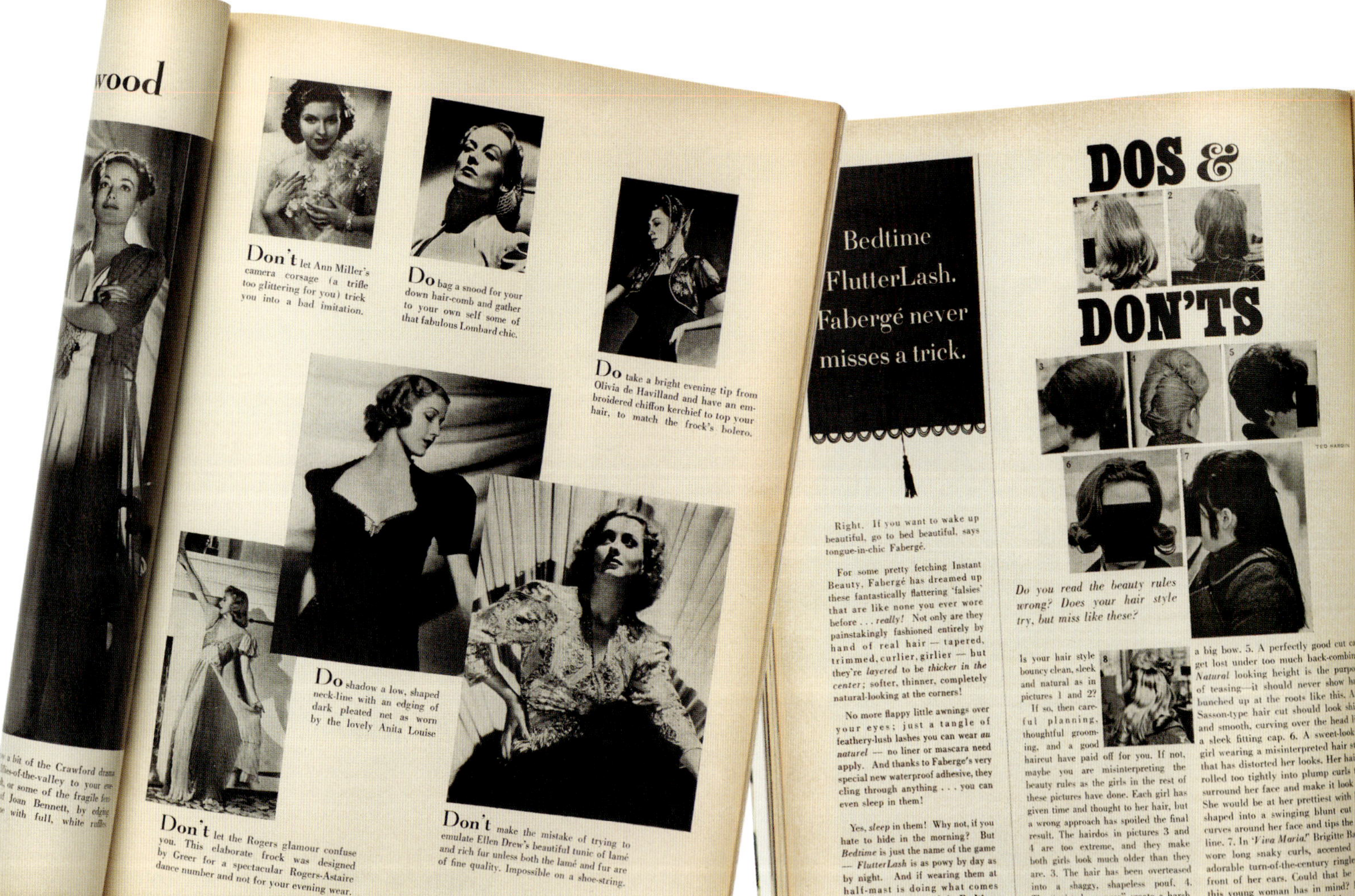

Glamour's 1992 tongue-in-cheek history book, collecting 50 years of American women's fashion sense.

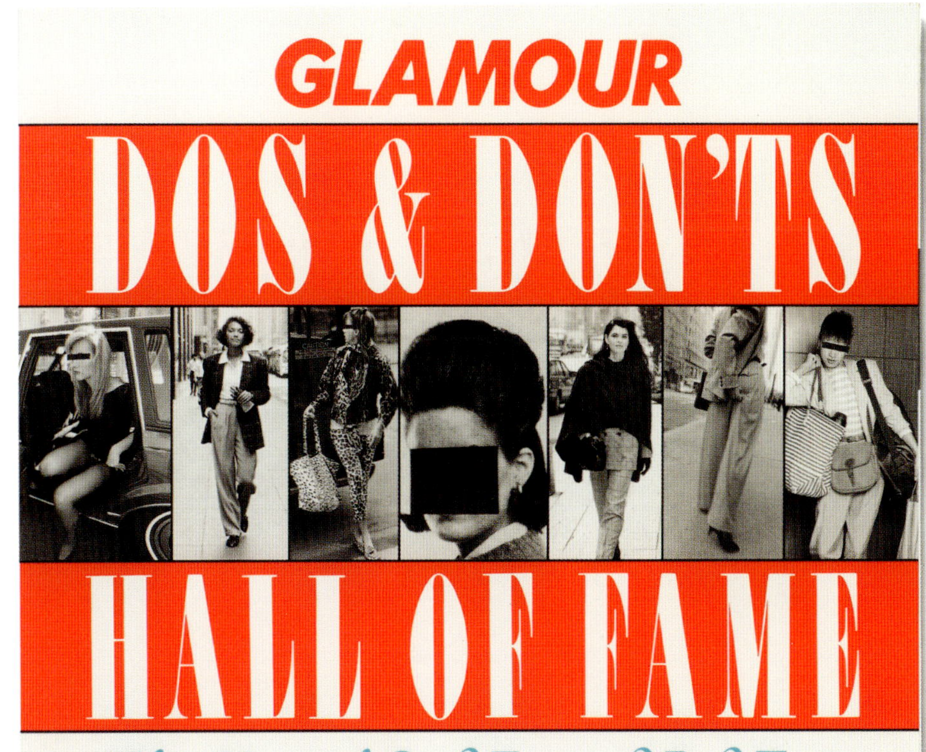

From left, Dos and Don'ts from the very first issue of *Glamour*, April 1939. The Dos and Don'ts of hair, April 1966, and of stockings, May 1985.

IN THE AUGHTS AND EARLY 2010S, Dos and Don'ts became even more influential—expanding from fashion to cover readers' sex lives, dating lives, and advice from celebrities like Gabrielle Union (her Dos and Don'ts for love) and Olivia Wilde (on turning 30). But as the culture evolved, so did *Glamour*—it became less appealing to single women out for getting things "wrong," even if it was done in a gently comic way, and even though many of the Don'ts were actually posed by *Glamour* staffers. By the time Dos and Don'ts were phased out—the last column appeared in the April 2018 issue—it was no longer about what not to wear, but only what *to* wear. It had been an extraordinary and extended run, but time was finally called.

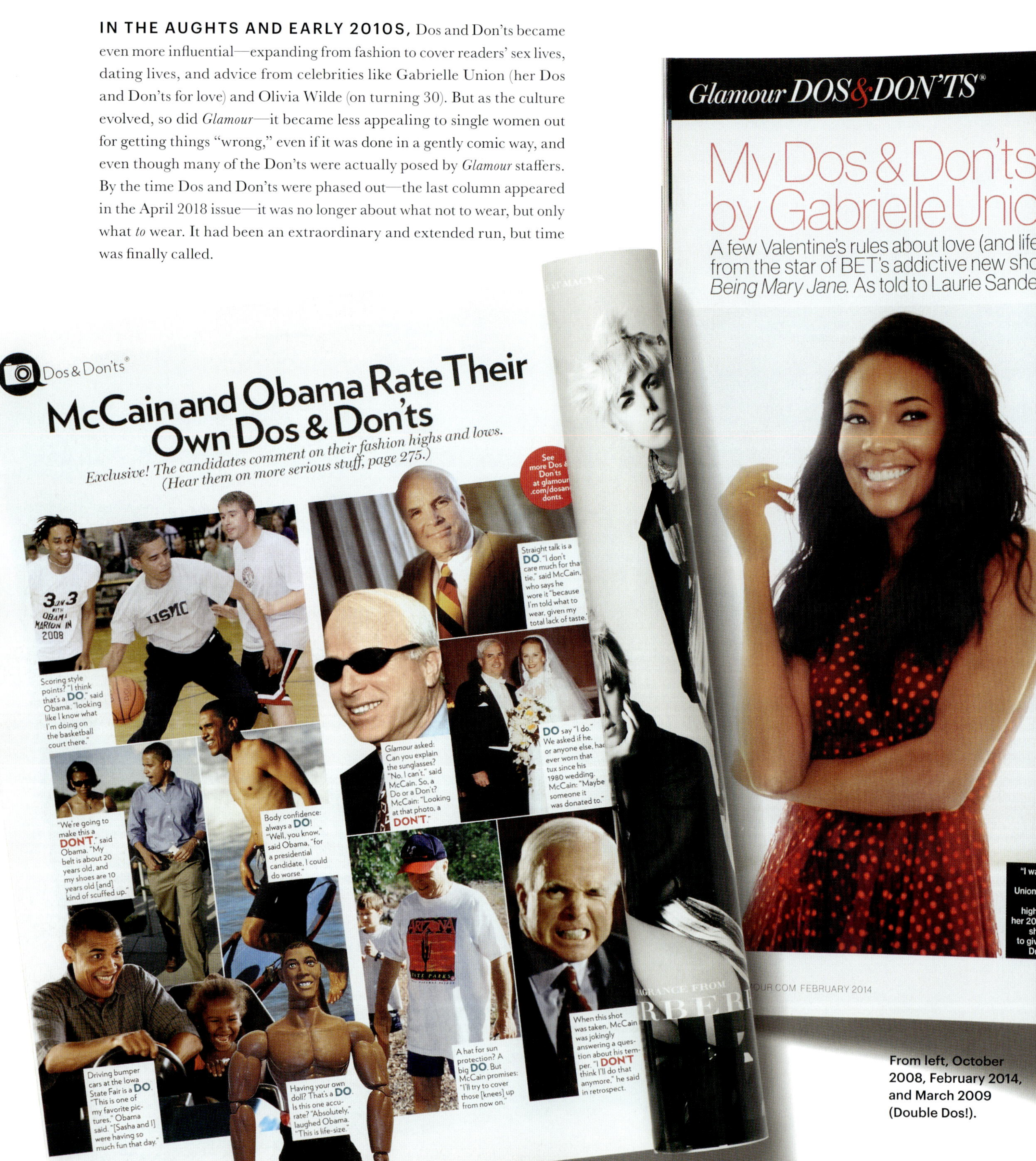

From left, October 2008, February 2014, and March 2009 (Double Dos!).

"MY DOS AND DON'TS" BY GABRIELLE UNION, FEBRUARY 2014

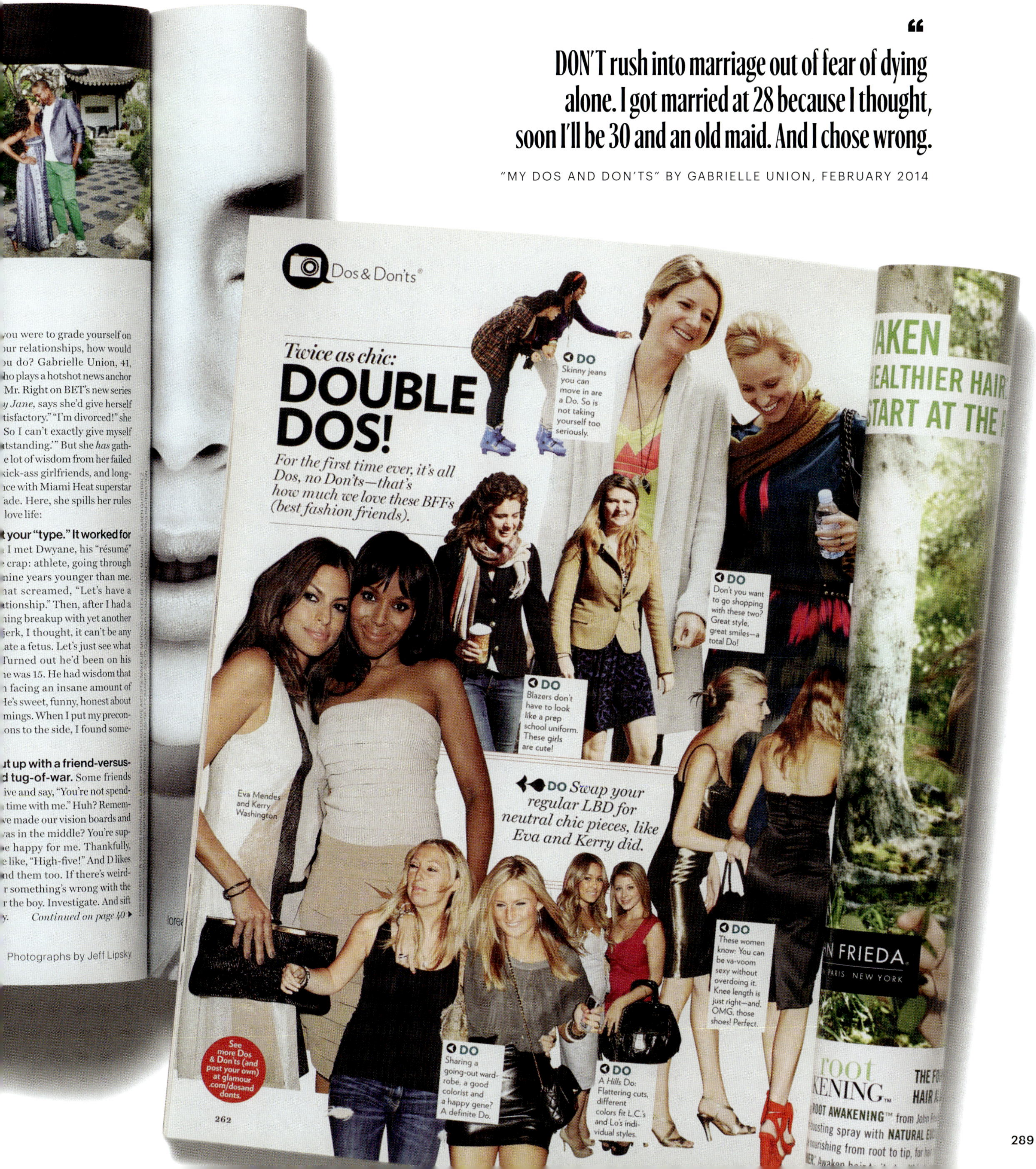

you were to grade yourself on
ur relationships, how would
u do? Gabrielle Union, 41,
ho plays a hotshot news anchor
Mr. Right on BET's new series
y Jane, says she'd give herself
tisfactory." "I'm divorced!" she
So I can't exactly give myself
tstanding.'" But she *has* gathe-
e lot of wisdom from her failed
kick-ass girlfriends, and long-
nce with Miami Heat superstar
ade. Here, she spills her rules
love life:

t your "type." It worked for
I met Dwyane, his "résumé"
crap: athlete, going through
nine years younger than me.
at screamed, "Let's have a
ationship." Then, after I had a
ning breakup with yet another
jerk, I thought, it can't be any
ate a fetus. Let's just see what
Turned out he'd been on his
e was 15. He had wisdom that
facing an insane amount of
He's sweet, funny, honest about
mings. When I put my precon-
ons to the side, I found some-

t up with a friend-versus-
d tug-of-war. Some friends
ive and say, "You're not spend-
time with me." Huh? Remem-
we made our vision boards and
as in the middle? You're sup-
e happy for me. Thankfully,
like, "High-five!" And D likes
nd them too. If there's weird-
something's wrong with the
r the boy. Investigate. And sift
y.

Continued on page 40 ▶

Photographs by Jeff Lipsky

Dos & Don'ts®

Twice as chic:
DOUBLE DOS!

For the first time ever, it's all Dos, no Don'ts—that's how much we love these BFFs (best fashion friends).

DO Skinny jeans you can move in are a Do. So is not taking yourself too seriously.

DO Don't you want to go shopping with these two? Great style, great smiles—a total Do!

DO Blazers don't have to look like a prep school uniform. These girls are cute!

♠ DO *Swap your regular LBD for neutral chic pieces, like Eva and Kerry did.*

Eva Mendes and Kerry Washington

DO These women know: You can be va-voom sexy without overdoing it. Knee length is just right—and. OMG, those shoes! Perfect.

See more Dos & Don'ts (and post your own) at glamour.com/dosand donts.

DO Sharing a going-out wardrobe, a good colorist and a happy gene? A definite Do.

DO A Hills Do: Flattering cuts, different colors fit L.C.'s and Lo's individual styles.

262

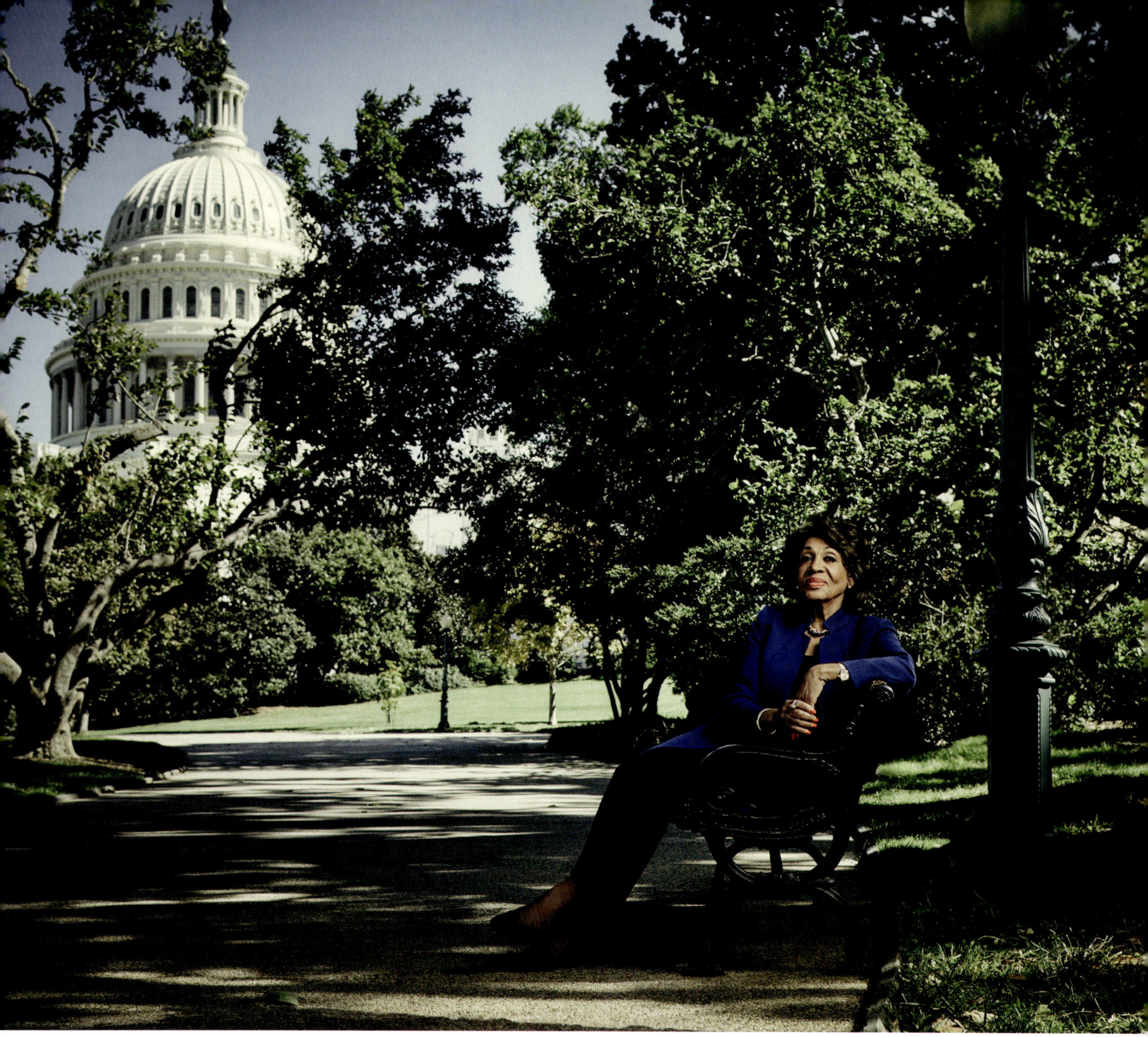

BETWEEN 2009 AND 2023, THE PERCENTAGE OF WOMEN among political leaders grew significantly. Women in the Senate increased from 17 percent to 25 percent, and in the House of Representatives from 17 percent to 28 percent. In the same time period, a quarter of all state governors were now women. While this still doesn't reflect the population as a whole, these were a huge steps forward, and *Glamour*, having long championed the importance of women's representation in politics, chronicled this shift—interviewing and photographing longtime congresswoman Maxine Waters, senators Elizabeth Warren and Kirsten Gillibrand (who both ran for the 2020 Democratic presidential nomination), businesswoman Carly Fiorina (who ran for the 2016 Republican presidential nomination), and many more. Here is a selection of the most memorable.

↑

Representative Maxine Waters of California.
Photographed by Jason Bell, December 2017.

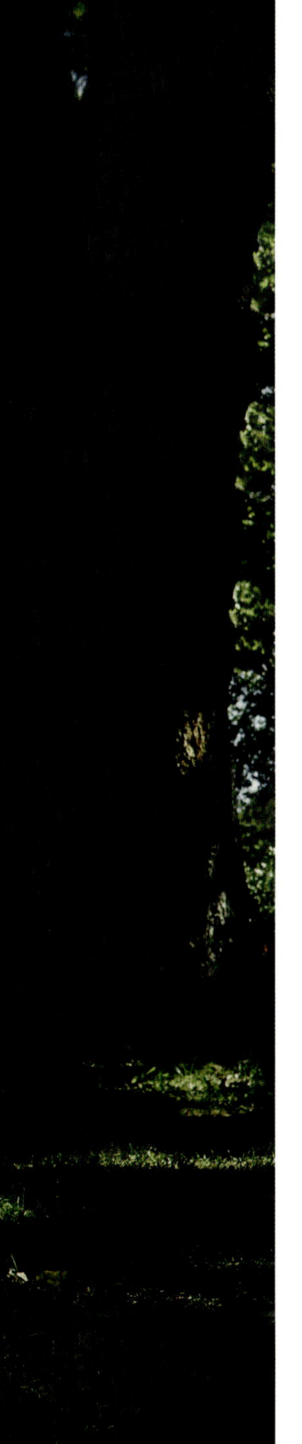

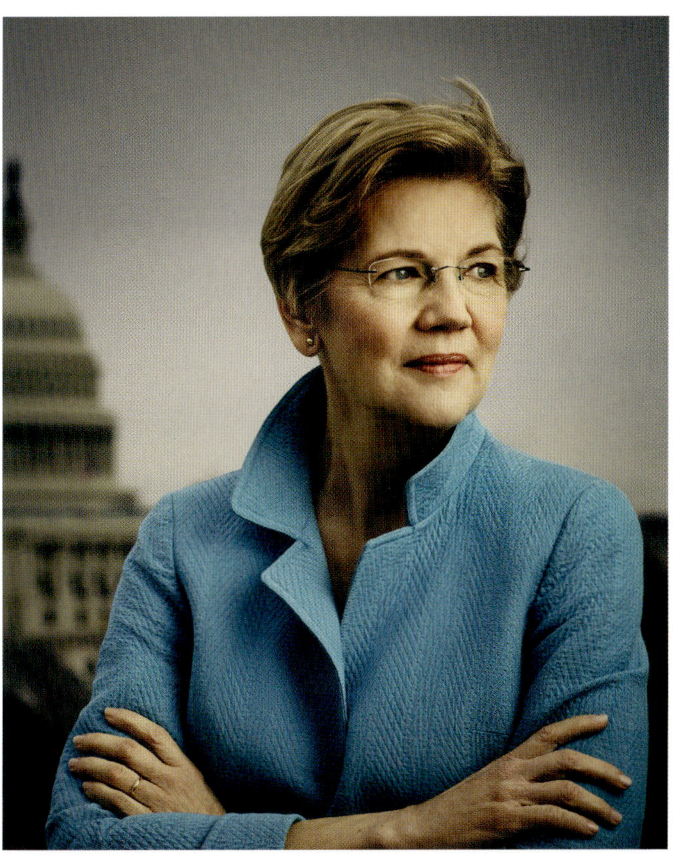

Senator Elizabeth Warren of Massachusetts. *Photographed by Jason Bell, May 2017.*

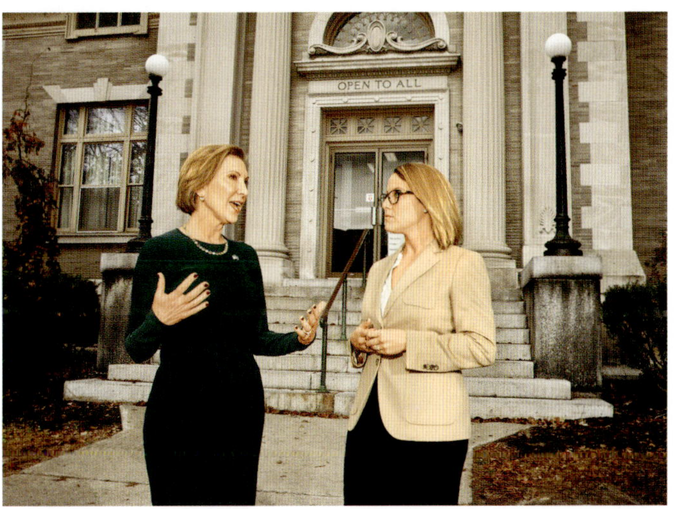

2016 Republican presidential candidate Carly Fiorina (left) talks with *Glamour* reporter Sarah Cupp. *Photographed by Jonno Rattman, February 2016.*

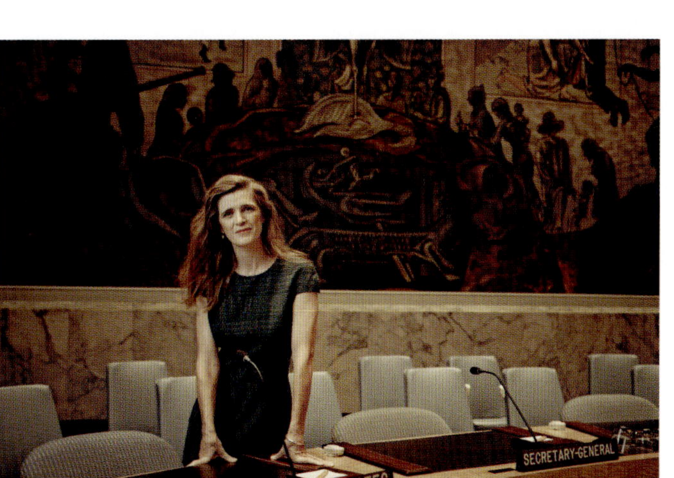

Then US ambassador to the United Nations Samantha Power. *Photographed by Jason Bell, December 2014.*

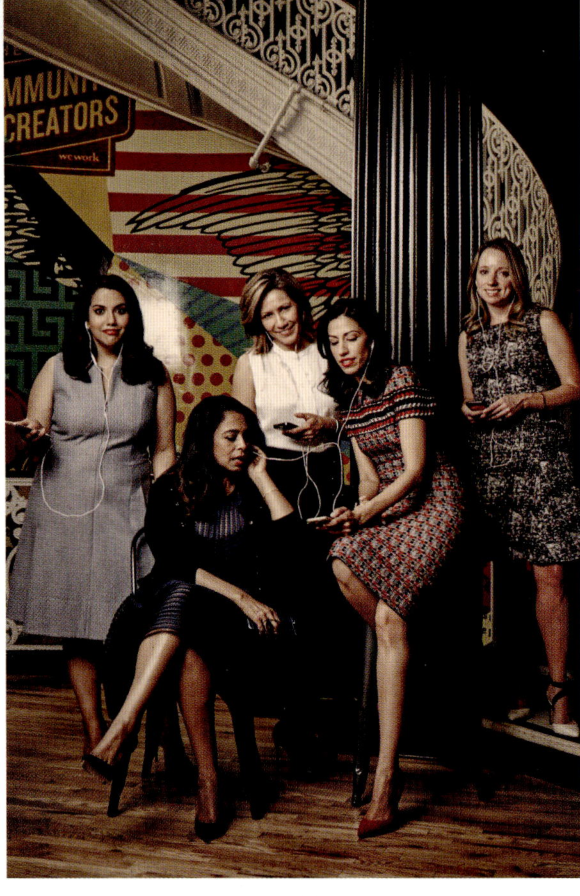

←

2016 Hillary for America campaign workers. From left, Aditi Nangia, Maya Harris, Amanda Renteria, Huma Abedin, and Kate Dowd. *Photographed by Jason Bell, September 2015.*

↓

Then US ambassador to the United Nations Nikki Haley in the UN General Assembly room in New York City. *Photographed by Winnie Au, November 2017.*

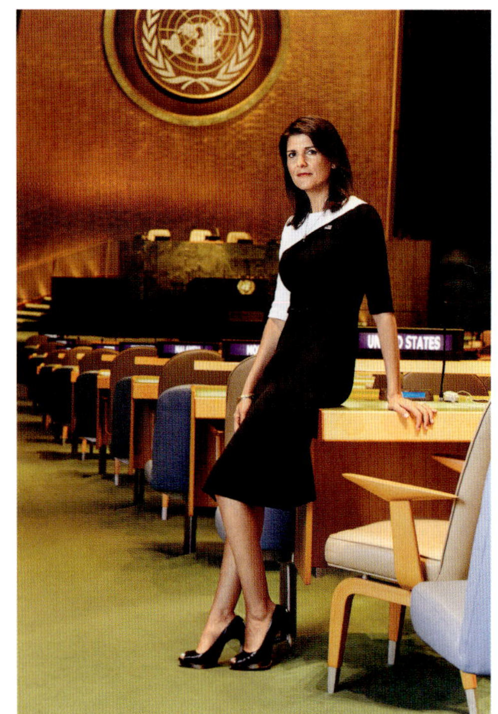

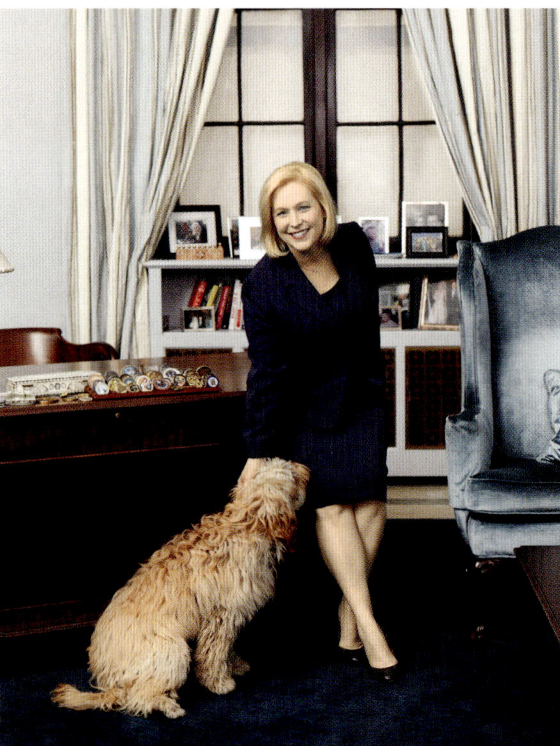

↑

Senator Kirsten Gillibrand of New York. *Photographed by Winnie Au, April 2018.*

→

Then contender for the Alabama House Arlene Easley (seated) and judge Marshell Jackson Hatcher. *Photographed by Shaniqwa Jarvis, June/July 2018.*

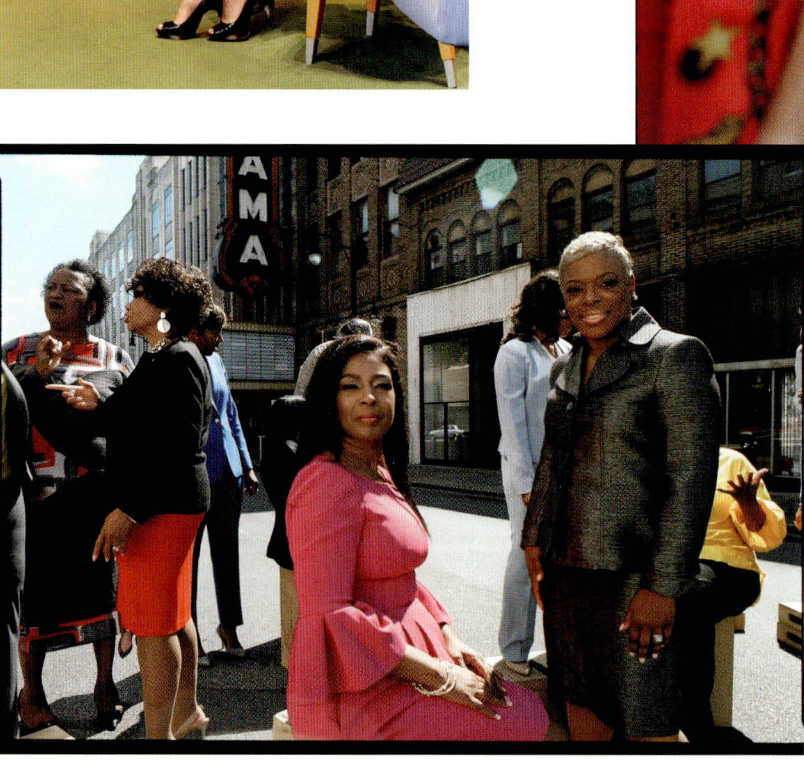

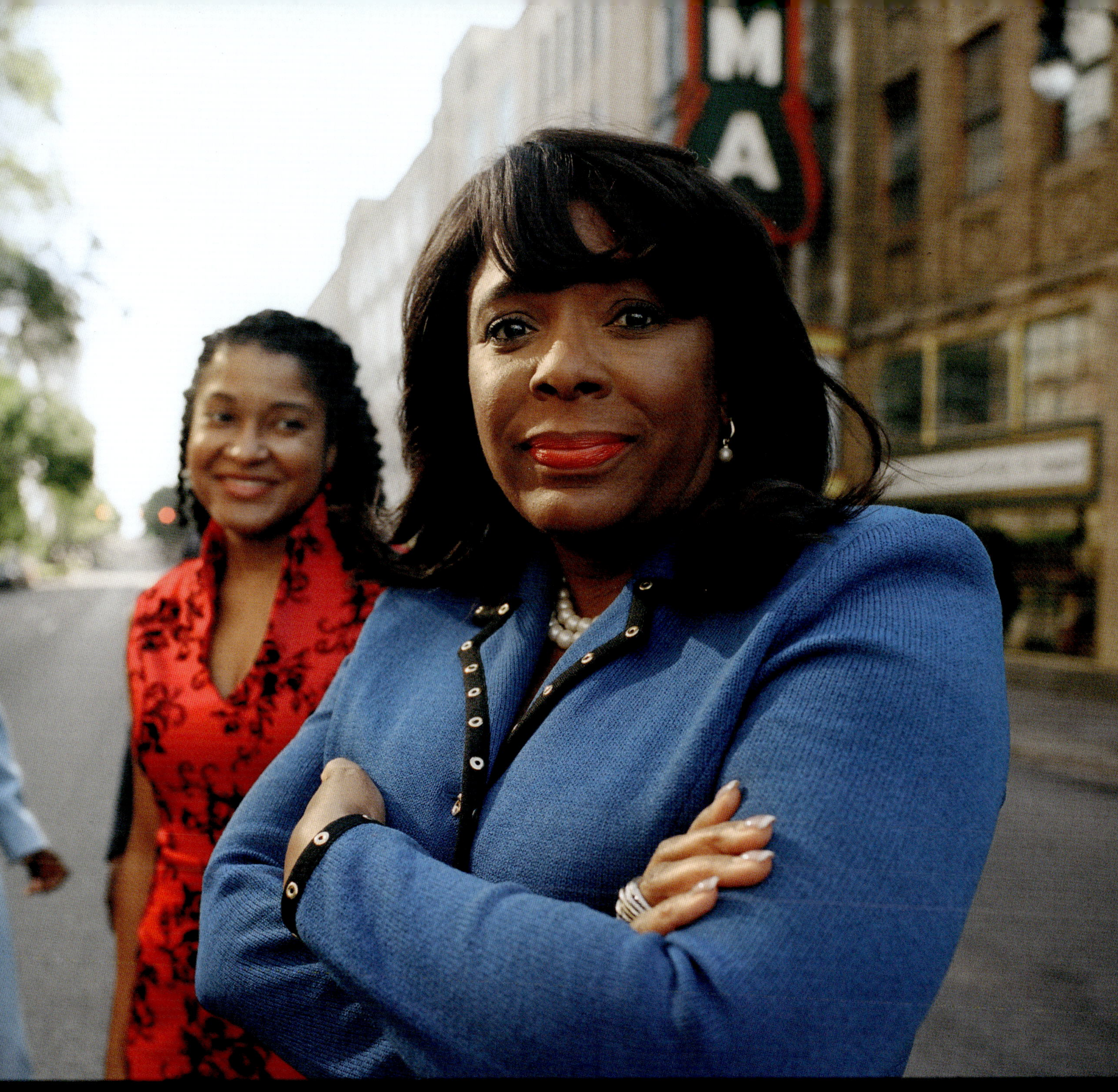

↑
Miranda Joseph and Congresswoman Terri Sewell of Alabama.
Photographed by Shaniqwa Jarvis, June/July 2018.

IN 2018, AN UNPRECEDENTED GROUNDSWELL of at least 70 Black women launched electoral campaigns across Alabama for local, state, and national offices. That year, *Glamour* documented their work in an article that appeared in print and online. Representative Terri Sewell, pictured above, was the first Black woman to represent Alabama in Congress when she was elected in 2011. She recalled, "As a congressional intern during the late eighties, I remember walking the halls of the Capitol and not seeing many black women in any role, let alone as elected officials. When I was first elected, making my voice heard as a black woman surrounded by older white men was a challenge. This year we're proving the strength of our voice at the ballot box."

Talk

Edited by **Emily Mahaney**

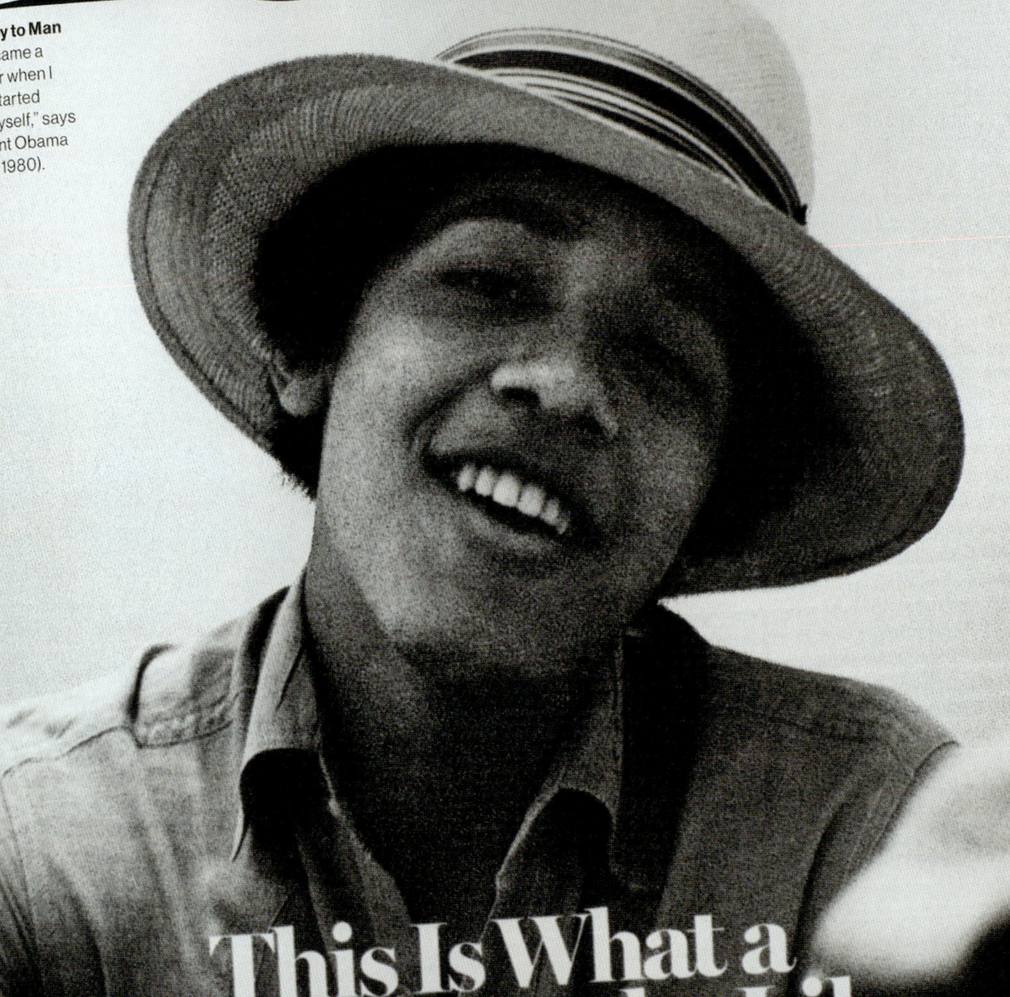

From Boy to Man
"Life became a lot easier when I simply started being myself," says President Obama (here in 1980).

This Is What a Feminist Looks Like

In his final months in office, President Barack Obama reflects on "tough guys," "bossy girls," and how stereotypes limit us *all*.

Obama for *Glamour*

In the final months of his presidency, Barack Obama penned an essay for *Glamour* in which he shared his most extensive remarks on feminism and the importance of equality. The piece was covered around the world, and its message stands the test of time. We reprint it here.

THERE ARE A LOT OF TOUGH ASPECTS to being President. But there are some perks too. Meeting extraordinary people across the country. Holding an office where you get to make a difference in the life of our nation. Air Force One.

But perhaps the greatest unexpected gift of this job has been living above the store. For many years my life was consumed by long commutes—from my home in Chicago to Springfield, Illinois, as a state senator, and then to Washington, D.C., as a United States senator. It's often meant I had to work even harder to be the kind of husband and father I want to be.

But for the past seven and a half years, that commute has been reduced to 45 seconds—the time it takes to walk from my living room to the Oval Office. As a result, I've been able to spend a lot more time watching my daughters grow up into smart, funny, kind, wonderful young women.

That isn't always easy, either—watching them prepare to leave the nest. But one thing that makes me optimistic for them is that this is an extraordinary time to be a woman. The progress we've made in the past 100 years, 50 years, and, yes, even the past eight years has made life significantly better for my daughters than it was for my grandmothers. And I say that not just as President but also as a feminist.

In my lifetime we've gone from a job market that basically confined women to a handful of often poorly paid positions to a moment when women not only make up roughly half the workforce but are leading in every sector, from sports to space, from Hollywood to the Supreme Court. I've witnessed how women have won the freedom to make your own choices about how you'll live your lives—about your bodies, your educations, your careers, your finances. Gone are the days when you needed a husband to get a credit card. In fact, more women than ever, married or single, are financially independent.

So we shouldn't downplay how far we've come. That would do a disservice to all those who spent their lives fighting for justice. At the same time, there's still a lot of work we need to do to improve the prospects of women and girls here and around the world. And while I'll keep working on good policies—from equal pay for equal work to protecting reproductive rights—there are some changes that have nothing to do with passing new laws.

In fact, the most important change may be the toughest of all—and that's changing ourselves.

This is something I spoke about at length in June at the first ever White House Summit on the United State of Women. As far as we've come, all too often we are still boxed in by stereotypes about how men and women should behave. One of my heroines is Congresswoman Shirley Chisholm, who was the first African American to run for a major party's presidential nomination. She once said, "The emotional, sexual, and psychological stereotyping of females begins when the doctor says, 'It's a girl.'" We know that these stereotypes affect how girls see themselves starting at a very young age, making them feel that if they don't look or act a certain way, they are somehow less worthy. In fact, gender stereotypes affect all of us, regardless of our gender, gender identity, or sexual orientation.

Now, the most important people in my life have always been women. I was raised by a single mom, who spent much of her career working to empower women in developing countries. I watched as my grandmother, who helped raise me, worked her way up at a bank only to hit a glass ceiling. I've seen how Michelle has balanced the demands of a busy ➡

career and raising a family. Like many working mothers, she worried about the expectations and judgments of how she should handle the trade-offs, knowing that few people would question my choices. And the reality was that when our girls were young, I was often away from home serving in the state legislature, while also juggling my teaching responsibilities as a law professor. I can look back now and see that, while I helped out, it was usually on my schedule and on my terms. The burden disproportionately and unfairly fell on Michelle.

So I'd like to think that I've been pretty aware of the unique challenges women face—it's what has shaped my own feminism. But I also have to admit that when you're the father of two daughters, you become even more aware of how gender stereotypes pervade our society. You see the subtle and not-so-subtle social cues transmitted through culture. You feel the enormous pressure girls are under to look and behave and even think a certain way. And those same stereotypes affected my own consciousness as a young man.

Growing up without a dad, I spent a lot of time trying to figure out who I was, how the world perceived me, and what kind of man I wanted to be. It's easy to absorb all kinds of messages from society about masculinity and come to believe that there's a right way and a wrong way to be a man. But as I got older, I realized that my ideas about being a tough guy or cool guy just weren't me. They were a manifestation of my youth and insecurity. Life became a lot easier when I simply started being myself.

So we need to break through these limitations. We need to keep changing the attitude that raises our girls to be demure and our boys to be assertive, that criticizes our daughters for speaking out and our sons for shedding a tear. We need to keep changing the attitude that punishes women for their sexuality and rewards men for theirs.

We need to keep changing the attitude that permits the routine harassment of women, whether they're walking down the street or daring to go online. We need to keep changing the attitude that teaches men to feel threatened by the presence and success of women.

We need to keep changing the attitude that congratulates men for changing a diaper, stigmatizes full-time dads, and penalizes working mothers. We need to keep changing the attitude that values being confident, competitive, and ambitious in the workplace—unless you're a woman. Then you're being too bossy, and suddenly the very qualities you thought were necessary for success end up holding you back.

We need to keep changing a culture that shines a particularly unforgiving light on women and girls of color. Michelle has often spoken about this. Even after achieving success in her own right, she still held doubts; she had to worry about whether she looked the right way or was acting the right way—whether she was being too assertive or too "angry."

That's what twenty-first century feminism is about: the idea that when everybody is equal, we are all more free.

PRESIDENT BARACK OBAMA

As a parent, helping your kids to rise above these constraints is a constant learning process. Michelle and I have raised our daughters to speak up when they see a double standard or feel unfairly judged based on their gender or race—or when they notice that happening to someone else. It's important for them to see role models out in the world who climb to the highest levels of whatever field they choose. And yes, it's important that their dad is a feminist, because now that's what they expect of all men.

It is absolutely men's responsibility to fight sexism too. And as spouses and partners and boyfriends, we need to work hard and be deliberate about creating truly equal relationships.

The good news is that everywhere I go across the country, and around the world, I see people pushing back against dated assumptions about gender roles. From the young men who've joined our It's On Us campaign to end campus sexual assault, to the young women who became the first female Army Rangers in our nation's history, your generation refuses to be bound by old ways of thinking. And you're helping all of us understand that forcing people to adhere to outmoded, rigid notions of identity isn't good for anybody—men, women, gay, straight, transgender, or otherwise. These stereotypes limit our ability to simply be ourselves.

This fall we enter a historic election. Two hundred and forty years after our nation's founding, and almost a century after women finally won the right to vote, for the first time ever, a woman is a major political party's presidential nominee. No matter your political views, this is a historic moment for America. And it's just one more example of how far women have come on the long journey toward equality.

I want all of our daughters and sons to see that this, too, is their inheritance. I want them to know that it's never been just about the Benjamins; it's about the Tubmans too. And I want them to help do their part to ensure that America is a place where every single child can make of her life what she will.

That's what twenty-first century feminism is about: the idea that when everybody is equal, we are all more free.

→

Barack, Michelle, Sasha, and Malia embrace in November 2008.

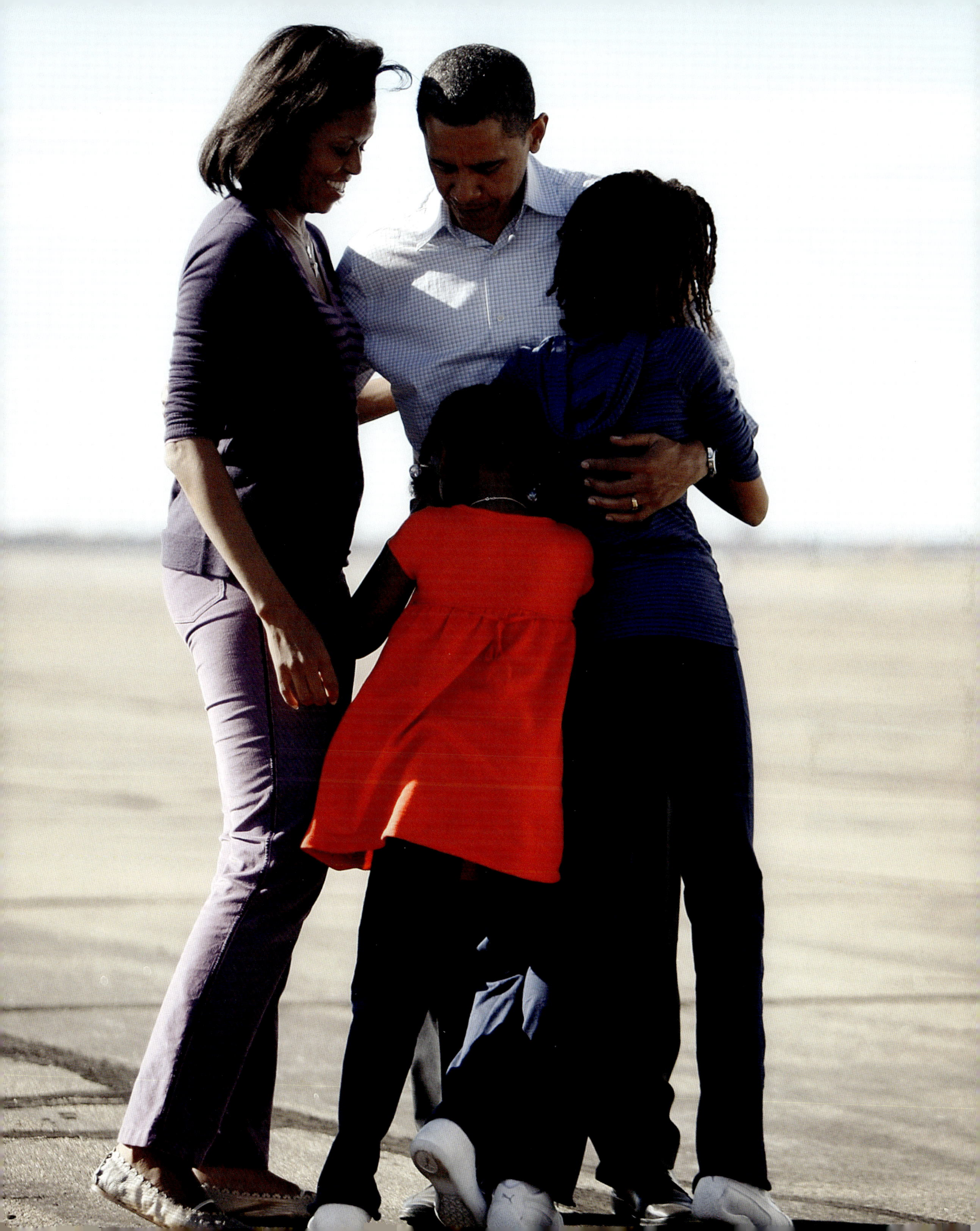

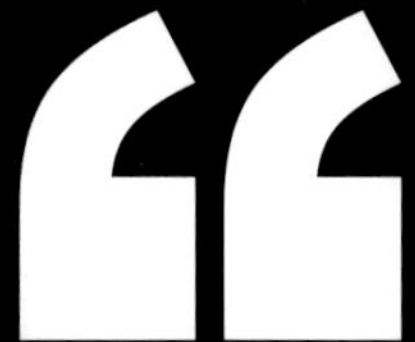

Run toward fear in the racial conversation. When your heart starts beating fast... step into it. Resist the impulse to circumnavigate. We think we can't be uncomfortable even for a second, when in fact, we can and we must if we want to move the needle on issues that have life-and-death consequences.

"IT'S TIME TO BREAK OUR 'COMFORTABLE SILENCE' ON RACE,"
ELIZABETH ALEXANDER, SEPTEMBER 2015

" Feminism is not 'one size fits all.' Sexism and oppression can be specific to class and race: For instance, African American women are often told their natural or braided hair is 'inappropriate' for work or school. It's important to understand that racism and sexism are inevitably intertwined. These are all our issues.

"THE DOS AND DON'TS OF BEING A FEMINIST " IN 2016" BY RASHIDA JONES, JUNE 2016

" FOR CISGENDER MEN WHO HAVE SEX WITH WOMEN, IT IS NOT JUST CRUEL BUT DELUDED TO ASSUME THAT CONTRACEPTION IS HER RESPONSIBILITY, THAT IF SHE GETS PREGNANT, SHE'LL HANDLE IT.

"MEN SHOULD ABSOLUTELY BE OBSESSED WITH CONTRACEPTION" BY JENNY SINGER, JULY 2022

" YOU MAY WONDER WHY PRONOUNS MATTER, OR FEEL LIKE IT'S A LOT TO ASK TO CALL SOMEONE SOMETHING OTHER THAN WHAT THEIR BIOLOGY CLEARLY LOOKS LIKE. THE THING IS, WHAT WE CALL SOMEONE CHANGES HOW WE SEE AND TREAT THEM. BECAUSE MAN, WOMAN, OR SMACK IN THE GORGEOUS GRAY ZONE OF ANDROGYNY, EVERYONE LOVES TO BE ACKNOWLEDGED AND GIVEN THE OPPORTUNITY TO WEIGH IN ON HOW THEY ARE DISCUSSED.

"HE, SHE, THEY?" BY IO TILLET WRIGHT, MARCH 2017

" Don't be bogged down by your past.... Consider your baggage (bad boyfriends, job setbacks, body issues) lost by the airline of life, leaving you empty-handed at your new destination with only one choice: Go shopping.

"THE DOS AND DON'TS OF TURNING 30" BY OLIVIA WILDE, SEPTEMBER 2013

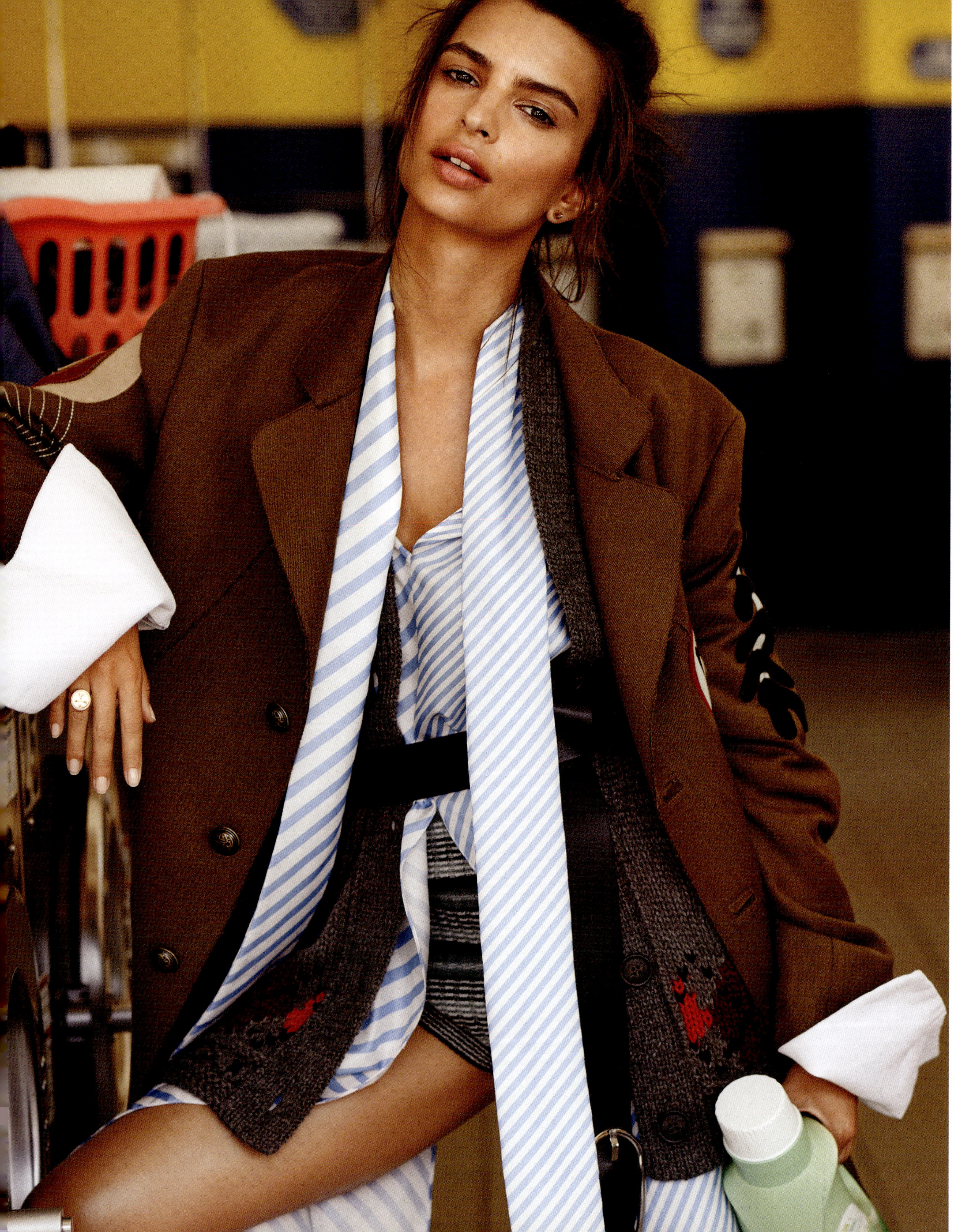

The Feminist Debate

AS WOMEN IN AMERICA took charge of their careers, finances, relationships, and sexuality in ways that women growing up in previous decades could only have hoped for, a heated debate around what feminism stood for arose. Could you be a feminist and pose in your underwear? Could you preach sex and sexual liberation, and still fight sexism? It may seem like a no-brainer today (for why shouldn't women embrace all parts of themselves, as long as they are not being coerced?), but in the early 2010s, it provoked fierce arguments. It came to a head in *Glamour* in 2014, the year Gloria Steinem—a figurehead of the '70s feminist movement—turned 80. In January of that year, the actor Rashida Jones wrote a column for the magazine in which she criticized the pornification of culture. "I understand that owning and expressing our sexuality is a huge step forward for women," she argued. "But, in my opinion, we are at a point of oversaturation.… I consider myself a feminist. I think all women have the right to express their desires. But I will look at women with influence—millionaire women who use their 'sexiness' to make money—and ask some questions." Her column generated such a huge response, both in support and against, that *Glamour* conducted a survey of 1,000 readers to get their views—50 percent said they didn't like stars stripping down, although 63 percent also blamed the media for pressuring female stars to bare all.

One person who disagreed was model and author Emily Ratajkowski. The cover star of *Glamour*'s October 2016 issue, she argued that women and men were being held to different—unequal—standards when it came to their sexuality. "The ideal feminist world shouldn't be one where women suppress their human instincts for attention and desire," she wrote in an essay for the magazine. "We shouldn't be weighed down with the responsibility of explaining our every move. We shouldn't have to apologize for wanting attention either. We don't owe anyone an explanation. It's not our responsibility to change the way we are seen—it's society's responsibility to change the way it sees *us*."

←

Emily Ratajkowski.
*Photographed by
Carter Smith,
October 2016.*

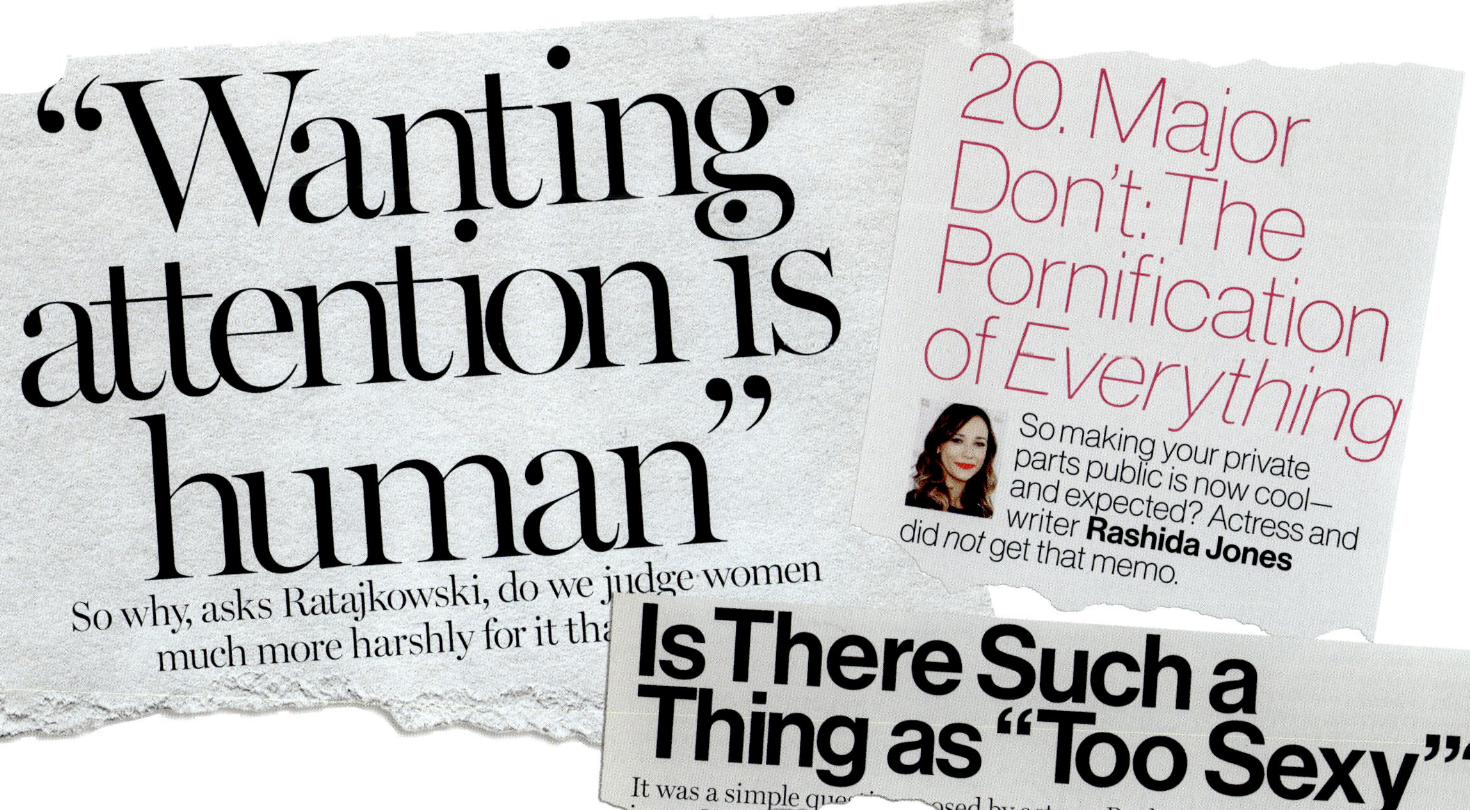

2010 ONWARDS SAW *Glamour* commit to more inclusive fashion. The magazine published standalone fashion supplements "Chic at Any Size" and "Size 12 and Up." It introduced a new monthly feature, "Style Your Size," and ensured shopping advice covered women of all sizes. When *Glamour*'s new editor in chief Samantha Barry took over in 2018, her first cover as editor in chief featured Melissa McCarthy, who proudly did not fit the sample size mold. In September 2019 Barry commissioned a fashion issue cover celebrating "The New Supers"—models of the future, all size 12 and above. On its release, she told CBS News, "They're sizes 12 to 16, but they represent so much more than that. Sixty-eight percent of women in America are over a size 14, but they're only seen in 2 percent of media." In that same issue, the staff of the magazine also launched a series called The "F" Word. As *Glamour*'s then senior beauty editor Lindsay Schallon, the author of the main piece, wrote, "F stands for 'fat.' Yes, fat, and I don't mean that pejoratively. Women in the body-positive space are reclaiming the term for what it is, simply an adjective that describes their physical attributes. No longer is it—or should it be—a dirty word…. Our goal…is not to ostracize. What we're hoping to do now is move forward and break down the barriers holding us all back, so we can have truly honest conversations about our bodies." It was a bold, and positive, reclaiming of a term that had been used largely negatively—even by *Glamour* itself in previous eras (see page 76). But, no longer.

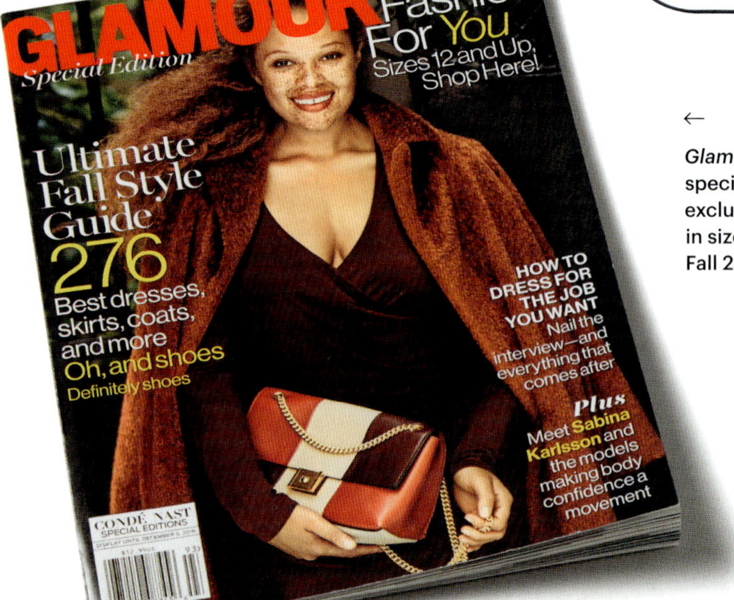

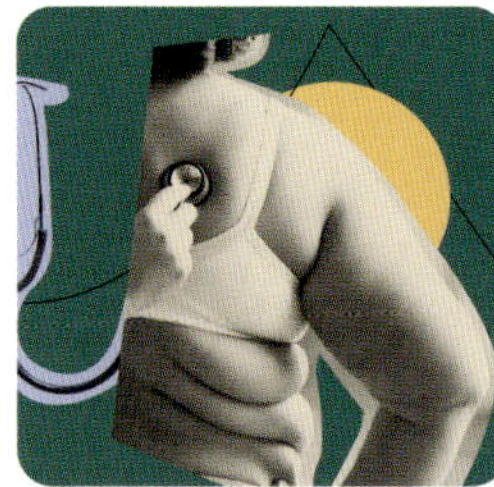
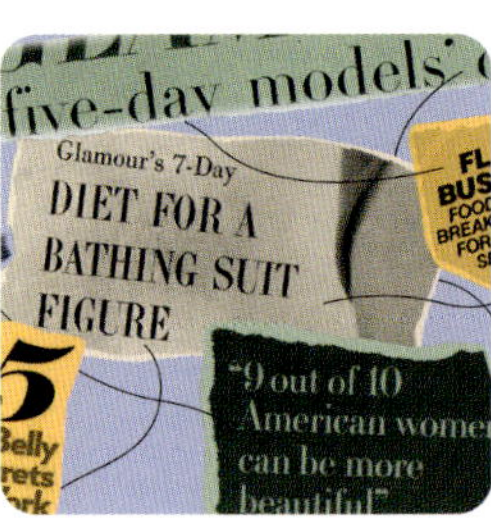
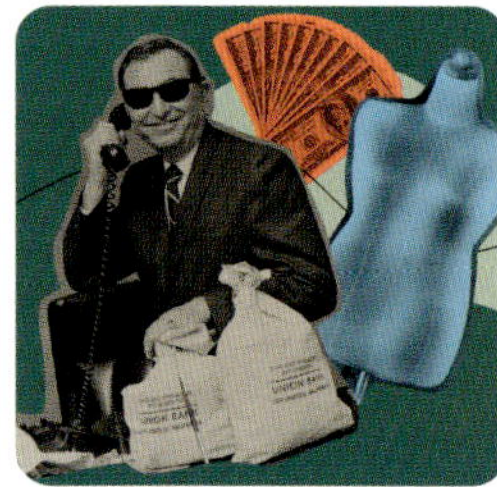

The 'F' Word

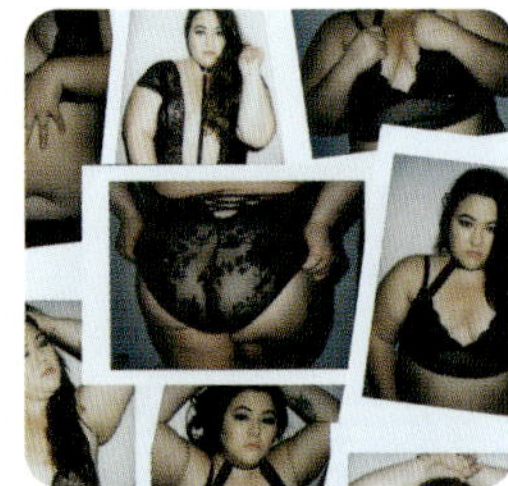
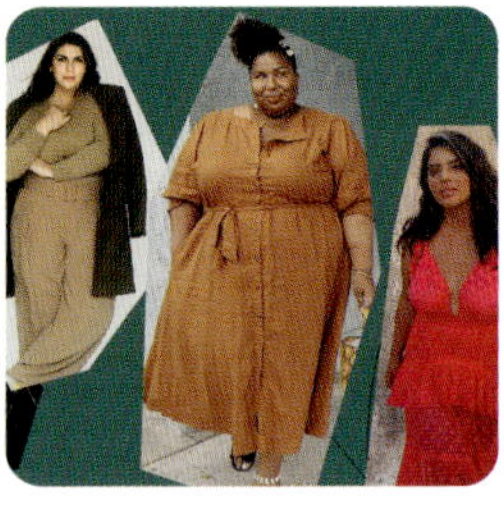
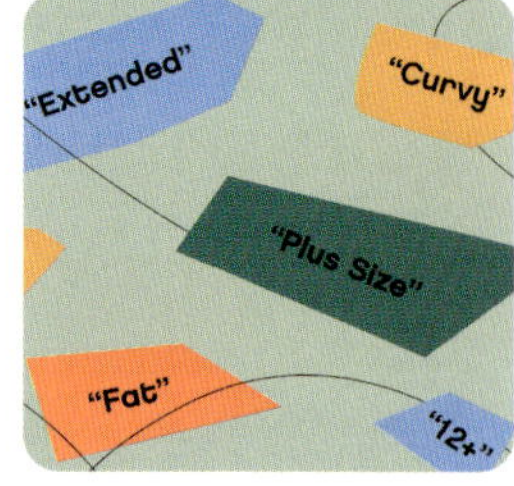

←
Glamour's second special issue focused exclusively on fashion in sizes 12 and up, Fall 2016.

↑
Glamour's The "F" Word package, launched in 2019.

→
Models wearing sports bras and fitness pants for *Glamour*'s Plus-Size Fashion Awards. *Photographed for Glamour.com, August 2019.*

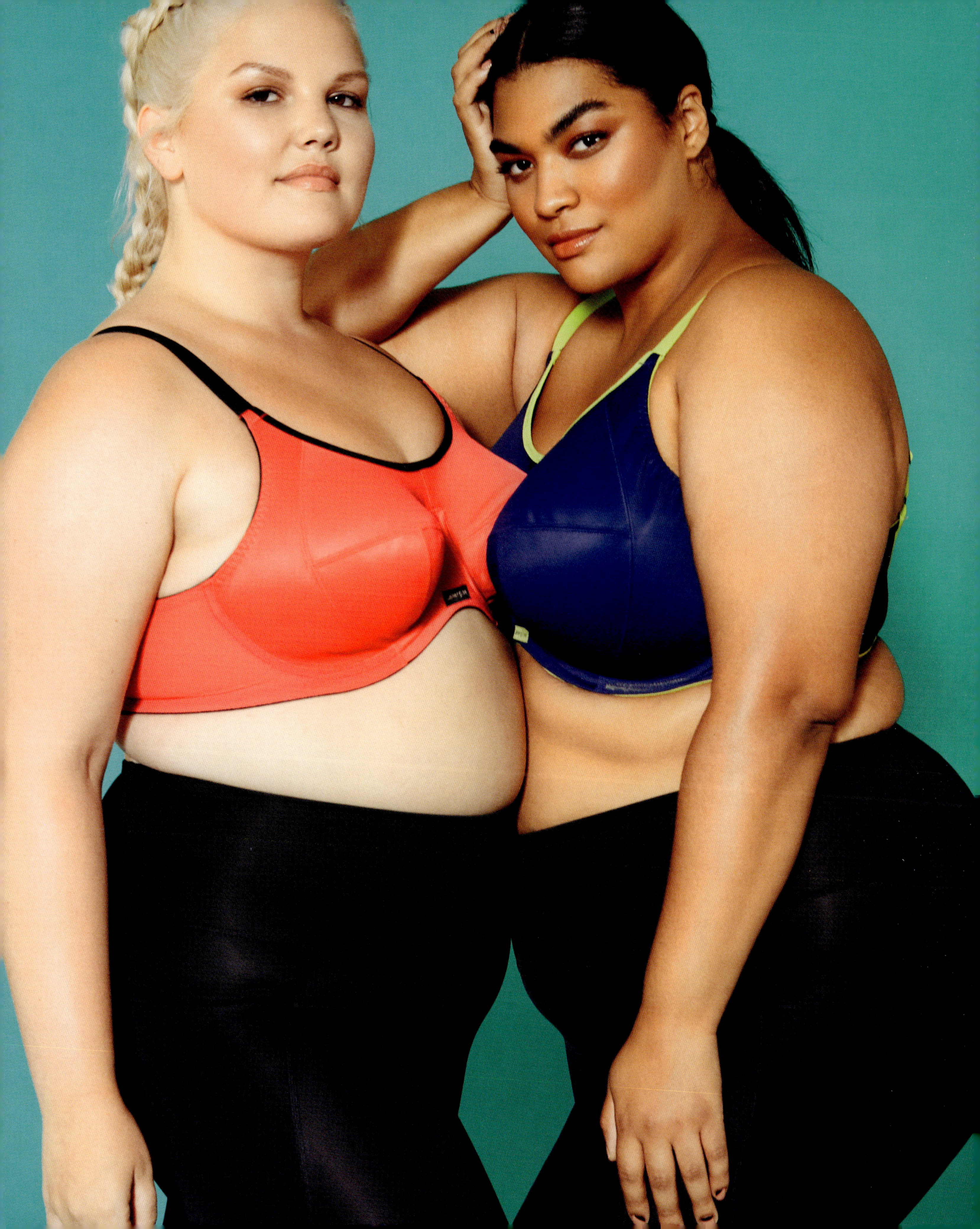

Samantha Barry

In January 2018, at a time of enormous cultural and societal change, Samantha Barry was appointed *Glamour*'s seventh editor in chief. With audiences accessing information in new ways, the magazine had to evolve. Here, Barry shares the story of *Glamour*'s transition to digital.

"My background was in radio, television, and social media. For over a decade, before I joined Glamour in 2018, I worked to create content that was available instantly. And increasingly, that's how people wanted to access content: immediately, and on devices that they carried around in their pockets. It's the art of storytelling that I wanted to evolve when I made the decision in January 2019, alongside the company, to take *Glamour* fully digital. It wasn't something I came to lightly. *Glamour* has such an extraordinary history in print. We were there for women during the war, when they were stepping into the workplace in record numbers, and we were by their side as they fought for reproductive rights, for their right to buy a house without a man, to choose whether to get married or not, or raise children or not. We also always met them where they were. As a young journalist, I consumed endless print magazines and newspapers. Whenever I was in an airport, I'd buy every magazine on the shelves, and then read every word. Then, like so many women, I started to access the information I wanted from different places—I read long-form pieces on my phone on the subway to work, I checked social media first thing in the morning to get up to date on what people were talking about, I listened to podcasts on the way home. It's not that I had stopped enjoying the content that newspapers and magazines put out there (I still love to read print), but I was finding it in different places. It was finding me in different places. I feel honored that I spent a year—from January 2018 to January 2019—working on *Glamour* in print. It taught me so much about the title, its history, and what it meant to devoted readers. But so many of them were now online, where everything was to a timeline of a minute, or even a millisecond. Moving to digital offered a chance for us to break new ground—to report faster, more interactively, and more immersively.

It was a tough transition, but I was also so excited and optimistic about new ways of storytelling—be that our podcasts, our videos, our online features, our social media, or leading the way in live event coverage—that I knew it was ultimately the right decision. I remember the wedding of Harry and Meghan, the Duke and Duchess of Sussex, in May 2018. I got the whole team in the office early, brought in British food and snacks, set up a huge television so everyone could watch, and we knocked it out of the park. We had enormous traffic, the team rallied together, and I think everyone understood the power of what we could achieve as a digital brand. Today, we continue to evolve our storytelling with new multimedia formats, and we are still entertaining our readers with fashion, beauty, and entertainment, and fighting for women's rights as *Glamour* always has—be that through our award-winning campaigning for paid family leave, or our reportage from countries in conflict like Ukraine and Afghanistan. Just this time, we can reach them in real time.

I would like to think that in 2039, on the hundredth anniversary of this title, that our readers look to us and feel that we're as relevant—if not more relevant—to women's lives than we've ever been."

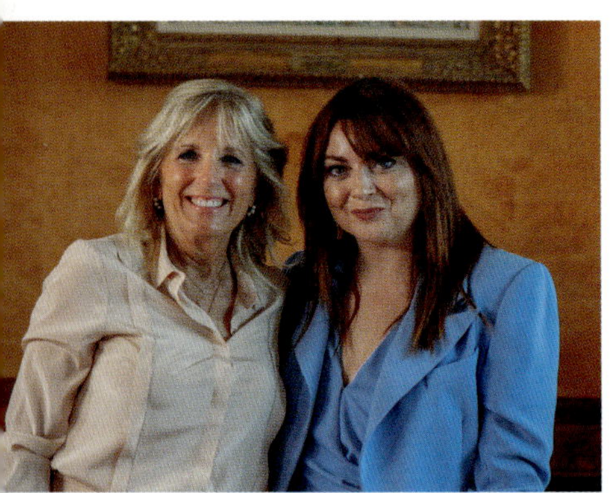

↓

Amal Clooney and Barry at a pop-up legal clinic in central Malawi. *Photographed by Thoko Chikondi, December 2023.*

↑

Samantha Barry with Jill Biden during an exclusive interview at the White House. *Photographed by Calla Kessler, June 2021.*

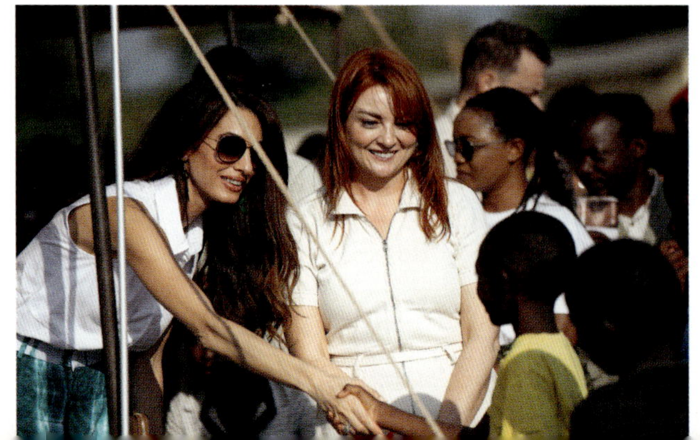

→

Barry in her sixth year as editor in chief. *Photographed by Rick Wenner, 2023.*

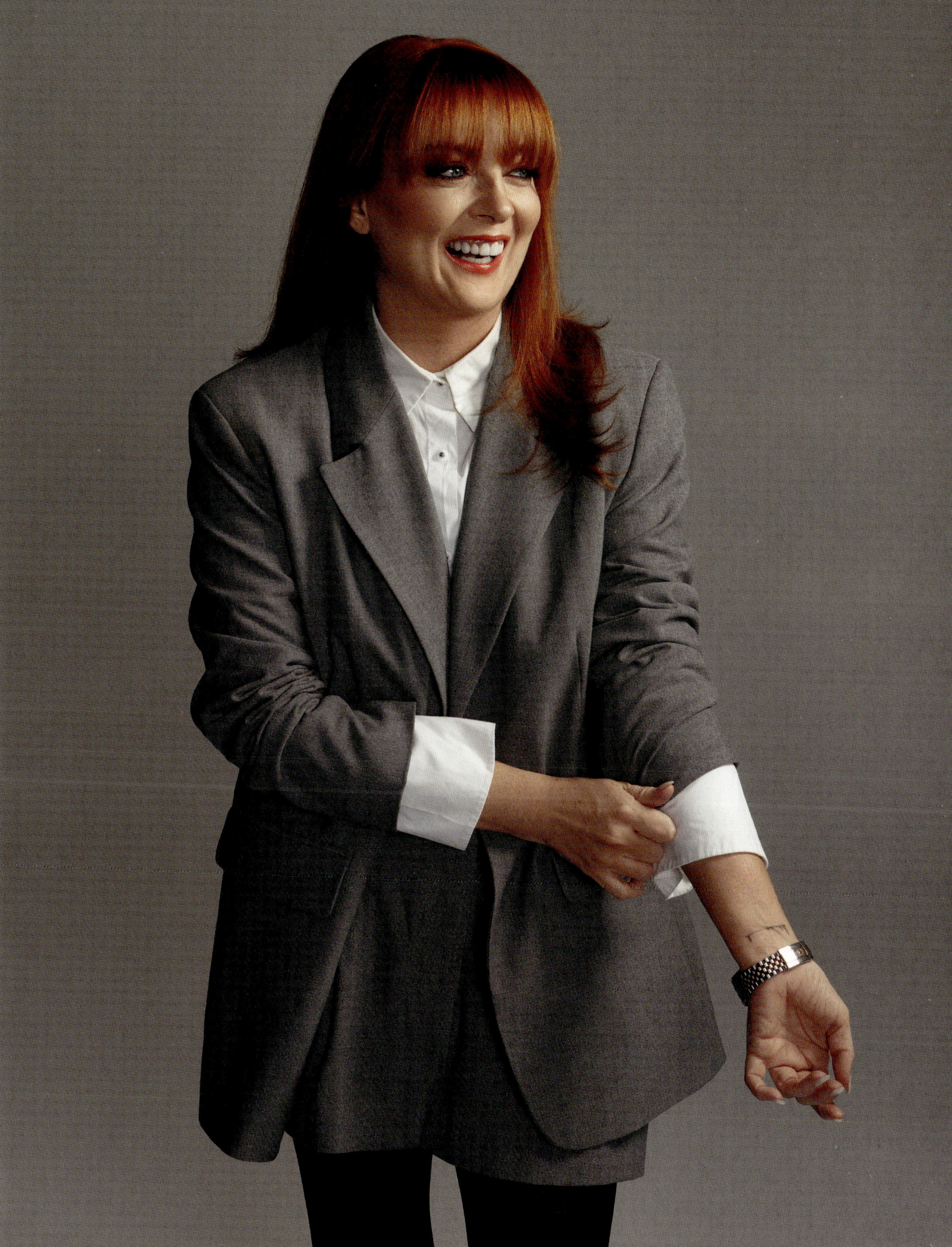

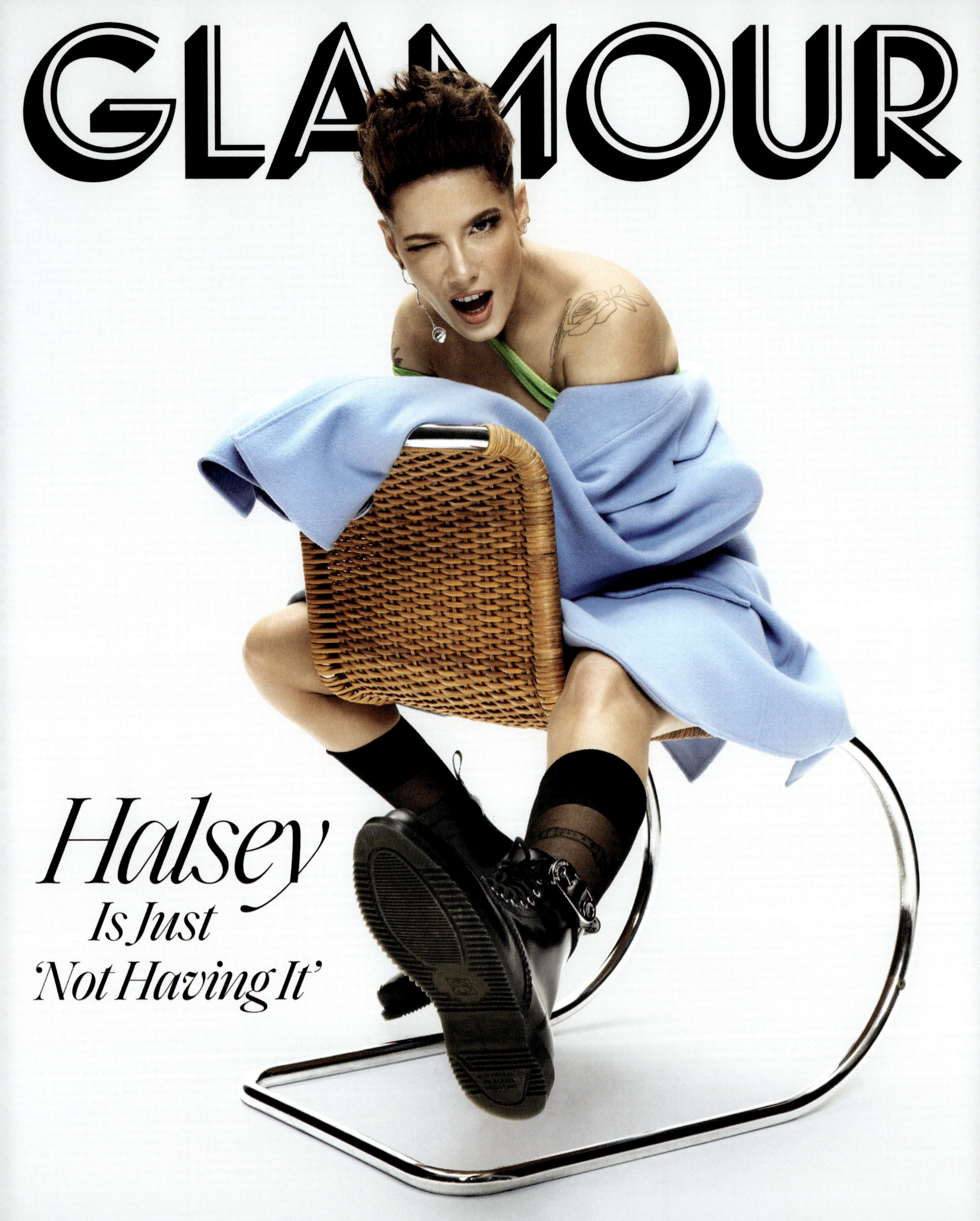

GLAMOUR
Halsey
Is Just
'Not Having It'

Glamour Goes Digital

JANUARY 2019 MARKED THE LAST MONTHLY
print issue of *Glamour*. It was a brave and exciting decision. While Glamour had long been interacting with readers off the printed page—the career councils and events of the 1940s and 1950s, the annual Women of the Year live summits in New York City, a conversation to mark International Day of the Girl with Michelle Obama in Washington, DC—readers were increasingly in the digital world, and it was time to meet them there. The leap online enabled new formats—not just a website, but a thriving digital video and social offering, and the creation of a suite of hit podcasts, including *Broken Harts*, examining a tragic murder and the true story behind a seemingly "perfect" family.

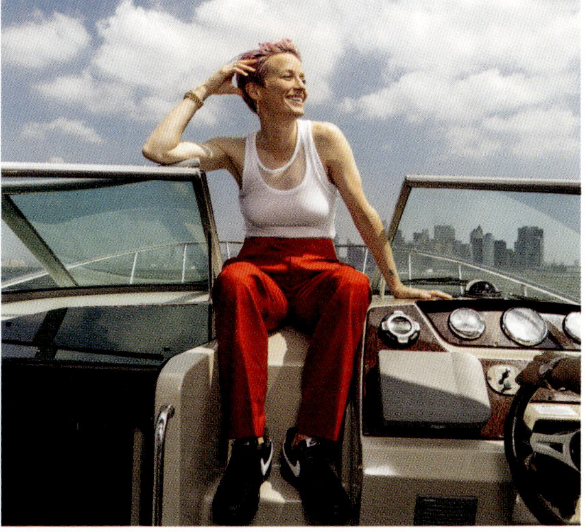

← Halsey on *Glamour*'s first digital cover, January 2019.

↙ Amber Heard on *Glamour*'s final monthly print issue, January 2019.

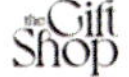

Glamour's *Broken Harts* podcast. *Photographed by Holly Andres, December 2018.*

← The website, where Glamour continues evolving.

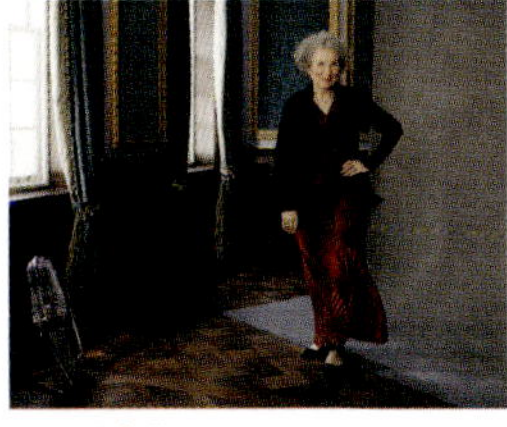

Margaret Atwood's Crystal Ball Is Scarily Accurate

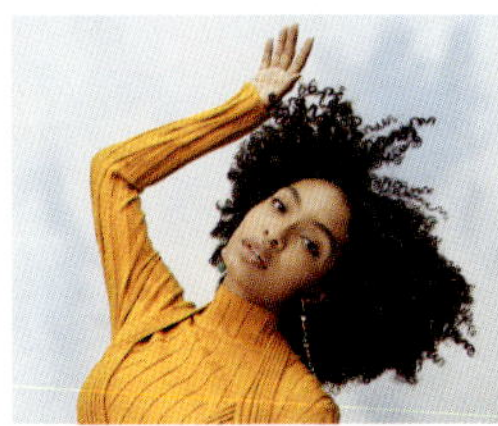

Yara Shahidi: 'My Metric for Success Is Having an Impact on Something Greater Than Myself'

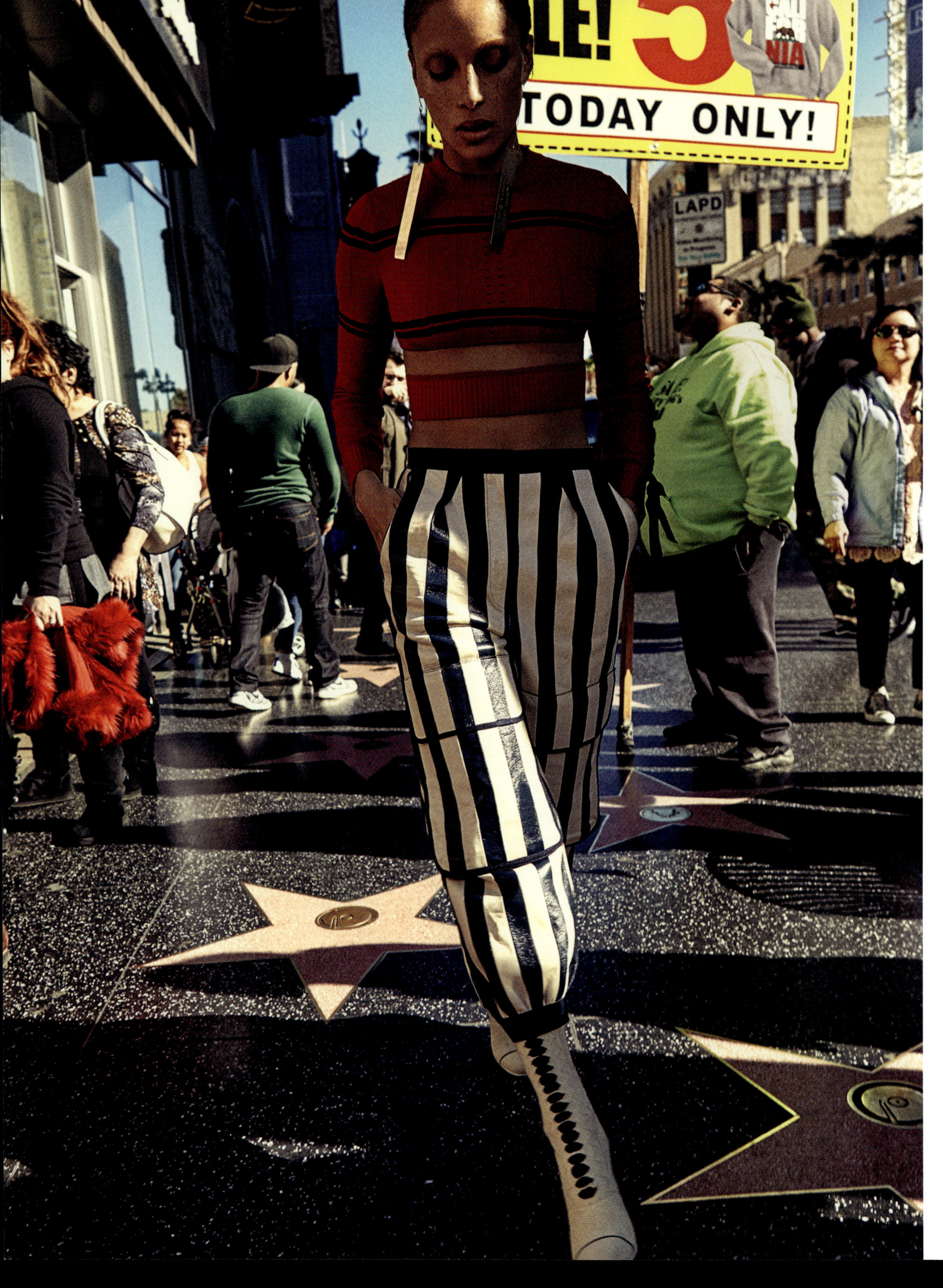
LE! 5
TODAY ONLY!
CALI
FOR
NIA
LAPD

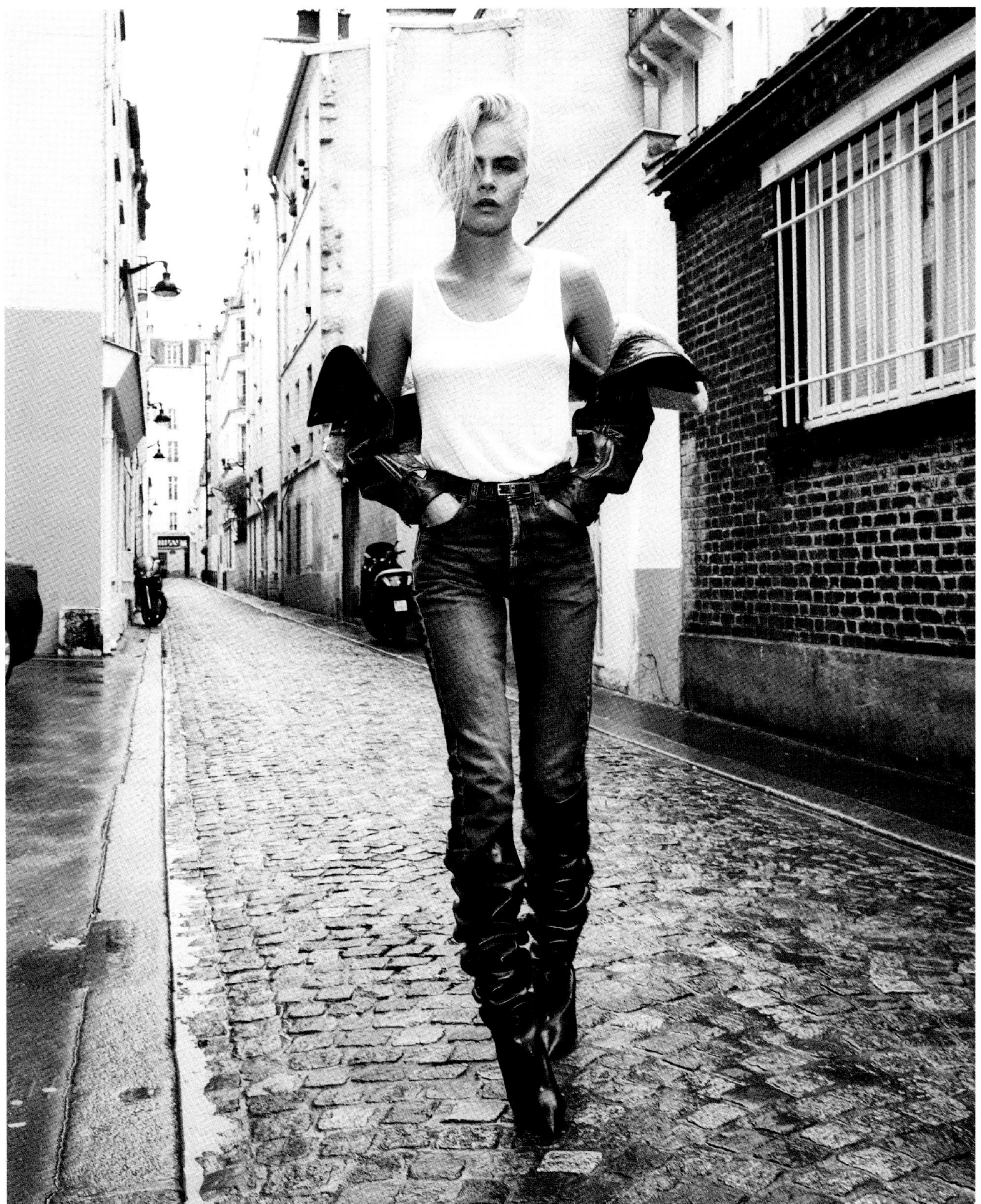

FROM CARA DELEVINGNE AND ADWOA ABOAH

to Gigi Hadid, Ashley Graham, and Halima Aden, this era of *Glamour* celebrated some of the most notable women in fashion. What set them apart? Using their voices to speak about issues beyond fashion—whether that be body inclusivity, religious representation, or mental health. Here are some of the most iconic shoots they starred in.

←

Adwoa Aboah on Hollywood's Walk of Fame, wearing a Fendi ensemble. *Photographed by Robbie Fimmano, March 2017.*

↑

Cara Delevingne in Paris, dressed in head to toe Saint Laurent by Anthony Vaccarello. *Photographed by Patrick Demarchelier, August 2017.*

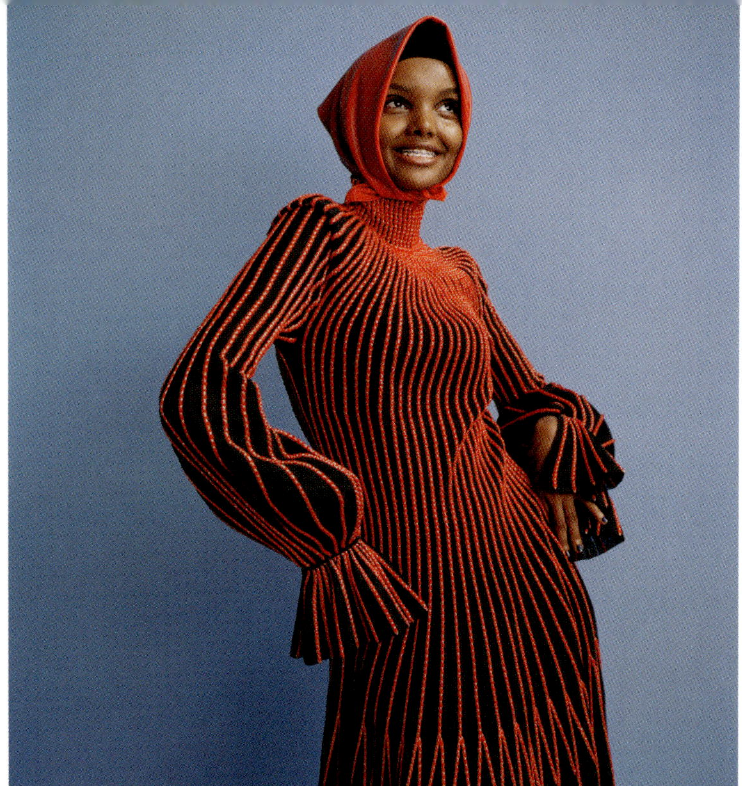

Former Kenyan refugee Halima Aden, who in 2016 was the first woman to wear a hijab in the Miss Minnesota USA pageant, wears an Alexander McQueen dress, David Menkes leather scarf, and Hijab-ista underscarf. *Photographed by Benjamin Vnuk, September 2017.*

Model and disability activist Jillian Mercado wears a Rodarte top and pants with Miu Miu shoes. *Photographed by Miguel Reveriego, September 2016.*

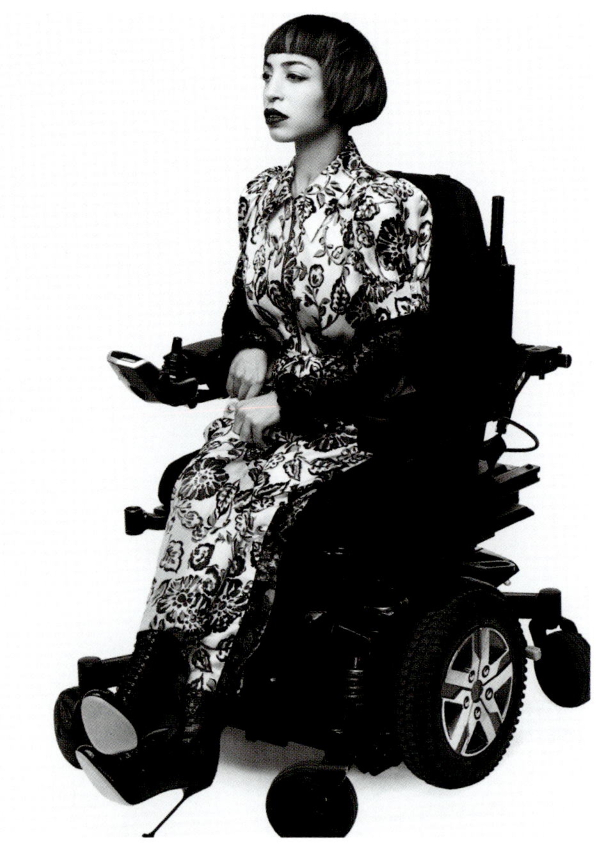

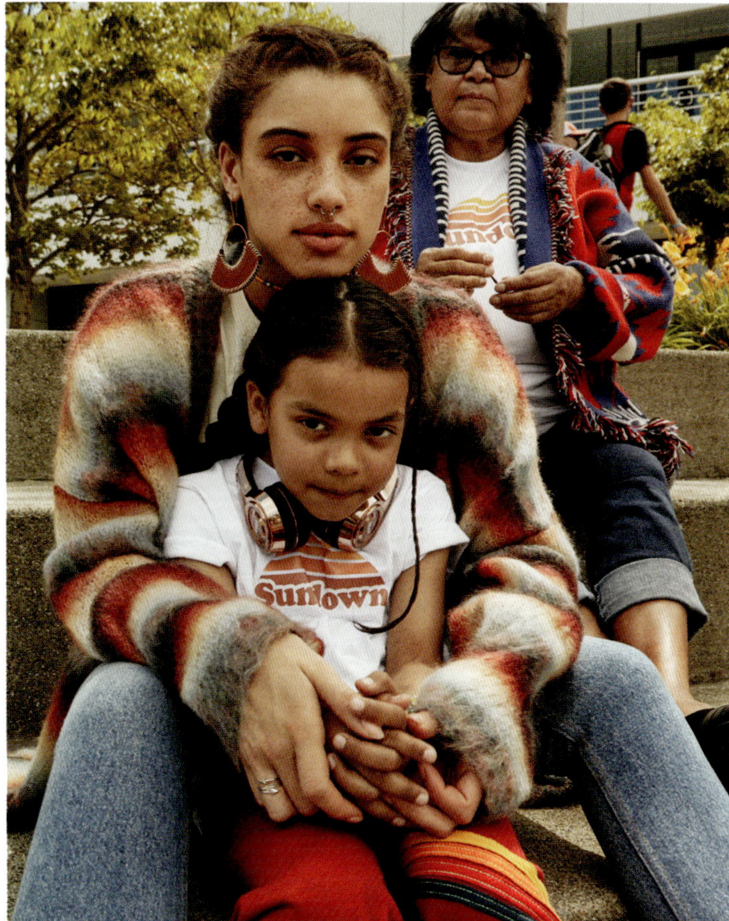

Native American model Khadijha Red Thunder with her brother, Sundown, and her grandmother, Margaret. *Photographed by Victor Demarchelier, September 2017.*

Model Ashley Graham wears a Michael Kors Collection bralette and skirt. *Photographed by Nathaniel Goldberg, July 2017.*

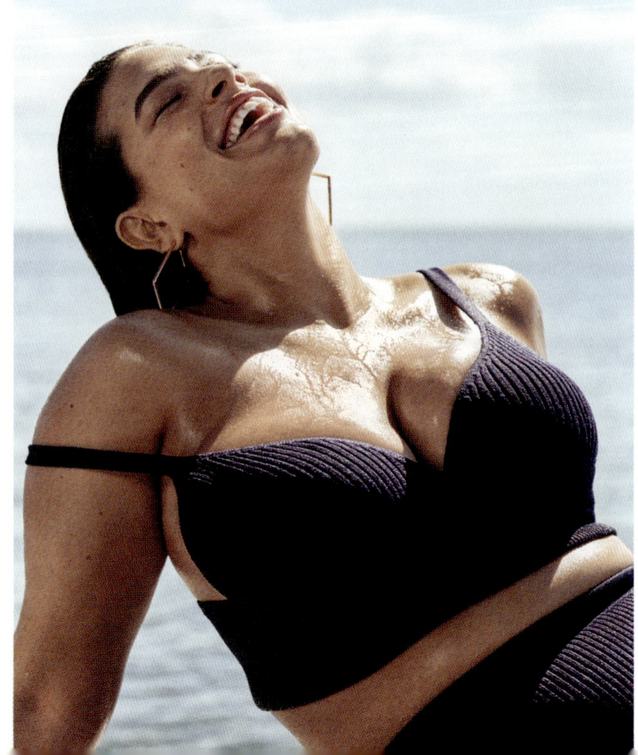

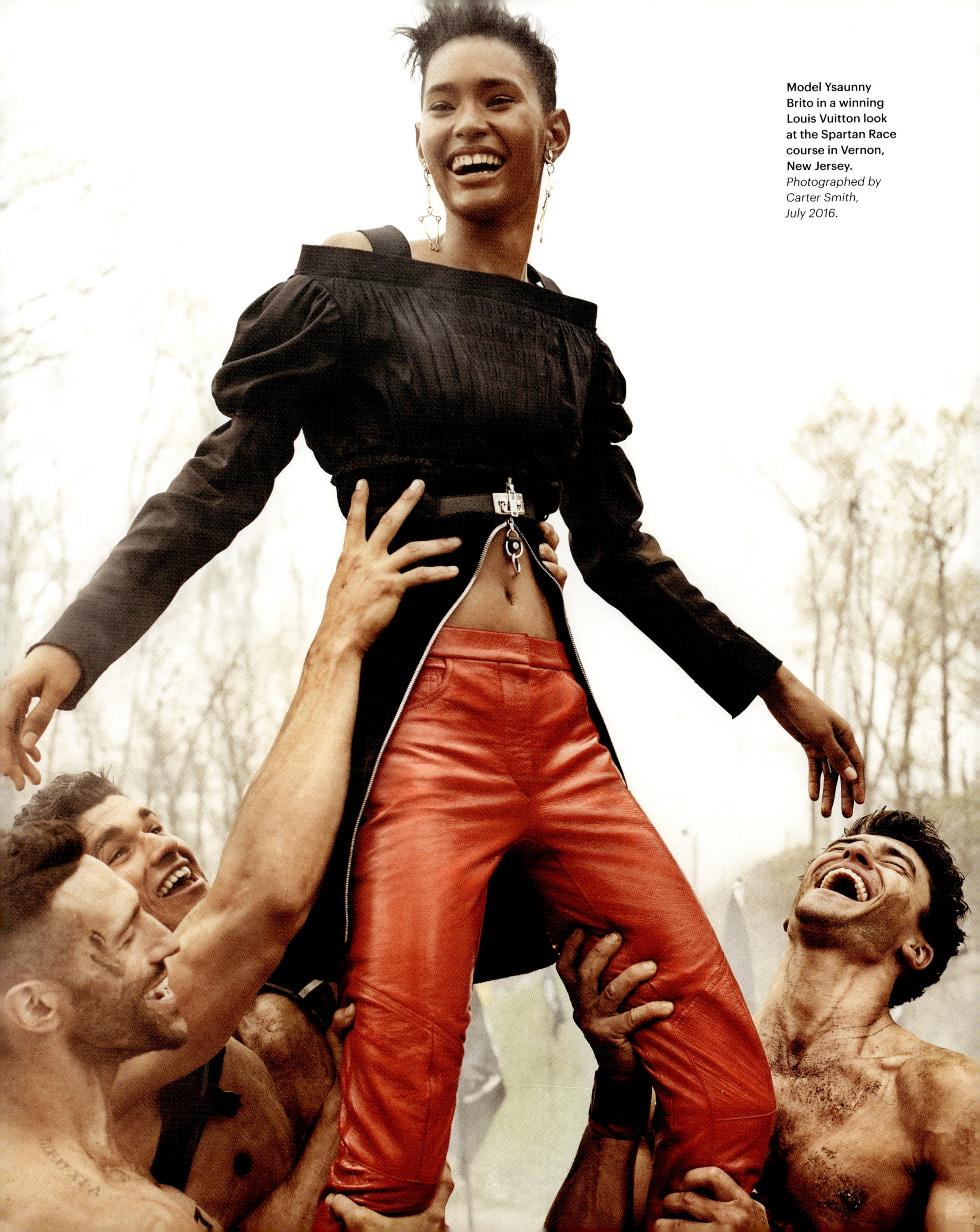

Model Ysaunny Brito in a winning Louis Vuitton look at the Spartan Race course in Vernon, New Jersey. *Photographed by Carter Smith, July 2016.*

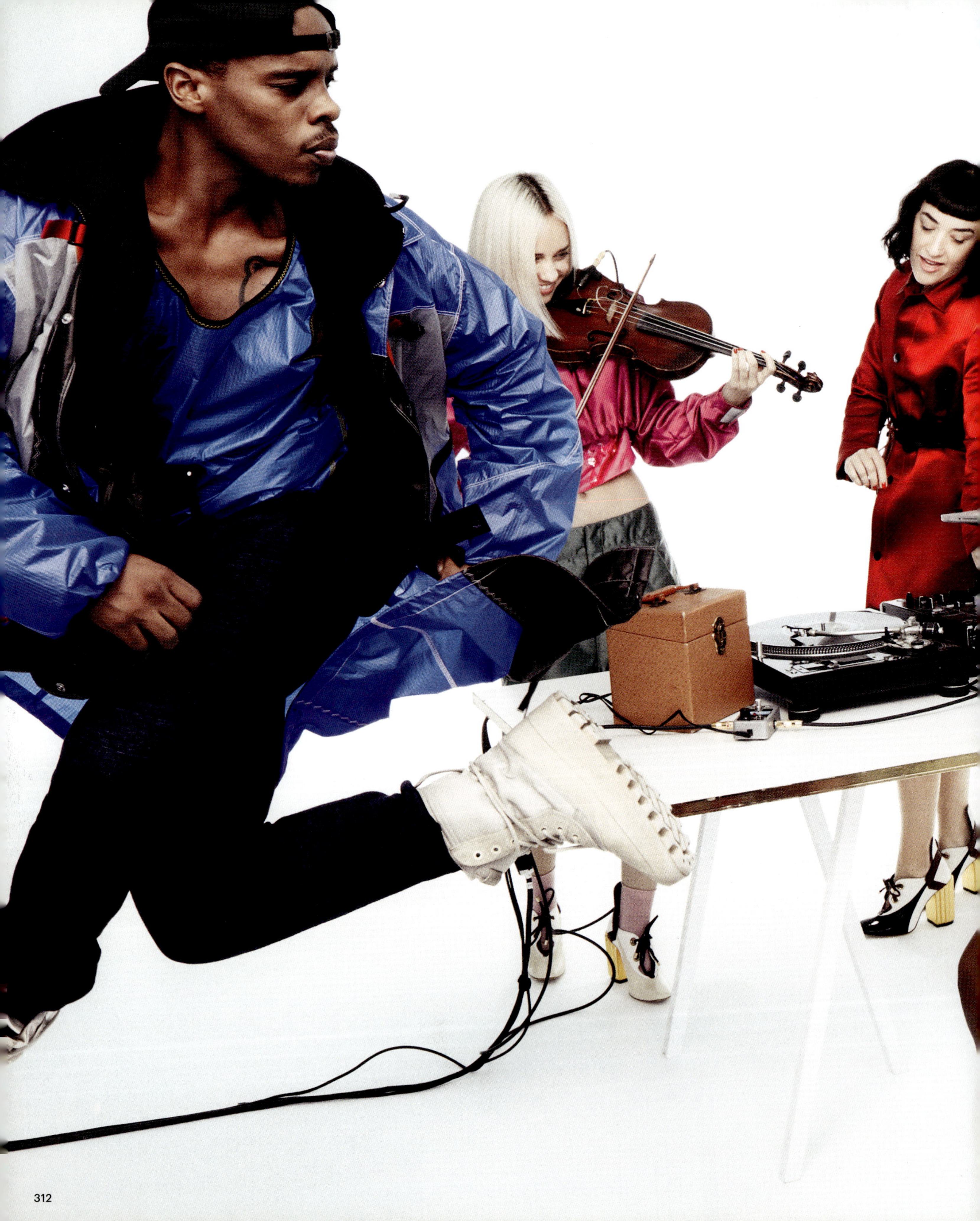

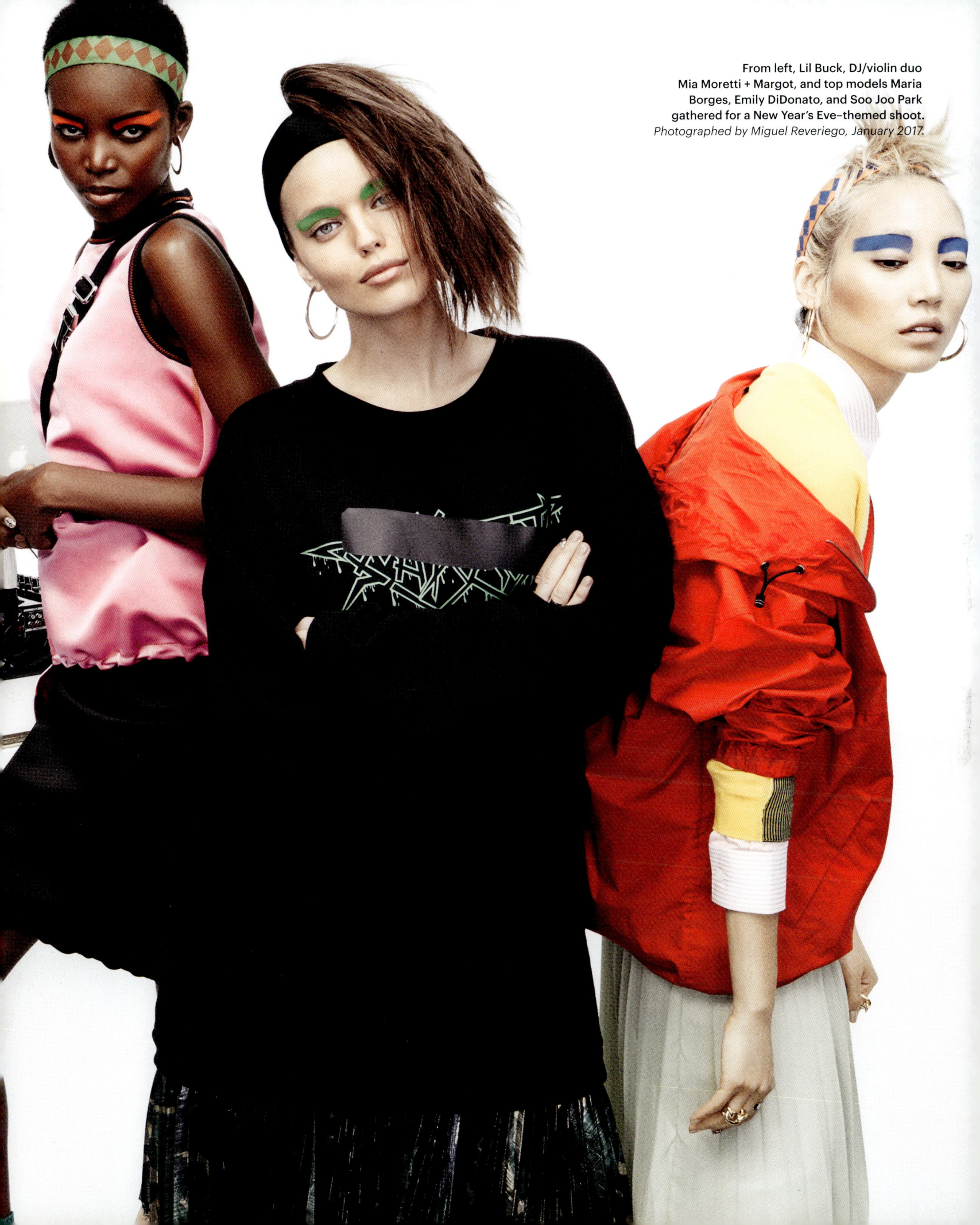

From left, Lil Buck, DJ/violin duo Mia Moretti + Margot, and top models Maria Borges, Emily DiDonato, and Soo Joo Park gathered for a New Year's Eve–themed shoot. *Photographed by Miguel Reveriego, January 2017.*

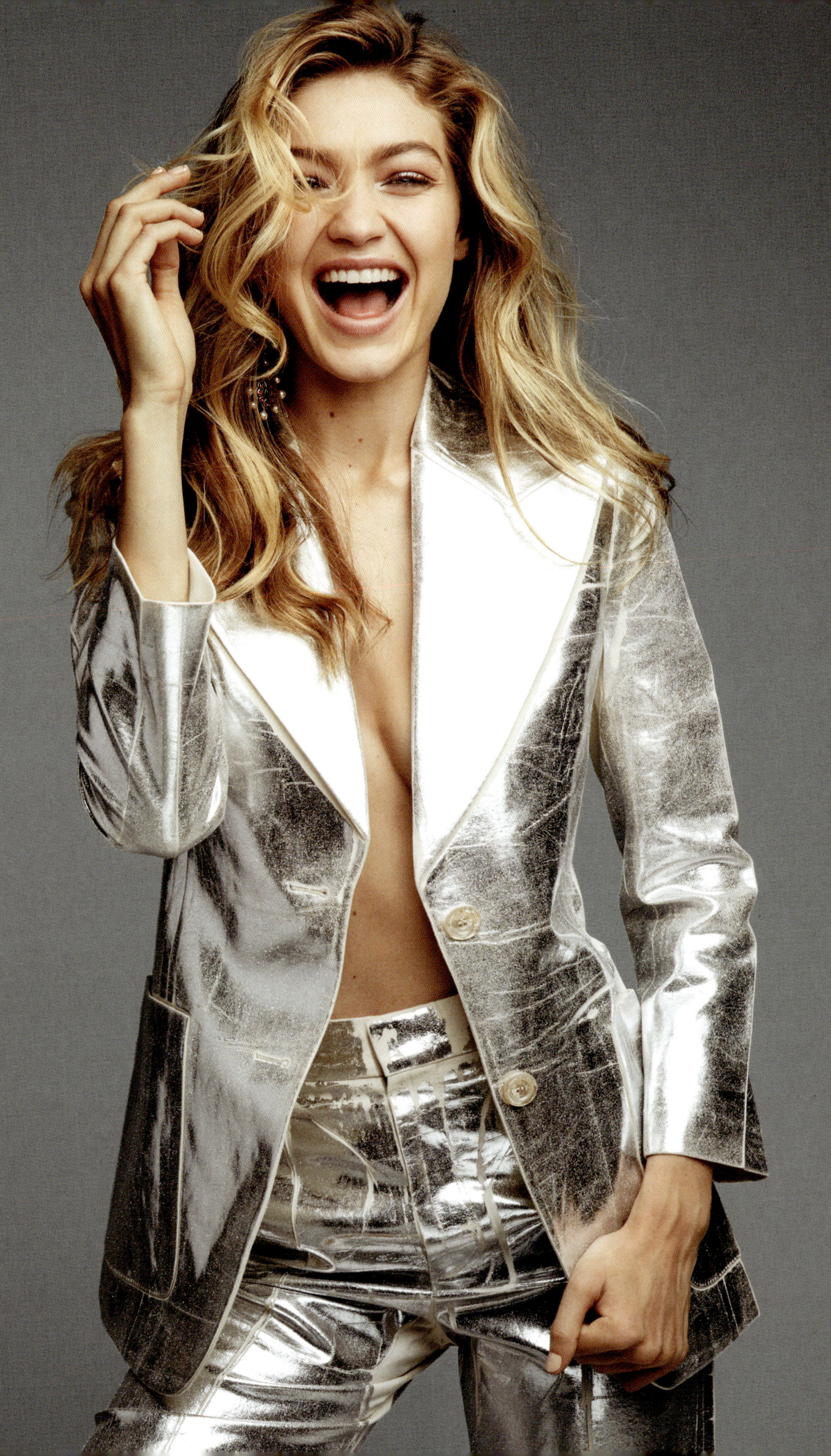

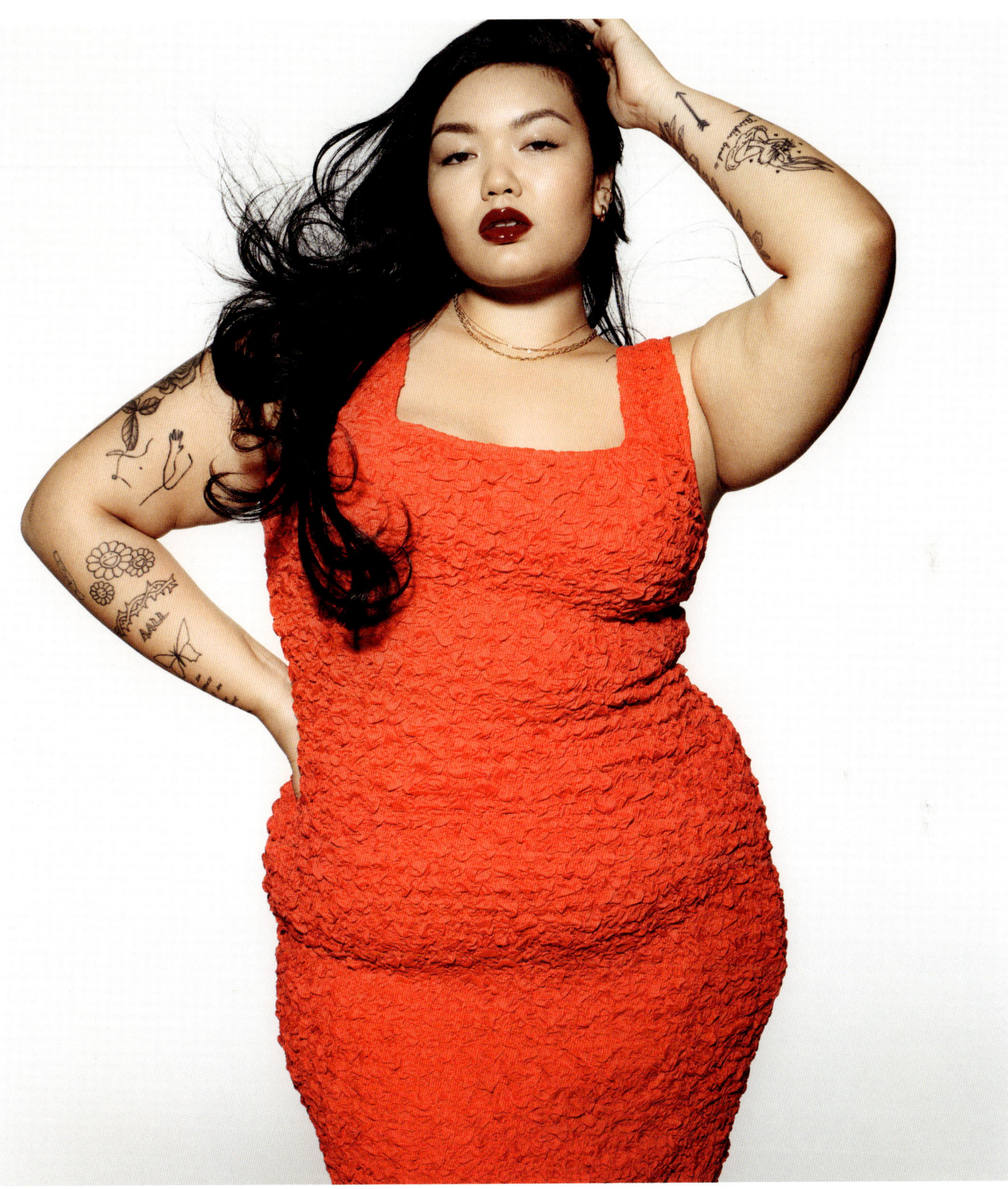

**Gigi Hadid wearing a Gucci
jacket, pants, and earrings.**
*Photographed by Patrick
Demarchelier, December 2017.*

Model Lovisa Lager.
*Photographed by Jason Kim,
March 2022.*

Come as You Are

IN MAY 2017, THE ICONIC supermodel Pat Cleveland told *Glamour*: "You have to see your flaws as the most beautiful things about you." She continued: "I had a friend in Hollywood who did her nose in her thirties, and years later she looked at my nose and said, 'I wish I still had my nose.' You can't be somebody else." Her words set the tone for a whole issue that celebrated women of every age—from teen to septuagenarian—and of every unique kind of beauty. And it was a theme that permeated *Glamour* throughout this new era: women celebrated for who they were, and for breaking societal molds rather than conforming to them.

↓

"When it comes to age and beauty, there's always been a double standard for women," Debbie Harry told *Glamour* in 2017. *Photographed by Sebastian Kim, May 2017.*

↗

Model Benny Harlem and his daughter Jaxyn. *Photographed by Olivia Malone, February 2018.*

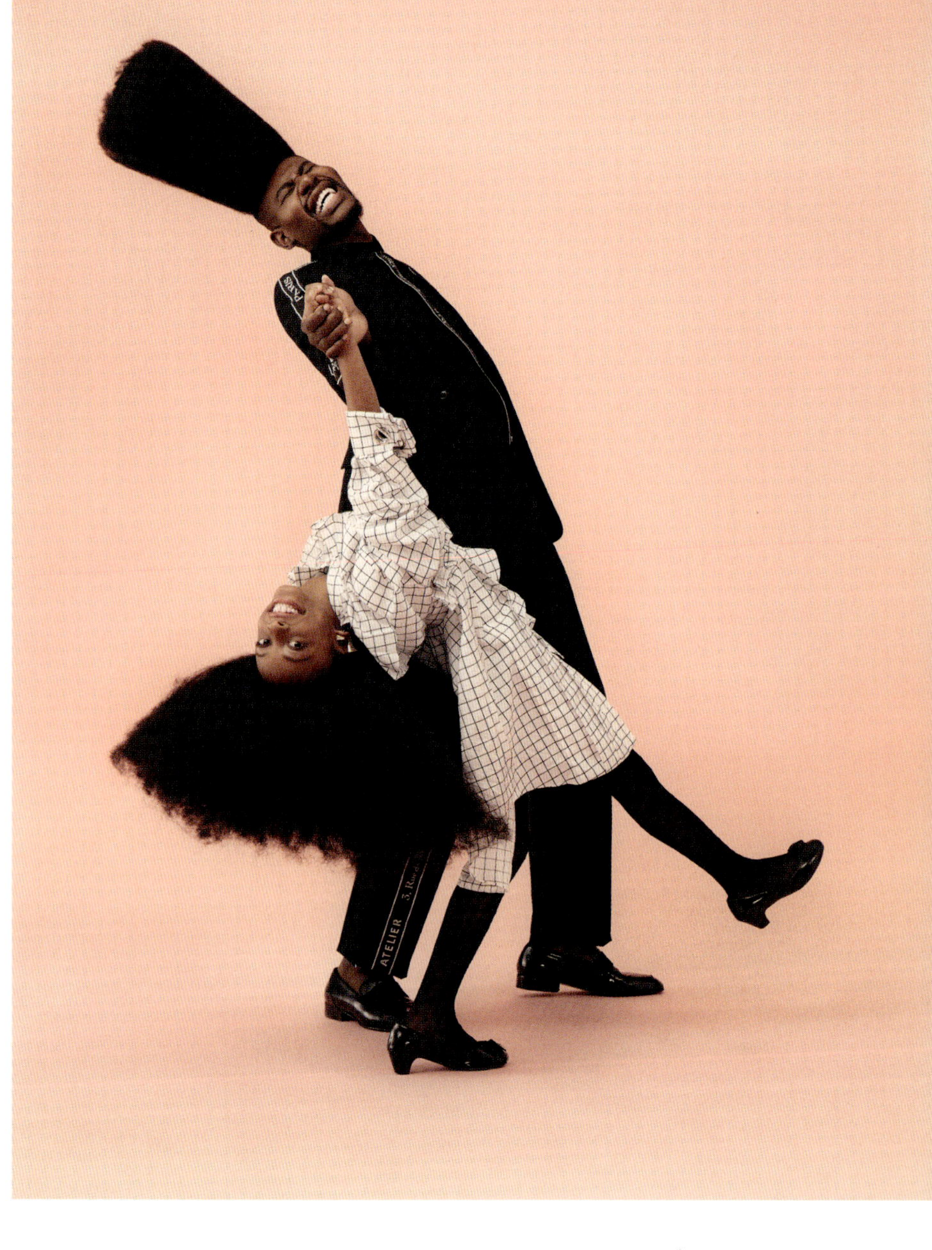

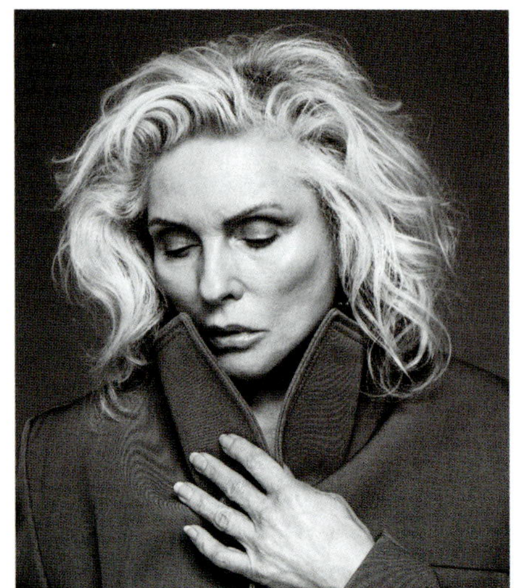

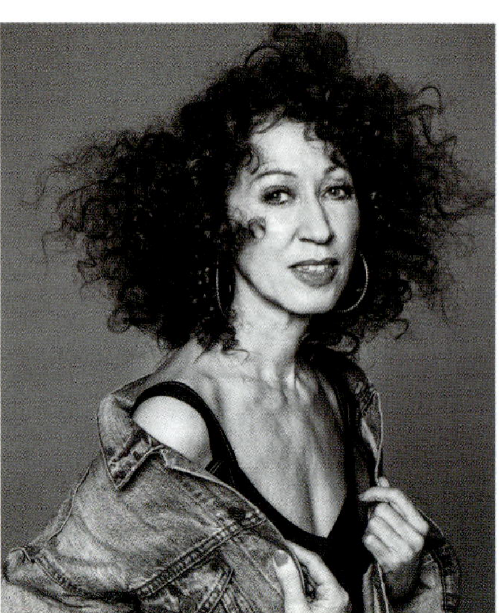

←

"Find ways to wake up every morning and say, 'Oh. I'm alive!'" said Pat Cleveland. *Photographed by Sebastian Kim, May 2017.*

→

Slick Woods told *Glamour*, "I didn't think that I was ever going to be able to make money without conforming." *Photographed by Jason Kibbler, May 2018.*

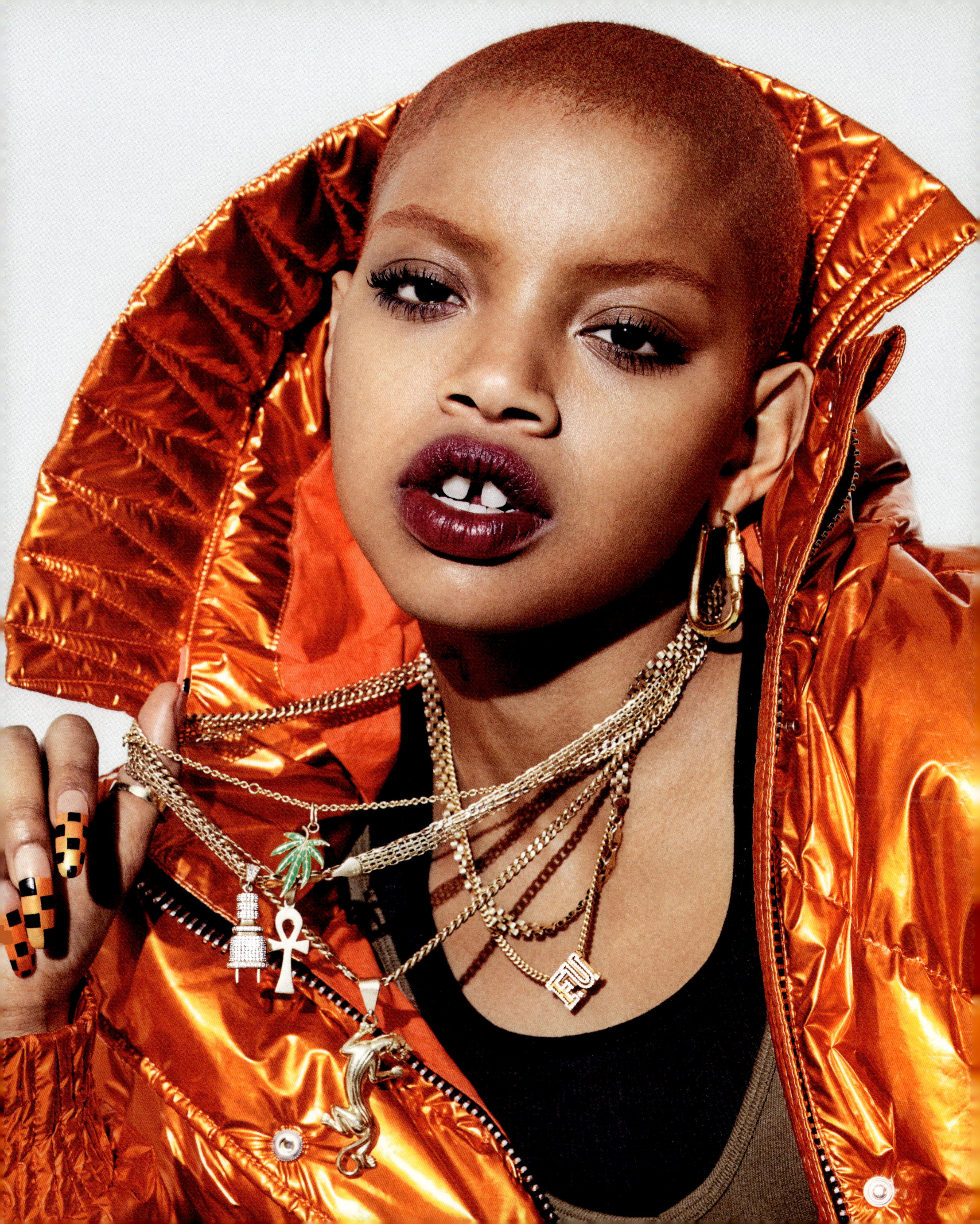

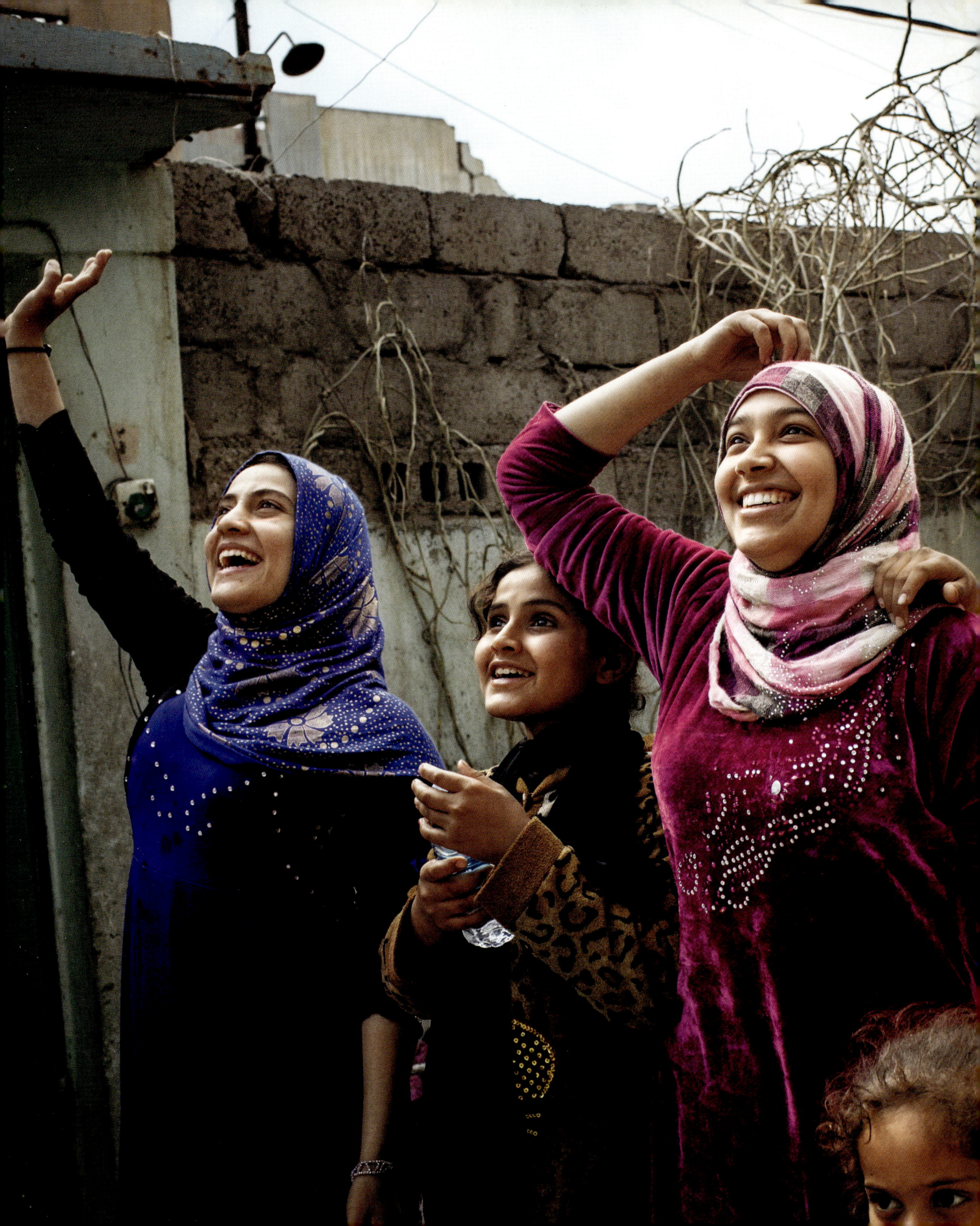

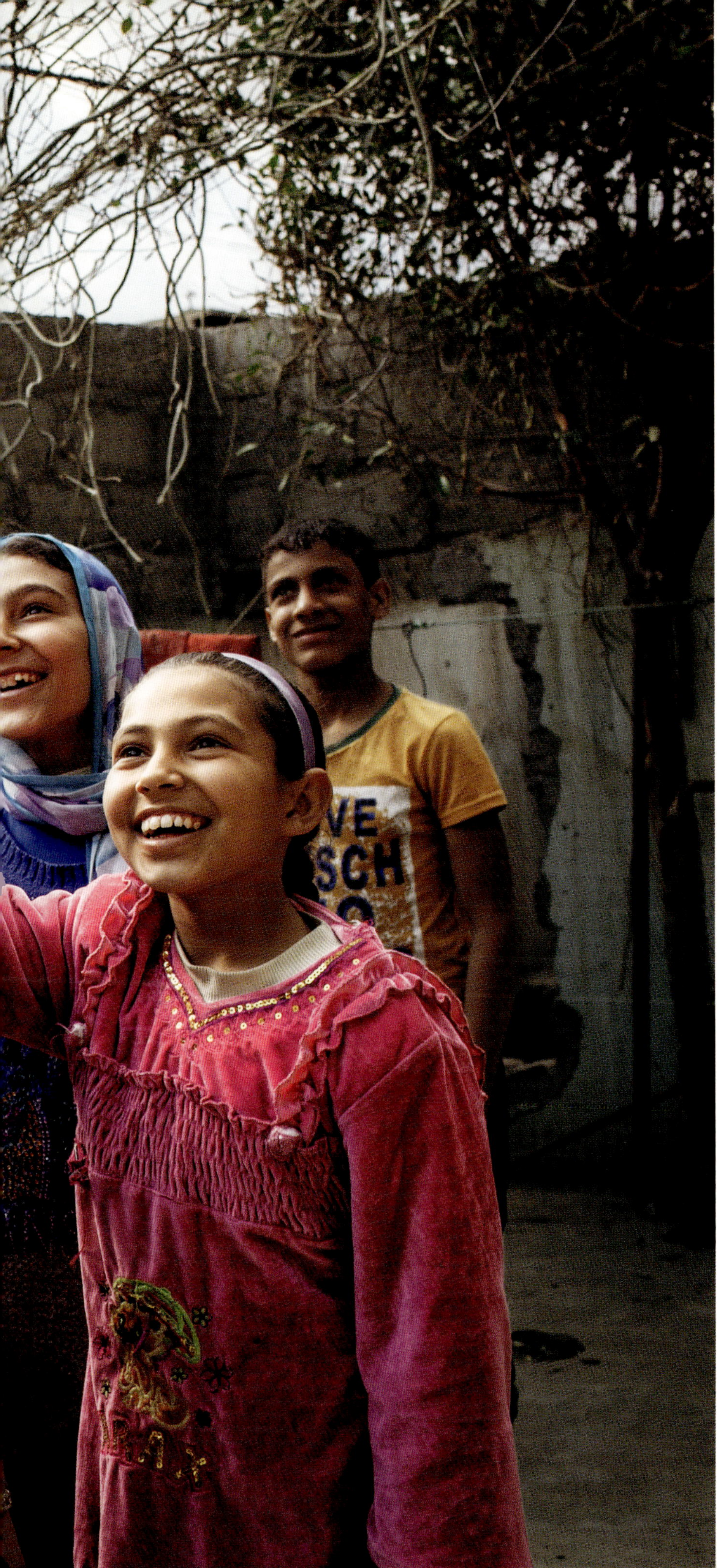

2017

WHEN PHOTOJOURNALIST ERIN TRIEB ARRIVED IN MOSUL FOR *Glamour* in mid-March 2017, neighborhoods were erupting in gunfire, and bombs screamed from the sky. Iraqi forces had rallied to liberate the city in October 2016, and families could finally embrace freedom after years of ISIS rule, but the situation remained deadly. Residents were terrified that ISIS would come back and retaliate. Amidst the chaos, *Glamour*, continuing its long-term commitment to telling stories about women's experiences around the world, and Trieb wanted to know what it felt like for women to taste their first moments of freedom. "These women's stories were so much more harrowing than I expected," Trieb told *Glamour*. "They had hit rock bottom, were starving to death, traumatized. And yet, defiantly, they survived." Two of the young girls Trieb met were cousins: Miami Fares, 18 (center, in pink), and Hojran Adnan, 16 (far left). Recalling life under the tyranny of ISIS, Hojran said: "They can cut your head off if you do anything wrong." But when Trieb met them, just a week after they had left their house, their neighbors were throwing a party. Playing music, singing, and dancing for the first time in three years, Miami told Trieb: "We let out three years of anxiety!" Yet restrictions still remained. "Even now, if I want to visit a friend or walk down a street alone, my family won't allow it," she continued. "But a boy can do whatever he wants. We want to remove these restrictions. We want to live a normal life."

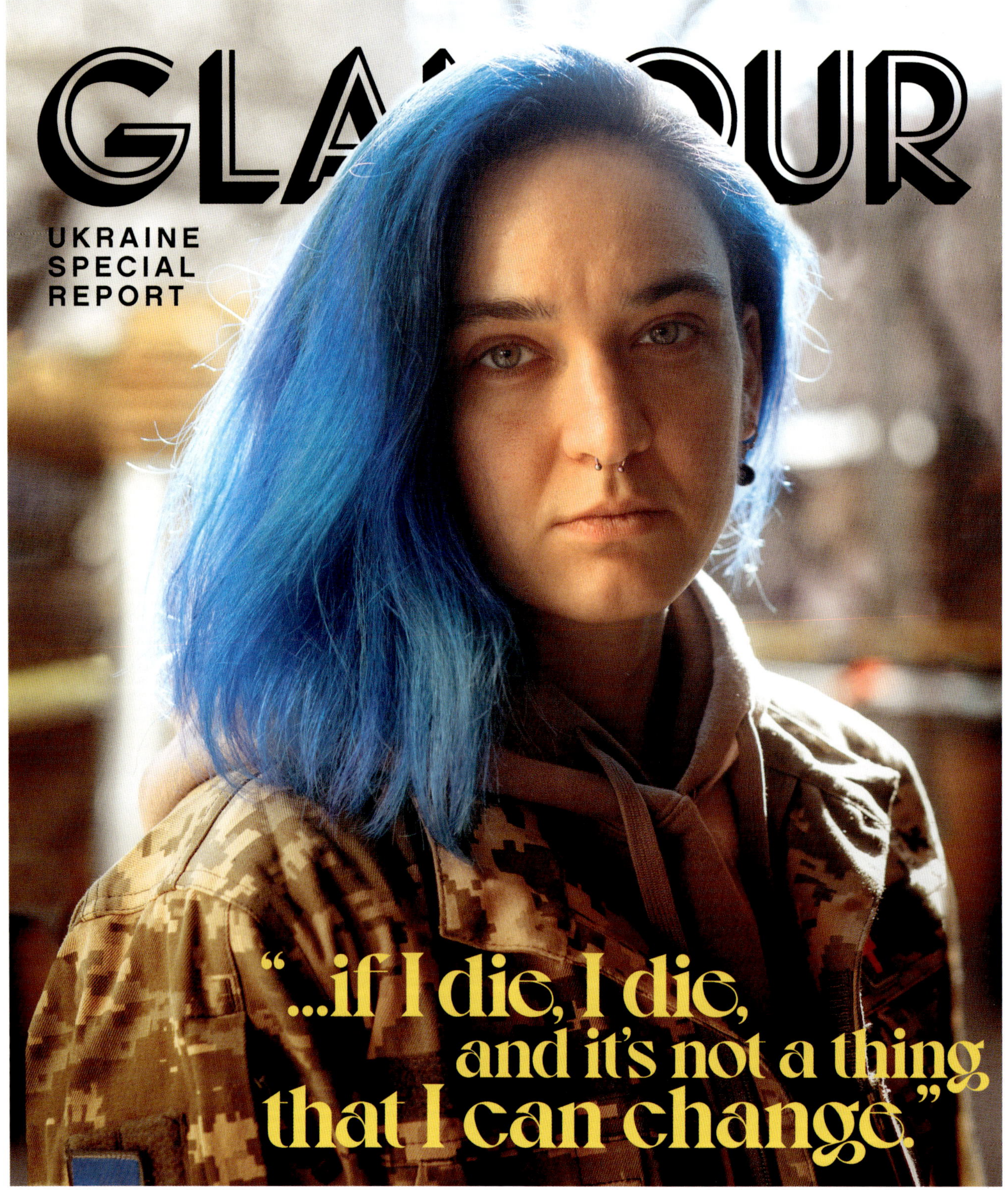

DURING THIS MODERN ERA, *GLAMOUR*'**S ON-THE-GROUND COVERAGE OF WOMEN ACTIVISTS** at home and abroad became a quickening drumbeat, in print and online, bringing stories of immense courage, resistance against oppression, and the fight for racial equality to *Glamour*'s millions of readers. In 2014, for example, *Glamour* traveled to Nigeria with Taliban survivor and Nobel Prize winner Malala Yousafzai to meet with the families of girls kidnapped by Boko Haram. In 2016, the magazine profiled eight survivors of gun violence fighting to make mass shootings history. In 2018, the women who helped expose sexual abuse by Larry Nassar, former team doctor for the US women's national gymnastics team, were honored as Women of the Year. *Glamour*'s special 2020 Our Hair issue highlighted the anti-Black hair discrimination faced by women in workplaces around the US, and urged readers to sign a petition calling for the passing of the Crown Act—making hair discrimination illegal. This work, often heartbreaking to read and difficult to report, but of vital importance, signaled the title's ongoing commitment to telling deeply reported stories about game-changing women.

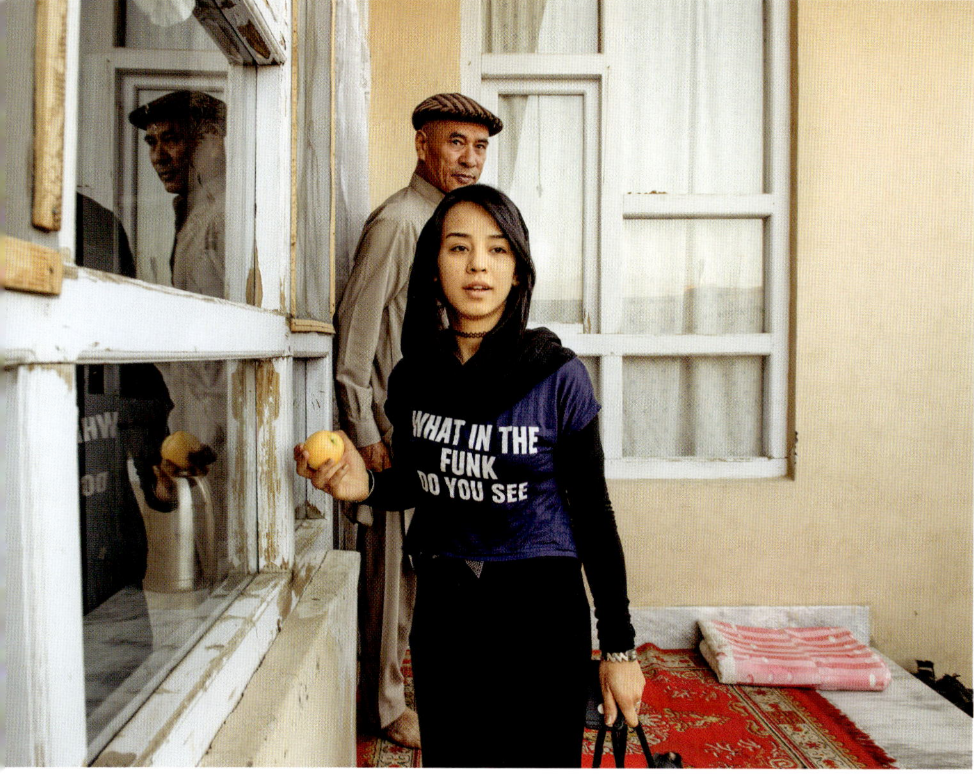

←

TV anchor Shabana Noori's story was covered by *Glamour* in 2018. She was a reporter for ZANTV—the first all-female women's news channel in Afghanistan—and Noori and her colleagues risked their lives to do their work. Noori is pictured here with her father, Ghulam Mohammad. *Photographed by Kiana Hayeri, March 2018*.

←

In February 2022, Vladimir Putin ordered the invasion of Ukraine. It marked the beginning of a conflict that is ongoing at press time. Photojournalist Erin Trieb was in Ukraine and documented stories of the impact of war on women in Kyiv. *Glamour* published her report as a special April 2022 cover. Featured on the front page was medical doctor Oksana Hnatiuk, who had enlisted in the country's civilian volunteer military unit.

→

Eight survivors of gun violence came together in 2016 to speak out against the cycle of mass shootings. From left, Sherrie Lawson, a survivor of the Washington Navy Yard shooting, September 16, 2013; Heather Egeland, a survivor of the shooting at Columbine High School, Colorado, April 20, 1999; Jennifer Hammer, also a Columbine survivor; Missy Jenkins Smith, a survivor of the Heath High School shooting, Kentucky, December 1, 1997; Chloe Quinn, a survivor of the Umpqua Community College shooting, Oregon, October 1, 2015; Mary Reed and her daughter, Emma McMahon, survivors of the Safeway parking lot shooting, Arizona, January 8, 2011; and Kristina Anderson, a survivor of the Virginia Tech shooting, April 16, 2007. *Photographed by Jason Schmidt, March 2016.*

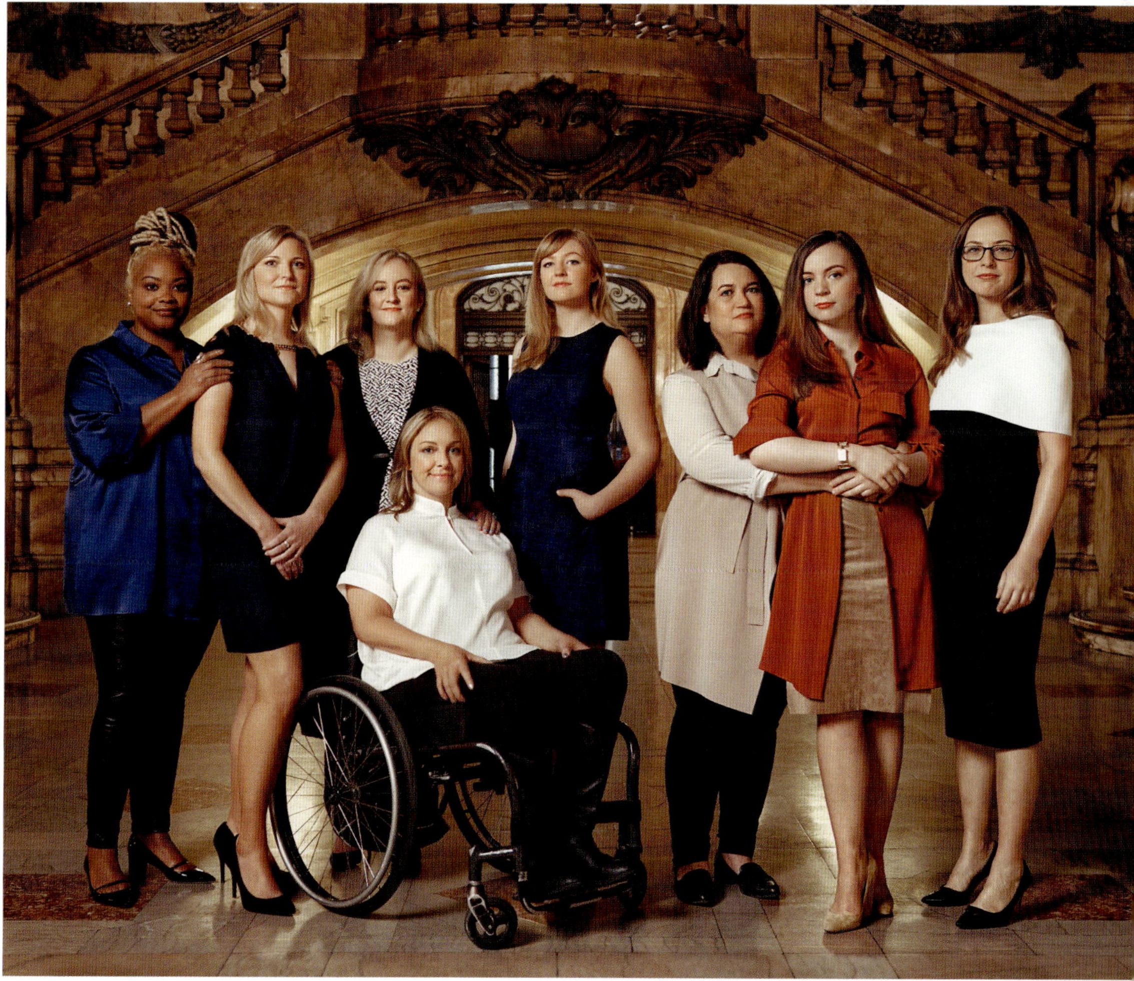

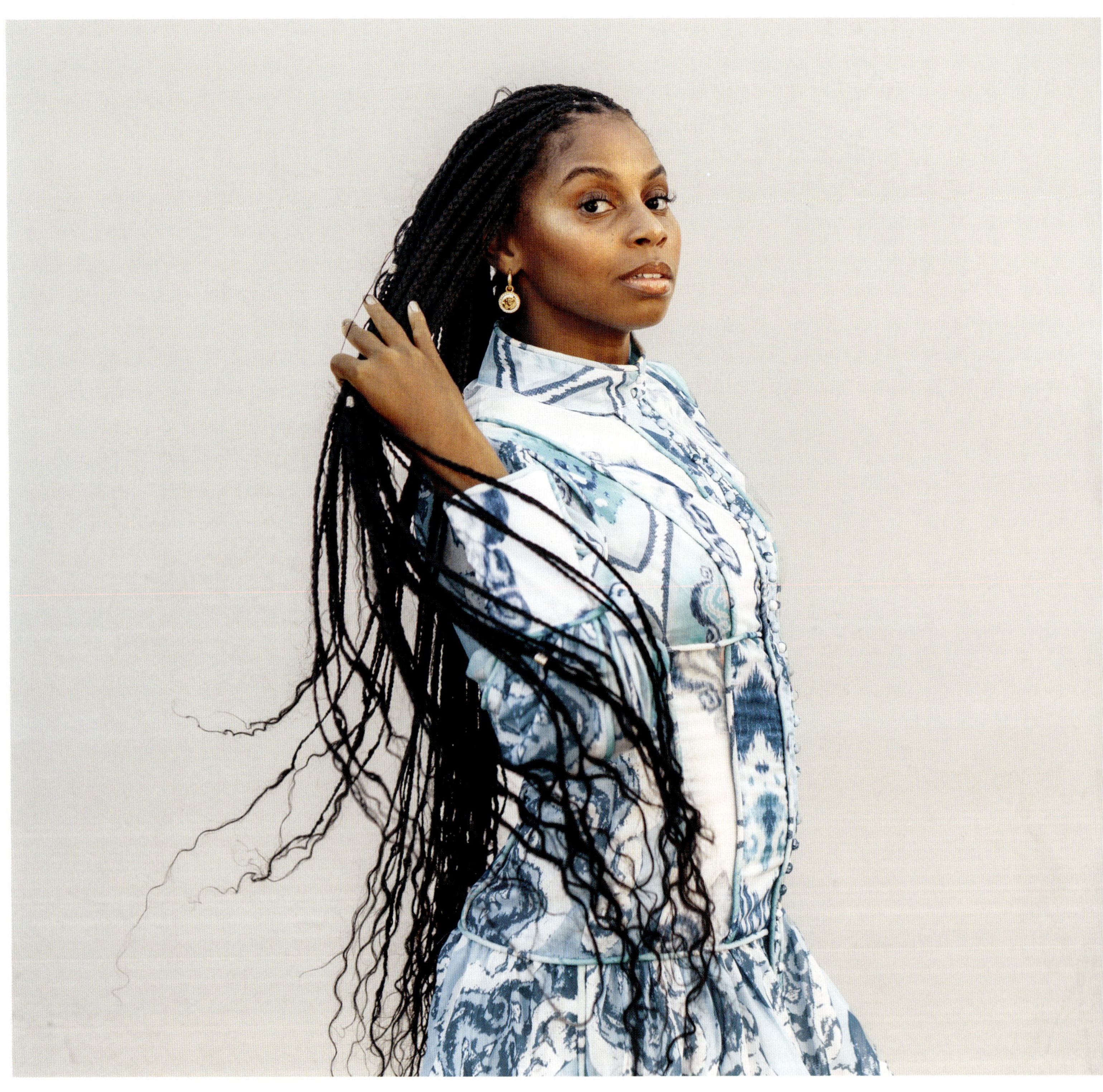

↑

The journalist Ashley Alese Edwards spearheaded *Glamour*'s Our Hair issue, tackling the "insidious policing of Black hair by workplaces." The cover story featured six women fighting back against the discrimination they had faced and calling for legal protection against hair discrimination—which is racist, if it even needs to be said. Pictured here, Farryn Johnson, who shared her story about being fired for coloring her hair. *Photographed by Bethany Mollenkof, August 2020.*

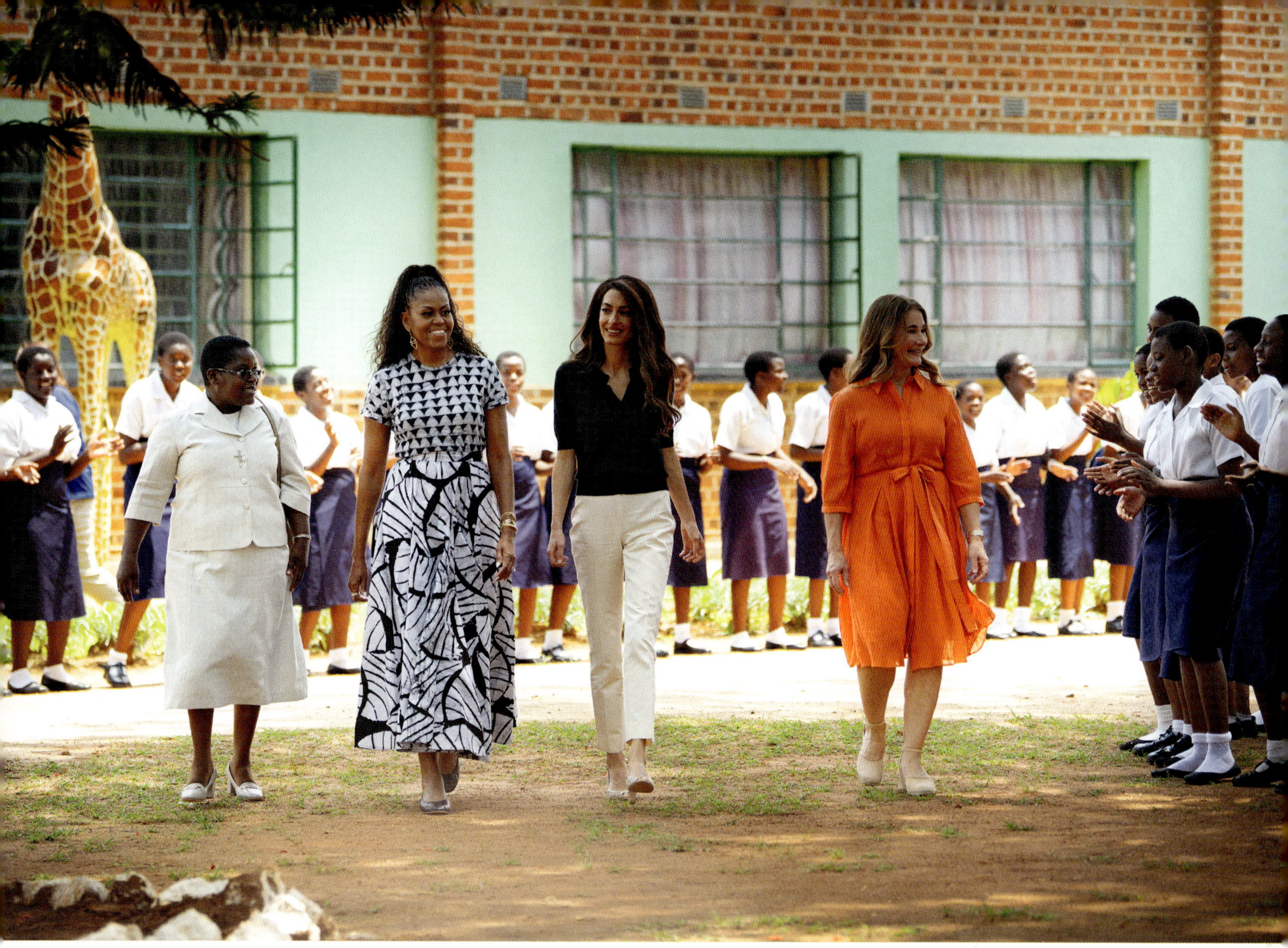

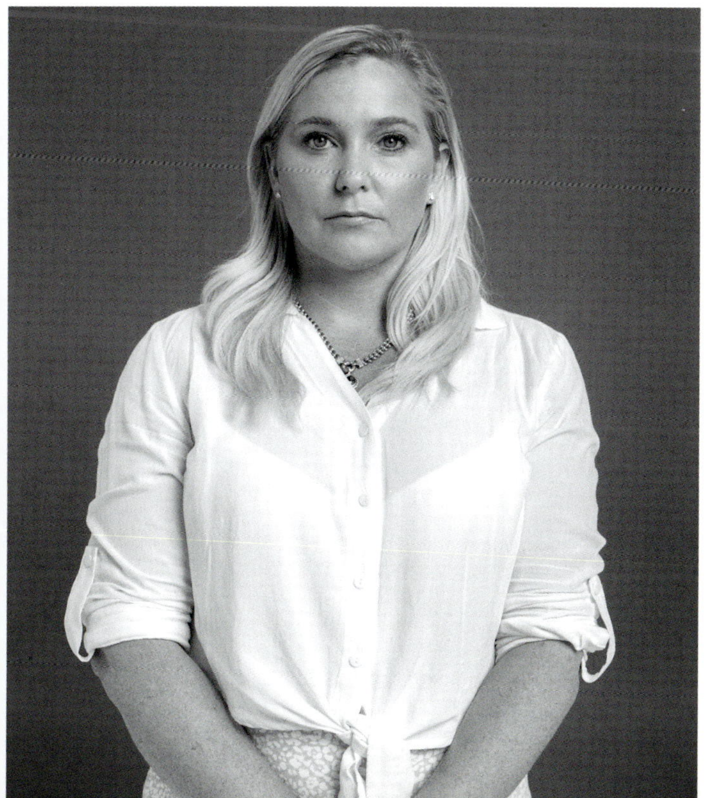

↑

In November 2023, former first lady Michelle Obama, human rights lawyer Amal Clooney, and philanthropist Melinda French Gates combined forces, traveling to Malawi and South Africa to launch a project aiming to end child marriage around the world. *Glamour* accompanied the three women to report on their work and meet the young girls fighting to create a better future for themselves. *Photographed by Thoko Chikondi, November 2023.*

←

Survivors of abuser Jeffrey Epstein gathered in New York in 2019 to share their stories with *Glamour* in a hard-hitting but vital report. Virginia Giuffre, pictured left, has had her life picked apart after coming forward about the abuse she suffered, but told *Glamour*, "This is not our shame. They did something wrong." *Photographed by Cassie Basford, December 2019.*

#PassPaidLeave

THE U.S. IS ONE OF ONLY SEVEN COUNTRIES in the entire world with no national paid family or maternity leave policy, and one in four women have returned to work within two weeks of giving birth as a result. When a government bid in late 2021 to fund just four weeks of paid leave failed, *Glamour* decided to follow eight women—with varying access to leave—through the first 28 days postpartum. The goal? To showcase the impact of a paid leave policy—devastating for those who lack it, beneficial for those who have it— and to launch a national campaign to demand Congress pass it. It was a groundbreaking project that not only won the prestigious Public Interest category at the National Magazine Awards, but set in motion a chain of events that launched a nationwide advertising campaign, an advocacy day in Washington, DC, and laid the foundation for an ongoing partnership with nonpartisan campaign group Paid Leave for All to press for the creation of the country's first paid leave law.

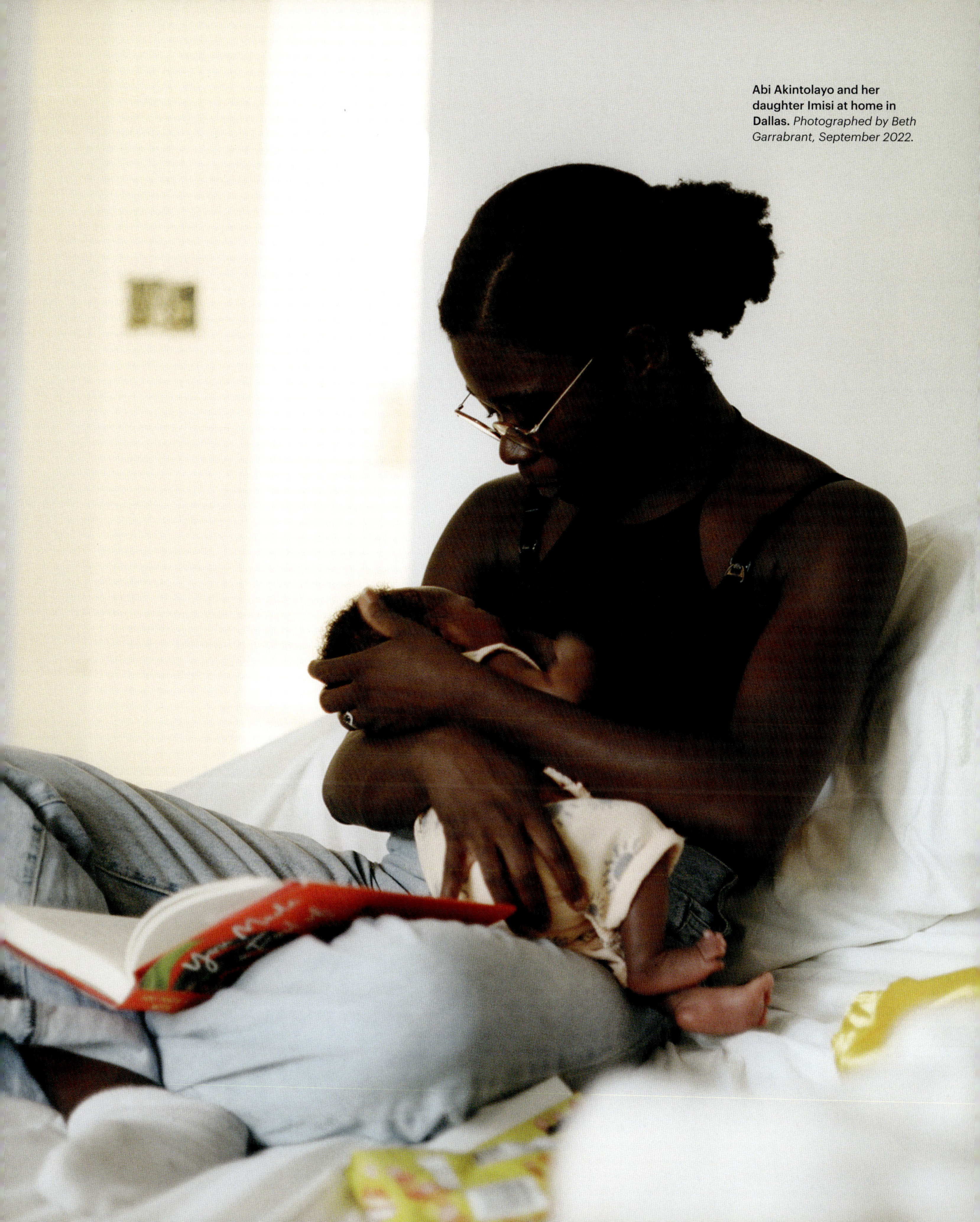

Abi Akintolayo and her daughter Imisi at home in Dallas. *Photographed by Beth Garrabrant, September 2022.*

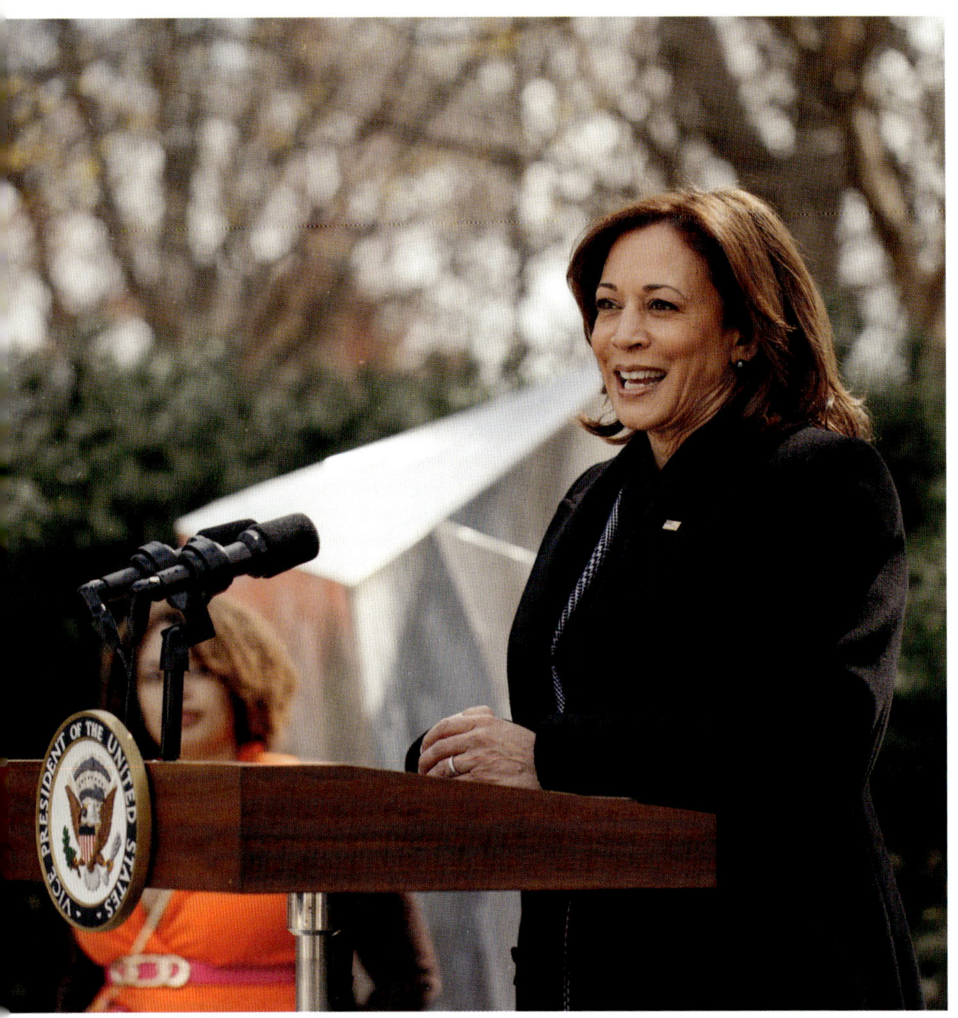

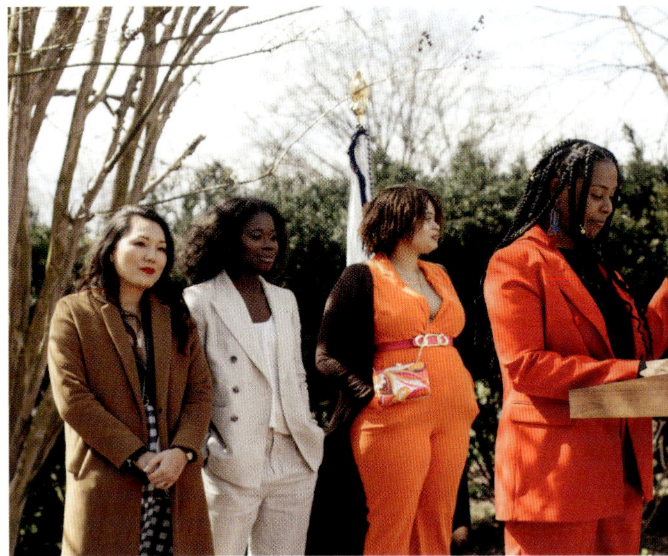

←

In recognition of its campaign to pass paid leave, Vice President Kamala Harris invited Glamour to cohost a Women's History Month brunch with her at the vice president's residence. She gave a speech on the importance of passing paid leave and increasing women's economic empowerment. *Photographed by Lauren Cowart, March 2023.*

↓

Karina Garcia, one of the women featured in *Glamour*'s award-winning 28 Days package, shared her own paid leave story and introduced the vice president at the Women's History Month brunch. *Photographed by Lauren Cowart, March 2023.*

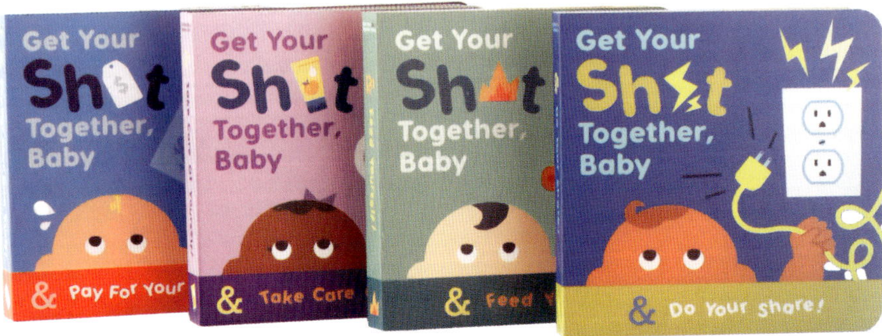

↑

Glamour partnered with Paid Leave for All to create a spoof advertising campaign to highlight the ludicrousness of the lack of paid family leave in America. Working with award-winning advertising agency Mother, Glamour and Paid Leave for All created a set of four books teaching babies how to look after themselves (with their parents forced back to work with no paid leave), and took over four huge screens in Times Square for a month.

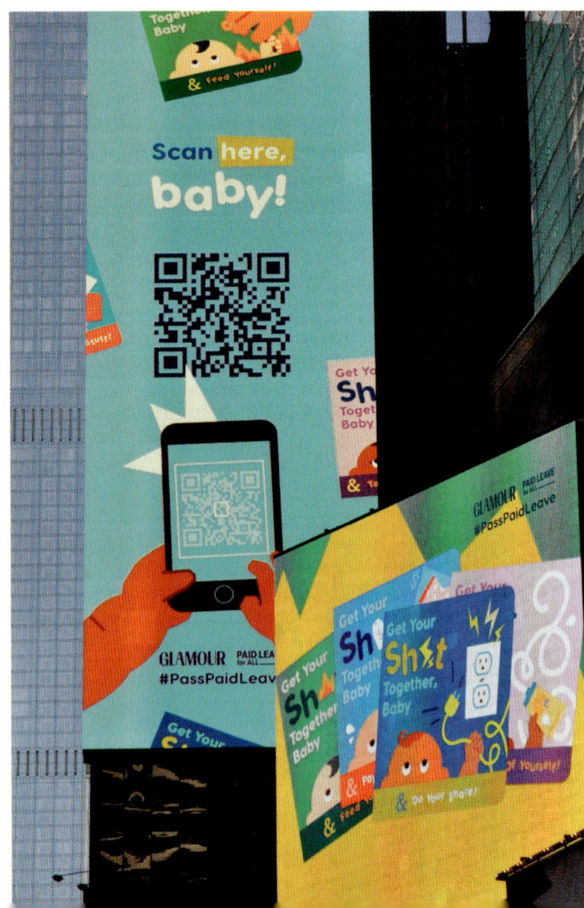

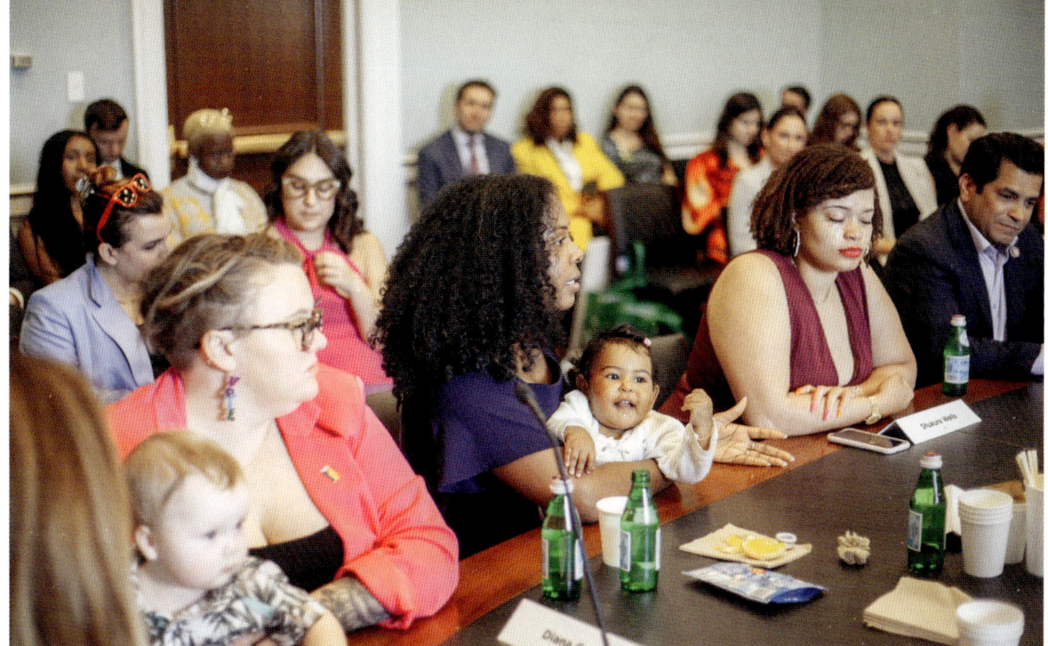

Mothers from *Glamour*'s 28 Days project meet with House representatives, including Jimmy Gomez of California, to call for paid leave for all. *Photographed by Alexandra Folino, May 2023.*

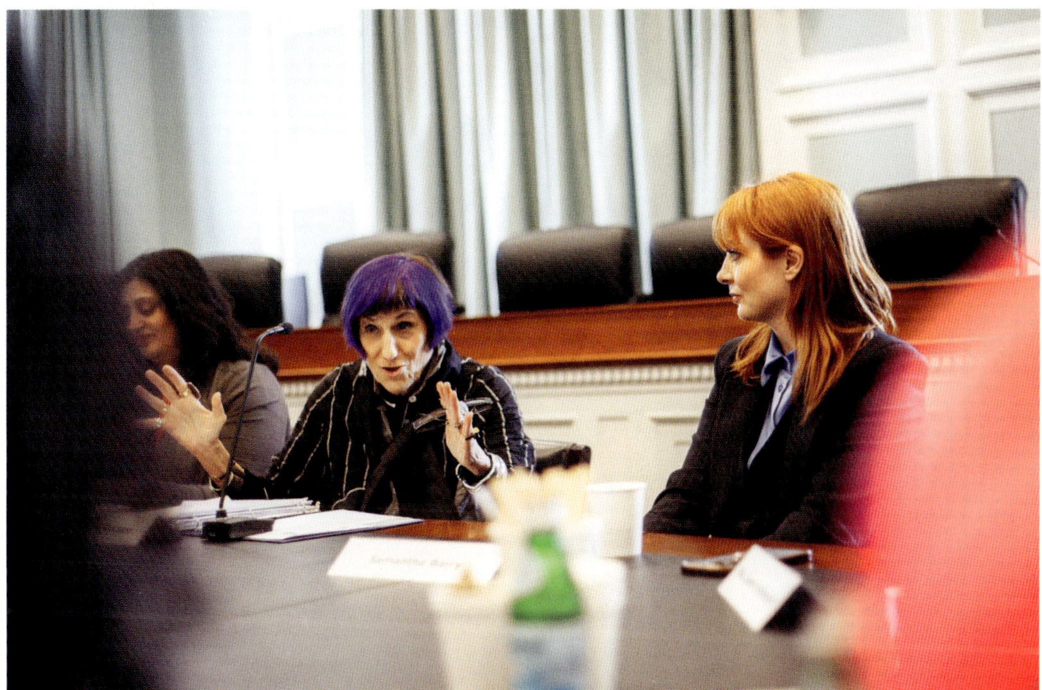

Representative Rosa DeLauro of Connecticut gives the opening speech at Glamour's round table in Washington, DC. *Photographed by Alexandra Folino, May 2023.*

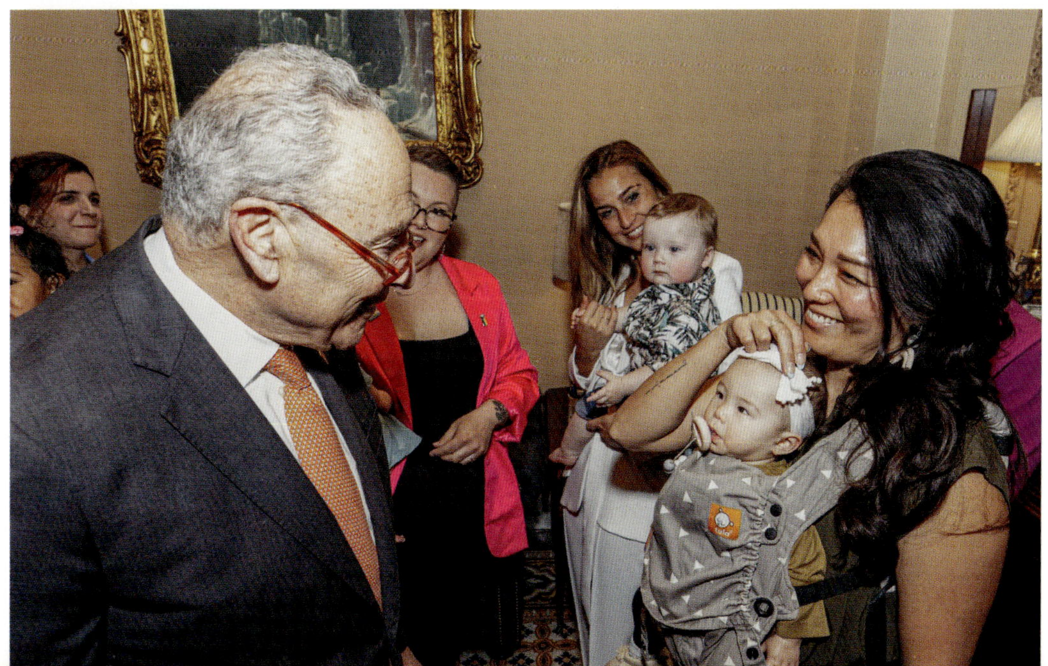

Senator Chuck Schumer of New York meets Tiffany Motrek, a mother from *Glamour*'s 28 Days project, offering his support for Glamour's paid leave campaign.

Acknowledgments

A special thank you to every single person who has worked for and contributed to *Glamour* from 1939 to today. This book is a celebration of your passion, creativity, and dedication to creating such an important publication. Without all of you, this book wouldn't exist. The same goes to *Glamour*'s readers. We know how much *Glamour* means to you, and your continued patronage powers us.

The deepest gratitude to *Glamour*'s editors in chief, past and present—Alice Thompson, Elizabeth Penrose, Kathleen Aston Casey, Ruth Whitney, Bonnie Fuller, Cindi Leive, and Samantha Barry—who have built such an inspiring women's title. Samantha, thank you especially for your support for this book, and for your clear vision that drives *Glamour* every day.

To the team who brought this book to life. Thank you.

Natasha Pearlman, your unwavering belief in the significance of this book means that these stories aren't just relics of the past, but impactful narratives that resonate today. Without your leadership, passion, and commitment, this book's journey wouldn't have even begun.

Ruhama Wolle and Anna Moeslein, your months of research and your thoughtful words and interviews shone a light on vital issues, and spotlighted the outsize contributions of women like Rosemary Bray, Ruth Whitney, Beverly Johnson, and more.

Alexandra Folino, your design is exceptional, and this book's unique and evocative cover is a testament to your talent, hard work, and vision.

For every extraordinary moment in history in the pages of this book, we needed an equally extraordinary image, and for that thanks go to Kathryne Hall and Isaac Lobel. You made 85 years of visual research appear effortless, though it was anything but. And more than that, your work significantly guided our writing.

This book would truly not have been possible without the belief and support of Eilish Morley and Ivan Shaw. Thank you for working on this when it was just the germ of an idea and also helping to bring together an incredible team to pull this off.

And a special thank you to Anna Wintour, for your leadership and guidance throughout the process, and your belief in this project.

Nicole Stuart, you have been our production rock. Thank you for guiding us through and ensuring that we met deadlines that sometimes felt impossible. Emma Baker, thank you for your masterful work, and for becoming a *Glamour* historian alongside us. To Robin Aigner, Christy Walker, Steve George, Michael Brownell, John Banta, and Jim Gomez, the biggest thanks for your careful planning, direction, and editing, and for believing in the importance of this work.

Cynthia Cathcart, the deepest gratitude for your passion and archival knowledge of *Glamour* and Condé Nast. We can't think of a question you didn't know the answer to off the top of your head.

Monique Wilson, thank you for your invaluable research and work helping to shape the early chapters, and to Ashley Latona and Zachary Vietze for your support in the Condé Nast archives. Many thanks to Christopher Donnellan, Terence Keegan, Toni Boyd, and Lindsay Lander for your support.

Thank you especially to Alison Ward Frank, Caitlin Brody, and Gabrielle Seo for your constant support, and contributions to so many of *Glamour*'s iconic covers.

To Rebecca Kaplan, thank you for sharing our passion for celebrating the achievements of women. And to Juliet Dore, Darilyn Carnes, Annalea Manalili, Denise LaCongo, Diane Shaw, Danielle Youngsmith, Gabby Fisher, and Danielle Kolodkin, thank you for all your work getting the book off to print and out into the world, and your thoughtful notes and edits.

A deep gratitude is due to Philip Whitney, Ruth Whitney's son, and Steven Galbraith, curator at the RIT Libraries, who gave us access to so many important historic speeches, letters, and artifacts. To Rosemary Bray, Nena Thurman, Katiti Kironde, and Beverly Johnson, it was an honor to speak with you about your experiences with *Glamour*, and to hear how much the publication has meant to you. Thank you for your enormous contributions to *Glamour*'s legacy.

To Patty Sicular and Dana Brockman, thank you both for your encyclopedic knowledge of *Glamour*'s cover models, and to Patty for connecting us to so many important contributors.

And of course, to all our models, cover stars, and those who shared their stories with *Glamour,* as well as every single person who has worked for and contributed to *Glamour* since its inception, through nearly 1,000 printed issues and beyond, this book honors and celebrates you.

Thank you for believing in the magic of magazines, and a future where the possibilities of storytelling are limitless.

Thank You.

Photography Credits

Magazines throughout photographed by Josephine Schiele.

7   Arthur Gareev

8–9   From left: Constantin Joffé, Sante Forlano (2), Rico Puhlmann

10–11   From left: Steve Prezant, Mark Seliger, Patrick Demarchelier, Miguel Reveriego

14   Covers, from left: George Hurrell, Gjon Mili

15   Stephen Colhoun (1953), Frances McLaughlin-Gill (cover), Sante Forlano (1957)

16   Bottom, from left: Frances McLaughlin-Gill, Jack Ward, Mike Reinhardt, William Connors

17   Claude Mougin (Houston), Courtesy of Philip Whitney (group)

18   Clockwise from top right: Riccardo Tinelli, Ronnie Andren, Nina Berman/Redux

19   Clockwise from top: Lauren Dukoff, Alyssa Schukar, Danielle Levitt

20   Josephine Schiele

27   *Glamour* Staff

28   George Hurrell

29   *Glamour* Staff

34   John Rawlings

37   Clockwise from top: Myron Davis/The LIFE Picture Collection/Shutterstock, *Glamour* Staff, Alfred T. Palmer/Library of Congress

41   Gjon Mili

45   John Rawlings

51   Norman Parkinson/Iconic Images

54   Roger Kahan

59   Dagmar

63   RIT Cary Graphic Design Archives, Cipe Pineles Papers

66   Alexander Paal

68   John Rawlings (top), Gjon Mili (bottom)

69   John Rawlings

70   Gjon Mili

71   From top: Diane and Allan Arbus, Constantin Joffé (2)

76   Sante Forlano (cover), Frances McLaughlin-Gill

78   Sante Forlano (top), Diane and Allan Arbus

79   Richard Heimann

84–85   Diane and Allan Arbus

96   Lionel Kazan

98   Joseph Leombruno and Jack Bodi

101   Leonard Balish (top)

104   Frances McLaughlin-Gill

105   Frances McLaughlin-Gill (2), Karen Radkai (Fonda)

106   Milton Greene (2), Tom Palumbo (bottom)

PHOTOGRAPHY CREDITS, CONTINUED

217   Stephen Lovekin/Getty Images, Timothy Greenfield-Sanders/Contour RA by Getty Images (Morrison)

221   Zoë Ghertner/Art Partner/Courtesy of Vogue

222   Michelle Watt/Trunk Archive

224   Clockwise from top left: Brigitte Lacombe, Andrew Macpherson, Mark Abrahams, Ellen Von Unwerth/Trunk Archive, Matthias Vriens, Norman Jean Roy

225   Clockwise from top left: Patrick Demarchelier, Tom Munro (2), Danielle Levitt, Josefina Santos, Emman Montalvan, Gillian Laub, Miguel Reveriego, Emma Summerton (Kidman)

230   Clockwise from top left: Firooz Zahedi, Mark Abrahams, James White, Matthias Vriens

231   Mark Abrahams

238–239 Ronnie Andren, Alan Tannenbaum (Bush cutout)

245   Mario Tama/Getty Images

246   AP Photo/Suzanne Plunkett (top), Matt Moyer/Corbis/Getty Images

253   Kate Powers (top), Museum of Fine Arts, Houston/The Edith A. and Percy S. Straus Collection/Bridgeman Images

254   Davies+Starr

255   Deborah Jaffe

265   Drew Riker, Bud Fraker/MPTV (Hepburn)

267   Walter Chin (inset)

269   Clockwise from top right: Paul Lange, Rico Puhlmann, Christophe Jouany, Wayne Maser, Mike Reinhardt, Walter Chin, William Connors, Walter Chin, Susan Wood, Walter Chin/Trunk Archive, Patrick Demarchelier

270   Anne Keenan Higgins/Illo Reps

271   Paul Costello

280   Steven Pan

281   Getty Images

282   Clockwise from top right: Emma Summerton, Patrick Demarchelier, Steven Pan, Norman Jean Roy, Nathaniel Goldberg

283   Terry Tsiolis

284   Lauren Dukoff, Karen Radkai (backdrop)

285   Clockwise from top right: Radka Leitmeritz, Hannah Whitaker, AB+DM, Danielle Levitt, Billy Kidd, Kennedi Carter

288   Getty Images, Jeff Lipsky (Union), Ronnie Andren (Conrad and Bosworth)

294   Lisa Jack/Contour by Getty Images

297   Joe Raedle/Getty Images

302   Tom Schirmacher (cover), Getty Images

306   Eric Ray Davidson

307   Jason Kibbler (cover), Getty Images, Holly Andres (Harts)

326   Courtesy of Mother Los Angeles (books), Rachel Pickus

327   Courtesy of the Senate Democratic Media Center

Glamour Editor in Chief: Samantha Barry
Text: Natasha Pearlman, Ruhama Wolle, Anna Moeslein
Designer: Alexandra Folino
Photo Editor: Kathryne Hall
Photo Research: Isaac Lobel
Production: Nicole Stuart, Steve George
Copyediting: Robin Aigner, Michael Brownell
Research: John Banta, Emma Baker

Abrams Editor: Rebecca Kaplan
Design Managers: Danielle Youngsmith and Darilyn Lowe Carnes
Managing Editor: Annalea Manalili
Production Manager: Denise LaCongo

Library of Congress Control Number: 2024933817

ISBN: 978-1-4197-6705-0
eISBN: 979-8-88707-523-5

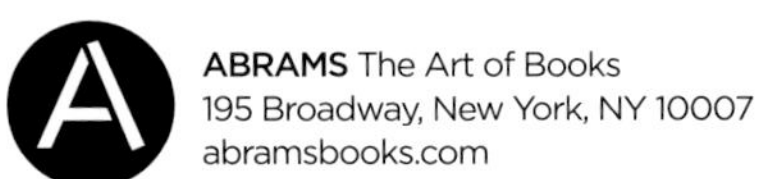
ABRAMS The Art of Books
195 Broadway, New York, NY 10007
abramsbooks.com

CALCULATED COOLNESS

for the girl with a job

DOS & DON'TS

SHE DRAFTS HERSELF FOR DEFENSE

how to do anything better guide

Your Job is our job

A New Magazine

PUT YOURSELF FIRST

WHERE THE GIRLS GO!

PROTEST

Viewpoint

No more waiting our turn

A MORTGAGE WITHOUT A MAN

ON YOUR OWN

Have I got Glamour?